Urban Issues
Eighth Edition

CQ Press, an imprint of SAGE, is the leading publisher of books, periodicals, and electronic products on American government and international affairs. CQ Press consistently ranks among the top commercial publishers in terms of quality, as evidenced by the numerous awards its products have won over the years. CQ Press owes its existence to Nelson Poynter, former publisher of the *St. Petersburg Times,* and his wife Henrietta, with whom he founded Congressional Quarterly in 1945. Poynter established CQ with the mission of promoting democracy through education and in 1975 founded the Modern Media Institute, renamed The Poynter Institute for Media Studies after his death. The Poynter Institute (*www.poynter.org*) is a nonprofit organization dedicated to training journalists and media leaders.

In 2008, CQ Press was acquired by SAGE, a leading international publisher of journals, books, and electronic media for academic, educational, and professional markets. Since 1965, SAGE has helped inform and educate a global community of scholars, practitioners, researchers, and students spanning a wide range of subject areas, including business, humanities, social sciences, and science, technology, and medicine. A privately owned corporation, SAGE has offices in Los Angeles, London, New Delhi, and Singapore, in addition to the Washington DC office of CQ Press.

Urban Issues

SELECTIONS FROM *CQ RESEARCHER*

EIGHTH EDITION

FOR INFORMATION:

CQ Press

An Imprint of SAGE Publications, Inc.

2455 Teller Road

Thousand Oaks, California 91320

E-mail: order@sagepub.com

SAGE Publications Ltd.

1 Oliver's Yard

55 City Road

London EC1Y 1SP

United Kingdom

SAGE Publications India Pvt. Ltd.

B 1/I 1 Mohan Cooperative Industrial Area

Mathura Road, New Delhi 110 044

India

SAGE Publications Asia-Pacific Pte. Ltd.

3 Church Street

#10-04 Samsung Hub

Singapore 049483

Acquisitions Editor: Michael Kerns

Editorial Assistant: Zachary Hoskins

Production Editor: Kelly DeRosa

Copy Editor: Diane DiMura

Typesetter: C&M Digitals (P) Ltd.

Cover Designer: Michael Dubowe

Marketing Manager: Amy Whitaker

Copyright © 2017 by CQ Press, an Imprint of SAGE Publications, Inc. CQ Press is a registered trademark of Congressional Quarterly, Inc.

All rights reserved. No part of this book may be reproduced or utilized in any form or by any means, electronic or mechanical, including photocopying, recording, or by any information storage and retrieval system, without permission in writing from the publisher.

Printed in the United States of America

Library of Congress Control Number: 2016949850

ISBN 978-1-5063-4361-7

This book is printed on acid-free paper.

16 17 18 19 20 10 9 8 7 6 5 4 3 2 1

Contents

ANNOTATED CONTENTS ix
PREFACE xiii
CONTRIBUTORS xvii

EDUCATION

1. Dropout Rate 1
Is societal change needed for
  graduation rates to rise? 4
Are successful local dropout
  programs viable nationwide? 7
Are the federal government's
  efforts to raise graduation
  rates working? 8
Background 9
  Early Origins 9
  "Waste We Cannot Afford" 9
  Seeking Solutions 11
  Research and Action 14
Current Situation 15
  Washington Gridlock 15
  Fewer "Dropout Factories" 17
  Concern Over Standards 18
Outlook: Striving for 90 Percent 18
Notes 19
Bibliography 22

2. Race and Education 25
Was court-ordered school
  desegregation effective? 27
Have charter schools and
  school choice laws increased
  racial separation? 29
Has teacher tenure contributed
  to racial disparities in education? 31
Background 33
  Legal Segregation 33
  Brown v. Board of Education 35
  Desegregation 35
  Integration Declines 35
Current Situation 40
  Education Challenges 40
  Enforcing Civil Rights 42
  State Action 43
Outlook: Changes Coming? 43
Notes 44
Bibliography 47

LAND USE AND URBAN DEVELOPMENT

3. Coastal Development 49
Should state and local governments
  block coastal development? 52

v

Can the federal flood insurance program be fixed?	54
Does New York City need floodgates?	55
Background	56
Wealth and Trade Centers	56
Rush to the Shore	60
Coasts Under Pressure	60
In Harm's Way	61
Current Situation	63
Clashing Signals	63
Flood Insurance Fraud?	65
Rising Seas	65
Outlook: Resilient Coastlines	66
Notes	66
Bibliography	70

4. Air Pollution and Climate Change — 73

Is President Obama's Clean Power Plan good policy?	76
Is the EPA's new ozone standard good policy?	78
Can renewable energy become a major contributor to the power industry?	79
Background	80
Early Air Pollution	80
Carbon Dioxide Measured	81
Clean Air Act	83
Acid Rain	83
Regulating Emissions	84
Current Situation	88
Global Negotiations	88
Court Fight	89
Outlook: Obama Agenda	91
Notes	92
Bibliography	95

LAW ENFORCEMENT

5. Police Tactics — 98

Do SWAT teams and military tactics and weaponry have a place in policing?	101
Has police use of military-style tactics increased tensions with minority communities?	102
Do body cameras prevent police misconduct?	106
Background	112
Troops in the Streets	112
War on Drugs	112
Drawing Fire	113
New Tensions	114
Current Situation	117
Stemming the Flow	117
Troubled Cities	117
Outlook: Re-engineering Police Culture	118
Notes	120
Bibliography	125

6. Racial Profiling — 127

Are racial- and ethnic-profiling prevalent in U.S. law enforcement today?	130
Do aggressive stop-and-frisk tactics help reduce crime?	133
Should courts take a leading role in combating police racial and ethnic profiling?	134
Background	135
"A Difficult History"	135
An 'Indefensible' Practice	136
'Deliberate Indifference'?	141
Current Situation	143
Pressure for Change	143
Mixed Results for Prosecutors	145
Outlook: Regaining Trust?	146
Notes	147
Bibliography	149

7. Fighting Gangs — 152

Is the gang threat growing?	155
Is banning street gangs from congregating an effective anti-gang strategy?	156
Can former gang members help quell street violence?	157
Background	159
Immigrant Gangs	159
Postwar Gangs	160
Birth of Modern Gangs	163
Current Situation	165
Gangs on the Internet	165
Policy Progress	168

Outlook: Growing Sophistication	170
Notes	171
Bibliography	174

RACE, CLASS, AND ETHNICITY

8. Racial Conflict — 177
- Would improving police interactions with African-Americans significantly advance race relations in America? — 180
- Would new laws and government programs reduce institutional racism? — 182
- Does government need to recommit to school desegregation? — 183
- Background — 184
  - Slavery and Jim Crow — 184
  - 'White Affirmative Action' — 185
  - Civil Rights — 187
  - Economic Shifts — 192
- Current Situation — 193
  - Police on Trial — 193
  - Campus Revolts — 195
- Outlook: Hope and Fear — 195
- Notes — 196
- Bibliography — 200

9. Housing the Homeless — 203
- Does unemployment cause most homelessness? — 206
- Is Housing First the best way to keep people from reverting to homelessness? — 207
- Should homeless families receive bigger or longer-lasting housing subsidies? — 208
- Background — 209
  - "I Ain't Got No Home" — 209
  - Emptying Asylums — 210
  - The "New Homeless" — 211
  - New Strategies — 213
- Current Situation — 218
  - Arresting the Problem — 218
  - Alternate Approach — 220
- Outlook: "A Human Right" — 220
- Notes — 221
- Bibliography — 225

10. Wealth and Inequality — 227
- Does income inequality hamper economic growth? — 231
- Are parental background and inheritance becoming more important for success? — 233
- Should the wealthy be taxed more? — 235
- Background — 237
  - 'Fatal Ailment' — 237
  - Postwar Prosperity — 239
  - The Great Switch — 244
- Current Situation — 245
  - Proposed Fixes — 245
  - Executive Pay — 249
- Outlook: 'Oligarchic Evolution' — 249
- Notes — 250
- Bibliography — 256

11. Housing Discrimination — 259
- Are current government policies contributing to residential segregation? — 262
- Are current real estate and lending practices contributing to residential segregation? — 264
- Can local officials do more to reduce racial segregation in housing? — 265
- Background — 266
  - Separate Worlds — 266
  - Slow Changes — 269
  - Unsettled Times — 271
- Current Situation — 274
  - Stepping Up Efforts — 274
  - Squaring Off in Court — 276
- Outlook: Political Challenges — 277
- Notes — 278
- Bibliography — 280

12. Fighting Urban Poverty — 283
- Would more federal aid reduce poverty in urban areas? — 286
- Do federal housing programs alleviate urban poverty? — 288
- Should the business community play a larger role in solving urban poverty? — 290

Background	291	Workplace Issues	298
Expanding Slums	291	Presidential Candidates	300
Depression Era	292	Outlook: Economy Is Key	301
"War on Poverty"	294	Notes	301
Recession Takes Root	297	Bibliography	305
Current Situation	297		
Promise Zones	297		

Annotated Contents

EDUCATION

Dropout Rate
The U.S. public high school graduation rate has risen to 80 percent, but more than 700,000 teens still drop out each year. Experts say dropouts create an economic and societal burden because they are ill-prepared to participate in an increasingly sophisticated global economy. The dropout rate is highly uneven, with students who are poor, disabled or still learning English more likely to leave school. Much of the problem can be traced to factors such as poverty, family instability and dangerous neighborhoods. But many critics also fault schools for failing to engage students and Congress for resisting adequate funding for schools. At the same time, conservatives and the Obama administration are locked in a debate about the proper role of Washington in shaping school policy. The federal government aims to increase the graduation rate to 90 percent in coming years, but critics say meeting that goal demands major educational reforms and the money to pay for them.

Race and Education
American public education underwent a profound transformation in the second half of the 20th century. Spurred by the 1954 Supreme Court ruling in *Brown v. Board of Education* that separate schools for black and white students are "inherently unequal," schools were integrated to a degree unknown in the nation's history. But in the 1980s a more conservative high court limited the impact of desegregation orders, and judges began releasing many

school districts from court-ordered desegregation plans. Critics say the resulting changes have led to resegregation in schools that threatens to limit the educational opportunities of poorer, minority students and undermines racial understanding. But other analysts say the problem is overstated or that claims of resegregation unfairly imply that minority children cannot achieve academically unless they are in the same classroom with white students. The debate surrounding school integration and equal access to quality education is likely to play an important role in shaping the future of American society.

LAND USE AND URBAN DEVELOPMENT

Coastal Development

When Superstorm Sandy wreaked havoc along the East coast in October 2012, it revived longstanding debates about coastal development. Sandy killed 72 people in the United States and caused more than $70 billion in damages, ranking it as one of the most destructive storms in U.S. history. Future storms could be even worse because of climate change, which is raising global sea levels. In New York City, which suffered severe flooding and damage, officials are pursuing many strategies to make the city more resilient, including reinforcing the shoreline and retrofitting buildings. Some experts argue that to make coastlines better able to withstand extreme weather, storm-damaged houses in vulnerable zones should not be rebuilt. Meanwhile, critics blame the federal flood insurance program, designed to help homeowners who cannot get private coverage, for subsidizing risky development with taxpayer dollars. Advocates say the program protects homeowners against catastrophic loss, but many New York and New Jersey residents say they have received payments far smaller than the actual damage to their homes.

Air Pollution and Climate Change

Air pollution kills 3.3 million people a year world-wide, including 55,000 Americans, according to a recent study by an international group of scientists. Moreover, airborne pollutants, especially carbon dioxide (CO_2), are contributing to global climate change. In response, President Obama, frustrated by congressional inaction, has used his executive authority to institute a sweeping plan aimed at limiting CO_2 emissions from coal-fired power plants, curbing smog-causing ozone and encouraging the growth of renewable energy. Industry officials are challenging Obama's Clean Power Plan in court, arguing the regulations are too costly and that market forces are enough to bring about reductions in pollution. Environmental advocates dismiss those claims and say the administration should have gone further in tightening emission standards. Meanwhile, the United States and almost all the other nations on Earth began climate talks in Paris last year to seek consensus on ways to curb emissions to stave off further warming of the planet.

LAW ENFORCEMENT

Police Tactics

The killing in August 2014 of an unarmed, black 18-year-old by police in Ferguson, Mo., has intensified a long-simmering debate over how police do their jobs. The shooting of Michael Brown by white officer Darren Wilson has led to angry and sometimes violent protests, initially heightened when police in military-style gear and armored vehicles responded to the unrest. The tactics highlighted what some criticize as the "militarization" of America's police forces, fueled by a Pentagon program that supplies local police with surplus weapons and vehicles. Others say police overuse SWAT teams to serve warrants and enforce drug laws. The Ferguson shooting and other recent high-profile police killings of unarmed African-Americans also has ignited a national outcry against what many say is disproportionate police action against black males. Police respond that low-income communities of all races have the highest crime rates and that they need military-style equipment to defend themselves in a heavily armed society.

Racial Profiling

The long debate over racial and ethnic profiling by police in pedestrian and traffic stops has intensified over the past two years with several deaths of African Americans under questionable circumstances in encounters with officers. The deaths have helped spawn the growing "Black Lives Matter" movement even as polls have registered growing distrust of police among African Americans. Some of the deaths have resulted in criminal charges against officers, but prosecutions face significant difficulties. Meanwhile, the Obama administration and police professional associations are urging reforms to improve police-community relations and to minimize the use of excessive force. Many states have enacted laws or procedures to monitor or reduce racial profiling, while courts are also being urged to control the practice. But some observers fear that less aggressive police tactics in minority neighborhoods may be contributing to a spike in violent crime.

Fighting Gangs

After years of decline, homicide and gun violence are surging in U.S. cities, and many law enforcement officials say street gangs are a major reason for the increase. Gang membership has soared in recent years, and crimes committed by gangs have expanded beyond drug dealing and murder to migrant smuggling, sex trafficking and counterfeiting. Gang leaders are using the Internet and social media to communicate, recruit members and threaten rival groups. Meanwhile, gangs are spreading to smaller cities, suburbs and even rural areas. Legal injunctions — restraining orders that bar gang members from congregating publicly — have curbed criminal activity in some localities, but critics say the tactic violates civil liberties, is applied in a racially biased manner and unfairly stigmatizes innocent young people. Countering the gang threat requires a multipronged strategy, many experts say, that combines tough policing with anti-poverty programs that seek to keep youths from falling into the gang lifestyle.

RACE, CLASS, AND ETHNICITY

Racial Conflict

Race-centered conflicts in several U.S. cities have led to the strongest calls for policy reforms since the turbulent civil rights era of the 1960s. Propelled largely by videos of violent police confrontations with African-Americans, protesters have taken to the streets in Chicago, New York and other cities demanding changes in police tactics. Meanwhile, students—black and white—at several major universities have pressured school presidents to deal aggressively with racist incidents on campus. And activists in the emerging Black Lives Matter movement are charging that "institutional racism" persists in public institutions and laws a half century after legally sanctioned discrimination was banned. Critics of that view argue that moral failings in the black community—and not institutional racism—explain why many African-Americans lack parity with whites in such areas as wealth, employment, housing and educational attainment. But those who cite institutional racism say enormous socioeconomic gaps and entrenched housing and school segregation patterns stem from societal decisions that far outweigh individuals' life choices.

Housing the Homeless

Although homelessness has fallen almost continuously since 2007, about 1.5 million Americans use a shelter in a given year — and advocates for the homeless say that figure badly understates the problem. Unemployment, cuts in funding for mental health care and the psychological effects of war on veterans all have helped fuel the homeless crisis. The Obama administration vowed to eliminate homelessness among families by 2020. But experts are divided on whether "rapid rehousing" programs that provide short-term rental aid will keep individuals and families from becoming homeless again. Meanwhile, many cities are trying to banish the homeless from their downtowns by enacting anti-vagrancy laws — an approach opposed by those who say living on the street should not be treated as a crime.

Wealth and Inequality

The very richest now claim a share of the world's wealth not seen since the Gilded Age of the late 1800s and early 1900s. The world's top 1 percent owns about half of global wealth and the bottom half less than 5 percent, according to French economist and best-selling author Thomas Piketty. Income inequality, once a fringe political topic, has become a major issue in the presidential campaign, fueled by the populist anger of candidates Bernie Sanders and Donald Trump. While Sanders targeted big banks and the top 0.1 percent, millionaire Trump blames free trade agreements with China and Mexico for disappearing jobs and stagnating wages. Democrats, including presidential candidate Hillary Clinton, want to help struggling middle-class and low-income Americans by raising the minimum wage, providing preschool education and taxing the rich. But conservative economists say taxes on wealth would punish entrepreneurialism and stifle economic growth, arguing that wealth at the top translates into investment that creates jobs at the bottom.

Housing Discrimination
Almost 50 years after enactment of the Fair Housing Act, racial segregation in housing persists in the United States, in large cities and suburbs alike. Fair-housing advocacy groups blame the federal government for lax enforcement of the law and state and local housing agencies for limited efforts to disperse affordable housing into predominantly white neighborhoods. They also cite federal studies and court cases that show continuing discrimination against African-Americans, in particular by mortgage bankers, landlords and real estate brokers. The Supreme Court cheered fair-housing advocates with a decision last June endorsing broad application of the law against policies that have a "disparate impact" on minorities. The Department of Housing and Urban Development (HUD) followed with a rule aimed at requiring communities to do more to advance fair-housing policies, but local resistance may slow those efforts. Meanwhile, complaints of housing discrimination against individuals with disabilities now account for a majority of the cases HUD receives each year.

Fighting Urban Poverty
This year's unrest in Ferguson, Mo., and Baltimore, arising from alleged police misconduct in the deaths of black men, cast a light on impoverished conditions not only in those cities but in urban areas throughout the country. From Philadelphia and New York to Kansas City and Los Angeles, joblessness, poor schools, crime, blight, high incarceration rates and segregated housing patterns have helped drive millions of Americans — many of them minorities — into poverty. In some localities, up to a third of the residents subsist below the federal poverty line. Many experts say economic growth is essential to combat urban poverty. But beyond that, policymakers are divided on how to help the poor, with some advocating a higher minimum wage and more government social programs and others stressing personal responsibility and economic incentives to spur business growth in inner cities. With Congress gridlocked, some states and cities are moving on their own to help the urban poor, including increasing the minimum wage.

Preface

As the daily news constantly reminds us, coming to terms with the full complexity and variety of issues that confront America's urban areas is no small feat. Does income inequality hamper economic growth? Are racial- and ethnic-profiling prevalent in U.S. law enforcement today? Is societal change needed for graduation rates to rise? In order to promote change and hopefully reach viable resolution, scholars, students and policymakers must strive to understand the context and content of each of these urban issues. It is such understanding that eventually enables students to define their roles as active participants in urban policy.

With the view that only an objective examination that synthesizes all competing viewpoints can lead to sound analysis, this eighth edition of *Urban Issues* provides comprehensive and unbiased coverage of today's most pressing policy problems. This book is a compilation of 12 recent reports from *CQ Researcher*, a weekly policy backgrounder that brings into focus key issues on the public agenda. It enables instructors to fairly and comprehensively uncover opposing sides of each issue, and illustrate just how significantly they impact citizens and the government they elect. *CQ Researcher* fully explains difficult concepts in plain English. Each article chronicles and analyzes past legislative and judicial action as well as current and possible future maneuvering. Each report addresses how issues affect all levels of government, whether at the local, state or federal level, and also the lives and futures of all citizens. *Urban Issues* is designed to promote in-depth discussion, facilitate further research and help readers think critically and formulate their own positions on these crucial issues.

This collection is organized into four subject areas that span a range of important urban policy concerns: Education; Land Use and Urban Development; Law Enforcement; and Race, Class, and Ethnicity. These pieces were chosen to expose students to a wide range of issues, from debates over race and education to the militarization of local police forces. We are gratified to know that Urban Issues has found a following in a wide range of departments of political science, sociology, public administration and urban planning, and hope that this new edition continues to meet readers' needs.

CQ RESEARCHER

CQ Researcher was founded in 1923 as *Editorial Research Reports* and was sold primarily to newspapers as a research tool. The magazine was renamed and redesigned in 1991 as *CQ Researcher*. Today, students are its primary audience. While still used by hundreds of journalists and newspapers, many of which reprint portions of the reports, the *Researcher's* main subscribers are now high school, college and public libraries. In 2002, *Researcher* won the American Bar Association's coveted Silver Gavel award for magazine excellence for a series of nine reports on civil liberties and other legal issues.

Researcher writers — all highly experienced journalists — sometimes compare the experience of writing a *Researcher* report to drafting a college term paper. Indeed, there are many similarities. Each report is as long as many term papers — about 11,000 words — and is written by one person without any significant outside help. One of the key differences is that writers interview leading experts, scholars and government officials for each issue.

Like students, the writers begin the creative process by choosing a topic. Working with the *Researcher's* editors, the writer identifies a controversial subject that has important public policy implications. After a topic is selected, the writer embarks on one to two weeks of intense research. Newspaper and magazine articles are clipped or downloaded, books are ordered and information is gathered from a wide variety of sources, including interest groups, universities and the government. Once the writers are well informed, they develop a detailed outline, and begin the interview process. Each report requires a minimum of ten to fifteen interviews with academics, officials, lobbyists and people working in the field. Only after all interviews are completed does the writing begin.

CHAPTER FORMAT

Each issue of *CQ Researcher*, and therefore each selection in this book, is structured in the same way. Each begins with an overview, which briefly summarizes the areas that will be explored in greater detail in the rest of the chapter. The next section chronicles important and current debates on the topic under discussion and is structured around a number of key questions, such as "Would raising the federal minimum wage mean job losses? Can government end homelessness?" and "Are public schools failing?" These questions are usually the subject of much debate among practitioners and scholars in the field. Hence, the answers presented are never conclusive but detail the range of opinion on the topic.

Next, the "Background" section provides a history of the issue being examined. This retrospective covers important legislative measures, executive actions and court decisions that illustrate how current policy has evolved. Then the "Current Situation" section examines contemporary policy issues, legislation under consideration and legal action being taken. Each selection concludes with an "Outlook" section, which addresses possible regulation, court rulings, and initiatives from Capitol Hill and the White House over the next five to ten years.

Each report contains features that augment the main text: two to three sidebars that examine issues related to the topic at hand, a pro versus con debate between two experts, a chronology of key dates and events and an annotated bibliography detailing major sources used by the writer.

ACKNOWLEDGMENTS

We wish to thank many people for helping to make this collection a reality. Thomas J. Billitteri, managing editor of *CQ Researcher*, gave us his enthusiastic support and cooperation as we developed this eighth edition. He and his talented staff of editors have amassed a first-class library of *Researcher* reports, and we are fortunate to have access to that rich cache. We also thankfully acknowledge the advice and feedback from current readers and are gratified by their satisfaction with the book.

Some readers may be learning about *CQ Researcher* for the first time. We expect that many readers will want regular access to this excellent weekly research tool. For subscription information or a no-obligation free trial of *CQ Researcher*, please contact CQ Press at www.cqpress.com or toll-free at 1-866-4CQ-PRESS (1-866-427-7737).

We hope that you will be pleased by the eighth edition of *Urban Issues*. We welcome your feedback and suggestions for future editions. Please direct comments to Michael Kerns, Senior Acquisitions Editor for Political Science, CQ Press, 2600 Virginia Avenue, N.W., Suite 600, Washington, DC 20037, or *Michael.Kerns@sagepub.com.*

The Editors of CQ Press

Contributors

Jill U. Adams writes a health column for *The Washington Post* and reports on health, biomedical research and environmental issues for magazines such as *Audubon, Scientific American* and *Science*. She holds a Ph.D. in pharmacology from Emory University.

Sarah Glazer contributes regularly to *CQ Researcher*. Her articles on health, education and social-policy issues also have appeared in *The New York Times* and *The Washington Post*. Her recent *CQ Researcher* reports include "Treating Autism" and "Treating Schizophrenia." She graduated from the University of Chicago with a B.A. in American history.

Christina Hoag, a freelance writer based in California, covered gangs and urban affairs for The Associated Press in Los Angeles and has written about gangs in El Salvador. She is co-author of *Peace in the Hood: Working with Gang Members to End the Violence* (2014).

Kenneth Jost has written 170 reports for *CQ Researcher* since 1991 on topics ranging from legal affairs and social policy to national security and international relations. He is the author of *The Supreme Court Yearbook* and *Supreme Court From A to Z* (both CQ Press). He is an honors graduate of Harvard College and Georgetown Law School, where he teaches media law as an adjunct professor. He also writes the blog *Jost on Justice* (http://jostonjustice.blogspot.com). His earlier reports include "Racial Diversity in Public Schools" (September 2007) and "School Desegregation" (April 2004).

Reed Karaim, a freelance writer in Tucson, Arizona, has written for *The Washington Post*, *U.S. News & World Report*, *Smithsonian*, *American Scholar*, *USA Weekend* and other publications. He is the author of the novel, *If Men Were Angels*, which was selected for the Barnes & Noble Discover Great New Writers series. He is also the winner of the Robin Goldstein Award for Outstanding Regional Reporting and other journalism honors. Karaim is a graduate of North Dakota State University in Fargo.

Peter Katel is a *CQ Researcher* contributing writer who previously reported on Haiti and Latin America for *Time* and *Newsweek* and covered the Southwest for newspapers in New Mexico. He has received several journalism awards, including the Bartolomé Mitre Award for coverage of drug trafficking from the Inter-American Press Association. He holds an A.B. in university studies from the University of New Mexico. His recent reports include "U.S. Global Engagement" and "Central American Gangs."

Robert Kiener is a freelance writer based in Vermont whose work has appeared in *The London Sunday Times*, *The Christian Science Monitor*, *The Washington Post*, *Reader's Digest*, Time Life Books and other publications. For more than two decades he worked as an editor and correspondent in Guam, Hong Kong, Canada and England. He holds an M.A. in Asian studies from Hong Kong University and an M.Phil. in international relations from England's Cambridge University.

Jane Fullerton Lemons is a freelance writer from Northern Virginia with more than 25 years of journalism experience. A former Washington bureau chief for the *Arkansas Democrat-Gazette* and *Farm Journal* magazine, she has covered the White House, Congress, food policy and health care. She is currently seeking a master's degree in creative nonfiction from Goucher College in Towson, Maryland.

Jennifer Weeks is a Massachusetts freelance writer who specializes in energy, the environment and science. She has written for *The Washington Post*, *Audubon*, *Popular Mechanics* and other magazines and previously was a policy analyst, congressional staffer and lobbyist. She has an A.B. degree from Williams College and master's degrees from the University of North Carolina and Harvard. Her recent CQ Researcher reports include "Gulf Coast Restoration" and "Energy Policy."

1 Dropout Rate

Robert Keiner

Brandon Campbell, 20, studies online at the Boston Re-engagement Center on Jan. 8, 2013, for courses he needed to get his high school diploma. Dropout rates are highest among students who are poor, disabled or still learning English, and those who are black or Hispanic. In today's demanding job market, dropouts could be doomed to what Education Secretary Arne Duncan calls continued "poverty and misery."

From *CQ Researcher*, June 13, 2014.

The nation has achieved a "profound milestone," Secretary of Education Arne Duncan told a Washington audience in April — the national on-time public high school graduation rate is at its highest level ever. "As a country we owe a debt of gratitude to the teachers, students and families whose hard work has helped us reach an 80 percent graduation rate," he said.[1]

However, the assembled educators, researchers, policy advocates and high school students also heard words of caution. "We cannot coast when we have big hills to climb," said Alma Powell, chairwoman of America's Promise Alliance, an education foundation started by her husband, retired Gen. Colin L. Powell, former chairman of the Joint Chiefs of Staff.[2]

As Duncan explained, the 80 percent graduation rate translates into one in five students dropping out — 718,000 high school students a year.[3] That's nearly 4,000 students every school day. Even though the U.S. graduation rate has been improving for more than a decade, rising from 71.7 percent in 2000, it's still one of the lowest in the developed world. And it is still short of the long-held government goal of 90 percent by 2020.

Overwhelmingly, dropout rates are highest among those who are poor, disabled or still learning English. Today's dropouts, many of whom may be unemployable in an ever-more-demanding job market, could be doomed to what Duncan called continued "poverty and misery." They will also become an increasing economic and societal burden on the rest of the nation because a technical and global economy has little room for workers without high school diplomas, many say. The search for solutions to the U.S.

27 States Meet or Exceed National Graduation Rate

Public high school graduation rates in 27 states equaled or exceeded the national average of 80 percent in 2011-12. Ranking highest was Iowa (89 percent), followed by Nebraska, Texas, Vermont and Wisconsin (88 percent). The District of Columbia was lowest, at 59 percent, followed by Nevada (63 percent).

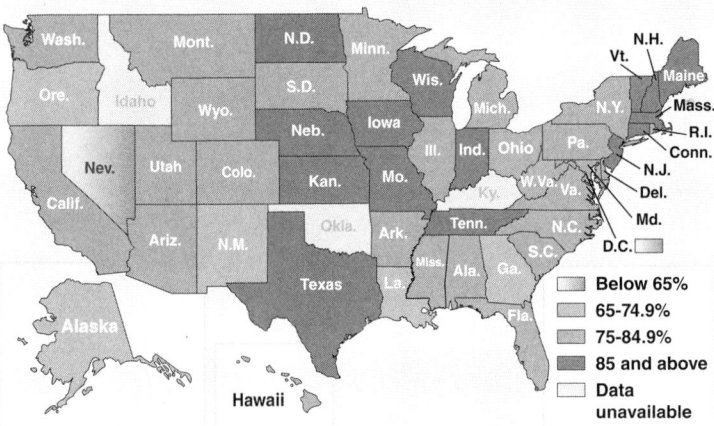

Public High School Graduation Rates, 2011-12

Source: Marie Stetser and Robert Stillwell, "Public High School Four-Year On-Time Graduation Rates and Event Dropout Rates: School Years 2010-11 and 2011-12," U.S. Department of Education and National Center for Education Statistics, April 2014, pp. 9-10, http://tinyurl.com/km2k6jp

dropout problem, an issue that has vexed educators, administrators and politicians for decades, raises questions about how to determine what works and how to pay for it. It also fuels debate about the proper role of the federal government in education, traditionally guided at the local and state levels.

"Twenty years ago a high school dropout could find a job that paid a living wage. Today that's impossible," says Russell W. Rumberger, a professor of education at the University of California, Santa Barbara (UCSB), and director of the California Dropout Research Project, which has published scores of research reports about the issue. "There are no jobs. That's why dropping out is a crisis."

The consequences are not just economic. "Our communities created public schools to develop citizens and to sustain our democracy," wrote Diane Ravitch, a New York University education professor and public education advocate. ". . . When public education is in danger, democracy is jeopardized. We cannot afford that risk."[4]

The dropout crisis is especially acute among blacks and Hispanics. "We still have many school districts where it looks like apartheid in America," said Daniel J. Losen, director of the Center for Civil Rights Remedies at the University of California, Los Angeles.[5]

Although some of the nation's weakest high schools have improved or have been closed over the last several years, there are still some 1,300 "dropout factories," defined as schools that graduate fewer than 60 percent of their students.[6]

Ron Haskins, co-director of the Center on Children and Families at the Brookings Institution, a liberal-leaning Washington, D.C., think tank, says, "You cannot separate the problems of schools and society. You have to work on both at the same time, and we are. But the gap between the poor and the rich is increasing."

Alma Powell and Duncan were featured speakers at a day-long discussion of the report "Building a Grad-Nation 2014," an annual update on dropout prevention issued by Powell's group together with several other education policy organizations.[7] That report and others presented statistics that underline the differences in graduation rates:

• Low-income students are woefully behind their better-off peers. For example, in Minnesota just 59 percent of low-income students graduated, compared with 87 percent of their wealthier peers. In many states, roughly one-third of low-income students did not graduate in 2012.[8]

• English-language learners, at 59 percent, and special-education students, at 61 percent, had below-average graduation rates.[9]

• Black students graduated at a 69 percent rate and Hispanics at 73 percent, compared with whites at 86 percent and Asian-Americans at 88 percent. In some cities the statistics were even more dismal. For example, only 59 percent of students in the largely black Washington, D.C., public school system graduated.[10]

- Graduation rates also varied widely among states; while 93 percent of Vermont's students graduated, only 59 percent of Nevada's did.[11]

Dropouts cost the nation in a variety of ways. Over a lifetime, a typical high school dropout earns an estimated $260,000 less than a graduate.[12] Those lower earnings cost federal and state governments more than $50 billion annually in income tax that would have been paid if all dropouts graduated.[13] High school dropouts live shorter lives — by six to nine years — than graduates and are disproportionately affected by heart disease, diabetes and obesity; 80 percent of dropouts depend on government for health care assistance.[14] Dropouts are 67 percent of the inmates in state prisons, 56 percent of federal inmates and 69 percent of inmates in local jails.[15]

The global nature of the economy magnifies the cost of the dropout problem, according to Robert Rothman, a senior fellow at the Alliance for Excellent Education, a Washington education policy and advocacy group. "Students from Baltimore and Boston no longer compete against each other for jobs; instead, their rivals are well-educated students from Sydney and Singapore," he wrote. "But as globalization has progressed, American educational progress has stagnated. . . . Given that human capital is a prerequisite for success in the global economy, U.S. economic competitiveness is unsustainable with poorly prepared students feeding into the workforce."[16]

Rothman cited an estimate from the Paris-based Organisation for Economic Co-operation and Development (OECD), which conducts economic research on industrialized countries, that if the United States brought all students up to a minimum level of proficiency, the country would add as much as $72 trillion to its gross domestic product over the lifetime of a child born in 2010.[17]

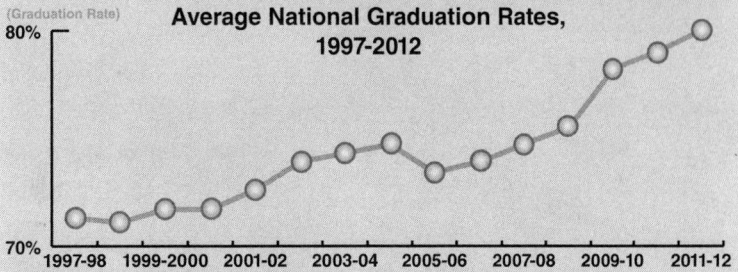

Graduation Rate Peaks in 2012

The public high school graduation rate climbed nearly 10 percentage points during the past 15 years to a high of 80 percent in 2011-12.

Note: The methodology for reporting graduation rates was standardized nationally in the 2010-11 academic year; earlier calculations used a slightly different definition of a freshman class.

Sources: "Digest of Education Statistics, Table 124," U.S. Department of Education, National Center for Education Statistics, October 2012 (1997-2010 data), http://tinyurl.com/jvonwls; Marie Stetser and Robert Stillwell, "Public High School Four-Year On-Time Graduation Rates and Event Dropout Rates: School Years 2010-11 and 2011-12," U.S. Department of Education and National Center for Education Statistics, April 2014 (2010-12 data), http://tinyurl.com/km2k6jp

Even with the recent improvement in graduation numbers, the United States ranks 21st among 28 industrialized countries in the proportion of youth who complete high school, according to the OECD.[18] In the 1970s, the United States ranked first.

Experts agree that a large part of the dropout problem can be traced to social, economic and cultural factors that adversely affect some students, such as poverty, a troubled home atmosphere and dangerous neighborhoods. High dropout rates can't necessarily be blamed on the education system, says Maria Ferguson, executive director of the Center on Education Policy at George Washington University. "Often they are caused by other factors." Until problems such as extreme poverty and high crime are remedied and the special needs of at-risk students are addressed, some education experts say, too many students will drop out.

Some national and state programs, such as one-on-one intervention and mentoring for at-risk students,

Education Secretary Arne Duncan is upbeat about the nation's efforts to improve secondary education. "The progress, while incremental, indicates that local leaders and educators are leading the way to raising standards and achievement and driving innovation over the next few years."

have produced improved graduation rates. However, many such programs are expensive and time-consuming, and experts question whether they can be duplicated across the country.

Officials in the Obama administration, the latest in a long line to attempt to solve the high school dropout problem, have frequently spoken out on the issue. Indeed, in his first State of the Union address, President Obama declared that "dropping out of high school is no longer an option" and described the nation's high dropout rate as "a prescription for economic decline."[19]

He has continued to discuss the problem in subsequent speeches. In an effort to cut the number of dropouts, he has suggested all states raise the legal dropout age to 18, although the suggestion has not gained much traction.[20] Eighteen states allow students to leave school before the age of 18.[21]

However, education legislation is stalled in Congress, despite pleas for action on key issues. Because of political gridlock and other factors, "most policy makers and education leaders have little hope any of these will be passed soon," says Ferguson.

As politicians, researchers and educators look for ways to raise the graduation rate, here are some of the questions they are asking:

Is societal change needed for graduation rates to rise?

Poverty is the strongest predictor of a school's dropout rate. Students from low-income families are five times more likely to drop out than students from high-income families.[22] In all but six states, the graduation rate for low-income students is below the national average.[23] Education experts say that in many cases, especially among minority and poor communities, sociological and cultural factors — such as disinterested or overburdened parents, crime and safety issues — also lead students to drop out.

Since the mid-1960s, when Congress enacted the Elementary and Secondary Education Act (ESEA) to fund schools based on the proportion of low-income children enrolled, educators have been debating whether graduation rates can improve without a corresponding improvement in poverty and related issues.

"Graduation rates may be inching up, but there are still huge gaps between underserved students and students in richer school systems," says Ferguson at George Washington. "The reality is that we have a ZIP code-funded public education system and will never have a truly level playing field." Much of U.S. school funding comes from locally collected property and other taxes, so funding varies widely, depending on the incomes of families in a school's district.

Mary Clare Reim, a research assistant at the Center for Policy Innovation at the conservative Heritage Foundation think tank in Washington, wrote, "Too many young students are trapped in failing public schools simply because of where they were born. Place of birth should not be a life sentence to low economic mobility."[24]

Ferguson says, "We have to do the best we can to improve our lowest-funded school systems or we won't see real increases in graduation rates." Available

"Why We Dropped Out"

High school dropouts from high-poverty areas cite a variety of reasons for leaving school, including gang influence, street violence, boredom, family health issues and a lack of support from parents or teachers. Researchers from the Center for Promise at Tufts University conducted group interviews last year with more than 200 dropouts in 16 high-poverty urban communities across the country. Here are excerpts:

"Seeing my homeboy stabbed to death, multiple deaths, having a cousin that was murdered when I was 5, just a lot of things. I started hanging around with the wrong people, gang members getting into crap like . . . just a lot of stuff." — Sara

"I eventually dropped out just 'cause the bills weren't getting paid and I knew I could pay the bills, step up. I never took on responsibility like that before in my life." — Aaron

"Never had my mom in my life; she was always on drugs. It was just me growing up watching over my little brothers while she was out in the street doing her thing. So me and my other brothers grew up too quick, took responsibility, we just — it was too late to go back to school." — Thomas

"I just didn't like school. It wasn't because I'm dumb. I get sick just entering the building. I feel like I'm in prison. It's how the school was set up." — Jeff

"I got shot in my leg, and they started sending me homework from school . . . and I was doin' it and all of a sudden I started drinking and I got a little bit depressed, and just tired of it, you know, I don't want to do it no more, and I just quit." — Paul

"Everybody I was around smoked weed. Everybody I was around didn't go to school. So it was either go to school by yourself or stay around here and smoke with my friends." — Ernest

"I learn really hands-on and if it's shown to me in a really creative way then I get it right away. But, in traditional high school you sit down and read a book and hopefully you learn this. . . . Once I got into high school and that's all I was doing, I started hating reading." — Sharif

"The gangs showed me love, showed me the ropes, showed me how to get money. After that I was like, what do I need school for?" — Carl

The teachers "weren't sure what to do with me, how to help me. . . . I was moving around foster homes a lot so it's like you didn't get any support anywhere. After a while I just stopped going to class, stopped doing homework, skipped school and got into doing drugs and things like that." — Denise

"Even though I was taking extra-credit classes and doing after-school work, they didn't give me any of my extra credits or any credits from the credit-recovery program. So, then I just kind of fell off, I figured there was no point in trying." — Donald

"The teachers wouldn't even acknowledge me. I would say I'm behind, can you do this for me? . . . A lot of teachers didn't even know my name, it got really bad and came to the point where I wasn't going to graduate." — Arielys

"In school I was reckless because no one cared and no one said anything. If someone was there to push me, maybe we would have all stayed in school." — Vivian

"When I turned 18 I [aged out of foster care] and became homeless and that's where it all started. It just went downhill. I withdrew myself because I had nowhere to go." — Mandy

Source: "Don't Call Them Dropouts: Understanding the Experiences of Young People who Leave High School Before Graduation," America's Promise Alliance and its Center for Promise, Tufts University, May 20, 2014, http://tinyurl.com/mpawcm7

funds should be concentrated on low-income schools, she says.

But increased funding is not always the answer, argues Martha Bruckner, superintendent of schools in Council Bluffs, Iowa, where nearly 70 percent of the district's approximately 9,000 students are from low-income families, and graduation rates have jumped from 68 percent to 84.5 percent over the last eight

Blacks, Hispanics Lag Behind Whites, Asians

In the 2011-12 school year, 80 percent of public high school students graduated within four years. However, the graduation rate was considerably lower for American Indians, blacks and Hispanics than for whites or Asian-Americans.

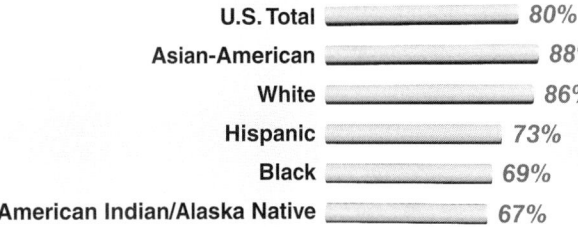

Four-Year Graduation Rates, by Race/Ethnicity, 2011-12

U.S. Total	80%
Asian-American	88%
White	86%
Hispanic	73%
Black	69%
American Indian/Alaska Native	67%

Source: Marie Stetser and Robert Stillwell, "Public High School Four-Year On-Time Graduation Rates and Event Dropout Rates: School Years 2010-11 and 2011-12," U.S. Department of Education and National Center for Education Statistics, April 2014, pp. 9-10, http://tinyurl.com/km2k6jp

years. "Poverty is a problem, but it's not insurmountable," she says.

Six years ago the Council Bluffs school district put in place a strategic plan with the objective of "guaranteeing" every student a high school diploma. It included a range of targeted programs that appointed "graduation coaches" for mentoring at-risk students, such as those who became pregnant or had poor attendance. This one-on-one intervention made students more accountable to their teachers and, Bruckner says, helped them learn the value of completing school. In addition, an attendance facilitator worked with each of the district's schools to increase school attendance.

"We also reached out into the community and enlisted the aid of concerned parents as volunteers," Bruckner says. "A lot of what we are doing is instilling pride in students, and their parents, in earning a high school diploma. I think too many people have used poverty as an excuse for our nation's high dropout rates. Instead of waiting for the government to cure poverty, we say education is the key to reducing poverty."

Some educators say asking schools to solve or even merely compensate for societal problems may be asking too much. "No matter how much we improve our public schools, they alone cannot solve the deeply rooted, systemic problems of our society," according to New York University's Ravitch, who once advocated conservative-backed reforms such as school choice but has since become a vocal opponent of such policies. "The failure of public policy is not the failure of the public schools."[25] Her 2013 book *Reign of Error* denounces what she calls "the hoax of the privatization movement" — or what she sees as an effort by school reformers to turn public education over to the private sector.

Others say that schools must find ways to deal with the situations that students face. "High school dropout rates are often not the main problem but an indicator of other problems," says Rumberger at UCSB. "These are often examples of society failing kids, not kids failing schools. The challenge is to improve schools so they can better compensate for the inequalities or handicaps of these at-risk students. That's a way to raise graduation rates." In his book *Dropping Out: Why Students Drop Out of High School and What Can Be Done About It*, he advocates targeting help to the poorest schools and most vulnerable students early in elementary school, among other steps.

Bob Wise, former governor of West Virginia and now president of the Alliance for Excellent Education, says the nation cannot use economic and social problems as an excuse to avoid trying to improve the educational system. "Certainly, low-income children need improved health care and better support systems, but we cannot wait for these societal fixes to be done to work on education," he says. "We have to get on with working on education. If all we do is provide better housing and health care for people who don't have an education, they will remain in the economic straits they are in."

Some point to the improvement in graduation rates over the last decade as evidence that the situation can improve despite poverty and in the face of other socio-economic problems. "Poverty matters, but schools and teachers can make a lot of difference in the face of poverty," says Frederick M. Hess, a resident scholar and director of education policy studies at the American

Enterprise Institute (AEI), a conservative Washington think tank.

"We lived through a powerful recession, and [graduation] rates still went up," says Robert Balfanz, a research scientist at the Center for Social Organization of Schools at Johns Hopkins University, who has worked with low-performing schools nationally, many in poor neighborhoods. He points to successful programs designed to support at-risk students and says, "Poverty is admittedly a significant driver of these low graduation rates, but the evidence shows that things can happen at the school level that can modify that to some extent."

Bruckner in Council Bluffs agrees. "Teachers, working in tandem with their students, parents and the local community, can make a quantifiable difference," Bruckner says. "Our district is proof of that."

Are successful local dropout programs viable nationwide?

Hundreds of programs to reduce dropout rates have been created over the last decade. These include big-budget, statewide education reform programs such as Florida's, which raised the state's graduation rate 21 percent between 1999 and 2010. They also include big-city programs such as Children First in New York City, where schools are graded A through F based in part on student progress, and the high school graduation rate rose 42 percent in eight years; as well as district- or local-level programs such as those in Council Bluffs and Darlington County, S.C., with 10,500 students.[26]

While some of these programs have shown promising results, it is still unclear whether they could be sustainable and scalable nationwide. Funding can be difficult to obtain, and there is little research on which programs are most effective.

In Darlington County, a rural, low-income region where 22 percent of the population is below the national poverty level and per capita annual income is only $20,000, turnaround has been dramatic.[27] In five years the county has boosted its graduation rate from 70 percent to 93.4 percent, the highest in South Carolina.[28] The county's education reforms included one-on-one intervention for struggling students plus a dropout-prevention facilitator in each school who focuses on at-risk students. The district also introduced a more comprehensive K-12 reading curriculum, self-directed learning at the high school level (where students may choose from various courses in a curriculum) and a strict attendance policy.

"Happily, we are seeing models that are duplicable nationwide," says Wise, the former West Virginia governor. But there's no magic formula that can be applied to any high school. "You have to look carefully at what's happening in a community and what each school's particular needs are," he says. For example, while one school could use non-union staff in an intervention program, another might be restricted to employing only union personnel and thus face higher costs. Also, programs can be duplicated more successfully if demographics are similar.

Funding is a frequently cited problem. "These programs are inevitably costly, and many are most needed in under-funded school districts with low tax bases," says George Washington University's Ferguson. "Teachers, mentors and tutors cost money, and it is often difficult to convince taxpayers to pay up."

In Council Bluffs, Bruckner says, dropout prevention programs are funded by a $2.5 million per year state grant, plus a foundation grant of $250,000, which works out to about $300 per student. In Darlington County, Eddie Ingram, the superintendent of schools, says that they spend $383,000 per year on salaries for people whose primary responsibility is dropout intervention.

Unreliability of funding is also a problem. UCSB's Rumberger notes that programs featuring expensive advocates or monitors for at-risk students are often paid by federal or state grants, rather than from local school funds. "What happens when that grant money runs out, as it usually does, in a year or two?" he asks. "Governments and foundations need to better focus on how these programs can be sustained in the current fiscally restrained climate after the funding expires."

For example, the federal government in 2010 funded the Striving Readers Comprehensive Literacy Program, meant to help states develop literacy programs. "Congress in its wisdom funded the program, then a year later eliminated it and restarted it the following year," says Phillip Lovell, vice president for policy and advocacy/comprehensive school reform at the Alliance for Excellent Education. "No business would ever do such a thing." The level of uncertainty created by Washington's gridlock "is a real impediment to reform."

It's wrong to focus on short-term costs, says Wise. "We cannot not afford to transform our schools. It's a case of 'pay me now or pay me later.' If we don't fund education now, we'll pay later in the form of increased health care costs, social welfare costs, low earnings and more."

While programs such as Darlington County's might succeed in other school systems, there is a lack of research on which dropout prevention programs work best, says Rumberger. "The federal government is very weak on measuring the effectiveness, and especially the cost effectiveness, of many intervention programs." Citing a lack of research funding, he notes, "We educators don't do enough research on those factors." Ferguson, too, says a shortage of research funding prevents more schools from adopting reform programs.

But Haskins at Brookings disagrees, noting that the federal Institute of Education Sciences "is well-funded, and they are doing high-quality education research, as are the schools taking part in the federal program Investing in Innovation." In that program, school districts and nonprofits compete for grants to develop and test new ideas.

Some education officials praise the federal government for its role in pressing states to agree to a standardized, uniform calculation of graduation rates. "It's impossible to know how you're doing if you don't have good numbers," says Lovell.

While the initial call for this statistical reform came in a 2005 report from the nation's governors, the federal government took the lead in the ensuing years by making use of that method a part of state education-accountability systems linked to federal aid.[29] Says Balfanz, at Johns Hopkins, "This reform would have died if the federal government didn't push it forward."

Complaints about the lack of research aren't new. A 2008 report from the National Education Association (NEA), the nation's largest teachers union, noted, "For at least a decade, researchers have reported the dearth of rigorous evaluations of the effectiveness of educational programs in general, and of dropout prevention and intervention programs in particular. This makes it difficult to identify high-quality model programs or the components that make them effective."[30]

Says AEI's Hess, an advocate of local control of schools, "I'd rather that Congress increase funding for education research instead of funding federal programs that seek to dictate how states and local governments run their schools."

Are the federal government's efforts to raise graduation rates working?

Between 2009 and 2013, the Obama administration distributed $5.1 billion to states to improve academic performance at about 1,500 struggling high schools. These School Improvement Grants constitute the largest-ever federal aid targeted at failing schools, many of them so-called dropout factories.

Results have been mixed, however: Students at a third of the schools did the same or worse than before the funding; the others improved, but at a rate similar to that of all U.S. students during the same time.

"You can't help but look at the results and be discouraged. We didn't spend $5 billion of taxpayer's money for incremental change," said Andrew Smarick, a former federal education official and a partner at Bellwether Education Partners, a Massachusetts consulting firm.[31]

Education Secretary Duncan disagreed: "The progress, while incremental, indicates that local leaders and educators are leading the way to raising standards and achievement and driving innovation over the next few years."[32]

Balfanz, whose research was largely responsible for identifying the phenomenon of dropout factories and helping to popularize the term, says the federal money helped prove that troubled schools could be reformed. "We used to think these problems were intractable," he says. "Now we can see some of these schools can be turned around." The number of dropout factories fell from 2,007 in 2002 to 1,359 in 2012.[33]

While some applaud Washington's funding for education programs, such as the School Improvement Grants and other initiatives, others claim these programs are the latest in a succession of actions that give Washington too much say in education policy, historically a state and local matter. "One of the biggest questions that will affect education policy is how big a role do we want the federal government to have in education," says Ferguson. Debate over the issue often splits along ideological lines, with Republicans generally calling for a reduced federal role and Democrats a larger one.

Critics of Washington's education-reform efforts claim that with the advent of No Child Left Behind, the federal school reform law that went into effect in 2002, and the more recent Race to the Top programs, which tie federal money to adoption of national education standards, the federal government has taken a direct hand in mandating education policy. Over time, "the U.S. secretary of Education became the nation's superintendent of schools, telling every district and every school what was required of them to receive federal funding," said critic Ravitch at NYU.[34]

Critics also note that Washington provides only about 10 percent of the nation's education budget, while state and local governments fund the rest. "We've seen 50 years of federal attempts to move the needle on graduation rates with little results," says Lindsey Burke, a policy analyst at the conservative Heritage Foundation think tank in Washington. "There's a pattern of large-scale federal education reform programs, such as Head Start and others, that are failing in their stated mission. This is an issue better left to the states and local districts, especially because Washington is only a 10 percent stakeholder in education."

Ravitch and others say federal "interference" in state and local education policy harms the national graduation rate instead of helping it. They say the galaxy of practices often lumped together as "school reform," many supported by the Obama administration — practices such as charter schools, performance-based pay for teachers and extensive standardized testing — are distractions. It's time, they say, to let teachers teach. "If Uncle Sam is going to be involved in schooling, his role should be constructive and constrained. And recently it hasn't been," says Hess at AEI.

Brookings' Haskins counters, "Schools just haven't been doing their job for decades. I think politics is driving some arguments. I don't see any danger that the feds are going to take over the schools; they may have been a little heavy-handed . . . but leaving the performance of the schools to the states and localities does not do the job."

Lovell of the Alliance for Excellent Education says, "If schools could fix this problem by themselves, why are we now applauding a graduation rate where one-fifth of our students are [still] failing to graduate?"

While the graduation rate has been inching up, it is still too early to determine the effects of relatively recent federal programs, such as Race to the Top. Says George Washington's Ferguson, "Until we sort out the federal role, it will be difficult to make any lasting progress."

BACKGROUND

Early Origins

Although the history of U.S. schools goes back to 1635, when the Boston Latin Grammar School opened, early schools were vastly different from those today. The first high schools were private and reserved for the privileged few in a time when most people had little schooling.

The nation's first public high school, Boston's English Classical School, did not open until 1821; others followed in New England and New York. Still, at a time when jobs generally didn't require high school diplomas, only a small part of the population attended high school and fewer graduated. In 1870, 50,000 students were attending 500 public high schools across the country, and just 2 percent of the nation's 17-year-olds graduated.[35]

"It can be said that the modern public high school was born when the Michigan Supreme Court ruled in 1874 that taxes could be levied to support public high schools as well as elementary schools," according to a history of high school prepared for the U.S. Department of Education.[36] Tax-supported schools became common, enrollment was opened to girls and working-class children attended to learn skilled trades.

By 1940, for the first time in the nation's history, half of all high school students were graduating. A decade later, that number had jumped to about two-thirds.[37] With these higher numbers, the high school diploma came to be seen a valuable credential and for many jobs, a requirement.

"Waste We Cannot Afford"

As more students attended high school, more inevitably left school before graduating, but the issue of "dropouts" did not receive major national attention until the 1960s. "Educators and others may have been worried about attrition before 1960, but few defined it as a crisis," according to Sherman Dorn, an education professor at the University of South Florida in Tampa who has written about the history of the issue.[38]

The Soviet Union's 1957 launch of *Sputnik*, the first spacecraft to orbit Earth, began the space race and fueled concerns that America and American education were slipping behind the Soviet Union. The failure of many students to graduate from high school soon became a national issue. "How American education solves the

CHRONOLOGY

1940s-1980s *With high school open to all, concept of "dropout" emerges.*

1940 Almost 80 percent of high-school-age teens are enrolled, and half of 17-year-olds are high school graduates.

1954 Supreme Court's landmark *Brown v. Board of Education* decision holds racial segregation in public schools unconstitutional.

1962 The National Education Association's Project on School Dropouts is one of the first to explore the dropout issue.

1963 President John F. Kennedy initiates campaign to publicize the dropout issue.

1965 Congress passes Elementary and Secondary Education Assistance Act, first broad federal funding for public schools, targeted largely at the poorest schools.

1983 The widely discussed report "A Nation at Risk" depicts the U.S. education system as failing and students lagging behind those in other industrialized countries, but does not directly deal with dropouts.

1988 George H. W. Bush elected president; vows to be the "education president."

1989 Congress kills Bush education initiative; president's "education summit" produces few concrete results. Bush pledges to raise the graduation rate to 90 percent by 2000.

1990-2000 *Nation's focus on education and dropouts sharpens.*

1991 Congress kills Bush's America 2000 legislation, which calls for national standards and student assessments.

1994 Congress passes President Bill Clinton's Goals 2000 initiative calling for states to develop education standards. . . . Improving America's Schools Act ties federal funds to adoption of standards.

1997 Former presidents hold President's Summit on America's Future, drawing attention to the dropout crisis. . . . America's Promise Alliance, a partnership of groups focused on education policy, evolves from the summit.

2000 U.S. Army launches Operation Graduation ad campaign to encourage at-risk students and dropouts to complete high school.

2001-Present *Reform movement goes national, creates backlash.*

2001 No Child Left Behind Act, centerpiece of national school reform, calls for annual testing in reading and math, with penalties for failing schools. Schools must comply in order to receive federal funds. Launched with bipartisan support, the law becomes increasingly controversial over time.

2004 Johns Hopkins University researchers publish report that describes "dropout factories" with graduation rates below 60 percent.

2005 All states agree to use a single method to track graduation rates. . . . Bill & Melinda Gates Foundation steps up dropout program funding.

2008 Barack Obama elected president after campaigning on education platform. . . . Review of 22 dropout-prevention programs finds none raise graduation rates.

2009 In his first State of the Union speech, Obama says, "Dropping out of high school is no longer an option." . . . Congress approves $4.35 billion for Race to the Top grants for states with education reform plans; 41 states compete for grants.

2010 America's Promise Alliance launches Grad Nation Initiative, focusing on dropout prevention.

2011 With changes to No Child Left Behind stalled in Congress, Obama administration grants waivers of the law's requirements to states that make changes such as tying teacher evaluations to test scores. Opponents say the administration is using federal money to impose its policies.

2013 Administrators of the GED, the widely used high school equivalency test, announce tests will increase in price and have to be taken on computers; some states drop the GEDs.

2014 National high school graduation rate hits 80 percent in 2012.

problem of school dropouts... may well determine America's future," said Daniel Schreiber, who in the early 1960s was director of the National Education Association's Project on School Dropouts.[39]

The term "dropout" entered the national consciousness. In 1960, *Life* magazine described the consequences: "Leaving school is usually one more step on a treadmill of discouragement, failure and escape. But the individual tragedy is also a national waste."[40]

Sociologist Lucius F. Cervantes saw even more dire consequences, writing in 1965, "It is from this hard core of dropouts that a high proportion of the gangsters, hoodlums, drug addicted, government-dependent-prone, irresponsible and illegitimate parents of tomorrow will be inevitably recruited."[41]

Concern extended beyond academic researchers. President John F. Kennedy initiated a national campaign in 1963 to publicize the dropout issue and help local school districts identify and help potential dropouts. Noting that four out of 10 fifth-graders did not finish high school, he called the dropout problem a "waste we cannot afford."[42] In 1965, as part of President Lyndon B. Johnson's War on Poverty, Congress enacted the Elementary and Secondary Education Act (ESEA) to allocate federal funds to schools and districts based on the proportion of low-income children enrolled, thus aiming to improve the chances that poor children would graduate.

However, few of the dropout prevention programs in the 1960s were successful. "The programs rarely fulfilled their advocates' wishes, either in scope or in nature of programs. Constrained by budget limits, informal protocol, and often contradictory demands of sponsors and clients, programs failed to eliminate dropping out," according to Dorn.[43]

Although the U.S. Department of Education was created in 1979, at a time of growing discussion about the importance of education, the dropout issue did not receive as much attention during the 1970s and '80s as it had during the 1960s. Indeed, the 1983 "A Nation at Risk" report, which many educators cite as the impetus for the modern era of education reform, warned of a "rising tide of mediocrity" in the public schools "that threatens our very future as a nation and a people." It called for more rigorous graduation requirements, but did not even mention the dropout issue.[44]

Between 1988 and 1995 only 89 of the nation's approximately 15,000 school districts won federal grants for dropout prevention.[45] Even some generously funded dropout prevention programs recorded poor results. For example, New York City's school system spent more than $120 million between 1985 and 1989 on a prevention program. More than half of its participants left school by the third year of the program, and fewer than 40 percent improved attendance.[46] As the Heritage Foundation noted, "The study's most significant finding is that it made no difference whether students participated only one year or for the full three years.... At a cost of more than $8,000 per student, this program failed to assist even half of the participants."[47]

However, beginning in the 1980s, the mission of high school had begun to shift, according to Johns Hopkins researcher Balfanz. "In response to the nation's transition from an industrial to an information economy, academic preparation once again became a priority. No longer an end point in the public education system, the American high school is now being asked to prepare all its students for postsecondary schooling and training required for full economic and social participation in U.S. society. In short, it is being challenged to make good on its potential and become an avenue of advancement for all."[48]

Seeking Solutions

In 1989, newly inaugurated President George H. W. Bush, who had promised during his campaign to become an "education president," organized an education summit of the nation's governors. The meeting resulted in a commitment to a set of "national performance goals" to be achieved by 2000. Among them was raising the graduation rate to 90 percent by 2000, announced in Bush's State of the Union address in 1990, when the graduation rate was 71 percent.[49]

Graduation rates did not improve markedly, however, and education reform received little support during the remainder of the Bush administration. "Four years into his presidency — and three years after expectations had been raised with the education summit — no substantial education legislation had been enacted," according to a summary of the history of federal education policy prepared by the New York State Archives for a continuing research project on the history of education policy.[50]

GED Gets a Modern Makeover

Critics say the venerable high school equivalency test is on borrowed time

The General Educational Development (GED) test, the 72-year-old measure of high school equivalency for dropouts, recently underwent a major transformation — more than a decade since it was last revised.

The new version, introduced early this year, was designed to better align the GED with the new Common Core curriculum standards, be more rigorous and better evaluate "career and college readiness skills" than its predecessor.

However, some educators say the revised test is too difficult, expensive and inconvenient to take, and recent research has many questioning its value.

Created in 1942 and largely used after World War II by veterans who had not had a chance to finish high school, the "second-chance" test since then has helped both veterans and civilians qualify for jobs, higher education and education loans. One out of seven high school credentials is a GED certificate, and in 2011 about 723,000 students took the tests; their average age was 26.[1]

The revised test emphasizes critical thinking and includes more questions on science and more writing than the previous version. For example, test-takers will now have to analyze literature and form arguments to answer essay questions.

Some adult educators worry that it will take at least a year to prepare students for the overhauled test. As one education writer noted, teachers "worry that their students, who are already beaten down and vulnerable, will give up."[2] One potential test-taker told *USA Today*, "We're already trying to cram in four years of education. Now you're trying to cram in more."[3]

Proponents of the new GED say it is an improvement on the previous version because it promotes critical thinking — for example, by requiring essay answers instead of relying solely on multiple choice. "How many apples and oranges? That's not the kind of question that employers ask anymore," said Lynn Bartlett, at Sunrise Tech Center near Sacramento, Calif. "Our instructional model is changing to match the new reality, the new vocabulary. . . . So when students earn the GED, it says they've accomplished something that's needed in today's economy and workplace."[4]

The new GED will better prepare students for jobs, maintains C. T. Turner, director of public affairs at the GED Testing Service. "If we don't provide them something of value, and they don't have the information and skills they need, we are setting them up for failure."[5]

The test will also be more expensive, with fees jumping in some states from $65 to $120 (Massachusetts), $35 to $130 (North Carolina) and $95 to $160 (Georgia). Jeff Putthoff, a Jesuit priest who is founder and executive director of Hopeworks N' Camden, a New Jersey-based youth development organization, wrote, "The monetary hurdle is now huge. Besides having to travel significant distance and incur the cost of trains, tolls or parking, the fee to take the test has increased by nearly 300 percent. For the poorest among us the challenge to become employable is that much harder. How does one get the money to take the test needed to get a job to earn money?"[6]

The new test also will be offered exclusively on computers, which some educators say will create a barrier for some students, especially those lacking ready access to a

Like Bush, President Bill Clinton, during his 1992 campaign, emphasized education. His Goals 2000: The Educate America Act, signed into law in March 1994, reiterated the target of a 90 percent graduation rate by 2000. The measure also called for states to develop educational standards but gave them control over the content of those standards. Initially the law required the federal government to approve standards, but that condition was dropped after critics said Washington was trying to impose a nationwide curriculum on local school districts.[51]

Another 1994 law, the Improving America's Schools Act, which reauthorized the Elementary and Secondary Education Act, required states to adopt education standards

computer. "For someone who doesn't have access to technology on a daily basis, we have to spend a lot of time on just the basic mechanics of using a mouse and moving around the screen," said Lecester Johnson, executive director of the Academy of Hope, an adult education center in Washington, D.C.[7]

In addition, some researchers question the value of getting a GED. According to a study by James Heckman, a Nobel Prize-winning economist at the University of Chicago, typical GED holders don't earn any more during their lifetimes than the typical high school dropout. His study also showed that the availability of the GED may influence capable students to drop out and apply for the less-onerous GED exam instead of studying for a high school diploma. (One-quarter of the nation's 673,000 GED recipients in 2012 were 18 or younger.) He recommends raising the minimum age for taking the GED from 17 to 20 to dissuade students from dropping out of school in hopes of taking the "easier" GED.[8]

Given concerns about the difficulty, cost, inconvenience and value of the GED, it's not surprising that at least nine states have decided to stop offering GED testing as an alternative to a high school diploma.[9] Meanwhile, some private companies are offering less expensive pencil and paper alternatives to the GED.

States determine which tests they will offer, according to Brian Belardi, director of media relations for McGraw-Hill, which publishes one of the competing tests. His company's test is recognized in seven states as an official equivalency test, he says — in three exclusively instead of the GED, and in four as one alternative.

"Angst is the good word" to describe the current GED situation, said Lennox McLendon, executive director of the National Adult Education Professional Development Consortium.[10]

— *Robert Kiener*

Graduates move their tassels after receiving their GED certificates from a Denver Rescue Mission education program. Participants typically overcome such obstacles as homelessness or unemployment.

[1] Caralee J. Adams, "New GED tests stir concerns, draw competitors," *Education Week*, June 6, 2013, http://tinyurl.com/nohbv44.

[2] Kavitha Cardoza, "The GED test is about to get much harder, and much more expensive," *The Atlantic*, Oct. 8, 2013, http://tinyurl.com/m8hkdua.

[3] Michael Auslen, "GED test takers to study harder, pay more," *USA Today*, July 24, 2013, http://tinyurl.com/pzqb8xq.

[4] Loretta Kalb, "New GED test requires computer skills, more knowledge," *The Sacramento Bee*, Jan. 13, 2014, www.sacbee.com/2014/01/13/6069988/new-ged-testing-requires-computer.html.

[5] Cardoza, *op. cit.*

[6] Jeff Putthoff, S.J., "GED overhaul diminishing hope," *The Huffington Post*, April 2, 2014, http://tinyurl.com/o759dea.

[7] *Ibid.*

[8] Whet Moser, "How to fix the GED," *Chicago Magazine*, April 10, 2014, http://tinyurl.com/kjxjfre.

[9] Kimberly Hefling, "GED test overhauled; some states opt for new exam," The Associated Press, Jan. 1, 2014, http://tinyurl.com/lohqv3q.

[10] *Ibid.*

in order to receive federal funds. The act also required assessments of students at some point between grades three and five and again in high school. The two laws gave the federal government authority to enforce teaching standards, but the Clinton administration never used its power to take money away from states that did not comply.[52]

Research examining the dropout issue also evolved during the 1980s and '90s. Much early research had been based on the belief that dropping out was the student's fault and supported this belief with an examination of demographic and behavioral characteristics of these students.[53] In the 1990s, however, researchers broadened the scope of their research, in particular to

President George W. Bush proposed the No Child Left Behind Act three days after his Jan. 20, 2001, inauguration. Passed with bipartisan support, the law called for annual testing in reading and math, with penalties for schools that failed to achieve "adequate yearly progress." The law greatly expanded the federal government's power over the nation's education system. Above, the president speaks on the law at the public Gen. Philip Kearny School in Philadelphia on Jan. 8, 2009.

include longitudinal studies — based on data collected over time — to see how students fared in different environments. By following students over time, researchers gained greater insight, for example, into the weight of economic and social factors on dropping out.

By the late 1990s, with rising interest in school reform, numerous private organizations, think tanks and university-based research institutes had been established to formulate and help implement school-reform programs, including dropout prevention efforts. Among these were the Center for Educational Innovation-Public Education Association, Colin Powell's America's Promise Alliance, the Council for Basic Education, the Manhattan Institute's Center for Civic Innovation, the Center for Education Reform and many more.

Research and Action

Federal attention to education policy increased in the 21st century. Three days into his presidency, in January 2001, President George W. Bush announced his first legislative proposal — the No Child Left Behind Act (NCLB), which passed that year with bipartisan support. The law, signed by Bush in January 2002, called for annual testing in reading and math with penalties for schools that failed to achieve "adequate yearly progress." Federal funding was tied to the law's requirements. The NCLB greatly expanded the federal government's power over the nation's education system. A primary objective of the legislation was increasing high school graduation rates. Continuing debate over the measure, its requirements and its effects still shapes the national discussion about education.

Philanthropic organizations, such as the Bill & Melinda Gates Foundation, the Walmart Foundation and the Carnegie Foundation, invested in reform strategies that sought to increase high school achievement and improve graduation rates. In February 2005, the Gates Foundation pledged $15 million to improve the nation's "obsolete" high schools over time. As Microsoft cofounder-turned-philanthropist Bill Gates explained, "By obsolete, I don't just mean that our high schools are broken, flawed and underfunded — though a case could be made for every one of those points. By obsolete, I mean that our high schools — even when they're working exactly as designed — cannot teach our kids what they need to know today. . . . The poor performance of our high schools in preparing students for college is a major reason why the United States has now dropped from first to fifth in the percentage of young adults with a college degree."[54]

In President Obama's first State of the Union address, in February 2009, when he declared that dropping out was "no longer an option," he called for efforts to increase the graduation rate. That month, Congress approved $4.35 billion in federal stimulus money for a competitive school grant program called Race to the Top, which offered schools and districts federal grants for reform programs that were innovative and could be measured for their effectiveness.[55] Likewise, the federal Investing in Innovation fund, created at the same time, provided $650 million to schools to expand innovative reforms.

Because the administration required states and school districts to enact certain education policies to qualify for the funding, such as promising to adopt formal standards for content and testing in subjects such as math and English, some critics claimed that Race to the Top gave the federal government even more control over education matters.

Said New York University's Ravitch, "The Obama administration pretended that states participated of their

CURRENT SITUATION

Washington Gridlock

As with legislation on numerous other issues, several federal education policy measures are stalled in the gridlock among the Democratic administration, the Democratic-controlled Senate and the Republican-controlled House of Representatives. In addition to reauthorization of No Child Left Behind (NCLB), stalled legislation includes funding for measures that support children with disabilities, career and technical education, educational research and more.

"Despite the president's request during his recent State of the Union address that Congress get moving on passing education legislation, it doesn't look like anything will be happening soon," says Ferguson at George Washington.

Education experts cite a growing disconnect between the administration and Congress, and within Congress itself, regarding the extent of the federal role in education. Broadly speaking, Republicans favor little federal involvement in education policy while Democrats believe the federal government has a role in telling states how to identify and fix low-performing schools.

Microsoft cofounder Bill Gates and his wife, Melinda, head the Bill & Melinda Gates Foundation, a major contributor of funding for education initiatives. In 2005 the foundation pledged $15 million to improve the nation's "obsolete" high schools. "The poor performance of our high schools in preparing students for college is a major reason why the United States has dropped from first to fifth in the percentage of young adults with a college degree," Bill Gates said then.

own volition, thus maintaining the fiction that Race to the Top was 'voluntary' and that the federal government was not calling the tune."[56]

Although educators, politicians and others say NCLB should be changed, they sharply disagree on how. Although the law has not been reauthorized since 2007, its provisions remain in force.[57]

Beginning in 2011, the administration permitted states to apply for waivers from NCLB requirements and still receive federal funding. To get a waiver, a state must agree to adopt policies such as tying teacher evaluations to good test scores. Forty-two states and the District of Columbia had received waivers as of early 2014.[58]

Republicans complained that the waivers were a violation of executive power and accused Education Secretary Duncan and the administration of circumventing congressional authority. They also argued the program forces states to adopt education policies favored by the administration. In 2011 Duncan said he was offering waivers because Congress had failed to rewrite NCLB, which he termed a "slow motion train wreck." He added, "The current law serves as a disincentive to higher standards, rather than as an incentive."[59]

President Obama examines a student project at the Pathways in Technology Early College High School, in Brooklyn, part of the New York City public school system, on Oct. 25, 2013. If the United States brought all high school students up to minimum proficiency levels, as much as $72 trillion would be added to the country's gross domestic product over the lifetime of a child born in 2010, an international research organization estimated.

AT ISSUE

Should all states raise the high school dropout age to 18?

YES

Bob Wise
President, Alliance for Excellent Education; former governor, West Virginia

Written for CQ Researcher, June 2014

All states should raise the legal high school dropout age to 18, but not because it will automatically increase graduation rates — it won't. Rather they should do it because of the message it sends students, parents, the public and the state about the critical importance of a high school diploma in today's global economy.

Fifty years ago, high school dropouts could still land well-paying jobs and support their families. But times have changed. Today, jobs that require relatively little education are disappearing. According to research from the Georgetown University Center on Education and the Workforce, only about 10 percent of jobs are open to high school dropouts, compared with more than 30 percent in 1973.

Still, hundreds of thousands of students continue to drop out of high school every year. But passing a law that forces students to continue going to school must be only a first legislative action, not the final one. In fact, research from the Brookings Institution finds that states with higher compulsory school attendance ages do not have higher graduation rates than states with lower age requirements. Raising the compulsory age does little to address the root causes of why students drop out, which include difficult transitions from middle school to high school, an absence of basic reading and math skills and a lack of engagement.

As states debate whether to increase the compulsory school age, they must also provide the kind of education that engages students and give them a reason to want stay in school. Requiring compulsory attendance also means that state legislators need to plan for the additional classrooms, teachers and other resources needed to serve additional students who are now staying in school. Ensuring that all students have access to effective teachers and rigorous and engaging content is a good place to start — as is additional support, both academic and social — for students who have fallen behind.

Raising the compulsory attendance age can be a powerful motivational tool to express commitment to high school graduation, but only if it's accompanied by supporting policies and resources. While a legislative mandate increasing the compulsory school age can force students to attend school, it can't force them to learn. Provided that policymakers understand this important distinction, raising the dropout age to 18 can be one of the tools in their toolbox to increase high school graduation rates.

NO

Franklin Schargel
Schargel Consulting Group; author of 12 education reform books including Creating Safe Schools: A Guide for School Leaders, Teachers, Counselors and Parents

Written for CQ Researcher, June 2014

If America is to be globally competitive, it must have a high-performing, highly trained, technologically prepared workforce. And that means, at minimum, a high school diploma. I believe all students should stay in school until they graduate. However, that does not mean that all states should require that students remain in school until they are 18.

U.S. education is primarily a state and local responsibility. But President Obama and a number of state legislatures believe that the dropout age should be raised to 18. There is little data to indicate that will reduce dropout rates, according to a report by the Rennie Center for Education Research and Policy. "Our review revealed that there is little research to support the effectiveness of compulsory attendance laws in achieving these goals," said the report.

Some states that require students to stay in school until age 18 have some of the nation's highest graduation rates (such as Nebraska and Wisconsin, both with 88 percent graduating) and some of the lowest, such as New Mexico (70 percent) and the District of Columbia (59 percent). So it is not the age of mandatory attendance that determines the dropout rate, but other factors. Simply mandating that young people remain in school without addressing the causes for their leaving will accomplish little.

There are five reasons children leave school prior to graduation:

- The childrens' bad decisions — getting pregnant, becoming involved in alcohol or drugs, committing crimes.
- The families they come from — low income, dropouts themselves, a clash of cultures between families and schools.
- The communities they come from — places where there are gangs, violence and drugs.
- The schools they attend, which are toxic to learning.
- The teachers they have — we give the least experienced, least trained teachers the most difficult students.

If we wish to eliminate dropouts we need to deal with these causes. By raising the dropout age, we add additional costs, for additional classrooms, teachers, support personnel and alternative online courses. This is foolhardy, especially when so many states have already cut into the marrow of education. Changing the dropout age is a simplistic, sound-bite solution to a complex problem.

"We sorely need a smarter, more coherent vision of the federal role in K-12 education," wrote Hess, director of education policy studies at the American Enterprise Institute (AEI), and Linda Darling-Hammond, a professor of education at Stanford. "Yet both parties find themselves hemmed in. Republicans are stuck debating whether, rather than how, the federal government ought to be involved in education, while Democrats are squeezed between superintendents, school boards and teachers' unions that want money with no strings, and activists with little patience for concerns about federal overreach."[60]

Two recent pieces of legislation illustrate the ideological differences. The Republican-sponsored Student Success Act seeks to reduce the federal role in education policy. As its backers said, "House Republicans are determined to put an end to the Obama administration's overreach in our nation's classrooms and empower communities to fix our broken education system. For too long, states and school districts have been inundated with federal intervention and bureaucratic red tape that has done little to improve student performance."[61]

The Senate bill, the Democratic-sponsored Strengthening America's Schools Act of 2013, includes federal oversight of school programs and would establish requirements that schools and districts must meet in order to receive federal funding. Unlike the House bill, the Senate measure gives the federal government a supervisory role.

"There's a world of difference between the two bills," says Lovell at the Alliance for Excellent Education.

Congressional Republicans have complained that by offering NCLB waivers, Education Secretary Duncan and the administration are "leapfrogging" Congress to create their own version of the law. Sen. Lamar Alexander, R-Tenn., the top Republican on the Senate Education Committee and a former secretary of Education (1991-93), recently said, "Too often, this administration has turned competitive grants into federal mandates."[62]

However, Duncan said, "To avoid getting bogged down by the dysfunctionality of Washington, I had to go directly to the states who are teaching the kids and to the employers who are hiring them."[63]

"Maybe Duncan has not helped by offering waivers, but what was he going to do?" asks George Washington's Ferguson. "Congress was doing nothing about education reform to improve graduation rates, and he wanted to act. The Congress said 'How dare you!' and we have a stalemate."

A student addresses a meeting in Washington in April to discuss the 2014 "Building a GradNation" report, an annual update on dropout prevention efforts issued by America's Promise Alliance, an education policy organization started by retired Gen. Colin Powell, and other policy groups. This year's report underscored the differences in nationwide graduation rates. Blacks, for example, graduate at a 69 percent rate and Hispanics at 73 percent, compared with whites at 86 percent and Asian-Americans at 88 percent.

Fewer "Dropout Factories"

A bright point in the April 2014 "Building a GradNation" report was the continued decline in the number of what have been called dropout factories — high schools with graduation rates of 60 percent or lower. Over the last decade, such schools, which are responsible for an outsized proportion of students who do not graduate, have been targeted for reform or closure.

The number of these schools has declined from 2,007 in 2002 to 1,359 in 2012. There were still a million students attending the schools, but that was down from 2.2 million in 2002. Some schools improved their graduation rate, some closed and some had so many students transfer to other schools that they were no longer required to report graduation results to the government.

In 2004, almost half of the nation's African-American high school students and nearly 40 percent of Hispanic students were enrolled in such schools. By 2012 those levels had fallen to 23 percent and 15 percent, respectively.[64]

Balfanz of Johns Hopkins, who wrote a groundbreaking report on dropout factories in 2004, says, "Once the word got out about these dropout factories, there was a concerted effort by the government, communities, businesses and foundations to make changes."

Concern Over Standards

With the recent rise in graduation rates, many educators and administrators say they are cautiously optimistic about the state of the nation's high schools. The caution stems from concern about the quality of the education some students are receiving. "The numbers tell us that more students are graduating, but we don't know much about the quality of those diplomas," says Rumberger at the University of California-Santa Barbara. "More students may have a diploma, but how prepared are they to enter the workforce? We don't know if they are just barely passing or doing better."

Some recent test results are causing educators concern. For example, average reading scores from the just-released 2013 National Assessment of Educational Progress (NAEP) — the "Nation's Report Card" — have not improved from 2009 — and are lower than results from 1992.[65] Based on approximately 92,000 students' test results nationwide, the 2013 scores showed that only 38 percent of the country's high school seniors were reading at or above the "proficient" level and that only 26 percent scored at or above "proficient" in mathematics.

According to David Driscoll, chairman of the National Assessment Governing Board, which oversees the content and operation of NAEP, the findings are particularly troubling for further student success. "Achievement at this very critical point in a student's life must be improved to ensure success after high school," he said.[66]

Nevertheless, some states are reducing long-held requirements for graduation, a move that critics call "dumbing down" the high school curriculum. Florida stopped requiring students to study chemistry, physics and Algebra II to graduate, and Texas dropped its Algebra II requirement. Washington state dropped requirements that students study a foreign language. Nevada lowered the score needed to pass a high school math proficiency exam from 300 (out of 500) to 242.[67]

Some see the state changes as a rebellion against the Common Core standards, a curriculum developed by the nation's governors that is being phased in nationally.[68] Conservatives have charged that the standards — which set national benchmarks for what students should learn in reading, writing and math in each grade — interfere with local control of education. Some educators complain that they put too much emphasis on testing.

Opponents of Common Core's "college-prep" curriculum also say high schools should provide education suitable for all students, not just those who intend to go to college. Democratic New Mexico state Rep. Mimi Stewart, a retired teacher who introduced a bill to let students graduate without passing state exams or taking Algebra II, said, "We are supposed to be doing college and career readiness, not college and college readiness."[69]

Critics claim it is a mistake to lower standards. "If we are making it much easier for people to receive that diploma, I'm not confident it will translate into successful life outcomes," says AEI's Hess.

Others say that with American students falling further behind many of their counterparts in industrialized nations in subjects such as science, mathematics and reading comprehension, lower standards will widen the gap. "The U.S. system of education and training is inadequate in the new global environment," wrote journalist Fareed Zakaria, who specializes in international affairs.[70] He and others warn that raising standards, not lowering them, is the only way the United States can compete globally.

OUTLOOK

Striving for 90 Percent

Some optimists say U.S. graduation rates are on track to improve. "Four successive presidents have set high goals for graduation rates only to see them fall short of the mark," says Balfanz, the Johns Hopkins researcher. "But after years of flat-lining graduation rates, it looks like we finally have a shot at reaching that much-talked-about 90 percent graduation rate. Identifying, then improving, dropout factories was a start; now we have to keep working to increase how we support at-risk, low-income students."

The stakes are huge. According to the Alliance for Excellent Education, one of the sponsors of the "Building a Grad-Nation" report, reaching the 90 percent goal for high school graduates nationwide would create as many as 65,700 jobs and boost the national economy by as much as $10.9 billion.[71]

But there is no way the nation can reach the goal without meeting several tough challenges. "The recent numbers look good, but there is a lot of unevenness in the graduation rates," says Lovell at the Alliance for Excellent Education. "We need to focus on accountability, awareness and reform if we want to get to 90 percent."

According to Balfanz and other authors of the GradNation report, the country must:

- Close the opportunity gap. Graduation gaps between low-income students and their middle-to-higher-income peers reach nearly 30 percentage points in some states.
- Target students with disabilities, who represent 13 percent of all students.
- Reform or reinvent urban high schools so they help drive graduation rates higher than current 50- and 60-percent levels, so black and Hispanic students don't languish behind.
- Ensure big states, such as California, which has 13 percent of all students and 20 percent of all the nation's low-income students, continue to make significant progress.

"I think our chances are good," says Wise, the former West Virginia governor. He is enthusiastic about models being developed to redesign high schools and to provide more individual intervention and guidance and more cooperation between educators and the business community. He is especially optimistic about how technology could boost graduation rates: "Technology will be a game changer. For example, tech will provide data systems to allow teachers to be like doctors, knowing exactly in what areas a student is strong and where they need help."

The federal government's role will affect the future. "Funding is key, especially because the income gap between low-income school communities and high-income areas will probably keep growing," says George Washington's Ferguson.

Others warn that as long as Washington is gridlocked, education will suffer. "The president's shining a light on the dropout issue has been a great start," says Balfanz, "but Congress has to come together on education issues."

The effect of the Common Core standards on dropout rates is still unknown. Some educators think that if the new curriculum is more rigorous than that offered in the past, more students will drop out. Speaking of the new program's tests, Andrew Hacker, a political scientist and professor emeritus in the political science department at Queens College in New York City, said, "There's going to be a huge failure rate. It's going to exacerbate the . . . dropout rate we have among high school students already."[72]

Others disagree, predicting that while there may be a temporary decline in graduation rates at the beginning, as some students become frustrated, in time the effect will be fewer dropouts. The New York State Department of Education points to research that shows students want to be more challenged in school, saying that seven out of 10 students who dropped out said they were not motivated or inspired to work hard in high school.[73]

Rumberger at the University of California-Santa Barbara stresses the need for more research on the efficacy and cost-effectiveness of intervention and reform programs. "Setting specific targets, such as [the] 90 percent graduation rate, is less useful than making a more fundamental commitment to improving the lives of children and strengthening the families, schools and communities that serve them," he says.

NOTES

1. Lyndsey Layton, "High school graduation rates at historic high," *The Washington Post*, April 28, 2014, http://tinyurl.com/nezh2mz.
2. "GradNation Summit focused on increased grad rate, reaching last 20 percent," America's Promise Alliance, April 28, 2014, http://tinyurl.com/on57r7l.
3. Arne Duncan, "Remarks to Grad Nation Summit 2014," April 28, 2014, http://tinyurl.com/ngz6zb6.
4. Diane Ravitch, *Reign of Error* (2013), p. 324.
5. Lalita Clozel, "National high school graduation rate exceeds 80% for the first time," *Los Angeles Times*, April 28, 2014, http://tinyurl.com/oyadaz6.
6. Amanda Paulson, "U.S. graduation rates hit historic high," *The Christian Science Monitor*, April 28, 2014, http://tinyurl.com/qzjf2mc.
7. "Building a GradNation," Civic Enterprises, April 2014, http://tinyurl.com/p35yk2q.
8. Marie Stetser and Robert Stilwell, "Public High School Four Year on Time Graduation Rates and Event Dropout Rates: School Years 2010-2011 and

2011-2012, National Center for Education Statistics, April 2014, p. 4, http://nces.ed.gov/pubs2014/2014391.pdf.

9. *Ibid.*

10. *Ibid.*

11. *Ibid.*

12. "Education and the economy: quick facts," National Education Association, http://tinyurl.com/oyzbuff.

13. *Ibid.*

14. "Healthier and Wealthier: Decreasing Health Care Costs by Increasing Educational Attainment," Alliance for Excellent Education, November 2006, http://tinyurl.com/pbah9fr; and "Summary Health Statistics for U.S. Adults: National Health Interview Survey, 2011," U.S. Department of Health and Human Services, 2011, http://tinyurl.com/oxfmuqb.

15. "Saving futures, saving dollars," Alliance for Excellent Education, September 2013, http://tinyurl.com/kx5sw9k.

16. Robert Rothman, "How Does the United States Stack Up? International Comparisons of Academic Achievement," Alliance for Excellent Education, January 2014, http://tinyurl.com/of52rub.

17. E. Hanushek and L. Woessmann, "The High Cost of Low Educational Performance," Organisation for Economic Co-Operation and Development, 2010, http://tinyurl.com/kphp3uq.

18. "OECD countries with the highest high school graduation rates," Aneki.com Rankings and Records, http://tinyurl.com/lmslqp3.

19. "Remarks of President Barack Obama — Address to Joint Session of Congress," The White House, Feb. 24, 2009, http://tinyurl.com/dc8oob.

20. Shannon McFarland, "Obama Proposal to Raise Dropout Age Falls Flat," The Associated Press, June 16, 2012, http://tinyurl.com/musz4wc.

21. "Dropout Crisis Facts," America's Promise Alliance, http://tinyurl.com/myr3xch.

22. Chris Chapman, Jennifer Laird, Nicole Ifill and Angelina Kewal Ramani, "Trends in high school dropout and completion rates in the United States: 1972-2009." National Center for Education Statistics, Institute of Education Sciences, U.S. Department of Education, 2012, p. 6, http://tinyurl.com/3vuwwzt.

23. "Building a GradNation," *op. cit.*, pp. 16-17.

24. Mary Clare Reim, "Barriers to high school completion creates barriers to economic mobility," The Heritage Foundation, May 15, 2014, http://tinyurl.com/l4o4ufg.

25. Ravitch, *op. cit.*, p. 324.

26. "Florida's Education Revolution," Foundation for Excellence in Education, 2013, http://tinyurl.com/msux4p5; Alyssa Zauderer and James Ford, "City graduation rates reach all time high, so why is de Blasio still critical of Bloomberg's education policies?," *Pix 11*, Dec. 4, 2013, http://tinyurl.com/lceblcn; and "Children First Intensive," New York City Department of Education, undated, http://tinyurl.com/mhljy2x.

27. "Darlington County, South Carolina," U.S. Census Bureau, undated, http://tinyurl.com/mo45ro8.

28. "How we compare with other districts in the state," Darlington County School District, undated, http://tinyurl.com/buovqhv.

29. "Graduation Counts: A Report of the NGA Task Force on State High School Graduation Data," National Governors Association, 2005, www.nga.org/files/live/sites/NGA/files/pdf/0507GRAD.PDF.

30. Marcella R. Dianda, "Preventing Future High School Dropouts: An Advocacy and Action Guide for NEA State and Local Affiliates, National Education Association, p. 77, November 2008, http://tinyurl.com/o26cn4b.

31. Lyndsey Layton, "Federal analysis of school grants shows mixed results," *The Washington Post*, Nov. 21, 2013, http://tinyurl.com/oguvump.

32. *Ibid.*

33. "Building a GradNation," *op. cit.*

34. Ravitch, *op. cit.*, p. 282.

35. Ernest L. Boyer, *High School: A Report on Secondary Education in America* (1983), p. 49.

36. "From There to Here: The Road to Reform of American High Schools," The High School Leadership Summit, http://tinyurl.com/o8yxvz.
37. National Assessment of Adult Literacy, National Center for Education Statistics, http://tinyurl.com/2vpfm8.
38. Sherman Dorn, *Creating the Dropout* (1996), p. 51.
39. *Ibid.*, p. 65.
40. *Ibid.*, p. 66.
41. "Understanding Dropouts," *op. cit.*, p. 11; and Dorn, *op. cit.*, p. 69.
42. Margaret Spellings and Edward M. Kennedy, "National epidemic, economic necessity," *Politico*, May 11, 2007, http://tinyurl.com/nkd4cjn.
43. Dorn, *op. cit.*, p. 81.
44. "A Nation at Risk: The Imperative for Educational Reform," National Commission on Excellence in Education, April 1983, http://tinyurl.com/2878wlj.
45. "School Dropouts: Education could play a stronger role in identifying and disseminating promising prevention strategies," U.S. General Accounting Office, February 2002, p. 5, http://tinyurl.com/mdt5sop; and "Number of public school districts and public and private elementary and secondary schools: Selected years, 1869-70 through 2010-11," *Digest of Education Statistics*, National Center for Education Statistics, 2012, http://tinyurl.com/m5x2a47.
46. Joseph Berger, "Dropout Plans Not Working, Study Finds," *The New York Times*, May 16, 1990, http://tinyurl.com/lmg44pm.
47. Michael J. McLaughlin, "High school dropouts: How much of a crisis?" The Heritage Foundation, Aug. 3, 1990, http://tinyurl.com/klycvzb.
48. Robert Balfanz, "Can the American High School Become an Avenue of Advancement for All?" *The Future of Children*, Spring 2009, http://tinyurl.com/l69h9kw.
49. "Federal education policy and the states, 1945-2009: A brief synopsis," States' Impact on Federal Education Policy Project, New York State Archives, Albany, January 2006, revised November 2009, p. 56, www.archives.nysed.gov/edpolicy/altformats/ed_background_overview_essay.pdf; and "Public High School Graduation Rates," National Center for Higher Education Management Systems, undated, www.higheredinfo.org/dbrowser/?year=1990&level=nation&mode=map&state=0&submeasure=36.
50. *Ibid.*, p. 59 (New York State Archives).
51. For background, see Charles S. Clark, "Education Standards," *CQ Researcher*, March 11, 1994, pp. 217-240; and Kathy Koch, "National Education Standards," *CQ Researcher*, May 14, 1999, pp. 401-424.
52. For background, see Kenneth Jost, "Revising No Child Left Behind," *CQ Researcher*, April 16, 2010, pp. 337-360.
53. Karen E. Stout and Sandra L. Christenson, "Staying on Track for High School Graduation: Promoting Student Engagement," *The Prevention Researcher*, Vol. 16 (3), September 2009, pp. 17-20, www.tpronline.org/article.cfm/Staying_on_Track_for_High_School_Graduation.
54. "Bill Gates, "National Education Summit on High Schools," Bill & Melinda Gates Foundation, Feb. 26, 2005, http://tinyurl.com/l7defsg.
55. Race to the Top Fund, U.S. Department of Education, undated, http://tinyurl.com/ygr6mw9.
56. Ravitch, *op. cit.*, p. 281.
57. Jost, *op. cit.*
58. "NCLB Waivers: A State-By-State Breakdown," *Education Week*, updated Feb. 25, 2014, http://tinyurl.com/n474jeb.
59. Sam Dillon, "Overriding a key education law," *The New York Times*, Aug. 8, 2011, http://tinyurl.com/42zxnhl.
60. Frederick M. Hess and Linda Darling-Hammond, "How to Rescue Education Reform," *The New York Times*, Dec. 5, 2011, http://tinyurl.com/lk38qv5.

61. "Fact Sheets — HR5: The Student Success Act," U.S. House of Representatives Education and the Workforce Committee, June 6, 2013.
62. Alyson Klein, "Obama Administration to Face Hurdles on Vulnerable Programs," *Education Week*, April 23, 2014, http://tinyurl.com/ngbxdpq.
63. Monica Langley, "U.S. Schools Chief Arne Duncan Labors to Straddle Political Divide," *The Wall Street Journal*, July 21, 2013, http://tinyurl.com/k8onla8.
64. "Building a GradNation," *op. cit.*
65. "Are the nation's twelfth-graders making progress in mathematics and reading?" *The Nation's Report Card*, undated, http://tinyurl.com/n29nv37; data retrieved from U.S. Department of Education, Institute of Education Sciences, National Center for Education Statistics, National Assessment of Educational Progress (NAEP), 1992-2013 Mathematics and Reading Assessments.
66. Allison Nielsen, "Stagnant NAEP Scores Raise Concerns for High School Seniors," *Sunshine State News*, May 8, 2014, http://tinyurl.com/ol8u22r.
67. Stephanie Simon, "The school standards rebellion," *Politico*, Feb. 14, 2014, http://tinyurl.com/nnelzwf; and Trevon Milliard, "Education board lowers math test minimum passing score," *Las Vegas Review-Journal*, Feb. 26, 2014, http://tinyurl.com/kdk8rtd.
68. Simon, *op. cit.*
69. *Ibid.*
70. Fareed Zakaria, "America's educational failings," *The Washington Post*, May 1, 2014, http://tinyurl.com/qzgosc6.
71. "Building a Grad Nation: With High School Graduation Rate Over 80 Percent, Nation on Track to Meet 90 Percent Goal by 2020, New Report Finds," Straight A's: Public Education Policy And Progress, Alliance for Excellent Education, Vol. 14, (8), April 29, 2014, http://tinyurl.com/p6mlgea.
72. "Education Standards and the Common Core," On Point with Tom Ashbrook, WBUR, Dec. 6, 2013, http://tinyurl.com/k2dbqes.
73. "Common Core State Standards — Frequently Asked Questions," *EngageNY*, undated, http://tinyurl.com/okkwqvp.

BIBLIOGRAPHY

Selected Sources

Books

Dorn, Sherman, *Creating the Dropout: An Institutional and Social History of School Failure*, **Praeger, 1996.**
Written by a longtime educator and historian, this well-researched and readable book examines the dropout problem in the United States and how concerns over — and efforts to change it — have evolved from the 1800s to the modern day.

Ravitch, Diane, *Reign of Error: The Hoax of the Privatization Movement and the Danger to America's Public Schools*, **Alfred A. Knopf, 2013.**
The well-known education historian and former assistant secretary of Education under President George H. W. Bush argues that the real crisis in American schools is not academic but rather related to efforts to privatize schools and transform education into a profit-oriented venture.

Rumberger, Russell, *Dropping Out: Why Students Drop Out of High School and What Can Be Done About It*, **Harvard University Press, 2011.**
A professor of education at the Gevirtz Graduate School of Education at the University of California, Santa Barbara, and director of the California Dropout Research Project, provides a scholarly, well-researched yet accessible examination of the nation's dropout crisis.

Articles

Adams, Caralee, "Challenges ahead as push continues to improve high school graduation rate," *Education Week*, **May 5, 2014, http://tinyurl.com/nlr4c2p.**
Although many have applauded the recent rise in the national graduation rate, improving the rate poses challenges.

Cardoza, Kavitha, "The GED test is about to get much harder, and much more expensive," *The Atlantic*, **Oct. 8, 2013, http://tinyurl.com/m8hkdua.**
This excellent summary of recent changes to the GED test explains how the changes may affect those seeking to obtain the certification.

Ferguson, Maria, "Amid the chaos of Washington lies opportunity," *Phi Delta Kappan*, April 2014, http://tinyurl.com/o7xgbdb.

The executive director of the Center on Education Policy at George Washington University, Washington, D.C., examines how congressional gridlock is holding up reauthorization of numerous education bills.

Gallagher, Noel K., "Maine high schools revamping graduation requirements," *Portland Press Herald* (Maine), May 28, 2014, http://tinyurl.com/pjelyx2.

Officials in Portland, Maine, are proposing changes to graduation requirements that are part of a statewide move toward proficiency-based diplomas, such as mandating that every future high school student complete an in-depth capstone project and apply to a post-secondary school or a job certification program in order to receive a diploma.

Layton, Lyndsey, "High school graduation rates at historic high," *The Washington Post*, April 28, 2014, http://tinyurl.com/nezh2mz.

Federal statistics track graduation rates.

McNeil, Michele, "Arne Duncan vows push on range of education priorities," *Education Week*, April 23, 2014, www.edweek.org/ew/articles/2014/04/23/29secretary.h33.html.

The Education secretary explains how the Obama administration hopes to affect education policy during the remainder of his term.

Simon, Stephanie, "The school standards rebellion," *Politico*, Feb. 14, 2014, http://tinyurl.com/kbprkt8.

States, some of which have objected to the Common Core standards, are changing their own academic standards.

Reports and Studies

"Building a Grad Nation: Progress and Challenge in Ending the High School Dropout Epidemic," Civic Enterprises, April 2014, http://tinyurl.com/p35yk2q.

This annual report, produced by a coalition of advocacy groups and researchers at Johns Hopkins University, provides a comprehensive examination of national trends in the graduation rate.

"The Condition of Education," National Center for Education Statistics, http://tinyurl.com/l2jw65t.

Produced by the U.S. government's primary entity for collecting and analyzing data related to education, this report includes an assessment of K-12 education factors and an examination of factors affecting public high school graduation rates.

"Diplomas Count — Second Chances: Turning Dropouts into Graduates," *Education Week* and the Editorial Projects in Education Research Center, June 6, 2013, http://tinyurl.com/nq8fbm9.

A multifaceted report examines trends in graduation rates and changes in GED testing and includes features on individual education reform projects as well as graduation statistics for all 50 states.

"Don't Call Them Dropouts," America's Promise Alliance, May 20, 2014, http://tinyurl.com/ndhcpua.

Researchers associated with Tufts University and the America's Promise Alliance, an education policy coalition, interviewed more than 200 young people, and surveyed almost 3,000 more, to determine reasons that students say they left high school.

For More Information

Alliance for Excellent Education, 1201 Connecticut Ave., N.W., Suite 901, Washington, DC 20036; 202-828-0828; www.all4ed.org. Promotes high school transformation to ensure preparedness of students for postsecondary education and success in life.

American Educational Research Association, 1430 K St., N.W., Suite 1200, Washington, DC 20005; 202-238-3200; www.aera.net. National research society encouraging scholarly research in efforts to improve education.

American Enterprise Institute, 1150 17th St., N.W., Washington, DC 20036; 202-862-5800; www.aei.org. Conservative think tank promoting school choice and accountability in education.

American Federation of Teachers, 555 New Jersey Ave., N.W., Washington, DC 20001; 202-879-4400; www.aft.org. Union and AFL-CIO affiliate representing 1.5 million teachers.

America's Promise Alliance, 1100 Vermont Ave., N.W., Suite 900, Washington, DC 20005; 202-657-0600; www.americaspromise.org. Partnership that brings together organizations helping young people in education and other fields.

Center on Education Policy, 2140 Pennsylvania Ave., N.W., Rm. 103, Washington, DC 20037; 202-994-9050; www.cep-dc.org. National advocate for public education and more effective public schools.

Education Trust, 1250 H St., N.W., Suite 700, Washington, DC 20005; 202-293-1217; www.edtrust.org. Nonprofit that works to close the achievement gap among minorities and low-income families.

National Dropout Prevention Center, Clemson University, 209 Martin St., Clemson, SC 29631-1555; 864-656-2599; www.dropoutprevention.org. Research center that works to increase graduation rates.

National Education Association, 1201 16th St., N.W., Washington, DC 20036; 202-833-4000; www.nea.org. Nation's largest teachers union, representing 3 million teachers and other school employees.

2
Race and Education

Reed Karaim

Linda Brown (left) with her parents, Leola and Oliver, and her little sister Terry Lynn stand in front of their house in Topeka, Kan., in 1954, the year the U.S. Supreme Court ruled in the *Brown v. Board of Education* case that separate schools for black and shite children are "inherently unequal." The Browns sued the Kansas Board of Education when Linda wasn't allowed to attend a nearby school because she was black.

From *CQ Researcher*,
June 13, 2014.

Central High School in Tuscaloosa, Ala., once was considered a national example of successful school desegregation. Created in 1979 after a federal judge ordered the city's two segregated high schools to merge, Central High had an integrated student body that won state academic and athletic competitions.[1]

The court order, and others like it elsewhere, stemmed from the U.S. Supreme Court's landmark 1954 *Brown v. Board of Education* ruling, which held unanimously that separate schools for blacks and whites are "inherently unequal."

Central High was not without problems, partly because it was large and partly because of persistent claims that black and white students were held to different academic expectations.

"But despite these challenges, large numbers of black students studied the same robust curriculum as white students, and students of both races mixed peacefully and thrived," according to reporter Nikole Hannah-Jones, who wrote a lengthy study of Central High's history for the nonprofit investigative journalism site *ProPublica*.[2]

However, after a federal judge released the school district from its desegregation order in 2000 — saying federal oversight no longer was deemed necessary — Tuscaloosa dramatically reorganized its school system, partly in an effort to keep white families from leaving, a phenomenon known as "white flight." Two new high schools were created, and Central High's attendance zone was redrawn to encompass just the city's African-American west end. The student population, once about a third white, is now 99 percent black.[3]

South Has High Concentration of Poor Students

The states with the highest proportions of low-income students — as measured by those receiving free or reduced-price school lunches — are primarily in the South. Civil rights advocates say schools often become segregated according to poverty rates as well as race.

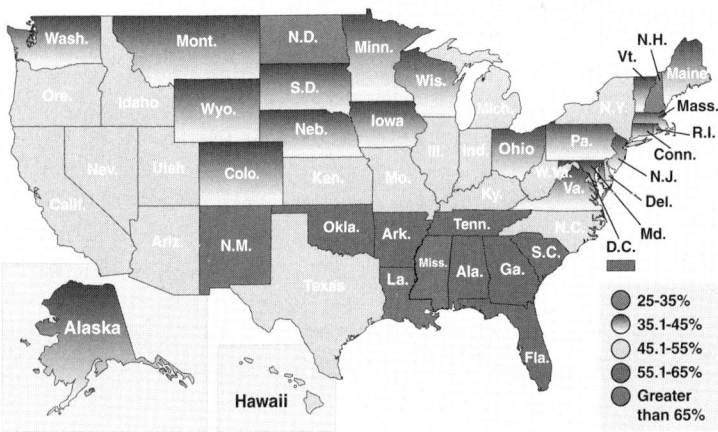

Percentage of Students Receiving Free/Reduced-Price Lunch (2010-2011, by State)

Legend: 25-35%, 35.1-45%, 45.1-55%, 55.1-65%, Greater than 65%

Source: "Public Elementary/Secondary School Universe Survey," National Center for Education Statistics, Common Core of Data (CCD), U.S. Department of Education, 2010-11 and 2011-12, http://tinyurl.com/lwuxfpf

The changes in Central High and the Tuscaloosa school system are examples of what many education experts have described as the resegregation of U.S. public schools.

School integration peaked in 1988 and has been declining ever since, according to a study published in May by the Civil Rights Project at the University of California, Los Angeles (UCLA). In 2011, only 23.2 percent of black students attended schools in which a majority of students were white — a smaller percentage than in 1968.[4] Moreover, the study found that resegregation is occurring in schools across the country. Since 1991, "all regions have experienced an increase in the percentage of black students in 90-100 percent minority schools," a common definition of a highly segregated school.[5]

Some analysts have called U.S. public schools with overwhelming minority populations "apartheid schools," likening them to schools in South Africa in 1948-1994, when racial segregation was officially mandated nationwide.[6] But other observers say the idea that U.S. schools are resegregating is overstated or that many of the changes are largely a reflection of the country's shifting demographics as the white population shrinks as a share of the whole.[7]

The increasing concentration of minorities in some schools also has spurred concern about the disparity in resources available to affluent and poor schools, which often have significant minority populations, and about the quality of education received by minority students.

The Civil Rights Project study also found that Latino students, particularly Mexican-Americans, are significantly more racially isolated than in the 1960s. This has been largely spurred by the rapid growth of the Latino population, according to scholars, which has dramatically affected public schools. From 1968 to 2011, white enrollment in public schools fell by 28 percent, while black enrollment climbed 19 percent and Latino enrollment rose by a stunning 495 percent.[8]

Those students increasingly are concentrated in urban centers or largely Latino neighborhoods. The change has been most significant in the West, where integration of whites and Latinos had been substantial in the 1960s, but has declined significantly since.[9]

"There's no doubt school segregation is increasing in terms of declining contact between African-American and Latino students and white students — it's been happening for nearly a quarter of a century for black students, for half a century for Latino students," says Gary Orfield, co-director of the UCLA Civil Rights Project.

He and other scholars see a combination of factors at play, starting with the termination of many court-ordered desegregation plans that followed a conservative tilt in the federal courts in the 1980s and '90s.[10] They also cite the growth of charter schools and the school choice movement, which they say leads to economic and racial separation.

Other analysts say Orfield and others have exaggerated the shift toward greater racial imbalance in schools, and that the imbalance may be reversing. In a 2013 study of trends in 350 metropolitan areas from 1993 to 2009, two university researchers found that "worsening segregation over the 1990s has given way to a period of modest integration among all racial/ethnic groups since 1998."[11] However, they added, reintegration has been most modest in the South and in cities with large increases in racial or ethnic diversity.

Abigail and Stephan Thernstrom, conservative scholars who have written extensively on race relations, say characterizing schools with heavy black or Hispanic populations as segregated is "a gross misuse of the term." Segregation referred to laws that set up separate school systems for white and black students during the so-called Jim Crow era — from the late 1800s until the 1960s — when African-Americans were restricted to separate restaurants, water fountains, bathrooms and schools — and to the back of public buses.[12]

Today's public schools remain far more diverse than before integration, the Thernstroms say, and the growth in the percentage of schools with a mostly minority population is largely the result of the growth of U.S. minority populations. "The promise of *Brown v. Board of Education* has been fulfilled. Nothing resembling the Jim Crow South has re-emerged, and it never will," the couple wrote in an article commemorating the 60th anniversary of the *Brown* decision.[13]

Most court-ordered desegregation occurred in the South, and Orfield and other analysts emphasize that the region's schools are more integrated than before the process began. "You're not moving back to pre-*Brown* levels where white kids and black kids aren't allowed to go to the same schools, you're moving back to something in between," says Sean Reardon, an education professor specializing in poverty and inequality of education at California's Stanford University.

In sharp contrast to the years before court-ordered school desegregation, the Northeast now has the highest concentration of black students in schools with a 90- to 100-percent minority population.[14] In fact, New York state now has the nation's most segregated schools, led by New York City, with its stark neighborhood disparities in race and income.[15]

"Segregation is typically segregation by both race and poverty," the Civil Rights Project noted.[16]

Some critics blame teacher tenure rules, which can make it more difficult to fire underperforming teachers, for some of the educational disadvantages experienced by minority and poor students. But other analysts say the real problem is state and local school financing, which usually is based on property taxes, leaving schools in poorer neighborhoods underfunded.

The teacher tenure issue came before a California court in June when Students Matter, an educational reform group founded by Silicon Valley entrepreneur David Welch, backed a lawsuit on behalf of Beatriz Vergara and eight other California students against the state's laws governing teacher job security. Los Angeles Superior Court Judge Rolf M. Treu ruled the laws unconstitutional, saying they unduly harm poor and minority students. Appeals are expected to continue for years.[17]

An underlying question concerning racial separation in schools is how much integration benefits students. Several studies have found educational benefits for minority students in mixed classrooms, but some conservative scholars dispute their methodology and consider the results mixed.

Orfield believes the results are clear. "Lots of data shows that there's basically no risk for middle-class kids to go to integrated schools, but there is a gain for poorer kids," he says. He and other educators say there are also less easily quantifiable benefits for all children.

"You understand each other better. You understand your society better. You understand how to think in a more complex way because you're more exposed to alternative views," he says. "All these things are related to diversity."

As scholars and analysts consider the impact of the changing racial composition of U.S. schools, here are some of the questions they are debating:

Was court-ordered school desegregation effective?

Before the Supreme Court ruled in 1954 that separate schools were inherently unequal, segregation was the law throughout the South and in some Northern and Western states. No black children in the South were

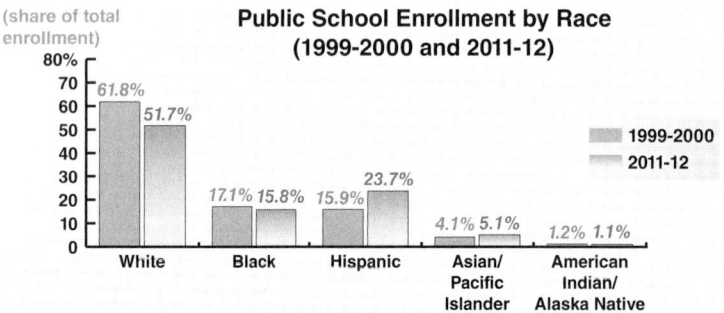

Percentage of Hispanic Students Rises

As a percentage of total public student enrollment — including charters — white and black enrollment fell between the 1999 and 2012 school years, while Hispanic enrollment rose by nearly 8 points.

Source: "Number and percentage distribution of public elementary and secondary students and schools, by traditional or charter school status and selected characteristics: Selected years, 1999-2000 through 2011-12," National Center for Education Statistics, U.S. Department of Education, http://tinyurl.com/mzqay8l

enrolled in predominantly white schools. But by 1988, nearly 44 percent of all African-American students attending Southern schools were in majority-white schools, and the region's schools had become the most integrated in the country.[18]

Despite the retreat over the last two decades, the region remains more integrated than the rest of the nation, and several analysts point to that as proof that court-ordered desegregation had a lasting impact. "For me, that's a huge legacy, particularly in the South," says Erica Frankenberg, an assistant professor of education policy studies at Pennsylvania State University in State College. "Still today, it's the most desegregated area. That's a great sign of progress."

But Richard Rothstein, an author and research associate at the Economic Policy Institute, a Washington think tank that studies issues affecting low- and middle-income people, says the retreat from the high point of desegregation was inevitable without an effort to address the underlying reasons black and white children went to different schools: housing discrimination and economic inequality.

Brown "changed things temporarily, but attempting to deal with school desegregation without addressing the segregation of neighborhoods in which schools are located is bound to fail. It can't succeed," says Rothstein. He adds that after lawyer Thurgood Marshall, who would later join the Supreme Court, won the *Brown* case on behalf of the National Association for the Advancement of Colored People (NAACP), he said the group would turn its attention to housing. "Had they pursued housing desegregation, they would have accomplished more than they did by pursuing school desegregation," Rothstein concludes.

Dennis Parker, director of the Racial Justice Program at the American Civil Liberties Union (ACLU), shares others' frustration at what they see as the limited benefits of court-ordered desegregation. However, he says, "When people say desegregation didn't work because we still have an achievement gap [between races] or because we didn't address economic or housing discrimination, I think that's an unfair burden to place on a single kind of litigation — the burden of addressing the whole range of racial problems that bedevil the United States. . . . *Brown* ended the system of apartheid that existed in the United States, and that is a huge thing. And for many students it created education opportunities that weren't there before, and that's a huge thing."

However, William Jelani Cobb, an associate professor of history and director of the Africana Studies Institute at the University of Connecticut in Storrs, views court-ordered desegregation as ultimately a failure. The idea that forcing schools to desegregate could permanently change the educational and social inequalities faced by African-American children was naïve, he says.

"When we talk segregation, we mistakenly think that it's one thing. It's not," Cobb says. "Segregation is more like a hydra, where you cut off one head and two more rise."

By inspiring white flight to suburbs or private schools, Cobb says, the ruling allowed racism and segregation to transmute into more complicated and insidious forms. "We look at it now, and the way it's operating is more sophisticated, such that a Supreme Court decision would not change it," he says. "It would have to be a much broader societal change."

The academic performance of students — particularly minority students — in integrated schools is central to the debate on the effectiveness of desegregation. Many educators cite extensive research on the benefits of integration. According to a 2014 study published by the National Bureau of Economic Research, black students who attended a school under a court-ordered integration plan were more likely to graduate, attend college and earn more money than black students who attended segregated schools. They were even healthier, on average, the study found.[19] The achievement gap between black and white students also declined significantly during the height of court-ordered desegregation.[20]

Researchers point out that the results were not caused simply by mixing races but also were tied to the shift in resources that came with integrating students of different races and economic classes. "School systems that had spent a pittance on all-black schools were now obliged to invest considerably more on African-American students' education after the schools became integrated," wrote David L. Kirp, a professor of public policy at the University of California, Berkeley.[21]

But several conservative scholars have criticized such studies. "I think the benefits of racial and ethnic balancing are frequently exaggerated. . . . Just because a school has a lot of racial and ethnic minority students doesn't mean it's a bad school and doesn't mean the kids there are incapable of learning just because they don't have enough white kids sitting next to them," says Roger Clegg, a former Justice Department official in the Ronald Reagan and George H. W. Bush administrations who heads the Center for Equal Opportunity, a conservative research and educational organization in Falls Church, Va.

Terry Stoops, director of education studies at the John Locke Foundation, a free market-oriented think tank in Raleigh, N.C., gives the Supreme Court credit for identifying a "very real problem in society" — the inequality of racially separate educational institutions. But he considers the educational benefits of integration to minority children unclear, although he says, "there probably is a larger societal benefit."

More critically, he says the focus on racial numbers diverted energy from what should have been the primary goal. "I think racial integration became an end unto itself, and there was a failure to focus on improving education, improving the quality of education available," says Stoops. "So we're left to wonder if the cost [through forced busing and the disruption of neighborhood schools] was justified."

But Charles Clotfelter, an economist and professor of public policy and law at Duke University in Durham, N.C., examined the consequences of school desegregation in his book, *After Brown: The Rise and Retreat of School Desegregation*. He concluded it measurably increased inter-racial contact, preparing students of all races and ethnicities for living in a diverse society.

"In the light of the large declines in racial isolation, one is almost compelled to judge the policy a success, perhaps a great success, for the changes accomplished in its wake were undeniably significant," he wrote. "Yet that judgment inevitably will be tempered by the failure of school desegregation to achieve *more*."[22]

Have charter schools and school choice laws increased racial separation?

The last 20 years have brought not only a decline in racial integration in schools but also another significant shift in public education: the rise of the charter school and school choice movement.

Charter schools, which can be started by individuals, groups or companies, are public schools that receive taxpayer funding but are generally not subject to the same rules and are freer to experiment with different approaches to education. The idea was developed by Massachusetts educator Ray Budde and first received significant attention when it was proposed by American Federation of Teachers President Albert Shanker in a 1988 speech at the National Press Club.[23]

Three years later, Minnesota became the first state to pass a charter school law.[24] Last school year, there were more than 6,000 charter schools in the United States, enrolling nearly 2.3 million students, according to the National Alliance for Public Charter Schools.[25]

The requirements for charter schools differ by state, and the schools take a wide range of approaches to education, so generalizations are difficult. But along the Eastern Seaboard, many charters have opened in urban cores where they enroll predominantly African-American students. A 2010 study by UCLA's Civil Rights Project of

An old-fashioned tug of war energizes soon-to-be kindergarteners at a public school enrollment carnival at Garfield Elementary School in Washington, D.C., on June 5, 2014. With traditional public schools in Washington losing students to the growing number of local charter schools, schools officials are stepping up efforts to recruit new students.

charter schools in 40 states, the District of Columbia and several dozen metropolitan areas found significant racial isolation among students in charter schools.[26]

"We certainly see much higher rates of racial segregation than we see in traditional public schools," says Penn State's Frankenberg, the lead author of the study. "And the important context there is that segregation in traditional public schools has been increasing since the 1980s, so it's not like that's a low figure."

Charter school advocates counter that studies have shown students in many charter schools with predominantly or exclusively minority enrollments are performing better than students in traditional public schools. A 2013 study covering 26 states and New York City by Stanford University's Center for Research on Education Outcomes found that "students in poverty, black students and those who are English-language learners" who attend charter schools posted the most impressive gains compared with their peers in traditional public schools.[27]

Some supporters say these results render questions of racial isolation insignificant. "If the education that children get in those schools is better than if they had gone to one with a more politically correct racial and ethnic balance, if the school is more rigorous or offers the curriculum that students want, why does it matter that the racial makeup is different than [some civil rights activists] would like?" asks the Center for Equal Opportunity's Clegg.

But charter school critics say such results can be misleading because some charter schools cherry-pick their students, avoiding lower-achieving or problem students, an option not available to traditional public schools. "Some push out students who threaten their test averages," wrote Diane Ravitch, a historian of education at New York University and outspoken critic of the charter school movement. "Last year [2012], the federal [Government] Accountability Office issued a report chastising charters for avoiding students with disabilities, and the ACLU is suing charters in New Orleans for that reason."[28]

The Civil Rights Project also found that in the West and parts of the Midwest and South, charter schools were disproportionately white compared with traditional public schools, suggesting they may be expediting white flight from public schools where minority populations are growing.[29]

"Charters are either very white places or very non-white places," said Myron Orfield, director of the Institute on Metropolitan Opportunity at the University of Minnesota in Minneapolis. Charters are "an accelerant to the normal segregation of public schools."[30]

However, Andre Perry, dean of the College of Urban Education at Davenport University in Grand Rapids, Mich., a former chief executive of a small charter network in New Orleans, says charter schools simply reflect larger societal trends. "I just don't see charter schools as this unique structure that causes resegregation," Perry says. "If you ask why schools aren't integrated, you have to look at housing policy, tax policy, culture, a number of factors. It's not school type that drives our behaviors."

The growth of charter schools is connected to a broader school choice movement that supports giving families greater freedom to choose what schools their children attend. Among other things, the movement supports tax credits or state-funded vouchers to help students pay for private schools and open-enrollment laws that allow parents to pick among public schools.

In 2006, Greg Forster, a senior researcher for the Friedman Foundation for School Choice, a think tank and advocacy group founded by Nobel Prize-winning free-market economist Milton Friedman and his wife, Rose, reviewed studies of school choice programs in

Cleveland, Milwaukee and Washington, D.C. He concluded that students were using vouchers to move to private schools that were more integrated than their public school counterparts.

"Private schools have a much greater potential to desegregate students because they break down geographic barriers, drawing students together across neighborhood boundaries," he wrote. Without vouchers, many families cannot afford private schools, but "vouchers overcome the monetary barrier, enabling private schools to make desegregation a reality," Forster concluded.[31]

However, a more recent 2013 study by the University of Minnesota found that the state's open-enrollment program in public schools resulted in greater segregation in Minneapolis-St. Paul, the state's major metropolitan area. Under the open-enrollment program, more white students than students of color were leaving racially diverse districts to enroll in predominantly white districts, the study found.[32]

UCLA's Orfield says the evidence indicates that unless school choice plans incorporate provisions to encourage the economically disadvantaged and minority populations to participate, they will inevitably favor populations that have the resources to take better advantage of all their options, leading to disproportionately white student bodies.

"We've learned what works in terms of school choice," he says. "Getting out good information to parents, having a goal of including all the different racial and ethnic groups, free transportation, which is absolutely essential, welcoming the kids into the school, all these can make choice into an integrated approach. But if you just have choice, the only thing you provide kids is another segregated school."

Has teacher tenure contributed to racial disparities in education?

The *Vergara v. State of California* lawsuit focused national attention on the role that teacher tenure laws

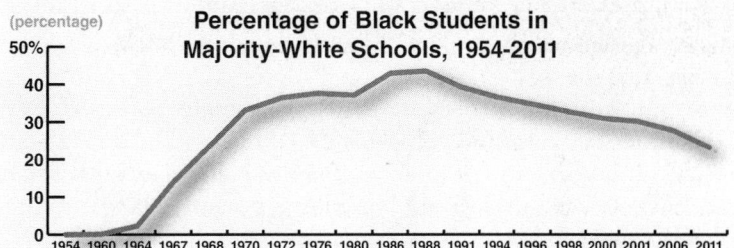

Public School Integration Peaked in 1988

The share of black students attending majority-white public schools grew rapidly after 1964 — when Congress passed the Civil Rights Act — peaking at 43.5 percent in 1988. The proportion has fallen steadily since then, including in 1991, when the Supreme Court ruled that courts could terminate successful desegregation plans.

Percentage of Black Students in Majority-White Schools, 1954-2011

Source: Gary Orfield, et al., "Brown at 60: Great Progress, a Long Retreat and an Uncertain Future," The Civil Rights Project, May 15, 2014, p. 10, http://tinyurl.com/n9cok4e

play in expanding disparities in educational opportunity and achievement between the races. Students Matter, the education reform and advocacy group, filed the suit on behalf of Beatriz Vergara and eight other California students, who claimed the state's laws governing teacher retention and firing — tenure laws — violated the state constitution's guarantee of equal educational opportunity.

Superior Court Judge Treu agreed, ruling that the laws "impose a real and appreciable impact on students' fundamental right to equality of education and they impose a disproportionate burden on poor and minority students."[33]

Treu's ruling, however, has done little to quell the debate. California teachers' unions, which strongly support tenure, vowed to continue the fight, and lengthy appeals are likely. Likewise, Students Matter and similar advocacy groups are planning more lawsuits in other states. For instance, the group recently joined a lawsuit in New York alleging that teacher job protections mean some students receive an inferior education.[34]

Felix Schein, a spokesperson for Students Matter, says the group was founded to improve public education through litigation but did not start out targeting teacher tenure. However, it soon became clear, Schein says, that the system placed some children at a severe disadvantage.

California's laws make it too difficult to dismiss underperforming teachers once they have been granted tenure, he says, so administrators resort to what has become known as "the dance of the lemons," bouncing the worst teachers from school to school. Because the poorest schools have difficulty retaining teachers, they too often end up with the teachers no else wants.

"If you're a poor African-American or Latino, you're much more likely to get a chronically underperforming teacher," Schein says.

In addition, "first in, first out" rules for retaining teachers, he says, mean that younger, talented teachers are laid off before teachers with more seniority, even if the senior teachers are performing poorly. Because schools with large minority populations are often in neighborhoods with limited financial resources, this, too, affects them disproportionately, Schein says.

"When you look at who was receiving reduction-in-force notices, huge numbers were being sent to schools that were primarily majority minority," he says.

But Jim Finberg, the lead attorney in the *Vergara* case for the California Teachers Association, the state's largest teacher's union, says teachers are being unfairly blamed for problems over which they have no control. "There is an achievement gap in this country, but it is not caused by tenure statutes or the dismissal statutes, it's caused by the fact that poor, inner-city schools are under-resourced, and higher-crime schools and the teachers in those schools don't get support," he says.

Studies have shown that if a school district provides sufficient resources to poorer schools with high minority populations and supports its teachers, it can close the achievement gap, Finberg says. "You put your strongest principals in those schools and you will attract good teachers and keep them," he says. "Working conditions in schools are the single biggest factor when it comes to keeping teachers."

Jeff Seymour, a former school superintendent in El Monte, Calif., who testified on behalf of the state, told the court that administrators engaging in the "dance of the lemons" were not doing their job, and there were other ways to deal with subpar teachers, such as helping them find ways to succeed.

He defended teacher tenure, saying it gives teachers the job security to try creative ways to reach students. "It also protects teachers who are good teachers from arbitrary behavior on the part of principals who come in and may have a very set view of how a school should be run and are not willing to look at the success of those teachers and make their judgments after that," Seymour said.[35]

But Bhavini Bhakta, an elementary teacher who lost positions in four schools over eight years, including a year she won a school's Golden Apple Teacher of the Year Award, testified on behalf of the plaintiffs that California's "first-in, first-out" retention rules discouraged young teachers. "I just felt like no matter what work I did in the classroom, or how hard I worked, none of it mattered because the seniority date mattered way more than how much I did for kids, or what principals would say about me, or what parents would say about me, [or] my love for it," Bhakta testified. "None of it mattered, nothing . . . all that mattered was my hire date."[36]

New York University's Ravitch, however, has questioned the logic behind eliminating rules that protect senior teachers. "Is there any evidence that firing experienced teachers raises student achievement? Well, actually, no," Ravitch wrote in her education blog.[37]

Yet a study by researchers at Stanford and the University of Virginia in Charlottesville found that when New York City established a more rigorous performance review before granting tenure, the less-effective teachers left the system. Fewer teachers at schools with a larger proportion of black students were granted tenure, prompting the authors to conclude that the change was likely to benefit black students. "[It's] likely replacement teachers will be more effective than . . . teachers who leave, leading to an improvement of teaching in these schools" said James H. Wyckoff, a co-author and education professor at the University of Virginia.[38]

Tenure rules also have been an issue in North Carolina, home to the John Locke Foundation. Director Stoops says reforming tenure law is "necessary, but insufficient."

He adds: "Even if you take away tenure, the number of low-performing teachers who will be taken out of poor-performing schools is probably rather low. We also need to look at teacher training, teacher recruitment, whether our [teacher licensing requirements] provide a barrier to individuals in the private sectors.

"All these issues are intertwined in raising the quality of our teachers."

BACKGROUND
Legal Segregation

The separate educational systems that existed for black children and white children across a swath of America before *Brown v. Board of Education* were part of a larger system of legal segregation. Following the post-Civil War Reconstruction Era, Southern states re-established a system of white privilege using laws that separated whites from people of color in schools, housing, businesses and public facilities.[39]

In 1892 blacks in New Orleans challenged a law that required railroads to provide "equal but separate accommodations for the white, and colored, races."[40] Homer Plessy, a black shoemaker, agreed to be arrested for refusing to move from a seat reserved for whites. The case made its way to the Supreme Court in 1896, and in its infamous *Plessy v. Ferguson* ruling the court, with only one dissenting vote, held that "separate but equal" facilities were constitutional.[41]

Twenty states eventually passed laws separating students by race. They included the Southern states of the old Confederacy, several neighboring states as well as Wyoming, New Mexico and Arizona in the West.[42]

Most Northern states did not have laws requiring segregated schools, but the races remained largely segregated by custom and housing patterns. The Economic Policy Institute's Rothstein says those housing patterns were in large part created, and continue to be affected, by government policies that encouraged segregation in housing, particularly after World War II. For example, when Levittown, N.Y.,

Then and Now
White students at Central High School in Littel Rock, Ark., try to stop African-American students from entering the school on Sept. 9, 1957 (top). That year Arkansas Gov. Orval Faubus forcibly resisted integration in the state in the wake of the Supreme court's landmark *Brown v. Board of Education* ruling in 1954. President Dwight D. Eisenhower called in federal troops to enforce school integration in Little Rock. More recently, police officers in Raleigh, N.C., forcibly removed a pro-busing advocate from a Wake County school board meeting on school busing on March 23, 2010 (bottom). The board voted to stop busing students for diversity and took the first steps toward setting up a community-based system of student assignment.

CHRONOLOGY

1950s *Supreme Court declares segregated schools unconstitutional, but Southern states resist integration.*

1954 In *Brown v. Board of Education*, the Supreme Court rules segregated schools are "inherently unequal" but does not set a desegregation deadline.

1957 After Arkansas Gov. Orval Faubus forcibly resists integration, President Dwight D. Eisenhower deploys federal troops to enforce the integration, by nine African-American students, of Little Rock's Central High School.

1960s *Civil rights reform and school desegregation accelerate.*

1963 An estimated 250,000 Americans rally for civil rights in the March on Washington, during which the Rev. Martin Luther King Jr. gives his "I have a dream" speech.

1964 President Lyndon B. Johnson signs Civil Rights Act of 1964, which prohibits discrimination based on race, color, religion or national origin and empowers federal government to sue to desegregate schools.

1969 In a case concerning Mississippi schools, the Supreme Court declares its previous desegregation standard — with "all deliberate speed" — is no longer permissible, and the schools must desegregate immediately (*Alexander v. Holmes County Bd. of Ed.*).

1970s *Student busing speeds desegregation, but later court rulings limit the reach of desegregation orders.*

1971 In *Swann v. Charlotte-Mecklenburg Board of Education*, the Supreme Court upholds busing to integrate schools.

1973 The Supreme Court finds that Denver intentionally segregated Mexican-American and black students from white students (*Keyes v. Denver School District No. 1*).

1974 In a Detroit case, the Supreme Court blocks metropolitan-wide integration plans, limiting desegregation of racially isolated urban districts (*Milliken v. Bradley*).

1980s *School integration peaks.*

1986 Federal court finds that once a school district meets certain conditions it can be released from its court-ordered desegregation plan and returned to local control.

1988 School integration reaches all-time high; almost 44 percent of black students attend majority-white schools.

1990s *A more conservative Supreme Court makes it easier for school districts to exit desegregation orders.*

1991 Emphasizing that court orders are not intended "to operate in perpetuity," the Supreme Court, in a case concerning Oklahoma City, makes it easier for school systems to fulfill desegregation decrees. The Oklahoma City school system abandons desegregation and returns to neighborhood schools (*Board of Education of Oklahoma City v. Dowell*).

1995 Supreme Court sets new goal for desegregation: the return of schools to local control, saying judicial remedies were intended to be "limited in time and extent."

2000-Present *Studies indicate schools have become more segregated; Supreme Court changes integration rules.*

2003 Harvard's Civil Rights Project finds that schools were more segregated in 2000 than in 1970 when busing began.

2004 Nation marks 50th anniversary of *Brown v. Board of Education*.

2007 In a case concerning Seattle and Louisville, the Supreme Court rules that schools can no longer take a student's race into explicit account for purposes of integration (*Parents Involved in Community Schools v. Seattle School District No. 1*).

2014 California judge rules teacher tenure rules violate state constitution by denying minority and poorer children equal access to quality education.

the first modern suburb, was built on Long Island after World War II, many of the homes were sold to returning veterans — but only white veterans. At the time, he adds, the Federal Housing Administration would not insure mortgages to African-Americans.

"Most of the policy designed to segregate metropolitan areas came from the federal government," says Rothstein. And segregated neighborhoods meant largely segregated schools.

Brown v. Board of Education

In the 1930s, the NAACP and the law school at Howard University, a leading historically black institution in Washington, D.C., began a campaign to bring down the idea of separate but equal facilities through a series of legal challenges.[43]

But the University of Connecticut's Cobb says black leaders settled on overturning *Plessy v. Ferguson* only after repeated failures to get the United States to live up to the "equal" part of separate but equal.

"There was a lot of ambivalence. The extended narrative is that African-Americans were eager for desegregation, and that's not entirely true," Cobb says. "They spent years on cases trying to equalize [education]. They realized that was never going to get the results they wanted. The idea was that the only way you could prevent unequal education was to sit black kids next to the white kids, but [integration] wasn't the first priority, it was equality."

These challenges would finally lead to *Brown v. Board of Education*, which the Supreme Court decided in 1954. In a decision that would transform American society, the court ruled unanimously that segregated schools were unconstitutional. In his opinion, Chief Justice Earl Warren wrote, "We conclude that in the field of public education the doctrine of 'separate but equal' has no place. Separate educational facilities are inherently unequal."[44]

However, the court did not immediately set a timetable for desegregation. After more hearings, it declared in 1955 that desegregation was to proceed with "all deliberate speed."[45] The ambiguity of that directive led to protracted battles over desegregation.

Desegregation

Despite the *Brown* decision in 1954, there was little immediate change in the racial composition of school systems across the South or elsewhere. The year of the ruling, zero percent of black students in the South were in majority-white schools. By 1960, only 0.1 percent were.[46]

With many Southern politicians vowing to preserve segregation, even small changes came with difficulty. In a particularly high-profile incident, when Arkansas Gov. Orval Faubus used National Guard troops to block integration of Central High School in Little Rock in 1957, President Dwight D. Eisenhower deployed federal troops to protect nine African-American students from an angry white crowd as they entered the school.[47]

The number of integrated schools began to climb in 1964, the year Congress passed the Civil Rights Act, which outlawed discrimination based on race, color, sex, religion or national origin in many facets of society, including public education.[48]

In 1969, the Supreme Court abandoned its previous "all deliberate speed" standard and declared that schools must desegregate immediately.[49]

Two years later, in *Swann v. Charlotte-Mecklenburg* [North Carolina] *Board of Education*, the court upheld the busing of students to schools outside of their neighborhoods as a tool of desegregation, along with other potential remedies.

By 1970, a third of African-American children in the South were attending schools with a majority of white students. That percentage would continue to climb until 1988, when nearly 44 percent of African-American children would be in majority-white schools.[50]

By then, further court rulings and a shift in the American political climate had set the stage for a slow retreat from school desegregation.

Integration Declines

School busing for desegregation generated strong resistance, and not just in the South. Lengthy political and legal battles were fought over busing in Seattle, Denver, Detroit, Boston and other cities.[51]

In Detroit, the Ku Klux Klan blew up empty buses in the white suburb of Pontiac to prevent them from being used to integrate schools.[52] In Boston, African-American children arriving at newly integrated schools were greeted by angry white mobs that tried to block their entry.[53]

Charter Schools' Performance Varies

"Charter schools are benefiting low-income, disadvantaged students."

Judged by their numbers, charter schools are one of the great educational success stories of the last 25 years. In 1990 there were no U.S. charter schools. Last school year, about 2.3 million students attended more than 6,000 charters, and they now account for nearly 6 percent of all public schools.[1]

But since the charter movement began, that growth has been accompanied by a heated debate about whether charter schools really do a better job of educating children than traditional public schools. With charter schools flourishing in minority, inner-city neighborhoods in Eastern cities and doing well in mostly white suburban communities in the West and Midwest, the debate has relevance to questions of racial balance in schools.

Charter schools, which receive taxpayer funding like traditional public schools but generally do not have to follow the same rules, were intended to encourage innovation in education. While outstanding charter schools have existed from the beginning, early studies found education quality varied widely. Some of the most credible studies found that charters performed no better or slightly worse, on average, than traditional schools, based on tests and other measures of academic progress.[2]

Two new studies indicate charters have been making gains, while another indicates their performance remains on a par with traditional schools.

The most comprehensive study, by Stanford University's Center for Research on Education Outcomes, compared the standardized test scores of charter school students in 25 states and the District of Columbia with the scores of similar students in the traditional public schools the students would have otherwise attended. "The results reveal that the charter school sector is getting better on average and that charter schools are benefiting low-income, disadvantaged, and special education students," said Margaret Raymond, center director.[3]

The study found results improved compared with 2009, when the center conducted a similar study of 16 states. The earlier study found that only 17 percent of charter schools showed academic gains significantly better than traditional schools, while 37 percent showed gains that were worse.[4] The other 46 percent performed about the same as their counterparts. "The issue of quality is the most pressing problem that the charter school movement faces," Raymond said at the time.

In the new study, however, 25 percent of the charters were better than traditional schools in reading and 29 percent in math. Nineteen percent of charters were worse for reading and 31 percent for math. The study also found that African-American students and those living in poverty or who are learning English made some of the most impressive gains.[5]

Critics were quick to point out the largest share of charters still performed no better than their traditional

President Richard M. Nixon, elected in 1968, opposed forced school busing. While vowing to uphold the law, he ordered administration officials to work with school districts to minimize busing.[54] Nixon also would end up filling four Supreme Court vacancies by the end of 1971, making the court more conservative.

In 1974, the court established a limit on court-ordered busing that many analysts believe marked the beginning of the end of school desegregation in many metropolitan areas and increased white flight to the suburbs. In *Milliken v. Bradley*, the court ruled 5-4 against a Detroit desegregation plan that would have bused large numbers of black children between the city and 53 separate school districts in the largely white suburbs.[55] The ruling stated the suburbs did not have to be part of a larger desegregation plan because there was no evidence that they had violated the law within their districts. It also emphasized the importance of local control of schools and said desegregation did not require "any particular racial balance in each school, grade or classroom."[56]

counterparts. "The message here, no matter how it is framed, is that 20 years after the start of the charter school movement, even with all the private energy and public policy cheerleading it has engendered, students in charter schools roughly perform the same as students in the rest of public education — not the leaps and bounds that were promised," said Randi Weingarten, president of the American Federation of Teachers, whose 1.6 million members include about 8,000 charter school employees.[6]

Providing further support to critics, a comparison of test scores in Chicago conducted by the *Chicago Sun-Times* and the Medill Data Project at Northwestern University showed little difference in performance between the two kinds of schools.[7]

But a study of six major Boston charters found they were doing significantly better in important measures of post-high school academic success. Charters boosted the frequency of Advanced Placement test-taking, college entrance-exam scores and the chances that students qualified for exam-based college scholarships, the study found.[8]

In conjunction with the Stanford study, the results indicate successful charter schools are doing an above-average job of educating students, but vary greatly in student achievement. "As welcome as these changes are, more work remains to be done to ensure that all charter schools provide their students high-quality education," said Raymond.[9]

— *Reed Karaim*

Ninth-graders take a break between classes at Shasta charter public high school in Daly City, Calif., where the "blended learning model" lets students learn at their own pace in a big, open classroom.

[1] "National Data on the Public Charter School Movement," National Alliance for Public Charter Schools, http://dashboard.publiccharters.org/dashboard/home.

[2] "America's Charter Schools: Results from the NAEP 2003 Study," The National Assessment of Education Progress, U.S. Department of Education, December 2004, http://tinyurl.com/3xark37. Also see

[3] "Multiple Choice: Charter School Performance in 16 States," Center for Research on Education Outcomes, Stanford University, June 2009, http://tinyurl.com/lz8nrh.

[3] "Charter Schools Make Gains, According to 26-State Study," Center for Research on Education Outcomes, Stanford University, June 2013, http://tinyurl.com/ox2p84b.

[4] "Multiple Choice: Charter School Performance in 16 States," *op. cit.*

[5] "Charter Schools Make Gains, According to 26-state study," *op. cit.*

[6] "AFT Statement on CREDO Charter School Study," American Federation of Teachers, June 25, 2013, http://tinyurl.com/mzz75hj.

[7] Darnell Little, "Charter schools show little difference in school performance," *The Chicago Sun-Times*, April 7, 2014, http://tinyurl.com/lpkamw8.

[8] "Charter Schools and the Road to College Readiness: The Effects on College Preparation, Attendance and Choice," The Boston Foundation and NewSchools Venture Fund, May 2013, http://tinyurl.com/mz6v4qv.

[9] "Charter Schools Make Gains, According to 26-state study," *op. cit.*

Civil rights lawyers continued to pursue school desegregation cases in the 1970s and '80s and won victories in several cities, but in some cases the federal government opposed those efforts.[57]

In the 1980s and '90s, federal judges began to release school districts from court-ordered desegregation plans, finding that they had achieved their objectives. "Under the Reagan administration, there was suddenly an effort to close down these cases," says Rothstein of the Economic Policy Institute.

"The Justice Department actually went around to school districts suggesting that they move to dismiss cases."

More than 200 large and medium-sized school districts were released from desegregation orders from 1991 to 2010, according to a study by Stanford University's School of Education.[58]

Once the schools were released from the plans, racial segregation rose, the study found. "There are some districts where you see a sudden jump in segregation

Louisville Schools Strive to Integrate

In 2007 the Supreme Court struck down the school system's desegregation plan.

At a time when studies indicate U.S. schools are resegregating, the efforts of Kentucky's Jefferson County school district to preserve diversity reveal the challenges of maintaining an integrated school system in today's legal and political environment.

Jefferson County, which includes Louisville and its suburbs, has more than 101,000 students from a wide variety of ethnic, racial and socio-economic backgrounds.[1] For about 7,000 students, who speak 107 different languages at home, English is a second language, says Linda Duncan, a longtime school board member. About two-thirds of the students receive a free or subsidized lunch, and some 13,000 have no fixed address, she says.

School integration in the district began in 1975, when a federal judge ordered the largely white county school system and largely black city system to consolidate to achieve greater racial balance. Amid angry protests by white residents, Jefferson County began busing students to schools around the district to comply with the order.

By the 1990s, the system was considered the nation's most racially integrated.[2] But over time, white flight and other demographic shifts made it more difficult for the district to maintain racial balance. In 1998, a group of African-American families sued the district, frustrated that their children could not get into the historically black Central High because the school was struggling to maintain the required ratio of white students. Two years later a judge released the district from its desegregation plan.

A 2012 study of U.S. school districts by Stanford University's School of Education found that among the more than 200 districts that have been released from a court-ordered desegregation plan, there usually was a return to racial segregation.[3] But Louisville's civic leaders decided they did not want to turn back.

"The desegregation plan actually had a lot of support in the community," says Sheldon Berman, who would become superintendent of the Jefferson County system a few years later. "It actually created an attitude . . . about addressing race in an effective way."

However, some families — still upset with the school choices available to their children — objected and filed another lawsuit. In 2007 the Supreme Court struck down the Louisville plan in a landmark 5-4 decision. Writing for the majority, Chief Justice John Roberts said schools that never segregated on the basis of race "or that have removed the vestiges of past segregation, such as Jefferson County" must stop assigning students to school explicitly on the basis of race.[4]

Berman became Jefferson County superintendent two days after the ruling. The decision, he notes, could have meant the end of 32 years of school desegregation. Instead, Berman says, the school board initiated an intense community discussion, utilizing public forums, opinion polling and online surveys. The dialogue established that most parents and community members favored a continuing commitment to diversity.

In a document titled "No Retreat," the district outlined a new plan that no longer assigned students explicitly based on race. Instead, it created six geographic subdivisions, each with 12 to 15 elementary schools, with diverse student populations

after the release from the court order," says Reardon, the lead researcher. "But the more common pattern is this sort of slow, gradual increase in segregation, in ways that are . . . consistent with a slow return to neighborhood schools and neighborhood levels of segregation."

But some school districts worked to maintain their desegregation plans even after being released from the court orders.

In Kentucky, the Jefferson County School District, which includes Louisville and surrounding suburbs, was released from its original court order in 2000. But civic leaders and school administrators remained committed to desegregation, despite opposition from some parents, and implemented a voluntary student-assignment plan in an effort to maintain school integration.

That plan was struck down by a 2007 Supreme Court ruling that declared school districts could no longer

based on race, household income and adult educational attainment. To attract a broad range of students from across socio-economic and racial lines, the plan called for converting several inner city schools into magnet schools.[5]

The plan won national recognition from scholars and the media for finding a way to maintain diversity that didn't violate the Supreme Court ruling. Daniel Kiel, a University of Memphis law professor who specializes in race and education, called the plan "a model for districts seeking to capture the educational benefits of diverse schools."[6]

But the plan had opponents, including a group of Jefferson County parents who sued to block it. Families were upset with the distance some children still had to travel, Duncan says. "Time on the bus was a big problem," she says. Berman contends that discontent came primarily from some families in the district's wealthier east side, who were unhappy with how the plan connected their area to poorer, urban neighborhoods.

The plan became a political issue in both the next mayoral and gubernatorial elections. The board finally decided on a revised approach, which Berman says he felt would leave the district's schools more segregated than he could accept. He took a job with an Oregon school district in 2011.

That revised plan, to be phased in over the next four years, creates smaller geographic clusters of elementary schools. It will allow more children to attend schools closer to home, Duncan says, but it will also leave schools in some poorer, minority neighborhoods with largely minority populations.

Berman credits the district for not abandoning its effort completely, but he is pessimistic about the future of integration in Jefferson County and the nation as a whole. "Without federal leadership we're not going to make any changes . . .," he says. "We're back to a system that divides us."

Duncan is more optimistic. "I think we're maintaining the idea of having diverse schools," she says. "I think we value diversity, and we're committed to it. But I think diversity is a lot more these days than African-American diversity."

Wilt Elementary School, in southern Jefferson County, could be considered an example of that new diversity. Its student body is 19 percent black, 60 percent white and 20 percent Hispanic, Asian or another race. The students speak 11 different languages.[7]

Jefferson County is using a variety of approaches, including specialized programs and high-achieving magnet schools, especially for middle and high school students, to maintain diversity. But the system is complicated, Duncan says, and depends more on personal choice. And while some schools are becoming less integrated, she says, "I do believe we're going to maintain diverse schools. I do not see us going back to segregated schools. No way."

— *Reed Karaim*

---

[1] "Data Management and Research Department," Jefferson County Public Schools, http://tinyurl.com/m97vak7.

[2] Sarah Garland, *Divided We Fail: The Story of the African American Community that Ended the Era of School Desegregation* (2013), p. 19.

[3] Daniel S. Levine, "Schools resegregate after being freed from judicial oversight, Stanford study shows," *Stanford News*, Dec. 5, 2012, http://tinyurl.com/a2a6ens.

[4] *Parents Involved in Community Schools v. Seattle School District No. 1*, 551 U.S. 701 (2007), http://tinyurl.com/72nzlyk.

[5] "No Retreat: The JCPS Commitment to School Integration," Jefferson County Public Schools, http://tinyurl.com/p3op4pw.

[6] Sheldon Berman, "Student Assignment Under Louisville's 2008 Plan," *School Administrator*, December 2013, http://tinyurl.com/k9g52qs.

[7] Lesli A. Maxwell, "Ky. District 'Keeps Faith' on School Desegregation," *Education Week*, May 13, 2014, http://tinyurl.com/lzr5joo.

---

explicitly take the race of students into account when attempting to integrate schools. "The way to stop discrimination on the basis of race is to stop discriminating on the basis of race," said Chief Justice John Roberts, who wrote the majority opinion.[59]

Roberts proclaimed the court's decision true to the spirit of *Brown v. Board of Education*. Justice John Paul Stevens, who wrote a dissenting opinion, disagreed sharply, saying Roberts' decision "rewrites the history of one of this court's most important decisions."[60]

Today, 60 years after the Supreme Court's 1954 ruling, many analysts see the country retreating from its commitment to desegregation. "The bottom line is that children of color are still far more likely to find themselves in schools that are segregated by race or ethnicity and are much more likely to be involved in schools with high poverty concentration," says the ACLU's Parker.

Former CNN anchor Campbell Brown, founder of the Partnership for Educational Justice, announces the organization's legal challenge to New York City's teacher tenure laws on July 28, 2014. The group contends that tenure fosters weak teaching that is having a negative effect on minority and poor students. "Often, the teachers who are ineffective end up concentrated in the most disadvantaged neighborhoods in the poorest schools where the kids need the most help," she said.

CURRENT SITUATION

Education Challenges

The debate about American public education no longer revolves around integration as it did in the 1960s and '70s. Instead it is focused largely on standardized testing, school and teacher accountability and the growing school choice movement.

Yet many of these issues continue to involve questions of racial equity, made more pressing by the changing U.S. student population. For the first time, the nation's 99,000 public schools this fall are projected to have more minority students than non-Hispanic whites, according to the National Center for Education Statistics.[61] Non-Hispanic whites will still be the largest group in schools, but taken together, other groups will make up slightly more than 50 percent of the school population. The second-largest group will be Hispanic students, expected to make up nearly a quarter of the population, while African-Americans will make up about 15 percent.[62]

The challenge to teacher tenure laws also appears to be gaining strength. In July, the advocacy group Partnership for Educational Justice, founded by former CNN anchor Campbell Brown, announced it was challenging New York City's teacher tenure laws in court, citing the effect weak teaching was having on minority and poor students.

"Often the teachers who are ineffective end up concentrated in the most disadvantaged neighborhoods in the poorest schools where the kids need the most help," Brown said.[63]

Those comments echoed a key argument used by Students Matter, the advocacy group that pushed its successful case against teacher tenure laws in California. Students Matter recently joined the New York lawsuit and is considering initiating action in Minnesota, New Mexico and Washington state, says spokesperson Schein.

The National Education Association (NEA), the nation's largest teachers' union, has denounced the efforts as attempts by corporate interests working to privatize public education by undermining teachers' unions.[64] California's teachers' unions are appealing the *Vergara* ruling.

"This will not be the last word," said Weingarten, of the American Federation of Teachers.[65]

Students in poorer schools also face challenges due to fewer resources when it comes to taking standardized tests, which are used to determine both whether students are on track and whether schools are succeeding. State standardized achievement tests became a significant part of the American education landscape with passage of the No Child Left Behind Act in 2001. The Obama administration, which supports standardized testing to measure student progress and hold educators accountable for their performance, announced in June that it would expand the use of standardized testing for special-needs students and Native Americans.[66]

In a detailed analysis published in July in *The Atlantic*, Meredith Broussard, a data-journalism professor at Temple University in Philadelphia, examined the challenge faced by students in poorer schools taking standardized achievement tests. She found that the testing companies publish textbooks containing the answers and the wording to express them most likely to be judged correct. But many poorer schools cannot afford those texts, leaving their students and teachers at a significant disadvantage.[67]

AT ISSUE

Are U.S. schools becoming resegregated?

YES Dennis Parker
Director, Racial Justice Program, American Civil Liberties Union

Written for *CQ Researcher*, August 2014

Looking at the persistent isolation of students of color in American schools, it is difficult to believe that six decades have passed since the U.S. Supreme Court condemned legally imposed racial segregation in *Brown v. Board of Education*.

After initial massive resistance to the court's mandate, there was a significant reduction in segregation, particularly in the South, where most school desegregation cases occurred. However, more recently, ongoing discrimination and the effects of complex institutional and structural bias have threatened those gains, leaving the nation more diverse overall but with more of its students confined to segregated schools.

In districts, primarily in the South, that experienced the greatest progress in desegregating because of legal action, release from court supervision has been accompanied by steadily increasing resegregation, beginning almost immediately after dismissal. In the North, housing segregation sustained racially segregated schools, resulting in a concentration of the nation's most segregated schools in Northern cities. As a result, an increasing percentage of blacks and Latinos attend racially and ethnically segregated schools. Particularly disturbing: These segregated schools are far more likely to have a high poverty concentration.

Arguments that segregated schools are the benign result of personal housing choices are wrong and dangerous. The legal ban on segregation does not change the powerful forces that continue to segregate students by race and ethnicity and isolate students of color from equal educational opportunity. Government and private enforcers of fair housing laws have demonstrated the continuing existence of housing discrimination and a range of other discriminatory factors, such as a long history of predatory lending, which have disproportionately limited the choices of people of color.

But regardless of the cause of segregation, its impact is often devastating. All students are deprived of the benefits of diversity in education. But the deprivations associated with segregation are most sharply felt by students who have been deprived of opportunity historically. Students in racially, ethnically and economically isolated schools are condemned to institutions with fewer resources, fewer experienced, certified teachers and more pressure on the schools due to the additional costs associated with educating disadvantaged students.

Passively allowing the resegregation of U.S. schools unfairly disadvantages the students who could benefit most from quality education and disserves the nation as a whole. We owe more to our children and to ourselves.

NO Roger Clegg
President and General Counsel, Center for Equal Opportunity

Written for *CQ Researcher*, August 2014

No child today attends a segregated public school. Not one. "Segregation" means telling children they cannot attend the same school as children of a different color. It does not mean a failure to have socially engineered racial balance.

It is true that there are educational disparities across racial lines, but racial imbalances in classrooms have little if anything to do with this. Black children do not need a certain number of white children in a classroom in order to learn.

The real reasons that racial disparities exist are ignored by those who complain about "resegregation."

When you think about it, a child's environment has three major components — parents, schools and peers — and in all three respects African-American children face more hurdles. They are more likely to grow up in single-parent homes, go to substandard schools and have peers who are, to put it mildly, unsupportive of academic achievement.

But the left is slow to acknowledge that out-of-wedlock births are a bad thing or that anti-"acting white" peer pressure exists. They will admit that substandard schools are a problem, but resist (partly because of recalcitrant teacher unions) the most promising reforms: competition among schools, merit pay for teachers and more choice for parents and children.

The only way to bring schools into the politically correct racial balance that the left wants is not by ignoring students' skin color, but by using it to sort, assign and bus them. This is flatly inconsistent with *Brown v. Board of Education*, which prohibited race-based student assignments.

In addition, there is no increase in racial imbalance in schools. In *No Excuses: Closing the Racial Gap in Learning*, Stephan and Abigail Thernstrom conclude that "minority students are not becoming more racially isolated; white students typically attend schools that are much more racially and ethnically diverse than 30 years ago, and the modest decline in the exposure of black and Hispanic children to whites is solely due to the declining share of white children in the school-age population." And race is no proxy for disadvantage.

Nor is there any validity in the left's premise that more racial balance means better education. To quote the Thernstroms again: "The most sophisticated research on the subject does not find that having white classmates notably improves the academic achievement of blacks and Hispanics."

So forget racial bean-counting and focus on improving our schools.

Opposition to standardized testing is growing. Many opponents, such as Fairtest.org and other groups, say the tests are racially biased. The NEA stepped up its public disagreement with the Obama administration over testing in July, when it called on Education Secretary Arne Duncan to resign.[68]

NEA President Lily Eskelsen García harshly criticized the idea that teachers working in schools that can differ widely in resources and student demographics should be judged by the performance of their classes on standardized tests. "It's stupid. It's absurd. It's non-defensible," García said.[69]

Public schools are financed with federal, state and local funds. The federal government's contribution is about 12 percent of expenditures, but the amount provided by state and local governments varies widely by state.[70] In states that depend largely on local property taxes, significant differences between wealthy and poorer school districts exist. Wealthier districts can spend three times as much per student as nearby poorer districts. Wealthier states also generally spend more per student.[71]

Opposition to standardized tests is also growing as some school districts reject the use of the Common Core, a set of math and English language standards for students in kindergarten through 12th grade. Contrary to widely held beliefs, the standards were not developed by the federal government, but rather by the bipartisan National Governors Association Center for Best Practices and the Council of Chief State School Officers. However, the Obama administration has supported them through its Race to the Top education initiative, which aims to improve achievement by providing points toward federal grants for states that adopt the Common Core.[72]

Many conservatives oppose Common Core because they believe it reduces local control of education, while other groups say the standards do not put the proper emphasis on certain topics or areas of learning.[73]

Enforcing Civil Rights

The Obama administration gets mixed reviews on enforcement of existing school desegregation orders and addressing racial inequality in education.

The ACLU's Parker says desegregation "has not been a priority" of the administration. "Criticism has been made that programs like Race to the Top do not sufficiently take desegregation and racial diversity into account," he says. "It would be useful if the federal government made those [issues] part of their consideration, so the schools receiving grants actively encouraged integration."

But Jim Eichner, managing director of the Advancement Project, a Washington-based civil rights organization, credits the administration for its work in areas important to the organization, specifically harsher punishments, including arrests, handed out to students of color compared to whites for minor school disciplinary infractions.

"I would certainly give them very high marks on school discipline," Eichner says. "They've really done a lot on that." The Justice Department has worked with school districts to reform disciplinary policies, he says, and earlier this year the Education and Justice departments issued guidance on the degree to which discrimination in discipline violates the Civil Rights Act.

"It made a huge difference to have the federal government say not only is discriminatory discipline a big deal, but it can be a violation of federal law," says Eichner.[74]

On Aug. 19, the Los Angeles Unified School District announced it will arrest fewer students in school discipline cases. A report by a civil rights group last year found that Los Angeles students were more likely to receive a criminal citation for discipline infractions than students in Chicago, Philadelphia or New York. And other studies had found that black and Latino students were far more likely than whites to face harsh disciplinary procedures in Los Angeles.

"We're talking about schoolyard fights that a couple of decades ago nobody would have ever thought would lead to arrest," said Ruth Cusick, an education rights lawyer for Public Counsel, a nonprofit group that helped draft the new policies. "The criminalizing of this behavior only goes on in low-income communities."[75]

In addition, the Advancement Project is mounting a campaign against school closings that the organization claims have disproportionately affected students of color. "We're also encouraged that [the administration] has recently agreed to look at the school closing issue," Eichner says.

Although hundreds of school districts have been released from federal court desegregation orders, many orders are still in place. Approximately half the almost 500 school districts that were under court order to desegregate in 1990 had been released by 2012, according to a Stanford University study.[76]

The Justice and Education departments don't actively track desegregation orders and are uncertain how many are still in force. "We didn't even have records," said Russlynn H. Ali, the Education Department's assistant secretary for civil rights in President Obama's first term. The department is now asking districts to report whether they are operating under an order or desegregation plan.[77]

An investigation by *Politico*, the political news website, found that the Justice Department used its authority to enforce desegregation orders to intervene in local decisions at least 43 times during Obama's first term. In a case in Beaufort County, S.C., the department intervened when a nearly all-white charter school was about to open. A revised plan for student recruitment and enrollment significantly boosted minority attendance.[78]

The Justice Department also worked out an agreement with the Tucson, Ariz., school district to bring back a Mexican-American studies program last year as a step toward conforming with a court-ordered desegregation program. In a battle that attracted national attention, the district had eliminated the program after the state, which said the program violated a state law that prohibits ethnic studies, threatened to withhold funding.[79]

State Action

The movement to encourage charters and choice continues unabated, despite debate over whether they are of benefit to minority groups.

An annual assessment released by the National Alliance for Public Charter Schools found that 12 states increased their support for charters in 2013, while three — Mississippi, New Hampshire and Texas — raised or removed caps on the number of charter schools allowed.[80]

States seem to be even more active this year. According to the National Council of State Legislatures' online database, 28 states have already enacted 71 new bills covering a wide range of charter school activities, including many that provide new financing options or make it easier for charters to open.[81]

Fifteen states also enacted laws governing other school choice measures, including several intended to expand the use of school vouchers. But states are not spending more on education overall. A study by *FiveThirtyEight*, statistician Nate Silver's website, found that state spending per student fell sharply from 2007 to 2010 as a result of the recession and did not significantly recover from 2010 to 2012, the most recent year for which data are available.[82]

The reduced state education spending, when combined with reductions in federal support for public education that came as federal stimulus funds ran out, led total school spending to fall in 2012 for the first time since 1977. The study found that urban districts have been particularly hard hit, with nearly 90 percent spending less per student in 2012 than when the recession ended in 2009.[83]

OUTLOOK
Changes Coming?

Many experts believe the nation's attitudes concerning race and education could be changing.

When it comes to school segregation, "if you draw a straight line from what's happening, it's going to get worse and worse," says UCLA's Orfield.

But the public mood could change, he says, noting that the Supreme Court is generally divided 5-4 on issues of racial integration, so a change in one member could return the court to its earlier stance supporting more aggressive school desegregation and "bring the issue back to life."

Penn State's Frankenberg is one of several education experts who believe a broader approach is needed to bring about lasting change. "If we really want to [desegregate] our schools, we need to make desegregation a more essential issue and not peripheral," she says. "But we also need to think about desegregating other parts of our society."

Also looking at segregation through a larger lens, the University of Connecticut's Cobb says, "The most pernicious thing in our contemporary politics as it pertains to race is the ascendant culture of white grievance," in which whites see themselves as victims of pro-minority laws. As long as that remains a powerful force in contemporary politics, he says, "we'll remain exactly where we are."

However, Cobb notes, desegregation hit its stride during the era of civil rights reform in the 1960s, fed by protests and activism among young people determined to change the system. That mass movement occurred only after African-Americans reached a level of frustration in which they believed they had no choice but to upend the system. He believes the nation could be reaching a similar moment as minority groups face a level of unequal treatment that leads to large-scale social and political action.

But the Center for Equal Opportunity's Clegg says that rather than focusing on race, the future of education depends on continuing to open the field to competition. "If we focus on improving education and we forget about racial and ethnic bean counting and we refuse to see the challenges through the distorting prism of race," he says, "then I'm optimistic."

On the other hand, the Advancement Project's Eichner says changes in the U.S. population are likely to have a significant impact on the politics of public education in the next few decades as the nation's white majority disappears before the middle of the century. Continuing high levels of immigration and the rapidly growing Latino population, which has so far been less attracted to charter schools, will result in dramatic shifts in the racial composition of the school-age population.[84]

In addition, says Schein of Students Matter, "Changes in demographics bring changes in policies. So there could be a dramatic change in the way public education looks in the next generation."

The ACLU's Parker is encouraged by the ongoing public debate about education. "I've been seeing more discussions about how you can educate kids. I've been seeing more programs that are designed to deal with issues.

"There's more of a recognition that there is a real crisis in American education, and so I'm hopeful we will find a way to deal with some of the larger problems in our education system that affect everyone, but particularly the inequalities and the way they affect some students," he says.

"There's a lot going on," he continues. "You have to be hopeful."

NOTES

1. Nikole Hannah-Jones, "Segregation Now; In Tuscaloosa today, nearly one in three black students attends a school that looks as if *Brown v. Board of Education* never happened," *ProPublica*, April 16, 2014, http://tinyurl.com/o7zoyox.

2. *Ibid.*

3. *Ibid.*

4. Gary Orfield, Erica Frankenberg, *et al.*, "*Brown* at 60: Great Progress, a Long Retreat and an Uncertain Future," The Civil Rights Project, May 15, 2014, p. 10, http://tinyurl.com/n9cok4e.

5. *Ibid.*

6. Paul Tractenberg, Gary Orfield and Greg Flaxman, "New Jersey's Apartheid and Intensely Segregated Urban Schools: Powerful Evidence of an Inefficient and Unconstitutional State Education System," Institute on Education Law and Policy, Rutgers University, October 2013, http://tinyurl.com/pdql4po.

7. Abigail and Stephan Thernstrom, "Brown at 60: An American success story," *The Wall Street Journal*, May 13, 2013, http://tinyurl.com/nmq2wp8.

8. Orfield and Frankenberg, *op. cit.*, p. 23.

9. *Ibid.*, p. 2.

10. For background, see Sarah Glazer, "Wealth and Inequality," *CQ Researcher*, April 18, 2014, pp. 337-360; and Marcia Clemmitt, "Income Inequality," *CQ Researcher*, Dec. 3, 2010, pp. 989-1012.

11. Kori J. Stroub and Meredith P. Richards, "From Resegregation to Reintegration: Trends in the Racial/Ethnic Segregation of Metropolitan Public Schools, 1993–2009," *American Educational Research Journal*, June 2013, http://tinyurl.com/qbpp3np.

12. Abigail and Stephen Thernstrom, *op. cit.*

13. *Ibid.*

14. Orfield and Frankenberg, *et al.*, *op. cit.*, p. 18.

15. John Kucsera, "New York State's Extreme School Segregation: Inequality, Inaction and a Damaged Future," The Civil Rights Project, UCLA, March 26, 2014, http://tinyurl.com/kl9ff48.

16. Orfield and Frankenberg, *et al.*, *op. cit.*, p. 2.
17. Howard Blume and Stephen Ceasar, "California teacher tenure is struck down: Expect years of appeals," *Los Angeles Times*, June 11, 2014, http://tinyurl.com/mwoyl68.
18. Orfield and Frankenberg, *op. cit.*, p. 10.
19. Rucker C. Johnson, "Long-Run Impacts of School Desegregation & School Quality on Adult Attainments," National Bureau of Economic Research, May 2014, http://tinyurl.com/katral3.
20. David L. Kirp, "Making Schools Work," *The New York Times*, May 19, 2012, http://tinyurl.com/osmyh77.
21. *Ibid.*
22. Charles T. Clotfelter, *After Brown: The Rise and Retreat of School Desegregation* (2004), p. 7.
23. Richard D. Kahlenberg, "The Charter School Idea Turns 20," *Education Week*, March 25, 2008, http://tinyurl.com/2fchqn.
24. "Fast Facts: Charter Schools," National Center for Education Statistics, http://tinyurl.com/m9o5nz5.
25. "National Data on the Public Charter School Movement," National Alliance for Public Charter Schools, undated, http://tinyurl.com/meeq2cg.
26. Erica Frankenberg, *et al.*, "Choice without Equity: Charter School Segregation and the Need for Civil Rights Standards," The Civil Rights Project, January 2010, http://tinyurl.com/2bby5fs.
27. "The National Charter School Study 2013," The Center for Research on Educational Outcomes, Stanford University, June 25, 2013, http://tinyurl.com/nhrnlhx.
28. Diane Ravitch, "The Charter School Mistake," *Los Angeles Times*, Oct. 10, 2013, http://tinyurl.com/ku7cjc6.
29. Frankenberg, *et al.*, *op. cit.*
30. Sarah Butrymowicz, "A new round of segregation plays out in charter schools," *The Hechinger Report*, July 15, 2013, http://tinyurl.com/py6gbto.
31. Greg Forster, "Freedom from Racial Barriers: The Empirical Evidence on Vouchers and Segregation," *School Choice Issues*, October 2006, http://tinyurl.com/mw24npu.
32. Cynthia Boyd, "Minnesota's new 'white flight': school open-enrollment program," *Minnpost*, Jan. 11, 2013, www.minnpost.com/community-sketchbook/2013/01/minnesota-s-new-white-flight-school-open-enrollment-program.
33. The complete text of the ruling is available through the Students Matter website: http://tinyurl.com/n225maa.
34. Ben Chapman and Stephen Rex Brown, "California millionaire joins fight against teacher tenure in New York," *The New York Daily News*, Aug. 6, 2014, http://tinyurl.com/l8dw22s.
35. "*Vergara* Trial: Superintendent Jeff Seymour Supports Teachers," California Teachers, March 28, 2014, http://tinyurl.com/kgwjzq7.
36. Bhavini Bhakta on "Last-In, First-Out" Layoffs — *Vergara v. California* Trial Day 7," Students Matter videos, Feb. 14, 2014, http://tinyurl.com/klqol4m.
37. Diane Ravitch, "What Do Celebrities and Superstars Know about Teaching," *Diane Ravitch's blog: A site to discuss better education for all*, Aug. 8, 2014, http://tinyurl.com/led4q8k.
38. "Tenure Reform Increases Voluntary Attrition of Less Effective Teachers in NYC, New Study Finds," Center for Education Policy Analysis, Stanford University, June 11, 2014, http://tinyurl.com/lmashlj.
39. "Separate is not Equal: *Brown v. Board of Education*," Smithsonian Museum of American History, http://tinyurl.com/37jyagd.
40. *Ibid.*
41. *Ibid.*
42. "The Rise and Fall of Jim Crow, Interactive Maps," PBS, http://tinyurl.com/n5hytmr.
43. "Separate is not Equal: *Brown v. Board of Education*," *op. cit.*
44. "History of *Brown v. Board of Education*," United States Courts website, http://tinyurl.com/o87rthw.
45. *Ibid.*
46. Orfield and Frankenberg, *op. cit.*, p. 10.
47. "Integration of Central High School," *History.com*, http://tinyurl.com/mkqldy5.
48. *Ibid.*

49. "*Brown v. Board*: Timeline of School Integration in the U.S.," Teaching Tolerance, a project of the Southern Poverty Law Center, http://tinyurl.com/nyqlcq7.
50. Orfield and Frankenberg, *op. cit.*, p. 10.
51. James Brook, "Court says Denver can end forced busing," *The New York Times*, Sept. 17, 1995, http://tinyurl.com/k2pdtop; "Busing in Seattle: A Well-Intentioned Failure," *Historylink.org*, http://tinyurl.com/lync9bt.
52. Sarah Alvarez, "How Court's Bus Ruling Sealed Differences In Detroit Schools," NPR, Nov. 19, 2013, http://tinyurl.com/omkwpuh.
53. Delores Handy, "40 Years Later, Boston Looks Back On Busing Crisis," WBUR, Boston NPR, March 30, 2012, http://tinyurl.com/mxrdbyo.
54. Richard Nixon, "Statement about the busing of schoolchildren," The American Presidency Project, Aug. 3, 1971, http://tinyurl.com/lyz272n.
55. Samantha Meinke, "*Milliken v. Bradley*: The Northern Battle for Desegregation," *Michigan Bar Journal*, September 2011, http://tinyurl.com/mts2ssy.
56. *Ibid.*
57. "School Desegregation and Equal Educational Opportunity," The Leadership Conference on Civil and Human Rights, undated, http://tinyurl.com/yfdcszy.
58. Daniel S. Levine, "Schools resegregate after being freed from judicial oversight, Stanford study shows," *Stanford News*, Dec. 5, 2012, http://tinyurl.com/a2a6ens.
59. Linda Greenhouse, "Justices Limit the Use of Race in School Plans for Integration," *The New York Times*, June 29 2007, http://tinyurl.com/mlpv8yu.
60. *Ibid.*
61. "Fast Facts," National Center for Education Statistics, http://tinyurl.com/o26wtr. Also see "White students to no longer be majority in U.S. public schools," CBS News, Aug. 10, 2014, http://tinyurl.com/mmjfjer.
62. *Ibid.*
63. "Inside City Hall: Campbell Brown & Keoni Wright Discuss Teacher Tenure," Partnership for Educational Justice, Aug. 6, 2014, http://tinyurl.com/myj8tp2.
64. "NEA President: California ruling allows corporate interests to trump students' needs," National Education Foundation, June 10, 2014, http://tinyurl.com/ln7cbp7.
65. "Teachers unions vow to fight *Vergara* decision, others celebrate," *The LA School Report*, June 10, 2014, http://tinyurl.com/kv8a9sw.
66. Valerie Strauss, "Obama expands use of standardized tests for special-needs and American Indian students," *The Washington Post*, June 27, 2014, http://tinyurl.com/n9k77yf.
67. Meredith Broussard, "Why Poor Schools Can't Win at Standardized Testing," *The Atlantic*, July 15, 2014, http://tinyurl.com/qhmnq4k.
68. Leana Heltin and Stephen Sawchuck, "NEA Calls for Secretary Duncan's Resignation," *Education Week*, July 4, 2014, http://tinyurl.com/otmslxm.
69. Jeff Bryant, " 'Stupid, absurd, non-defensible': New NEA president Lily Eskelsen García on the problem with Arne Duncan, standardized tests and the war on teachers," *Salon*, July 30, 2014, http://tinyurl.com/qgy7cqz.
70. "Federal, State, and Local K-12 School Finance Overview," Federal Education Budget Project, April 21, 2014, http://tinyurl.com/c9kadh5.
71. *Ibid.*
72. Amy Golod, "Common Core: Myths and Facts," *U.S. News & World Report*, March 4, 2014, http://tinyurl.com/kxw37dh.
73. *Ibid.*
74. For background, see Anne Farris Rosen, "School Discipline," *CQ Researcher*, May 9, 2014, pp. 409-432.
75. Jennifer Medina, "Los Angeles to Reduce Arrest Rate in Schools," *The New York Times*, Aug. 18, 2014, http://tinyurl.com/kst2yxq.
76. Levine, *op. cit.*
77. Nirvi Shah and Maggie Severns, "60 years on: Education, segregation and the Obama White House," *Politico*, May 17, 2014, http://tinyurl.com/lumj4oz.

78. Ibid.
79. Ted Robbins, "Tucson Revives Mexican-American Studies Program," NPR, July 24, 2013, http://tinyurl.com/kyy5k9z.
80. "New National Rankings Find States Are Strengthening Charter School Laws," The National Alliance for Charter Schools, Jan. 29, 2014, http://tinyurl.com/mavgvuu.
81. "Education Bill Tracking Database," National Council of State Legislatures, www.ncls.org/research/education-bill-tracking-database.aspx.
80. Ben Casselman, "Public Schools are Hurting More in the Recovery Than in the Recession," *FiveThirtyEight*, June 10, 2014, http://tinyurl.com/or5lws9.
81. Ibid.
82. "Census: White majority in U.S. gone by 2043," NBC News, June 13, 2013, http://tinyurl.com/m5pgahy.

BIBLIOGRAPHY

Selected Sources
Books

Frankenberg, Erica, and Gary Orfield, eds., *The Resegregation of Suburban Schools: A Hidden Crisis in American Education,* **Harvard Education Press, 2012.**
Two leading school-segregation scholars provide a collection of essays documenting growing school segregation in the United States and potential solutions.

Garland, Sarah, *Divided We Fail: The Story of An African American Community that Ended the Era of School Desegregation,* **Beacon Press, 2013.**
A veteran education journalist looks at the battle over desegregation at Central High in Louisville, Ky., initiated by some African-American families who preferred to send their kids to traditionally black schools, opening the door to the Supreme Court's 2007 ruling that largely ended court-ordered race-based desegregation.

Kluger, Richard, *Simple Justice: The History of Brown v. Board of Education and Black America's Struggle for Equality,* **Vintage, 2004.**
A Pulitzer Prize-winning author traces the history of racial integration efforts that culminated in the 1954 *Brown v. Board of Education* Supreme Court ruling desegregating schools; includes a chapter updating developments.

Tatum, Beverly Daniel, *Can We Talk About Race? And Other Conversations in an Era of School Resegregation,* **Beacon Press, 2007.**
The president of historically black Spelman College examines the impact of segregation in public schools, along with the implications of continued segregation for the future of an increasingly multiracial country.

Articles

Bloom, Howard, and Stephen Ceasar, "California teacher tenure is struck down: Expect years of appeals," *Los Angeles Times,* **June 11, 2014, http://tinyurl.com/mwoyl68.**
A Los Angeles County Superior Court judge struck down teacher tenure in California public schools, ruling, in part, that tenure laws put minority students at a disadvantage by saddling them with a disproportionate number of bad teachers.

Cobb, Jelani, "The Failure of Desegregation," *The New Yorker,* **April 16, 2014, http://tinyurl.com/lxu86ct.**
A history professor and director of the Institute for African American Studies at the University of Connecticut argues that court-ordered school desegregation failed to account for the deeper roots of racial separation.

Hannah-Jones, Nikole, "The Resegregation of America's Schools," *ProPublica,* **April 16, 2014, http://tinyurl.com/lxqnfsp.**
Part of an ongoing series titled "Segregation Now: Investigating America's racial divide in education, housing and beyond," this story examines school resegregation in Tuscaloosa, Ala., where the public school system once was considered an example of successful integration.

Rich, Motoko, "School Data Finds Pattern of Inequality Along Racial Lines," *The New York Times,* **March 21, 2014, http://tinyurl.com/k8stumj.**
The Department of Education's Office for Civil Rights has found that racial minorities in the nation's public

schools were more likely to be taught by less experienced teachers and less likely to have access to advanced classes.

Shah, Nirvi, and Maggie Severns, "60 years on: Education, segregation and the Obama White House," *Politico*, **May 17, 2014, http://tinyurl.com/lumj4oz.**
Reporters examine the Obama administration's efforts on school desegregation and the current state of court-ordered desegregation.

Studies and Reports

Orfield, Gary, Erica Frankenberg, *et al.*, **"*Brown* at 60: Great Progress, a Long Retreat and an Uncertain Future," The Civil Rights Project, May 15, 2014, http://tinyurl.com/q8v3t6b.**
To mark the 60th anniversary of the Supreme Court's landmark desegregation ruling, *Brown v. Board of Education*, UCLA's Civil Rights Project assessed the current state of school segregation.

Reardon, Sean, Elena Grewal, *et al.*, **"*Brown* fades: the end of court-ordered school desegregation and the resegregation of American public schools,"** *Journal of Policy Analysis and Management*, **Fall 2012, http://tinyurl.com/met7hhx.**
In an analysis of more than 200 school districts released from court desegregation orders, Stanford University researchers found that racial segregation increased gradually once the districts no longer had to follow court orders.

Suitts, Steve, *et al.*, **"A New Majority: Low Income Students in the South and Nation," Southern Education Foundation, October 2013, http://tinyurl.com/lc7le4l.**
A study by a nonprofit organization seeking to advance educational equity and excellence in the South found that the majority of public school children in one-third of the states were in low-income families, a dramatic increase in the last decade.

For More Information

The Advancement Project, 1220 L St., N.W., Suite 850, Washington, DC 20005; 202-728-9558; www.advancementproject.org/content/home. Civil rights organization that aims to help communities "dismantle and reform . . . policies that undermine the promise of democracy."

Center for Equal Opportunity, 7700 Leesburg Pike, Suite 231, Falls Church, VA 22043; 703-442-0066; www.ceousa.org. Conservative think tank that promotes "a color-blind society."

The Civil Rights Project, 8370 Math Sciences, Box 951521, Los Angeles, CA 90095; http://civilrightsproject.ucla.edu. Seeks to help renew the civil rights movement by deepening the understanding of issues related to racial and ethnic equity.

National Alliance for Public Charter Schools, 1101 15th St., N.W., Suite 1010, Washington, DC 20005; 202-289-2700; www.publiccharters.org. Advocates for the quality, growth and sustainability of charter schools and maintains a national database of charter school laws and related information.

National Education Association, 1201 16th St., N.W., Washington, DC 20036; 202-833-4000; www.nea.org. Labor union representing teachers and other education professionals; advocates for public education and teachers' rights.

Office for Civil Rights, U.S. Department of Education, Lyndon Baines Johnson Department of Education Building, 400 Maryland Ave., S.W., Washington, DC 20202; 800-421-3481; www2.ed.gov/about/offices/list/ocr/index.html. Works to ensure equal access to education and enforces civil rights laws.

Students Matter, 325 Sharon Park Drive, No. 521, Menlo Park, CA 94025; http://studentsmatter.org. Nonprofit founded by Silicon Valley entrepreneur David Welch; sponsors litigation to promote access to quality public education.

3
Coastal Development

Jennifer Weeks

Gary Silberman surveys the damage to his home wrought by Superstorm Sandy in October 2012 in Lindenhurst, N.Y., located on the south side of Long Island. Sandy caused an estimated $70 billion in damages, making it the second-costliest storm in U.S. history and reviving a longstanding debate over coastal development. Critics say government policies encourage construction — and constant reconstruction — in storm- and flood-prone areas, endangering people and property and harming critical wetlands and estuaries.

From *CQ Researcher*,
February 22, 2013; updated May 2016.

Before Superstorm Sandy barreled up the Atlantic coast in October 2012, the worst flooding John Schreiber had experienced was a year earlier, when Hurricane Irene left three inches of water standing in a back room of his house on the south shore of Long Island. Schreiber's neighborhood was laced with canals, including one directly behind his property.

But Sandy was the most intense storm to hit New York and New Jersey in 40 years, even though it had been downgraded to a tropical storm by the time it made landfall near Atlantic City on October 29.[1] Striking at high tide during a full moon, it pushed flood waters as much as nine feet above average high-tide marks.[2] Four feet of water poured into Schreiber's back room and flowed through the ground level of his home.

Nearly four months after Sandy, up to half of the houses on Schreiber's block were still vacant.

"People have ripped out the insides and are waiting for contractors to put in new Sheetrock, or plumbing, or floors," he said. A retired teacher, Schreiber estimated that he had spent $20,000 of his savings to tear out damaged walls and floors and replace appliances.

It could have been worse. Sandy killed 72 people in the United States and 75 in the Caribbean.[3] High winds knocked out electricity for more than 8.5 million homes in 16 states and the District of Columbia. Heavy flooding in New Jersey and New York damaged or destroyed more than 650,000 homes and swamped thousands of businesses.[4]

Damages from Sandy totaled an estimated $71.4 billion, according to the National Oceanic and Atmospheric

Floodgates Proposed for New York Harbor

Engineers have proposed two separate designs for floodgates to block storm surges in New York Harbor. Both systems would require a barrier across the Upper East River to close off surges from Long Island Sound. A three-gate system would place short barriers between New Jersey and Staten Island and from Staten Island to Brooklyn. The alternative system would include a five-mile-long barrier stretching from the Gateway National Recreation Area in New Jersey to the Rockaway Peninsula on Long Island. Cost estimates for the structures range from $7 billion to $29 billion.

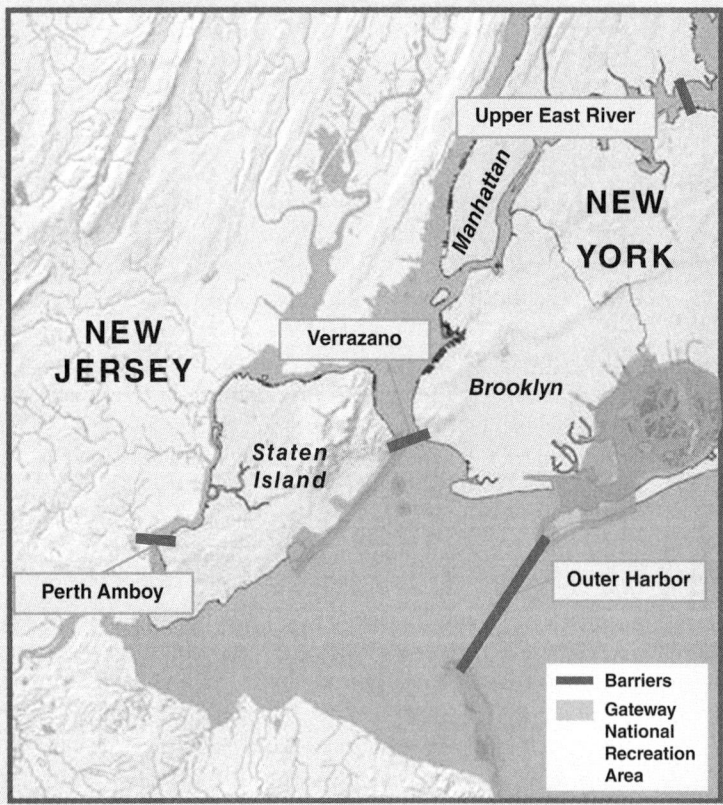

Storm Surge Barriers Proposed for New York Harbor

Source: "Recommendations to Improve the Strength and Resilience of the Empire State's Infrastructure," NYS 2100 Commission, January 2013, p. 121; map adapted with permission from the American Society of Civil Engineers

Administration (NOAA).[5] That makes it the second-costliest storm in U.S. history, exceeded only by Hurricane Katrina, which caused damage worth $128 billion (in 2012 adjusted dollars) after striking the Gulf Coast in August 2005.[6]

Sandy's devastation revived a long-standing debate over development in coastal areas. Critics of coastal development, including many scientists and environmentalists and even some free-market advocates, say government policies encourage construction in storm- and flood-prone areas. This puts people and property directly in harm's way. Coastal development also harms beaches and coastal wetlands and estuaries, which are highly productive ecosystems that provide habitat for fish, shellfish and birds — including many endangered species — and provide natural storm buffers for inland areas. Thus, the critics contend, government policies should be changed to encourage homes and businesses to move out of harm's way and make it harder to build along the shore in the future.[7]

"Sandy was a wake-up call for New York and New Jersey," says Robert Young, a coastal geologist and director of the Program for the Study of Developed Shorelines at Western Carolina University. "Scientific panels had been prodding people to get ready for [a direct hit] for some time, but most of that advice was ignored." In Young's view, most zones of the Atlantic and Gulf Coasts are equally vulnerable. "Everyone should be concerned about storm risks," he warns.

Multiple government programs directly or indirectly subsidize coastal development, including federal flood insurance, post-storm disaster aid and federal cost-sharing for beach restoration projects. Some of these measures provide benefits beyond their immediate scope. For example, states that write plans for managing their coastlines can receive federal grants to redevelop urban waterfronts or protect coastal resources — steps that make those areas more enjoyable for both residents and visitors.

But other programs encourage harmful overdevelopment. A prime example is the federally administered National Flood Insurance Program (NFIP), created in 1968. Conventional homeowners' insurance policies do not cover flooding because private insurers consider the risk too high, so the federal program insures coastal properties for less than what the private sector would charge.

NFIP is allowed to borrow funds from the U.S. Treasury when claims from major storms exceed premiums that the program collects from policyholders. The program has been on the U.S. Government Accountability Office's "high risk" list since 2006 because it owes the Treasury billions of dollars — $24 billion as of the end of 2014 — to pay for claims from Katrina and Sandy.[8]

Flood insurance advocates say the NFIP saves the federal government money because premiums help pay for flood relief. "I'm certainly glad I had it," said Schreiber, who expected his flood insurance to pay all or most of his Sandy repair costs. Moreover, to participate in the program communities must adopt and enforce floodplain management regulations designed to reduce losses — for example, elevating new homes in flood zones above the level of a 100-year flood.[9] But critics argue that the program subsidizes development in flood-prone areas. They want to privatize NFIP so owners pay the full cost of protecting risky properties.

Development Concerns Spawn National Seashores

Concerns over heavy development in coastal regions have led Congress to designate 10 areas in the National Park System as National Seashores. The designation protects the areas from new development.

Federally Designated National Seashores

National Seashore	Location	Year est.	Acreage
Cape Hatteras	North Carolina	1953	30,351
Located in the Outer Banks. Known for beaches, waterfowl, fishing and points of historical interest, including the iconic Cape Hatteras Lighthouse. Includes 6,000-acre Pea Island National Wildlife Refuge.			
Assateague Island	Maryland, Virginia	1965	39,727
Known for sandy beaches, waterfowl and wild horses. Includes 9,000-acre Chincoteague National Wildlife Refuge.			
Cape Lookout	North Carolina	1966	28,243
Composed of three islands in the Outer Banks. Islands have two historic villages and the Cape Lookout Lighthouse. Camping, fishing and hiking are traditional recreational activities.			
Cape Cod	Massachusetts	1966	43,608
National Seashore located on the outer part of the cape. Includes archaeological sites, lighthouses and the Marconi Station Site, where trans-Atlantic wireless communication began in 1903.			
Padre Island	Texas	1968	130,434
World's longest undeveloped barrier island. Known for fishing and abundant bird and marine life. U.S. military used island as a bombing range during World War II.			
Gulf Islands	Florida, Mississippi	1971	137,991
Includes four historic forts used for Civil War defense. Once home to Apache Indians. Includes the Naval Live Oaks Reservation, which has been set aside for tree preservation.			
Point Reyes	California	1972	71,068
San Francisco-area peninsula with beaches backed by tall cliffs, lagoons, forested ridges and offshore bird and sea lion colonies. Occupied by elk and elephant seals.			
Cumberland Island	Georgia	1972	36,415
Largest of Georgia's Golden Isles. Once home to Native Americans, missionaries and slaves.			
Canaveral	Florida	1975	57,662
Barrier island includes multiple bird species in lagoon habitats. Kennedy Space Center occupies southern end.			
Fire Island	New York	1984	19,579
Known for beaches and dunes. Includes the estate of William Floyd, a signer of the Declaration of Independence.			

Source: "The National Parks: Index 2009-2011," National Park Service, 2011, www.nps.gov/history/history/online_books/nps/index2009_11.pdf

The federal government also provides billions of dollars in emergency aid to states and communities during and after major disasters such as storms, tornadoes, or earthquakes. Under the Stafford Act, passed in 1988, the federal government pays 100 percent of eligible housing assistance and at least 75 percent of costs for removing debris and repairing or replacing public facilities.[10] President Obama issued major disaster declarations for Sandy that covered all or part of 12 states and the District of Columbia, making them eligible for federal disaster aid.[11]

Beyond pork-barrel spending, observers see a bigger problem: Disaster relief money often does not require recipients to make new homes, businesses or other structures safer or move them out of harm's way, even though such steps (known as risk mitigation) can reduce future damage. Under the Stafford Act, funds can be used only to upgrade structures to meet stricter building codes or zoning standards if a state or local government adopted such requirements before the disaster.[12]

"After disasters, we usually build back almost exactly what was there before, and I think that's what we're going to find after Sandy," says Steve Ellis, vice president of Taxpayers for Common Sense, a nonpartisan fiscal watchdog group in Washington.

For example, he notes, the Sandy relief bill includes $5 billion for the Army Corps of Engineers, which constructs and maintains dams, waterways, and navigation channels. The Corps also manages "beach replenishment" projects — pumping sand from offshore onto beaches to restore eroded dunes. Many coastal communities see beach replenishment as a shield against storm damage because dunes can absorb some of the force from storm surges. But critics say replenishment does not last and can harm the environment. For example, pumping fine sediments onto beaches can make water murky, and building new dunes can bury sensitive wildlife habitats.[13]

The Sandy relief bill directs the Corps to help restore navigation channels, beaches and other damaged infrastructure to pre-storm conditions. "It aims to put beaches back, but they won't last," says Young. Instead, he and other coastal experts say, the hardest-hit areas should not be reconstructed.

Climate change will exacerbate coastal flooding by warming the oceans, which causes seawater to expand, and melting glaciers and ice caps on land.[14] These processes raise global sea levels. According to recent climate change assessments, global sea levels will rise roughly one to four feet this century.[15] But the increases will not be uniform. According to the U.S. Geological Survey, sea levels are rising at three to four times the global rate along the Atlantic coast from North Carolina to Massachusetts because of such factors as ocean currents, water temperature and salinity.[16]

As politicians, scientists and coastal communities consider where and how to rebuild after Superstorm Sandy, here are some issues they are considering:

Should state and local governments block coastal development?

Many scientists say that as climate change raises sea levels, it will make storms — the main cause of coastal erosion — more catastrophic.[17] Thus, governments should limit development near the water's edge, contend many environmentalists, coastal scientists, and taxpayer watchdog groups. And in zones hit hard by storms like Sandy, they say that now is the time to move development back from coastlines.

"We should strongly discourage the reconstruction of destroyed or badly damaged beachfront homes in New Jersey and New York," Orrin H. Pilkey, emeritus professor of earth sciences at Duke University and longtime critic of shoreline development, wrote three weeks after Sandy. "This is tough medicine to be sure, and taxpayers may be forced to compensate homeowners. But it should save taxpayers money in the long run by ending this cycle of repairing or rebuilding properties in the path of future storms."[18]

Typically, homeowners and communities want to rebuild damaged structures wherever possible. "Most people still see coastal property as highly desirable even if they face repetitive damage," says Grover Fugate, executive director of the Rhode Island Coastal Resources Management Council, a state regulatory agency. "Property owners want to keep holding the line until they've got no more property to build on. Local communities will push for development because vacation homes are gravy for towns — they generate high taxes and don't require a lot of municipal services, since they're only occupied for part of the year."

In the wake of Sandy, New Jersey Gov. Christie initially dismissed the need to regulate where or how owners could rebuild. "I think, in the main, that's a local decision, and the localities need to make that decision themselves," Christie said just a few days after the storm.[19] But in December 2012, FEMA released updated flood hazard maps for the Jersey shore showing that flood waters could rise one to five feet higher than previous versions of the maps had indicated. (FEMA had begun updating its maps of flood-prone areas before Sandy hit.)

In January 2013, Christie ordered the immediate adoption of the new maps as the state rebuilding standard. The order did not block owners from rebuilding in high-risk zones, but if people do not mitigate flood risks — for example, by raising their homes on posts or pilings — they will face sharp increases in flood insurance premiums. Raising houses, Christie said, is "what we need to do to build a 21st-century Jersey shore."[20]

Democratic New York Gov. Andrew Cuomo urged Sandy victims to consider raising their houses, but he also advocated a second option: selling damaged homes in high-risk areas to the state, which would demolish them and leave the properties undeveloped. "At one point you have to say maybe Mother Nature doesn't want you here," Cuomo said in late January 2013. Sales would be voluntary, the governor emphasized: "I'm not saying anybody should sell, but you should think about it."[21]

After Sandy, New York bought out homes in several highly vulnerable neighborhoods on Staten Island where many houses had been swept away or damaged beyond repair.[22] But then the state started offering individual homeowners the option to sell their houses, which would be rebuilt to modern standards, or stay in place and elevate their homes, As of spring 2016, 6,000 properties citywide had qualified for repairs or reconstruction under the Build It Back program; of these, nearly half were finished or under construction.[23]

States can use eminent domain (the right to take private property for a public use) to ban redevelopment or require owners to abandon developed property in areas where flood risks are extreme.[24] Such actions would likely generate "takings" claims — lawsuits citing the Fifth Amendment's ban on depriving citizens of their property without due process of law and seeking compensation from the state. But J. Peter Byrne, a law professor at Georgetown University, says less-drastic options exist for steering development away from flood-prone areas and preventing landowners from "hardening" coastal areas with such fixtures as seawalls, which block the natural shifting of sand and actually promote erosion.

"When the California Coastal Commission [a state regulatory agency] awards permits for new housing, it adds a provision that limits owners' ability to harden shorelines," says Byrne. "You could imagine going a step further and letting owners rebuild, but limiting it to one time if some specific fraction of the property was destroyed again. That's a limit on future development, not current activities. Governments could justify it as protecting public health and safety by reducing risks of future shoreline damage."

Rhode Island imposes multiple limits on shoreline development, including bans on constructing seawalls and other hard shoreline protection structures and building on dunes. The state assumes for planning purposes that sea levels will rise three to five feet by 2100. Many of the development restrictions, adopted in the 1980s, are controversial today. "With each storm we're challenged because people obviously want to protect their homes, and many of our policies don't let them," says Fugate. "But if states are really concerned about public finances and public safety and health, they've got to address this issue aggressively."

Some states are less willing to acknowledge risks from climate change. In 2010, North Carolina's Coastal Resources Commission advised coastal communities to plan for three feet or more of sea-level rise by 2100. Local critics assailed the recommendation, arguing that it would limit development. In 2012, the state's Republican-majority legislature passed a bill barring the commission from planning on anything beyond historic rates of change. After the measure was widely mocked as an attempt to outlaw science, the legislature amended the bill, directing the commission to study the issue until 2016 without defining rates of sea-level change.[25]

Scientists produced a new analysis for the state in 2015, again projecting that sea levels would rise, but only looking 30 years ahead, so the forecast was not as extreme as the earlier report. Politicians and businesspeople praised the report: one real estate lobbyist called it "not only a scientific approach but just plain common sense."[26]

Can the federal flood insurance program be fixed?

The National Flood Insurance Program offers discounted coverage for homes and businesses in areas at moderate to high risk of flooding. It is intended to save taxpayers money by providing affordable insurance in zones where private insurance companies will not write policies, reducing the need for massive federal-aid legislation every time a big flood occurs.

But critics say people who live in flood-prone areas should have to pay insurance rates that reflect the actual risk to their properties. About one-fourth of NFIP policies insure "grandfathered" properties that predate the program. These policies cost only 40 to 45 percent as much as full-risk premiums. Moreover, since the NFIP was designed to provide affordable flood protection, even the rates NFIP considers full-price premiums are cheaper than what private insurers would charge.

Those subsidies encourage risky development, critics argue. "Before federal flood insurance, people built beach shacks that they could afford to lose," says David Helvarg, president of the Blue Frontier Campaign, an ocean conservation advocacy group. "But once the federal government started providing insurance that the private sector wouldn't offer, it was easy to get mortgages, and that triggered a [coastal] development boom."

Insurers say that without the NFIP, many people in flood zones would not be able to afford coverage.

"When you underwrite this risk correctly, it's very expensive," says John Prible, vice president for government affairs with the Independent Insurance Agents and Brokers of America (IIABA). "You don't want to drive people away by making it too expensive. Some people say they'll self-insure instead by setting the money aside to mitigate risks" — in other words, they'll pay to protect the property themselves.

"But they don't usually follow through," Prible says. "That's why insurance exists."

For the NFIP's first several decades, damage reimbursements to policy holders were funded by premiums on policies. But when Hurricanes Katrina and Rita hit the Gulf Coast in 2005, damage was so widespread that the program had to borrow money from the Treasury to pay claims. Before Sandy struck, the NFIP already owed the Treasury $18 billion. It received nearly $10 billion in additional borrowing authority to pay claims from Sandy.

Insurance premiums are based on flooding risk in the zone where a property is located. To help property owners and mortgage lenders judge flood risks, FEMA, which administers the NFIP, has produced maps of flood-risk areas across the United States. All homes and businesses in high-risk areas must be covered by flood insurance to qualify for federally regulated or insured mortgages. In fact, however, the NFIP currently insures only about 25 percent of eligible households in these areas, totaling roughly 5.6 million policies.[27]

"Some consumers buy coverage when they get their mortgage, but then let it lapse," says Prible. "And a lot of older homes in coastal areas are paid off and don't have mortgages."

In July 2012, Congress passed the Biggert-Waters Flood Insurance Reform Act, which reauthorized the NFIP for five years and took steps that were intended to stabilize the program. For example, it voted to let premiums rise by 20 percent yearly (increases previously had been capped at 10 percent) and to phase out subsidies for second homes, business properties, and homes that have suffered repeated losses.[28]

One extreme case was the Alabama beach community of Dauphin Island, which has been hit repeatedly by hurricanes over the past 30 years. Dauphin Island has only about 1,300 year-round residents, but owners there have received $72 million in payments from the NFIP.[29]

Updates to FEMA's flood-hazard maps also raised premiums for some owners whose communities had become high-risk zones due to climate change, sea level rise, and increased development in flood plains.

Observers widely agreed that higher premiums were an essential step toward stabilizing the NFIP. But when homeowners started receiving higher premium bills — and, in some cases, confusing information about which zone their homes were in on new flood risk maps — a fierce backlash developed. Some owners who rebuilt and elevated homes damaged by Sandy still saw their premiums increase from a few thousand dollars per year to over $30,000.[30]

Objections poured in from coastal states. "Uncertainty hangs over thousands of homes. By many accounts, sales have stalled in low-lying areas, sellers are dropping prices, and real-estate closings are becoming more complex," Florida Gov. Rick Scott wrote to President Obama in

January 2014. "Act now and undo the effects of this mistaken law before it cripples Florida's real-estate market, harms even more Floridians, and reverses our state's burgeoning economic recovery."[31]

In March 2014, Congress passed the Homeowner Flood Insurance Affordability Act, which repealed some portions of the Biggert-Waters Act and amended others. The law restored some rate subsidies and the practice of grandfathering, which was to have been phased out under the 2012 law.[32]

Critics argued that the reversal was shortsighted and only delayed further crises for the NFIP. "While politically expedient today, this abdication of responsibility by Congress is going to come back and bite them and taxpayers when the next disaster strikes," said Ellis of Taxpayers for Common Sense. "Everyone knows this program is not fiscally sound or even viable in the near term."[33]

Ocean waves crash over the seawall in Winthrop, Mass., on Feb. 9, 2013, as a powerful winter storm swept through New England, dumping more than two feet of snow in some areas and knocking out power to at least 600,000 homes.

Does New York City need floodgates?

As New York City pursues a broad range of upgrades to prepare for future coastal storms, officials are considering many large-scale investments, some of which will take years to complete. One controversial proposal is to build large floodgates that could block major storm surges from entering New York Harbor.

These systems already are used in Europe. London, Rotterdam, and St. Petersburg, Russia, are all protected by large storm-surge barriers on nearby rivers, and Venice is building a flood control system to close off its lagoon. In the United States, smaller gates protect Stamford, Conn., and Providence, R.I. William Merrell, a professor of marine science at Texas A&M University, has proposed building a floodgate that would close off Galveston Bay during storms. The "Ike Dike" — named for 2008's Hurricane Ike, which caused $30 billion in damage around Houston — would cost an estimated $6 billion.[34] So far it has not attracted high-level support or federal funding.[35]

In recent years, engineers have proposed two designs for floodgates in New York Harbor. One would be a two-gate system, with barriers reaching from New Jersey to Staten Island and from Staten Island to Brooklyn. Alternatively, the city could build a five-mile barrier stretching from New Jersey to the Rockaway Peninsula on Long Island. Either approach would require an additional barrier to close off surges from Long Island Sound up the East River. Cost estimates for either range from $7 billion to $29 billion.[36]

The New York City Panel on Climate Change (NPCC), a high-level advisory group convened by Mayor Bloomberg, examined the city's vulnerability to climate change and in 2010 recommended steps to adapt to rising sea levels. The panel concluded that floodgates were worth considering but would require "very extensive study," especially since other, smaller-scale strategies were available.[37]

"Key research questions need to be answered," says Radley Horton, a research scientist at Columbia University's Center for Climate Systems Research and adviser to the NPCC. "How do you test a system like this? How do you minimize the risk that it will fail? Will it create a false sense of security and encourage people to live close to the coast? What will its environmental impacts be? What happens to people who live just outside of the barrier, where flood risks will increase?"

After Sandy, Gov. Cuomo convened another expert group, the NYS 2100 Commission, to recommend ways to make the entire state more resilient against future storms. In January 2013, the group called for an in-depth study on building floodgates for New York Harbor. A barrier from New Jersey to the Rockaways "likely would have prevented the flooding of the

> **Defining Flood Risks for Landowners**
>
> Maps prepared by the Federal Emergency Management Agency designate the level of flood risk in low-lying areas of the country. Government officials, insurance agents and lenders use the designations to set flood insurance rates and premiums and determine whether a home or business owner must buy flood insurance to obtain a federally insured mortgage. To enable residents to buy flood insurance, communities in these zones must participate in the National Flood Insurance Program (NFIP) by adopting and enforcing minimum standards for development in floodplains.
>
> - **High risk areas** — Zones expected to flood once every 100 years (also known as 100-year flood areas). This risk translates to a 1 percent chance of flooding in any given year, or roughly 1 in 4 odds over the life of a 30-year mortgage. All home and business owners in these zones must buy flood insurance in order to qualify for federally regulated or insured mortgages.
>
> - **Moderate risk areas** — Zones that typically lie between 100-year and 500-year flood lines (1 to 0.2 percent chance of flooding in any given year), or that lie in 100-year flood zones but are protected by levees. Flood insurance in these zones is not generally required as a condition for federally regulated mortgages, although some states or lenders may require it.
>
> - **Low risk areas** — Zones typically above the 500-year flood line. Flood insurance in these zones is not generally required as a condition for federally regulated mortgages.
>
> Source: https://msc.fema.gov/webapp/wcs/stores/servlet/info?storeId=10001&catalogId=10001&langId=-1&content=floodZones&title=FEMA percent 2520Flood percent 2520Zone percent 2520Designations

A 2014 study by experts from the Netherlands and the United States calculated that the most cost-effective way to make New York more resilient against flooding was to work though building codes, adding requirements such as elevating new buildings and protecting critical infrastructure systems like the electricity grid. The scientists recommended studying storm surge barriers but putting off a decision on building them for as long as 25 years, until more data was available on rates of sea level rise.[39]

For now, the city is investing in more modest steps, such as reinforcing shorelines around lower and midtown Manhattan, creating parks as bugger zones that can soak up flood waters, and redesigning power stations, subway tunnels and other critical facilities to make them more floodproof.[40]

"There won't be one silver bullet to solve this problem. We need a robust mixture of tools and strategies, from elevating buildings to long-term retreat in vulnerable areas," says Timothy Beatley, a professor of urban and environmental planning at the University of Virginia who has written about making coastal areas more resilient against disasters.

subways, tunnels, airports, wastewater treatments plants and other critical infrastructure" that occurred during Sandy, the group stated.

But the panel also noted shortcomings. Surge barriers would not protect the city against flooding from rainfall or high water on the East or Hudson Rivers. And because they would be closed only when a major storm was expected, the barriers would not prevent rising sea levels from gradually inundating low-lying coastal sites. Finally, surge barriers could have major impacts on the ecology of New York Harbor and on shipping and recreation around the harbor.[38]

BACKGROUND
Wealth and Trade Centers

For more than two centuries, scholars have observed that coastal areas tend to attract more wealth, investment, and people than inland zones. Scottish economist Adam Smith pointed out this correlation in his landmark work, *The Wealth of Nations* (1776), and it still holds true: Coastal economies prosper because they have direct connections to international shipping routes, which are the cheapest way to move goods around the globe.[41]

CHRONOLOGY

1900-1960 *Industry, ports, and military bases spread along large sections of U.S. coastlines.*

1900 Hurricane inundates Galveston, Texas, killing between 6,000 and 12,000 people.

1922 First U.S. beach replenishment program launched at Coney Island, N.Y.

1940 After France falls to Nazi Germany, United States launches a massive military expansion along its coasts, including new naval bases, shipyards and port facilities.

1956 Federal Aid Highway Act authorizes construction of the Interstate Highway System, boosting tourist travel to coastal resorts.

1960-1980 *Economic growth spurs increased tourism, putting new pressure on coastal areas and raising concerns about overdevelopment.*

1968 Congress creates National Flood Insurance Program (NFIP) after Hurricane Betsy inflicts heavy damage on Gulf Coast. The program offers coverage to homeowners, renters, and businesses in communities that adopt measures to mitigate flood risks.

1969 Stratton Commission on management of U.S. coastal resources warns that these zones are threatened by heavy development and calls for better coastal zone management.

1970 National Oceanic and Atmospheric Administration (NOAA) created to protect and manage marine resources.

1972 Congress enacts Coastal Zone Management Act to help states along the nation's coasts manage growth in coastal areas. . . . California voters pass Proposition 20, creating a state commission to regulate coastal development.

1973 NFIP is amended to require homes and buildings in high-risk flood areas to have flood insurance in order to receive a federally regulated or insured mortgage.

1980-2000 *Growth outstrips conservation measures in many coastal areas.*

1982 Congress passes Coastal Barriers Resources Act, banning federal subsidies for development on 186 Atlantic and Gulf Coast barrier islands.

1988 Congress passes Stafford Act (named after its sponsor, Sen. Robert T. Stafford, R-VT), establishing a system of federal aid to state and local governments after natural disasters.

1992 In *Lucas v. South Carolina Coastal Council*, U.S. Supreme Court rules that forbidding all use of private land in a potential flood zone amounts to a "taking" of private land, so the government must pay the owner. . . . Hurricane Andrew hits Miami, causing $25 billion in damages, according to a 1993 National Hurricane Center report.

2001-2016 *Storms inflict heavy damage in many coastal zones.*

2005 Hurricanes Katrina and Rita strike Gulf Coast, inflicting $117 billion in damages.

2006 Congress raises NFIP borrowing authority to $20 billion.

2008 Hurricane Ike causes $27 billion in damage to the Texas coast.

2012 Congress reauthorizes NFIP through 2017 with higher premiums. . . . Superstorm Sandy strikes East Coast, causing an estimated $50 billion in damages.

2013 Congress raises NFIP borrowing authority to $30 billion and approves $50.5 billion in emergency aid for Hurricane Sandy victims.

2014 Congress reverses and extends some flood insurance premium increases enacted in 2012 after thousands of homeowners protest sharp rate increases.

2015 FEMA allows all Sandy claimants to appeal their payments after several thousand sue, arguing insurers deliberately underpaid them for storm damage.

2016 FEMA announces reforms to tighten controls over private insurers who write flood insurance policies and make it easier to appeal settlements.

Cities Seek Ways to Block Rising Oceans

Movable gates are part of broader protection systems.

Some cities vulnerable to flooding from storms and rising sea levels are building a variety of structures to block or mitigate the damage. They range from 10 massive movable gates in the Thames River near London to Rotterdam's "Climate Proof" system, which includes a large set of flood gates and innovative features such as water plazas and floating buildings.

London is about 40 miles from the coast, spreading along both sides of the Thames River. Because the Thames flows into the North Sea, its lower section is affected by tides, and high tides have flooded London throughout its history. The Thames Barrier, a line of 10 movable gates that can be raised to block storm surges, has been closed 176 times since its completion in 1982. More than half of those incidents have occurred since 2000.[1]

When the system is open, the gates lie on the river bottom, allowing ships to pass over them; when activated, they rotate upward, forming a solid wall.[2] The gates are the largest element of a system of barriers and locks that protects London and downriver communities from floods.

In 2012, the United Kingdom's Environment Agency released its Thames Estuary 2100 Plan, which sets out strategies for protecting lives and property along the Thames from growing flood risks through 2100. The document is based on scientists' estimates that climate change will raise global sea levels by about three feet by 2100, but the plan can be adapted for higher levels. It projects that many existing flood control structures will be raised or upgraded between 2035 and 2050 and that a new Thames Barrier may have to be constructed between 2050 and 2070 if oceans rise to even higher levels.[3]

Venice, which dates back to the Middle Ages, was built on 118 small islands in a marshy lagoon adjacent to the Adriatic Sea and straddling the mouths of two rivers. Once a commercial and naval power, Venice today is a major tourist destination — famous for its network of canals, plied by colorful gondoliers. But Venice is sinking as sea levels are rising. About 100 times a year, floods inundate stores, restaurants and popular sites such as the Piazza San Marco, the city's main square.

Since 2003, Venice has been building 78 metal sea gates (named MOSE, from the Italian for the Biblical prophet Moses) that can be raised to close off three inlets connecting its lagoon to the Adriatic. Other elements of the project include restoring nearby beaches, dunes and salt marshes; reinforcing fragile buildings; and reducing oil tanker traffic in the lagoon. The project is estimated to cost about $6.5 billion.[4]

The barrier, which is years behind schedule, is currently projected to enter operation in 2016, but that date is likely to slip still further. In 2014, Venice's mayor, Giorgio Orsoni, and 35 others were arrested on charges of bribery, corruption, and money laundering in connection with the dam project.[5]

Rotterdam, the second-largest city in the Netherlands (population 600,000), lies near the North Sea, much of it on land that is below sea level. Rotterdam also is near the Rhine-Meuse-Scheldt Delta, where three rivers converge and flow into the North Sea, so it is vulnerable to flooding from the river, the ocean and heavy rains, all of which can overwhelm the city's drainage systems and pumping stations.

Rotterdam is protected by the massive Maeslant Barrier, a movable gate that closes off the New Waterway, a large shipping canal linking the Port of Rotterdam to the North Sea. When the barrier is open, the storm doors are

---

Only 5 percent of the population in colonial America lived in major cities, the largest of which were the port cities of Boston, Philadelphia, New York, and Charleston, S.C. Those cities' trade links to Europe made them commercial, political, and cultural centers.[42]

Acquiring new ports was a priority during Westward expansion. In 1803, President Thomas Jefferson approved spending up to $10 million — an enormous sum at that time — to buy New Orleans from France. Eventually, the United States ended up purchasing not only New Orleans but the entire Louisiana Territory for $15 million, nearly doubling the size of the country. Jefferson then sent the Lewis and Clark expedition west to find a route to the Pacific Ocean.

concealed in docks on both sides of the canal. If water levels in the canal rise to a specified level, the doors swing out horizontally into the canal and sink, blocking the channel.[6] The system has been activated only once, in 2007.

The Maeslant Barrier is one element of the Netherlands's elaborate Delta Works, a system of river dams and storm-surge barriers developed after 1953, when a hurricane storm surge broke through 89 dikes, killing nearly 2,000 people and contaminating 772 square miles of fertile farmland with salt water. Such massive damage has not recurred, although the Netherlands experienced heavy river flooding in 1993 and 1995.

Maintaining barriers and dikes is a top national priority in the Netherlands, but designers also are exploring innovative flood-control techniques. Rotterdam's "Climate Proof" initiative is designed to make the city resilient to flooding and heat stress caused by climate change.

Rotterdam is building a series of "water plazas" — parks that are set below grade that serve as mini reservoirs, storing water during heavy storms. The city also subsidizes construction of green rooftops — covered with plantings that absorb water — and is planning a district of floating buildings where people can live, work and shop on the water.[7]

— *Jennifer Weeks*

The Thames Barrier — a line of 10 movable gates that can be raised from the river bottom to form a solid wall that blocks storm surges — is part of a system of barriers and locks that protects London and downriver communities from floods.

---

[1] "21st Century Challenges: The Thames Barrier," Royal Geographic Society, https://www.21stcenturychallenges.org/focus/the-thames-barrier/; Emma Glanfield and Anthony Joseph, "Huge Parts of London Flooded After Thames Bursts its Banks Due to Massive Tides and Heavy Rain," *The Daily Mail*, February 13, 2016, http://www.dailymail.co.uk/news/article-3444778/Flood-warnings-Londoners-Thames-Barrier-remains-closed.html.

[2] Video at http://www.dailymail.co.uk/news/article-2253624/Thames-Barrier-shuts-time-years-prevent-flooding-London-fresh-Atlantic-storm-promises-rain.html#axzz2KFHYuGAE.

[3] "Thames Estuary 2100 Plan," U.K. Environment Agency, November 2012, http://webarchive.nationalarchives.gov.uk/20140328084622/http://www.environment-agency.gov.uk/static/documents/Leisure/SE_TE2100_briefing.pdf.

[4] Giulia Lasagi, "Italy Goes Big to Save Venice as it Sinks Into the Sea," *The Christian Science Monitor*, April 13, 2012, http://www.csmonitor.com/World/Global-News/2012/0413/Italy-goes-big-to-save-Venice-as-it-sinks-into-the-sea.

[5] Rachel Sanderson, "Venice Mayor Giorgio Orsoni Arrested on Bribery Charges Over Dam," *The Financial Times*, June 14, 2014, http://www.ft.com/intl/cms/s/0/87bd7cd2-ebcc-11e3-8cef-00144feabdc0.html#axzz4AjA0tJcl.

[6] "Maeslant Barrier," http://www.deltawerken.com/The-functioning/463.html.

[7] For details, see "Rotterdam Climate Proof: Connecting water with opportunities," by John Jacobs (June 12, 2012),

http://tudelft.nl/fileadmin/UD/MenC/Support/Internet/TU%20Website/TU%20Delft/Images/Onderzoek/DRI_Environment/Water_City/Rotterdam_Climate_Proof_introduction.pdf.

Naval blockades during the War of 1812 and the Civil War highlighted the economic importance of port cities. The U.S. Army Corps of Engineers, established in 1802, built forts and military batteries along the Atlantic and Gulf Coasts, and later along the Pacific Coast. The Corps also constructed canals, lighthouses, piers, and other harbor facilities and mapped navigation routes to support more trade and travel.

The Corps' mission turned to flood prevention after disasters in 1927 and 1928 — including devastating flooding along the Mississippi River and hurricanes in South Florida that killed thousands and flooded hundreds of acres. The Corps began building massive dike systems in flood-prone areas, enabling landowners there to build homes and farms. The disasters of the 1920s also led private companies to stop providing flood insurance because it had become too costly.[43]

After the Civil War, industrialization accelerated in Northern states, but growth lagged in the devastated South. Millions of Americans and new immigrants moved to cities seeking jobs. But urban life in the late 1800s was noisy, polluted, and crowded. Coasts offered fresh air and open space.

During the Gilded Age (1877-1893), wealthy industrialists transformed the port town of Newport, R.I., into a summer playground, building so-called "cottages" that actually were opulent mansions. In winter, they traveled by train to new, grand beach resorts in Florida. Meanwhile, less wealthy city dwellers escaped to such havens as Cape Cod, Mass.; Cape May, N.J.; and Ocean City, Md. Working-class beachgoers took subways to Coney Island at Brooklyn's southern tip or to Boston's Revere Beach.

In the 1920s, as wages rose and cars became widely available, middle-class Americans began traveling for pleasure, fueling development along Florida and Southern California beaches.

Trade and economic production stagnated during the Great Depression. But as war loomed in Europe, President Franklin D. Roosevelt (1933-1945) began mobilizing industry and rebuilding U.S. military forces. After France fell to Nazi Germany in 1940, the U.S. War Department launched a major expansion, building or modernizing military bases, shipyards, supply depots, and other facilities across the nation. From Alaska to Florida, military construction transformed many sleepy coastal areas into industrial hubs.

Rush to the Shore

After World War II, the U.S. economy expanded sharply as soldiers returned to civilian life and weapons factories shifted to producing cars and consumer goods. Leisure travel became affordable for middle- and working-class families. In 1956, President Dwight D. Eisenhower commissioned a new interstate highway system, which made many coastal regions more accessible. Low-cost mortgages for veterans helped to spur a wave of homebuilding, including new construction in coastal areas.

As beaches became increasingly popular destinations, the federal government took a larger role in beach replenishment projects — moving sand and sediment to rebuild eroded shorelines. Before World War II, such projects were rare and were funded by state governments and local communities. But in 1946, Congress authorized the Army Corps of Engineers to help restore public beaches and the federal government to pay up to a third of the costs. In 1956, Congress allowed the Corps to participate in private-beach replenishment projects that showed substantial public benefits. And in 1962, Congress raised the federal cost-sharing limit for beach restoration to 50 percent.[44]

In 1965, Hurricane Betsy struck the Gulf Coast, flooding 164,000 homes in New Orleans and killing 76 people.[45] The scale of the damage spurred Congress in 1968 to create the National Flood Insurance Program. Initially, purchasing flood insurance was voluntary. But after Hurricane Agnes hit the East Coast in 1972, killing 122 and causing $2.1 billion in damage, it became clear that many coastal residents had not bought policies.[46]

In 1973, Congress made flood insurance mandatory for federally backed mortgages in high-risk flood areas. But because many eligible owners found ways around the requirement, problems persisted in the program.

Nonetheless, Americans continued moving to the coasts. The population of counties along the Atlantic, Pacific and Gulf Coasts rose from 47 million in 1960 to 89 million in 2010, an 89 percent increase. In contrast, the overall U.S. population grew by 72 percent during that period.[47] About the same time, the average population density of coastal counties, excluding Alaska, rose from 260 people per square mile in 1960 to 479 in 2008.[48]

Coasts Under Pressure

During the second half of the 20th century, intense coastal development began to alarm observers who worried that scenic areas would be covered with houses, roads, and billboards. Between 1953 and 1984, conservationists persuaded Congress to add 10 swaths of unspoiled coasts and islands to the National Park System as National Seashores, protecting them from any new development. Seven of the sites were located along the Atlantic Coast, two on the Gulf Coast, and one in California.

By the late 1960s, many national leaders were becoming concerned about negative impacts of unfettered development across the United States. In 1969, a congressionally mandated commission called for more strategic management of U.S. fisheries, waters, and coastlines.[49] The commission, chaired by Ford Foundation President Julius Stratton, called coastal zones "in many respects . . . the Nation's most valuable geographic feature" and warned that they were at risk.

"Rapidly intensifying use of coastal areas already has outrun the capabilities of local governments to plan their orderly development and to resolve conflicts," the commission reported. Trade, industry, fishing, recreation, the armed forces, and other uses were all competing for coastal space, but responsibility for managing coasts was spread among many agencies with no one in charge.[50]

To fill this gap the commission urged Congress to pass a coastal management law that would set priorities, create a new agency to manage oceanic and atmospheric issues (recognizing that oceans and atmosphere interacted to shape global weather and climate patterns), and authorize the federal government to help states pay for coastal-management policies.

Almost simultaneously in 1969, an undersea wellhead near Santa Barbara, Calif., blew out and leaked 200,000 gallons of oil, contaminating 35 miles of coastline and killing seabirds, seals, and dolphins. The Santa Barbara oil spill helped to catalyze the first Earth Day rally in April 1970 and led to state and federal bans on new offshore drilling.

Also in 1970, Congress voted to establish the National Oceanic and Atmospheric Administration (NOAA) within the Department of Commerce to manage U.S. fisheries, monitor the climate, forecast weather, and restore U.S. coastlines. And in 1972, Congress enacted the Coastal Zone Management Act, which encouraged coastal states to develop plans for managing and protecting their coasts. The law also created a National Estuarine Reserve Research System to research and conserve large estuaries (bodies of water where salt and fresh water meet), such as the Chesapeake Bay. Many of these zones, which are ecologically rich and harbor many species of fish and birds, had been heavily polluted and threatened by shoreline development.

The Coastal Zone Management Act gave states grants for coastal protection if they adopted a management

An iconic roller coaster in Seaside Heights, N.J., sits offshore after Superstorm Sandy struck the community last October. Storm damage along New Jersey's coast was unprecedented in the state's history, according to the National Hurricane Center. Sandy inundated seaside towns with water and sand, swept houses from their foundations and destroyed cars, boats, and boardwalks.

plan. But some states regulated coastal development more aggressively than others. The act "doesn't set standards for what should be in coastal management plans, so it's pretty toothless," says Georgetown's Byrne.

Congress took a more forceful approach with the 1982 Coastal Barrier Resources Act, which severely limited development on barrier islands along the Atlantic and Gulf Coasts. The law recognized that these islands were unique land forms and protected the mainland against storms. Buildings constructed or substantially improved on the islands after the law went into effect were ineligible for federal flood insurance, and FEMA disaster aid was limited to emergencies that threatened lives or public health and safety.[51]

"In the last six years alone, the federal government has spent more than $800 million to aid development and redevelopment of coastal barriers," President Ronald Reagan said. "By signing [the act] into law today, this administration is acting to halt this subsidy spiral."[52]

In Harm's Way

Through the 1980s and 1990s, as Americans continued to flock to the coasts, every storm put more lives and property at risk. After heavy flooding along the Mississippi River in the early 1990s, Congress tightened penalties for lenders who failed to enforce flood insurance requirements, and FEMA began a public education

Interest Grows in "Soft" Shoreline Engineering

"This approach improves the quality of life in cities."

As state and local governments address coastal flooding hazards, some are trying an innovative concept called soft shoreline engineering. It uses plants and other natural materials to stabilize shorelines, rather than hard structures such as concrete retaining walls or banks of riprap (broken stones or chunks of concrete).

Soft engineering projects include restoring marshes and offshore shellfish beds and creating buffer zones of native plants that thrive in floodplains.

Advocates of soft engineering say it is often cheaper than hard engineered strategies and does not interfere with natural ecological processes, such as the transport of sediments along shorelines. Soft techniques also protect upland areas from storms and floods: Shellfish reefs can act as barriers against storm surges, and marshes soak up floodwaters, releasing them slowly after storms have passed.

Soft shoreline engineering also complements city initiatives to reclaim urban waterfronts and make them more attractive and accessible. "We're developing more parks and finding more ways for people to connect with water," says Timothy Beatley, a professor of urban and environmental planning at the University of Virginia. "This approach improves the quality of life in cities and makes them more adaptable at the same time."

The U.S. Fish and Wildlife Service has cooperated with local partners in the United States and Canada on more than 50 soft engineering projects along the Detroit River and the western shoreline of Lake Erie — a highly urbanized area where heavy industry once occupied most waterfront zones. The projects have removed old dams, restored flood plains and created new habitat for birds and passages for fish.[1]

Experts want soft engineering projects monitored and measured so officials can determine whether the projects are producing the ecological benefits they were designed to achieve. One review of 38 projects around Detroit found that only six had carried out any kind of post-construction monitoring, and those projects only measured impacts for a year or two. Damaged ecosystems often need more time to recover.[2]

A provocative exhibit at New York's Museum of Modern Art in 2010 presented a radical vision of soft shoreline engineering for the city. The exhibit, titled "Rising Currents," challenged five teams to design soft engineering structures that could protect zones around New York Harbor during an extreme flood. Their proposals included waterfront parks, restored oyster reefs, parks set in basins designed to hold floodwaters, and streets paved with absorptive tiles to filter runoff.[3]

After Hurricane Sandy flooded lower Manhattan in October, leaving millions of residents homeless or without

---

campaign to boost enrollment. Coverage rose from about 1.5 million policies in the mid-1970s to 4 million in 1997, and the value of property insured increased from $165 billion in 1978 to $703 billion in 2000.[53]

In 2005, Hurricanes Katrina and Rita struck the Gulf Coast, devastating communities from Texas to the Florida Panhandle. Together the storms killed nearly 1,900 people and caused more than $120 billion in damages.[54] Congress was forced to increase the NFIP's federal borrowing authority from $1.5 billion to $20.8 billion to cover claims. The U.S. Government Accountability Office, Congress's oversight agency, warned that the program was not financially sound and might never be able to repay its loans to the Treasury.[55]

Images of a flooded New Orleans after Katrina drove home the message that large storms could devastate major cities. Planners and environmental advocates warned that the same thing could happen along the East Coast, especially as climate change raises sea levels. Several task forces in 2005, 2006, and 2010 forecast that a direct hit on New York City by a major storm could cause massive damage and disrupt transportation systems and financial markets. But even after Tropical Storm Irene flooded parts of the city's subway system in 2011, New York leaders did not take aggressive steps to floodproof the city.[56]

utilities and transportation, the designers looked like prophets.

"It was sort of an, 'Oh my god, we were so right' moment when all the electrical transformers started to blow up," said Susannah Drake, a landscape architect and team leader. "They need my waterproof vaults to put all the infrastructure under the sidewalks."[4]

As the exhibit showed, soft shoreline engineering alone cannot immunize cities from heavy floods. "It's smaller-scale infrastructure that you do along with other changes to the built environment," says Beatley.

Beach replenishment is another form of soft shoreline engineering that is widely used in areas with heavy coastal development, especially along the Atlantic Coast. But since replenishment involves simply pumping sand onto beaches, it is a temporary solution. "If a community decides to manage erosion that way, they will be doing it forever," says Robert Young, a coastal geologist and director of the Program for the Study of Developed Shorelines at Western Carolina University.

After Sandy, many observers contended that dunes (including both engineered and natural dunes) had protected some coastal communities from the full force of the storm and mitigated the damage.[5] But Young wants more analysis. "Those claims need to be tested scientifically before we assume they're true," he says.

Even if communities and taxpayers are willing to pay for replenishing beaches over and over after storms, there may be another limit — the supply of sand. Atlantic coastal communities that invest heavily in beach engineering are having trouble finding enough sand of suitable quality close to shore.[6]

"We are always looking for sand," said Margaret Kearney, president of the nonprofit Duxbury Beach Reservation, Inc., in Massachusetts.[7]

— *Jennifer Weeks*

---

[1] For examples, see "Soft Shoreline Engineering," U.S. Fish & Wildlife Service, https://www.fws.gov/refuge/detroit_river/what_we_do/resource_management/soft_shoreline_engineering.html.

[2] John H. Hartig, Michael A. Zarull, and Anna Cook, "Soft Shoreline Engineering Survey of Ecological Effectiveness," *Ecological Engineering*, Vol. 37, 2011, pp. 1231-1238.

[3] For details see "Rising Currents: Projects for New York's Waterfront," Museum of Modern Art, www.moma.org/visit/calendar/exhibitions/1031.

[4] Brad McKee, "In New York, Drying Out," *Landscape Architecture Magazine*, November 1, 2012, http://landscapearchitecturemagazine.org/2012/11/01/in-new-york-drying-out/.

[5] For example, see Evan Lehmann, "Superstorm Sandy Settles Long-Standing Argument over the Value of Dunes," Scientific American.com, December 11, 2012, http://www.scientificamerican.com/article.cfm?id=superstorm-sandy-settles-long-standing-argument-over-the-value-of-dunes; and Janet Babin, "Beach Dunes Spark a Battle After Sandy," WNYC Radio, December 12, 2012, http://www.wnyc.org/story/257497-beach_dunes_spark_battle_after_sandy/.

[6] Lizette Alvarez, "Where Sand is Gold, the Reserves Are Running Dry," *The New York Times*, August 24, 2013, http://www.nytimes.com/2013/08/25/us/where-sand-is-gold-the-coffers-are-running-dry-in-florida.html.

[7] Beth Daley, "'Sand Wars' Come to New England Coast," *The Boston Globe*, December 15, 2014.

CURRENT SITUATION

Clashing Signals

As New York and New Jersey continue to recover from Sandy, many observers say clearer signals from the federal government would help states manage development in hazardous areas. Even when officials propose limits, as Gov. Cuomo has done in New York State, critics argue that many federal policies promote coastal development without considering flooding and storm hazards.

"The Federal Highway Administration doesn't have any directives requiring it to assess flood risks before it rebuilds a highway," says Stiles of Wetlands Watch. "Federal tax credits and development incentives don't differentiate between coastal and inland locations. There are no drivers [policy directions] that anticipate risk over the useful lives of building projects."

One meaningful change, Stiles asserts, would be for FEMA to start considering sea-level rise projections in its flood hazard maps. FEMA is studying how climate change could affect the National Flood Insurance Program and already has concluded that sea-level rise could significantly increase the number of high-risk flood areas across the nation this century.[57] However, sea-level rise is not factored into FEMA's mapping practices, so it is likely underestimating the geographic breadth and

AT ISSUE

Should the National Flood Insurance Program Be Privatized?

YES

R. J. Lehmann
Senior Fellow, The R Street Institute

Written for *CQ Researcher*, February 2013

The National Flood Insurance Program (NFIP), in a sense, is responsible for the modern American suburb. Construction of the Interstate Highway System, easy mortgage insurance from the Veterans Administration and Federal Housing Administration, and a host of federal, state and local rules favoring low-density residential development all played a role in the nation's post-war suburbanization, to be sure. But the 1968 creation of the NFIP really changed the landscape, literally, by allowing acres of lush river valleys and miles of coastal land to be transformed into manicured lawns and beachfront cottages.

Unfortunately, after nearly 45 years the NFIP is unsustainable, with some $30 billion in debt that it has no means to repay. With some 5.6 million policyholders across the country, the program also has sparked development in the most risk-prone and environmentally sensitive regions, threatening innumerable endangered species, depleting wetlands, and overdeveloping barrier islands that serve as natural buffers against hurricanes.

Today, global warming and rising sea levels appear likely to make future floods and tropical storms both more frequent and more severe. To prepare for that, a functioning private market must be part of the solution. When property owners don't bear the full cost of the risks they face, they are encouraged to take on more. Transitioning to a private, risk-based insurance market for floods will not be easy, but it is a challenge private insurers can meet, just as they have done in countries such as the United Kingdom and Australia. Advances in mapping, risk modeling, and the ability to spread risk across the globe means that most of the logistical problems the insurance industry once faced in underwriting floods have been long solved.

Private flood insurance would be expensive, although not nearly as expensive as continually rebuilding flood-prone communities that have no incentive to adapt and mitigate risk because that risk is borne by others. Some policyholders may need financial assistance to harden their homes against flooding, pay their premiums or move to higher ground. But research by the Institute for Policy Integrity shows that the NFIP's benefits currently flow overwhelmingly to the rich, with the wealthiest counties filing 3.5 times more claims and receiving $1 billion more in NFIP payments between 1998 and 2008 than the poorest counties.

The NFIP has helped shape the country, for good and for ill. To tackle long-term challenges, both budgetary and environmental, it must be phased out.

NO

Jon Jensen
Chair, Government Affairs Committee, Independent Insurance Agents and Brokers of America

From testimony before the Subcommittee on Economic Policy, Senate Committee on Banking, Housing and Urban Affairs, May 9, 2012

The Independent Insurance Agents and Brokers of America (IIABA) believes that the NFIP provides a vital service to people and places that have been hit by a natural disaster. The private insurance industry has been, and continues to be, largely unable to underwrite flood insurance because of the catastrophic nature of these losses. Therefore, the NFIP is virtually the only way for people to protect against the loss of their home or business due to flood damage.

Prior to the introduction of the program in 1968, the federal government spent increasing sums . . . on disaster assistance to flood victims. Since then, the NFIP has saved disaster assistance money and provided a more reliable system of payments for people whose properties have suffered flood damage. It is also important to note that for almost two decades, up until the 2005 hurricane season, no taxpayer money had been used to support the NFIP; rather, the NFIP was able to support itself using the funds from the premiums it collected every year. . . .

Despite our strong support of the NFIP, we also recognize that the program is far from perfect, which was made . . . clear by the devastating 2005 hurricane season. . . . While IIABA is confident that the NFIP will recover, it is important that Congress shore up the NFIP's financial foundation and use this opportunity to enact needed reforms to ensure the long-term sustainability of the program. . . .

Some observers have argued that the program should be eliminated or completely privatized. These arguments center on the assumption that the private market could step in and offer flood insurance coverage. However, the IIABA has met with many insurance carriers who categorically state that the private market is simply unable to underwrite this inherently difficult catastrophic risk, especially in the most high-risk zones where it is needed.

IIABA would always prefer to utilize the private market, and our members would almost certainly prefer to work directly with private insurance carriers rather than a government agency. However, where there is a failure in the marketplace, as there is in the case of flood insurance, we believe it is imperative that the government step in to ensure that consumers have the protection they need. . . . We see no evidence that the private marketplace is any more prepared or capable of underwriting flood risk in 2012 than . . . in 1968.

severity of flood risks.[58] In contrast, the Army Corps of Engineers requires project managers to consider potential sea-level change in every coastal activity.[59]

"If FEMA started using sea-level rise projections like the Corps, we would see changes," says Stiles. "State plans are written to FEMA standards, so raising that bar would make a big difference."

Other experts cite disaster relief under the Stafford Act as a major driver of coastal development. "The Stafford Act aid puts back roads, power lines and water lines after storms, which promotes rebuilding of homes," says Young of Western Carolina University. "If coastal communities had to replace that infrastructure themselves, their tax rates would be incredibly high, and property values would be very different."

Major disaster declarations under the Stafford Act have increased in recent years, from an average of 18 per year in the 1960s to 56 per year between 2000 and 2009. (These numbers include storms, flooding, tornadoes, and other events, not just coastal storms.) Some politicians have suggested that states are requesting disaster declarations more frequently in order to obtain more federal aid.

But analysts say many factors could be driving the increase. For example, population growth and economic development have put more people and property in harm's way.[60]

As Congress debates federal budget policy, some observers have proposed limiting Stafford Act aid. Matt Mayer, a visiting fellow at the conservative Heritage Foundation, recommends cutting the federal portion of shared costs for all FEMA declarations to no more than 25 percent.[61] The Congressional Research Service suggests a more moderate option: reducing to 50 percent the federal share of aid for communities that don't require storm mitigation. The aid helps pay for measures to reduce harm from future disasters, such as installing flood control barriers or raising the height of homes.[62]

Flood Insurance Fraud?

In New York and New Jersey, thousands of residents who held policies purchased under NFIP say the program shortchanged them, paying out much less than the actual damaged they suffered. Under NFIP, people who buy maximum coverage can receive up to $250,000 for flood damage. But many claimants received only a fraction of that amount, even when independent assessors said they were due much more money.

"I did not realize that the game was stacked against us, and there really was no way to win," said Doug Quinn, who received $90,000 for damage to his house in Toms River, N.J. during Sandy, even after state officials told Quinn the damage was so severe that the house had to be demolished.[63]

After several thousand Sandy victims sued FEMA, saying the agency had deliberately lowballed their claims, the agency agreed in 2015 to reopen every post-Sandy flood claim. But complaints continued to mount. Several inspectors who had worked for FEMA told congressional investigators and reporters that engineers who worked for private insurance companies that wrote NFIP policies had altered their reports to hide or devalue damage.[64]

Insurers denied that they had deliberately underpaid claims. "There's always going to be the case in the event of a major catastrophic event where . . . [victims] will believe that they are due more than, in fact, the claims was ultimately adjusted for," said Insurance Information Institute president Robert Hartwig.[65] But in May 2016, FEMA announced that it would oversee insurance companies that wrote NFIP policies more closely and make it easier for homeowners to appeal claims decisions.[66]

"These are the right steps to build out this foundation and turn this program around," said Roy Wright, who took over management of the NFIP at FEMA in 2015. "And we have a lot more work to go."[67]

Some members of Congress are skeptical that FEMA can fix the program. "It is too little, too late," said New Jersey Democratic Sen. Robert Menendez. "FEMA has basically turned over this program to the private insurance companies." Menendez and other senators were reportedly considering either completely privatizing the flood insurance program or having FEMA run it directly, without relying on private insurers.[68]

Rising Seas

Estimating how quickly sea-level rise will accelerate in coming decades due to climate change has been a highly complex issue for climate scientists in recent years.

When the Intergovernmental Panel on Climate Change (IPCC, the international scientific body that evaluates climate science) published its last major assessment in 2013, it estimated that warming of Earth's surface would raise global sea levels 10 to 384 inches by 2100.[69] But more recent studies indicate that these numbers may be low.

In 2015, NASA scientists warned that IPCC projections did not include water from melting glaciers at the North and South Poles. Sea levels "might rise half a meter per century, or several meters per century. We just don't know," said NASA glaciologist Eric Rignot."[70]

Other research shows that sea levels are not rising uniformly. The U.S. Geological Survey reported that sea levels along the U.S. East Coast, from North Carolina to Massachusetts, are rising 2 to 3.7 millimeters (0.08 to 0.15 inches) per year — three to four times faster than globally — due to changes in ocean circulation patterns. Cities in this zone will be highly vulnerable to flooding during storms, the scientists said.[71]

"We've learned in the past several years that impacts are more severe than we previously thought," says Columbia University climate scientist Radley Horton. "Now the worst-case scenario projects that global sea levels could rise as much as six feet by 2100. The biggest remaining uncertainty is what will happen to that land ice in Greenland and West Antarctica. We know it won't all melt, but even if 5 to 10 percent melts, that will have a big impact."

OUTLOOK
Resilient Coastlines

Although the long-term impacts of Sandy are still unfolding, scientists and environmentalists say the giant storm may lead to new thinking about coastal development — if leaders and communities recognize that Sandy was not a fluke.

"This is a teachable moment, and it could make people start rethinking unsustainable practices before the next storm," says Stiles of Wetlands Watch.

To drive lasting change, experts widely agree that laws and policies should be amended to reduce incentives for coastal development. "We should end subsidies for rebuilding in the most vulnerable coastal areas, including programs like beach nourishment," says Western Carolina University's Young. "You could do it in an organized way — for example, by tapering off funding over a decade, or giving people one or two strikes [before making them ineligible for money to rebuild]. If communities had to deal with these issues themselves, they would make better decisions."

Flooding in New York City during Sandy was a warning for coastal cities. "We need to find ways to make cities livable in the aftermath of big storms," says Beatley of the University of Virginia. "People may have to live without power or water for some time, so we should be designing structures with features like natural day lighting and ventilation. That will make them more resilient."

Some states and cities are already taking Sandy as a warning. Boston, Mass. is conducting surveys of all buildings and subway lines in flood zones and requiring developers to address climate change risks when applying for building permits.[72]

In fact, coastal experts say reducing risky practices makes political sense. "This ought to be an issue where environmentalists and fiscal conservatives can agree on doing things differently," says Young. "Rebuilding in flood zones is an easy decision when owners are spending other people's money. We shouldn't be taking all the economic risk for them."

In a study published early in 2016, researchers at the University of Georgia combined data about population growth in coastal regions with sea-level rise projections and estimated that if sea levels rise at catastrophic rates — for example, if Antarctic ice sheets collapse, as some scientists say could occur — up to 13 million people could be at risk from flooding, nearly half of them in Florida.[73]

Experts warn that if states fail to plan for rising seas now, they will pay in the long run. "There are three ways to respond to climate change: You can adapt, mitigate, or suffer," says Fugate of Rhode Island's Coastal Resources Management Council. "The less mitigation you do, the more adaptation and suffering you'll have to do. And the longer you wait, the more expensive mitigation and adaptation become."

NOTES

1. Sandy set records for low pressure (measured in millibars) in Atlantic City and other nearby locations. Lower pressure at the center of hurricanes and tropical storms corresponds to stronger storms.

1. See Andrew Freedman, "Statistics Show Hurricane Sandy's Extraordinary Intensity," Climate Central, November 1, 2012, http://www.climatecentral.org/news/statistics-show-just-how-intense-hurricane-sandy-was-15196.
2. Ibid.
3. See Eric S. Blake, Todd B. Kimberlain, Robert J. Berg, John P. Cangialosi, and John L. Beven, II "Tropical Cyclone Report: Hurricane Sandy," National Hurricane Center, February 12, 2013, p. 14, and Tables 8, 9, p. 120, http://www.nhc.noaa.gov/data/tcr/AL182012_Sandy.pdf.
4. Ibid.
5. NOAA, "The thirty costliest mainland United States tropical cyclones 1900-2013," http://www.aoml.noaa.gov/hrd/tcfaq/costliesttable.html.
6. "Report: Sandy Was USA's Second-Costliest Hurricane," Associated Press, February 12, 2013, http://www.usatoday.com/story/weather/2013/02/12/hurricane-sandy-weather-katrina/1912941/.
7. For background, see Adriel Bettelheim, "Coastal Development," *CQ Researcher*, August 21, 1998, pp. 721-744.
8. U.S. Government Accountability Office, "Key Issues: High Risk: National Flood Insurance Program," http://www.gao.gov/highrisk/national_flood_insurance/why_did_study.
9. "The NFIP Floodplain Management Requirements," Federal Emergency Management Agency, http://www.fema.gov/pdf/floodplain/nfip_sg_unit_5.pdf. A 100-year flood is one that has a 1 percent chance of flooding in any given year.
10. "Understanding the Stafford Act: Its Effect on Public Entities," Public Risk Management Association, http://www.primacentral.org/resources/Stafford%20Act%20FAQs.pdf.
11. "Disaster Declarations," Federal Emergency Management Agency, http://www.fema.gov/disasters.
12. J. Wylie Donald, "Will Climate Change Considerations Affect Rebuilding After Sandy?" Climatelawyers.com, November 27, 2012, http://climatelawyers.com/post/2012/11/27/Will-Climate-Change-Considerations-Affect-Rebuilding-After-Sandy-The-Short-Answer-is-Yes.aspx.
13. For example, see Serge Dedina, "Hurricane Sandy, Climate Change, Sand Replenishment and Surf," Encinitas Patch, October 31, 2012, http://patch.com/california/imperialbeach/hurricane-sandy-climate-change-sand-replenishment-surf; and Kate Spinner, "Beach Renourishment May Harm Ecosystem," *Sarasota Herald-Tribune*, February 19, 2012, http://www.heraldtribune.com/article/20120219/article/120219439?tc=ar.
14. For background, see Chanan Tigay, "Extreme Weather," *CQ Researcher*, September 9, 2011, pp. 733-756; Reed Karaim, "Climate Change," *CQ Global Researcher*, February 1, 2010, pp. 25-50; and Colin Woodard, "Curbing Climate Change," *CQ Global Researcher*, February 1, 2007, pp. 25-48.
15. U.S. Environmental Protection Agency, "Future Climate Change," https://www3.epa.gov/climatechange/science/future.html#sealevel.
16. Melanie Gade, "Sea-Level Rise Accelerating on U.S. Atlantic Coast," Sound Waves (U.S. Geological Survey), September/October 2012, http://soundwaves.usgs.gov/2012/10/research.html.
17. For example, see Kerry Emanuel, *What We Know about Climate Change*, 2nd ed. (MIT Press, 2012); "'Storm of the Century' May Become 'Storm of the Decade,'" ScienceDaily, February 23, 2012, https://www.sciencedaily.com/releases/2012/02/120223133216.htm.
18. Orrin H. Pilkey, "We Need to Retreat From the Beach," *The New York Times*, November 15, 2012, http://www.nytimes.com/2012/11/15/opinion/a-beachfront-retreat.html.
19. Anna Sale, "Christie and Cuomo's Dueling Visions for Post-Sandy Rebuilding," WNYC Radio, November 23, 2012, http://www.wnyc.org/articles/its-free-country/2012/nov/23/christie-and-cuomos-dueling-visions-post-sandy-rebuilding/.
20. Todd B. Bates, "N.J. Sandy Rebuilding Rules: Go Higher or Pay More," *USA Today*, January 25, 2013, http://www.usatoday.com/story/news/nation/2013/01/25/sandy-rebuilding-flood-maps/1863761/.
21. Ken Lovett, "NY Could Buy Out Flood Zones' Hurricane Sandy Victims: Gov. Cuomo," New York

Daily News, January 24, 2013, http://www.nydailynews.com/blogs/dailypolitics/2013/01/state-could-buy-out-flood-zones-hurricane-sandy-victims-gov-cuomo?print=true.

22. For updates see Fox Beach 165, http://foxbeach165.com/,

23. Matt A.V. Chaban, "Staten Island Homes Finally Go Up, and Up For Auction, In Hurricane's Wake," *The New York Times*, March 7, 2016, http://www.nytimes.com/2016/03/08/nyregion/staten-island-homes-finally-go-up-and-up-for-auction-in-hurricanes-wake.html.

24. For background, see Kenneth Jost, "Property Rights," *CQ Researcher*, March 4, 2005, pp. 197-220.

25. Rob Young, "Shoot the Messenger: Carolina's Costly Mistake on Sea Level Rise," Yale Environment 360, June 18, 2012, http://e360.yale.edu/feature/north_carolina_costly_mistake_on_climate_change/2543/; Alan I. Leshner and William L. Chameides, "N.C. Can't Outlaw Global Climate Change," *Raleigh News & Observer*, August 1, 2012, http://www.aaas.org/sites/default/files/migrate/uploads/0801newsobserver_leshner_chameides.pdf.

26. Dave Dewitt, "The State that 'Outlawed Climate Change' Accepts Latest Sea-level Rise Report," WUNC.org, May 4, 2015, http://wunc.org/post/state-outlawed-climate-change-accepts-latest-sea-level-rise-report#stream/0.

27. See Jessica Grannis, "Analysis of How the Flood Insurance Reform Act of 2012 (H.R. 4348) May Affect State and Local Adaptation Efforts," Georgetown Climate Center, August 1, 2012, http://www.law.georgetown.edu/academics/academic-programs/clinical-programs/our-clinics/HIP/upload/GCC_Analysis-of-the-Flood-Insurance-Reform-Act-of-2012_8-14-12.pdf.

28. For details see FEMA, "Impact of National Flood Insurance Program (NFIP) Program Changes," April 2013, http://www.fema.gov/media-library-data/20130726-1909-25045-0554/bw12_sec_205_207_factsheet4_13_2013.pdf.

29. Justin Gillis and Felicity Barringer, "As Coasts Rebuild and U.S. Pays, Repeatedly, the Critics Ask Why," *The New York Times*, November 18, 2012, www.nytimes.com/2012/11/19/science/earth/as-coasts-rebuild-and-us-pays-again-critics-stop-to-ask-why.html?pagewanted=all.

30. Erin O'Neill, ""Union Beach couple gets $33k insurance bill after raising home above new federal flood standards," NJ.com, July 27, 2014, http://www.nj.com/monmouth/index.ssf/2014/07/union_beach_homeowners_get_33k_flood_insurance_bill_after_raising_home_above_new_federal_requirement.html.

31. Letter online at http://www.flgov.com/2014/01/09/gov-scott-obama-failing-to-delay-nfip-law-that-hurts-floridians-yet-delayed-healthcare-law/.

32. FEMA, "Homeowner Flood Insurance Affordability Act Overview," April 3, 2014, http://www.fema.gov/media-library-data/1396551935597-4048b68f6d695a6eb6e6e7118d3ce464/HFIAA_Overview_FINAL_03282014.pdf.

33. Kate Sheppard, "Congress Just Undid the 1 Good Thing It's Done on Climate Change," Huffington Post, March 17, 2014, http://www.huffingtonpost.com/2014/03/17/congress-flood-insurance_n_4981226.html.

34. For details see Texas A&M University, "Ike Dike," http://www.tamug.edu/ikedike/.

35. Eric Berger, "Ike Dike May Be Among Sandy's Casualties," Houston Chronicle, Nov. 4, 2012, www.chron.com/news/houston-texas/houston/article/Ike-Dike-may-be-among-Sandy-s-casualties-4005871.php.

36. "Recommendations to Improve the Strength and Resilience of the Empire State's Infrastructure," NYS 2100 Commission, January 2013, p. 121, http://www.rockefellerfoundation.org/uploads/files/7c012997-176f-4e80-bf9c-b473ae9bbbf3.pdf.

37. New York City Panel on Climate Change, "Climate Change Adaptation in New York City: Building a Risk Management Response," *Annals of the New York Academy of Sciences*, Vol. 1196, 2010, p. 76, http://onlinelibrary.wiley.com/doi/10.1111/j.1749-6632.2009.05318.x/pdf.

38. "Recommendations to Improve the Strength and Resilience of the Empire State's Infrastructure," op. cit., p. 123.

39. Jeroen C. J. H. Aerts, W. J. Wouter Botzen, Kerry Emanuel, Ning Lin, Hans de Moel1, Erwann O. Michel-Kerjan, "Evaluating Flood Resilience Strategies for Coastal Megacities," *Science*, Vol. 344, May 2, 2014, pp. 473-475.

40. Alan Feuer, "Building for the Next Big Storm," *The New York Times*, October 25, 2014, http://www.nytimes.com/2014/10/26/nyregion/after-hurricane-sandy-new-york-rebuilds-for-the-future.html?_r=0; Winnie Hu, "New York City to Get $176 Million From U.S. for Storm Protections," *The New York Times*, January 18, 2016, http://www.nytimes.com/2016/01/19/nyregion/new-york-city-to-get-176-million-from-us-for-storm-protections.html.

41. Jeffrey D. Sachs, Andrew D. Mellinger, and John L. Gallup, "The Geography of Poverty and Wealth," *Scientific American*, March 2001, http://www.earth.columbia.edu/sitefiles/file/about/director/documents/sciam0301.pdf; Jared Diamond, "What Makes Countries Rich or Poor?' New York Review of Books, June 7, 2012, www.nybooks.com/articles/archives/2012/jun/07/what-makes-countries-rich-or-poor/?pagination=false.

42. "Becoming American: The British Atlantic Colonies, 1690-1763," National Humanities Center, http://nationalhumanitiescenter.org/pds/becomingamer/growth/text2/text2read.htm.

43. See "Unit 2: National Flood Insurance Program," Federal Emergency Management Administration, pp. 2-3, http://www.fema.gov/pdf/floodplain/nfip_sg_unit_2.pdf.

44. Sen. Tom Coburn, "Washed Out to Sea: How Congress Prioritizes Beach Pork Over National Needs," May 2009, pp. 9-10, http://www.coburn.senate.gov/public/index.cfm?a=Files.Serve&File_id=e12c6935-f034-4d9e-b7b3-093cf98a4ff9.

45. "Hurricanes: Science and Society," http://www.hurricanescience.org/history/storms/1960s/betsy/.

46. Facts on Hurricane Agnes from "Hurricane Agnes," National Oceanic and Atmospheric Administration, http://www.nhc.noaa.gov/outreach/history/#agnes.

47. U.S. Census Bureau figures.

48. "Coastline Population Trends in the United States: 1960 to 2008," U.S. Census Bureau, p. 24, www.census.gov/prod/2010pubs/p25-1139.pdf.

49. For background, see Mary. H. Cooper, "Threatened Fisheries," *CQ Researcher*, August 2, 2002, pp. 617-648.

50. "Our Nation and the Sea: A Plan for National Action," Commission on Marine Science, Engineering and Resources," January 1969, pp. 49-57, http://www.lib.noaa.gov/noaainfo/heritage/stratton/title.html.

51. "Coastal Barrier Resources Act Fact Sheet," Federal Emergency Management Agency, http://www.fema.gov/library/viewRecord.do?id=3818.

52. "Statement on Signing the Coastal Barrier Resources Act," Oct.18, 1982, http://www.presidency.ucsb.edu/ws/index.php?pid=41879.

53. Erwann O. Michel-Kerjan, "Catastrophe Economics: The National Flood Insurance Program," *Journal of Economic Perspectives*, Vol. 24 (4) (Fall 2010), p. 169, https://www.aeaweb.org/articles?id=10.1257/jep.24.4.165.

54. See reports for hurricanes Katrina and Rita at http://www.nhc.noaa.gov/data/tcr/AL122005_Katrina.pdf and http://www.nhc.noaa.gov/data/tcr/AL182005_Rita.pdf.

55. "Federal Emergency Management Agency: Ongoing Challenges Facing the National Flood Insurance Program" GAO-08-118T, U.S. Government Accountability Office, Oct. 2, 2007, p. 6, www.gao.gov/assets/120/117930.pdf.

56. David W. Chen and Mireya Navarro, "For Years, Warnings That It Could Happen Here," *The New York Times*, October 30, 2012, http://www.nytimes.com/2012/10/31/nyregion/for-years-warnings-that-storm-damage-could-ravage-new-york.html; "New York Superstorm Warnings Went Unheeded for Decades, Observers Say," The Associated Press, December 9, 2012, www.insurancejournal.com/news/east/2012/12/09/273239.htm.

57. "FEMA Climate Change Adaptation Policy Statement," January 23, 2012, p. 2, item IV.A.2, https://www.fema.gov/media-library/assets/documents/33082.

58. FEMA, "Coastal Flood Hazard Mapping Questions," updated November 18, 2015, http://www.fema.gov/coastal-frequently-asked-questions#How is FEMA accounting for sea level

rise and climate change on the FIRMs? Does sea level rise/climate change affect the FIRMs?

59. Current guidance is at http://planning.usace.army.mil/toolbox/library/ECs/EC11652212Nov2011.pdf.

60. Bruce R. Lindsay and Francis X. McCarthy, "Stafford Act Declarations 1953-2011: Trends and Analyses, and Implications for Congress," Congressional Research Service, Aug. 31, 2012, pp. 8-13, www.fas.org/sgp/crs/homesec/R42702.pdf.

61. Matt A. Mayer, "Hurricane Sandy: Disaster Aid Request Too Big," Heritage Foundation, Dec. 13, 2012, www.heritage.org/research/reports/2012/12/hurricane-sandy-disaster-aid-request-too-big.

62. Lindsay and McCarthy, op. cit., p. 25.

63. "Business of Disaster: Insurance Firms Profited $400 Million After Sandy," National Public Radio, May 24, 2016, http://www.npr.org/2016/05/24/478868270/business-of-disaster-insurance-firms-profited-400-million-after-sandy.

64. Emmarie Muetteman, "New Jersey Representative, Citing Fraud, Calls on Congress to Investigate FEMA," The New York Times, April 28, 2016, http://www.nytimes.com/2016/04/29/nyregion/new-jersey-congressman-citing-fraud-calls-on-congress-to-investigate-fema.html; National Public Radio, "Business of disaster," op. cit.

65. National Public Radio, "Business of Disaster," op. cit.

66. Priyanka Boghani, "FEMA Announces Reforms to National Flood Insurance Program," PBS.org, May 24, 2016, http://www.pbs.org/wgbh/frontline/article/fema-announces-reforms-to-national-flood-insurance-program/.

67. "Lawmakers to FEMA: Flood Plan Overhaul is 'Too Little, Too Late,'" National Public Radio, June 3, 2016, http://www.npr.org/templates/transcript/transcript.php?storyId=480600851.

68. Ibid.

69. Intergovernmental Panel on Climate Change, Climate Change 2013: The Physical Science, Summary for Policymakers (2013), p. 25, http://www.climatechange2013.org/images/report/WG1AR5_SPM_FINAL.pdf (estimate converted from a range of 26-98 centimeters into inches).

70. Tim Folger, "Oceans Will Rise Much More than Predicted, NASA Says," National Geographic, August 27, 2015, http://news.nationalgeographic.com/2015/08/150827-NASA-climate-oceans-seas-greenland/.

71. Melanie Gade, "Sea-Level Rise Accelerating on U.S. Atlantic Coast," Sound Waves, U.S. Geological Survey, Sept./Oct. 2012, http://soundwaves.usgs.gov/2012/10/research.html.

72. "Mayor Menino Announces Comprehensive Actions to Better Prepare Boston for Storms Like Sandy," Feb. 5, 2013, www.cityofboston.gov/news/default.aspx?id=5959.

73. Oliver Milman, "13 Million Along U.S. Coast Could See Homes Swamped by 2100, Study Shows," The Guardian, March 14, 2016, http://www.theguardian.com/environment/2016/mar/14/climate-change-us-coast-homes-2100-great-migration.

BIBLIOGRAPHY

Books

Helvarg, David, *The Golden Shore: California's Love Affair with the Sea*, St. Martin's Press, 2013.
A journalist and ocean conservation advocate recounts the history of California's scenic 1,100-mile coastline and steps that Californians are taking to protect it.

Kahrl, Andrew W., *The Land Was Ours: African American Beaches from Jim Crow to the Sunbelt South*, Harvard University Press, 2012.
A professor of history at Marquette University describes how coastal development in mid-Atlantic and southern states after 1950 pushed many African-Americans off their land.

Pilkey, Orrin M., William J. Neal, James Andrew Graham Cooper, and Joseph T. Kelley, *The World's Beaches: A Global Guide to the Science of the Shoreline*, University of California Press, 2011.
Four prominent academic experts in earth science and coastal studies explain waves, tides, winds and other forces that make and alter beaches.

Articles

"Shifting Sands: Sandy's Lessons in Coastal Geology," U.S. Geological Survey, November 15, 2012, https://www.usgs.gov/blogs/features/usgs_top_story/shifting-sands-sandys-lessons-in-coastal-geology/?from=textlink.
Damage from Hurricane Sandy left large sections of the East Coast more vulnerable to future storms. Adapting to those changes by relocating buildings may be more effective than trying to rebuild dunes that move naturally.

Florida, Richard, and Sarah Johnson, "Making Our Coastal Cities More Resilient Can't Wait," *The Atlantic Cities*, November 1, 2012, http://www.theatlanticcities.com/jobs-and-economy/2012/11/making-our-cities-more-resilient-cant-wait/3758/.
Coastal cities are critical economic engines, so making them more resistant to natural disasters is urgent.

Frazier, Ian, "The Toll," *The New Yorker*, February 11-18, 2013, http://www.newyorker.com/reporting/2013/02/11/130211fa_fact_frazier.
Staten Island bore much of the force of Sandy and was the site of 23 deaths.

Klinenberg, Eric, "Adaptation," *The New Yorker*, January 7, 2013, http://www.newyorker.com/magazine/2013/01/07/adaptation-2.
Rotterdam and Singapore offer lessons for U.S. cities in flood-proofing.

Rudolf, John, et al., "Hurricane Sandy Damage Amplified by Breakneck Development of Coast," *The Huffington Post*, Nov. 12, 2012, www.huffingtonpost.com/2012/11/12/hurricane-sandy-damage_n_2114525.html.
New York and New Jersey had allowed intensive development in areas that were heavily damaged by Hurricane Sandy, despite known risks from direct storm hits.

Salkeld, Luke, and Ray Massey, "Thames Barrier Shuts for the First Time in Two Years to Prevent Flooding in London as Fresh Atlantic Storm Promises Yet More Rain," *Daily Mail*, December 27, 2012, http://www.dailymail.co.uk/news/article-2253624/Thames-Barrier-shuts-time-years-prevent-flooding-London-fresh-Atlantic-storm-promises-rain.html.
Britain's wettest year on record led to activation of London's floodgates in late December.

Wallack, Todd, "Homeowners Question the Use of Storm Models," *The Boston Globe*, January 6, 2013, http://www.bostonglobe.com/business/2013/01/06/air-worldwide-tracked-sandy-now-says-monster-storm-will-strike-new-england-someday/NrEB3QX7RxOxY30GmXXhvK/story.html.
Weather-modeling companies generate storm risk estimates that insurers use to set rates for homeowners.

Reports and Studies

"Recommendations to Improve the Strength and Resilience of the Empire State's Infrastructure," NYS 2100 Commission, January 2013, http://www.rockefellerfoundation.org/uploads/files/7c012997-176f-4e80-bf9c-b473ae9bbbf3.pdf.
An expert panel convened by Gov. Andrew Cuomo after Hurricane Sandy to guide rebuilding and preparation for future disasters lists short-, medium- and long-term priorities to guide rebuilding.

Burkett, Virginia, and Margaret Davidson, eds., *Coastal Impacts, Adaptations, and Vulnerabilities: A Technical Input to the 2013 National Climate Assessment*, Island Press, 2013, http://downloads.usgcrp.gov/NCA/technicalinputreports/Burkett_Davidson_Coasts_Final_.pdf.
A review by the U.S. Global Change Research Program, part of a periodic national climate study, finds that coastal U.S. communities will face many challenges adapting to climate change in the coming years.

Kousky, Carolyn, and Erwann Michel-Kerjan, "Hurricane Sandy, Storm Surge, and the National Flood Insurance Program: A Primer on New York and New Jersey," Issue Brief 12-08, Resources for the Future/Wharton Risk Center, November 2012, http://www.rff.org/RFF/Documents/RFF-IB-12-08.pdf.
A Washington, D.C. think tank and the Wharton School of Business estimate that the National Flood Insurance Program will need to increase its borrowing authority to pay claims in New York and New Jersey from Hurricane Sandy.

For More Information

Federal Emergency Management Agency, 500 C St., S.W., Washington, DC 20472; 202-646-2500; www.fema.gov. Part of the Department of Homeland Security that helps federal, state, and local governments, private organizations, and the public prepare for and respond to natural and manmade disasters; manages National Flood Insurance Program.

Independent Insurance Agents and Brokers of America, 127 South Peyton St., Alexandria, VA 22314; 800-221-7917; www.iiaba.org. A national alliance of independent insurance agents and brokers.

Office of Ocean and Coastal Resource Management, National Oceanic and Atmospheric Administration, 1305 East-West Highway, Silver Spring, MD 20910; 301-713-3155; http://coastalmanagement.noaa.gov. An office of the federal government's "oceans agency" that helps keep America's coastlines healthy and resilient.

Program for the Study of Developed Shorelines, Western Carolina University, Belk 294, Cullowhee, NC 28734; 828-227-7519; http://www.wcu.edu/1037.asp. Analyzes coastal management issues and advocates for the long-term sustainability of coastal ecosystems.

Wetlands Watch, P.O. Box 9335, Norfolk, VA 23505; 757-623-4835; http://www.wetlandswatch.org. Nonprofit advocacy group working to save wetlands in Virginia.

4

Air Pollution and Climate Change

Jill U. Adams

The smog-shrouded Los Angeles skyline sets the scene for tourists taking a selfie on May 31, 2015. More than 3 million people a year die as a result of air pollution, including 55,000 Americans. The United States and most of the world's other nations met in Paris in November 2015 to establish policies to curb polluting emissions that are dangerously warming the planet.

From *CQ Researcher*,
June 13, 2014.

In the battle to clean up the nation's air, progress is as hazy as the Los Angeles skyline on a hot, smoggy day.

In the past 15 years, the city has cut ozone* — the main component of smog — by more than one-third and fine-particle pollution, or soot, by about half.[1]

For car-clogged California, which has some of the nation's worst air pollution, that is a significant step forward. Yet the Los Angeles region ranked No. 1 in a 2015 listing of U.S. cities with the worst air quality, including the most ozone pollution and the third most soot, according to the American Lung Association.[2]

The good news/bad news in Los Angeles reflects the complexity of the air pollution fight in the United States and worldwide.[3]

The days of pedestrians in U.S. cities being unable to see across a smoggy street are largely over, but air pollution remains the world's biggest environmental health risk, with some of the worst problems in developing nations such as China and India.[4]

Air pollution kills 3.3 million people a year, including 55,000 in the United States, mostly from strokes and heart attacks, according to a study by scientists from the United States, Europe and the Middle East, published in September.[5] Worldwide, air pollution is implicated in nearly one in eight premature deaths from respiratory and cardiovascular diseases, as well as in many

---

*Ozone, a major component of smog, is created when hydrocarbons, nitrogen oxides and other pollutants emitted by cars, power plants and factories mix in the air on hot, sunny days.

cancers, according to the World Health Organization.⁶ And the International Agency for Research on Cancer said evidence shows a causal link between air pollution and lung cancer and a heightened risk of bladder cancer.⁷

Air pollution also poses other, potentially catastrophic, consequences for global climate change. It is inextricably bound up with global climate change because of pollutants in the atmosphere known as greenhouse gases. Produced largely by burning coal and oil, these gases, including carbon dioxide (CO_2), contribute to the greenhouse, or warming, effect in the Earth's atmosphere.

A widely cited figure suggested in 2009 by former NASA climate scientist James Hansen set a CO_2 level of 350 parts per million (ppm) as a threshold for Earth's safety. Any level above that will lead to dangerous warming not seen since the Pliocene era (5.3 million to 2.6 million years ago), Hansen warned. In May 2013, the level reached 400 ppm at a monitoring station in Hawaii for the first time, and this year it appears that 400 will be the new normal, the World Meteorological Organization announced in early November. The planet's temperature will rise at least 2 degrees by the end of the century, according to current projections, and an increase topping that could lead to a host of environmental crises, including flooding from rising sea levels and catastrophic weather events.⁸

On Nov. 30, the United States and 195 other countries will attend the 21st United Nations Climate Change Conference in Paris, or COP21. The conference will set global targets for reducing carbon emissions and mitigating climate change. Participating countries already have pledged to reduce their emissions, but experts say that is only a start. "Paris must be the floor, not the ceiling, for collective ambition," said United Nations Secretary-General Ban Ki-moon of South Korea.⁹

Domestic politics, including in the United States, may limit how far national leaders can go in addressing climate change. Frustrated by congressional inaction on the environment, convinced that climate change is at a crisis point and determined to set an example for other nations in the run-up to COP21, President Obama used his executive power in early August to issue regulations setting strict carbon-emission limits for states. Claiming authority under the 1970 Clean Air Act, he said his Clean Power Plan will cut carbon dioxide emissions from power plants and other industrial sources by 32 percent from 2005 levels by 2030.¹⁰

Obama's plan has raised a slew of objections from all sides: The power industry, manufacturers and conservatives condemn it as a jobs-killer, unneeded and in violation of the Clean Air Act, and they have sued to block its implementation. Environmentalists applaud the plan's goals but say it doesn't go far enough. The opposing views crystallize a fierce debate over what should be done about climate change, carbon dioxide emissions and air pollution.

Carbon emissions actually have been decreasing in the United States in recent years as the power grid increasingly is fed by sources other than coal and oil.¹¹ Natural gas supplies are plentiful and cheap, and the renewable energy sector — including wind and solar power — is growing rapidly. In addition, so-called clean-coal technologies promise to further curb carbon emissions once they are more widely deployed. These technologies, such as carbon capture, "clean" coal by capturing its emissions before they enter the atmosphere.¹²

The Clean Power Plan defines carbon dioxide as a pollutant under the Clean Air Act and sets limits on carbon emissions produced by electricity-generating power plants, the source of about 37 percent of U.S. carbon emissions, the most of any sector.¹³ Transportation is second, contributing 31 percent, and industry third, at 15 percent.¹⁴

Proponents cite studies showing the Clean Power Plan will lead to 3,600 fewer premature deaths in the United States and 90,000 fewer childhood asthma attacks. The plan also will boost investment in renewable energy technologies, backers say. And it provides flexibility by phasing in the stricter standards and letting states decide how to meet their reductions — whether by using more clean energy, increasing efficiency or trading emission credits (plants whose emissions are below allowable levels can "sell" their credits for unused emissions to those plants unable to meet their targets).¹⁵

"It's a simple idea that will change the world: Cut carbon pollution today so our kids won't inherit climate chaos tomorrow," said Rhea Suh, president of the Natural Resources Defense Council, an environmental advocacy group. "That's what this historic plan will achieve. . . . Now we are going to fight with everything

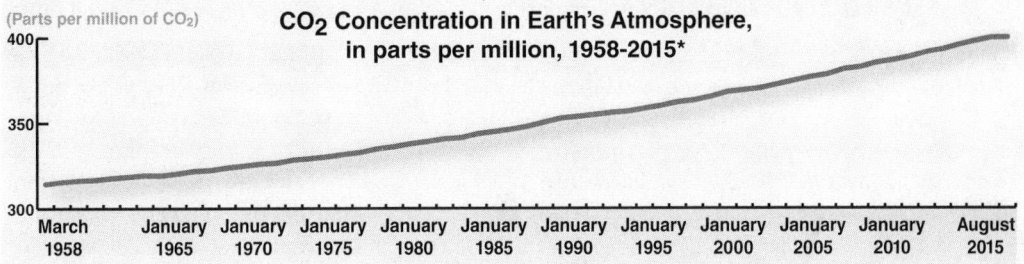

Carbon Dioxide Levels Accelerating

Concentrations of carbon dioxide (CO_2) in Earth's atmosphere reached 400 parts per million (ppm) for the first time in 2013, but when CO_2 hit 400 ppm again this year, scientists said that level would be the new normal, and well over the 350 ppm that is considered the threshold for Earth's safety. CO_2 levels have risen 27 percent since 1958, when scientists first began measuring them.

*March 1958 through August 2015, seasonally adjusted.

Source: C. D. Keeling et. al, "Exchanges of atmospheric CO_2 and 13 CO_2 with the terrestrial biosphere and oceans from 1978 to 2000," Scripps Institution of Oceanography, University of California San Diego, accessed Nov. 3, 2015, http://tinyurl.com/nalmrzlc; caption information from Philip Bump, "So Much for 350: The Atmosphere's Carbon Dioxide Tops 400," The Wire, April 29, 2013, http://tinyurl.com/oka5nkj

we've got to ensure the plan moves forward and provides the necessary momentum for unified global action."[16]

Opponents, including states that produce and burn coal and dozens of energy companies, say the Clean Power Plan is an economic vise, harming industries that provide a necessary product — electric power. Twenty-five states and several industry groups are suing to block the plan, arguing that Obama overstepped his executive power by illegally basing his plan on an obscure provision of the Clean Air Act and that the plan will drive up utility rates for homeowners and businesses and slash jobs in the power industry.[17]

Mike Dugan, president and CEO of the American Coalition for Clean Coal Electricity, rejects the Clean Power Plan in its finalized form, as published by the EPA. "Even in the face of damning analyses and scathing opposition from across the country, [the Environmental Protection Agency's] final carbon rule reveals what we've said for months — this agency is pursuing an illegal plan that will drive up electricity costs and put people out of work," said Dugan. "This rule fails across the board, but most troubling is that it fails the millions of families and businesses who rely on affordable electricity to help them keep food on the table and the lights on."[18]

Opponents also say the new regulations are unneeded because carbon emissions are already falling. Natural gas is providing new incentives for utilities to switch from coal. Although it is a fossil fuel, natural gas produces fewer emissions than coal and oil when it burns.

Environmentalists say government regulations are necessary to further reduce carbon emissions. They also note that the gains in lower emissions thus far are not uniform. Recent data from the Energy Information Administration show that from 2000 to 2013 carbon emissions increased in 13 states — mostly in the Plains, where oil and gas drilling has been booming — with Nebraska recording the biggest rise.[19]

A second component of Obama's effort to improve air quality is a tougher ozone standard, announced by the EPA on Oct. 1. It will require states and counties to lower their ozone levels from 75 parts per billion (ppb) to 70 ppb in the next five to 22 years (the amount of time depends on the state and the severity of that state's ozone problem).

Ground-level ozone is a pollutant regulated by the Clean Air Act, primarily because of its harmful effects on human health. In contrast, the ozone layer in the upper atmosphere (the stratosphere) protects life on Earth by blocking much of the sun's ultraviolet light.

Ozone Pollution Hits California Cities Hardest

Largely because of auto emissions, California contains a majority of the top 15 cities in the United States with the worst pollution from ozone, the main component of smog.

Top 15 Ozone-Polluted Cities, 2011-2013

Rank	City	State
1	Los Angeles-Long Beach	California
2	Visalia-Porterville-Hanford	California
3	Bakersfield	California
4	Fresno-Madera	California
5	Sacramento-Roseville	California
6	Houston-The Woodlands	Texas
7	Dallas-Fort Worth	Texas
8	Modesto-Merced	California
9	Las Vegas-Henderson	Nevada
10	Phoenix-Mesa-Scottsdale	Arizona
11	New York-Newark	New York-New Jersey
12	Tulsa-Muskogee-Bartlesville	Oklahoma
13	Denver-Aurora	Colorado
14	El Centro	California
15	Oklahoma City-Shawnee	Oklahoma

Source: "State of the Air 2015," American Lung Association, 2015, http://tinyurl.com/pl98d94

Under the Clean Air Act, ground-level ozone standards are supposed to be revisited every five years or so. Although the new standard was expected, the U.S. Chamber of Commerce, the National Association of Manufacturers (NAM) and other opponents said it will hurt the economy. "Manufacturers have been leading the way in lowering ozone levels; yet, the Obama administration forges on with a regulation that will stunt growth, production and job creation," said Jay Timmons, president and CEO of NAM.[20]

But environmental advocates such as the group Clear Air Watch and medical associations such as the American Lung Association (ALA) say the new standard doesn't go far enough. "Given the health threats from ozone, greater health protections are clearly needed," said Harold Wimmer, president and CEO of the ALA. "The level chosen of 70 parts per billion simply does not reflect what the science shows is necessary to truly protect public health."[21]

As controversy swirls around Obama's regulatory plans and the best way to improve air quality, here are some of the questions being debated:

Is President Obama's Clean Power Plan good policy?

When Obama announced his Clean Power Plan on Aug. 3, he said its primary purpose was to reduce the nation's greenhouse emissions. Lowering the amount of carbon dioxide that power-generating plants release into the atmosphere, he said, is one step in addressing climate change. Obama called the plan a moral obligation, a public health issue and a matter of national security.[22]

Environmental advocacy groups hailed the plan, whose emission limits will phase in over eight years beginning in 2022, as a "game-changer," a "great start" and "the most significant step in U.S. history toward reducing the pollution that causes climate change."[23] Critics had an opposite reaction: The Clean Power Plan, they said, will be costly to implement and represents government overreach at its worst. They contend Obama should have worked through Congress instead of issuing an executive order.

The limits in the plan "exceed the EPA's legal authority under the Clean Air Act," Republican Gov. Mike Pence of Indiana wrote Obama in a June 24 letter, when the plan was in proposal phase. Besides threatening jobs and the supply of energy, Pence continued, "your plan ignores the separation of powers enshrined in our nation's Constitution."[24]

Ann Weeks, senior counsel and legal director for the Clean Air Task Force, a Boston-based nonprofit that advocates for reductions in air pollution, says the rule aims for a maximum decrease in carbon dioxide while not being overly burdensome in terms of cost. "It's an ambitious standard that looks forward to what can be achieved over the regulatory period — eight years," she says. "The rule applies to existing sources and new sources. States are directed to make plans to accomplish this in a cost-effective way."

"The Clean Power Plan will sharply reduce carbon pollution and other dangerous air pollutants by shifting our electric power system toward cleaner energy sources at a steady but achievable pace," wrote David Doniger and Derek Murrow of the Natural Resources Defense Council. "Enforceable carbon pollution limits will kick in starting in 2022 and ramp up into full effect by 2030."[25]

Although she praises Obama for acting, Weeks says, "We could have done this years ago. We could have had more leadership. Canada has had these standards in place for a while."

Opponents say the Clean Power Plan will be too costly for industry to implement. Building a power-generating plant is expensive, and it takes decades for a company to recover the up-front investment, says Christi Tezak, managing director of research at ClearView Energy Partners, an independent research firm in Washington that analyzes U.S. energy policy. With the new rule, "we may be pulling offline a perfectly serviceable power plant before it's paid for," she says. "It's like wanting a shiny new car, but you haven't paid off your last car yet."

Closing older plants that have been paid off carries costs as well, says Arnold Reitze, a law professor at the University of Utah in Salt Lake City who has 50 years of air pollution litigation experience. Such plants produce "very inexpensive electricity" because they incur only fuel and operating costs, he says. "You can't build a new plant and sell electricity at prices like that."

Opponents also argue that the new regulations are unnecessary and unfairly penalize the coal industry. "We're fine with market forces," says Paul Bailey, senior vice president for federal affairs and policy at the American Coalition for Clean Coal Electricity. The falling price of natural gas has already tipped the balance against coal. But with new regulations on power plant emissions, including the Clean Power Plan and a new rule on mercury and other toxic emissions, it's as if "EPA has their finger on the scale," Bailey says.

Giving the EPA such power is dangerous for another reason, Bailey and other foes of the Clean Power Plan say: Market forces, not the government, do the best job of picking winners and losers in the energy sector.

Protesters at the White House demand an end to coal mining by so-called mountaintop removal on Sept. 27, 2010. President Obama used his executive authority in August to institute a sweeping plan to limit CO2 emissions from coal-fired power plants, curb smog-causing ozone and encourage the growth of renewable energy sources. Industry officials say Obama's Clean Power Plan requires industry changes that will be too costly and that market forces can achieve reductions in pollution.

They point to Solyndra, the California-based maker of solar cells that went bankrupt in August 2011 despite receiving a $535 million loan guarantee from the Department of Energy only two years earlier. President Obama enthusiastically praised the company during a 2010 visit to Solyndra, touting it as a model of clean energy and a job creator, only for the company to fail. Industry and free-market advocates say the loan wasted taxpayer money and unfairly backed renewable energy over traditional energy sources. Solyndra, they say, offers dramatic evidence as to why the government should not intervene in the energy marketplace.[26]

Besides, Bailey says, targeting coal and the traditional energy sector will lead to higher electricity prices. "And when energy prices go up, it harms those at the low end of the economic spectrum," he says.

Environmentalists counter that Solyndra was an aberration, that the marketplace has its own shortcomings, and that government has played an important role in encouraging nascent industries. Although they concede that market forces are helping to lower carbon emissions, they say the market alone is not enough to achieve the reductions needed. "For us, the [Clean Power Plan] provides the opportunity to lock in" falling levels of carbon, emissions of which are down 15 percent from 10 years ago, says Nicholas Bianco, director of regulatory analysis and strategic partnerships for the Environmental Defense Fund, an environmental advocacy group. "Otherwise, there's no guarantee that these trends will continue."

Is the EPA's new ozone standard good policy?

When EPA Administrator Gina McCarthy announced in August that the national ozone standard would be tightened, she said, "While the days are gone when cities like Los Angeles were so smoggy that people had trouble seeing across the street, science tells us that ozone is still making people sick and we still have work to do."[27]

The agency contends the health benefits of the tougher standard, effective Dec. 28, far outweigh the costs. The new standard will require municipalities to enforce pollution-limiting strategies, such as implementing pollution-control technologies on vehicles, factories and power plants, shutting down pollution-emitting plants and freezing new development, including transportation projects and new industrial facilities.

The EPA estimates that economic costs to businesses will run a total of $1.4 billion per year for modifying some plants and potentially shutting down others, but that $2.9 billion to $5.9 billion will be saved each year due to fewer missed days of work and school, emergency room visits and premature deaths.[28]

While proponents praised the EPA for tightening the standard, many wanted the agency to go further. Scientific advisory panels have recommended standards as demanding as 60 ppb, based on evidence that higher levels of ozone harm public health. "Disappointing is too mild a term," said Frank O'Donnell, president of the advocacy group Clean Air Watch. "The big polluters won this time, for the most part."[29]

Opponents were unhappy, too, but they recognized that things could have been worse. "Today, the Obama administration finalized a rule that is overly burdensome, costly and misguided," said Timmons of the National Association of Manufacturers. "For months, the administration threatened to impose on manufacturers an even harsher rule, with even more devastating consequences. After an unprecedented level of outreach by manufacturers and other stakeholders, the worst-case scenario was avoided."[30]

Whether it's the ozone standard or carbon emission restrictions, Tezak of ClearView Energy Partners asks, "Are we doing something that's nice to have, or are we doing something that's smart?" If an old plant is to be taken offline at some point in the future, she says, perhaps it's wiser to work within that longer timeline and get to the same pollution reductions without people losing their investments.

"The new regulations simply change the rate of change," says Robert Hebner, director of the Center for Electromechanics at the University of Texas, Austin, which researches energy storage and power generation. Hebner, who experienced similar policy debates when he served at the Office of Management and Budget in 1990, sees the new ozone and carbon regulations as being on "the trailing edge," because the energy sector has been moving away from coal for some time. "They're replacing it with so-called clean coal, increasing the use of natural gas and renewables," he says. "And it's working."

Ozone levels have decreased by about a third from 1980 to 2014, according to EPA records. "Why the urgent need now, then, to impose such a draconian new regulatory scheme?" asked David Johnson, CEO of a family-owned clay products manufacturing company in Appalachian, Ohio.[31]

Ozone primarily affects the airways and the lungs. As people inhale the pollutant it can irritate the lining of the throat, causing inflammation; trigger coughing and shortness of breath; and decrease lung function. In susceptible individuals, ozone can spark serious asthma attacks, heart attacks and premature death. Children, the elderly and people with asthma or respiratory illnesses are particularly sensitive to ozone.[32]

A 2010 analysis of the medical literature by a scientific advisory panel convened by the EPA quantified the impact of different levels of ozone in terms of illness and premature deaths. The panel determined that tightening the standard from 75 ppb to 70 ppb would prevent about 2,200 heart attacks, 23,000 asthma attacks and 1,500 to 4,300 premature deaths per year. A change from 75 ppb to 60 ppb would dramatically improve those numbers even more — averting 5,300 heart attacks, 58,000 asthma attacks and 4,000 to 12,000 premature deaths.[33]

Clean Air Watch's O'Donnell said numbers like that are why he is disappointed in the new ozone standard: "EPA has taken a baby step, when what was really needed is a giant stride to protect people's health from dirty air," he said. "It is really a missed opportunity."[34]

Can renewable energy become a major contributor to the power industry?

Many experts say generating more electricity from renewable energy sources is a good idea because it would improve air quality and slow climate change. But they disagree over how soon that can happen.

Already solar and wind power are experiencing record growth, but their overall contributions to the energy sector remain small.

Solar energy has been growing spectacularly. In 2010, it provided 2,300 megawatts of electricity in the United States; compared with more than 12,000 in 2014, or enough to power about 1.2 million homes.* Even so, solar power accounts for only 1 percent of electricity generated in the United States.[35]

Wind energy's growth also has been robust, rising from 40,000 megawatts of capacity in 2010 to more than 65,000 in 2014 — about 4 percent of the electricity generated in the United States.[36]

The energy industry sees these trends continuing at least for the next four years, according to a survey conducted by the global energy consulting firm DNV GL. One in two respondents said they thought that by 2030 renewables would be generating 70 percent of the energy in markets that have actively adopted green technologies (primarily in Europe and North America).[37]

"We've seen an explosion in both solar and wind generation throughout the country — some 43 percent of all new electricity generated was from these cleaner fuel sources," said Suh of the Natural Resources Defense Council. "That's going to [rise] further under this new framework that the president has unveiled," she added, referring to the Clean Power

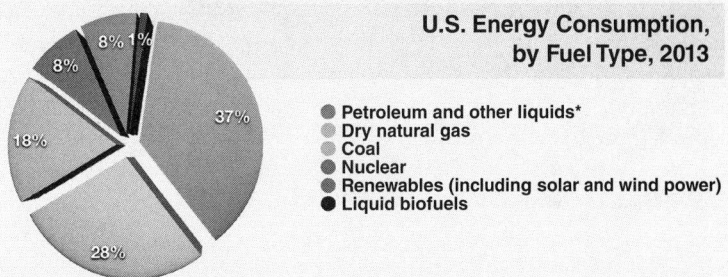

Fossil Fuels Supply Most U.S. Energy

Coal and petroleum — fossil fuels that emit large amounts of carbon dioxide when burned — produced more than half the energy consumed in the United States in 2013. Natural gas, a cleaner-burning fossil fuel, represented more than a fourth, while biofuels, nuclear power and renewables supplied less than a fifth.

U.S. Energy Consumption, by Fuel Type, 2013

- Petroleum and other liquids*
- Dry natural gas
- Coal
- Nuclear
- Renewables (including solar and wind power)
- Liquid biofuels

* Includes crude oil, refined petroleum products, natural gas liquids used in petroleum production and liquids derived from other hydrocarbon sources.

Source: "Annual Energy Outlook 2015," U.S. Energy Information Administration, April 2015, p. 15, http://tinyurl.com/o5bohzb

Plan and its incentives for increasing renewable energy by offering emissions credits.[38]

Renewable technology is a big industry in some surprising places, such as Colorado, Illinois and North Carolina, Suh said. "It's not necessarily just the hotbeds of solar energy like Southern California or the Southwest. It's really an opportunity throughout the country that we're seeing in the development of clean energy technologies."[39]

Those tracking the investment market also see a coming boom. *Bloomberg New Energy Finance* predicts wind and solar will generate 18 percent of North America's electricity by 2030 — more than triple this year's 5 percent, driven by a desire to diversify energy sources, improving economics for green technologies and new policies, such as the Clean Power Plan. Rooftop solar panels will achieve a 10 percent share of the U.S. energy mix in the same time frame, according to Bloomberg.[40]

Other analyses are less optimistic. In a detailed look at the U.S. energy market, *Forbes* magazine found that a bump in natural gas prices — as occurred during a January 2014 polar vortex, when temperatures throughout much of the nation plunged and demand for heat spiked — forced oil-burning backup generators into service and triggered some gas-to-coal switching. The

---

*One megawatt can power 1,000 homes.

Computer monitors at the PacifiCorp Transmissions Grid Operations Center in Portland, Ore., help technicians control the delivery of electricity to customers throughout the Western United States. The utility firm, a subsidiary of Warren Buffett's Berkshire Hathaway Energy, is a major user of wind turbines to produce clean energy.

lesson, *Forbes* said: Local and short-term conditions can squeeze the system in ways that favor old, standby energy sources.[41]

The Clean Air Task Force's Weeks questions how big a boost the Clean Power Plan will actually give the clean-energy industry. Technical limitations remain, she says, "including the fact that we don't have an advanced [energy] storage system."

Energy analyst Tezak agrees the storage issue is critical. "The wind doesn't always blow and the sun doesn't always shine," she says. Yet public utilities have an obligation to provide power around the clock when solar or wind power is unavailable, she says.

Grid problems are cropping up in some places. "In Arizona, there's so much solar [energy]," Tezak says, that it's costing utilities revenue. Homeowners with rooftop solar panels might owe nothing on their monthly bill. And yet those homeowners are getting a service — use of the electric grid on cloudy days. Utilities are scrambling to come up with new rate structures to charge for that benefit.

These problems aren't intractable, says energy expert Hebner. "But is it difficult? Yes. It needs money to get it done," he says, referring to improved storage and grid upgrades. He cites Florida as a place where old and new energy sources are beginning to play nicely together. "For instance, Florida Power & Light is making progress — they're combining natural gas and solar," he says. Other regions are integrating natural gas and wind power, where both those sources are competitive in price.

However, if natural gas prices continue to drop, the renewable energy sector's growth could slow, because its prices would be less competitive, analysts say.

Some states have set ambitious goals to reduce reliance on fossil fuels and increase renewables. California wants to cut fossil fuel use by a third by 2020. New York's energy plan says renewable sources, which currently provide about 11 percent of the state's energy, could meet up to 40 percent by 2030.

Environmental advocates say investments in renewable energy make economic sense. Although jobs may be lost in the fossil fuel sector, other jobs will be created in solar and wind, they say. Between January 2011 and June 2014, the renewable sector (solar, wind, biomass and geothermal) gained 1,800 jobs, with solar power leading the way, according to the Bureau of Labor Statistics (BLS). The number of solar jobs tripled during that period, although the wind sector still employs twice as many as solar, the BLS said.[42]

Government policies can help shift the balance toward renewables, many experts say. "Look at Germany, where there's enormous solar installations but virtually no sun," said Kevin Book, managing director of research at the energy research firm ClearView Energy Partners. "What's the thing that moved solar there? Well, it was government incentive programs."[43]

BACKGROUND

Early Air Pollution

As early as the 13th century, a national leader tried to curb air pollution by restricting the use of fossil fuels. England's King Edward banned the burning of coal in London because of the smoke it created.[44] However, the ban was largely ineffective, although it may have reduced burning for a while.

By the 17th century, the ill effects of coal smoke were widely recognized, although Londoners' dependence on coal outweighed concerns about health. As energy policy expert Barbara Freese, who wrote a history of coal, noted, "Coal's pollution may have been killing them slowly, but a lack of heat would have killed them quickly."[45]

In the late 18th and early 19th centuries, coal helped fuel the Industrial Revolution in England. The newly invented steam engine, the building of mechanized factories and the growing use of locomotives — all powered by coal — helped transform society. "Thanks in large part to its coal — and its ability to turn that coal into motion as well as heat — Britain would remain the most powerful nation in the world until the end of the 19th century," Freese said.[46]

As the Industrial Revolution spread to other countries, including the fledgling United States, air pollution from soot and smog worsened. The United States had thick forests from which to harvest wood, but it didn't take long before Americans discovered rich coal deposits — including huge coal fields under the Appalachian Mountains and in Illinois and Missouri, states half the size of Europe itself.[47]

Industrialization and coal spurred urbanization in places such as Pittsburgh, which began growing as an industrial town in the late 1700s and became noted for its sooty gloom, even in daytime.[48] Early studies in Germany and the United States documented the existence of lung-related illnesses, including pneumonia, in smoky areas. And yet, "few people then could imagine a world not heavily dependent on coal," according to Freese. "In 1910 natural gas and oil still represented less than 10 percent of the nation's energy supplies, slightly less than wood."[49]

Carbon Dioxide Measured

In the late 1800s a few scientists began to examine the factors determining temperatures on Earth. French physicist Joseph Fourier postulated that the Earth's atmosphere acted like a greenhouse, allowing heat radiation from the sun to be trapped near the planet's surface. In 1862, Irish physicist John Tyndall wrote: "As a dam built across a river causes a local deepening of the stream, so our atmosphere, thrown as a barrier across the terrestrial infrared rays, produces a local heightening of the temperature at the Earth's surface."[50]

Tyndall wondered what components in the atmosphere caused the trapping. With laboratory experiments, he showed that nitrogen and oxygen, the atmosphere's most abundant gases, were transparent to heat rays. In contrast, carbon dioxide-containing coal gas — piped into the laboratory for heat — blocked heat radiation as a solid material might. Tyndall not only determined that carbon dioxide was responsible, but he also found that naturally occurring (and very low) concentrations of carbon dioxide were enough to trap heat radiation in surface air.[51]

The impact of the Ice Age — the opposite of global warming — also captured the imagination of scientists at the time. Geological evidence in North America and Europe showed that glaciers covered much of the two continents 20,000 years earlier. Faced with such evidence, scientists set about theorizing how the Earth's climate could change so dramatically.

In 1896, Swedish scientist Svante Arrhenius reasoned that several geologic and atmospheric events interacted to chill the Earth in a sustained way. Volcanic eruptions add carbon dioxide to the air and can cause warming, in turn leading to more moisture in the atmosphere and a greenhouse effect. What if the opposite happened? A particularly quiet volcanic stretch, Arrhenius suspected, could lead to a drop in carbon dioxide, which might mean cooler temperatures and less atmospheric water vapor, which would mean even less heat trapped near Earth's surface — a vicious cycle of cooling.[52]

Four decades later Englishman Guy Stewart Callendar documented rising temperatures in many different locations on Earth and expanded on Arrhenius' work to study the greenhouse effect of carbon dioxide in the atmosphere. In 1938, Callendar, an engineer by training, presented his data and a new theory to the Royal Meteorological Society in London: that humans were contributing to global warming by burning fossil fuels.[53]

Much of this early work was speculation. What evidence existed came from controlled laboratory experiments and did not include the many dozens of factors that influence the planet's temperature and climate — not the least of which was how much carbon dioxide the oceans can absorb.[54]

By the 1950s, scientists began measuring carbon dioxide in the atmosphere and in ocean surface waters. Some government funding was secured in 1957-58, when researchers worked together during the International Geophysical Year — a yearlong effort to design ambitious interdisciplinary projects. One involved setting up an instrument atop the volcanic Mauna Loa peak in Hawaii, where Charles David Keeling, a young American scientist, could measure carbon

CHRONOLOGY

1700s-1930s *Industrialization ramps up and is implicated in climate change.*

1780s-90s Industrial Revolution spreads, replacing handicraft industries with polluting factories.

1862 Irish physicist John Tyndall describes how the Earth's atmosphere acts as a greenhouse, holding warmth close to the ground.

1896 Swedish scientist Svante Arrhenius theorizes on the geophysical events that brought about the ice age, including reduced atmospheric carbon dioxide.

1938 English engineer Guy Stewart Callendar asserts that burning fossil fuels adds enough carbon dioxide to the atmosphere to affect global temperatures.

1950s-1960s *Geophysics advances include research into pollution, monitoring of the air and new environmental regulations.*

1957-58 International Geophysical Year brings researchers together to explore interdisciplinary questions about Earth science.

1958 Mauna Loa Observatory in Hawaii begins recording atmospheric carbon dioxide concentrations.

1960s Scientists blame coal-burning emissions for acidifying rain and harming fish populations and forests in the Northeast United States and Scandinavia.

1967 Air Quality Act establishes first emission standards in the United States.

1970s *New agencies and regulations address air pollution.*

1970 Nixon administration creates the National Oceanic and Atmospheric Administration and Environmental Protection Agency (EPA). . . . Congress passes Clean Air Act, bringing all previous clean air efforts under one federal statute.

1979 European and North American countries at the United Nations Convention on Long-Range Transboundary Air Pollution agree to cut fossil fuel emissions.

1990s *United States curbs some air pollution.*

1990 In its first report, the new International Panel on Climate Change says the world has been warming. . . . Congress amends Clean Air Act to control acid rain and prohibit leaded gasoline (to reduce lead emissions).

1995 A cap-and-trade scheme to reduce sulfur dioxide emissions, and thereby acid rain, goes into effect in the United States.

1997 Kyoto Protocol sets targets for industrialized nations to reduce greenhouse gas emissions, but Congress never ratifies it. . . . EPA lowers ozone standard to 80 parts per billion (ppb) for public health reasons.

2000-Present *Regulators seek further reductions in carbon emissions and ozone.*

2007 U.S. Supreme Court says EPA must regulate carbon emissions from cars.

2008 EPA lowers the ozone standard to 75 ppb, even though a scientific advisory panel wanted a lower standard — 60 ppb to 65 ppb.

2009 Legislation to create a cap-and-trade mechanism for carbon emissions passes the House but dies in the Senate.

2014 President Obama, citing authority under the Clean Air Act, announces the Clean Power Plan, which regulates carbon emissions from power plants. . . . EPA lowers ozone standard to 70 ppb.

2015 Twenty-five states and industry groups challenge Clean Power Plan. . . . Obama rejects Keystone XL oil pipeline to carry Canadian crude oil to the Gulf of Mexico. . . . World leaders to meet in Paris Nov. 30 for 21st U.N. Climate Change Conference (COP21).

dioxide concentrations in the atmosphere far away from human sources of the gas.[55] (The Mauna Loa observatory still monitors carbon dioxide levels.[56])

Clean Air Act

Several forces led to passage of the Clean Air Act in 1970, including decades of serious smog events that forced people to face the dangers of industrial pollution.

In 1948, a thick cloud of smog formed in Donora, Pa., an industrial town of 14,000, and lingered for five days. The pollution was implicated in the sickening of 6,000 people and the deaths of 20. In 1952, similarly, London's "Killer Fog" killed more than 3,000.[57] Serious smog problems also arose in Los Angeles, where auto pollution gets trapped by the mountain ranges surrounding the city.[58]

Early iterations of the Clean Air Act — both called the Air Pollution Control Act — were passed in 1955 and 1963; both provided funding for research and sought to promote public health and welfare. The 1965 act also funded efforts to curb air pollution from motor vehicles and industrial smokestacks. In 1967, an amendment called the Air Quality Act divided the nation into Air Quality Control Regions, in which states monitored air quality in their regions. The 1967 act also established national emission standards for industry, to be enforced by states.[59]

Pushed by Republican President Richard M. Nixon, the Clean Air Act of 1970 overhauled these previous efforts and pulled together federal anti-pollution programs. It included National Ambient Air Quality Standards for six pollutants: carbon monoxide (CO), nitrogen dioxide (NO_2), ozone (O_3), sulfur dioxide (SO_2), particulate matter (particles 10 micrometers or less in size) and lead.[60] The act's New Source Performance Standards strictly regulated new sources of air pollution, applicable to new facilities as well as expansions of old ones. With clear emissions limits established, the act allowed citizens to sue violators of the standards.[61]

The EPA, created by Nixon the same year, was charged with implementing the new law. The first Earth Day also took place in 1970, the brainchild of Sen. Gaylord Nelson, a Wisconsin Democrat.[62]

Congress revised and expanded the Clean Air Act in 1990, granting even broader authority to the EPA to implement and enforce regulations reducing air pollutant emissions.[63]

Acid Rain

The Clean Air Act also targeted acid rain. Concern over the environmental scourge began in the 1960s, when scientists puzzled over the disappearance of once-plentiful fish species in Swedish and upstate New York lakes. Large stands of trees also were dying in the same areas. Through dogged research, scientists learned that sulfur dioxide emissions from coal-burning power plants were leading to the acidification of rain, making it lethal to fish and trees. The problem crossed state and national borders: Wind-blown pollution from Germany and Britain was poisoning Scandinavia, and pollution from the industrial Midwest in the United States was harming the Northeast and Canada.[64]

Fossil fuels are the main contributor to acid rain, although natural sources such as volcanoes are also a cause. In the United States, coal-fired electric power plants account for about two-thirds of all sulfur dioxide.[65]

"As the evidence linking acid rain to coal poured in, the response of the electric and coal industries was to deny the link, to question the motives of those investigating the connection and always to call for more research," coal historian Freese noted. "In October 1980, the head of the National Coal Association dismissed acid rain as 'a campaign of misleading publicity which seems designed to gain public support for new legislative and regulatory measures.'"[66]

In 1979, governments from Europe and North America met at the United Nations Convention on Long-range Transboundary Air Pollution, where they agreed to cut fossil fuel emissions. The initial agreement funded monitoring efforts; a protocol added in 1985 called for a 30 percent decrease in sulfur dioxide emissions.[67] During the presidency of Republican Ronald Reagan, however, the federal government took no regulatory action against acid rain. "By the end of the Reagan administration [in January 1989], Congress had put forward and slapped down 70 different acid rain bills, and frustration ran so deep that Canada's prime minister bleakly joked about declaring war on the United States," wrote one observer of the period.[68]

Still, sulfur dioxide emissions were gradually dropping because of regulations already in the Clean Air Act. It wasn't until 1990 that Congress passed amendments to the act that included a goal to reduce sulfur dioxide emissions by half over the next 20 years.

Wearable Monitors Track Pollution

Scientists debate the reliability of personal sensing devices.

To better understand how cars and trucks contribute to air pollution, environmental scientist Mark Nieuwenhuijsen and his colleagues turned to some unusual helpers — 54 Barcelona schoolchildren ages 7 to 11.

The scientists, who work for the Centre for Research in Environmental Epidemiology, a public research institution in the Spanish city, placed small pollution sensors on the children's clothing, enabling them to collect data on black carbon — a form of soot — common in diesel fumes.[1]

The study is part of a trend in which researchers use wearable monitors to track air pollution in various locations, and at different times of day, so they can gain a more accurate picture of black carbon and other forms of pollution than fixed monitors provide. The scientists also want to better understand individuals' exposure to pollution: A major shortcoming of fixed pollution-monitoring stations, they say, is their inability to track pollution's effects on people in a variety of settings.

Relying only on fixed monitors means "researchers take data from a couple of monitors in a city and assume that everyone in the city has that level of exposure," says Nieuwenhuijsen. However, "the level of a pollutant at a background monitoring station might be quite different than near a major roadway."

A study by academic and government scientists from the United States and Canada found that air quality conditions in Detroit neighborhoods were not well represented by the nearby state of Michigan fixed station. The researchers fitted 65 non-smoking adults in the Detroit area with pollution-monitoring vests, which participants wore for five consecutive days. The participants' blood pressure, checked each evening, increased as the vest monitor showed increases in pollution. The fixed monitor, located two to 18 miles from where participants lived and worked, showed no such correlation between pollutant levels and blood pressure.[2]

In the Barcelona study, which monitored the children around the clock on two typical weekdays during 2012 and 2013, black carbon exposure was low when the children were at home, somewhat higher when they were in school and two to three times higher when they were traveling to and from school.[3]

Small sensors used in other studies can track a range of pollutants, including nitrogen oxides, carbon monoxide and ozone. But critics question their reliability, saying that cheap ones do not work well and that small devices can give inaccurate readings.

Top-of-the-line devices like the ones that Nieuwenhuijsen uses in his studies cost more than $8,000 each. Midrange devices cost about $1,000. But simple sensors can be built from scratch from online instructions for as little as $50 or bought assembled for about $250.

The 1990 amendment, which had bipartisan support, included a creative market mechanism called cap-and-trade. While the new regulation required cutting all sulfur emissions in half, it allowed individual companies to determine how and where to make those cuts: If a power plant emitted less than its cap, it could sell its remaining allowance to another plant, which would use it to keep under its own cap.[69]

The Environmental Defense Fund helped come up with the idea and worked with the new administration of Republican President George H. W. Bush to create the legislation implementing cap-and-trade.[70]

The cap on acid-rain-producing emissions took effect in 1995 and had an immediate impact, reducing emissions by 3 million tons in the first year, according to the EPA. Eight years later, the EPA reported that costs to industry averaged $1 billion to $2 billion per year — a quarter of what the agency had predicted and only a tiny fraction of what utility executives had feared.[71] In addition, the health of Adirondack lakes in New York state rebounded, visibility in national parks improved and harms to human health decreased, according to the Environmental Defense Fund.[72]

Regulating Emissions

In 2007, in response to a suit brought by environmental organizations, the Supreme Court ruled that the EPA had authority to regulate carbon dioxide and other greenhouse

The low-cost sensors target the consumer market and are less reliable and accurate as the top-of-the-line ones, Nieuwenhuijsen says. Moreover, he says, small handheld or wearable sensors, even the pricey ones, tend to be sensitive to changes in temperature and humidity, which can affect results. Environmental researchers typically conduct quality checks to validate the monitors' data.

Ben Barratt, an air-quality scientist at King's College in London, said inaccurate information can invalidate data comparisons. "Monitoring air pollution levels is far more involved than the manufacturers and suppliers of cheap sensors suggest," he said.[4]

But other scientists say the lower-cost versions have virtues, such as allowing researchers to deploy more monitors to track small variations in pollutant concentrations. "The fact that you can buy 50 low-cost sensors for the cost of one [top-of-the-line] sensor is a tremendously powerful thing," said Joshua Apte, an air quality engineer at the University of Texas, Austin.[5]

University of Pennsylvania researchers used multiple pocket-sized monitors to detect black carbon in 17 locations outside homes, schools and parks in a Philadelphia neighborhood located between a major highway and a shipping port. Higher soot levels were recorded closer to the highway and during morning and evening rush hours, moreso than at other times of day or by weather factors.[6]

A number of devices are on the market; one is the Air Quality Egg, made by Ithaca, N.Y.-based Wicked Device, for consumers who want to detect pollution in their immediate environment and to send that information to a central database and a grassroots community online forum for sharing air pollution experiences and information.

Scientists are taking advantage of citizen scientists in Europe to better understand local variation in air pollution in cities such as Athens, London, Rome and Manchester, England. "This is a project that means anyone with the right phone can take part in a real life science experiment, that will produce real data and help us know more about our environment," said University of Manchester chemistry professor Carl Percival.[7]

— *Jill U. Adams*

---

[1] Mark J. Nieuwenhuijsen *et al.*, "Variability in and Agreement between Modeled and Personal Continuously Measured Black Carbon Levels Using Novel Smartphone and Sensor Technologies," *Environmental Science & Technology*, Jan. 26, 2015, pp. 2977–2982, http://tinyurl.com/prd37lp.

[2] Robert D. Brook *et al.*, "Differences in Blood Pressure and Vascular Responses Associated with Ambient Fine Particulate Matter Exposures Measure at the Personal versus Community Level," *Occupational and Environmental Medicine*, March 2011, pp. 224–230, http://tinyurl.com/nuosltu.

[3] Nieuwenhuijsen *et al.*, *op. cit.*

[4] Kat Austen, "Environmental science: Pollution patrol," *Nature News*, Jan. 8, 2015, pp. 136–138, http://tinyurl.com/ny2ufbk.

[5] *Ibid.*

[6] Michelle C. Kondo *et al.*, "Black carbon concentrations in a goods-movement neighborhood of Philadelphia, PA," *Environmental Monitoring and Assessment*, July 2014, pp. 4605–4618, http://tinyurl.com/nhpue48.

[7] Quoted in "Citizen science project to measure air pollution," Manchester University press release, Sept. 9, 2015, http://tinyurl.com/p6tfkvr.

---

gases as air pollutants under the Clean Air Act. In the wake of that decision, the EPA concluded that greenhouse emissions did indeed endanger public health and welfare, and in 2010 it issued a final rule on limiting the pollutants from motor vehicles.[73]

Meanwhile, the Democratic-controlled House of Representatives passed a bill to cap carbon emissions from all sources in 2009, modeled on the same cap-and-trade mechanism that had proved successful in reducing acid rain.[74] However, the legislation, popularly called the Waxman-Markey bill (for co-sponsors Rep. Henry Waxman, D-Calif., and Sen. Edward Markey, D-Mass.), died in the Senate.

Many observers blamed Republican opposition and industry lobbying for the bill's failure. But the severe recession — preceded by the 2008 Wall Street meltdown and the bursting of the housing bubble — also contributed to the Senate defeat.[75]

Once the courts determined that carbon dioxide was a pollutant that could be regulated under the Clean Air Act, the EPA began considering how to regulate carbon emissions, which eventually led to Obama's Clean Power Plan.

However, despite efforts in the United States and abroad to mitigate climate change, global temperatures are still rising. The 10 hottest years on record have

Germany's Push for Renewables Generates Debate

Supporters see it as a model, critics a warning.

An ambitious plan by Germany to reduce air pollution by phasing out nuclear power and switching to renewable energy is garnering both high praise and bitter criticism.

To its advocates, the *energiewende* — or energy transition — has lowered carbon emissions, created jobs and strengthened Germany's economy. To its critics, the effort has sent domestic energy prices soaring and harmed both utilities and the economy.

Both sides agree *energiewende* is bold: Renewable energy from wind, solar and biomass is supplying more than 30 percent of Germany's electricity, up from 5 percent 15 years ago. Germany wants to increase renewable energy's share of the nation's power supply to about 45 percent by 2025, 60 percent by 2035 and 80 percent by 2050.[1] The nation also seeks to reduce its carbon emissions by 40 percent from 1990 levels by 2020, a far more aggressive goal than the European Union's target of 20 percent.[2]

In contrast, the Obama administration's Clean Power Plan focuses not on renewables but on reducing power plant carbon emissions by 32 percent from 2005 levels by 2030. The energy industry can meet that target by adopting so-called clean-coal technology or switching to natural gas, without necessarily boosting renewable-energy contributions, according to a White House statement.[3]

Germany began weaning itself from fossil fuels in 1999, when the Ecological Tax Reform Act increased taxes on oil and gas and placed a levy on electricity. Higher energy prices helped force the nation to become more energy-efficient and to seek alternative-energy solutions.[4]

In 2014, the German parliament passed comprehensive legislation to decrease carbon emissions, back renewable energy projects and wean the nation from nuclear power, an effort that some international energy experts praised as the world's most far-reaching green power initiative. Economic incentives included feed-in tariffs, which are guaranteed above-market prices for the energy produced by renewable suppliers.[5]

"The German example reveals that, while aligning politics, policies and governance structure for such a transition is a heavy lift requiring robust agenda-setting efforts, implementation occurs quickly and with overwhelming economic benefits once these pieces are in place," wrote Peter Sopher, a policy analyst with the Environmental Defense Fund, an environmental advocacy group in Washington. "Energiewende is creating jobs, raising GDP [gross domestic product] and attracting business."[6]

But some analysts call Germany's plan a costly mistake, saying the price of energy is too high and the country has a glut of unused power. "Germany's renewable energy producers enjoy a guaranteed minimum price for their energy. So they can successfully produce and sell it at a guaranteed price, regardless of what customers want," said Fred Roeder, a Berlin-based economic consultant who now works for the Washington, D.C.-based PR firm Young Voices. "Many farmers and municipalities are producing green energy no one actually needs but are entitled to sell it. In the end, consumers have to pay for it. These policies caused a doubling of energy prices for German consumers over 10 years."[7]

Critics also say the push for renewables has hurt German utilities. "A reckoning is at hand, and nowhere is that clearer than in Germany," wrote *New York Times* economics writer Justin Gillis. "Even as the country sets records nearly every month for renewable power production, the changes have devastated its utility companies, whose profits from power generation have collapsed."[8]

Indeed, by guaranteeing above-market prices for renewable energy, the feed-in tariffs have fostered growth in that sector at the expense of traditional utilities. Recognizing the problem, the government has proposed to roll back those incentives, putting green energy producers in more direct competition with coal-powered energy plants and rebalancing the economic playing field.[9]

Renewable energy in Germany comes from rooftop photovoltaic panels, which contribute 90 percent of the solar energy consumed.[10] In addition, producers are building offshore wind farms in the North and Baltic seas, where the winds blows more regularly than on land.[11] Eight offshore wind farms are in operation and still growing; the country's target is to produce 6,500 megawatts a year from wind by 2020.[12] Germany set a record for a single day's renewable energy use on July 25, when 78 percent of its electricity came from renewable sources.[13]

Despite such a milestone, many analysts predict that, even with its aggressive renewable energy plan, Germany will struggle to meet its carbon emissions goal because the number of cars and other vehicles is rising, and coal still accounts for about 44 percent of the nation's energy.[14]

Political will in Germany has helped the country forge this new path. No one expected to pull it off without a hitch, said Patrick Graichen, who leads a Berlin energy think tank. "The question is: How can we turn the energy transition into a success story?" he said.[15]

— *Jill U. Adams*

German Economy Minister and Vice Chancellor Sigmar Gabriel visits an offshore wind farm in the Baltic Ocean on Aug. 5, 2014, near Barhoeft, Germany.

---

[1]Matthias Lang and Annette Lang, "Overview Renewable Energy Sources Act," "German Energy Blog," 2014, http://tinyurl.com/ol9yycl. Ari Phillips, "Germany Just Got 78 Percent Of Its Electricity From Renewable Sources," Climate Progress, July 29, 2015, http://tinyurl.com/oxp2gk2."

[2]Vera Eckert, "German CO2 emissions in 2014 down 4.1 pct in EU trade scheme," Reuters, May 22, 2015, http://tinyurl.com/ochpvjp.

[3]"Fact Sheet: President Obama to Announce Historic Carbon Pollution Standards for Power Plants," White House press release, Aug. 3, 2015, http://tinyurl.com/nzjl5qh.

[4]Ralph Buehler *et al.*, "How Germany Became Europe's Green Leader: A Look at Four Decades of Sustainable Policymaking," *The Solutions Journal*, October 2011, http://tinyurl.com/3b38t5s.

[5]Peter Dinkloh, "EEG 2.0 — A new legal framework for the German energy transition," *Clean Energy Wire*, Aug. 1, 2014, http://tinyurl.com/qgnu5wl.

[6]Peter Sopher, "Germany is revolutionizing how we use energy . . . and the U.S. could learn a thing or two," "Energy Exchange," Environmental Defense Fund, May 14, 2014, http://tinyurl.com/py6lgrp. Peter Sopher, "While critics debate energiewende, Germany is gaining a global advantage," "Energy Exchange," Environmental Defense Fund, Oct. 6, 2014, http://tinyurl.com/ptgrsee.

[7]Fred Roeder, "What the U.S. can learn from Germany's green energy debacle," *Forbes*, Nov. 7, 2013, http://tinyurl.com/pttrj3x.

[8]Justin Gillis, "Sun and Wind Alter Global Landscape, Leaving Utilities Behind," *The New York Times*, Sept. 13, 2014, http://tinyurl.com/pmld8ej.

[9]Dinkloh, *op. cit.*

[10]"Germany Breaks Solar Power Records Again," *Permaculture*, June 23, 2014, http://tinyurl.com/nlc3y94.

[11]Gillis, *op cit.*

[12]Jorg Luyken, "German offshore wind power breaks records," *The Local*, July 20, 2015, http://tinyurl.com/pre59nz.

[13]Phillips, *op. cit.*

[14]Robert Kunzig, "Germany Could Be a Model for How We'll Get Power in the Future," *National Geographic*, Oct. 15, 2015, http://tinyurl.com/pmldlcn.

[15]Gillis, *op. cit.*

Rep. Diana DeGette, D-Colo., questions a U.S. Volkswagen official on Oct. 8, 2015, during an Energy and Commerce subcommittee investigating admitted cheating by VW on emissions tests of its diesel-powered cars. In November, as an apology for its cheating, VW offered $1,000 in gift cards and vouchers to the owners of more than 400,000 diesel-powered VWs in the United States.

occurred since 1998; last year was the hottest and 2015 will likely surpass it.[76] The Greenland and Antarctic ice sheets are shrinking. Sea levels have risen by more than six inches in the last century. And evidence is building that climate change is behind an increasing number of extreme weather events.[77]

CURRENT SITUATION

Global Negotiations

Although President Obama faces domestic opposition to his Clean Power Plan, he is positioning the United States as a willing partner in global efforts to combat carbon emissions. On Nov. 6, he formally rejected the 1,179-mile Keystone XL pipeline, partly out of fears the pipeline, which would have carried carbon-heavy petroleum from the Canadian oil sands to the Gulf Coast, would have contributed to global warming by encouraging the extraction of more oil.[78] In June, he hosted Brazilian President Dilma Rousseff, and the two leaders agreed to increase the amount of electricity their countries generate from renewable sources to 20 percent by 2030, a doubling for Brazil and a tripling for the United States.[79]

When Chinese President Xi Jinping visited Washington in September, he and Obama agreed to tighten carbon emission targets, with the Chinese leadership saying it will use cap-and-trade to achieve reductions.[80] The meeting solidified pledges the two countries made last November. Experts hope the pledges by the two giant economies will help participating nations reach agreement on emission reductions at the United Nations Conference on Climate Change in Paris at the end of this month.[81]

Aside from its impact on climate change, air pollution overall remains a serious global problem. It kills 3.3 million more people worldwide than HIV and malaria combined, according to an international team of researchers in one of the most detailed reports to date. Published in the journal *Nature*, the study said if current trends hold, the rate of air pollution deaths can be expected to double in only 35 years. China leads in air pollution-related deaths, with an estimated 1.4 million; India and Pakistan follow with 645,000 and 110,000 respectively. The United States is seventh with 55,000 deaths.[82]

Burning of coal, wood and animal dung for heat and cooking, incineration of trash and the use of diesel generators contribute to air pollution in developing countries. The *Nature* study estimated that more than 30 percent of deaths in China and 50 percent of those in India can be attributed to such residential and commercial activity. In contrast, auto and truck pollution was a bigger problem in the United States and Germany, accounting for about 20 percent of premature deaths.[83]

Besides its cap-and-trade program, China hints that it may take the drastic step of barring construction of more coal-fired plants.[84] India lags other nations in anti-pollution programs but is preparing to take the first step — measuring pollutant levels in the air of 10 cities, including Delhi, Agra and Bangalore.[85]

In Europe, vehicular pollution is fouling urban air, experts say, with illegal actions by Volkswagen contributing to the problem. The German-based automaker admitted cheating on government-mandated emissions tests by installing "shielding" software in diesel-powered cars. During the tests, the software switched on pollution controls that limit emissions of nitrogen oxides, but the controls were disabled by the software when owners drove their VWs on the road. Nitrogen oxides, ozone and particulate matter are often above legal limits in large

European cities, such as Paris and London, where many cars run on diesel. Some experts say that if Volkswagen's clean diesel fleet had performed as advertised, urban pollution would be less severe.[86]

Canada represents an international bright spot.[87] It ranks among the least-polluted countries. Ontario and Quebec — the country's two largest and most populated provinces — have committed to a cap-and-trade program designed to help reduce carbon emissions by 15 percent to 20 percent below 1990 levels by 2020. Although other provinces have not signed on to cap-and-trade, many have set ambitious targets for carbon emission reductions. British Columbia aims to cut emissions to a third below 2007 levels by 2020, and Saskatchewan wants to reach 20 percent below 2006 levels by 2020.[88]

Canada also has the world's first large-scale carbon capture and storage power plant, a coal-burning power plant that captures carbon dioxide before it escapes the smokestack and pumps it underground, where it is stored. "It just went online," says the Clean Air Task Force's Weeks. According to the plant owners, the technology will cut carbon emissions from the plant by up to 90 percent and prevent 1 million tons of the greenhouse gas from entering the atmosphere each year — the equivalent of taking 250,000 cars off the road.[89]

Carbon-capture technology is expensive, however. A carbon-capture power plant in Texas had been scheduled to go online this year, but progress has stalled, in large part because of economics. The current low prices of oil and natural gas make the costly investment in clean-coal technology seem risky. And current economics favor power companies switching to cleaner-burning natural gas over investments in costly new technology.[90]

Court Fight

In the United States, further progress in cutting carbon emissions may hinge on the courts. Two and a half months after Obama announced the Clean Power Plan, the final rule was published in the *Federal Register*, which makes the regulation official. The same day, 25 states, including coal producers such as West Virginia and Ohio, and industry groups filed lawsuits challenging the rule.[91]

The power industry argues that the Clean Power Plan overreaches because the EPA wrote it to regulate the power sector as a whole rather than at the source — power plant by power plant.[92] "The EPA has gone way beyond its

A man eats dinner at the Christ's Hands soup kitchen and food pantry in Harlan, Ky. Thousands of coal miners in Kentucky and throughout the Appalachian region have lost jobs in recent years as mines have shut down in the face of concern about pollution and safety and the rising use of renewable energy sources.

statutory authority," says Jeff Holmstead, who was an EPA lawyer during the George W. Bush administration and is now at the Washington-based law firm Bracewell & Giuliani and often represents energy companies. "All the companies I deal with are concerned about greenhouse gases. And pretty much all of them think that the Clean Power Plan is not a lawful way of doing this."

Much of the dispute focuses on Section 111(d) of the original Clean Air Act, which requires states to develop standards of performance for smokestack pollutants not covered elsewhere in the act. It's a catch-all clause, written to cover harmful pollutants identified after 1970. But, argues Holmstead, carbon dioxide is already covered elsewhere in the Clean Air Act. "EPA has the authority to regulate carbon dioxide, but they can't regulate it under two sections — 112 and 111," he says. (Section 212 covers hazardous air pollutants, including carbon species.)

An Environmental Defense Fund analysis disagreed, stating that "standards under Section 112 must not be 'interpreted, construed or applied to diminish or replace' more stringent requirements under Section 111 — a strong indication that Congress intended for Section 112 to work seamlessly with, not displace, Section 111(d)."[93]

Environmental advocates say the Clean Air Act provides strong legal footing for the Clean Power Plan. "The courts have been quite clear on this matter — carbon dioxide is a pollutant and EPA has the authority to regulate it," the Environmental Defense Fund's Bianco says.

AT ISSUE

Is the Clean Power Plan good policy?

YES
David Doniger
Director, Climate and Clean Air Program, Natural Resources Defense Council

Written for *CQ Researcher*, November 2015

The Clean Power Plan is good policy because it is grounded in federal law, backed by Supreme Court rulings, protects public health and addresses the central, and growing, environmental challenge of our time — climate change.

Congress passed and President Richard M. Nixon signed the Clean Air Act in 1970, creating the nation's fundamental law to address air pollution. In 2007, the Supreme Court ruled that the Environmental Protection Agency (EPA) could limit greenhouse gases if those gases endangered the public's health or welfare. Then, in 2011, the high court ruled that the EPA had the authority to curb pollution from the nation's fleet of power plants under Section 111(d).

Under President Obama's direction, the EPA drafted the Clean Power Plan using that provision. It requires each state, with EPA assistance, to develop "standards of performance" for existing stationary sources such as power plants, and to draft a plan to reach those standards. The performance standards seek to limit emissions through the best system available, taking into account the costs of achieving that reduction.

Our country limits arsenic, lead, soot and other air pollutants, but not the dangerous carbon pollution driving climate change. The Clean Power Plan builds on those policies by setting the first limits on carbon pollution from power plants, the nation's biggest source of carbon emissions. The plan will sharply reduce carbon pollution and other dangerous air pollutants by shifting our electric power system toward cleaner energy sources at a steady but achievable pace, reaching a 32 percent reduction in carbon emissions by 2030.

The Clean Power Plan is also good policy because it is fair and flexible. States and power providers can design their most cost-effective pathway to reduce pollution, and without disrupting the reliability of the nation's energy supply. Reining in power plant pollution will speed America's transition away from fossil fuels, protect our health, help safeguard future generations from the worst effects of climate change and position the United States for global leadership on climate change — all valuable outcomes of sound policy.

The hallmark of good policy is whether it delivers substantial benefits, at reasonable cost, to the American people. The Clean Power Plan exceeds that test. We need it now because it's the most powerful step our country can take to reduce the threat of climate change before it's too late.

NO
Jeff Holmstead
Partner, Bracewell & Giuliani; former assistant administrator, Office of Air and Radiation, Environmental Protection Agency

Written for *CQ Researcher*, November 2015

Regardless of how you feel about climate change, you should be troubled by the Clean Power Plan (CPP). Across the U.S. political spectrum, there has traditionally been a commitment to the rule of law — the notion that public officials, including the president, must act within the authority they have been given by duly elected legislatures and not by executive fiat. The CPP flies in the face of this tradition.

White House officials say they want climate change to be a "legacy issue" for the president. Historically, presidents have secured such a legacy by working with Congress to pass legislation. But when it comes to climate change, the administration has never done the hard work necessary to pass major legislation. To be sure, the president has called for climate change legislation, but the administration never actually developed a legislative proposal or made serious efforts to engage Congress or hammer out a compromise. This stands in stark contrast to the effort the first Bush administration made to secure passage of the 1990 Clean Air Act amendments — the last major piece of environmental legislation adopted in the United States.

Instead of working with Congress, the Obama administration claims to have discovered all the authority it needs to restructure the U.S. electricity system in a short, 45-year-old provision of the Clean Air Act. This obscure provision allows the EPA, under certain limited circumstances, to require states to set an emission standard for individual facilities within their borders based on the best system that can be used to control emissions at such a facility. But the administration makes the remarkable assertion that it gives the EPA authority to shut down coal-fired power plants throughout the country and require wind and solar plants be built to replace them.

The Supreme Court will almost certainly reject the administration's attempt to restructure the electricity system based on a few words in the Clean Air Act. In a recent case that partially invalidated another EPA regulation dealing with climate change, the court went out of its way to state: "When an agency claims to discover in a long-extant statute an unheralded power to regulate 'a significant portion of the American economy,' we typically greet its announcement with a measure of skepticism. We expect Congress to speak clearly if it wishes to assign to an agency decisions of vast 'economic and political significance.'" The Clean Power Plan clearly fails this test.

A three-judge panel of the U.S. Court of Appeals for the District of Columbia will consider the lawsuits and issue a ruling. Because the decision by the panel can be appealed to the Supreme Court, the process could take years. In the meantime, some of the same states suing the Obama administration have started drafting plans to comply with the new regulations.[94]

Natural gas, meanwhile, is poised to assume an ever-larger proportion of U.S. power generation. Indeed, for two months in 2015, natural gas generated more electricity than coal, according to the U.S. Energy Information Administration. Many people in industry expect this to become routine. "You just can't go with new coal [plants] at this point in time," said Charles Patton, president of Appalachian Power, a utility that provides electricity for parts of West Virginia, Virginia and Tennessee. "It is just not economically feasible to do so."[95]

OUTLOOK

Obama Agenda

With the Clean Power Plan headed to court, stakeholders are as divided on their predictions as they are on whether the rule is good policy.

"We're very confident that it will survive review," says environmental advocate Doniger.

"It's very likely that it will be overturned, if not in the D.C. Circuit Court, then by the U.S. Supreme Court," says energy industry lawyer Holmstead.

The University of Utah's Reitze says, "It will probably survive. The questionable provisions that were in there were dropped, and the final rule has much stronger legal footing."

"For the next three years, we're going to be involved in lawsuits," says the Clean Air Task Force's Weeks. At the same time, she says, "the states will be moving forward with their plans, and we'll see more movement toward clean solutions." This may mean natural gas replacing coal at power plants, improved carbon capture and more renewables, Week says.

"Companies and industries are looking at solutions," Weeks says, no matter how they see the outcome of legal challenges to the Clean Power Plan. "It's like the stages of grief," she says, describing how companies react to new regulations. "First they say, 'We can't do it! It's too costly! Let's fight back!' With time, they come to grips with their new reality. And eventually they say, 'Wow, that wasn't so bad.' This is exactly what happened with sulfur emissions in the 1970s."

The Clean Power Plan may also become a campaign issue in the 2016 presidential race. Predictably, presidential candidates' opinions of the Clean Power Plan fall along party lines. Democrats support Obama's rule and its goals of mitigating climate change and spurring growth in renewable energy sources. Republicans lambast the rule as job-killing and harmful to families faced with higher electricity bills.

Doniger says voters' views are more nuanced than politicians indicate. "A wide range of polling in blue, purple and even red states consistently shows strong support — usually 60 to 70 percent — for EPA standards to limit dangerous carbon pollution from power plants and other industries," he wrote in his blog. "Support levels are strong — often majorities, even among Republicans — even when respondents are prompted with dire messages of economic impact."[96]

Political observers point out that swing states such as Ohio remain central to the 2016 presidential race, and yet it was one of the hardest-hit states in terms of the Clean Power Plan's goals: Ohio must cut carbon emissions by 37 percent from its 2012 levels. Ohio Gov. and Republican presidential candidate John Kasich calls the Clean Power Plan "an unemployment plan" for his state, which relies on coal for 67 percent of its energy.[97]

If a Republican is elected president, the new administration will likely try to do away with the rule. However, undoing a rule is not as simple as it sounds. "To actually repeal a rule that has already been finalized, EPA would have to go through a new rule-making process, which takes years," said environmental writer Ben Adler. "And it would be challenged in court, forcing the agency to demonstrate a 'rational basis' for its action."[98]

A Republican president could choose not to enforce the regulation, or he or she could approve state plans that do not meet their carbon-reduction targets. The Clean Power Plan says the EPA will create compliance plans for states that come up short, but a Republican administration is not likely to push that action along either.[99]

Much of this debate — how to cut emissions without harming the economy — is also playing out globally. After the Paris talks conclude, individual countries could be forced to deal with recalcitrant legislatures and constituencies and find ways to implement the pledges they made at the conference. Some climate experts warn the Paris pledges will fall short anyway. The main goal, according to scientists, is to prevent global temperatures from rising 2 degrees Celsius by the end of the century. That's the amount that Earth can withstand and still stave off the most catastrophic consequences of climate change, they say.[100]

Failure could mean frequent extreme weather events such as the heat waves, stronger hurricanes and tsunamis already occurring. Marine ecosystems would be stressed to the point of collapse, according to the Intergovernmental Panel on Climate Change. Food and water security, infrastructure and human health will be threatened.[101]

"At 1 degree we are already experiencing damages," says Anders Levermann, a professor of climate science at the Potsdam Institute for Climate Impact Research in Germany. "Sea-level rise in the long term . . . is somewhere in the vicinity of 2 meters. That puts cities like New York, Calcutta and Shanghai in difficult positions, and they need to protect themselves."

NOTES

1. Tony Barboza, "L.A., Central Valley have worst air quality, American Lung Association says," *Los Angeles Times*, April 29, 2014, http://tinyurl.com/pye5eo6.
2. "State of the Air 2015," American Lung Association, 2015, http://tinyurl.com/pl98d94.
3. J. Lielveld *et al*, "The contribution of outdoor air pollution sources to premature mortality on a global scale," *Nature*, Sept. 17, 2015, http://tinyurl.com/pvw9dm5.
4. Chris Buckley, "China Burns Much More Coal Than Reported, Complicating Climate Talks," *The New York Times*, Nov. 3, 2015, http://tinyurl.com/ocu7jef.
5. Lieveled, *op. cit*.
6. Sushmi Dey, "Air pollution is world's top environmental health risk, WHO says," *The Economic Times*, June 2, 2015, http://tinyurl.com/nmmswcj.
7. Stacy Simon, "World Health Organization: Outdoor Air Pollution Causes Cancer," American Cancer Society, Oct. 17, 2013, http://tinyurl.com/oby8too.
8. Andrew C. Revkin, "Starting Later This Year, 400 and Up is Likely to Be the New Normal for CO2 Measurements," *The New York Times*, Oct. 22, 2015, http://tinyurl.com/p6mk9ng; Joby Warrick, "Greenhouse gases hit new milestone, fueling worries about climate change," *The Washington Post*, Nov. 8, 2015, http://tinyurl.com/otsq2dv.
9. Justin Gillis and Somini Sengupta, "Limited Progress Seen Even as More Nations Step Up on Climate," *The New York Times*, Sept. 28, 2015, http://tinyurl.com/q7vb89t.
10. "Fact Sheet: President Obama to Announce Historic Carbon Pollution Standards for Power Plants," press release, The White House, Aug. 3, 2015, http://tinyurl.com/nzjl5qh.
11. "Overview of Greenhouse Gases," Environmental Protection Agency, undated, http://tinyurl.com/nuuf3x4.
12. "'Clean Coal' Technologies, Carbon Capture & Sequestration," World Nuclear Association, August 2015, http://tinyurl.com/nnepfmv.
13. David Doniger, "The Clean Air Act and Climate Change: Where We've Been and Where We're Going," "Switchboard," Natural Resources Defense Council, Nov. 18, 2014, http://tinyurl.com/q3x6swq.
14. Environmental Protection Agency, *op. cit*.
15. "Fact Sheet: President Obama to Announce Historic Carbon Pollution Standards for Power Plants," *op. cit*.
16. "The Clean Power Plan: An Idea that will Change the World," press release, Natural Resources Defense Council, Aug. 3, 2015, http://tinyurl.com/nnhexby.
17. Valerie Volcovici and Lawrence Hurley, "States, business groups challenge Obama's carbon rules in court," Reuters, Oct. 23, 2015, http://tinyurl.com/ncjmadm.
18. "ACCCE Blasts Finalized EPA Carbon Emissions Rule," press release, American Coalition for Clean Coal Electricity, Aug. 3, 2015, http://tinyurl.com/oxdzfk7.

19. "Energy-Related Carbon Dioxide Emissions at the State Level, 2000-2013," Energy Information Administration, Oct. 26, 2015, http://tinyurl.com/cxtk7l6.

20. Mallory Micetich, "NAM Launches New Ozone Ads Highlighting Progress of Manufacturing and Bipartisan Opposition to Proposed Regulation," press release, National Association of Manufacturers, Sept. 25, 2015, http://tinyurl.com/nzxk86e.

21. "American Lung Association Responds to EPA Ozone Standard Update, Impact on Public Health," American Lung Association press release, Oct. 1, 2015, http://tinyurl.com/qc52gvt.

22. Colleen McCain Nelson and Amy Harder, "Obama Announces Rule to Cut Carbon Emissions from Power Plants," *The Wall Street Journal*, Aug. 3, 2015, http://tinyurl.com/phv8ckg.

23. David Doniger and Derek Murrow, "Understanding the EPA's Clean Power Plan," "Switchboard," Natural Resources Defense Council, Aug. 11, 2015, http://tinyurl.com/ompe9n4; Ann Weeks and Jay Duffy, "Let's Go EPA — Remain Strong on Power Plant Rules!" "Ahead of the Curve," Clean Air Task Force, June 15, 2015, http://tinyurl.com/on3ye8g; and "A new national Clean Power Plan," Environmental Defense Fund, undated, http://tinyurl.com/q5aj4oy.

24. "Indiana Gov. Michael R. Pence to President Obama," *Scribd*, June 24, 2015, http://tinyurl.com/oefbywo.

25. Doniger and Murrow, *op. cit.*

26. "Solyndra scandal timeline," *The Washington Post*, December 2011, http://tinyurl.com/l54e7jz.

27. Juliet Eilperin and Joby Warrick, "Obama administration tightens smog limits but satisfies few," *The Washington Post*, Oct. 1, 2015, http://tinyurl.com/nbzzujz.

28. Coral Davenport, "New Limit for Smog-Causing Emissions Isn't as Strict as Many Had Expected," *The New York Times*, Oct. 1, 2015, http://tinyurl.com/o4ru35s.

29. *Ibid.*

30. *Ibid.*

31. David W. Johnson, "Ozone standard will be crippling," *The Times and Democrat* (Orangeburg, S.C.), Sept. 29, 2015, http://tinyurl.com/ooodtbs.

32. Jill U. Adams, "A closer look: Setting a 'safer' ozone level," *Los Angeles Times*, Sept. 26, 2011, http://tinyurl.com/nz2r6dx.

33. "Fact Sheet: Supplement to the Regulatory Impact Analysis for Ozone," Environmental Protection Agency, Jan. 7, 2010, http://tinyurl.com/pgnfv83.

34. Frank O'Donnell, "Clean Air Watch Reaction to EPA Smog Decision," press release, Clean Air Watch, Oct. 1, 2015, http://tinyurl.com/nf8wgxr.

35. Daniel Cusick and Climate Wire, "Solar Power Grows 400 Percent in Only 4 Years," *Scientific American*, April 24, 2014, http://tinyurl.com/melak56.

36. "Wind Energy Facts at a Glance," American Wind Energy Association, undated, http://tinyurl.com/mg2ofvs. "Wind Energy Facts at a Glance," American Wind Energy Association, undated, http://tinyurl.com/mg2ofvs.

37. Etienne te Brake, "DNV GL Survey: 82 percent of global industry respondents say electricity system can be 70 percent renewable by 2050," DNV GL, March 18, 2015, http://tinyurl.com/orsagdx.

38. Quoted in "President Obama Announces New Limits on Power Plant Carbon Emissions," "The Diane Rehm Show," Aug. 4, 2015, http://tinyurl.com/prfydx8.

39. *Ibid.*

40. Tristan Edis, "Bloomberg sees a solar power takeover," *Business Spectator*, July 2, 2014, http://tinyurl.com/o2c43qz.

41. Christopher Helman, "Solar Power is Booming, But Will Never Replace Coal. Here's Why," *Forbes*, April 24, 2014, http://tinyurl.com/lgdxpl2.

42. Robert McManmon, "Power sector employment declines, except for renewable electricity generators," *Today in Energy*, Dec. 19, 2014, http://tinyurl.com/kc4ee9t.

43. "The Diane Rehm Show," *op. cit.*

44. David Urbinato, "London's Historic 'Pea-Soupers,'" *EPA Journal*, Summer 1994, http://tinyurl.com/on2cz37.

45. Barbara Freese, *Coal: A Human History* (2003), pp. 40-41.
46. *Ibid.*, pp. 43-69.
47. *Ibid.*, p. 105.
48. *Ibid.*, pp. 108-109.
49. *Ibid.*, pp. 153.
50. Spencer R. Weart, *The Discovery of Global Warming* (2008), pp. 2-4.
51. *Ibid.*
52. *Ibid.*, pp. 4-5, 53.
53. *Ibid.*, p. 2.
54. *Ibid.*, pp. 26-27.
55. *Ibid.*, pp. 33-35.
56. "The Keeling Curve," Scripps Institution of Oceanography, Nov. 3, 2015, http://tinyurl.com/lrvgj2z.
57. "Understanding the Clean Air Act," Environmental Protection Agency, "Plain English Guide to the Clean Air Act," Sept. 10, 2015, http://tinyurl.com/o57gt7y.
58. Sarah Gardner, "LA Smog: the battle against air pollution," "Marketplace," July 14, 2014, http://tinyurl.com/mfudhkl.
59. James R. Fleming and Bethany R. Knorr, "History of the Clean Air Act," American Meteorological Society, 1999, http://tinyurl.com/oonadp2.
60. "Clean Air Act Requirements and History," Environmental Protection Agency, http://tinyurl.com/o2me86d.
61. Fleming and Knorr, *op. cit.*
62. "Understanding the Clean Air Act," *op. cit.*
63. *Ibid.*
64. Freese, *op. cit.*, p. 169.
65. "What is Acid Rain?" Environmental Protection Agency, Dec. 4, 2012, http://tinyurl.com/ogt4ct7.
66. Freese, *op. cit.*, p. 170.
67. "The 1979 Geneva Convention on Long-range Transboundary Air Pollution," United Nations Economic Commission for Europe, undated, http://tinyurl.com/nnmd4hj; Rachel Rothschild, "Acid Wash," *Foreign Affairs*, Aug. 24, 2015, http://tinyurl.com/ods6myj.
68. Richard Coniff, "The Political History of Cap and Trade," *Smithsonian*, August 2009, http://tinyurl.com/prvwx42.
69. "Acid Rain: The power of markets to help the planet," Environmental Defense Fund, undated, http://tinyurl.com/o7p27bd.
70. Coniff, *op. cit.*
71. "Cap and Trade: Acid Rain Program Results," Environmental Protection Agency, undated, http://tinyurl.com/neunfa6; Coniff, *op. cit.*
72. "Acid Rain: The power of markets to help the planet," *op. cit.*
73. "Background and History of EPA Regulation of Greenhouse Gas Emissions Under the Clean Air Act," National Association of Clean Air Agencies, July 19, 2011, http://tinyurl.com/owo497l.
74. Chris Arnold, "GOP Demonizes Once Favored Cap-And-Trade Policy," NPR, June 3, 2014, http://tinyurl.com/py5sto9.
75. Daniel J. Weiss, "Anatomy of a Senate Climate Bill Death," Center for American Progress, Oct. 12, 2010, http://tinyurl.com/psrbpjz.
76. Justin Gillis, "2015 Likely to Be Hottest Year Ever Recorded," *The New York Times*, Oct. 21, 2015, http://tinyurl.com/po7949b.
77. "Climate change: How do we know?" NASA, undated, http://tinyurl.com/yhsnaz8.
78. Coral Davenport, "Citing Climate Change, Obama Rejects Construction of Keystone XL Oil Pipeline," *The New York Times*, Nov. 6, 2015, http://tinyurl.com/qaqkcbg.
79. Coral Davenport, "Global Climate Pact Gains Momentum as China, U.S. and Brazil Detail Plans," *The New York Times*, June 30, 2015, http://tinyurl.com/ofhonn3.
80. David Stanway, "China-US deal sets bar low ahead of Paris climate talks," Reuters, Sept. 28, 2015, http://tinyurl.com/naxtsal.
81. *Ibid.*
82. Lieleveld *et al.*, *op. cit.*
83. Michael Jerrett, "The death toll from air-pollution sources," *Nature*, Sept. 17, 2015, http://tinyurl.com/pz9pmz4.

84. Keith Johnson, "China's Leaner and Greener 5-year Plan," *Foreign Policy*, Oct. 30, 2015, http://tinyurl.com/q6zu7bn.

85. Andrew Freedman, "India, home to the world's most polluted city, launches air quality index," *Mashable*, April 6, 2015, http://tinyurl.com/pahf2os.

86. Matthew Dalton, "Volkswagen Scandal Puts Spotlight on Europe's Dirty Air," *The Wall Street Journal*, Oct. 13, 2015, http://tinyurl.com/p73cxdt; Tom Krisher, "AP News Guide: A look at the Volkswagen emissions scandal," *The Washington Post*, Nov. 5, 2015, http://tinyurl.com/pnkxpaz.

87. "Canada's air quality 3rd best in the world," *CBC News*, Sept. 26, 2011, http://tinyurl.com/qhmpewh.

88. Kazi Stastna, "How Canada's provinces are tackling greenhouse gas emissions," *CBC News*, April 14, 2015, http://tinyurl.com/mtu8u7g.

89. Suzanne Goldenberg, "Canada switches on world's first carbon capture power plant," *The Guardian*, Oct. 1, 2014, http://tinyurl.com/l9qtkd4.

90. Jordan Blum, "Low oil prices cloud futures of clean coal and carbon capture," *Houston Chronicle*, Oct. 2, 2015, http://tinyurl.com/p6dccz3.

91. Valerie Volcovici and Lawrence Hurley, "States, business groups challenge Obama's carbon rules in court," Reuters, Oct. 23, 2015, http://tinyurl.com/ncjmadm.

92. *Ibid.*

93. Tomas Carbonell, "Misguided Legal Attacks on Clear Power Plan Seek to Undermine Clean Air Act, Public Participation," "Climate 411," Environmental Defense Fund, Feb. 13, 2015, http://tinyurl.com/qhs7vwc.

94. Volcovici and Hurley, *op. cit.*; Coral Davenport, "Numerous States Prepare Lawsuits Against Obama's Climate Policy," *The New York Times*, Oct. 22, 2015, http://tinyurl.com/nu5xd8a.

95. Chris Mooney, "How super low natural gas prices are reshaping how we get our power," *The Washington Post*, Oct. 28, 2015, http://tinyurl.com/oaqv8tp.

96. Doniger, "The Clean Air Act and Climate Change," *op. cit.*

97. Philip A. Wallach, "Will the Clean Power Plan Swing the 2016 Presidential Election?" "FixGov" blog, Brookings Institution, Aug. 11, 2015, http://tinyurl.com/pfmokc3.

98. Ben Adler, "Here's how a Republican president could undermine the Clean Power Plan," *Grist*, Aug. 5, 2015, http://tinyurl.com/oe2cdpv.

99. *Ibid.*

100. Robin McKie, "World will pass crucial 2C global warming limit, experts warn," *The Guardian*, Oct. 10, 2015, http://tinyurl.com/p234y6x.

101. Roz Pidcock, "What happens if we overshoot the two degree target for limiting global warming?" *Carbon Brief*, Oct. 12, 2014, http://tinyurl.com/nw8c2vd.

BIBLIOGRAPHY

Selected Sources
Books

Freese, Barbara, *Coal: A Human History*, Perseus Publishing, 2003.
A former Minnesota assistant attorney general who helped enforce the state's air-pollution laws traces the use of coal over centuries, including during the Industrial Revolution.

Jacobson, Mark Z., *Air Pollution and Global Warming: History, Science, and Solutions*, Cambridge University Press, 2012.
A Stanford University professor of civil and environmental engineering integrates scientific study and policy approaches in a textbook addressing the modern problems of air pollution.

Lenart, Melanie, *Life in the Hothouse: How a Living Planet Survives Climate Change*, University of Arizona Press, 2010.
An environmental scientist and writer describes how the Earth responds to changes in climate.

McDaniel, Carl N., *Wisdom for a Livable Planet*, Trinity University Press, 2005.
A Rensselaer Polytechnic University biology professor profiles eight environmental activists who have worked to improve the environment.

Weart, Spencer R., *The Discovery of Global Warming*, Harvard University Press, 2008.

An historian trained in physics details the history of climate-change research.

Articles

Coniff, Richard, "The Political History of Cap and Trade," *Smithsonian Magazine*, August 2009, http://tinyurl.com/prvwx42.
A business journalist details how environmentalists and free-market conservatives created a mechanism for trading emissions credits.

Eilperin, Juliet, and Joby Warrick, "Obama administration tightens smog limits but satisfies few," *The Washington Post*, Oct. 1, 2015, http://tinyurl.com/nbzzujz.
Environmentalists say a stricter EPA ozone standard does not go far enough.

Jerrett, Michael, "The death toll from air-pollution sources," *Nature*, Sept. 17, 2015, http://tinyurl.com/pz9pmz4.
A University of California-Los Angeles environmental health sciences professor analyzes the latest study on worldwide deaths from air pollution.

McBride, James, "Modernizing the U.S. Energy Grid," Council on Foreign Relations, Aug. 3, 2015, http://tinyurl.com/phw5hwp.
A writer for a think tank provides background on how the nation's power grid works and what needs to change as wind and solar energy comes online.

Nelson, Colleen McCain, and Amy Harder, "Obama Announces Rule to Cut Carbon Emissions from Power Plants," *The Wall Street Journal*, Aug. 3, 2015, http://tinyurl.com/phv8ckg.
President Obama unveils the Clean Power Plan aimed at tightening carbon dioxide emissions.

Nuccitelli, Dana, "Is the fossil fuel industry, like the tobacco industry, guilty of racketeering?" *The Guardian*, Sept. 29, 2015, http://tinyurl.com/of9ubvh.
ExxonMobil scientists warned about the dangers of climate change years before the company began attacking climate research, *InsideClimate News* alleges.

Pearce, Fred, "Will the Paris Climate Talks Be Too Little and Too Late?" *Yale Environment 360*, Sept. 14, 2015, http://tinyurl.com/nche5uc.
An environmental consultant takes a broad look at the global political scene on climate change and reducing carbon emissions in advance of the 2015 United Nations Climate Change Conference in Paris.

Powell, Alvin, "Air Pollution's Invisible Toll," *Environment@Harvard*, June 9, 2014, http://tinyurl.com/ndh2ten.
A study documents the health effects of air pollution over two decades in six American cities.

Reports and Studies

"Advancing the Science of Climate Change," National Academy of Sciences, 2010, http://tinyurl.com/a3u2xu8.
The research group provides an in-depth look at the scientific evidence for climate change.

"Climate Change 2014: Synthesis Report Summary for Policymakers," Intergovernmental Panel on Climate Change, 2014, http://tinyurl.com/q4jnuxj.
The Intergovernmental Panel on Climate Change presents the latest in a series of reports on how humans are accelerating climate change.

"Issue Brief: What to Expect in Clean Power Plan Litigation," Natural Resources Defense Council, 2015, http://tinyurl.com/pdu3dbq.
The environmental advocacy group reports on the legal aspects of challenges to the Clean Power Plan.

"State of the Air 2015," American Lung Association, 2015, http://tinyurl.com/o9mvuen.
The health advocacy group presents its latest report on ozone and particle pollution in the United States.

For More Information

American Coalition for Clean Coal Electricity, 1152 15th St., N.W., Suite 400, Washington, DC 20005; 202-459-4800; www.americaspower.org. Partnership organization of the coal industry; advocates for the responsible use of coal.

Clean Air Task Force, 18 Tremont St., Suite 530, Boston, MA 02108; 617-292-0234; www.catf.us. Nonprofit environmental group that provides research and analysis aimed at finding solutions for climate change.

Energy Institute at the University of Texas, Flawn Academic Center, FAC 428, 2304 Whitis Ave., Stop C2400, Austin, TX 78712; 512-475-8447; http://energy.utexas.edu. Academic center that provides research and develops technology that aims to inform and improve energy policy.

Environmental Defense Fund, 257 Park Ave., South, New York, NY 10010; 800-684-3322; www.edf.org. Environmental advocacy organization that seeks ways to protect the environment.

Intergovernmental Panel on Climate Change, c/o World Meteorological Organization, 7bis Avenue de la Paix, C.P. 2300, CH 1211 Geneva 2, Switzerland; +41-22-730-8208; www.ipcc.ch/index.htm. U.N body assessing global climate change.

National Association of Manufacturers, 733 10th St., N.W., Suite 700, Washington, DC 20001; 800-814-8468; www.nam.org. Trade association representing small and large American manufacturers.

Natural Resources Defense Council, 40 W. 20th St., New York, NY 10011; 212-727-2700; www.nrdc.org. Nonprofit group that conducts public education on environmental issues, such as how to combat global climate change.

U.S. Environmental Protection Agency, 1200 Pennsylvania Ave., N.W., Washington, DC 20460; 202-272-0167; http://www3.epa.gov. Federal agency that develops and enforces regulations to support environmental legislation enacted by Congress. Also awards grants and publishes information related to environmental issues in the United States.

5

Police Tactics

Peter Katel

Demonstrators block Cleveland's Public Square on Nov. 25 during a protest over the fatal shooting of 12-year-old Tamir Rice, an African-American shot by a white Cleveland police officer after waving and reportedly reaching for a toy gun at a city park. A video of the shooting shows a police car driving up next to the boy, who was shot two seconds later.

From *CQ Researcher*, December 12, 2014.

The images packed a powerful punch: men in battle dress, carrying automatic rifles, riding in armored personnel carriers and throwing noise-and-light producing "flash-bang" grenades to disperse crowds.[1]

The show of paramilitary might was happening not at a mass street demonstration in Cairo or Rio de Janeiro but the St. Louis, Mo., suburb of Ferguson. It came in response to angry, sometimes violent, protests against the death in August of Michael Brown, an unarmed 18-year-old shot to death by a city policeman.

Public and political indignation over the shooting exploded at the military appearance of the Ferguson police, helping to fuel days-long protests in the town and deepen suspicion and fear of law enforcement. "There's no question in my mind that the idea that all of this equipment . . . contributed to a mentality among the peaceful protesters that they were being treated as the enemy," Missouri Sen. Claire McClaskill, a Democrat, said in a Senate Homeland Security Committee hearing last September.[2]

The Ferguson shooting and its continuing aftermath struck a raw nerve, aggravated by a string of shootings, some fatal, arising from police-citizen encounters in several cities, including New York; Albuquerque, N.M.; Columbia, S.C.; and Beavercreek, Ohio. In the Ohio case, a Walmart shopper in the Dayton suburb was seen talking on his cellphone while walking the aisles, holding a BB gun he had taken down from a shelf. Police, responding to a 911 call, shot him dead. In New York, Eric Garner died in a police chokehold — gasping "I can't breathe" — after verbally protesting an arrest for selling single cigarettes on the street. A grand jury declined to indict the officer involved, prompting widespread protests.³

Garner was black, and the officer who choked him was white. The Walmart shopper, John Crawford III, was black, and the two officers who shot him were white. The Ferguson shooting presented the same racial pattern — as do other, but not all — of the episodes prompting current controversies over police tactics. "Ferguson laid bare . . . a simmering distrust that exists between too many police departments and too many communities of color," President Obama said at the White House. "When any part of the American family does not feel like it is being treated fairly, that's a problem for all of us."⁴

Even some police professionals say the appearance of militarization is eroding public trust in law enforcement. "Perception is reality," said Mark Lomax, executive director of the National Tactical Officers Association — a professional organization for police special weapons and tactics (SWAT) team members. "Right now, the perception is there's a militarization of policing, which becomes a reality to a lot of people."⁵

Controversy over police tactics also intersects with intensified debate over drug laws and how they are enforced. Critics, including some former law enforcement officials, say the nation's decades-long "war on drugs" — which often involves raids by helmeted, flash-bang grenade-throwing SWAT teams — has been misguided and dangerous. The military terminology associated with U.S. anti-drug policy "evokes images of friends and foes and enemies of the police and enemies of society," says former Seattle Police Chief Norm Stamper. "If you're talking about a 16-year-old nonviolent drug offender, he's not the enemy."

In Washington much of the furor over police tactics has centered on a 23-year-old program for transferring Defense Department surplus gear to police departments, a once-informal system that expanded along with the drug war. The program is now known as "1033" after the relevant section of federal law.

Since 1990, the Pentagon has shifted more than $5.1 billion worth of surplus equipment to local and federal law enforcement entities — 96 percent of it nonlethal supplies such as office furniture, tents and forklifts, but also some 90,000 pistols and assault rifles and 600 armored vehicles. Data show big increases in equipment transfers in 2012 and 2013, when the wars in Iraq and Afghanistan were winding down.⁶

Critics say the gear encourages military-style tactics against civilians. "Cutting off the supply of military weaponry to our civilian police is the least we

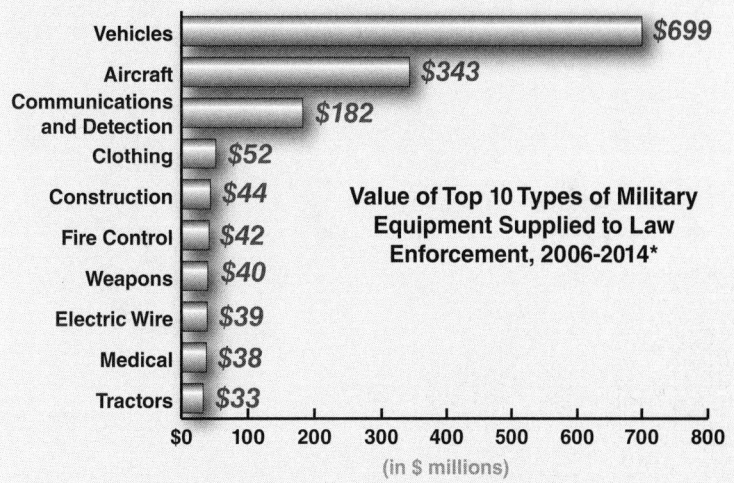

Vehicles, Aircraft Top List of Military Supplies

The Department of Defense has supplied local police departments with more than $1.5 billion worth of surplus equipment over the past eight years. Most of the hardware was vehicles, including armored ones, aircraft and communications and detection equipment. Only $40 million worth of the equipment was for weapons.

Value of Top 10 Types of Military Equipment Supplied to Law Enforcement, 2006-2014*

Type	Value (in $ millions)
Vehicles	$699
Aircraft	$343
Communications and Detection	$182
Clothing	$52
Construction	$44
Fire Control	$42
Weapons	$40
Electric Wire	$39
Medical	$38
Tractors	$33

* Spending data from 2006 through April 2014

Source: Analysis by David Eads and Tyler Fisher, "MRAPs And Bayonets: What We Know About The Pentagon's 1033 Program," NPR, Sept. 2, 2014, http://tinyurl.com/p3a4fqj; original data for 1033 program expenditures located at "LESO Program data," Defense Logistics Agency, http://tinyurl.com/n7koanr

Most SWAT Deployments Are for Search Warrants

Police departments executed four out of five SWAT team deployments to serve search warrants in 2011 and 2012, according to a civil liberties organization's study of 20 law enforcement agencies. Another 17 percent of deployments were for other purposes, such as protecting visiting officials, responding to emergencies and pursuing fleeing suspects.

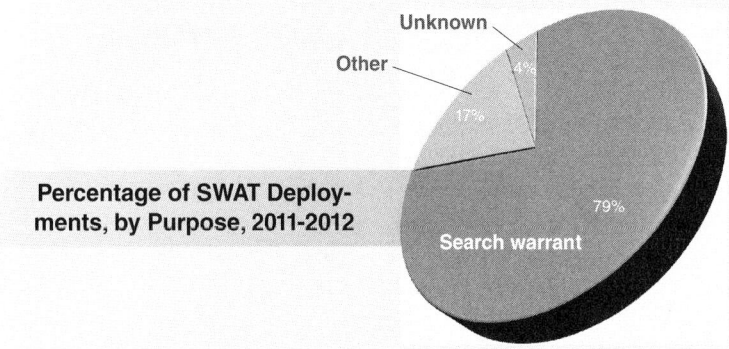

Percentage of SWAT Deployments, by Purpose, 2011-2012

Source: "War Comes Home: The Excessive Militarization of American Policing," American Civil Liberties Union, June 2014, p. 31, http://tinyurl.com/myxzoju

could do to begin the process of reining in police militarization and attempting to make clear the increasingly blurred distinction between the military and police," Peter Kraska, chair of criminal justice studies at Eastern Kentucky University in Richmond, Ky., told the Senate Homeland Security Committee in September. Kraska pioneered studies of police SWAT teams, first created in 1967 to deal with high-risk episodes such as hostage rescues.[7]

But police defenders call increased militarization a myth. Unlike the military, "SWAT teams do not engage the enemy with the purpose of destroying them; they are trained to protect life," says Chuck Canterbury, national president of the Fraternal Order of Police, the nation's largest law-enforcement union, and former operations chief of the county police department in Conway, S.C. "The majority of SWAT calls end with nobody injured; if the military had a record like that, they'd be losing the war."

And much of the Pentagon equipment, such as high-wheeled trucks and forklifts, are used in disaster-recovery missions, Alan Estevez, the Defense undersecretary in charge of the surplus equipment system, told a Senate committee in September.[8]

But during the early days of 1033, the Justice Department didn't cite disaster relief as a prime justification for the program. "The best examples of law enforcement and military participation in common missions are the 'wars' being waged against narcotics and terrorism," a 1997 Justice Department report on developing weapons and technology for military and police use stated.[9]

Among those tools were flash-bang grenades. They are part of SWAT team toolkits but have caused at least seven unintended deaths, including of a police officer, and burn injuries prompting a total of $2.1 million in settlements in two cases in 2010 and 2011.[10]

Last May, SWAT officers from Georgia's Habersham County and Cornelia city threw a flash-bang grenade into a house during a 3 a.m. drug raid, causing third-degree burns on a 19-month-old child and blowing a hole in his chest. The raiders were seeking a relative who wasn't home.[11]

County Sheriff Joey Terrell said authorities didn't know children were present but argued drug raids call for SWAT deployment. Drug dealers, he said, "are no better than a domestic terrorist, . . . and I think we should treat them as such."[12]

With many drug dealers today being heavily armed, drug raids can be extremely dangerous for cops. In 2012, a member of an Ogden, Utah, drug strike force was killed and five others were wounded during a raid on a house to serve a search warrant on a small-scale marijuana case suspect, who fired at police.[13]

SWAT teams are used predominantly to serve search warrants, mostly in drug cases. According to an American Civil Liberties Union (ACLU) survey, 79 percent of SWAT deployments in 2011–12 involved searches — 62 percent of them for drugs.[14]

Concern that SWAT teams are being wrongly assigned to duties that don't require a high-intensity approach runs through police circles. Inappropriate SWAT deployments are "more prevalent in smaller agencies," says Charles "Sid" Heal, a retired Los Angeles County Sheriff's Department officer who commanded a SWAT unit. "They may get 12 callouts a year, and they have to justify their existence." Raiding a "dime-bag dealer" does not require a tactical team, but SWAT raids against high-level drug dealers are fully justified, Heal says, given the long sentences they face if arrested. "They've got nothing to lose," he adds.

Officers face other dangerous enemies as well. Last September, a sniper killed a Pennsylvania state trooper as he ended his shift. And in Albuquerque last year, an AK-47-wielding gunman with "cop killer" tattooed on his knuckles shot and gravely wounded a sheriff's deputy before being shot to death.[15]

Part of the Albuquerque gunfight was captured on officers' body-worn cameras. Support is growing for widespread use of the devices because, supporters say, both police and citizens tend to behave better when they are being recorded.

But some experts warn against placing too much faith in cameras — or in military gear. "There is a time and place for police to . . . use military weapons and tactics to end a threat to human life," former Seattle chief Stamper says, but "there are no strings attached, no training requirements or certification that the local agency is going to use that equipment under very carefully circumscribed circumstances."

As law enforcement officials, Congress and the public weigh the use of aggressive tactics and military-style equipment by police, here are some of the questions under debate:

Do SWAT teams and military tactics and weaponry have a place in policing?

Debate over militarization was well underway before recent media reports on the 1033 program and its transfers of military guns and personnel carriers to local police departments.

Much of that early debate focused on the formation of SWAT teams.

Los Angeles formed the first SWAT team, in 1967, prompted by violent events that included a sniper attack on the University of Texas at Austin campus. By the late 1990s, about 89 percent of departments in cities with 50,000 people or more had SWAT units, a rate that experts say holds true today.[16]

An upswing in the number of heavily armed criminals, mass shootings and other emergencies prompted the spread of tactical units, concluded a 2002 California commission study of the state's SWAT operations. Most countries would send a national police force to such emergencies, the study found, but U.S. law leaves most policing duties to cities, counties and states.

"It became clear that a new method of response to such complex, high-risk and often high-energy situations was needed," the study said. "Over the years, SWAT has evolved into the management of barricaded suspect situations, the service of high-risk warrants, dignitary protection and the actual rescue of hostages."[17]

The commission was formed after an 11-year-old boy was accidentally killed during a 2000 SWAT raid conducted with FBI and Drug Enforcement Administration (DEA) agents in Modesto, Calif. Then-state Attorney General Bill Lockyer was "concerned about the potential erosion of community confidence in local law enforcement agencies caused by such tragedies," the commission said.[18]

But SWAT teams are increasingly active, according to Kraska of Eastern Kentucky University, who found an increase of 57,000 SWAT deployments between 1980 and 2007.[19]

Moreover, Lomax, of the National Tactical Officers Association, told a Senate committee: "It is not uncommon for agencies to take receipt of such [military] equipment and receive little or no training on how to utilize it, when to deploy it and, equally as important, when not to deploy it."[20]

Critics including the ACLU and Radley Balko, a *Washington Post* blogger and one of the earliest critics of the expansion and growing use of SWAT teams, argues that many of them are being used to serve run-of-the-mill search and arrest warrants, unnecessarily using overwhelming force. "We see SWAT teams now in white-collar crimes, even regulatory crimes, [such as] barbering without a license" Balko, told an Albuquerque audience in November. He cited an 11th Circuit U.S. Court of Appeals decision in September that SWAT raids on Orlando, Fla., barbershops were unconstitutional.[21]

Police, as well as police critics, say many SWAT teams are misdirected to routine duties. A 2011 policy paper published by the Alexandria, Va.-based International Association of Chiefs of Police said serving search warrants was the "most common" task of SWAT teams — with some departments sending them to every search. That policy represented "overuse of a team created to deal with high-risk interventions," the paper said.[22]

Some specialists trace what they call an overreliance on SWAT to an eagerness to acquire military equipment. "Once you get the equipment you have to develop the military mindset to use it," says sociologist Peter Moskos, a former Baltimore police officer and professor in the Law, Police Science and Criminal Justice Administration department at John Jay College of Criminal Justice in New York. "You can have the mindset without equipment, but you can do less damage."

Weapons trainers, who teach police officers that "it's a war out there, everyone is out to get you," also foster a military mentality, says Moskos. "That is not a realistic fear."

But Canterbury, of the Fraternal Order of Police, says given the fundamental difference between military and police missions, military equipment — even attention-getting mine-resistant vehicles — have effectively been demilitarized for police use. "They don't have military weapons or computer systems on them," he says. "They're nothing but an armored vehicle once law enforcement gets them."

Richard Greenleaf, director of the criminal justice major at Elmhurst College in Elmhurst, Ill., and a former sergeant in the Albuquerque Police Department, doesn't question the view that police are militarizing. But he also says police are rightly danger-conscious because of the nation's high rate of gun ownership.[23]

"America has more guns per capita than any other country in the whole world, and many of them are very powerful," Greenleaf says. "You can't not think about that when you think about the militarization of the police."

For many policing experts, an event that confirmed the need for SWAT teams as well as heavier armament for regular patrol cops was a 44-minute shootout in North Hollywood, Calif., in 1997 in which two body-armor-wearing bank robbers with several assault rifles, plus handguns, exchanged nearly 2,000 rounds with officers, including some SWAT team members. The robbers were killed, but no police died. "Patrol officers had never before been engaged in such a protracted, high-intensity firefight," Bob Parker, a former Omaha SWAT commander, wrote in *Police* magazine.[24]

Stamper, the former Seattle police chief, was in the San Diego Police Department when a gunman killed 21 people at a McDonald's restaurant there before a police sniper killed him.[25] Stamper says military capabilities are essential, but they are being overused. He largely blames politicians who constantly depicted drug enforcement in military terms. "It started with 'drug war,' " he says. "And there is a macho dimension to this that can't be denied. It's boys with toys."

Police departments that routinely use SWAT teams to serve drug-case warrants should return to standard procedures that would make most raids unnecessary, Stamper argues. "Why have 14 cops for one low-level offender?" he asks. "What about surveillance — watching for the suspect to come out? He comes out, goes into his car, and you conduct a routine traffic stop."

Heal, the former Los Angeles County Sheriff's Department commander, agrees that with low-level drug dealers, the best option is to determine "if you can do a door-knock and tell a guy to come out."

Nevertheless, he says, such determinations are subjective, with no easy formulas to apply. And in the case of higher-level traffickers, "Whether people want to believe it or not, drug dealers are inherently dangerous," Heal says. "I don't know of a single one anywhere I wouldn't consider them a threat."

Has police use of military-style tactics increased tensions with minority communities?

The community-police conflict that erupted in Ferguson after the shooting death of Brown illustrated, again, that controversies over police conduct often involve a racial dimension. Recent Justice Department investigations of police departments found discriminatory conduct toward African-Americans, and in some cases Latinos, in Maricopa County, Ariz.; East Haven, Conn.; New Orleans; Newark; Alamance County, N.C., and Portland, Ore.[26]

An analysis by the investigative news website ProPublica of fatal police shootings of teenagers ages 15–19 concluded that in 2010–2012, black teens were killed at a rate of 31.17 per million, compared to 1.47 per million among white teens.[27]

ProPublica acknowledged that the FBI data it used, which include victims' race — and which show 1,217 fatal police shootings overall, adults and minors, in those years — were "terribly incomplete." Indeed a *Wall Street Journal* investigation counted at least 1,800 deaths at police hands but found only 1,242 recorded in police department records. Some experts argued that though a racial disproportion exists, ProPublica's use of the data vastly overstated the trend. Moskos of John Jay College of Criminal Justice calculated, using the same data, that if ProPublica had analyzed 15 years of available statistics instead of three years, the results would show that black youths were nine times likelier — instead of 21 times likelier — to be killed by police than young white people — "a huge difference," Moskos wrote. The underlying data also showed 62 police shootings of all teenagers in 2010–2012 reported to the FBI. One of the ProPublica reporters said that the analysis focused on recent years because "the disparity is growing."[28]

In addition to the killings of Brown and Garner, other recent police-involved deaths of African-Americans include:

- John Crawford III, 22, shot dead by police in a Beavercreek, Ohio, Walmart, while talking on his cellphone and walking the aisles holding a BB gun he had taken down from a shelf;
- Akai Gurley, 28, a resident of a Brooklyn public housing project, who was shot while walking down a darkened stairway. Police called the shooting, by a rookie officer, unintentional; and
- Tamir Rice, a 12-year-old Cleveland boy who was shot after waving and then reportedly reaching for a toy pistol that resembled a real one.[29]

For many politicians and ordinary citizens, the deaths were only the latest illustrations of what they call police over-aggressiveness — if not hostility — when it comes to black men. President Obama is one of many to weigh in on the topic. "Too many young men of color feel targeted by law enforcement," Obama said in a speech to the Congressional Black Caucus in September. "We know that, statistically, in everything from enforcing drug policy to applying the death penalty to pulling people over, there are significant racial disparities."[30]

The deaths above did not arise from drug cases, but drug enforcement usually comes up in discussions of police and race. Police critics say drug-war tactics are one

Protesters in Los Angeles stage a sit-in on Nov. 25, one day after a grand jury decided not to indict Darren Wilson, the white Ferguson, Mo., police officer who shot and killed Michael Brown. The demonstration was one of dozens around the country since August in response to several recent cases in which unarmed African-American males have been killed by white police officers, two of whom were not indicted.

of the issues underlying the outcry over Brown's death. "The war on drugs and war on crime have been predominantly waged in racial and ethnic minority communities and too often against African-Americans," Hilary Shelton, the NAACP's senior vice president for advocacy, told the Senate Homeland Security Committee in September.[31]

A leading African-American political figure, the Rev. Al Sharpton of New York, connected the deaths of Brown and Garner to police action against minor offenses. Brown died after being stopped for walking in the street. The shooter, Officer Darren Wilson — who has resigned — said he believed Brown and a friend might have stolen cigarillos from a nearby store, although police initially said Wilson didn't know of that incident.

"Both of them were victims of this aggressive policing of alleged low-level crime," Sharpton said.[32]

Police Say 'Shoot to Wound' Is Not an Option

"If you point a gun at a police officer, you have punched your ticket."

Police veterans are of one mind when someone — a politician, a journalist, a member of the public — asks why police don't shoot to wound when they open fire, especially on an unarmed civilian.

Following the fatal shooting of Michael Brown by a Ferguson, Mo., police officer, the question came from CNN anchor Wolf Blitzer: "Why do they have to shoot to kill? . . . Why can't they shoot to injure, shall we say?"[1]

The question may seem reasonable — especially after an unarmed citizen dies in a police shooting.

In 2010, following one such death, New York state Assemblywoman Annette Robinson of Brooklyn proposed legislation that would have required a police officer to use deadly force "with the intent to stop, rather than kill." Robinson, who represents the largely African-American and low-income Bedford-Stuyvesant area, said she was responding to what she called a disproportionate number of police shootings of black men. "I do know that it happens, most often in the communities that I represent," she said, "and it happens too often."[2]

Specifically, Robinson proposed the legislation in response to the 2006 shooting death of Sean Bell, killed on his wedding day by undercover police who thought — mistakenly — that Bell and a friend, both black, were armed and about to commit a drive-by shooting.[3] But the bill died in committee amid heavy ridicule from police organizations.[4]

Police say officers in fast-moving confrontations have no time for precision shooting. "It works real well when you're shooting at a piece of paper," says Chuck Canterbury of Myrtle Beach, S.C., president of the national Fraternal Order of Police union. "We're not snipers. We're trained to point and shoot."

The objective, former police officers say, is not to kill, but to stop a threat to innocent human life. In practice, stopping a threat means shooting at the biggest target, which is the torso, what police trainers call the body's "center mass."

Former Seattle Police Chief Norm Stamper, a liberal critic of much police strategy, calls the idea that an officer can deliberately shoot to wound "a fallacy."

Police officers can be poor shots, he points out, especially in highly stressful situations. The New York Police Department reported that in 29 incidents in which officers fired their weapons, they hit at least one of their targets in only 64 percent of their shots. And in one incident, nine bystanders were injured when police fired 16 rounds at a man who had killed his ex-boss on a crowded sidewalk.[5]

Richard Greenleaf, director of the criminal justice major at Elmhurst College in Elmhurst, Ill., recalls from his days as an Albuquerque, N.M., police officer in the late 1970s and early '80s that colleagues who had been highly accurate shooters during training "in a real situation would miss 80 percent of the time."

Greenleaf says he was a bad shot on the range. But one night in 1981, he faced a man with a .22-caliber pistol who was running out of a convenience store he had just robbed. "I chased him to the back of the building," Greenleaf says. "He turned; I said, 'Oh, [no], he's going to shoot. I managed to hit him twice in three shots. He died. I do believe that if he had killed me, he would feel less remorse than I feel."

The next day, Greenleaf's girlfriend reported that a man walked into the bail bond company she ran and asked, "'Why didn't that cop wound him?'"

Says Greenleaf: "His perception was that I should have shot the gun out of his hand."

At least one country, Israel, recognizes shooting to wound as a tactic, at least for its military (human-rights activists criticize Israeli police for shooting to kill).[6] But specially trained Israel Defense Forces (IDF) troops must go to great lengths to make such shots, which is why those tactics would be impractical for police.

"It is 10 times harder to shoot someone in the leg than to simply kill him," an ex-IDF sniper, using a pseudonym, wrote in a long account of lying in wait to wound a target at the border fence between Gaza and Israel. "The leg is narrow, easily concealed by the land and always moving."[7]

Moreover, the target must be standing. "If we shoot while he is sitting, the bullet could hit his thigh and kill him," the ex-sniper wrote. Thigh wounds can involve the femoral artery, with fatal consequences.[8]

U.S. police do have alternatives to guns, depending on the circumstances. The Taser, a device that can temporarily disable an adversary with an electric discharge, is perhaps the most widely known alternative.

But Tasers can be problematic as well. Last March, an 18-year-old Miami artist, Israel "Reefa" Hernandez, died after Miami Beach police shot him with a Taser. He had tried to run away after they saw him painting graffiti on a vacant building. The Miami-Dade medical examiner concluded that his heart failed after an "energy device discharge."[9]

In Albuquerque, a Justice Department investigation this year into improper use of force concluded that officers "frequently misused" Tasers against people who were merely ignoring orders or who posed little danger. In one case, officers fired at a man who had doused himself with gasoline. The Taser discharges set him on fire, although he survived.[10]

Donald E. Wilkes Jr., an emeritus law professor at the University of Georgia, and Athens, Ga., lawyer Lauren Farmer have compiled 618 media accounts of deaths apparently caused by police Taser discharges from 2001 through Oct. 13, 2013.[11]

Police experts are unanimous that intensive training on when to use force is essential. Former Seattle chief Stamper cited a rookie police officer's fatal shooting in November of 12-year-old Tamir Rice in Cleveland, Ohio. Rice had been waving a toy pistol. A video of the shooting — showing a police car driving up next to the boy, who was shot two seconds later — demonstrates that the shooting never had to happen, Stamper concludes, saying the officer could have taken cover behind his car and evaluated the situation more calmly.[12]

"A more mature, experienced, confident police officer would have better understood what he was facing," Stamper says.

At the same time, he says Rice's parents never should have let him outside with a replica pistol, and schools and police should ensure that children know an essential fact of life: No one seen to pose a mortal threat in the presence of police should expect to walk away, or even to survive.

"If you point a gun at a police officer, you have punched your ticket," Stamper says. "I don't care if it's a toy gun. At a minimum you are going to get two shots to the chest."

— *Peter Katel*

---

[1] Quoted in Ahiza Garcia, "Wolf Blitzer: Why Can't Ferguson Police Just 'Shoot To Injure?'" *Talking Points Memo*, Aug. 15, 2014, http://tinyurl.com/p8bv42l.

[2] Quoted in Brendan Scott, "'Don't Kill' Pol in a Cop-Out — Admits: I'm No Expert," *New York Post*, May 26, 2010, http://tinyurl.com/ngaq6lx.

[3] "An act to amend the penal law, in relation to the use of deadly force by police officers," New York State Assembly, Jan. 22, 2009, http://tinyurl.com/nbclrau; Murray Weiss, "Cops furious at 'don't kill' bill," *New York Post*, May 25, 2010, http://tinyurl.com/m34xej8; Matt Flegenheimer and Al Baker, "Officer in Bell Killing Is Fired," *The New York Times*, March 23, 2012, http://tinyurl.com/oy5792m.

[4] "NY AO2952 — 2009-2010, General Assembly," http://tinyurl.com/ndc3xe5. Murray Weiss, "Cops furious at 'don't kill' bill," *New York Post*, May 25, 2010, http://tinyurl.com/m34xej8.

[5] "Annual Firearms Discharge Report," New York City Police Department, 2013, pp. 21, 27, http://tinyurl.com/mprloo3.

[6] Edo Konrad, "Intellectuals call for investigation into police shooting of Arab youth," *+972 Magazine*, Nov. 13, 2014, http://tinyurl.com/pha8ktp.

[7] Gershon Morris, "Israeli Sniper's Anguished Look Into Crosshairs," *Jewish Daily Forward*, March 21, 2014, http://tinyurl.com/mcr2vy7.

[8] *Ibid.*; Ed Nowicki, "Training for Gunshot Wound Treatment," *Law and Order*, April 2009, http://tinyurl.com/n8ashyf.

[9] Michael E. Miller, "Israel 'Reefa' Hernandez Died by Taser," *Miami New Times*, March 13, 2014, http://tinyurl.com/lz88jry; Michael E. Miller, "Teenager Israel Hernandez Dies after Miami Beach Cops Catch Him Tagging, Taser Him," *Miami New Times*, Aug. 7, 2014, http://tinyurl.com/mlwgmda.

[10] "Civil Investigation of the Albuquerque Police Department," U.S. Department of Justice, April 10, 2014, p. 3, http://tinyurl.com/n6bubpo; Patrick Lohmann, "APD guilty of Taser abuse," *Albuquerque Journal*, April 11, 2014, http://tinyurl.com/kbsgmlg.

[11] Donald E. Wilkes Jr. and Lauren Farmer, "Fatal Police Taserings, List and Annexures," December 2013, http://tinyurl.com/lnlsjh5.

[12] Emma G. Fitzsimmons, "Video Shows Cleveland Officer Shot Boy in 2 Seconds," *The New York Times*, Nov. 26, 2014, http://tinyurl.com/pajhjnl.

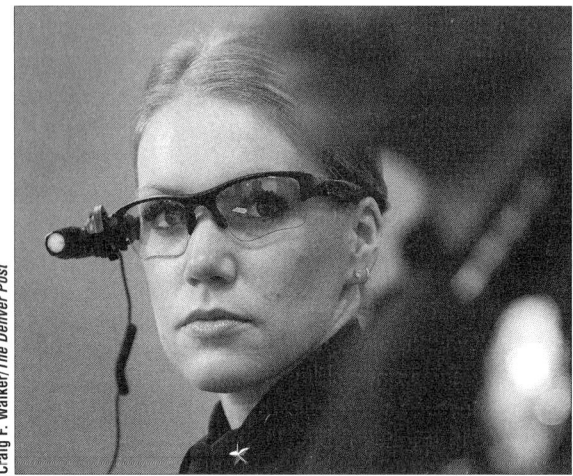

Denver police commander Magen Dodge displays a body camera during a press conference on Aug. 27. Denver Police hope to equip 800 officers, including all patrol and traffic officers, with "bodycams" by 2015. Many police critics, and some officers, say the cameras can help resolve problems between citizens and police. But some law enforcement officers worry they will have limited value, and possibly limit officers' discretion.

Sharpton's role as a nationwide police critic is especially irritating to police who resent being portrayed as overly focused on African-Americans. "Al Sharpton is a race-baiter," says Canterbury of the FOP. He questioned why Sharpton hadn't visited Chicago, where 10 other black men were killed in crimes in the eight days before Brown was shot.[33]

In fact, Sharpton held a meeting in Chicago last year to address gun violence in the city's black neighborhoods. And in speaking at Brown's funeral, he said: "We've got to be straight up in our community, too. We have to be outraged at . . . our killing and shooting and running around gun-toting each other."[34]

Poverty, not race, is what focuses police attention on some communities, Canterbury says. "How about talking about poverty-stricken communities? Whether they're white, black, Hispanic, when you have a neighborhood that has high unemployment, high infant mortality, a high percentage of people who are on public assistance or have been on public assistance, when they don't see any chance of getting out of their circumstances, drugs are the only way they see to escape."

Some cities do deploy intensive patrols of poor neighborhoods, focusing on violations that affect quality of life. But whether that so-called "broken windows" strategy reduces crime is a long-running, unresolved debate among criminologists.[35]

Former Seattle police chief Stamper says police don't get orders to round up African-Americans. However, "You see wildly disproportionate numbers of young people, poor people, people of color apprehended, jailed — if not imprisoned — as a result of low-level, nonviolent drug offenses."

Race is an inescapable part of the picture, he argues. "We've ended up with a lot of young people of color on street corners doing hand-to-hand deals," he says. "They're low-hanging fruit. You get a lot of complaints about that behavior, and the police are called and do buy-and-busts and scoop up hundreds of thousands of offenders who fall into that demography."

Moskos, of the John Jay College of Criminal Justice, wrote about police and race in a memoir about a year he spent on the Baltimore police force patrolling poor African-American neighborhoods. He rebuts what he calls the "standard liberal line" that black people are shot because they're black.[36] "A cop is not shooting a black person," Moskos says. "A cop is shooting a person because he is afraid, justly or not."

Do body cameras prevent police misconduct?

Aside from race, another thread running through controversies over police tactics has been the explosive growth of documentary evidence in the form of digital imagery — still and video.

Some of this video evidence comes from police cameras, mounted on squad car dashboards or — more recently — worn on officers' bodies. Many police critics, and some officers, say the so-called "bodycams" offer a technological solution to problems that arise between police and citizens.

"We won't have to play this game of witnesses' memories and secret grand jury procedures," Benjamin Crump, the lawyer for Brown's family, said after the grand jury's decision not to indict Wilson for Brown's death, which was not recorded. "It would just be transparent, and we could see it ourselves, and we could hold people accountable when they have interactions with citizens."[37]

Obama embraced the growing movement calling for more bodycams, proposing spending $75 million over three years to provide up to 50,000 of the devices for local police departments. Technology, he said, can "enhance trust between communities and the police."[38]

Among the police-citizen encounters, some fatal, captured on video from body or dashboard cameras in recent years are:

- A Hamilton, Mont., police officer in 2010 shot and killed a fleeing driver who had fired on the officer during a routine traffic stop;
- A New Mexico State Police officer in 2013 shot at a minivan containing young children, hitting no one;
- Albuquerque Police Department officers in 2014 shot dead homeless, mentally ill James Boyd, who the video showed was preparing to surrender;
- A Salt Lake City officer this year shot and killed a man reported to have a gun, who first refused to raise his hands, then lifted his shirt and reached for his waistband; he turned out to be unarmed.[39]

Body cameras — attached to an officer's belt, lapel or helmet — were introduced in Britain in 2005.[40] In Rialto, Calif., citizen complaints against officers dropped 88 percent from the previous 12 months after some officers began wearing them two years ago. "When you put a camera on a police officer, they tend to behave a little better, follow the rules a little better," Rialto's police chief told *The New York Times*. "And if a citizen knows the officer is wearing a camera, chances are the citizen will behave a little better."[41]

Blacks Rate Police Poorly for Use of Force

Seven in 10 black Americans say police do a poor job of holding other officers accountable for misconduct and treating racial and ethnic groups equally. Additionally, 57 percent of blacks say police do a poor job of using the right amount of force. By comparison, only about one-quarter of whites say police do a poor job of holding officers accountable, treating racial groups equally and using the right amount of force.

Views on Police Job Performance, by Race, 2014

How well do you think police:

Hold other officers accountable for misconduct?

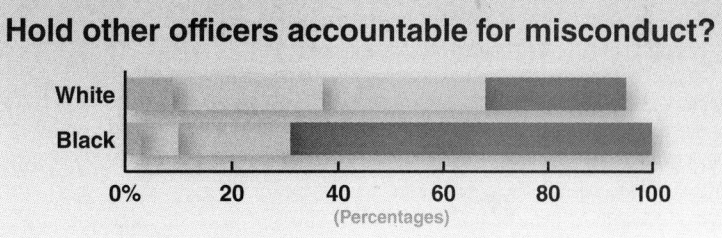

Treat racial and ethnic groups equally?

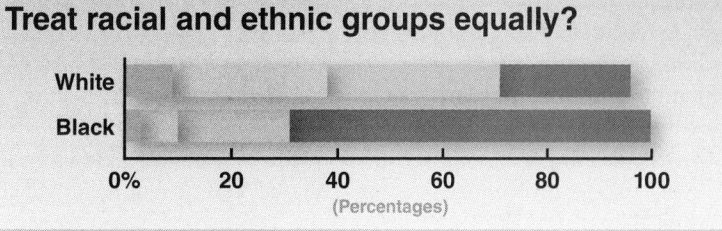

Use the right amount of force for each situation?

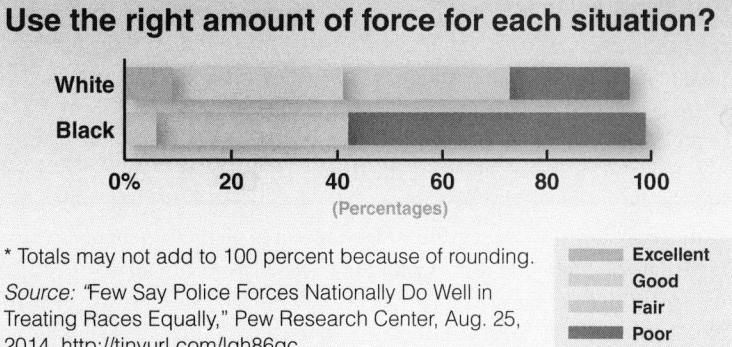

* Totals may not add to 100 percent because of rounding.

Source: "Few Say Police Forces Nationally Do Well in Treating Races Equally," Pew Research Center, Aug. 25, 2014, http://tinyurl.com/lgh86qc

Cameras are spreading to departments bigger than Rialto's 54 patrol officers.

New York City began experimenting with bodycams in September, after U.S. District Judge Shira Scheindlin ruled that the city's police department was stopping and

Looters flee with stolen shoes during widespread rioting in South-Central Los Angeles on April 30, 1992. The riots were sparked by the acquittals of three white police officers accused in the videotaped beating of black motorist Rodney King, the jury deadlocked on a fourth officer. More than 60 people died during the five days of rioting. Later that year, two of the officers were convicted of federal charges of violating King's civil rights; two were acquitted.

frisking a disproportionate number of black and Latino men, in violation of constitutional protections.[42]

Experts caution that good results from cameras depend on how departments use them — including specifying what kind of encounters should not be recorded, keeping a camera on until an interaction is over and obtaining consent to record crime victims.[43]

In Albuquerque, where officers began wearing lapel or belt cameras in 2010, the Justice Department found unsystematic use. "We . . . reviewed numerous reports where offices and supervisors on the scene failed to turn on their lapel cameras or belt tapes," the department said in a highly critical assessment of the department earlier this year.[44]

Indeed, shortly after the Justice Department issued its report, an Albuquerque officer shot and killed 19-year-old Mary Hawkes, claiming the suspected truck thief had pointed a pistol at him during a foot chase. The officer, Jeremy Dear, was wearing a camera, but no video of the shooting could be found.[45]

In early December, the Albuquerque department fired Dear for "insubordination," saying he had not complied with a policy to record all interactions with citizens. Officials said Dear claimed he had turned on the camera, but the camera manufacturer said it couldn't determine if the device malfunctioned, if Dear had turned it off or had never turned it on. Dear also had failed to record two previous incidents, police said. His lawyer, Thomas Grover, said Dear hadn't been told of the recording policy.[46]

Moskos at John Jay College of Criminal Justice said in an era of ubiquitous cellphone cameras, departments need to keep up with the times. "Often on these scenes, cops are the ones without cameras," Moskos says, which argues for police having their own — perhaps more complete — record of an incident.

Nevertheless, police suspicion of cameras is understandable, Moskos says "I think it's going to limit police discretion," he says. "Sometimes you just cut a guy a break. [But] what if that guy then goes out and kills someone?"

Police union president Canterbury cites research by a private firm in Mankato, Minn., that provides expert testimony in lawsuits against officers and police departments. Cameras respond better to dim light, for instance, than the human eye. But recording speed is slower than the eye.[47] "There are things an officer may see that the camera won't," Canterbury says.

He also cautions that citizens should realize that a lot of police video, including interviews with witnesses, will be public record and available to the media. "Will they make members of the public uncomfortable?" he asks. "Absolutely." And confidential witnesses could be identified.

Former Seattle police chief Stamper, who originally opposed body cameras and now supports them, warns that they may pose serious complications for officers and, indirectly, for citizens. "Assume you're working for a hard-ass sergeant who's all about numbers, numbers, and you're a cop who's community-oriented, committed to solving landlord-tenant disputes, [and] you spend time talking with people," Stamper says. "And you've got all this on film and the sergeant says, 'You want to be social worker or a cop?'"

With greater use of cameras inevitable, citizens and police will have to adjust, experts say. "They're going to have to come to the realization that no matter how good the camera, it can't incorporate everything," Stamper says.

CHRONOLOGY

1957-1969 *Military forces quell civil rights conflicts and urban uprisings, under exception to law barring domestic use of armed forces.*

1957 President Dwight D. Eisenhower sends Army troops to Little Rock, Ark., to enforce school desegregation.

1966 U.S. Marine veteran shoots 43 people, killing 13, from clock tower at University of Texas at Austin, prompting early fears of mass shootings.

1967 Army sent to Detroit to quell urban uprising. . . . Los Angeles forms the first police special weapons and tactics (SWAT) team.

1970-1989 *Drug war starts; military-law enforcement cooperation grows.*

1970 Congress authorizes "no-knock" searches when police suspect evidence could be destroyed if officers announce themselves.

1971 Armed forces and civil law enforcement agencies begin cooperating in drug enforcement, including small-scale loans of military equipment and personnel.

1974 Reports of abusive police searches prompt repeal of "no-knock" provision.

1981 Congress requires that the military hunt drug smugglers.

1989 Congress authorizes Defense Department to fund National Guard drug enforcement programs.

1990-1999 *Military-police cooperation broadened.*

1990 Congress begins formal program of providing military equipment to police departments for use in drug enforcement, later known as 1033 program.

1992 Massive, deadly riots break out in South-Central Los Angeles following acquittal of four police officers charged with brutal beating of black motorist Rodney King — a beating captured on video that was widely replayed on TV.

1996 Congress removes requirement police use surplus military equipment only in drug enforcement operations.

1999 Demonstrations against World Trade Organization meeting in Seattle met by forceful police response, including mass arrests and rubber bullets. . . . In notorious school shootings, two students attack Columbine High School in Colorado, leaving 13 dead.

2001-Present *Counter-terrorism duties assigned to police departments as a result of 9/11 attacks.*

2005 State Department calls "domestic preparedness" against terrorism a "staple of law enforcement operations."

2007 At least 80 percent of police departments have SWAT teams.

2009 Outrage follows video of transit officer shooting unarmed, prone young man in Oakland, Calif., subway station.

2011 Justice Department concludes that Maricopa County, Ariz., sheriff's department practices racial profiling and other unconstitutional actions, in one of about 20 investigations of U.S. police misconduct.

2013 Bill de Blasio elected mayor of New York City after opposing "stop-and-frisk" searches that disproportionately affect young black and Latino men.

2014 After 27 fatal shootings and other violent episodes by Albuquerque, N.M., Police Department since 2010, Justice Department reports that the department has violated constitutional limits on use of force. . . . Flash-bang grenade use in SWAT raid in Cornelia, Ga., gravely injures infant. . . . Video captures police chokehold death of Eric Garner in Staten Island, N.Y. . . . Ferguson, Mo., police officer shoots unarmed 18-year-old Michael Brown, sparking violent protests there and nationwide. . . . Military gear deployed against Ferguson demonstrators prompts congressional hearing on 1033 program and police militarization. . . . St. Louis County, Mo., grand jury declines to indict police officer Darren Wilson in death of Brown, leading to widespread protests and some violence and arson. . . . Cleveland police officer fatally shoots 12-year-old boy brandishing a toy pistol.

Police Face Danger in Everyday Situations

Even routine traffic stops can suddenly turn deadly.

Eric Frein allegedly lay in wait outside the Pennsylvania State Police Troop R building in Blooming Grove, holding a .308 caliber rifle with a scope. At about 10:50 p.m. on Sept. 12, when Cpl. Bryon Dickson was leaving the building in uniform, his colleagues inside saw him suddenly drop to the ground.[1]

A 38-year-old Marine Corps veteran, Dickson was dead at the scene. Trooper Alex Douglass, one of the officers who tried to help him, was shot in the pelvis.[2]

The ambush prompted a 48-day manhunt for Frein, who was captured on Oct. 30.[3] Pennsylvania prosecutors said Frein confessed to killing Dickson, calling the act an "assassination," though seemingly not aimed at any officer in particular. In a message to his parents that police reported finding on his computer, Frein wrote: "The time seems right for a spark to ignite a fire in the hearts of men."[4]

Dickson never had a chance.

His killing underscores the risks police officers face daily, even in environments that seem completely safe — including their own headquarters, as the Pennsylvania case illustrated. Experts say constant danger is one reason many law enforcement officers see potential threats lurking even in the most routine encounters, a sense of constant peril that can lead to misjudgments.

"Officer safety does matter," says Peter Moskos, an associate professor in the Department of Law, Police Science and Criminal Justice Administration at the John Jay College of Criminal Justice in New York and a former one-year member of the Baltimore Police Department. "But the job does have risks. If you always wanted to be safe, you'd never leave the police station."

Statistically, officer fatalities have decreased since their post-World War II peak of 280 in 1974. By late November this year, 113 officers had been killed or died in the line of duty (42 of them in traffic accidents). That figure was up from 100 in 2013, according to the National Law Enforcement Officers Memorial Fund, a Washington-based group that keeps records on police deaths dating back to 1791.[5]

James Glennon, a former commander in the DuPage County, Ill., Major Crimes Task Force and now owner of Lifeline Training, a company that runs instructional programs for police, says seemingly ordinary police business can hold the most danger. "We're not getting shot at bank robberies, really," he said. "We're getting shot at during bike theft investigations, traffic stops, evictions."[6]

A video taken by a police officer's dashboard-mounted camera and widely circulated in police circles shows a 2010 traffic stop in Hamilton, Mont. "How's it going tonight?" Officer Ross Jessop asked as he stepped up to the window of an SUV. After the conversation with driver Raymond Davis took a less friendly turn, Jessop asked, "How much have you had to drink tonight?"

"Plenty," Davis replied. Seconds later he pointed a revolver out the window, fired and then drove away. Jessop, who wasn't hit, shot 14 rounds at the vehicle, one of which killed Davis. A six-person coroner's inquest jury later found the shooting justified.[7]

But in Columbia, S.C., former State Police Lance Cpl. Sean Groubert has been charged with aggravated assault and battery after shooting Levar Jones during a traffic stop in September. That encounter, also captured on Groubert's dashboard camera, made equally dramatic viewing.

As the two men stood outside Jones' SUV at a gas station, Groubert said, "Your license, please." Jones immediately turned and leaned far into his car. As soon as Jones straightened up, Groubert fired at least four shots in rapid succession.

Jones, on the ground, sounding stunned and in pain, yells, "I just got my license! You said get my license!"[8]

"Well, you dove head-first back into your car," Groubert said.

"I'm sorry," said Jones, who survived the gunshot in his hip.[9]

A year earlier, Groubert and his partner had been shot at by a man in an incident that also began as a routine traffic stop. The two officers, who returned the man's fire, wounding him, received commendations for valor for their actions during the confrontation.[10]

Referring to the September shooting of Jones, Chuck Canterbury, president of the Fraternal Order of Police union and a retired Conway, S.C., police officer, says, "The guy did make a quick turn and go into the car." Noting that Groubert had come under fire before, he added, "If you've not been in a situation where someone pulled a gun on you . . . I will never second-guess him."

But David Klinger, a professor of criminal justice at the University of Missouri-St. Louis, said after the shooting that it could have been avoided if Groubert had not immediately demanded the license, but asked, "Do you have a driver's license?" At that point, Jones could have said he did, and it was in his car. "Then you can say, 'OK, sure, what I want you to do is slowly reach into the vehicle. . . . And then it's not a big issue."[11]

As in many other police-citizen encounters that end badly, race was part of the discussion. Groubert (who was fired and charged with aggravated assault and battery) is white and Jones is black.[12]

Gloria Browne-Marshall, a constitutional law professor at John Jay College of Criminal Justice, said, "It was almost as though the officer wanted to stop the man, anyway found a reason to stop him." (Groubert had said he stopped Jones for not wearing a seatbelt, but Jones said he removed it because he was pulling into the gas station.) "Deadly force is . . . happening when there's an African-American male."[13]

Leroy Smith, director of the South Carolina Department of Public Safety, called the shooting an "isolated incident." South Carolina State Rep. Joe Neal, former chairman of the Legislative Black Caucus, said the criminal charge against Groubert would lessen African-American anger over the shooting. "This is a good exercise in how the system can work," he said.[14]

— *Peter Katel*

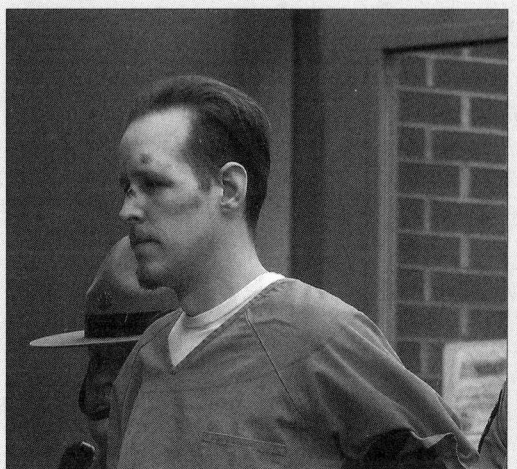

Eric Frein has been charged in the death of a Pennsylvania State Trooper last Sept. 12 in an ambush that underscored the daily risks faced by police. Frein was captured after a 48-day manhunt.

---

[1] "Affidavit of Probable Cause," Commonwealth of Pennsylvania, Pike County, Oct. 8, 2014, Docket Number CR-207-14, http://tinyurl.com/mcmmbyc.

[2] *Ibid.*

[3] "Eric Frein, Accused Killer of Pennsylvania Trooper, Arrested Using Slain Officer's Handcuffs," CNN Wire, Oct. 30, 2014, http://tinyurl.com/ltgknn2.

[4] Quoted in Pamela Lehman and Laurie Mason Schroeder, "Eric Frein in letter to mom and dad calls for 'revolution,' " *Morning Call*, Nov. 13, 2014, http://tinyurl.com/mb9n29q.

[5] "Preliminary 2014 Law Enforcement Officer Fatalities," "Officer Deaths by Year," National Law Enforcement Officers Memorial Fund, updated regularly, http://tinyurl.com/2b7co8f.

[6] Quoted in Crawford Coates, "Policing at the Level of Instinct," Calibre Press, Sept. 30, 2014, http://tinyurl.com/oa534bd.

[7] "Montana Officer Under Fire at Traffic Stop," LawOfficer, May 24, 2012, http://tinyurl.com/n5d92rn; Perry Backus, "Hamilton officer cleared in fatal shooting during January traffic stop," *Missoulian*, April 14, 2010, http://tinyurl.com/oeh75ob.

[8] John Monk, "Video Released: SC trooper charged with felony shooting at traffic stop over seat belt violation," *The Charlotte Observer*, Sept. 25, 2014, http://tinyurl.com/l5n86qd.

[9] *Ibid.*

[10] Jason Hanna, Martin Savidge and John Murgatroyd, "Video shows trooper shooting unarmed man, South Carolina police say," CNN, Sept. 26, 2014, http://tinyurl.com/k8tyvs5.

[11] "Transcript: Taking A Close Look at America's Police Force," WBUR, On Point with Tom Ashbrook, Oct. 1, 2014, http://tinyurl.com/ljmq7x7.

[12] John Monk, "Video Released: SC trooper charged with felony in shooting at traffic stop over seat belt violation," *The Charlotte Observer*, Sept. 25, 2014, http://tinyurl.com/mwberxs.

[13] "Transcript: . . .," *op. cit.*

[14] Quoted in *ibid.*; Cliff Leblanc, "Officials' silence on trooper shooting fuels anger, suspicion, demands for accounting," *The State*, Sept. 9, 2014, http://tinyurl.com/lolqp6b.

BACKGROUND

Troops in the Streets

Long before police militarization became a widely discussed issue, the military was used, on occasion, to enforce laws on U.S. soil.

The Posse Comitatus Act of 1878 placed limits on when the military could be used to enforce state or federal laws. It also prohibited the military from participating in emergencies, except when specifically authorized.[48] (State National Guard forces, first formally established in 1824, represented an exception, because they are under both federal and state authority; governors can deploy them to deal with natural disasters and civil disorders).[49]

Nearly 80 years after Congress passed the Posse Comitatus law, President Dwight D. Eisenhower federalized the Arkansas National Guard and ordered the 101st Airborne Division to Little Rock, to enforce a high school desegregation opposed by mobs of white segregationists. He acted under a law authorizing the military to take the place of local police if they could not protect individuals or if federal law was being violated.[50]

Although the Army in that case was sent in to do a job that police wouldn't or couldn't perform, the Defense Department and local and federal law enforcement agencies, broadly speaking, already enjoyed a cooperative relationship. The agencies had received surplus military helicopters, handheld radios and other devices from World War II and the Korean War.[51]

And in the 1960s and '70s, research funded by the Justice Department developed lightweight body armor made of Kevlar, a synthetic fiber, which became widely used by both the military and police.[52] During the same period, National Guard or Army troops were sent in to quell uprisings in black urban neighborhoods: in Los Angeles in 1965; Detroit in 1967; and Baltimore, Washington and Chicago in 1968 after the assassination of the Rev. Martin Luther King Jr.[53] In the Watts section of Los Angeles (and later in Detroit), residents protesting police tactics shot at police, troops and firefighters.

Police thinking was also influenced by a 1966 massacre at the University of Texas, Austin, in which a student, a Marine veteran, shot 43 people from the campus clock tower, killing 13. The sniper episode, coupled with the urban unrest, prompted the Los Angeles Police Department in 1967 to form the country's first SWAT team.[54]

The team came to public attention during a search-warrant raid on a Black Panther Party headquarters in Los Angeles that resulted in a four-hour-shoot-out with armed occupants (no one was killed).[55]

War on Drugs

As the Los Angeles innovation drew growing interest from other police departments, the country was entering the early stages of what became known as the "war on drugs." (President Richard M. Nixon, widely credited as the author of the phrase, was more specific, declaring "war against heroin addiction.")[56]

Legislatively, the war began when Congress — pushed by the Nixon administration — passed the Comprehensive Drug Abuse Prevention and Control Act in 1970. Among other things, it authorized "no-knock" searches if police believed that evidence might be destroyed — which came to be interpreted as any drug raid on a house. The measure would prove crucial to the development in smaller cities of SWAT teams as door-battering search units.[57] Four years later Congress repealed the "no-knock" authorization after a series of drug raids led to violence and abuse by police, triggering a political scandal.[58]

Nevertheless, starting in the 1980s, police conducting raids could obtain authorization not to announce they were at the door. In the 1990s, the U.S. Supreme Court upheld no-knock searches, ruling that the Fourth Amendment's protection against "unreasonable searches and seizures" did not flatly rule out unannounced searches. And, under a 1984 Supreme Court ruling, even when a search was found to be constitutionally unjustified, evidence seized can still be used against defendants.[59]

The military and police had begun cooperating in drug enforcement cases in the 1970s, a development that would reverberate decades later. From 1971 to 1981, the Army, Air Force and Navy carried out 140 joint missions with civilian law enforcement agencies and frequently provided "minor assistance," such as training, helping to transport suspected drug smugglers and lending equipment and personnel, according to the nonpartisan Government Accountability Office (GAO), then known as the General Accounting Office.[60]

During the Reagan administration, Congress brought military and police work into closer quarters. The Military Cooperation With Law Enforcement Act of 1981 ordered the armed forces to track suspected smugglers on sea and in the air and to open military intelligence files to police departments.[61]

The pace of military aid and equipment transfers to law enforcement increased in the ensuing years. In 1989, Congress authorized the Defense Department to fund state National Guard drug enforcement programs. And law enforcement agencies at all levels, including federal, could take "counterdrug" training at National Guard schools. Defense spending on such support services totaled $30 million in 1996-98.[62]

The military established a communications network for police in Alabama, Georgia, Louisiana and Mississippi to exchange and analyze counterdrug intelligence. It also provided $96 million in technology and equipment to state and local agencies; the equipment included cryptological, night-vision and chemical analysis devices and instruments.[63]

Drawing Fire

In the 1990s, military-style law enforcement operations became more controversial, particularly after two high-profile incidents — one in Ruby Ridge, Idaho, and one in Waco, Texas — involving federal agents.

The first incident involved a siege on the property of right-wing survivalist Randy Weaver, who was indicted in 1991 on a federal firearms charge after he refused to become an informant in a Bureau of Alcohol, Tobacco and Firearms (ATF) investigation of a white supremacist group.[64]

In 1992 federal agents were watching Weaver's property in a rural area of Idaho known as Ruby Ridge. After Weaver's dogs began barking a gunfight broke out in which a deputy

Citizen Anger

Police in Berkeley, Calif., clash with protesters on the fourth night of demonstrations sparked by recent grand jury decisions in police-involved deaths of African-American males (top). On Dec. 6, a man demands justice during the funeral service for Akai Gurley, an unarmed 28-year-old African-American man shot to death in a dark stairwell of a Brooklyn housing development by a rookie Asian-American police officer on patrol. He said his gun discharged unintentionally (bottom). Outrage spread across the political spectrum when a New York grand jury did not hand up an indictment in the death of cigarette seller Eric Garner, who was videotaped being wrestled to the ground by police officers and held in a chokehold. Calling the non-indictment "totally incomprehensible," conservative *Washington Post* columnist Charles Krauthammer said on Fox News, "The guy actually said, 'I can't breathe.'"

marshal and Weaver's 14-year-old son were killed. FBI snipers wounded a friend of Weaver's and killed Weaver's wife, who was inside the cabin.[65] A Justice Department investigation later concluded that the rules of engagement guiding the snipers were unconstitutional.[66]

The following year, an ATF attempt to serve an arrest warrant on a compound near Waco, Texas, occupied by the Branch Davidian religious sect led to a gunfight in which four agents were killed, 16 were wounded and an unknown number of compound residents were wounded or killed. A subsequent 51-day siege ended after Attorney General Janet Reno authorized the FBI to fire tear gas into the compound. The Branch Davidians responded by setting fires within the property, which eventually killed most of the 75 people inside, according to the Justice Department and some fire consultants.[67]

Six years later the FBI revealed that it had fired explosive, "pyrotechnic" tear gas rounds, whose hot canisters can cause fires, into the compound during the final assault. But an independent follow-up report said those munitions did not start the fatal fires.[68]

That early instance of the use of military-style munitions followed a national lesson in the power of civilian technology. In 1991, a man with a videotape camera recorded the furious beating of a Los Angeles motorist who had tried to flee officers after being stopped for driving about 100 mph. Rodney King, the man who fled and was caught, was kicked, hit with batons and fired on with a Taser, in vivid footage replayed endlessly on television.[69]

Four officers were indicted in connection with the beating and their trial moved to the predominantly white town of Simi Valley. In 1992, three were acquitted, and the jury deadlocked on the fourth. That decision set off five days of riots and looting in South Los Angeles in which more than 60 people died, 10 of them shot by law enforcement officers, and the others victims of rioters and of riot-related events such as trying to put out a rioter-caused fire, or a traffic accident at an intersection whose lights had failed.[70]

Later that year, a federal grand jury indicted the four officers for violating King's civil rights. Two were acquitted; the other two were convicted at trial and sentenced to 30 months in prison. In a civil trial, a federal court awarded King $3.8 million in compensatory damages from the city of Los Angeles.[71]

The 1990s also saw cooperation between the military and the police become formalized, especially in counterdrug activities. In the 1990–91 Defense Authorization Act, later continued until 1996, Congress authorized transfers of excess military gear — including loaned pistols and rifles and ammunition and gifts of non-military equipment — to state and federal agencies for drug enforcement.[72]

Meanwhile, the Justice and Defense departments in 1994 established a technology-sharing program.[73] The National Institute of Justice cited several reasons for the deal — one was that local law enforcement agencies needed the help to keep up with criminals and drug smugglers, who themselves were increasingly getting their hands on military gear. "Narcotics traffickers and smugglers use bulletproof vests, electro-optic devices that enable them to see at night and semiautomatic and even automatic weapons," making the transfer of military equipment to local law enforcement all the more necessary, the institute concluded.[74]

In 1997 Congress reauthorized the surplus equipment transfer system — now renamed the 1033 program — and removed the requirement that the equipment be used only in drug enforcement. However, Congress said it preferred that the gear be used for counterterrorism and antidrug activities.[75]

During the same period, the Clinton administration sent American troops on peacekeeping missions in Somalia, Haiti, Bosnia and Kosovo, with orders to limit harm to civilians and property. As a result, the armed forces developed an interest in nonlethal weapons, leading to production of the flash-bang grenades that SWAT teams now use.[76]

New Tensions

The events of Sept. 11, 2001 — the first mass-casualty terrorist strike by a foreign organization in the United States — marked an entirely new development in relations between American police and citizens. In the aftermath police departments nationwide, prompted by the federal government, added counterterrorism to their responsibilities.

"The continued threat of terrorism has thrust domestic preparedness obligations to the very top of the law enforcement agenda," a 2005 State Department report concluded. "This capacity must be considered . . . a staple of law enforcement operations."[77] The Homeland Security Department began providing grants to local police departments for antiterrorism equipment and training. By fiscal 2014, the program was totaling nearly $2 billion a year.[78]

Meanwhile, one theoretically nonlethal weapon developed under a Defense-Justice program — flash-bang grenades — was proving problematic in civilian use. Donald Wilkes Jr., a law professor emeritus at the University of Georgia, compiled — using 2003 Appellate Court decisions and media reports — a list of 39 incidents dating back to 1984 involving injuries and death from these grenades in SWAT raids.[79]

Three other developments after 9/11 have influenced the debate over police strategy and tactics:

- A large increase in the number of prison inmates since the 1980s has prompted growing criticism of mandatory sentencing laws, especially for nonviolent drug crimes.[80]
- The emergence of digital video technology, the proliferation of smartphones and security cameras and the rise of social media have led to a spate of videos posted online depicting sometimes deadly police-citizen confrontations.[81]
- A growing number of "active shooter" events in schools and public places has made police departments of all sizes aware of the need to be able to quickly respond to sudden attacks that threaten large numbers of lives.[82]

In the United States, images of police in tactical uniforms, carrying automatic rifles, became common in coverage, such as in the response to a 2012 massacre at Sandy Hook Elementary School in Newtown, Conn., and in the manhunt that followed a 2013 bombing during the Boston Marathon.

At the same time, controversy continued to grow over police conduct in minority communities. In a big-city election that received extensive coverage nationwide, liberal Bill de Blasio was elected mayor of New York, in part because he attacked the police department's controversial "stop-and-frisk" tactics, which disproportionately affect black and Latino young men, according to evidence from police data used by U.S. District Judge Scheindlin in ruling that the application of the stop-and-frisk program — though not the tactic itself — was unconstitutional.

"The city's highest officials have turned a blind eye to the evidence that officers are conducting stops in a racially discriminatory manner," she wrote in her decision.[83]

By the time de Blasio took office, use of the tactic had begun to fade, *The New York Times* reported in a data analysis. Police reported 33,699 stops in the second half of 2013 — less than 10 percent of the 337,410 recorded in the first half of 2012. But the videotaped death of cigarette seller Garner in an apparent police chokehold indicated to many that questionable police conduct didn't end with de Blasio's election.[84]

Police behavior is also a major factor in other cities. The Obama administration's Justice Department has opened more than two dozen investigations into possible civil rights violations by police departments in recent years after questions arose about whether police resort to force unnecessarily.[85]

The crucial event touching off the recent national debate over police tactics occurred Aug. 9 in Ferguson, Mo., when then-Officer Wilson shot Brown during a violent street confrontation.[86] By all accounts, the conflict began inside Wilson's patrol vehicle and continued with both men outside the car. According to conflicting accounts, Brown was either charging the officer or raising his arms in surrender.[87]

The latter account gave rise to the widely adopted slogan and arm gesture of protesters in Ferguson and elsewhere: "Hands up — don't shoot."[88]

Brown's death set off weeks of street protests in Ferguson, including looting and vandalism by a minority of demonstrators, as well as tear gas and rubber bullets from police. As conflict worsened between police outfitted with military garb and equipment and increasingly bitter and angry demonstrators, Missouri Gov. Jay Nixon put Highway Patrol Capt. Ronald S. Johnson in charge of the law enforcement response in Ferguson. Johnson, an African-American, set a new tone by marching with demonstrators, dressed in his standard uniform — no combat fatigues or helmet.

"We are going to have a different approach and have the approach that we're in this together," he said.[89]

AT ISSUE

Are U.S. police departments becoming dangerously militarized?

YES
Peter B. Kraska
Professor, School of Justice Studies, University of Eastern Kentucky

From written testimony to the Senate Committee on Homeland Security and Governmental Affairs, Sept. 9, 2014

The research I've been conducting, since 1989, has documented quantitatively and qualitatively the steady and certain march of U.S. civilian policing down the militarization continuum — culturally, materially, operationally and organizationally. This is not to imply that all police — nearly 20,000 unique departments — are heading in this direction. But the . . . evidence demonstrates a troubling and highly consequential overall trend.

What we saw played out in Ferguson was the application of a very common mindset, style of uniform and appearance and weaponry, used every day in the homes of private residences during SWAT raids — some departments conducting as many as 500 of these a year.

Only 20 years ago, forced investigative searches of private residences, using the military special-operations model employed during hostage rescues, was almost unheard of and would have been considered an extreme and unacceptable police tactic. It is critical to recognize that these are not forced-reaction situations necessitating use-of-force specialists; instead they are the result of police departments choosing to use an extreme and highly dangerous tactic, not for terrorists or hostage-takers, but for small-time drug possessors and dealers.

Of course a militarized response is sometimes necessary and even unavoidable if done in self defense or to protect lives in imminent danger. The bulk of U.S. SWAT activity . . ., however, constitute a proactive approach. Numerous departments are choosing, based no doubt to an extent on political pressures, to generate on their own initiative high-risk events.

I also learned that the paramilitary culture associated with SWAT teams is highly appealing to a certain segment of civilian police. . . . As with special-operations soldiers . . ., these units' members saw themselves as the elite police, involved in real crime-fighting and danger. A large network of for-profit training, weapons and equipment suppliers heavily promotes paramilitary culture at police shows, in police magazine advertisements and in training programs sponsored by gun manufacturers. . . . The "military special operations" culture — characterized by a distinct techno-warrior garb, heavy weaponry, sophisticated technology, hyper-masculinity and dangerous function — was nothing less than intoxicating for its participants.

Military gear and garb changes and reinforces a war-fighting mentality among civilian police, where marginalized populations become the enemy and the police perceive of themselves as the thin blue line between order and chaos that can only be controlled through military-model power.

NO
Charles "Sid" Heal
Retired Commander, Special Enforcement Bureau, Los Angeles Sheriff's Department; Retired U.S. Marine Corps Chief Warrant Officer

Written for *CQ Researcher*, December 2014

The allegation of militarization of U.S. police departments ignores the extremely diversified and highly segmented nature of local law enforcement. Each of the nearly 18,000 local agencies is independent and governed only by the laws of the land and the communities they serve. Even the most widespread and notorious examples fail to reflect the attitudes of the law enforcement community at large.

How does equipment or training or appearance make our protectors dangerous? Weapons and equipment are inanimate objects. Complaints that they are too "militaristic" in appearance is like complaining a welder's helmet is ugly or atrocious. All workers are entitled to the tools and protective gear needed for the hazards they confront.

The so-called 1033 program for providing surplus equipment to law enforcement agencies is periodically reviewed, but the hyperbole and mischaracterizations used to challenge it obfuscate meaningful scrutiny. Lack of availability of essential equipment from military sources will require replacement through costly civilian manufacturers.

Many of the criticisms that drive the current controversy were first expressed by law enforcement. Corrective measures should be based on measurable attributes rather than biased perceptions to avoid the narrow-minded "baby and the bathwater" demands suggested by extremists.

The counter-terrorist mission thrust upon domestic law enforcement as a result of the 9/11 attacks was neither sought nor welcomed. Furthermore, this new responsibility was "in addition to" and not "instead of." The law enforcement and security resources required by the U.S. Department of Homeland Security specifies weapons, equipment and protective clothing that is basically identical to that required by military organizations. Failing to provide these because of their appearance or origin is both abhorrent and stupid. The tools used to fight the "war on crime" are inadequate to fight the "war on terrorism."

The use of SWAT teams to serve high-risk warrants is not based on race, culture or type of crime but rather dangerous criminal behaviors. Criminals and terrorists have increasingly equipped themselves with high-powered weapons, explosive devices and protective armor and enjoy the advantages provided by choosing the time, location and circumstances for their nefarious activities. The self-appointed carpers who oversimplify and ignore the perilous realities of underestimating adversaries have been bereft of viable alternatives.

CURRENT SITUATION

Stemming the Flow

As Congress rushes to finish its year-end work before the Christmas recess, efforts in both chambers to restrict — though not end — the flow of military equipment to police departments remain on the table.

Obama entered the fray in early December, announcing that he would issue an executive order designed to ensure that the 1033 program is "transparent." The order will also be designed "to make sure that we're not building a militarized culture inside our local law enforcement."[90]

In Congress, even in a highly polarized political environment, bipartisan efforts are emerging to put more controls on the program. In the House, Democrat Hank Johnson of Georgia and Republican Raul Labrador of Idaho are pushing their Stop Militarizing Law Enforcement Act of 2014, which would limit the kinds of equipment the Pentagon can give or lend to law enforcement agencies. Labrador said the 1033 program was "introducing a military model of overwhelming force in our cities and towns."[91]

In case the legislation doesn't survive the lame-duck congressional session, Johnson asked the heads of the Armed Services committees in both chambers for a moratorium on transfers of some Pentagon equipment, saying Congress needs to "press pause . . . and revisit the merits of a militarized America."[92]

The bill would block transfer of what the sponsors called high-caliber weapons, grenade launchers, armed drones, armored vehicles and grenades or other explosives. Some of this material may already be blocked for police use. Current law, for instance, restricts weapons of more than 7.62 mm caliber, such as the AK-47 assault rifle.[93]

And the bill would end a requirement that police departments use Defense Department equipment within one year of receiving it. In the legislators' view, that encourages departments to use the gear inappropriately.

In the Senate, which will turn to Republican control next year, the sponsor of an identically titled bill on 1033 is Sen. Tom Coburn, an Oklahoma Republican. In a September hearing on the 1033 program he said: "Our Founders saw no role for the federal government in state and local police forces. We're on dangerous ground of undermining the very principles that built the country."[94]

SWAT team members prepare to arrest suspects believed to be armed in a house in Wichita, Kan., on Jan. 9, 2013. Critics of SWAT teams say they are overused, mostly to serve search and arrest warrants. But supporters say heavily armed SWAT teams are necessary because of the nation's widespread gun ownership.

Troubled Cities

A New York grand jury's decision on Dec. 3 not to indict the police officer whose chokehold led to cigarette seller Garner's death set off the second wave of autumn protests over police conduct.

"I can't breathe," marchers chanted in New York, echoing Garner's final words, captured on cellphone video. Demonstrators also took to the streets in Oakland and Los Angeles, Calif., following the grand jury's no-indictment of Officer Daniel Pantaleo.[95]

In response, Attorney General Eric Holder announced a Justice Department investigation of the Garner case. And Mayor de Blasio announced a police retraining program, including steps to de-escalate street confrontations.[96]

Patrick J. Lynch, president of the Patrolmen's Benevolent Association union said officers felt that the mayor had thrown them "under the bus." The mayor didn't say, Lynch added, "that you cannot resist arrest."[97] In the video Garner is seen loudly complaining to police about harassment, but never actively resists arrest.

However, the facts of Garner's death as shown on video brought some law-and-order conservatives to side — unlike in the Ferguson case — with police critics. Charles Krauthammer, a conservative *Washington Post* columnist, called Pantaleo's non-indictment "totally incomprehensible." Speaking on Fox News, Krauthammer said, "The guy actually said, 'I can't breathe.' "[98]

Critics see the use of Pentagon equipment, such as this mine-resistant ambush protected vehicle in Sanford, Maine, as unnecessary, especially by small police departments. But supporters say the vehicles serve many purposes, including disaster relief. In the past eight years, the Defense Department has distributed more than $1.5 billion worth of surplus equipment to local police, mainly vehicles, aircraft and communications and detection equipment.

But not all conservatives agreed. Republican Rep. Peter King of New York, who represents Long Island, said that Garner died because he was obese and asthmatic. "The police had no reason to know he was in serious condition."[99]

In a reminder that growing tension over police actions isn't limited to one or two places, Holder on the day following the Garner non-indictment announced that an 18-month investigation of the Cleveland police department found a pattern of "unnecessary and excessive use of deadly force" as well as African-Americans' repeated claims that police were "verbally and physically aggressive toward them because of their race."[100]

Cleveland — the city where a policeman had shot and killed 12-year-old Rice in late November after the boy was seen in a park waving a toy replica of a gun — agreed to formulate a consent decree with Justice under which police would be supervised by an independent monitor. Albuquerque reached that kind of agreement earlier this year; and 14 other cities have signed consent decrees in recent years.[101]

Developments in New York and Cleveland came the week after the St. Louis County grand jury's decision not to indict Wilson (now resigned from the police department) for Brown's death in Ferguson.

Immediately after county Prosecuting Attorney Robert P. McCulloch announced the decision in an evening press conference three days before Thanksgiving, protests broke out in downtown Ferguson. Although many were peaceful, violence-inclined groups torched about 12 businesses and burned some police cars, and gunfire could be heard during the disturbances.[102]

Street protests over the grand jury's decision spread beyond Ferguson and St. Louis to Oakland and San Francisco, Calif.; Chicago; New York; Washington, D.C.; and Seattle. Protesters demonstrated in shopping areas on "Black Friday," with protesters chanting, "If we don't get no justice, they don't get no profits."[103]

OUTLOOK
Re-engineering Police Culture

The debate over 21st-century police tactics should not be confused with a debate over police brutality, say critics of police adoption of military equipment, tactics and mentality.

"In the '60s and '70s cops were more brutal," says former officer Moskos of the John Jay College of Criminal Justice. "Cops are not allowed to beat people up like they used to. They may still have the attitude that 'you've got to do this or else,' but the 'else' is more limited. The rest of society has evolved; you would say it has progressed — if you're on that side — to the point where cops are not supposed to do that."

Former Seattle Police Chief Stamper characterizes old-school brutality as "punitive force" and says that today, "much of what we see as excessive force or police brutality is a perversion of officer safety tactics."

> "We are going to have a different approach and have the approach that we're in this together."
>
> — *Missouri Highway Patrol Capt. Ronald S. Johnson, on how he would direct the law enforcement response to the protests in Ferguson, MO.*

The idea that police live in constant danger reflects a drug war-spawned militarization that intensified after 9/11, Stamper says. "Many departments have treated low-level drug offenders as the enemy for so long that re-engineering the culture and structure of American policing is going to take generations."

Indeed, some police say, issues that give rise to protests and debates over police conduct are rooted in generations-old problems — not police tactics. "It's decades of racial disparity and economic disparity," Jeff Roorda, business manager of the St. Louis Police Officers Association, told CBS News. "It's not a problem with the police."[104]

Whether Justice Department investigations and police retraining programs will lead to rapid changes in interactions between police and minority group members, particularly black men, is far from clear. In angry and despairing tones that were echoed in remarks from protesters, Ta-Nehisi Coates, an influential essayist at *The Atlantic* magazine, wrote after the Ferguson non-indictment, "America does not really believe in nonviolence, so much as it believes in order. . . . The death of all our Michael Browns at the hands of people who are supposed to protect them originates in a force more powerful than any president: American society itself."[105]

Nevertheless, in Los Angeles, whose police department was once considered heavy-handed with minority communities, civil rights lawyer Constance Rice, who worked with the department in a reportedly successful reform program, argues that change is possible. Like other experts, she points to fear — rather than outright racism — as the key element in many police-citizen encounters that turn violent. "I have known cops who haven't had a racist bone in their bodies," Rice told NPR. "They weren't overtly racist. They weren't consciously racist. But you know what they had in their minds that made them act out and beat a black suspect unwarrantedly? They had fear. They were afraid of black men."[106]

On Dec. 9 the National Urban League, the 103-year-old African-American civil rights organization, issued a 10-point plan it said would help ease tensions between police and citizens, which included "comprehensive retraining" of all police, appointment of special prosecutors to investigate police misconduct and "widespread use" of dashboard and body cameras.[107]

Apart from conflicts reflecting race and class divides, "active shooter" mass-killing incidents — some of the most dangerous and stressful incidents that police

U.S. Attorney General Eric Holder embraces Missouri State Highway Patrol Capt. Ronald Johnson in Ferguson, Mo., on Aug. 20. Holder went to the troubled community to oversee the federal government's investigation into the shooting of 18-year-old Michael Brown by a police officer on Aug. 9. Johnson was widely credited with trying to defuse tensions through non-confrontational negotiations with protesters.

encounter — have been increasing in number since 2000, the FBI reported in September. And these are not likely to lessen officers' sense of ever-present peril.[108]

Former Los Angeles Sheriff's Department commander Heal notes that ordinary patrol officers may be rushed into highly dangerous "active shooter" incidents that were once reserved for SWAT teams because the new police tactical doctrine is that waiting costs too many lives. "More than 90 percent of victims are killed in the first eight minutes," Heal says.

And Fraternal Order of Police President Canterbury and other experts say military equipment, such as rifles and armored cars, are essential in dealing with mass shootings. The debate over the appropriateness of this gear for police raises the danger, Canterbury says, of "not having the equipment because of the perception that that's militarized policing."

On the nonmilitary equipment side, as a consensus forms that all police should wear body cameras, other technological approaches to policing issues are in the pipeline. In Santa Cruz, Calif., police are testing a pistol-borne sensor designed to immediately send out an alert when an officer unholsters or fires his gun.[109]

Data on how a weapon was used would help in post-incident investigations. "If we know the gun was holstered, that could resolve a critical element in the courtroom,"

Robert Stewart, CEO of Yardarm Technologies, a Capitola, Calif., start-up that is developing the sensor, told *PCWorld* magazine.[110]

Technology may be moving more quickly than social changes that could lessen police-citizen tensions. But, wherever the debate over militarization takes policing, experts agree the spotlight that mobile digital recording has focused on police practices is permanent and growing.

"In the age of social media," says Charles Wexler, executive director of the Police Executive Research Forum, "your actions get translated out there a thousandfold."

NOTES

1. John Eligon, "Anger, Hurt and Moments of Hope in Ferguson," *The New York Times*, Aug. 20, 2014, http://tinyurl.com/l8ps8qz.
2. "Police militarization," Google images, http://tinyurl.com/ppaqytz; "Sen. Thomas R. Carper Holds a Hearing on State and Local Law Enforcement Oversight, Panel 2," Senate Committee on Homeland Security and Governmental Affairs, Sept. 9, 2014, CQ Transcriptions LLC.
3. "Tracking the Events in the Wake of Michael Brown's Shooting," *The New York Times*, Aug. 9, 2014, http://tinyurl.com/q3rwm5j; "Beavercreek Wal-Mart police shooting: Does video tell whole story?" The Associated Press (via Cleveland.com), Sept. 30, 2014, http://tinyurl.com/pqhj2fu; J. David Goodman and Al Baker, "Wave of Protests After Grand Jury Doesn't Indict Officer in Eric Garner Chokehold Case," *The New York Times*, Dec. 3, 2014, http://tinyurl.com/nlx3dax; Dan McKay, "Video: Camper turning from officers when shot," *Albuquerque Journal*, March 22, 2014, http://tinyurl.com/ltuzozq; Coleen Heild, "Policing the police across the USA," *Albuquerque Journal*, Nov. 9, 2014, http://tinyurl.com/kp3h6h2.
4. "Remarks by the President After Meeting with Elected Officials, Community and Faith Leaders, and Law Enforcement Officials on How Communities and Law Enforcement Can Work Together to Build Trust to Strengthen Neighborhoods Across the Country," The White House, Dec. 1, 2014, http://tinyurl.com/nj7t6yh.
5. "Sen. Thomas R. Carper . . . ," *op. cit.*
6. Written Testimony, Alan Estevez, Principal Deputy Under Secretary of Defense for Acquisition Logistics and Technology, Senate Committee on Homeland Security and Governmental Affairs, Sept. 9, 2014, http://tinyurl.com/n9flmo8; Daniel H. Else, "The '1033 Program,' Department of Defense Support to Law Enforcement," Congressional Research Service, Aug. 28, 2014, pp. 1–2, http://tinyurl.com/l79spln; Arezou Rezvani, Jessica Pupovac, David Eads and Tyler Fisher, "MRAPs and Bayonets: What We Know About the Pentagon's 1033 Program," NPR, Sept. 2, 2014, http://tinyurl.com/p3a4fqj; Alicia Parlapiano, "The Flow of Money and Equipment to Local Police," *The New York Times*, updated Dec. 1, 2014, http://tinyurl.com/oeswx3y.
7. *Ibid.*; "Sen. Thomas R. Carper . . . ," *op. cit.*
8. Written Testimony, Alan Estevez, *op. cit.*
9. "Department of Justice and Department of Defense Joint Technology Program: Second Anniversary Report," National Institute of Justice, February 1997, http://tinyurl.com/m6vgdwe.
10. Corey Mitchell, "Disquiet builds nationwide over police flash-bang use," *Minneapolis Star-Tribune*, Dec. 31, 2011, http://tinyurl.com/kpgcjax.
11. "War Comes Home: The Excessive Militarization of American Policing," American Civil Liberties Union, June 2014, p. 15, http://tinyurl.com/lakqla6.
12. Quoted in Rob Moore, "Child burned by distraction device during raid," AccessNorthGa.com, May 29, 2014, http://tinyurl.com/mc3ac4j; David Beasley, "Georgia deputies cleared after stun grenade injured toddler," Reuters, Oct. 6, 2014, http://tinyurl.com/p7padk2.
13. Nate Carlisle, *et. al.*, "Ogden officer killed in firefight 'doing exactly what he wanted to do,' " *The Salt Lake Tribune*, Jan. 6, 2012, http://tinyurl.com/mznsutg; Jessica Miller, "Police detail what went wrong in fatal shootout with Matthew David Stewart," *The Salt Lake Tribune*, July 17, 2014, http://tinyurl.com/mloq29u.
14. "War Comes Home . . . ," *op. cit.*, pp. 27, 31.

15. John Bacon, "Pa. schools close in manhunt for accused cop killer," *USA Today*, Oct. 21, 2014, http://tinyurl.com/kjmvgrv; Leslie Linthicum, "A bullet, a rescue and a long road home," *Albuquerque Journal*, Dec. 22, 2013, http://tinyurl.com/nuz9g6x; "10/26/13: Officer Luke McPeek and Others Shoot Christopher Chase," *Albuquerque Journal*, 2014, http://tinyurl.com/p5z334c.
16. Peter B. Kraska, "Militarization and Policing — Its Relevance to 21st Century Police," *Policing*, 2007, http://tinyurl.com/nc3aazu.
17. "Commission on Special Weapons and Tactics (S.W.A.T.), Final Report," Attorney General's Commission on Special Weapons and Tactics, Sept. 10, 2002, p. 3, http://tinyurl.com/pvbzm9z.
18. *Ibid.*, p. 1; Radley Balko, *Rise of the Warrior Cop: The Militarization of America's Police Forces* (2014), pp. 248–249.
19. *Ibid.*, pp. 4, 7. Michael Rubinkam, "Trooper ambush suspect caught, death penalty eyed," The Associated Press, Oct. 31, 2014, http://tinyurl.com/of3cfps; Andrew Ba Tran and Luke Knox, "Map of school shootings from 2013–14," *The Boston Globe*, June 10, 2014, http://tinyurl.com/pywyqmr; "Boston Marathon Terror Attack Fast Facts," CNN, Nov. 1, 2014, http://tinyurl.com/q7ldwbc; Kraska testimony, *op. cit.*
20. "Sen. Thomas R. Carper . . . ," *op. cit.*
21. Debra Cassens Weiss, "SWAT-like raids for barber's license checks violated Constitution, 11th Circuit says," *ABA Journal*, Sept. 22, 2014, http://tinyurl.com/mozr9nb.
22. "Special Weapons and Tactics (SWAT), Concepts and Issues Paper," International Association of Chiefs of Police, March 2011, http://tinyurl.com/njfmadw.
23. "Gun Ownership Trends and Demographics," Pew Research Center, March 12, 2013, http://tinyurl.com/q822p6y; "Gun homicides and gun ownership by country," *The Washington Post*, Dec. 17, 2012, http://tinyurl.com/c53hytw.
24. Bob Parker, "How the North Hollywood Shootout Changed Patrol Arsenals," *Police Magazine*, Feb. 28, 2012, http://tinyurl.com/mppn9w2; Rick Orlov, "North Hollywood shootout, 15 years later," *Los Angeles Daily News*, Feb. 26, 2012, http://tinyurl.com/o9f2tg7.
25. Steve Bosh, "Survivors recount San Ysidro McDonald's massacre after 30 years," KUSI News, July 18, 2014, http://tinyurl.com/produ87.
26. "Special Litigation Section Cases and Matters, Law Enforcement Agencies," U.S. Justice Department, Civil Rights Division, http://tinyurl.com/lu76yt8.
27. Ryan Gabrielson, Ryann Grochowski Jones, Eric Sagara, "Deadly Force, in Black and White," *ProPublica*, October 2014, http://tinyurl.com/qfx6qmr.
28. "Quoted in William H. Freivogel, "How Many Police Kill Black Men? Without Database, We Can't Know," St. Louis Public Radio, Dec. 10, 2014, http://tinyurl.com/k3c85bb; *Ibid.*; Rob Barry and Coulter Jones, "Hundreds of Police Killings Are Uncounted in Federal Stats," *The Wall Street Journal*, Dec. 3, 2014, http://tinyurl.com/kra7pqj.
29. "Tracking the Events in the Wake of Michael Brown's Shooting," *op. cit.*; Paddock, Parascandola and Siemaszko, *op. cit.*; J. David Goodman, "In Brooklyn, 2 Young Men, a Dark Stairwell and a Gunshot," *The New York Times*, Nov. 23, 2014, http://tinyurl.com/opw75w9; Emma G. Fitzsimmons, "12-Year-Old Boy Dies After Police in Cleveland Shoot Him," *The New York Times*, Nov. 23, 2014, http://tinyurl.com/opw75w9; "Beavercreek Wal-Mart police shooting: Does video tell whole story?" The Associated Press (via Cleveland.com), Sept. 30, 2014, http://tinyurl.com/pqhj2fu.
30. "Remarks by the President at Congressional Black Caucus Awards Dinner," The White House, Sept. 28, 2014, http://tinyurl.com/occq8f5.
31. "Sen. Thomas R. Carper . . . ," *op. cit.*
32. Quoted in Erik Badia and Corky Siemaszko, "Rev. Al Sharpton accuses Ferguson, Mo., police chief of 'smear campaign' against Michael Brown," *New York Daily News*, Aug. 16, 2014, http://tinyurl.com/pqatdn8; Erik Eckholm, "Witness Told Grand Jury That Michael Brown Charged at Darren Wilson, Prosecutor Says," *The New York Times*, Nov. 24,

2014, http://tinyurl.com/ntyezrm; Trymaine Lee and Michele Richinick, "Police: Michael Brown stopped because he blocked traffic," MSNBC, Aug. 15, 2014, http://tinyurl.com/leltynp.

33. "Homicide Watch Chicago," *Chicago Sun-Times*, regularly updated, http://tinyurl.com/nlsfr2z; Amy Sherman, "A look at statistics on black-on-black murders," *PolitiFact Florida*, July 17, 2013, http://tinyurl.com/mhfw7f4.

34. Quoted in Steve Chapman, "Sharpton on black-on-black crime," *Chicago Tribune*, Aug. 28, 2014, http://tinyurl.com/k8sbp64; Jamelle Bouie, "Actually Blacks Do Care About Black Crime," *Slate*, Dec. 1, 2014, http://tinyurl.com/k7brpue.

35. "Broken Windows Policing," Center for Evidence-Based Crime Policy, George Mason University, undated, http://tinyurl.com/koravg6.

36. Peter Moskos, *Cop in the Hood: My Year Policing Baltimore's Eastern District* (2008).

37. Quoted in Michael B. Marois, "Body-Worn Cameras for Police Get Renewed Attention After Ferguson," Bloomberg News, Nov. 25, 2014, http://tinyurl.com/n4on8lv.

38. "Remarks by the President . . . ," *op. cit.*; Mark Landler, "Obama Offers New Standards on Police Gear," *The New York Times*, Dec. 1, 2014, http://tinyurl.com/lyde4wh.

39. Katti Gray and Dean Schabner, "UC Davis Pepper Spraying: Cops Suspended," ABC News, Nov. 20, 2011, http://tinyurl.com/7r9kk76; Matthew B. Stannard and Demian Bulwa, "BART shooting captured on video," *San Francisco Chronicle*, Jan. 7, 2009, http://tinyurl.com/bv89orh; Ryan Owens, "Cop's 'Heart Sank' on Realizing Shots Fired at Minivan Full of Kids," ABC News, Jan. 17, 2014, http://tinyurl.com/qe4wnct; Ryan Boetel, "APD detective who shot homeless camper James Boyd planning to retire," *Albuquerque Journal*, Nov. 18, 2014, http://tinyurl.com/lb9mtjn; Josh Sanburn, "Behind the Video of Eric Garner's Deadly Confrontation With New York Police," *Time*, July 22, 2014, http://tinyurl.com/oh94f6v; Pat Reavy, "Body cam helps justify fatal South Salt Lake police shooting," KSL.com, Sept. 30, 2014, http://tinyurl.com/q8z8pqn.

40. Michael D. White, "Police Officer Body-Worn Cameras: Assessing the Evidence," Office of Justice Programs, U.S. Justice Department, 2014, p. 16, http://tinyurl.com/q87pdtu.

41. Quoted in Ian Lovett, "In California, a Champion for Police Cameras," *The New York Times*, Aug. 21, 2013, http://tinyurl.com/k5mxafg.

42. Rocco Parascandola, "60 NYPD cops set to begin wearing body cameras in pilot program," *New York Daily News*, Sept. 4, 2014, http://tinyurl.com/qgqohaf.

43. "Implementing a Body-Worn Camera Program: Recommendations and Lessons Learned," Police Executive Research Forum, U.S. Justice Department, 2014, pp. 54–56, http://tinyurl.com/lxdg7ej.

44. "Findings of civil investigation," U.S. Justice Department, April 10, 2014, http://tinyurl.com/n6bubpo; Gwyneth Doland, "Police body cameras didn't provide accountability in New Mexico," Al Jazeera America, April 16, 2014, http://tinyurl.com/l8gowe9.

45. Patrick Lohmann, "No video of Mary Hawkes shooting, APD says," *Albuquerque Journal*, May 22, 2014, http://tinyurl.com/qzlorxz.

46. Quoted in Nicole Perez, "Officer who shot Mary Hawkes fired for insubordination," *Albuquerque Journal*, Dec. 1, 2014, http://tinyurl.com/paatg2a.

47. "10 limitations of body cams you need to know for your protection," Force Science Institute Ltd., undated, http://tinyurl.com/m94y3vw.

48. *Ibid.*, pp. 5–6.

49. Maj. Gen. Timothy J. Lowenberg, "The Role of the National Guard in National Defense and Homeland Security," National Guard Association of the United States, undated, http://tinyurl.com/qbmsnbd.

50. *Ibid.*, p. 40.

51. "Department of Justice and Department of Defense Joint Technology Program: Second Anniversary Report," National Institute of Justice, Department of Justice," February 1977, p. 2, http://tinyurl.com/qyemysa.

52. *Ibid.*; Jeremy Peace, "Stephanie L. Kwolek, Inventor of Kevlar, Is Dead at 90," *The New York Times*, June 20, 2014, http://tinyurl.com/nlhzb3l.

53. Charles Doyle and Jennifer K. Elsea, "The Posse Comitatus Act and Related Matters: The Use of the Military to Execute Civilian Law," Congressional Research Service, Aug. 16, 2012, pp. 35–36, http://tinyurl.com/l29a4ea.

54. Ibid., Balko, p. 62; "The UT Tower Shooting," *Texas Monthly*, undated, http://tinyurl.com/kaybz73.

55. Paul Clinton, "Daryl Gates and the origins of LAPD SWAT," *Police Magazine*, April 16, 2010, http://tinyurl.com/q2d95ql; Radley Balko, *Rise of the Warrior Cop: The Militarization of America's Police Forces* (2013), pp. 76–80; and "144 Hours in August 1965," Governor's Commission on the Los Angeles Riots, 1965, http://tinyurl.com/3zab8bg.

56. Richard Nixon, "Special Message to the Congress on Drug Abuse Prevention and Control, June 17, 1971," The American Presidency Project, University of California, Santa Barbara, http://tinyurl.com/l56dh26.

57. Ibid. Also see Radley Balko, *Rise of the Warrior Cop: The Militarization of America's Police Forces* (2014), pp. 81–134.

58. Ibid., Balko; Clinton, op. cit., p. 2.

59. Balko, op. cit., pp. 116–125; "War Comes Home: The Excessive Militarization of American Policing," ACLU, June 2014, http://tinyurl.com/lx56xmg; *U.S. v. Leon*, 488 U.S. 897 (1984), http://tinyurl.com/238nbgx.

60. Ronald F. Lauve, "Statement Before the Subcommittee on Crime, House Committee on the Judiciary on Military Cooperation With Civilian Law Enforcement Agencies," General Accounting Office, July 28, 1983, http://tinyurl.com/ouckbgl.

61. Balko, op. cit., pp. 96–97, 145–146.

62. "Crime Technology: Department of Defense Assistance to State and Local Law Enforcement Agencies," U.S. General Accounting Office, (now Government Accountability Office), October 1999, pp. 3–5, http://tinyurl.com/o5tfgev.

63. Ibid., pp. 7-9.

64. "Department of Justice Report on Internal Review Regarding the Ruby Ridge Hostage Situation and Shootings by Law Enforcement Personnel," U.S. Justice Department, 1994, Executive Summary, http://tinyurl.com/p8q988z; Balko, op. cit., pp. 200–201.

65. Ibid., Balko.

66. Ibid., "Department of Justice."

67. "Report to the Deputy Attorney General on the Events at Waco, Texas, February 28 to April 19, 1993, Executive Summary, http://tinyurl.com/o3yaxp7; Jim Hoft, "Author: Hillary Clinton Ordered Attack on David Koresh's Compound in Waco, Texas," *Free Republic*, March 4, 2014, http://tinyurl.com/ouqak4k.

68. "Final Report to the Deputy Attorney General Concerning the 1993 Confrontation at the Mt. Carmel Complex, Waco, Texas," Special Counsel John C. Danforth, Nov. 8, 2000, p. 29, http://tinyurl.com/nm59o2h; Matt Alsdorf, "Waco Twofer: Pyrotechnic Tear Gas and Delta Force," *Slate*, Sept. 2, 1999, http://tinyurl.com/ceduvf8.

69. Jennifer Medina, "Rodney King Dies a 47," *The New York Times*, June 17, 2012, http://tinyurl.com/8xdbzgc.

70. Ibid., "Los Angeles riots: Remember the 63 people who died," *Los Angeles Times*, April 26, 2012, http://tinyurl.com/ljb86rg; Linda Deutsch, "Rodney King's Death: Reporter Remembers Trial That Sparked Riots," The Associated Press, Aug. 18, 2012, http://tinyurl.com/n7a9fhl.

71. "Los Angeles Riots Fast Facts," CNN, May 3, 2014, http://tinyurl.com/njj82eh.

72. Daniel H. Else, "The '1033 Program,' " op. cit., pp. 1–2.

73. "Department of Justice and Department of Defense Joint Technology," op. cit., p. 1.

74. Ibid., pp. 5–6.

75. Else, op. cit.

76. "Department of Justice and Department of Defense Joint Technology," op. cit., pp. 5, 11; "War Comes Home," op. cit., pp. 2–3.

77. Lois M. Davis, et al., "Long-Term Effects of Law Enforcement's Post-9/11 Focus on Counterterrorism and Homeland Security," RAND Corp., 2010, p. xv, http://tinyurl.com/k3a2tas.

78. "DHS Announces Grant Allocations for Fiscal Year 2014 Preparedness Grants," U.S. Department of Homeland Security, July 25, 2014,

http://tinyurl.com/lphyxtd; Alicia Parlapiano, "The Flow of Money and Equipment to Local Police," *The New York Times*, updated Dec. 1, 2014, http://tinyurl.com/oeswx3y.

79. Donald E. Wilkes Jr., "Explosive Dynamic Entry," *Flagpole*, July 20, 2003, http://tinyurl.com/qeqzxoq.

80. Lisa D. Moore and Amy Elkavich, "Who's Using and Who's Doing Time: Incarceration, the War on Drugs, and Public Health," *American Journal of Public Health*, May, 2008, http://tinyurl.com/mnu-7awa; John Schmitt, Kris Warner, Sarika Gupta, "The High Budgetary Cost of Incarceration," Center for Economic and Policy Research, June 2010, http://tinyurl.com/27yos76.

81. "Social Media and Tactical Considerations for Law Enforcement," Community Oriented Policing Services, U.S. Justice Department and Police Executive Research Forum, 2013, http://tinyurl.com/karmhqx.

82. Tracy L. Frazzano and G. Matthew Snyder, "Hybrid Targeted Violence: Challenging Conventional 'Active Shooter' Response Strategies," Homeland Security Affairs, Naval Postgraduate School Center for Homeland Defense and Security, 2014, http://tinyurl.com/oeoj7rj.

83. Quoted in Joseph Goldstein, "Judge Rejects New York's Stop-and-Frisk Policy," *The New York Times*, Aug. 12, 2013, http://tinyurl.com/m826bvo; Michael Barbaro and David W. Chen, "De Blasio Is Elected New York City Mayor in Landslide," *The New York Times*, Nov. 5, 2013, http://tinyurl.com/ozbnwsu.

84. Mike Bostock and Ford Fessenden, "'Stop-and-Frisk' Is All but Gone From New York," *The New York Times*, Sept. 19, 2014, http://tinyurl.com/p7qma2a.

85. "Police Reform and Accountability Accomplishments Under Attorney General Eric Holder," U.S. Justice Department, Dec. 4, 2014, http://tinyurl.com/ocf4w5a.

86. Rachel Clarke and Christopher Lett, "What happened when Michael Brown met Officer Darren Wilson," CNN, Nov. 11, 2014, http://tinyurl.com/opdowzu.

87. *Ibid.*

88. Matt Pearce, "Protesters use hands-up gesture defiantly after Michael Brown shooting," *Los Angeles Times*, Aug. 12, 2014, http://tinyurl.com/ku56bs6.

89. Quoted in Elahe Izadi and Wesley Lowery, "Meet the Missouri Highway State Patrol captain who has taken over in Ferguson," *The Washington Post*, Aug. 15, 2014, http://tinyurl.com/nvscevv.

90. "Remarks by the President," *op. cit.*

91. Press release, "Reps. Johnson, Labrador introduce bill to de-militarize police," Website of Rep. Hank Johnson, Sept. 16, 2014, http://tinyurl.com/myz4s4p.

92. *Ibid.*

93. "M14 7.62mm Rifle," Federation of American Scientists, Military Analysis Network, updated Feb. 22, 2000, http://tinyurl.com/pghfqdm; Written Testimony, Alan Estevez, *op. cit.*, pp. 3–4.

94. "Sen. Thomas R. Carper Holds a Hearing," *op. cit.*

95. Vivian Yee, "'I Can't Breathe,' Is Echoed in Voices of Fury and Despair," *The New York Times*, Dec. 3, 2014, http://tinyurl.com/ndm9c3k; Bill Chapell, "Protests Spread in New York and Beyond Over Eric Garner Case," NPR, Dec. 3, 2014, http://tinyurl.com/pqj72rs.

96. Mollie Reilly, "Justice Department to Investigate Eric Garner's Death," *The Huffington Post*, Dec. 3, 2014, http://tinyurl.com/lngbeqn; Marc Santora, "Mayor de Blasio Calls for Retraining of New York Police Dept.," *The New York Times*, Dec. 4, 2014, http://tinyurl.com/o7uywau.

97. Quoted in Santora, *ibid.*

98. Quoted in Karen Tumulty, "Ferguson, Staten Island: Similar events bring very different reaction," *The Washington Post*, Dec. 4, 2014, http://tinyurl.com/mw9uykk.

99. Quoted in Nia-Malika Henderson, "Peter King blames asthma and obesity for Eric Garner's death. That's a problem for the GOP," *The Washington Post*, Dec. 4, 2014, http://tinyurl.com/mf6qcc9.

100. "Investigation of the Cleveland Division of Police," U.S. Department of Justice, Dec. 4, 2014, pp. 3, 49, http://tinyurl.com/keuaqgz.

101. Richard A. Oppel Jr., "Cleveland Police Abuse Pattern Cited by Justice Department," *The New York Times*, Dec. 4, 2014, http://tinyurl.com/mm97l4h; "Police Reform and Accountability

Accomplishments Under Attorney General Eric Holder," U.S. Justice Department, Dec. 4, 2014, http://tinyurl.com/ocf4w5a.

102. Ellen Wulfhorst, Daniel Wallis and Edward McAllister, "More troops deployed in Ferguson to guard against fresh riots," Reuters, Nov. 25, 2014, http://tinyurl.com/k5drrwa.

103. Quoted in John Eligon, "Protesters United Against Ferguson Decision, but Challenged in Unity," *The New York Times*, Nov. 28, 2014, http://tinyurl.com/m7sag4f.

104. Quoted in Matt Apuzzo, "Past Remarks by Loretta Lynch, Attorney General Nominee, Offer Insight on Race Issues," *The New York Times*, Dec. 2, 2014, http://tinyurl.com/mykozju.

105. Ta-Nehisi Coates, "Barack Obama, Ferguson, and the Evidence of Things Unsaid," *The Atlantic*, Nov. 26, 2014, http://tinyurl.com/mtjyjqz.

106. Quoted in "Civil Rights Attorney On How She Built Trust With Police," NPR, Dec. 5, 2014, http://tinyurl.com/l3s86oc.

107. "10-Point Justice Plan: National urban League Police Reform and Accountability Recommendations," National Urban League, December 2014, http://tinyurl.com/m2j2k7u.

108. "FBI Releases Study on Active Shooter Incidents," FBI, Sept. 24, 2014, http://tinyurl.com/nfm5pww.

109. Zach Miners, "Startup arms cops with Internet-connected 'smart' guns," *PCWorld*, Oct. 27, 2014, http://tinyurl.com/lmwmbht.

110. Quoted in *ibid*.

BIBLIOGRAPHY
Selected Sources
Books

Balko, Radley, *Rise of the Warrior Cop: The Militarization of America's Police Forces*, **PublicAffairs, 2014.**
A longtime critic of police tactics traces hardening of police methods to the spread of SWAT teams.

McCoy, Candace, ed., *Holding Police Accountable*, **Urban Institute Press, 2010.**
A group of academics, including two former police officers, examine changes in laws and procedures guiding police conduct.

Moskos, Peter, *Cop in the Hood: My Year Policing Baltimore's Eastern District*, **Princeton University Press, 2008.**
A former police officer who was trained as a sociologist examines his own and colleagues' actions and attitudes in policing poor, African-American neighborhoods.

Stamper, Norm, *Breaking Ranks: A Top Cop's Exposé of the Dark Side of American Policing*, **Nation Books, 2005.**
A career police officer who rose to Seattle police chief criticizes drug laws and drug enforcement.

Articles

Barrett, Devlin, "Attorney General Eric Holder Urges Broad Review of Police Tactics," *The Wall Street Journal*, **Oct. 8, 2014, http://tinyurl.com/nunrumb.**
The outgoing Justice Department chief calls for a thorough examination of police departments' policies and actions.

Devaney, Tim, "Senators blast DOD program that 'militarized police,' " *The Hill*, **Sept. 9, 2014, http://tinyurl.com/lxns2q6.**
Bipartisan criticism erupted at a Senate committee hearing on transfers to police departments of military gear.

Heal, Charles "Sid," "Swarming," *The Tactical Edge*, **Spring 2011, http://tinyurl.com/pke2bjb.**
A former Los Angeles Sheriff's Department commander analyzes a tactic in which police in a sudden emergency rush a shooter from several directions — a method Heal calls a departure from the military approach.

Lind, Dara, "How do police departments train cops to use force?," *Vox*, **Sept. 5, 2014, http://tinyurl.com/ncfnjjn.**
A justice system specialist details how officers are taught when and when not to shoot.

McKay, Dan, "Video: Camper turning from officers when shot," *Albuquerque Journal*, **March 22, 2014, http://tinyurl.com/ltuzozq.**
A video of police shooting to death a mentally disturbed man intensified criticism of an already troubled Albuquerque, N.M., police department.

Moore, Rob, "Child burned by distraction device during raid," *Access North Georgia*, May 29, 2014, http://tinyurl.com/mc3ac4j.

A county sheriff in charge of a disastrous SWAT raid in which an infant was gravely wounded by a flash-bang grenade says his men had had no information a child was in the house but defends the operation as based on available intelligence.

Nehring, Abbie, "'Less Lethal' Flash-Bangs Used in Ferguson Leave Some Feeling the Burn," *ProPublica*, Aug. 22, 2014, http://tinyurl.com/olovoph.

A journalist reports being burned by a flash-bang grenade used against demonstrators in Ferguson, Mo., and experts debate their use as crowd-control devices.

Proctor, Jeff, "Boyd shooter: 'Welcome to ROP; mistakes now cease to exist,' " *KRQE News*, Oct. 7, 2014, http://tinyurl.com/pqmhewu.

An investigative reporter recounts the little-known story of a specialized Albuquerque, N.M., Police Department unit — now disbanded — whose logo was a hangman's noose.

Swaine, Jon, "Doubts cast on witness's account of black man killed by police in Walmart," *The Guardian*, Sept. 7, 2014, http://tinyurl.com/k4g3gvg.

A U.S. correspondent for a London-based newspaper probes the evidence in a police shooting that left an unarmed man dead in a Walmart store in Beavercreek, Ohio, after picking up a BB rifle from a shelf and walking around the store with it.

Reports and Studies

Else, Daniel H., "The '1033 Program,' Department of Defense Support to Law Enforcement," Congressional Research Service, Aug. 28, 2014, http://tinyurl.com/l79spln.

A CRS specialist examines the requirements governing military equipment transfers to police.

"Police Under Attack: A Police Foundation Review of the Christopher Dorner Incident," Police Foundation, 2013, http://tinyurl.com/letwcga.

A team of career police officers working for a think tank analyzes and draws lessons from the 2013 manhunt for an ex-Los Angeles Police Department officer and U.S. Navy veteran who killed the daughter of a former superior, a police officer and a sheriff's deputy. Police shot at, but didn't kill, three civilians during the search.

"War Comes Home: The Excessive Militarization of American Policing," American Civil Liberties Union (ACLU), June 2014, http://tinyurl.com/nneqyrk.

The ACLU analyzes data from a small sample of police departments to conclude that U.S. police tactics and equipment are overly militarized.

For More Information

American Civil Liberties Union, 125 Broad St., New York, NY 10004; 212-549-2500; http://tinyurl.com/kghjobr. The rights-advocacy organization has published a series of detailed reports alleging police misconduct nationally and in several states and cities.

Law Enforcement Against Prohibition, 8730 Georgia Ave., Silver Spring, MD 20910; 301-565-0807; http://tinyurl.com/3ndoyw. The U.S.-based international organization of retired police officers, prosecutors and judges advocates legalizing and regulating drug use.

National Fraternal Order of Police, 701 Marriott Dr., Nashville, TN 37214; 615-399-0900; http://tinyurl.com/omy84xb. The nation's major police union advocates for its members on all issues affecting police safety and benefits.

National Tactical Officers Association, http://tinyurl.com/lrognsr. The main organization for SWAT team members offers training in crisis negotiation, hostage rescue, sniper shooting and other situations in which SWAT teams are mobilized.

Police Executive Research Forum, 1120 Connecticut Ave., N.W., Washington, DC 20036; 202-466-7820; http://tinyurl.com/kytrfy9. The think tank and consultancy recommends policies designed to improve police-community relations.

Police Foundation, 1201 Connecticut Ave., N.W., Washington, DC 20036; 202-833-1460; http://tinyurl.com/q85srua. Affiliated with three universities in the United States and United Kingdom, the foundation researches new developments affecting police departments and proposes strategies to deal with them.

U.S. Department of Justice, Civil Rights Division, 950 Pennsylvania Ave., N.W., Washington, DC 20530; 202-514-6255; http://tinyurl.com/lu76yt8. The division's Special Litigation Section has conducted detailed investigations and negotiated settlements — all available on the section's website — on police misconduct in numerous cities.

6
Racial Profiling

Kenneth Jost

Demonstrators in Los Angeles on July 16, 2013, protest the acquittal of white neighborhood watch volunteer George Zimmerman in the shooting death of Trayvon Martin, an unarmed black Florida 17-year-old. The verdict touched off a nationwide debate on racial profiling, which minority groups say is widespread.

San Francisco's police department had been under intense scrutiny for several months before a police sergeant shot and killed an unarmed African-American woman on the morning of May 19, 2016, as she drove away in what the sergeant suspected was a stolen vehicle. Within hours of Jessica Williams' death, Mayor Ed Lee fired Greg Suhr as chief of the 2,000-member force and replaced him on an interim basis with a veteran black deputy, Toney Chaplin.[1]

Suhr, who is white, was Lee's choice for the post in 2011 and had vowed as late as two days earlier to stay in the post. For months, Suhr had been defending the force and his leadership in the face of public protests, media headlines, and a Justice Department investigation over accusations of racial bigotry among the rank and file and racial profiling in traffic stops.*

The shake-up in San Francisco comes at a tumultuous time for police departments all around the county after issues of racial profiling and excessive force have spawned a nationwide protest movement under the name "Black Lives Matter." Suhr is the fourth police chief to lose his job within the previous 14 months in the wake of deaths of unarmed African-Americans that resulted from encounters with police.[2]

In San Francisco and each of the other cities — Chicago, Baltimore, and Ferguson, MO. — the fatalities touched off street

From *CQ Researcher*,
November 22, 2013; updated May 2016.

*The widely used term *racial profiling* in this report encompasses the targeting of an individual based on either race or ethnicity.

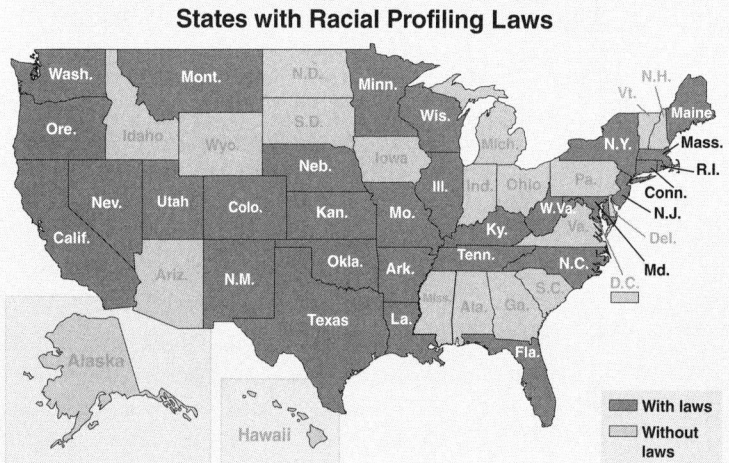

Majority of States Address Racial Profiling

At least 30 states have passed laws addressing racial profiling, according to the National Conference of State Legislatures. The laws vary widely. About half explicitly prohibit profiling. Others require law enforcement agencies to compile data on the race and ethnicity of drivers and pedestrians stopped by police and to develop policies and train officers on how to avoid profiling.

Sources: National Conference of State Legislatures, from unpublished compilation provided on request; Alejandro del Carmen, *Racial Profiling in America* (2008)

protests that underscored deep distrust between predominantly white police forces and in particular the cities' African-American communities. In San Francisco, as in the other cities, observers see the changes at the top as essential steps in efforts to restore confidence.

"Politically, it was necessary," John J. Pitney Jr., a political science professor at Claremont McKenna College in Pomona, Calif., told *The San Francisco Chronicle*. "The experience of other cities strongly suggests that without a firing the political pressure would become daunting. The mayor also undoubtedly considered the possibility of civil unrest, and that creates enormous problems of its own."[3]

Just one month earlier, an investigation by the *Chronicle* reported damaging evidence of racial profiling by San Francisco police in traffic stops — parallel to findings of racial profiling by police in many other U.S. municipalities. The newspaper's examination of traffic stops from 2013 through 2015 found that African-American and Latino drivers were stopped at much higher rates than white or Asian drivers but that searches of African-Americans and Latinos were much less likely to uncover evidence of crime than comparable searches of white or Asian drivers. "A lower hit rate for ethnic minorities is a red flag for bias," Lorie Fridell, an associate professor of criminology at the University of South Florida, told the *Chronicle*.[4]

Racial profiling is not only unfair to the individuals stopped but also unhealthy for police-community relations, experts say. "If the people you serve think you are going about it illegitimately, then there are going to be problems," says Jim Bueermann, president of the Police Foundation, a Washington-based think tank, and a former police chief in Redlands, Calif.

Anecdotal and statistical evidence indicating that police disproportionately stop and ticket African-American motorists compared to white drivers helped popularize the cynical phrase "driving while black." More substantively, that evidence has figured in court cases and legislation requiring law enforcement agencies to collect racial and ethnic data on traffic stops to identify possible racial profiling.

Public opinion polls indicate a widening gap of distrust between minority groups and police. In a survey in summer 2015, the Gallup organization found that 73 percent of African-Americans say that blacks are treated less fairly by police than whites are treated. The same figure was found in 2007, the highest level recorded in 20 years of asking that question. Only 34 percent of whites hold that view.[5]

Traditional civil rights groups representing African-Americans and Latinos agree that racial profiling is widespread among U.S. law enforcement agencies. "Absolutely," says Hilary Shelton, director of the Washington office of the NAACP, the century-old civil rights organization. "We're still getting reports and complaints of racial profiling still being quite prevalent."

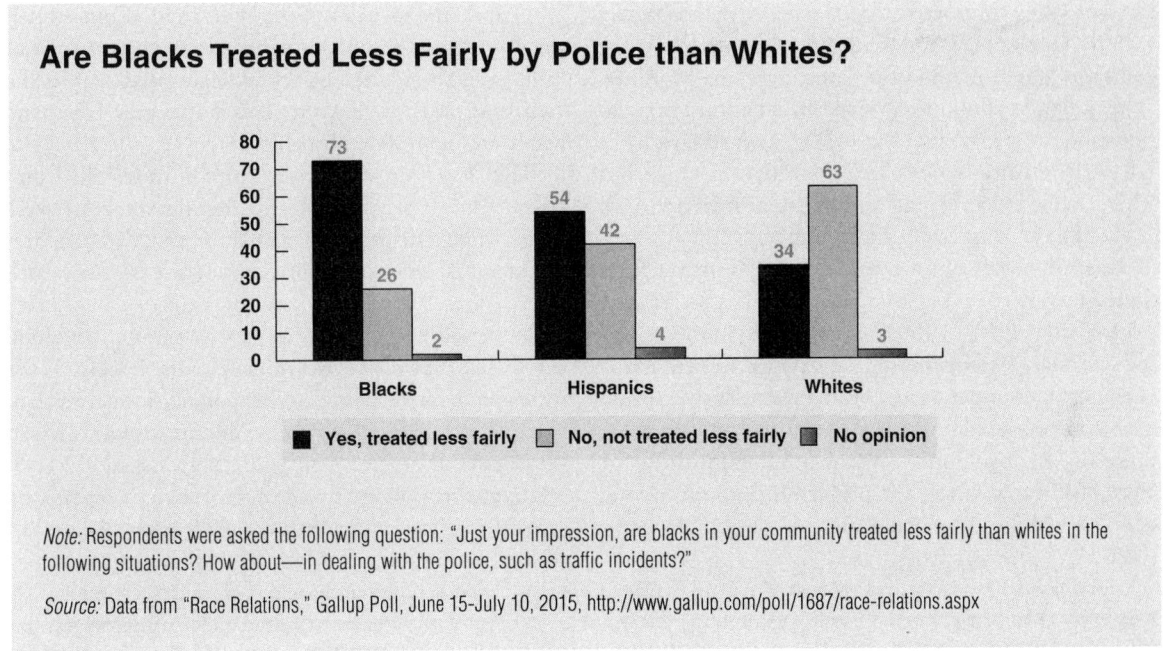

Are Blacks Treated Less Fairly by Police than Whites?

Note: Respondents were asked the following question: "Just your impression, are blacks in your community treated less fairly than whites in the following situations? How about — in dealing with the police, such as traffic incidents?"

Source: Data from "Race Relations," Gallup Poll, June 15-July 10, 2015, http://www.gallup.com/poll/1687/race-relations.aspx

Profiling of Latinos also has become "quite extensive," according to Thomas Saenz, president of the Mexican American Legal Defense and Educational Fund (MALDEF), especially now that police in some jurisdictions have been asked to engage in immigration enforcement. "They are forced to rely on stereotypes," Saenz explains, "and stereotypes in immigration particularly rest on ethnicity and race."

In New York City, a federal judge ordered extensive changes to the city's "stop and frisk" policy in minority neighborhoods under the then police commissioner in August 2013 after concluding the policies amounted to "indirect racial profiling." The newly installed mayor, Bill de Blasio, agreed to settle the suit early in 2014, but a report filed in federal court in February indicates that the new commissioner William Bratton is having difficulty getting rank-and-file officers to comply with the restrictions. Meanwhile, Bratton's predecessor, Raymond Kelly, is blaming an increase in homicides in the city on the sharp decline in stop-and-frisk activity.[6]

In a second closely watched profiling case, the tough-talking sheriff Joe Arpaio in Maricopa County, Ariz., is facing sanctions after being found in contempt of court in May. In a 162-page opinion issued on May 13, 2016, U.S. District Court Judge Murray Snow found Arpaio and three of his top aides guilty of "persistent disregard" for the court's orders prohibiting immigration patrols and requiring better training on constitutional rules for traffic stops. Arpaio, who has served as sheriff in Arizona's most populous county since 1993, faces possible penalties following a May 31 hearing before Snow.[7]

The extent of racial profiling — indeed, its very existence — is a subject of debate and inevitable uncertainty. In the New York stop-and-frisk case, the plaintiffs' evidence before Judge Shira Scheindlin — who retired from the bench in May — showed that 53 percent of those stopped were African-Americans and 32 percent Hispanics. Those figures were higher than their respective proportions in the city's overall population — 26 percent for African-Americans and 29 percent for Hispanics — but the then-mayor Michael Bloomberg and then-police commissioner Kelly insisted the apparent discrepancy reflects the demographics of criminal offenders.

Heather Mac Donald, a senior fellow at the conservative Manhattan Institute think tank who has followed the racial profiling controversy for more than a decade, agrees with the former New York City officials in disputing the commonly used method for detecting racial profiling. "Police actions continue to be measured against population ratios instead of crime ratios," McDonald says. "The relevant measure is not overall population ratios but where crime is happening and where officers are most likely to be encountering criminal force."

Brian Withrow, a professor of criminal justice at Texas State University in San Marcos who was a Texas state trooper from 1981 to 1993, says research on the issue is inconclusive despite continuing studies. "There hasn't been any substantial change in the research that would enable us to measure whether or not police officers are targeting African-Americans or other minorities for stops," Withrow says. "The problem is as it always has been an inability to measure the population of people subject to being stopped."

But David Harris, a professor at the University of Pittsburgh Law School and a leading critic of racial profiling since the late 1990s, says studies in New York, Philadelphia, and other cities "show very clearly that police cannot explain the racially disproportionate use of stop and frisk by any other factor." He says force is also used disproportionately against African-Americans and Latinos. "There's bias involved — implicit, conscious or not," he says.

In San Francisco, Williams, age 29, was shot and killed in the predominantly African-American Bayview community in the third police shooting death since December. Mario Woods, an African-American age 26, was shot by police 21 times on December 2, 2015, also in the Bayview area, after he refused officers' demand to drop a knife. Luis Gongora, a homeless Latino age 45, was shot and killed on April 7, 2016, in the city's gentrifying Mission District after allegedly lunging at officers with a knife.[8]

The seeming nationwide spate of police killings has roiled large cities such as Chicago, Cleveland, and New York and smaller cities such as Ferguson and North Charleston, S.C. The shooting death of the young African-American Michael Brown in Ferguson on Aug. 9, 2014, transformed the long simmering debate over racial profiling into an intense debate about police use of force by birthing the now familiar phrase, "Black Lives Matter."

Despite the focus of this nonhierarchical movement, the *Washington Post*'s comprehensive database of police killings in the United States indicates that half of the victims in 2015 were white, one-fourth were black and about one-sixth were Hispanic.

The *Post* reported, however, most of those killed after brandishing a weapon or threatening someone were white while a disproportionate number killed after less threatening behavior — three out of five — were black or Hispanic.[9]

Prompted by the events in Ferguson and other cities, the Police Executive Research Forum is calling for increased training about de-escalation, crisis intervention, and electronic weapon control to minimize loss of civilian life or risks to officers' lives. The report, issued in March 2016, credits police with "a step forward," however, by recognizing "the existence of racially biased policing and the serious threat it represents to building strong relationships between police and the communities they serve."[10]

Many of the deaths resulted in criminal investigations, and a few in criminal charges, but convictions have been relatively few. Some cases, however, have resulted in financial settlements to victims' families. As legal proceedings, official investigations, public protests, and news coverage continue, here are some of the questions being debated:

Are racial- and ethnic-profiling prevalent in U.S. law enforcement today?

As chief of police in the predominantly white northern New Jersey suburb of Wyckoff, Benjamin Fox told officers by memo that profiling, "racial or otherwise," has a place in law enforcement "if used fairly." The 40-year law enforcement veteran added that "black gang members from Teaneck commit burglaries in Wyckoff. That's why we check out suspicious black people in white neighborhoods."

Fox's memo, written in December 2014, surfaced in March 2016 after having been sent anonymously to the New Jersey affiliate of the American Civil Liberties Union (ACLU). The township committee responded on May 3 by voting to suspend Fox even with investigations under way by the Bergen County prosecutor and state attorney general's office.[11]

New Jersey is no stranger to racial profiling controversies. The state attorney general's office formally

Fatal Force: Police Killings in 2015

The *Washington Post* gathered information for a continuously updated data base on police killings in the United States and analyzed the killings by the race, age and gender of the victims and other circumstances, such as signs of mental illness, presence of weapons, and threat level. For 2015, almost exactly half of the 990 victims were white, slightly over one-fourth were black, and somewhat more than one-sixth were Hispanic. Nearly 80 percent of the victims had a deadly weapon and nearly 75 percent were attacking police before being killed.

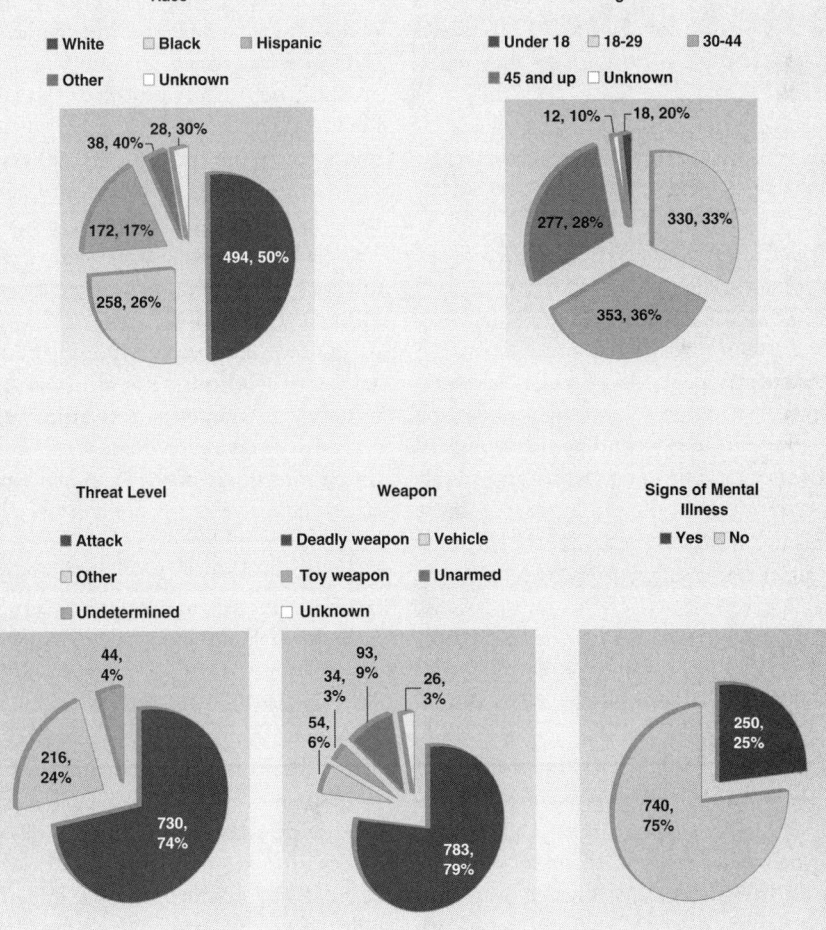

Source: Data from Fatal Force: A *Washington Post* database, https://www.washingtonpost.com/graphics/national/police-shootings/

On August 12, 2013, New York City Mayor Michael Bloomberg, left, and Police Commissioner Raymond W. Kelly responded to a blockbuster ruling by U.S. District Judge Shira Scheindlin that the city's aggressive stop-and-frisk policy violated the constitutional rights of minorities. The case was later settled under Mayor Bill de Blasio, and in 2015 police stops dropped to fewer than 3 percent of the peak number from 2011.

free, easy and it's the lowest common denominator," says Geoffrey Alpert, a professor of criminal justice at the University of South Carolina in Columbia. "And it's not worth its weight in anything in major cities and complex environments."

Creating the right baseline — for example, for traffic studies — can be "very difficult," Alpert explains. "We know who they pull over, we know to whom they give tickets, we know how long they keep them, but the problem is we don't know who the average driver is," he says. Alpert oversaw a study in Florida's Miami-Dade County that found what he termed "adverse results" at two of the eight intersections covered.

Withrow, the Texas State professor, notes as one methodological problem that it is often unclear whether police know the race of a driver before making a stop. Current studies, he says, attempt to look "more insightfully" at police conduct after motorists are pulled over. "We believe that a study of what happens during a stop provides much more insight into the mindset of a police officer," he explains.

In Texas, a newspaper investigation of traffic stops by state troopers found — as in San Francisco — that minority drivers were more likely than whites to be searched after being pulled over. Hispanics were 33 percent more likely to be searched than white drivers, according to the examination of five years' worth of stops by reporters for the *Austin American-Statesman*. A North Carolina newspaper's examination of traffic stops by 24 local police and sheriff's offices similarly found black male drivers more likely to be searched than white drivers even though whites were more likely to be found with contraband.[15]

Experts found the results of both investigations troubling. Texas troopers "are searching a higher percentage of Hispanics just because they appear to be Hispanic," Charles Epp, a University of Kansas professor and the author of *Pulled Over: How Police Stops Define Race and Citizenship*, told the Austin paper. Frank Baumgartner, a political science professor at the University of North Carolina in Chapel Hill, said the results of the investigation by the *News Record* in Greensboro were "an unwelcome reminder of the realities of race in America."

Alejandro del Carmen, chair of the Department of Criminology and Criminal Justice at the University of Texas at Arlington and a frequent instructor at police

acknowledged that state troopers had a policy of targeting black motorists in the 1990s following a study by a leading researcher on the issue. John Lamberth, a social psychologist turned private consultant who had formerly chaired the Department of Psychology at Temple University in Philadelphia, had produced a similar study earlier in the 1990s that also suggested racial profiling by state troopers in Maryland.[12]

The death of Michael Brown in Ferguson, a St. Louis suburb with a population about one-third white, prompted a Justice Department study that found blacks accounted for 85 percent of traffic stops, 90 percent of tickets and 93 percent of arrests. The study, issued in March 2015, concluded that Ferguson's police department routinely violated the rights of black residents.[13]

In New Jersey, a similar study of the predominantly white township of Bloomfield found that 78 percent of people answering tickets in municipal court were black or Latino. The police department disputed the conclusions of the study, which was conducted by researchers from Seton Hall Law School in Newark.[14]

Researchers agree that census data — commonly used for comparisons in news coverage — should not be used as a benchmark to compare police stops by race. "It's

academies in Texas, says aggregate studies are useful but fail to identify individual officers who engage in racial profiling. Overall, he believes racial profiling exists but is exaggerated.

"Racial profiling as a whole doesn't have the prevalence that the media would lead the public to believe, but it happens more often than the folks on the other spectrum say," del Carmen says. "Racism continues to be a problem in the law enforcement community."

Do aggressive stop-and-frisk tactics help reduce crime?

New York City police officers are stopping far fewer pedestrians for pat-down frisks under Mayor de Blasio and police commissioner Bratton than under the city's previous administration or before a federal court decision setting guidelines for the stops. Police stops numbered around 24,000 in 2015, according to a court-appointed monitor for the department — fewer than 3 percent of the peak number of 685,274 recorded in 2011.[16]

The number had risen roughly sevenfold over a 10-year period under the city's previous mayor, Bloomberg, and police commissioner Kelly, but had started to fall before they left office and has declined further under the new administration. As he was about to leave office, Kelly predicted that violent crime would go up in the city because of the judge's order to revamp stop-and-frisk policies. Overall, however, major crime is down in the city with a 5.8 percent decline during de Blasio's first two years in office despite a 5 percent increase in homicides in 2015 from the previous year.[17]

In her order, Scheindlin directed that officers record the basis for any stop, prohibited the consideration of race or ethnicity as a reason for a stop, and required the department to institute the use of body cameras to record police encounters. In his report to the judge now handling the case, Analisa Torres, the court-appointed monitor Peter Zimroth, a lawyer with a prominent New York firm, described compliance as a work in progress, with new training and monitoring under way. Zimroth

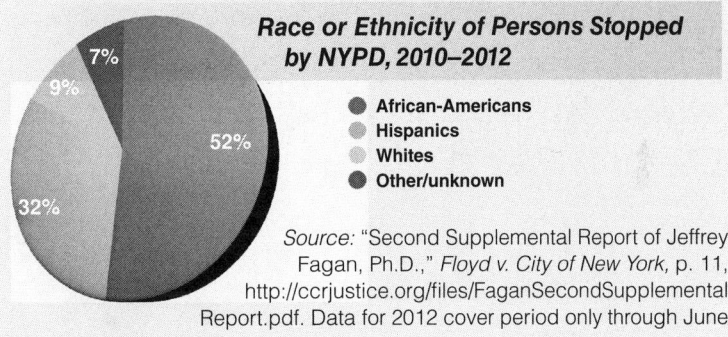

Blacks, Hispanics More Likely to Be Stopped

Of the approximately 1.6 million pedestrians stopped and questioned by New York City police officers during the period 2010-2012, more than half were African-American and nearly one in three were Hispanic. The statistics were compiled on behalf of the plaintiffs in the federal lawsuit Floyd v. City of New York.

Race or Ethnicity of Persons Stopped by NYPD, 2010–2012

- African-Americans: 52%
- Hispanics: 32%
- Whites: 9%
- Other/unknown: 7%

Source: "Second Supplemental Report of Jeffrey Fagan, Ph.D.," *Floyd v. City of New York*, p. 11, http://ccrjustice.org/files/FaganSecondSupplementalReport.pdf. Data for 2012 cover period only through June

described the efforts to guard against racial profiling as "complicated," with no decision yet on "yardsticks" to measure compliance.

The increased attention to police use of force is feeding fears of what law enforcement-minded observers are calling a "Ferguson effect" in deterring police from some proactive enforcement. The claimed phenomenon is sharply disputed but is drawing more attention with the latest statistics showing an increase in homicides in about half of the nation's biggest 50 cities. "Something is happening," FBI director James Comey remarked after seeing the statistics in mid-May 2016. Comey had earlier pointed to a possible "Ferguson effect" on police but avoided the term in his more recent remarks.[18]

The homicide statistics are far from uniform across the country. Chicago, Los Angeles, Dallas, and Las Vegas all recorded increases in the first three months of 2016 on top of increases in the previous year. Many other cities reported declines, however, including New York. The number of homicides in New York City fell to 68 in the first three months of 2016 compared to 85 for the same period the previous year — a 20 percent drop.[19]

Mac Donald, the Manhattan Institute expert, views the statistics as confirming the so-called Ferguson effect. "What we are seeing in cities with a high black

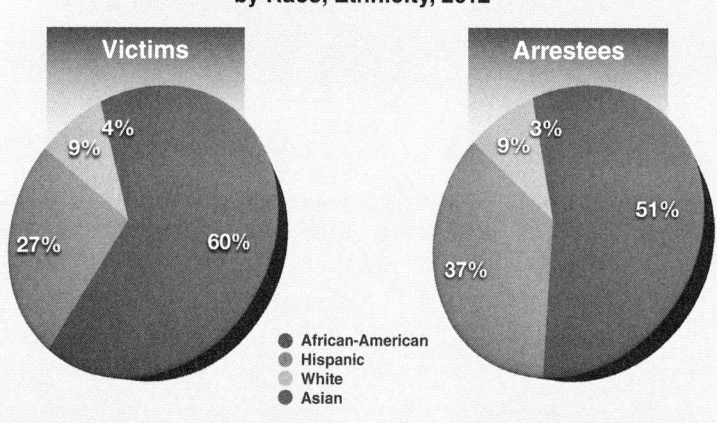

Most Victims, Arrestees Are Minorities

African-Americans and Hispanics were victims in nearly 90 percent of the murders or non-negligent manslaughters in New York City in 2012, according to the NYPD.

Murder Victims and Arrestees in New York City, by Race, Ethnicity, 2012

Victims: 60%, 27%, 9%, 4%
Arrestees: 51%, 37%, 9%, 3%

● African-American
● Hispanic
● White
● Asian

Source: "Crime and Enforcement Activity in New York, Jan. 1-Dec. 31, 2012," New York Police Department, www.nyc.gov/html/nypd/downloads/pdf/analysis_and_planning/2012_year_end_enforcement_report.pdf

population is a very worrisome de-policing effect," Mac Donald says. "Officers are doing less of the active policing. As a result, crime is going through the roof in urban areas."

In a detailed analysis of 2015 statistics, however, the Brennan Center for Law and Justice at New York University Law Center found no overall increase in crime nationwide, even compared to the historically low levels in recent years. The analysis, released in April 2016, reports that crime in the 30 largest cities was almost unchanged, with drops in two-thirds of the cities offset by a sharp increase in one city: Los Angeles.

The study acknowledged a 13 percent increase in homicides in the 30 cities, but minimized the change by noting the relatively small number of homicides overall. "Murder rates today are roughly the same as they were in 2012," the report adds. "In fact, they are slightly lower."[20]

Mac Donald credits the previous aggressive stop-and-frisk policies in New York City with contributing to the steady decline in crime during the 1990s. She argues the enforcement strategy benefited minority neighborhoods. "Police should be fighting crime," she says. "The most important thing is to bring safety to law-abiding residents of poor neighborhoods."

Other experts voiced doubts. "The objective of stop and frisk is to put a lot of police officers in high-crime areas to increase deterrence," says Withrow, the Texas State professor. "There are other ways to do that than stop-and-frisk searches."

Harris, the University of Pittsburgh professor, says the previous policies in New York were deliberately aimed at increasing the numbers. "The effect on driving crime down has been achieved and what you're doing is overenforcing," he says. "And that tends to drive a wedge between the police and the people you're serving."

The warnings about a change in tactics have not materialized, Harris adds. "Blood is not running in the streets," he says. "We're still at historically low levels of crime."

Should courts take a leading role in combating police racial and ethnic profiling?

The Arizona lawman who bills himself as the nation's "toughest sheriff" has been in federal court for the past eight years answering charges of racially profiling Latino drivers in his zeal to combat illegal immigration. Already under a court order to halt the practice, Joe Arpaio is now facing severe penalties after the federal judge overseeing the case found him in contempt for "persistent disregard" of the court's rulings.

U.S. District Court Judge Murray Snow issued a 162-page ruling on May 13, 2016, finding Arpaio and two of his top aides in civil contempt for violating the broad remedial order he issued in October 2013. Arpaio's lawyers disagreed with the ruling, but a lawyer for the American Civil Liberties Union of Arizona — which brought the suit along with the Mexican American Legal

Defense and Education Fund — praised the judge's action. "It's a damning finding — that they intentionally and repeatedly flouted the court's orders," said ACLU lawyer Cecilia Wang.[21]

Courts have played a leading role in combating racial profiling by police for more than two decades. Two of the earliest cases, in Maryland and New Jersey, resulted in ongoing federal court supervision of state police departments after the states agreed to changes to prevent the practice.[22] By contrast, New York City officials under Bloomberg and Kelly fought tooth-and-nail against accusations of racial profiling in stop-and-frisk policies until a new mayor, de Blasio, settled the case and worked with his police commissioner, Bratton, to comply with a judge's order to revamp the policies.

Racial profiling critics say the courts' role in combating the practice is useful and necessary. "That's what courts are set out to do, to determine whether police are acting within constitutional bounds," says Dennis Parker, national director of the ACLU's Racial Justice Program. Alejandro del Carmen, chair of the Department of Criminology and Criminal Justice at the University of Texas at Arlington, agrees. "Courts have the obligation and the moral and legal duty to intervene and to dissect, analyze and respond to concerns that the community may have with respect to racial profiling," del Carmen says.

Mac Donald — who criticized the New Jersey settlement in her book *Are Cops Racist?* — disagrees with the common technique of ongoing supervision by court-appointed monitors as "a tragic waste of resources." She also views the advancing practice of body-worn cameras as a waste. "I'm just not certain they would resolve the issues that are allegedly at stake here," she says. And she complains that Scheindlin, the former judge in the New York case, was guilty of "egregious calumnies" against the New York force in her decision.

Even while supporting the courts' role on the issues, some racial profiling critics say remedies may be more effective if crafted by law enforcement agencies themselves. "Courts have an important role to play, but they cannot be the sole enforcer of constitutional obligations to avoid racial discrimination," says Thomas Saenz, president of MALDEF. "It's important to have administrative processes short of going to court," he says, including an adequate opportunity to file complaints.

Harris, the University of Pittsburgh professor, says police react negatively to court supervision. "It's perceived as a judge who knows nothing, who's never done anything on the street, telling a police department what to do," he says.

"What I would like to see is the change coming primarily from law enforcement itself, from mayors and city governments, from state legislatures," Harris continues. "They are best positioned to know what's going on on the ground around them. They are in the best position to make changes that are likely to be accepted in the departments affected. That's where reform would be best hatched. And many police departments do things like that."

Jim Bueermann, president of the Police Foundation, a Washington-based research organization, and a retired police chief from Redlands, Calif., agrees on the limits of court-ordered changes. "You don't easily change a police department culture with a judicial ruling," Bueermann says. "Judges who think they're going to change a police department culture should spend time riding around in a police car, sitting down with officers in the station."

"Courts serve a very important role in controlling the power of the state, including the police department," says Withrow, the Texas State professor. "Courts play an essential role in improving policing. It doesn't seem like an improvement to cops, but in the long run it almost always results in improvement of policing."

BACKGROUND
"A Difficult History"

The term *racial profiling* is of recent coinage, but bias-based policing in the United States dates as far back as the revolutionary era with the religious profiling of Quakers seen as disloyal to the cause of independence. African-Americans have been subject to racial profiling from the days of slavery through the so-called Jim Crow era and up to modern times. Mexicans and other Latinos have been singled out for rough treatment by law enforcement since the time of Texas's independence. And immigration laws dating from the late 19th century amounted to racial or ethnic profiling against, among others, Asians and southern and eastern Europeans. "It's a very difficult history," says del Carmen, the University of Texas professor.[24]

The Continental Congress ordered the arrest and imprisonment of dozens of Pennsylvania Quakers suspected of disloyalty to the revolutionary cause in August 1777, according to an account by Emory University law professor Morgan Cloud.[25] No evidence was offered, no hearings were held, and some of those arrested were exiled to imprisonment in Virginia. The captives were released by April 1778, in part, Cloud says, because of objections to the procedures not only from their families but also from some political leaders.

African-Americans comprised around one-sixth of the country's population in the pre-Civil War era, the vast majority of them held in slavery, mainly but not exclusively in the South. Those who escaped — "runaway" slaves, as they were called — could be captured by private slave hunters under the Fugitive Slave Act, a 1793 law (strengthened in 1850) that offered few procedural protections. Free blacks had no immunity from capture, as dramatized in the 2013 movie *12 Years a Slave*; courts generally recognized a presumption that a black person was a slave.

The end of slavery merely transformed the legally and socially enforced profiling of African-Americans. The racial segregation laws of the Jim Crow era reflected the prevailing assumption that blacks were different from — and inferior to — whites. African-Americans suspected or accused of committing crimes could be subjected to abusive treatment by police or sheriffs' officers and to patently unjust proceedings in court. Worse was the threat of racially profiled vigilante justice: More than 3,400 African-Americans were lynched from the 1880s to 1950, according to a compilation by the Tuskegee Institute, the historically black college in Tuskegee, Ala. (renamed Tuskegee University in 1983).[26]

Mexicans and Mexican-Americans were also the victims of ethnic profiling from the time of Texas' independence from Mexico and its subsequent annexation by the United States. The Texas Rangers, founded in 1845 and the nation's first statewide police organization, was known, according to the University of Texas' del Carmen, for "brutal acts against Comanche tribes and thousands of Mexicans."[27] Mexican-Americans in Texas and the Southwest were subjected to the same kind of residential and educational segregation as African-Americans elsewhere. And in the 1930s, as many as two million people of Mexican descent were forced or pressured to leave the United States.

Federal immigration laws dating from the late 19th century reflected ethnic profiling at the national level. The first of the laws, passed in 1875, barred entry to "undesirables," who included Asians brought to the United States for forced labor or prostitution. Seven years later, the Chinese Exclusion Act prohibited all immigration of Chinese laborers. In the ensuing decades immigration officers enforced admission requirements, such as literacy tests, in ways that favored northern and western Europeans, del Carmen explains. The quota system enacted in the 1920s wrote those preferences into law.

The most notorious episode of ethnic profiling occurred during World War II with the internment of more than an estimated 110,000 persons of Japanese descent, most of them U.S. citizens. President Franklin D. Roosevelt authorized the internment in an executive order issued on Feb. 19, 1942, two-and-a-half months after Japan attacked Pearl Harbor, based on warnings from the military that the Japanese represented a national security threat. Today, those warnings are widely viewed as unfounded, the internment in ramshackle concentration camps in remote areas as shameful and the Supreme Court decision, *Korematsu v. United States* (1944), upholding the action as disgraceful.

Still, the court's decision in *Korematsu* established the principle that race-based restrictions in the law are "immediately suspect." Courts "must subject [such restrictions] to the most rigid scrutiny," Justice Hugo L. Black wrote for the 6-3 majority. "Pressing necessity may sometimes justify the existence of such restrictions," he continued. "Racial antagonism never can."[28] That principle laid the basis for courts, legislatures, and law enforcement agencies later in the 20th century to give greater scrutiny to racial and ethnic profiling.

An 'Indefensible' Practice

Racial and ethnic profiling emerged as an important issue late in the 20th century because of a confluence of factors. The civil rights revolution embodied the demand of African-Americans for equal treatment under the law, including by police. The rapid increase in the Latino population, especially from the 1980s, prompted analogous demands from Latino advocacy groups to eliminate discriminatory treatment. And the criminal law revolution wrought by the Supreme Court under Chief Justice Earl Warren

CHRONOLOGY

1960s–1970s *Civil rights movement targets racial inequality; Supreme Court forces changes in criminal justice systems.*

1968 The National Advisory Commission on Civil Disorders (Kerner Commission), charged with examining the causes of urban riots, urges more sensitive, diverse police forces. . . . Supreme Court approves limited stop-and-frisk authority (*Terry v. Ohio*, June 10).

1970s FBI develops "profiles" of airplane hijackers, serial killers.

1975, 1976 *Supreme Court limits use of race or ethnicity in roving Border Patrol stops but allows it at border checkpoints.*

1980s–1990s *Racial profiling emerges as issue.*

1989 Supreme Court approves use of drug courier profiles.

1995 Maryland State Police agree to prohibit stops based on racial drug courier profiles.

1996 Supreme Court allows traffic stops even if real purpose is drug enforcement.

1999 N.J. attorney general finds racial profiling by state troopers despite official policies prohibiting it; Justice Department appoints monitor; President Bill Clinton orders law enforcement agencies to compile race, ethnicity data to guard against profiling.

2000–Present *Racial profiling litigation increases; states pass laws addressing issue.*

2001 President George W. Bush promises to help end racial profiling; Al Qaeda hijackers attack United States; Muslims, Arabs rounded up in immigration sweeps, singled out in airport security checks, face widespread public suspicion.

2003 Bush administration bans racial, ethnic profiling in all federal law enforcement agencies, but allows exception for national security-related investigations; New York City settles racial profiling suit (*Daniels v. City of New York*); settlement approved by District Judge Shira Scheindlin.

2008 Center for Constitutional Rights files new stop-and-frisk suit against New York Police Department (NYPD) (*Floyd v. City of New York*), claiming violations of 2003 settlement in the Daniels case; new suit is assigned to Scheindlin as "related" case.

2009 Obama becomes first African-American president; Eric Holder becomes first black attorney general.

2012 White community-watch volunteer George Zimmerman kills unarmed black teenager Trayvon Martin in Sanford, Fla., touching off a nationwide debate on racial profiling; Zimmerman, charged with second-degree murder, is later acquitted; Muslim plaintiffs file federal suit to halt NYPD surveillance of mosques, Muslim neighborhoods; Federal judge dismisses FBI suit over informant's surveillance of mosques in Southern California.

2013 Federal judge finds Maricopa County Sheriff Joe Arpaio guilty of ethnic profiling of Latinos; orders appointment of monitor, other steps; Scheindlin finds NYPD guilty of racial profiling, Fourth Amendment violations in stop-and-frisk policies; orders appointment of monitor, test of body-worn cameras; Bill de Blasio, opponent of stop-and-frisk policies, elected New York City mayor.

2014 Mayor de Blasio agrees to settle stop-and-frisk suit; Eric Garner, African-American street peddler, dies from NYPD officer chokehold; Michael Brown, unarmed black teen, shot and killed by white officer in Ferguson, MO.; Tamir Rice fatally shot by Cleveland police officer while playing with toy gun; St. Louis County grand jury declines to indict Officer Darren Wilson in Brown's death.

2015 Freddie Gray dies of injuries sustained in Baltimore police custody; six officers face charges; North Charleston, S.C., officer Michael Slager indicted for murder in shooting of Walter Scott after traffic stop.

2016 Arpaio held in contempt of court.

Muslims Challenge 'Religious Profiling'

"We should not be singled out simply because of religion."

Sarah Abdurrahman was in a festive mood as she returned to the United States with friends and family in September 2013 after attending a friend's wedding in Canada.

But the good feelings died at the border as she and her traveling party, all U.S. citizens and all Muslims, suffered what the radio journalist later described as a painful and humiliating six-hour ordeal at the hands of U.S. Customs and Border Patrol (CPB) agents.

Abdurrahman, an assistant producer with the NPR program *On the Media*, said the agents detained the traveling party without explanation, refused to identify themselves, and questioned at least one of the travelers, Abdurrahman's husband, about his religious practices. She described the experience — and her fruitless efforts to get an explanation afterward — in a 20-minute report on the program.[1]

The episode typifies the seeming religious profiling that advocates for the United States' 6 million Muslims say has been common since al Qaeda's September 2011 attacks on the United States. Because of terrorism-inspired scrutiny at the federal, state, and local levels, many Muslims today worry that they may be monitored, interrogated, detained, or even arrested for no reason other than religion, according to officials with the San Francisco group Muslim Advocates.

"We're not saying mosques or Muslims should be off limits," explains Glenn Katon, the group's legal director. "It's that mosques should not be singled out; Muslims should not be singled out simply because of religion."

The complaints extend beyond individual anecdotes such as Abdurrahman's. Muslims are currently challenging in court broad surveillance programs maintained by the New York Police Department (NYPD) and by the FBI in Southern California. Both law enforcement agencies are accused of infringing religious liberties by infiltrating mosques without adequate justification. But so far none of the law enforcement practices has been ruled improper.

In California, Craig Monteilh posed as a Muslim convert under an assumed name for more than a year as a paid FBI informant, using audio and video recording devices to gather information. The American Civil Liberties Union (ACLU) of Southern California and the Council on American-Islamic Relations (CAIR) filed a civil rights suit against the FBI on behalf of Muslim community members in Orange County in regard to Monteilh's acknowledged infiltration of approximately 10 Southern California mosques. The government claimed the "state secrets" privilege in refusing to disclose details of Monteilh's surveillance in so-called Operation Flex. In August 2012, U.S. District Judge Cormac Carney dismissed the government as a defendant but allowed the suits against individual FBI agents and officials to proceed. ACLU lawyers appealed the decision; the appeal was argued before the Ninth U.S. Circuit Court of Appeals in December 2015.[2]

In New York, the NYPD faced three separate suits challenging its surveillance of mosques and Muslims as Fourth

---

subjected local and state law enforcement to greater scrutiny to comply with constitutional norms. Meanwhile, public concern about crime and, in particular, about illegal drugs led police and law enforcement agencies to adopt tactics often disproportionately aimed at African-Americans and Latinos — sometimes consciously.[29]

The Warren Court's major criminal law decisions — such as the *Miranda* ruling on police interrogation guidelines — benefited white and minority suspects and defendants alike. Despite criticism for supposedly "handcuffing" police, the Warren Court also gave police an important tool in its 1968 *Terry* decision upholding — with only one dissenting vote — the stop-and-frisk procedure. The court noted complaints of "harassment" by African-Americans, however, in stressing the need to limit the procedure to "the legitimate investigative sphere." Meanwhile, the so-called Kerner Commission, appointed by President Lyndon B. Johnson in response to urban riots of the mid-1960s, had issued a comprehensive report in 1968 recommending, among other steps, the hiring of more diverse and more sensitive police forces.[30]

The Supreme Court's initial encounter with the profiling issue came in a pair of immigration-related cases in the mid-1970s. In the first, the court in 1975 ruled that a roving Border Patrol car could not stop a vehicle solely

Amendment violations both in New York and across the state line in New Jersey. Lawyers for the New York-based Center for Constitutional Rights and the Muslim Advocates filed the first of the suits in federal district court in New Jersey in June 2012; the ACLU, along with the New York Civil Liberties Union (NYCLU) and a police accountability project at the City University of New York Law School, filed a comparable suit in federal district court in Brooklyn in June. The city settled the lawsuits in January 2016 by agreeing to appoint an independent civilian to monitor the police department's counterterrorism activities.[3]

In a third case, lawyers from the NYCLU charged the police with violating their own court-approved guidelines for initiating surveillance of political or religious organizations. The guidelines date back to a court-approved settlement of anti-spying litigation in the 1970s, but the NYPD got the rules eased in 2003 after claiming they hampered counterterrorism work.[4]

Separately, the ACLU sued the FBI under the Freedom of Information Act to try to obtain the agency's guidelines for counterterrorism investigations. In a ruling on Oct. 23, 2013, the federal appeals court in Philadelphia upheld the FBI's decision to limit disclosure of the requested documents because it would reveal investigative techniques.[5]

Abdurrahman was also stymied in her efforts to determine why her traveling party was detained when they re-entered the United States in September 2013. On the radio program, Abdurrahman said she filed a complaint about the incident with the Department of Homeland Security's Office of Civil Rights and Civil Liberties. The office rejected the complaint, she said, but the reasons for upholding the agents' actions were redacted in the notice of the decision.

The program quoted Munia Jabbar, an attorney with CAIR, that Muslims are often asked "really invasive" questions about religious practices when re-entering the United States. She says the questioning, as Abdurrahman's husband described, is improper. "You're singling people out because of their religion and then subjecting them to longer detentions and to humiliating questioning about stuff that they're allowed to do legally," she says.

Abdurrahman says the episode left her shaken. "I came out of the experience wondering what our rights are," she said.

— *Kenneth Jost*

---

[1] See "My Detainment Story: Or How I learned to Stop Feeling Safe in My Own Country and Hate the Border Agents," NPR, Sept. 20, 2013, http://www.wnyc.org/radio/#/ondemand/319368. For print coverage, see Harrison Jacobs, "American Muslim Reporter Describes 'Dehumanizing' Treatment at US Border," Business Insider, http://www.businessinsider.com/sarah-aburrahman-detained-at-us-border-2013-9.

[2] See Maura Dolan, "Is FBI liable in Muslim spying?," *Los Angeles Times*, December 21, 2015, p. A1.

[3] See Matt Apuzzo and Al Baker, "Sued Over Spying, New York Police Get Oversight," *The New York Times*, January 8, 2016, p. A1.

[4] The case is *Handschu v. Special Services Division*, http://www.nyclu.org/case/handschu-v-special-services-division-challenging-nypd-surveillance-practices-targeting-politica.

[5] *ACLU v. FBI*, 12-4345 (3d Cir., Oct. 23, 2013), http://www2.ca3.uscourts.gov/opinarch/124345p.pdf; for coverage, see Jason Grant, "ACLU denied access to FBI files on profiling," *The Star-Ledger* (Newark, N.J.), October 24, 2013, p. 11.

---

because the driver or passengers appeared to be of Mexican ancestry. Appearance was a "relevant factor," Justice Lewis F. Powell Jr. wrote, but not enough to "justify stopping all Mexican-Americans to ask if they are aliens." A year later, however, the court ruled that agents at a border checkpoint could select motorists for secondary inspection based solely on apparent Mexican ancestry.[31]

The formal art of "profiling" began in the 1970s, as police and the FBI tried to identify characteristics to spot in potential serial killers or airline hijackers. From those rare offenses, the practice expanded to the so-called war on drugs with the federal Drug Enforcement Administration's (DEA) development of a drug courier profile in the 1980s.

The DEA never published the profile, but evidence in some cases showed that profiles sometimes specifically referred to African-Americans or Hispanics. In any event, the open-ended characteristics gave agents broad discretion in selecting individuals to stop. The Supreme Court green-lighted the use of such profiles in a 1989 decision stemming from the search of a deplaning passenger at the Honolulu airport. By a 7-2 vote, the court found the combination of six listed factors justified the stop and search; the dissenters countered that none of the factors specifically pointed to criminal activity.[32]

Through the 1990s, evidence mounted that African-Americans were far and away the majority of motorists

"Black Lives Matter": A Growing Movement

Deaths in police encounters fuel protests

The death of an unarmed black teenager at the hands of a white police officer in the St. Louis suburb of Ferguson, Mo., gave birth to a diffuse protest movement that took the name "Black Lives Matter." Michael Brown's death came with racial tensions already somewhat high because of the chokehold death of an African-American man in a police encounter less than a month earlier in New York City.

With no formal hierarchy or designated leaders, the movement grew in media visibility and political impact with a succession of highly publicized deaths of African-Americans in police encounters. Here in chronological order are brief summaries of some of those incidents:[1]

Eric Garner, 43, died on July 17, 2014, on New York City's Staten Island after an NYPD officer who suspected him of selling untaxed cigarettes placed him in a prohibited chokehold for 15 to 19 seconds. Garner was heard on a video recorded on a passerby's cell phone to say, "I can't breathe." Officer Daniel Pantaleo and other officers did not attempt to administer CPR as they waited for seven minutes for an ambulance to arrive; Garner died an hour after arriving in hospital. A state grand jury declined to indict Pantaleo.

Michael Brown, 18, was shot and killed by Officer Darren Wilson on Aug. 9, 2014, in the racially mixed suburb of Ferguson under circumstances that remain sharply disputed even after a state grand jury declined on Nov. 24 to indict Wilson in the episode. In Wilson's version, he recognized Brown as a suspect in a robbery at a nearby pharmacy, struggled with the teenager as he was seated in his patrol car, and then, out of the car, shot as Brown was headed toward him, menacingly. Brown's companion related that Brown had his hands up in the air before the fatal shot was fired.

The death sparked unrest over a period of days, with a militarized response from authorities that fueled further protests. The U.S. Justice Department also declined to prosecute Wilson but issued a damning report in March 2015 accusing the city's police of a "pattern and practice" of racial profiling of African-Americans. Police Chief Thomas Jackson resigned within a week. The Brown family's wrongful death suit is awaiting trial in federal court in October 2016.

Laquan McDonald, 17, died after having been shot 16 times late on the evening of Oct. 20, 2014, by Chicago police officer Jason Van Dyke as he and others responded to a report of a man armed with a knife breaking into vehicles in a truck yard. McDonald, who had a record of juvenile arrests, allegedly refused the officers' demands to drop his knife. Cook County state's attorney Anita Alvarez released video of the incident a year later, on Nov. 24, 2015, only under a court order in a freedom-of-information suit by journalists; the video appeared to contradict the police accounts in some respects. Mayor Rahm Emanuel fired Chicago police superintendent Garry McCarthy a week later. Van Dyke is under indictment in state court for murder. The city paid McDonald's family $5 million to settle a civil suit. Alvarez was defeated in a Democratic Party primary on March 15, 2016, in her bid for a third term.

Tamir Rice, 12, was shot and killed during daytime hours on Nov. 22, 2014, as two Cleveland police officers

stopped in drug-related enforcement. A suit in Maryland by Robert Wilkins, an African-American lawyer, was the first to uncover hard evidence of targeting of African-Americans, as recounted by Harris, the University of Pittsburgh professor. A state police "Criminal Intelligence Report," disclosed during the suit and dated only days before Wilkins was stopped, included an explicit profile targeting African-Americans.

The data gathering that resulted from the settlement of Wilkins' suit showed that 72 percent of those stopped in Maryland were African-Americans. The litigation and newspaper investigations in New Jersey produced similar evidence that the vast majority of motorists stopped on the state's turnpikes were African-Americans.

Despite such evidence, the Supreme Court declined in 1996 to question the use of traffic stops as a pretext for drug enforcement. The decisions stemmed from the convictions of two African-Americans who had been found with drugs after police officers patrolling a "high-drug" area in Washington, D.C., stopped them ostensibly because of a taillight violation. Unanimously, the court said the officers' "ulterior

responded to a report of a young boy wielding a gun in a playground; the officers were not told that the caller had said that the supposed weapon was "probably fake," as in fact it was. Officer Timothy Loehmann opened fire on Rice almost immediately after arriving on the scene, purportedly because he saw Rice reaching inside his waistband as though for a weapon. Loehmann had joined the force eight months earlier following five months with the police department in nearby Independence, Ohio. A Cuyahoga County grand jury declined to indict either of the officers, but Loehmann resigned from the force. The Rice family has a wrongful death claim pending against the two officers and the city.

Walter Scott was a 50-year-old forklift operator and former Coast Guardsman who was shot and killed on April 4, 2015, as he fled from North Charleston, S.C., police officer Michael Slager following a traffic stop for a nonfunctioning brake light. Scott, who was unarmed, had outstanding warrants for failing to pay child support. Slager, then 33, a five-year veteran of the North Charleston force, was indicted in state court for murder on June 8, just two months later, and for a federal civil rights violation on May 11, 2016.

Freddie Gray, 25, died on April 19, 2015, of spinal cord injuries sustained a week earlier as he was being transported to Baltimore County jail following his arrest for possession of an allegedly illegal switchblade. Gray had served time in prison for a drug offense and was due in court in late April on a new drug charge. The death sparked riots in the city. Six officers face charges stemming from the arrest and subsequent death; the charges are variously based on an allegedly illegal arrest and alleged neglect in securing Gray in the van or summoning medical assistance. Mayor Stephanie Rawlings-Blake fired police chief Anthony Batts on July 8.

Officer Caesar Goodson faced the most serious charge, second-degree murder, along with other charges; he was acquitted in a bench trial June 23, 2016. Three others are charged with involuntary manslaughter and other offenses: Lt. Brian Rice, Sgt. Alicia White, and Officer William Porter. Two others were charged with assault, misconduct and false imprisonment: officers Edward Nero and William Porter. Porter's trial ended with a hung jury on Dec. 16, 2015, and he is scheduled to be retried. Nero was acquitted in a bench trial on May 23, 2016. Three of the defendants are white: Miller, Nero and Rice; Goodson, Porter and White are black. The city reached a $6.4 million settlement with Gray's family without admitting wrongdoing.

—Kenneth Jost

---

[1] Summaries drawn from well-documented Wikipedia entries.

Source for Eric Garner: Joseph Goldstein and Nate Schweber, "Man's Death After Chokehold Raises Old Issue for the Police," New York Times, July 18, 2014, http://www.nytimes.com/2014/07/19/nyregion/staten-island-man-dies-after-he-is-put-in-chokehold-during-arrest.html.

Source for Michael Brown: "Department of Justice Report Regarding the Criminal Investigation Into the Shooting Death of Michael Brown by Ferguson, Missouri Police Officer Darren Wilson," March 4, 2015, https://www.justice.gov/sites/default/files/opa/press-releases/attachments/2015/03/04/doj_report_on_shooting_of_michael_brown_1.pdf

Source for Laquan McDonald: Jason Meisner, Jeremy Gorner and Steve Schmadeke, "Chicago releases dash-cam video of fatal shooting after cop charged with murder," Chicago Tribune, November 24, 2015, http://www.chicagotribune.com/news/cat-chicago-cop-shooting-video-laquan-mcdonald-charges-20151124-story.html.

Source for Walter Scott: Chris Dixon and Tamar Lewin, "South Carolina Officer Faces Federal Charges in Fatal Shooting," New York Times, May 11, 2016, http://www.nytimes.com/2016/05/12/us/south-carolina-officer-faces-federal-charges-in-fatal-shooting.html.

Source for Freddie Gray: Jean Marbella. "Six Baltimore police officers charged in Freddie Gray's death," The Baltimore Sun, May 2, 2015, http://www.baltimoresun.com/news/maryland/freddie-gray/bs-md-freddie-gray-mainbar-20150501-story.html#page=1.

---

motives" did not matter as long as they had probable cause for the stop.[33]

President Bill Clinton cited the evidence of racial profiling in traffic stops, however, when he ordered federal law enforcement agencies in June 1999 to begin collecting data on the race or ethnicity of individuals they question, search, or arrest.[34] The Justice Department was to use the data to determine whether federal officers were engaging in racial profiling and, if so, what should be done to stop the practice. Clinton said he hoped state and local law enforcement agencies would adopt similar steps to try to eliminate what he called a "morally indefensible" practice. Racial profiling, he said, "is wrong, it is destructive and it must stop."

'Deliberate Indifference'?

The issue of racial and ethnic profiling gained new importance after the Sept. 11 terrorist attacks on the United States in 2001 as Muslims and people of Arab or South Asian background came under heightened attention — and suspicion — from law enforcement and the general public. Meanwhile, critics of racial profiling of

African-Americans and Latinos continued efforts in court and legislative bodies to combat the practice and drew important support from the Obama administration's stepped-up scrutiny of local police forces. And two incidents made racial profiling issues front-page news: the arrest of the prominent African-American scholar Henry Louis Gates Jr. at the door of his Cambridge, Mass., home in 2009 and the killing of Trayvon Martin, an unarmed black teenager, by a white community-watch volunteer in a gated community in Florida in 2012.

Just one month after taking office, President George W. Bush followed Clinton's example by promising in his State of the Union address on Feb. 27, 2001, that his administration would work to end racial profiling. Attorney General John Ashcroft echoed Bush's promise, describing the practice as "unconstitutional."[35] After 9/11, however, the government evidently focused attention on Muslims, Arab nationals, and Arab-Americans in investigating possible links to al Qaeda — the group responsible for the Sept. 11 attacks — within the United States. Immigration authorities rounded up hundreds of Middle Easterners.

Despite official denials, airport screeners appeared to be giving special attention to Muslims and Arabs; and some prominent commentators — including the Manhattan Institute's Mac Donald — forthrightly defended profiling as common-sense law enforcement.[36] When the Bush administration issued racial profiling guidelines in June 2003, it included an exception for national security-related investigations.[37] A decade later, Arab-American and Muslim groups continue to complain of heightened and unwarranted scrutiny from law enforcement — including a controversial special counterterrorism unit within the NYPD.

The New York City force had come under intense scrutiny for alleged racial profiling beginning in February 1999 with the shooting death of a Guinean immigrant, Amadou Diallo, at his front door in an ethnically diverse Bronx neighborhood. Plainclothes officers in the department's Street Crime Unit thought Diallo matched the description of a suspected rapist; when Diallo reached for his wallet as identification, the officers mistook it as a weapon and fired 41 rounds, killing him. The incident sparked raucous demonstrations and an unsuccessful prosecution of the four officers in a trial moved to Albany, N.Y., because of pretrial publicity.

The episode also led to a lawsuit by the Center for Constitutional Rights, accusing the NYPD of racial profiling and unlawful stop-and-frisk practices. The suit cited, among other evidence, a report by the New York attorney general's office that showed Street Crime Unit officers stopped 16 African-Americans for every arrest made. After lengthy discovery, the city disbanded the Street Crime Unit and, in September 2003, agreed to settle the suit — called *Daniels v. City of New York* — by promising to institute policies aimed at eliminating racial profiling. District Judge Scheindlin approved the settlement in December.[38]

Obama's election as the nation's first African-American president five years later was seen by some as marking a new era in race relations, but the Gates episode only six months after Obama's inauguration underlined the continuing points of contention between law enforcement and black Americans. Gates was charged with disorderly conduct on July 16, 2009, after a white Cambridge, Mass., police officer mistook him for a possible burglar. The charges were later dropped, and Obama hosted Gates and the officer for a so-called beer summit at the White House on July 30 to smooth things over.[39]

The killing of Martin by the white community-watch volunteer, George Zimmerman, on February 26, 2012, touched off a more protracted nationwide debate over possible racial profiling. Zimmerman, concerned about a rash of home burglaries in the largely white, gated community in Sanford, Fla., tailed Martin as the unarmed teenager was returning to his father's home and fatally wounded him during a scuffle.

Zimmerman was charged with second-degree murder and acquitted on July 13, 2013, under Florida's controversial so-called Stand Your Ground law, which eases rules for self-defense in criminal trials. The verdict prompted widespread protests by African-Americans.[40]

Meanwhile, NYPD's stop-and-frisk litigation had resumed in 2008, after the Center for Constitutional Rights accused the city of failing to comply with the 2003 settlement. Judge Scheindlin assumed jurisdiction over the new case, *Floyd*, since it was related to the *Daniels* case that she had previously tried. The assignment would underlie later complaints of bias by the city and others, including the Manhattan Institute's Mac Donald, and the appeals court's subsequent decision to order the case reassigned. The trial in the new case began on March 18, 2013 and closed two months later on May 20 after sharp arguments over the implications of opposing statistical studies and testimony from police officials.

Scheindlin issued her ruling on August 12. Out of the 4.4 million stops logged by police, Scheindlin found that at least 200,000 — about 5 percent — were unconstitutional, and that the actual figure was probably higher. She went on to find that blacks and Hispanics were more likely to be stopped than whites after controlling for other variables, that blacks were more likely to be arrested, and that blacks and Hispanics were more likely to be subjected to use of force. In all, Scheindlin concluded the data showed "deliberate indifference" on the city's part toward constitutional rights — a necessary finding to establish liability under federal civil rights law. Bloomberg appealed, but the city's newly elected mayor, de Blasio, agreed to settle the case shortly after taking office in January 2014.

Over the next two years, the issue of racial profiling became more urgent and more divisive because of a handful of highly publicized killings of African-Americans under disputed circumstances.

CURRENT SITUATION
Pressure for Change

Police agencies across the country are under pressure to improve relations with minority communities, address crime-breeding conditions in poverty neighborhoods and re-examine policies and practices on the use of force.

The Obama administration and leading police professional associations are taking steps to improve the gathering and reporting of racial data on police stops and arrests. Police departments in 50 mid-size to large cities have joined in an administration initiative launched in May 2015 to set up a publicly accessible data base on such practices as uses of force, police pedestrian and vehicle stops, and officer-involved shootings.

Police Foundation president Bueermann says the data will allow the public to "make their own analysis and make their own conclusion about whether police are biased in their actions." The foundation manages the portal for the site.[23]

The so-called Police Data Initiative came as part of a broad report by an Obama administration task force on policing created in December 2014. Among other steps recommended in the task force's report, the administration is providing guidance for departments to institute the use of body-worn cameras to record encounters with civilians. In announcing release of the report, Obama also said that the administration was banning the transfer of military-style equipment to local police departments — the kind of equipment that had stoked discontent when deployed in quelling disorder in Ferguson following the Michael Brown shooting.[24]

Separately, a leading police research group is urging police departments to train officers in steps to de-escalate encounters with civilians in order to minimize use of deadly force when the officers or bystanders are not themselves threatened. The 136-page report by the Police Executive Research Forum, issued in March, stresses that officer-involved shootings comprise "an infinitesimal fraction of the millions of interactions" between police and public, but warns that "even one bad encounter" can damage community trust.[25]

The report largely absolves officers of blames in "most" of what it calls the "controversial" episodes. "[T]he officers should not be faulted," the report says, in bold-faced type, "because their actions reflected the training they received." But the report also says that in the significant fraction of encounters that involve either mental illness or unarmed civilians, there is "significant potential for de-escalation and resolving encounters by means other than the use of deadly force."

Shelton, with the NAACP's Washington office, agrees on the need to re-examine use-of-force policies. "In some cases, the structure for the acceptable use of deadly force is not nearly comprehensive enough," he says. "It is not clear when it is truly necessary to use deadly force."

In cities with changes in police leadership, officials are promising changes in police practices and policies as well. In Ferguson, a new police chief greeted officers with a stern warning against misconduct at his swearing-in ceremony on May 9, 2016.

Delrish Moss, an African-American chosen from among four finalists after having served as spokesman for the Miami police department, threatened officers with being "removed or further prosecuted" if they performed their jobs "with malice." Moss recalled that he had had unpleasant encounters with police as a youth, including one incident in which an officer used a racial slur. As

AT ISSUE

Is racial profiling by police a serious problem in the United States?

YES
Dennis Parker
*Director, Racial Justice Program,
American Civil Liberties Union*

Written for *CQ Researcher*, November 2013

In their 2009 report, "The Persistence of Racial and Ethnic Profiling: A Follow-Up Report to the U.N. Committee on the Elimination of Racial Discrimination," the American Civil Liberties Union and the Rights Working Group concluded that despite "overwhelming evidence of its existence, often supported by official data, racial profiling continues to be a prevalent and egregious form of discrimination in the United States."

Time has not altered that conclusion. Numerous studies, data collection and individual anecdotes confirm that law enforcement agents continue to rely on race, color or national or ethnic origin as a basis for subjecting people to criminal investigations.

The cost of this reliance on race or ethnicity as a supposed indicator of likely criminal activity is high for individuals and society. Examples of the practice abound. After analyzing hundreds of thousands of police stops, a federal judge concluded that African-Americans and Latinos in New York City were far more likely than whites to be stopped by police when there was no reasonable suspicion of criminal activity and were less likely than whites to be found in possession of illegal items. Meanwhile, a federal court in Arizona found the Maricopa County Sheriff's Office relied on ethnicity in enforcing immigration laws in a way that was clearly unconstitutional. In both cases, the courts were so concerned about future violations that they ordered the use of impartial monitors to track compliance with remedies intended to stop the illegal practices.

Reliance on racial profiling is not limited to local law enforcement. Six states have adopted immigration enforcement laws that invite the profiling of Latinos. The federal government routinely relies on programs and practices that delegate immigration enforcement authority to state and local agencies, resulting in the unfair targeting of Latino, Arab, South Asian and Muslim people in the name of immigration control and national security.

Despite overwhelming evidence that racial profiling persists, the End Racial Profiling Act continues to languish in Congress. Until appropriate action is taken to address discriminatory profiling, people will continue to be subjected to the humiliation of repeated, unwarranted and intrusive stops and investigations, depriving them of their individual rights and undermining support for our criminal justice system.

The idea of basing law enforcement on actions rather than on race, ethnicity or religion is long overdue.

NO
Heather Mac Donald
Fellow, Manhattan Institute

Written for *CQ Researcher*, November 2013

There is no credible evidence that racial profiling is a serious problem among police forces. Studies that purport to show the contrary inevitably assume that police activity should match population ratios, rather than crime ratios. But urban policing today is driven by crime data: Officers are deployed to where city residents are most victimized by violence. Given the racial disparities in crime commission, the police cannot provide protection to neighborhoods that most need it without generating racially disproportionate enforcement numbers.

In New York City, for example, the per capita shooting rate in predominantly black Brownsville, Brooklyn, is 81 times higher than in Bay Ridge, Brooklyn, which is largely white and Asian. That disparity reflects Brownsville's gang saturation, which affects policing in myriad ways. Police presence will be much higher in gang-infested neighborhoods, and officers deployed there will try to disrupt gang activity with all available lawful tools, including the stopping and questioning of individuals suspected of criminal activity. Each shooting will trigger an intense police response, as officers seek to avert a retaliatory gang hit. Given the difference in shooting rates, it is no surprise that Brownsville's per capita police stop rate is 15 times higher than Bay Ridge's. If it were not, the police would not be targeting their resources equitably, according to need. Yet some advocates cite such stop disparities as prima facie proof of profiling.

Community requests for protection are the other determinant of police tactics. Last fall, I spoke with an elderly cancer amputee in the South Bronx. She was terrified to go down to her lobby to get her mail because of the youths hanging out there, smoking marijuana. Only when the police had been by to conduct trespass stops would she venture out: "When you see the police, everything's A-OK," she said. Police cannot respond to such requests for public order without producing racially disparate enforcement data that can be used against them in the next racial profiling lawsuit.

Young, black males are murdered at 10 times the rate of whites and Hispanics combined, usually killed by other minority males. The New York Police Department has brought the homicide victimization rate among the city's minorities down nearly 80 percent, yet young, black men are still 36 times more likely to be murdered than young, white males. Proactive policing is the best protection poor, minority neighborhoods have against violence and fear.

chief, Moss takes on responsibility for implementing reforms agreed to with the Justice Department in March 2016 that include better training and recordkeeping to monitor racial profiling.[26]

In Baltimore, the new police commissioner Kevin Davis is promising to cooperate with recommendations from a Justice Department probe of the department initiated in June 2015. Davis, a veteran white officer who served as deputy under the ousted African-American police commissioner Anthony Batts, says he expects the DOJ report to focus on discretionary arrests, stop-and-frisk encounters, and discipline investigations. "I welcome it," Davis said of the DOJ investigation in a remark to a reporter for the *Baltimore Sun* in December 2015. "It puts us in the position to hit the ground running."[27]

In Chicago, Emanuel replaced the white police superintendent Garry McCarthy with a veteran black officer, Kevin Davis, who grew up in Chicago's infamous Cabrini-Green public housing project. Among initial steps, Emanuel instituted a new policy of transparency on police-civilian encounters by ordering the release of videos, reports, and other materials from about 100 police incidents, including officer-involved shootings. Meanwhile, Johnson responded to the city's $2 million whistleblower suit by two police officers by promising to make it easier for officers to report misconduct against colleagues.[28]

In San Francisco, Mayor Lee says there should be "consequences" for the police sergeant in Williams' death because the shooting went against department policy that generally prohibits shooting at a vehicle except in limited circumstances. Lee's remark came in a meeting with the *San Francisco Chronicle* editorial board on May 26, 2016, the day before Sgt. Justin Erb, a 15-year veteran of the force, was identified as having fired the fatal shot.[29]

Mixed Results for Prosecutors

Prosecutors are having relatively little success in bringing criminal charges against police in many of the recent high-profile officer-involved deaths although some officers have been fired, suspended, or otherwise disciplined.

The mixed results for prosecutors are illustrated by the recent same-day announcements in two fatal shootings by police with charges brought in the killing of a stranded motorist in Florida but no charges against two officers for the death of a Minneapolis man under disputed circumstances.

Nouman Raja, a former Palm Beach Gardens officer, was charged on June 1 with manslaughter and attempted murder in the death of Corey Jones, an African-American musician, who was shot dead after Raja spotted him on the side of a roadway in the early morning hours of Oct. 18, 2015. Jones had called for roadside assistance after his car stalled, but Raja, in plainclothes, stopped to investigate and after a brief conversation recorded on Jones's cell phone fired six shots, one of them fatal.

Raja claimed that Jones, who had a gun and a legal permit to carry it, came at him with the weapon pointed. But Jones's body was found 64 feet away from his car and 40 feet away from his weapon, thus appearing to contradict Raja's version of events. Despite the charges, legal observers cautioned that the prosecution faces significant obstacles.[30]

In the Minneapolis case, the Justice Department announced on June 1 that no federal charges would be brought against officers Dustin Schwarze or Mark Ringgenberg for the fatal shooting of Jamar Clark on Nov. 15, 2015, as the white officers responded to a report of a disturbance at a party. Schwarze claimed that he fired the fatal shot after Clark, who was African-American, attempted to grab his gun. The Hennepin County state's attorney had previously found no basis for state criminal charges.[31]

Paul Butler, an outspoken African-American professor at Georgetown Law School in Washington, says prosecutions of police officers in episodes such as these often fail because of the broad discretion police enjoy under Supreme Court precedents. "Even when blacks are selectively targeted by police," Butler says, "it is often not against the law."

Despite the varying circumstances, the NAACP's Shelton agrees that the most controversial episodes have all had "elements of racial profiling." In the Baltimore case, for example, "the question is why Freddie Gray was singled out in the first place," he says.

Historically, police officers are prosecuted only rarely for fatal shootings and relatively few of those result in convictions, according to the *Washington Post*'s analysis of police use of deadly force from 2005 through the first few months of 2015. The *Post* counted 54 prosecutions in the previous 10 years with 21 cases ending in acquittals or dismissals, 14 in convictions or other dispositions and 19 cases then pending.[32]

Prosecutors have come up short so far in trials stemming from Gray's death even though six officers are facing charges. Officer Edward Nero was acquitted of assault and false imprisonment on May 23 in a bench trial before Circuit Judge Barry Williams. Nero and fellow officer Garret Miller were charged with assault on the basis of Gray's allegedly illegal arrest; Miller's case is still pending. Earlier, a jury failed on Dec. 16, 2015, to reach a verdict on involuntary manslaughter and other charges against officer William Porter, accused of failing to secure Gray in the police van and to summon medical help when needed. Williams declared a mistrial and a retrial scheduled to begin on July 7, 2016.[33]

Officer Caesar Goodson, the driver of the van, faced the most serious charges, second-degree murder and other counts, in the case; he was acquitted on June 23. Two other officers, Lt. Brian Rice and Sgt. Alicia White, are awaiting trial on involuntary manslaughter and other counts. Despite the lack of convictions, Shelton has no criticism of the way the case is being handled. "It's being done very methodically and very thoughtfully," he says.[34]

Two of the highest-profile episodes ended with no criminal charges after state grand juries declined to return indictments against the officers involved. In Ferguson, a St. Louis grand jury declined on Nov. 24, 2014, to bring any charges against Ferguson officer Darren Wilson in Michael Brown's death two months earlier; Wilson resigned from the force the next week, blaming threats on his life. In Cleveland, a Cuyahoga County grand jury declined on Dec. 28, 2015, to bring charges against officers Timothy Loehmann or Frank Garmback for the fatal shooting of the young boy Tamir Rice in November 2014. Loehmann and Garmback are facing administrative reviews, but prosecutor Timothy McGinty defended their actions in deciding not to seek an indictment.[35]

Among the most controversial cases, two officers are awaiting trials for fatal shootings in North Charleston, S.C., and Chicago. In Chicago, officer Jason Van Dyke was suspended from the force after his indictment in November 2015 for the shooting death of the teenager Laquan McDonald; no trial date has been set. In North Charleston, former officer Michael Slager is awaiting a state court trial on Oct. 31 for murder in the death of Walter Scott in April 2015; Slager was fired from the force, indicted on the state charge in June 2015, and then indicted on May 11, 2016, on federal civil rights and obstruction of justice counts.[36]

OUTLOOK

Regaining Trust?

When he created the White House task force on policing late in 2014, President Obama stressed the need for public confidence that law enforcement was being administered fairly for each and every community and demographic group. "When any part of the American family does not feel like it is being treated fairly," Obama said, "that's a problem for all of us."[37]

The distrust felt among many in the street turns back on police officers themselves. In the Police Executive Research Forum report on use of force, executive director Wexler writes of what he calls "upheaval" within the policing profession. "Officers who in the past exuded great pride in wearing the badge," Wexler writes, "now feel underappreciated by some members of the public, who seem to question their every move and motive."[38]

Four police chiefs lost their jobs within the past two years as a result of confidence gaps with the African-American communities in their cities that were exposed and widened by fatal encounters with civilians under questionable circumstances. In a report issued in April 2015, the police research group called for "honest conversations about race within the police department and with the public." The report goes on to call for devising enforcement strategies in consultation with affected communities and to criticize stop-and-frisk policies that emphasis the number instead of the quality of the stops.[39]

Mac Donald, the Manhattan Institute expert, complains that the issue of police shootings has been "distorted" by comparing the percentage of black victims with the total population instead of criminal offenders. "Any police killing of an unarmed civilian is a stomach-churning tragedy that police have to do all they can to prevent," she says. But the percentage of black victims — 25 percent, according to the *Washington Post*'s compilation for 2015 — is actually lower than would be projected from the racial breakdown of criminal offenders.

Epp, the University of Kansas expert, credits the Obama task force with "an interesting mix of reform proposals" that "if seriously adopted, would go some distance in addressing the problems of policing today." But he faults the report for treating racial profiling as a problem of individual officers more than one of policy. Butler, the Georgetown law professor, similarly views racial profiling as the result of policies known in police jargon as "order maintenance" — typically deployed in minority neighborhoods.

Withrow, the Texas State professor, expects to see significant changes in police department policies toward minority communities in the coming years. "We're going to see a concerted effort by police departments to engage minority communities in a substantial way," he says.

Police departments will step outside traditional policing and become more of a social actor in the community, Withrow predicts. "They will really attempt to go out and build communities," he continues. "They will do much more than just answer service calls. That is well outside the traditional policing role, but I think that's what we're going to see."

Bueermann, the Police Foundation president, agrees that police departments will be more responsive to community views than in the past. "There is an increasing voice in America about certain policing activities and I think there is an increasing sensitivity on the part of many police departments, of thoughtful, progressive leaders listening to what these people say and trying to make significant organizational changes," he says.

Policing as we have known it has not worked for everybody in this country," Bueermann adds, "and it needs to."

NOTES

1. Kevin Schultz, Vivian Ho, and Kimberly Veklerov, "S.F. police chief out," *The San Francisco Chronicle*, May 20, 2016, p. A1. Background also drawn from Joaquin Palomino and Bill Van Niekerken, "Timeline of Police Chief Greg Suhr's troubled tenure," ibid., p. A8.
2. See Julia Carrie Wong, "San Francisco police chief resigns in wake of shootings and scandals," *The Guardian*, May 19, 2016, http://www.theguardian.com/us-news/2016/may/19/san-francisco-police-greg-suhr-resigns-fatal-shooting-scandal?CMP=share_btn_tw.
3. Quoted in Emily Green, "Inevitable action: Lee had to replace chief to focus on reforms, analysts say," *The San Francisco Chronicle*, May 21, 2016, p. A1.
4. See Joaquin Palomino, "Racial disparities in SF traffic searches raise concerns of bias," *The San Francisco Chronicle*, April 10, 2016, p. A1.
5. Gallup Organization, Race Relations, http://www.gallup.com/poll/1687/race-relations.aspx (accessed June 2016).
6. See Al Baker, "City Police Still Struggle to Follow Stop-and-Frisk Rules, Report Says," *The New York Times*, Feb. 17, 2016, p. A17; J. David Goodman, "Bratton Battles His Predecessor on Crime Tally," ibid., December 30, 2015, p.A1.
7. See Walter Berry and Jacques Billeaud, "Sheriff Joe Arpaio of Arizona found in contempt of court," The Associated Press, May 14, 2016.
8. Joaquin Palomino and Bill Van Niekerken, "Timeline of Police Chief Greg Suhr's troubled tenure," *The San Francisco Chronicle*, May 20, 2016, p. A8.
9. See Kimberly Kindy, Marc Fisher, Julie Tate, and Todd Lindeman, "A Year of Reckoning: Police Fatally Shoot Nearly 1,000 in 2015," *The Washington Post*, December 26, 2015, http://www.washingtonpost.com/sf/investigative/2015/12/26/a-year-of-reckoning-police-fatally-shoot-nearly-1000/. The graphic includes a link to an earlier, related story: Sandhya Somashekhar, Wesley Lowery, Keith L. Alexander, Kimberly Kindy, and Julie Tate, "Black and Unarmed," *The Washington Post*, August 8, 2015, http://www.washingtonpost.com/sf/national/2015/08/08/black-and-unarmed/.
10. Police Executive Research Forum, "Guiding Principles on Use of Force," March 2016, http://www.policeforum.org/assets/guidingprinciples1.pdf, pp. 9, 117. See Chuck Wexler and Scott Thomson, "Making Policing Safer for Everyone," *The New York Times*, March 2, 2016, p. A29. Wexler is executive director of the forum; Thomson, president of the forum, is chief of the Camden County Police Department in New Jersey.

11. See Steve Janoski, "Wyckoff Suspends Police Chief," *The Record* (Bergen County, N.J.), May 4, 2016, p. L01; Salvador Rizzo, "Tough Battle to Eliminate Profiling," ibid., March 27, 2016, p. A1.

12. See David A. Harris, *Profiles in Injustice: Why Racial Profiling Cannot Work* (2002), pp. 53-60 (New Jersey), pp. 60-64 (Maryland).

13. See Matt Apuzzo, "Ferguson Police Routinely Violate Rights of Blacks, Justice Dept. Finds," *The New York Times*, March 3, 2015, http://www.nytimes.com/2015/03/04/us/justice-department-finds-pattern-of-police-bias-and-excessive-force-in-ferguson.html?_r=0.

14. See Jessica Mazzola, "ACLU Demands N.J. Police Track Racial Data," *The Star-Ledger* (Newark, N.J.), April 14, 2016, p. 28.

15. See Eric Dexheimer, Jeremy Schwartz, and Christian McDonald, "Data: DPS searches Hispanics more often," *Austin American-Statesman*, December 6, 2015, p. A1; See Margaret Moffett, "Data show black males more likely to be searched during traffic stops throughout North Carolina," *News and Record* (Greensboro, N.C.), November 22, 2015.

16. See Monitor's "Second Report," February 16, 2016, p.3, http://nypdmonitor.org/resourcesreports/monitor-reports/. For coverage, see Al Baker, "City Police Still Struggle to Follow Stop-and-Frisk Rules, Report Says," *The New York Times*, February 17, 2016, p. A17.

17. See Pervaiz Shallwani and Mark Morales, "NYC Officials Tout New Low in Crime, but Homicide, Rape, Robbery Rose," *The Wall Street Journal*, January 4, 2016, http://www.wsj.com/articles/nyc-officials-tout-new-low-in-crime-but-homicide-rape-robbery-rose-1451959203; J. David Goodman, "Bratton Battles His Predecessor on Crime Tally," *The New York Times*, December 30, 2015, p.A1; "New York Policing, by the Numbers," *The New York Times*, December 28, 2015, p. A18 (editorial).

18. See Mark Berman, "'We have a problem.' Homicides are up again this year in more than two dozen major U.S. cities," *Washington Post* blogs, May 14, 2016, http://www.washingtonpost.com/news/post-nation/wp/2016/05/14/we-have-a-problem-homicides-are-up-again-this-year-in-more-than-two-dozen-major-u-s-cities/.

19. See Mark Berman, "Police agencies say homicides are up this year in major cities," *The Washington Post*, May 16, 2016, p. A4; Eric Lichtblau and Monica Davey, "New Data on Homicide Rates Rekindles a Debate," *The New York Times*, May 14, 2016, p A11.

20. Ames Grawert and James Cullen, "Crime in 2015: A Final Analysis," April 20, 2016, https://www.brennancenter.org/sites/default/files/analysis/Crime_in_2015_A_Final_Analysis.pdf.

21. Quoted in Megan Cassidy, "Arpaio held in contempt," *The Arizona Republic* (Phoenix), May 14, 2016, p. A5. The ACLU of Arizona has a summary of the history of the case, *Ortega-Melendres v. Arpaio*, on its website and a link to the judge's decision: http://www.acluaz.org/sites/default/files/documents/Melendres%20Contempt%20Order%205_13_2016.pdf

22. See Paul W. Valentine, "Md. Settles Lawsuit Over Racial Profiles," *The Washington Post*, January 5, 1995, p. B1; David Kocieniewski, "U.S. Will Monitor New Jersey Police on Race Profiling," *The New York Times*, December 22, 1999, p. B1.

23. See Public Safety Open Data Portal, http://publicsafetydataportal.org/.

24. See Final Report of the President's Task Force on 21st Century Policing, May 2015, http://www.cops.usdoj.gov/PolicingTaskForce. For news coverage, see Julie Hirschfeld Davis and Michael D. Shear, "Obama Puts Focus on Police Success in Struggling City in New Jersey," *The New York Times*, May 19, 2015, p. A11; David Nakamura and Wesley Lowery, "U.S. to ban transfer of some military gear to local police," *The Washington Post*, May 19, 2015, p. A4.

25. Police Executive Research Forum, "Guiding Principles on Use of Force," March 2016, www.policeforum.org/assets/guidingprinciples1.pdf.

26. See Stephen Deere, "New Ferguson chief has no 'magic pill' for curing city's problems," *St. Louis Post-Dispatch*, May 10, 2016, p. A1; U.S.

Department of Justice, "Justice Department and City of Ferguson, Missouri, Resolve Lawsuit with Agreement to Reform Ferguson Police Department and Municipal Court to Ensure Constitutional Policing," March 17, 2016, https://www.justice.gov/opa/pr/justice-department-and-city-ferguson-missouri-resolve-lawsuit-agreement-reform-ferguson.

27. Mark Puente, "Davis stands firm for change: City's police chief begins reforms as he awaits results of Justice Dept. probe," *The Baltimore Sun*, December 6, 2015, p. 1A.

28. See Jeremy Gorner, "City to release materials from police shootings," *Chicago Tribune*, May 29, 2016, p. C14; Jeremy Gorner, "Top cop decries violence, broken justice system," ibid., June 1, 2016, p. C4.

29. See Lizzie Johnson, "S.F. sergeant who killed woman IDd," *The San Francisco Chronicle*, May 28, 2016, p. C1; Vivian Ho, "Lee wants action on police shooting, ibid., May 27, 2016, p. D1.

30. See Daphne Duret and Lawrence Mower, "State attorney charges ex-Gardens cop after grand jury finds fault," *Palm Beach Post*, June 2, 2016, p. 1A; Terry Spencer and Curt Anderson, "Convicting officer in Florida slaying may prove difficult," The Associated Press, June 2, 2016.

31. See Matt Furber and Richard Pérez-Peña, "No Federal Charges for Minneapolis Officers in Fatal Shooting of Black Man," *The New York Times*, June 2, 2016, p. A10.

32. "Police Officers Prosecuted for Use of Deadly Force," *The Washington Post*, April 11, 2015, https://www.washingtonpost.com/graphics/investigations/police-shootings/. The graphic includes a link to related story.

33. See Jean Marbella and Colin Campbell, "Response measured to Nero verdict," *The Baltimore Sun,* May 24, 2016, p. A5; Justin Fenton, "Porter's retrial set for June 13," ibid., December 22, 2015, p. 1A.

34. For other analysis, see Ian Duncan, "Experts say first verdict does not doom cases against five others," *The Baltimore Sun*, May 24, 2016, p. A1.

35. See David Hunn, "No charges for Wilson," *St. Louis Post-Dispatch*, November 25, 2014, p. A1; Cory Shaffer, "No charges for officers," *Plain Dealer* (Cleveland), December 29, 2015, p. A1.

36. See Christy Gutowski, "Backers dispute portrayal of Van Dyke as 'monster,'" *Chicago Tribune*, May 15, 2016, p. C1; John Monk, "Ex-North Charleston officer's indictment: Justice or scapegoating?" *The State* (Columbia, S.C.), May 11, 2016.

37. Quoted in Task Force, op. cit., p. 5.

38. Use of Force, op. cit., p. 4.

39. Police Executive Research Forum, "Constitutional Policing as a Cornerstone of Community Policing," April 2015, pp. 5, 14, http://ric-zai-inc.com/Publications/cops-p324-pub.pdf.

BIBLIOGRAPHY

Books

Del Carmen, Alejandro, *Racial Profiling in America*, **Pearson/Prentice Hall, 2008.**
The chairman of the Department of Criminology and Criminal Justice at the University of Texas-Arlington examines the historical and contemporary perspectives on racial and ethnic profiling in the United States. Includes chapter notes.

Epp, Charles S.; Steven Maynard-Moody, and Donald P. Haider-Markel, *Pulled Over: How Police Stops Define Race and Citizenship*, **University of Chicago Press, 2014.**
Three professors at the University of Kansas in Lawrence present results of research finding that black motorists are five times more likely to be subjected to "investigatory" traffic stops than white drivers. Includes detailed tables, notes. Epp and Maynard-Moody are professors in the School of Public Affairs and Administration and Haider-Markel, a professor of political science.

Glover, Karen S., *Racial Profiling: Research, Racism, and Resistance*, **Rowan & Littlefield, 2009.**
An assistant professor in the Department of Sociology, Criminology and Justice Studies at California State University-San Marcos examines racial profiling from the perspective of critical race theory through interviews

with minority group subjects who had been stopped by police officers. Includes chapter notes.

Harris, David A., *Profiles in Injustice: Why Racial Profiling Cannot Work***, New Press, 2002.**
A professor at the University of Pittsburgh School of Law, who was one of the first to comprehensively cover racial profiling, provides examples and continues with critical arguments on the purported justifications of the practice, as well as its costs and recommendations for reforms. The paperback edition issued in 2003 includes a chapter on post-9/11 ethnic profiling. Includes detailed notes.

Mac Donald, Heather, *Are Cops Racist? How the War Against Police Harms Black Americans***, Ivan R. Dee, 2002 [ebook issued 2010; reprinted 2010].**
A senior fellow at the Manhattan Institute, a conservative think tank, argues in a collection of magazine-length pieces that police do not engage in racial profiling and that the controversy hurts black Americans by impeding policing in minority neighborhoods.

Rice, Stephen K., and Michael D. White (eds.), *Race, Ethnicity, and Policing: New and Essential Readings***, New York University Press, 2010.**
The 22 separate essays on racial and ethnic profiling are divided into four parts: context, methods, research, and future. Rice is an associate professor in the Department of Criminal Justice, Seattle University; White is an associate professor at Arizona State University School of Criminology and Criminal Justice.

Articles

Harris, David A., "Picture This: Body-Worn Video Devices (Head Cams) as Tools for Ensuring Fourth Amendment Compliance by Police," *Texas Tech Law Review***, Vol. 43, No. 1 (2010), pp. 357-372, http://www.nlg-npap.org/reports/picture-body-worn-video-devices-head-cams-tools-ensuring-fourth-amendment-compliance-police.**
A University of Pittsburgh law professor proposes making video and audio recording of search-and-seizure incidents, as is done already in several cities, a routine police practice.

Williams, Rich, "Under Review: Policing in America," *State Legislatures Magazine***, December 2015, www.ncsl.org/research/civil-and-criminal-justice/policing-under-review.aspx.**
The article in the monthly magazine of the National Conference of State Legislatures details work by state lawmakers to address issues of racial profiling and use of force by law enforcement agencies.

Withrow, Brian L., and Jeffrey D. Dailey, "Racial Profiling and the Law," in Craig Hemmens (ed.), *Current Legal Issues in Criminal Justice* **(Oxford University Press, forthcoming 2014).**
The 11,000-word chapter gives a comprehensive, up-to-date account of law and litigation over racial profiling from the 1960s to the present. Withrow, a former Texas state trooper, is a professor of criminal justice at Texas State University in San Marcos; Dailey is an assistant professor of homeland and border security at Angelo State University, in San Angelo.

Reports and Studies

"Racial Profiling and the Use of Suspect Classifications in Law Enforcement Policy," Judiciary Subcommittee on the Constitution, Civil Rights, and Civil Liberties, U.S. House of Representatives, June 17, 2010, serial no. 111-131, https://www.gpo.gov/fdsys/pkg/CHRG-111hhrg56956/pdf/CHRG-111hhrg56956.pdf.
The hearing included testimony and statements from six witnesses, including representatives of the American Civil Liberties Union, Sikh Coalition, and Muslim Advocates. The committee website includes video and print transcript.

On the Web

"Fatal Force," a Washington Post database, https://www.washingtonpost.com/graphics/national/police-shootings-2016/.
The newspaper gathered information on 990 police killings in 2015 and 390 through first five months of 2016, with detailed statistical analyses: an invaluable resource.

For More Information

American Civil Liberties Union, 125 Broad St., New York, NY 10004; 212-549-2500; www.aclu.org. Monitors and sometimes brings lawsuits in cases involving racial profiling, use of force and other police-practices issues.

Fraternal Order of Police, Grand Lodge, 1410 Donelson Pike, A-17, Nashville, TN 37217; 615-399-0900; www.grandlodgefop.org. Largest membership organization representing rank-and-file law enforcement officers.

International Association of Chiefs of Police, 515 North Washington St., Alexandria, VA 22314; 703-836-6767; www.theiacp.org. Represents operating chief executives of international, federal, state and local law enforcement agencies of all sizes.

Major Cities Chiefs Police Association, https://majorcitieschiefs.com/about.php. Represents chiefs from 63 large American city or county police organizations.

Mexican American Legal Defense and Educational Fund, 634 S. Spring St., Los Angeles, CA; 213-629-2512; www.maldef.org. A leading civil rights organization for Latinos.

Muslim Advocates, 315 Montgomery St., 8th floor, San Francisco, CA 94104; 415-692-1484; www.muslimadvocates.org. Civil rights organization for Muslims, Arab and South Asian Americans.

NAACP, 4805 Mt. Hope Dr., Baltimore MD 21215; 410-580-5777; www.naacp.org. Century-old civil rights organization for African-Americans.

National Sheriffs' Association, 1450 Duke St., Alexandria, VA 22314; 1-800-424-7827; www.sheriffs.org. Represents and assists sheriffs' offices nationwide through education, training and information resources.

Police Foundation, 1201 Connecticut Ave., N.W., Washington, DC 20036-2636; 202-833-1460; www.policefoundation.org. Established by the Ford Foundation in 1970; sponsors research to support innovation and improvement in policing.

7

Fighting Gangs

Christina Hoag

Jorge Maya, an Army veteran who fought in Afghanistan, grew up among gang members in Chicago. Now he is a member of the Urban Warriors, a YMCA-sponsored program that seeks to reduce gang membership by pairing military veterans with youngsters who also grew up surrounded by gang members. Maya's tattoo shows the handprint of one of his daughters.

From *CQ Researcher*, October 9, 2015.

In a predawn raid in November 2014, authorities in Rockland County, N.Y., just north of Manhattan, arrested 26 members of a local gang affiliated with the Bloods, a notorious Los Angeles-based gang known for its violence.

But violence had nothing to do with the charges against the M-Block Crew — grand larceny and bank fraud. Police said the gang had amassed $500,000 from 14 banks by passing fake checks and phony money orders.[1]

The gang's success in targeting financial institutions is a sign of gangs' growing sophistication, experts say. "It's not just drugs and guns anymore," says Jorja Leap, a professor of social welfare at the University of California, Los Angeles (UCLA) who researches gangs. "Gangs are getting more astute."

Gangs pose a growing threat to public safety in the United States as their numbers rise and the range of their activities expands, many law enforcement agents and researchers say. In addition, gangs are becoming more technologically sophisticated, using the Internet to extend their reach and social media to recruit members. Gangs also are no longer just a big-city scourge. They are turning up in smaller cities, suburbs and even rural areas, where they are committing the same kinds of violent acts traditionally confined to urban cores. And gangs are becoming harder for police to detect because some are shunning such traditional gang markers as distinctive clothing colors, tattoos and hand signals.

Not all experts say the gang threat is growing, however. Gangs are simply evolving as society changes and law enforcement steps up its anti-gang efforts, says Alex Alonso, a Los Angeles-based gang researcher who runs Street-Gangs.com, a gang-issues website.

But many in law enforcement cite statistics showing that total gang membership, including street, prison and motorcycle gangs, is increasing nationwide. In 2011, membership totaled an estimated 1.4 million — up 40 percent from 2009, according to a report by the National Gang Intelligence Center (NGIC), a Justice Department unit that surveys several federal law enforcement agencies, including the FBI. During that two-year period, the report said, the number of U.S. gangs increased more than 50 percent — from 20,000 to 33,000.[2] *

Officials also point to a spike in homicides and shootings in more than 30 cities in 2015, reversing a years-long decline in violence.[4]

"Gangs are responsible for an average of 48 percent of violent crime in most jurisdictions and up to 90 percent in several others," according to the NGIC. "Major cities and suburban areas experience the most gang-related violence. Local neighborhood-based gangs and drug crews continue to pose the most significant criminal threat in most communities."

Deeming the situation urgent, big-city police chiefs met in Washington in August to discuss possible reasons for the surge.[5] In a survey of the 35 members in the Major Cities Chiefs Association, half, including the District of Columbia, reported an increase in gang and retaliatory violence.[6] Other key findings:

- 40 percent of respondents reported multiple firearms at shooting scenes, which resulted in more victims; and
- 30 percent saw spreading use of synthetic drugs as contributing to the violence.

The problem spans the nation, including the three biggest U.S. cities, all of which have entrenched gangs, law enforcement officials said. New York's killings were up 9 percent from January to August 2015 over the year-earlier period, while Chicago's were up 20 percent.[7] In Los Angeles, homicides were up 7 percent, and overall gang violence was up 15 percent.[8]

Smaller cities are also seeing a spike in violence. By early September, North Carolina's Charlotte-Mecklenburg region had had 43 homicides this year, more than in all of 2014. Over Labor Day weekend alone, police there reported 12 gang shootings that killed five people, including a 7-year-old boy.[9]

In Tampa, Fla., gangs are driving a rising murder rate, according to the Hillsborough County Sheriff's Department: 25 homicides occurred in the first eight months of 2015, compared with 28 in all of 2014.[10]

Experts say gangs are becoming more dangerous because of several trends.

Technology, they say, is exacerbating gang violence and helping to glamorize the lifestyle because it allows gang influence to spread faster and wider than when a gang issued a challenge to a rival the old-fashioned way — by scrawling graffiti in its rival's turf.

Gangs use their own websites, YouTube videos, Facebook and Twitter postings to spread gang culture. So do rap music, music videos and movies, says Al Valdez, a criminal justice professor at the University of California, Irvine.

Gang violence has always been cyclical, with rivalries flaring up unexpectedly, often for unknown reasons, Valdez says. "[But] technology has allowed gang culture to spread all over America."

Meanwhile, more gangs are seeking to avoid attention from authorities by pursuing nonviolent activities, such as prostitution and fraud — crimes that are lower priorities for police. Such activities are lucrative for the gangs, producing profits rather than headlines, says UCLA's Leap.

Leap says she has even encountered gang members who have moved away from their gang turf to evade police detection. "They don't live in the projects," she says. "They live outside the city and commute in."

Gangs also are using fewer visible tattoos, gang-style clothing, colors and hand signals, while communicating their business clandestinely via the Internet. "They call it going 'lo pro' for low profile," Valdez says.

Women and girls are participating more in gang crime as well, even taking on leadership roles, Leap says. Their participation can help gangs evade

---

*The 2011 data are the most recent available because the center's "2013 National Gang Report" did not contain any estimate as it received 25 percent fewer responses to its survey from law enforcement.[3]

Street Gangs on the Rebound

About 850,000 people belonged to 30,700 street gangs in 2012, according to the latest data from the U.S. Department of Justice. Gang membership and the number of gangs generally fell from 1996 through the early 2000s but then began edging higher, returning in 2012 to roughly their mid-1990s level.

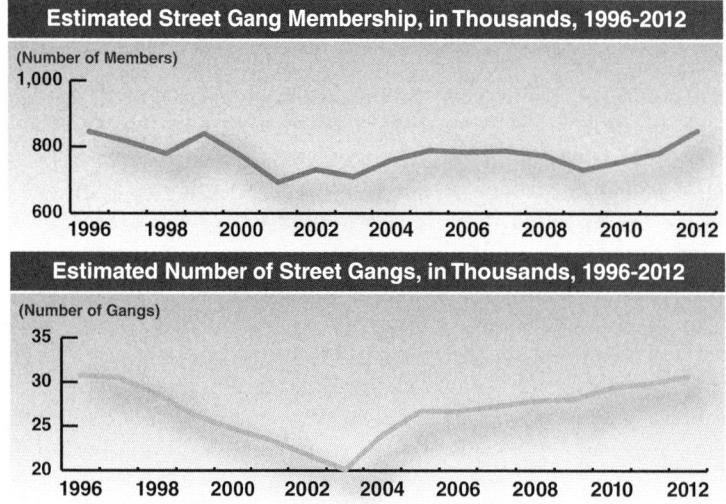

Source: "Measuring the Extent of Gang Problems," National Gang Center, December 2014, http://tinyurl.com/pov6n4o

detection because police often overlook females as potential criminals.

"The younger generation is coming up. They are savvier, more sophisticated and more lethal," she says.

Definitions of gangs differ among state and federal law enforcement agencies. The FBI's definition is most commonly used: A gang is a group of three or more persons with a common interest, bond or activity characterized by criminal or delinquent conduct.[11] Gangs encompass three types of criminal groups, according to the National Gang Intelligence Center: street gangs, which are predominantly black and Latino, are the most common, constituting 88 percent of total gang membership; prison gangs (9.5 percent), which operate inside correctional institutions; and outlaw motorcycle gangs (2.5 percent).[12]

Authorities do not consider organized crime syndicates such as the Mafia and Mexican drug trafficking cartels to be gangs. Such organizations have much older members and operate as hierarchical, highly structured, profit-driven businesses, experts say.

Some consider biker gangs, which typically have older, lifetime members, many of whom work in legitimate jobs, as better fitting the organized crime category. "The big 10 outlaw motorcycle gangs are, in fact, at that level," says George Knox, founder of the National Gang Crime Research Center, a private nonprofit database on gang issues. "They have written bylaws [and] their own lawyers; they're highly organized." Biker gangs are primarily white or Latino, although black motorcycle groups are becoming more numerous.[13]

Prison gangs — including the white supremacist Aryan Brotherhood, the Mexican Mafia and the Black Guerrilla Family — operate from inside correctional institutions, directing operations of affiliated street gangs.[14] Because members are already incarcerated and operate with minimal visibility, they are hard for police to thwart.[15]

Gangs have proved intractable against get-tough policies that law enforcement officials and policymakers have employed in recent decades.

Federal prosecutors can use the Racketeer Influenced and Corrupt Organizations (RICO) Act, passed in 1970 to prosecute the Mafia, to break up street gangs. At least eight states also allow cities to declare gangs a public nuisance and to use restraining orders — called gang injunctions — to bar members from congregating in public.[16] Many states have other anti-gang laws, such as California's 1988 Street Terrorism Enforcement and Prevention Act, which lengthens prison time for those convicted of gang-related crimes.[17]

Many experts say the answer to stopping gangs lies in preventing youths with no hope for the future from joining gangs by offering them anti-poverty programs that boost education and job training. "What drives the gang is issues of the underclass," says Knox. "But there's no consensus on what to do."

As gangs grow in size and influence, these are some of the questions that law enforcement officials, researchers and policymakers are asking:

Is the gang threat growing?

Gangs have long resorted to counterfeiting, extortion and other sideline activities to supplement income from their lucrative bread-and-butter business of drug trafficking. But some experts say today's gangs pose a greater threat because they are expanding their ancillary crimes, such as credit card fraud and prostitution, to evade detection by law enforcement.

Nonviolent crimes are generally a lower priority for police and often require complex investigations by under-resourced departments. For gangs, they also have the advantage of carrying less severe penalties if culprits are caught, specialists note.

"It's safer, and they make a lot more money," says Wes McBride, western spokesman for the Arizona-based National Alliance of Gang Investigators' Associations.

Others say gangs' criminal portfolios are not really broadening; rather, reporting of crime as "gang-related" is growing. Alonso of StreetGangs.com notes that cities can obtain extra funding to fight gang crime through various state and federal programs. Since 2001, for instance, the U.S. Justice Department's Project Safe Neighborhoods program has awarded $2 billion to police departments to help finance anti-gang initiatives.[18]

"More cities are reporting gang activity than ever before, but there's [money] in reporting gangs," he says. "Does Paducah, Ky., really have gangs, or do they want more resources?"

Scott Decker, a criminologist at Arizona State University, cites a different problem: The arrest of a gang member in connection with crimes such as prostitution or fraud does not necessarily mean a gang is involved, but police nevertheless tend to label such crimes as gang activities or gang-related.

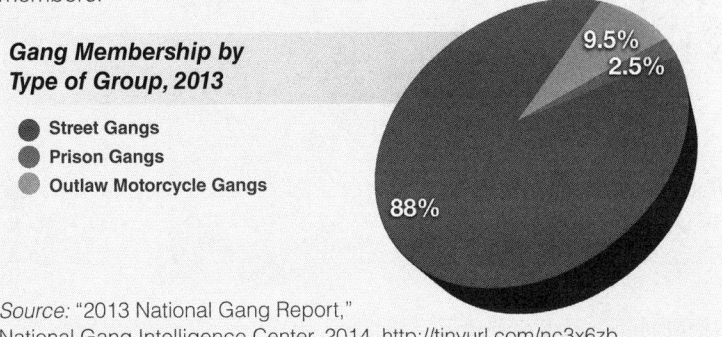

Street Gangs Most Prevalent

Street gangs dominated U.S. gang membership in 2013, according to the latest data from the National Gang Intelligence Center. Prison and outlaw motorcycle gangs accounted for about one in eight gang members.

Gang Membership by Type of Group, 2013

- Street Gangs
- Prison Gangs
- Outlaw Motorcycle Gangs

88% / 9.5% / 2.5%

Source: "2013 National Gang Report," National Gang Intelligence Center, 2014, http://tinyurl.com/nc3x6zb

The essence of street gangs has not changed, he says: Members' average age remains 17, and their principal activity is picking fights with rivals. "We've really seen a stabilization of the magnitude of gangs and their involvement in crime," Decker says.

Gauging gang crime is also difficult because of the problem of determining whether members acted on their own or at the behest of the gang. The 2014 "Texas Gang Threat Assessment Report," for instance, cited prostitution both by gangs acting collectively and gang members acting individually, making it tough to disentangle the two.[19]

In addition, the great variety of gangs makes categorizing their activities challenging. While the majority of street gangs are adolescent, turf-based groups that engage in "disorganized crime," as Decker calls it, a smaller number have older members who are more interested in profits than brawling, and they do not ally themselves with street gangs.

Street gangs are "too unreliable," McBride says. Yet authorities consider crime by these higher-level groups "gang crime."

Some gang crime goes unreported: Asian gangs, for example, keep a low profile, are not territorial and victimize members of their own communities, who tend not to report the crimes because of fear and language barriers, Valdez says.

Community activists promote peace among rival gangs in an area of Los Angeles known as "death alley" for its high homicide rate. Los Angeles emerged as the nation's modern gang capital in the 1970s. Black youths searching for both identity and money-making opportunities formed the Crips, while a splinter faction established the Bloods. The two groups developed an intense feud that continues today. Latino gangs in the city also strengthened during this period.

Despite these difficulties in tracking crime, evidence abounds of gang activities. Law enforcement reports indicate that human trafficking — which includes sex trafficking, forced labor and migrant smuggling — is a growth business for gangs. The 2013 National Gang Report said some 25 gangs became involved in sex and human trafficking to diversify their income.[20] Meanwhile, gang involvement in migrant smuggling along the Mexican border is a growing worry, according to the 2014 Texas Gang Threat Assessment Report.[21]

Global Centurion, an Arlington, Va.,-based foundation that is fighting human trafficking, said it has discovered more than 200 cases in which gang members were involved in human trafficking but noted that law enforcement officials largely overlook gangs' involvement in such crimes.[22]

Laura Lederer, executive director of Global Centurion, said human trafficking is becoming increasingly profitable. "Unlike selling drugs and weapons," she pointed out, "a human body may be sold repeatedly, [and] demand remains high, particularly for young girls."[23]

Some criminologists, however, say that although a few gangs engage in human trafficking, fraud and other crimes such as bootlegging IDs and DVDs, the problem is not widespread. But because it is out of the norm it attracts attention, they say.

Acts of violence remain at the heart of gang crime because that's how gangs derive their status, they note. "Violence is the language of gangs," says Valdez of the University of California. "It's still, 'The more you fear me, the more you respect me.'"

McBride says gangs have spread to small cities and rural areas in recent years, but the increase apparently is not systematic. Gangs are not dispatching members to form affiliates in a bid to win new territories, but individuals may move for employment purposes or to get away from a gang and end up forming a new one, he notes.

Alonso disputes the notion that gangs are a growing menace; they are simply changing with the times, he says. "It's an extension of, 'As the community goes, so does the gang,'" he says. "Everything's cyclical crime-wise."

Is banning street gangs from congregating an effective anti-gang strategy?

In 1987, a Los Angeles prosecutor hit upon a new legal tool to break up street gangs — banning gang members from congregating in public because they are a "public nuisance."[24]

The tactic, known as imposing "gang injunctions," has become common in California, Texas, Utah, Illinois, Florida, Minnesota, North Carolina and elsewhere to get gangs off street corners. But the injunctions generate debate over their effectiveness and potential harm to civil liberties.[25]

Injunctions — basically restraining orders filed by city or county prosecutors and approved by a judge — impose a variety of restrictions in a defined area. They can include a nighttime curfew or a ban on gang members associating with other gang members in public, wearing of clothing with gang-related symbols or colors, display of gang-related tattoos and a host of already-outlawed activity, such as using or selling drugs. If gang members violate the order, which are usually permanent, they can be cited for contempt of court.

Proponents say injunctions restore neighborhoods by clearing out gangs that intimidate residents walking along certain blocks, going to a corner store or playing in a park. They can also clean up streets by preventing graffiti and litter as well as noise at gang hangouts.

"When you drive crime off the streetscape, that has enormous dividends," says Lawrence Rosenthal, a law professor at Chapman University in Orange, Calif.

Opponents counter that injunctions simply drive gangs underground or force them to move while imposing significant restrictions on people's lives without affording them the chance to clear their name. "Most people stay in a gang two to three years, tops, between the ages of 15 to 18. Then they're on these injunctions for the rest of their lives, which seems pretty extreme without some periodic review," says Caitlin Sanderson, a staff attorney for the American Civil Liberties Union of Southern California.

Some type of hearing, either by prosecutors or courts, should be held to allow defendants to show evidence that they have left gang life and deserve to be removed from the injunction, she says.

Research shows that injunctions can make communities safer. A 2002 study by a University of Chicago urban policy professor who analyzed eight years of crime data found a 5 to 10 percent drop in violent crime in neighborhoods around Los Angeles with injunctions.[26] A 2011 study by a criminal justice professor at Worcester University and a San Diego County District Attorney's Office gang investigator showed a 14 percent drop in police calls in 25 Southern California injunction areas, with a drop of nearly 12 percent in serious-crime calls.[27]

Courts have upheld injunctions as constitutional. In a 1997 decision that has become a standard for prosecutors seeking injunctions, the California Supreme Court ruled that the First Amendment right to free association applies primarily to groups seeking religious and political expression. It does not extend to groups that plan to deprive others of their lawful rights by committing crime, the court said.[28]

Opponents, however, have successfully challenged the fairness of the injunctions.

In 2013, the Utah Supreme Court overturned an order barring 450 members of the Ogden Trece gang from congregating within a 25-square-mile area encompassing most of the city of Ogden because the suspected gang members had not been properly served with the injunction, says John Mejia, legal director of the American Civil Liberties Union of Utah. Ogden has not reinstated the injunction. "It was a poorly disguised attempt to exile [minority] youth from Ogden," he says.

In 2013, a federal appellate court struck down an injunction in Orange County, Calif., because people on the gang list had not been granted due process to challenge their designation as a gang member.[29] Police and prosecutors typically rely on their own discretion in drawing up such lists. Critics argue that this allows prosecutors to cast a wide net that can ensnare nongang members who may dress like gang members or be relatives of gang members and former members.

"It can be a violation to attend a family party with relatives who are or have been members of the same gang," says Sean Kennedy, executive director of the Center for Juvenile Law & Policy at Loyola Law School in Los Angeles. "It can also be a violation to study or work late because you will be traveling after curfew. The problem is especially troublesome because one remains on the gang injunction list long after he has 'aged out' of gang activities."

Some cities, including San Francisco, hold hearings for people on the gang list before the injunction takes effect, and Los Angeles allows people to present evidence that they are not in a gang, Sanderson says. "Injunctions tend to perpetuate the cycle of victimizing youths of color," she says. "They're not a good use of resources."

Some observers say injunctions boil down to the greater good for society vs. the civil liberties of a few. When someone is mistakenly identified as a gang member, that can and should be dealt with, says Stephen Morreale, a criminal justice professor at Worcester University in Massachusetts, but that doesn't mean cities should eliminate injunctions as an anti-gang tool.

"You don't throw the baby out with the bath water. Injunctions do reduce crime, at least in the short term, and they do disrupt the gang," Morreale says. "The more gangs get hassled for the little things, the less time they have for the big things."

Can former gang members help quell street violence?

When Anthony Porter turned 46, he came to a realization: He had spent nearly half his life in prison in what had become a ceaseless cycle of crime and punishment for a variety of drugs and weapons charges. He knew he had to change his life.

FBI Tracks Gang Activity

The FBI's Safe Streets program coordinates 163 teams of federal, state and local law enforcement officials who use wiretaps, financial analysis and other methods to investigate street gangs for racketeering and firearm- and drug-related crimes.

Gangs Targeted by FBI Safe Streets Program, by Region

Northeast
Latin Kings
Neighborhood-based gangs
Sureños
18th Street
MS-13
United Blood Nation

Southeast
Black Guerrilla Family
Crips
Folk Nation
Hells Angels
Latin Kings
Neighborhood-based gangs
Sureños
18th Street
MS-13
United Blood Nation

North Central
Bloods
Black P Stones
Crips
Gangster Disciples
Latin Kings
Neighborhood-based gangs
Norteños
Sureños
Vatos Locos

South Central
Barrio Azteca
Latin Kings
Neighborhood-based gangs
Sureños
18th Street
MS-13
Tango Blast
Texas Mexican Mafia
Texas Syndicate

West
Black Guerrilla Family
Bloods
Crips
Gangster Disciples
Mexican Mafia
Neighborhood-based gangs
Norteños
Sureños
18th Street
MS-13
Vagos

Source: "2013 National Gang Report," National Gang Intelligence Center, 2014, p. 70, http://tinyurl.com/nc3x6zb; "Violent Gang Task Forces," Federal Bureau of Investigation, undated, http://tinyurl.com/p4vf4k6; "Folk Nation Sets," Florida Department of Corrections, undated, http://tinyurl.com/oe7c2lp

"I was a true, hard-core gangbanger. I'd come home from prison and go wild in the streets against my enemies, the Crips, and go back to prison," says Porter, now 52, of Inglewood, Calif. With his mother in a gang and his father in prison, he says he didn't know any better: "It was just the environment that I was growing up in."

After his mother was shot and he saw several children get killed as innocent bystanders, he decided to use his experience as a gang member to do good: He became a gang interventionist working to stop the cycle of retaliation that drives gang violence.

Most often former gang members, gang interventionists arrive at the scenes of shootings ready to control crowds of onlookers, console grieving relatives and calm the victim's vengeful "homeboys."

"Their work is outside the [crime scene] tape," says Los Angeles Police Sgt. Curtis Woodle, a three-decade veteran of the city's gang-riddled Southside. "They do things that I, as a police officer, cannot do."

Gang interventionists work in several jurisdictions, including Seattle and Tacoma, Wash., and the District of Columbia. The model, which started in the 1990s, uses reformed gang members as community peacekeepers. Their activities range from mediating gang disputes and quelling rumors that can drive retribution to providing security for gang funerals, hospitalized victims and children walking to school in gang neighborhoods.

The concept hinges on former members' credibility with gangs, which police and social workers do not have. But problems can arise because interventionists must remain in contact with gangs, yet stay out of their criminal activities. Some do not.

Skeptics say intervention programs, many of which are run by ex-felons and financed publicly, can serve as fronts for gang activities. In July 2015, for example, Baltimore suspended its independent Safe Streets intervention program after police found guns and drugs in its office and arrested two employees.

It wasn't the first problem with the program. In 2010, a task force investigated allegations that Safe Streets was tied to the Black Guerrilla Family gang, but was unable to substantiate the accusations. Three years later, two of the program's outreach workers were arrested on drug and weapons charges.[30] Despite the problems, city officials consider Safe Streets successful, saying it remediated 136 incidents in the first half of 2015 that could have led to retaliation.[31]

In Chicago, the city in 2013 did not renew its year-long CeaseFire program, featured in a PBS "Frontline" show called "The Interrupters." Six of CeaseFire's 300 interrupters had returned to crime, reported the program director, who himself was arrested on domestic violence charges that were later dropped.[32]

Specialists say it can be difficult to determine when a gang member is sincere about leaving the criminal life because loyalty runs deep, often leading to lifetime affiliations although not necessarily active participation with gangs. "I'm not big on gang intervention because I'm not sure what an ex-gang member is," says McBride, a retired 26-year gang investigator with the Los Angeles County Sheriff's Department.

After problems surfaced with four city-funded intervention programs in Los Angeles in 2008-09 — including financial improprieties and the arrests of three interventionists on robbery, weapons and drugs charges — the city started a training course to weed out insincere interventionists and to school interventionists in topics such as negotiating and ethics.[33]

Research is scarce on the efficacy of intervention programs. A 2009 Northwestern University study of seven Chicago neighborhoods where CeaseFire interrupters worked showed mixed results. CeaseFire efforts resulted in a 16 to 21 percent decline in reports of gunshots in three neighborhoods; a decline in a fourth neighborhood was found to probably result from CeaseFire's work. But in three other areas the program had little or no effect on the number of gunshot reports, the study found.[34]

Some argue that the supposed successes of intervention are misleading. While interventionists can stop immediate violence, there's no guarantee that the cessation will last, says Decker of Arizona State University.

"If it holds down one retaliation, what happens to that retaliation in a week, a month, a year if [the gang members] don't have a job?" he says. Rehabilitation programs that offer jobs and skills training are a more permanent path to disrupting gang violence, Decker adds.

Proponents say it's unfair to expect interventionists to resolve such a long-entrenched social ill and note that thwarting even one retaliation can save numerous lives. "Interventionists aren't going to resolve a 40- to 50-year process of gang warfare," says Leap of UCLA. "[Those] are unrealistic expectations."

Interventionists can also be role models and mentors as no one else can, others say. Gangs "are very guarded as to who they let into their community," says Robert Hernandez, a senior lecturer at the University of Southern California, who teaches a course on gangs. "It's that trust factor that interventionists have."

LAPD's Woodle says police were initially wary about intervention, but it has become accepted. Now when something gang-related happens, "the captains and lieutenants ask, 'Have you contacted the intervention people?'" he says. "It's 21st-century policing."

Porter, who has undergone training as an interventionist, says it's one way he can make up for the harm he caused as a gang member. "I helped destroy the community. I was part of the problem, so I have the responsibility to make it better," he says.

BACKGROUND

Immigrant Gangs

Criminal gangs have been a scourge of society for centuries. Historians have tracked some of the earliest recorded gangs to loose bands of highwaymen operating in England in the 1600s and say such bands could have been in existence as far back as the 12th century.

Signs of more structured gangs, such as today's groups, appeared in London in the 17th century. They called themselves distinctive names such as the Mims, Hectors, Bugles and Dead Boys; wore ribbons of different colors to distinguish their factions; and established rivalries and fought among themselves while engaging in vandalism, such as destroying taverns and breaking windows.[35]

In the United States, gangs emerged in the colonies around 1783, just as the American Revolution was ending, but they were not criminal in nature. Rather, they were neighborhood groups fighting for territory in a generally more violent environment as the war wound down.[36]

Criminally motivated gangs took hold several decades later with the arrival of waves of poor European immigrants who formed ethnic gangs for protection and resorted to crime to make money. Since then, U.S. gang formation has largely been tied to immigration and to ethnic and racial divisions.[37]

As the initial stop for most European immigrants, New York City became the country's gang hub. Its first major gang, the Forty Thieves, emerged around 1825 on Manhattan's slum-ridden Lower East Side, then called Five Points and inhabited by low-skilled English, Irish and German laborers. The Forty Thieves had a defined

Six-year-old Elinyah Cavitt rests beside the casket of her father Ervin Devaunt Cavitt, who was shot and killed during an argument at a party that may have been gang related. His father, Jerald "Pee" Cavitt, is a prominent gang intervention worker in Los Angeles.

hierarchy, was known for violence and engaged in criminal enterprises.

In the ensuing decades, Five Points became home to a host of criminal gangs, many dominated by Irish immigrants, which also became involved in local politics. For a price, a gang would deliver sympathetic voters to the polls in city elections and likewise keep unsympathetic ones away.[38]

Chicago, the destination for many job-seeking immigrants, became the next gang center. In the latter half of the 19th century, the city saw a rise in Irish gangs who preyed on Polish, Jewish and German immigrants as well as blacks. From the 1870s on, Chicago gangs thrived on political patronage networks run by ward politicians.[39]

After the turn of the century, gang influence declined in the major cities. The highly structured Italian Mafia took control of many illicit businesses, including bootlegging during Prohibition, and second- and third-generation members moved to the suburbs.

Postwar Gangs

In the 1930s and '40s, Mexican immigrants formed gangs in Los Angeles, mostly on the city's east side. Gang historians note some key differences between these gangs and gangs elsewhere: Latino gangs established the concept of a gang's attachment to a neighborhood, or *barrio* in Spanish, and the use of graffiti to claim that neighborhood.[40]

With the help of two watershed events, Mexican gangs gathered widespread community support in Latino neighborhoods of East Los Angeles. One was the 1942 Sleepy Lagoon murder, in which 12 members of the 38th Street gang were convicted of killing a Mexican youngster, following a trial the community regarded as a kangaroo court.[41] The conviction was overturned a year later.

In 1943, the so-called Zoot Suit riots erupted — first in Los Angeles but later in other cities — when military personnel attacked Mexican gang members wearing "zoot suits" (baggy pants and tailored jackets with wide lapels). The service members, many of whom stripped the Mexicans of their suits in the middle of the street, felt it was unpatriotic to wear the extravagantly tailored outfits in wartime. The Mexican community viewed the riots as discriminatory.[42]

Before and after World War II, Los Angeles and major Northern cities saw the arrival of massive numbers of Southern blacks seeking jobs and a life free from discriminatory Jim Crow laws. Puerto Ricans and other Caribbean immigrants also arrived in New York and along the East Coast.

They were, however, met with restrictive covenants that barred blacks from buying homes in certain areas and other forms of housing discrimination that shunted them into highly segregated inner-city ghettoes.[43] Over the next decades, cities sought to house the poor in high-rise apartment blocks that became known as "projects," which formed dense concentrations of urban poverty. Both the ghettoes and housing projects created ripe conditions for gangs to flourish.[44]

Sociologist Sudhir Venkatesh studied gangs in one such project in the late 1980s, Chicago's infamous Robert Taylor Homes. The complex comprised 4,400 apartments housing 30,000 people, 90 percent of whom were on welfare. The project, demolished between 1998 and 2007, was controlled by the Black Kings gang, which engaged in drug dealing, extortion, prostitution, selling stolen goods and other schemes. "It was outlaw capitalism, and it ran hot, netting small fortunes for the bosses of the various gangs," Venkatesh wrote.[45]

Prison gangs also got their start during the postwar period. The white Aryan Brotherhood and Latino Mexican Mafia, which emerged in the California prison system in the late 1940s and '50s, respectively, endure today. From its prison base, the Mexican Mafia controls some 100,000

CHRONOLOGY

1800s *Immigration gives rise to ethnic and racially based gangs in U.S. cities.*

1820s The Forty Thieves, the nation's first gang, is formed in New York, consisting mostly of Irish immigrants. The Five Points area in Manhattan's Lower East Side becomes home to several gangs, many of which become involved in local politics.

1860s Chinese gangs control the U.S. opium trade. Chicago's first gangs develop among Irish, German and Lithuanian immigrants.

1900s-1950s *Sicilian Mafia eclipses urban street gangs as a criminal threat; black and Hispanic gangs form after World War II.*

1914 The Mafia, or La Cosa Nostra, begins controlling business through extortion and racketeering.

1915 New York City police declare first war on gangs and the Mafia.

1919 Al Capone moves to Chicago to evade police crackdown in New York and becomes one of the most violent gangsters in U.S. history; in 1931 he is convicted of tax evasion. . . . Prohibition fuels bootlegging by ethnic criminal gangs and the Mafia.

1943 Tensions between Mexican-American gangs and white servicemen spark the Zoot Suit riots in Los Angeles.

1950s Black and Hispanic gangs emerge in New York, Chicago and other Northern cities following the migration northward of Southern blacks and immigration by Caribbean islanders. The Mexican Mafia gang forms in California prisons.

1960s-1970s *Gangs become involved in the drug trade as distributors for importers.*

1964 White inmates at California's San Quentin prison form the racist Aryan Brotherhood gang.

1970 Passage of Racketeer Influenced Corrupt Organizations (RICO) Act allows prosecutors to go after organized crime and gangs.

1980s-1990s *Central America's civil wars lead to massive U.S. immigration and gang formation. The crack cocaine epidemic fuels gang drug wars.*

1980s Salvadoran immigrants in Los Angeles form the Mara Salvatrucha (MS-13) gang, which spreads across the U.S.

1987 Los Angeles enacts first "gang injunction," limiting the ability of gang members to congregate in public.

1996 Illegal Immigration Reform and Immigrant Responsibility Act leads to deportation of thousands of foreign-born gang members convicted of felonies.

2000s-Present *U.S. deportees establish MS-13 and 18th Street gangs in Central America; subsequent violence leads to massive migration to the United States.*

2000 Somali immigrants form gangs in Minneapolis and establish sex trafficking operations in the Midwest.

2005 Congress forms National Gang Intelligence Center to coordinate law enforcement's anti-gang efforts.

2009 Using RICO, Los Angeles conducts largest gang bust in U.S. history, after indicting 192 members of the Varrio Hawaiian Gardens, a Mexican-American street gang.

2010 The U.S. Justice Department's Criminal Division establishes the Organized Crime and Gang Section to coordinate federal efforts against gangs and the Mafia.

2014 After 30,000 California inmates stage a hunger strike against indefinite solitary confinement for gang leaders, officials scale back the practice.

2015 Several U.S. House members reintroduce bipartisan Prison Reduction Through Opportunities, Mentoring, Intervention, Support and Education (Youth PROMISE) Act to fund gang prevention and intervention programs.

Even Military Bases Are Vulnerable to Gangs

"The threat is too serious to discount."

Street corners and biker bars may be their usual haunts, but gang members also are cropping up on military bases. For example:

- In February 2015, an active duty Air Force captain serving at Fort Minot in North Dakota received 25 years in prison for running an off-base underage prostitution ring. The Air Force identified him as the leader of a violent street gang.[1]
- In 2012 a former Air Force senior airman was sentenced to 22 years in prison for the 2005 beating death of an Army sergeant who died while being initiated into a chapter of the Gangster Disciples, a gang with Chicago roots, near Ramstein Air Base in Germany. The airman, who was on active duty at the time of the killing, was the sixth soldier sentenced in the case.[2]

The gang problem is "not often addressed by military leadership because it's not seen as a discipline issue, but it's evolved as a problem," says Carter F. Smith, a lecturer at Middle Tennessee State University in Murfreesboro who served in the Army's Criminal Investigation Division.

The presence of gang members in the armed services is neither widespread nor organized, experts say — indeed, some dismiss the threat altogether. But many gang specialists say the issue nonetheless warrants close attention because gangs could commit violence or crimes at defense facilities. In addition, experts worry that gang members could exert power over other soldiers in ways that erode unit cohesion or supplant loyalty to the military with loyalty to the gang.

"The threat of gang members joining the military is too serious to discount," said the "2013 National Gang Report."[3]

The report identified 54 gangs with members who had served in the military. What's more, it said 16 law enforcement agencies reported a gang presence on military installations in their jurisdictions.[4]

Still, the rate of gang-related crime, ranging from assault and theft of military equipment to sale of illegal drugs was likely less than 1 percent of military felonies committed on or off base in 2011, the report said.[5]

Military officials have noticed increasing signs of a gang presence. In Afghanistan and Iraq, gang graffiti appeared on- and off-post, according to the "2011 National Gang Threat Assessment."[6]

Gang experts such as Arizona State University criminologist Scott Decker say they have seen photos that have been posted online of soldiers making gang signs.

The Department of Defense was concerned enough to update regulations in 2012 to specify that service personnel were barred from any activity relating to criminal gangs; the prohibition includes gang-related tattoos, posting online material about gangs and wearing gang colors and clothing.[7]

gang members in California and the Southwest, while the Aryan Brotherhood is chiefly known as a white supremacist group. They are just two of 34 gangs operating in the nation's prisons today.[46]

Outlaw motorcycle gangs emerged in this era as well. In 1948, World War II veteran Otto Friedli started a motorcycle club in Fontana, Calif., called the Hell's Angels, taking the name from World I and II bomber squadrons. The club appealed to other vets bored with civilian life. With a devil-may-care, anti-establishment philosophy, the Hells Angels has since spread to more than 30 countries and become an icon of popular culture, spawning several thousand biker gangs in the United States alone.[47]

As the civil rights movement got underway in the 1960s, gang activity and influence waned as minority groups turned to political movements such as the Black Panther Party and the Brown Berets (a Chicano movement) to fight discrimination. But as the turbulent Sixties wound down and political movements fell into disarray, gangs got a fresh boost both from disillusioned youth and the rising drug culture.

Military recruiters have also been trained to detect gang-related tattoos to prevent gang members from joining, says gang researcher Al Valdez at the University of California, Irvine.

In addition to gang members committing crimes, Smith says, some gangs are dispatching members with clean records to enlist in order to gain military skills, including tactical instruction and leadership training, that the gangs can use later. "They're learning how to put together and build weapons," Smith says. "It ups the ante of dangerousness in our communities."

On the other hand, Smith says, officers who have commanded troops later found to be gang members say they are good soldiers who take command well, likely because of their experience with gang hierarchy.

The 2013 gang report said 38 law enforcement agencies had found instances of gangs sending members to join up to gain weapons and combat expertise.[8]

To some extent, the presence of gang members in the military is natural because the soldier's life appeals to young males, who form the bulk of gang membership, says Decker, noting that gang members often join the armed forces as a way to escape a gang and improve their lives.

But they can backslide if they meet other gang members on bases and renew ties, according to the "2011 National Gang Threat Assessment."[9] "At the end of the day, they look around and say, 'Where's the adrenalin rush?'" Smith says. "They find another guy they share that bond with."

Some say the threat of gangs in the armed forces is exaggerated.

"It is absolutely overblown," says Alex Alonso, a gang researcher in Los Angeles who runs StreetGangs.com, a website dedicated to gang issues. "What type of gang members are really going to be in the military?"

Alonso says he served as an expert witness in a military trial in Alaska where three black and Latino servicemen involved in a bar brawl were accused of being in a gang because of clothing they wore. The gang charges were dismissed. "If they had been white, there would have no charge that they were in a gang," he says.

Others say the threat should not be downplayed. "The danger is their loyalty to the gang," Smith says. "It compromises the integrity of the military."

— *Christina Hoag*

---

[1] Kristin Davis, "AF: Missileer who ran 'violent street gang' gets 25 years," *Air Force Times*, Feb. 3, 2015, http://tinyurl.com/qaprkph.

[2] "Rico Williams sentenced to 22 years in 2005 slaying," WJLA-TV, April 20, 2012, http://tinyurl.com/otkwff2; Jeff Schogol, "Former airman convicted of murder in 2005 Gangster Disciples initiation death," *Stars and Stripes*, Nov. 15, 2010, http://tinyurl.com/27fvr6l.

[3] "2013 National Gang Report," National Gang Intelligence Center, 2013, p. 30, http://tinyurl.com/pdg694w.

[4] *Ibid.*, p. 29.

[5] *Ibid.*, p. 30.

[6] "2011 National Gang Threat Assessment," National Gang Intelligence Center, p. 35, http://tinyurl.com/nvo2enk.

[7] "2013 National Gang Report," *op. cit.*, p. 30.

[8] *Ibid.*, p. 29.

[9] "2011 National Gang Threat Assessment," *op. cit.*, p. 34.

Birth of Modern Gangs

In the 1970s, Los Angeles emerged as the nation's modern gang capital with the formation of gangs that would exert a national, and even international, influence into the next century. Gangs in Chicago, New York and other major cities surged anew during this period, but the Western organizations would have the most influence on the evolution of gangs over the next decades.

Black youths searching for both identity and money-making opportunities formed the Crips in South Los Angeles. A splinter faction of the Crips formed the Bloods. The two groups developed an intense feud that continues today.

Like the early English gangs, they adopted colors to differentiate themselves — blue for the Crips and red for Bloods. They also adopted the model of territoriality established by the early East Los Angeles gangs.[48] The word "hood," short for neighborhood, became synonymous with gangs, and gang subsets incorporated their location into their names, such as the Hoover Crips for Hoover Street in South Los Angeles. Wearing red in a

Crips hood, or blue in a Bloods area, was taken as a sign of disrespect and confrontation, as well as grounds for assault.

The gangs' appeal spread as they projected power, money and identity. In 1972, Los Angeles County had 18 black gangs; by 1980, it had 60 and by the 1990s, 270.[49] They expanded well beyond their hoods. Numerous gangs across the country today use Bloods or Crips monikers, whether officially affiliated with the Los Angeles gang or not: By 1994, more than 1,100 gangs in 115 cities used Bloods or Crips in their names.[50]

Latino gangs also strengthened during this era in Los Angeles. Non-Mexican Hispanics who were rejected by the Mexican gangs formed the 18th Street gang in the late Sixties. With a more open membership policy, the gang grew exponentially over the coming decade, even accepting members of other races.[51]

New York, the historical gang epicenter, saw its gangs wane into the 1980s. Experts cite several reasons, including less segregated and isolated public housing projects, gentrification of neighborhoods such as Harlem, and a drop-off in the number of organized gangs.[52] New York's competitive hip-hop movement also replaced gang warfare as an inner-city activity, according to Alonso's StreetGangs.com, which noted that gangs have made a slight comeback in more recent years.[53]

Immigration drove gang formation elsewhere. A wave of Asian arrivals beginning in the late 1960s resulted in Vietnamese, Korean, Filipino and Cambodian gangs springing up during the '70s and beyond. Incoming Pacific Islanders formed gangs, too. Asian gangs traditionally have been smaller and less territorially focused than black and Hispanic organizations in order to evade attention from law enforcement.[54]

A watershed in modern gang development was El Salvador's civil war, which began in 1979. Tens of thousands Salvadorans arrived in Los Angeles. Facing aggression from other Latino gangs, the Salvadorans formed the Mara Salvatrucha gang, also known as MS-13, and developed a bitter rivalry with the 18th Street gang. Over the next two decades, both gangs became notorious for their violence, as well as their heavy tattooing, often on the face and neck.[55]

The 1980s marked the arrival of a cheap, highly addictive form of smokeable cocaine — crack — that replaced the heroin of the 1970s. Gangs battled to control the lucrative drug trade, and drive-by shootings using military weapons such as AR-15 and AK-47 assault rifles became the preferred method of eliminating rivals. Homicides soared, particularly in urban communities. Between 1984 and 1994, the homicide rate for black males ages 14 to 17 more than doubled, while the rate for black males 18 to 24 increased almost as much.[56]

Law enforcement and politicians responded with a host of get-tough-on-crime measures, including three-strikes laws, which mandated lengthy prison sentences for three felony convictions, and mandatory minimum prison sentences.[57] The result was an extraordinary increase in the nation's prison population from less than 400,000 in 1980 to 1.6 million in 2013.[58]

In 1996, armed with the new Illegal Immigration Reform and Immigrant Responsibility Act, the government started large-scale deportations of foreign-born residents convicted of crimes, including gang members. By the late 1990s, deported members of the Mara Salvatrucha, also known as MS-13, and 18th Street had set up their gangs in El Salvador, Guatemala and Honduras. Because of weak law enforcement and entrenched poverty in those countries, the gangs have thrived on extortion, robbery and human trafficking there.[59]

Despite the violence of the 1990s, rap and hip-hop music popularized and glamourized the gang lifestyle. Permeating American youth culture were baggy pants and T-shirts and baseball caps worn sideways or backwards, plus the use of slang such as "bling" for shiny jewelry and "homies" and "homeboys" for friends.

As the 21st century arrived, popular culture helped spur gang formation in rural areas and smaller cities, such as Mobile, Ala., and Chattanooga, Tenn., gang experts say. New gangs also cropped up among newly arrived African immigrants. Somali and Sudanese gangs gravitated to Midwestern states, including Minnesota and Nebraska, where large communities of their compatriots had grown after early immigrants found jobs.[60]

In the early 2000s, Mexican drug cartels used mostly Latino gangs in the United States for retail drug distribution, leading to turf battles and outbreaks of gang violence, particularly in Chicago.[61] Gangs in northern Central America grew increasingly powerful, causing violence to soar in those countries. According to United Nations figures, in 2012 Honduras had the world's highest homicide rate, with 90 murders per 100,000 inhabitants, with El Salvador and Guatemala also high at 41 and 40 murders per 100,000 inhabitants, respectively. The U.S. homicide rate was just under 5.[62]

The repercussions of unchecked gang growth became clear in the 2010s. From 2013 to 2014, more than 100,000 Central Americans, mostly youths and many of them traveling solo, as well as mothers with small children, flooded the U.S. border. The reason many gave for fleeing: gang threats, intimidation and violence.[63]

The 2000s also ushered in a new type of gang, whose memberships are made up of mixed races, ethnicities and genders. These "hybrid" youth gangs do not ally themselves with any established group, instead drawing members from different gangs to form their own group. They are highly transient with few rules, making them difficult for law enforcement to track.[64]

"Hybrid gang culture is characterized by mixed racial and ethnic participation within a single gang, participation in multiple gangs by a single individual, vague rules and codes of conduct for gang members, use of symbols and colors from multiple — even rival — gangs, collaboration by rival gangs in criminal activities and the merger of smaller gangs into larger ones," researchers stated in a 2001 report.[65]

Members of one such group — the New World Order — were arrested on drugs and weapons charges in 2010 in Pontiac, Mich., together with members of the Almighty Latin King Nation, an established Hispanic gang. Police say hybrid groups pose a particular concern because they escalate violence in a bid to win attention and respect.[66]

In the 2010s, the U.S.-Mexico border emerged as a particular hot spot for gang activity. Texas officials reported more U.S.-based gangs forming alliances with Mexican drug cartels not only to smuggle narcotics and weapons but also people, including Central American gang members.[67]

Additionally, cartels are outsourcing crimes, including home invasions, assassinations and kidnappings, to U.S.-based gangs, the report said.[68]

Carolyn Torres, a high school teacher and grassroots activist with Chicanos Unidos, opposes the imposition of a gang injunction on Townsend Street in Santa Ana, CA. The Orange County District Attorney's office is seeking the injunction against the Townsend Street gang, which claims the area as its territory. Torres says drug rehabilitation, job re-entry and student programs are better solutions to gang violence than injunctions.

Law enforcement started to note more alliances between gangs, even traditional rivals, in an effort to strengthen drug distribution and profits.[69]

CURRENT SITUATION

Gangs on the Internet

Street gangs increasingly are moving online, taking advantage of social media and smartphones to bolster their own reputations and challenge rivals, and the new trend is sparking retaliatory violence, researchers say.

When police arrested 27 members of a Bronx, N.Y., gang in September on a 97-count indictment for a variety of crimes including two killings, one of the charges stemmed from a Facebook posting. The leader of the 6 Wilds, authorities said, had posted a hip-hop anthem describing how the gang has younger members commit most of the crimes because they would not face as much prison time as adults if they were caught.[70]

The incident was one example of how gangs are using the Internet. Another is "cyberbanging," which can involve turning rivals' Facebook photos upside down, posting

'Not Just Baby Mamas'

Females are leaving their fingerprints on gang culture.

Males dominate the gang world, but girls and women increasingly are asserting themselves in gangs throughout the nation. For example:

- When Boston police raided the Columbia Point Dawgs gang in June, those arrested on gun and drug charges included several women, one a leader of a gang faction.[1]
- In Fresno, Calif., three gang members — all women — were arrested in the same month on charges of robbing a Walmart.[2]
- In Dover, Del., a July 2015 raid netted 11 suspected members of the violent Bloods street gang, including two women who were booked on gun and drug charges.[3]

The arrests, researchers say, are signs that women's roles within gangs are expanding, with more females committing violent crimes and taking on leadership roles. "There's a paradigm shift, and no one knows why," says Al Valdez, a gang expert at the University of California, Irvine.

Gangs increasingly are using women as street "soldiers," according to a 2013 report by the National Gang Intelligence Center, which is composed of the FBI and other federal law enforcement agencies. In addition, law enforcement officials in Alabama, California and New York reported that female gang members are committing more violent acts, such as smash-and-grab burglaries and even murder, while 111 jurisdictions nationally (27 percent) reported active female gang members, the report said.[4]

"There's an increased presence of females. It's not in large numbers, it's subtle, but females are getting active as gang members," says Jorja Leap, a gang researcher at the University of California, Los Angeles. "They're not just baby mamas. They want to prove they're rough enough, tough enough, so they engage in the same behaviors as the men."

Other researchers agree that females are a presence in gangs, but not a big one. Estimates vary, but Arizona State University gang expert Scott Decker puts the figure at between 5 percent and 8 percent, even when older girls and women are counted.

Quantifying how many girls are involved in gangs is difficult, researchers say, because girls flow through the gangs more quickly than males: They tend to join at younger ages and stay for shorter periods, typically two years. The younger ones are generally less involved in money-making crimes, viewing gangs more as a social outlet, Decker says.

Girls gravitate toward gangs for many of the same reasons as boys: thrill-seeking, respect, protection and affirmation of identity.[5] But girls join gangs seeking safety

---

YouTube videos filmed in an opposing gang's turf and tweeting taunts and brags.[71]

"The Internet and social media are [among] the real drivers in changing gang culture," says Arizona State University's Decker, who has surveyed gang members extensively about their Internet use.

Gangs have their own websites and public and private Facebook pages, as well as Twitter, Instagram and YouTube accounts. They also communicate via smartphone apps such as Snapchat, where messages disappear after they've been read, and Yik Yak, where anyone within a few miles can view anonymous messages, according to researchers.

With the average age of street gang members at 17 and gang culture revolving around status and image, it is no surprise that gangs have embraced social media, Decker says. "Social media is an especially good vehicle to drive disrespect for rivals and respect for your own gang," he says.

Whereas gang members used to scrawl challenges and putdowns on a wall in an opposing gang's turf, now they find using the Internet safer and easier as well as more effective because they can spread their message faster and wider.[72]

Gang members increasingly incite cyber-disputes that end in bloody street confrontations. In Omaha,

and a surrogate family to a greater extent than boys. More than half of gang girls report they have been sexually assaulted, mostly by relatives, and three-fourths of female gang members said they had suffered physical abuse throughout their lives, usually by family members.[6]

However, gang life frequently offers the opposite of the protection the girls are seeking. "They get treated so badly by the guys. It's not a very attractive life," says Wes McBride, Western spokesman for the National Alliance of Gang Investigators' Associations.

All-female gangs usually are subsets of a larger male gang, although Valdez says researchers are seeing more independent "ROP" (run-your-own-program) gangs that can be more violent than typical female affiliates.

Male gangs typically employ women and girls in a variety of ways. Some perform only a sexual role, while others hide guns, drugs or fugitives, provide alibis or serve as drug couriers and sellers, lookouts or prostitutes to make money for the gang.

Women also obtain gun permits and buy weapons for gang members who may have criminal records, gather intelligence on other gangs and police activity and act as decoys and bait to lure rival gang members. Some take on leadership roles, particularly when men are incarcerated, because women tend to attract less attention from law enforcement.[7]

In 2015, the 39-year-old daughter of an incarcerated Mexican Mafia boss was sentenced to 15 years in prison for passing on her father's instructions, delivered during her monthly visits, to gang leaders in Los Angeles.[8]

Girls often leave gangs when they become pregnant, Leap says, but some expose their children to gang life. Nicola Daugherty, a former Los Angeles gang member, said she was so involved in gang culture that she brought up three of her seven children in the gang, a decision she now regrets. "I only taught my boys what I knew — gang-banging," she said.[9]

— *Christina Hoag*

---

[1] Milton J. Valencia, John R. Ellement and Astead W. Herndon, "48 charged in raid of violent Boston drug gang," *The Boston Globe*, June 18, 2015, http://tinyurl.com/pxxpjoc.

[2] "Fresno police arrest 3 women gang members in robbery case," *Fresno Bee*, July 19, 2015, http://tinyurl.com/oo2qxwt.

[3] Brittany Horn, "11 suspected Bloods Street Gang members arrested," Delaware Online, *The News Journal*, July 18, 2015, http://tinyurl.com/ndokb2c.

[4] "2013 National Gang Report," National Gang Intelligence Center, 2013, pp. 41-42, http://tinyurl.com/pdg694w.

[5] Meda Chesney-Lind, "How Can We Prevent Girls from Joining Gangs," Changing Course: Preventing Gang Membership, U.S. departments of Justice and Health and Human Services, September 2013, p. 122, http://tinyurl.com/ov9s8bq.

[6] *Ibid.*, p. 123.

[7] "2013 National Gang Report," *op. cit.*, pp. 41-42.

[8] Matt Hamilton, "Imprisoned gang leader's daughter sentenced in racketeering case," *Los Angeles Times*, March 23, 2015, http://tinyurl.com/ndcf4fn.

[9] Christina Hoag, "L.A.'s ex-gangsters train to go against the life," The Associated Press, April 18, 2010, http://tinyurl.com/npngnha.

---

police said rap videos that mock or threaten specific gangs and individual members have sparked numerous shootings.[73]

In Chicago, gangs taunt rivals by videoing themselves driving through their adversaries' neighborhood, including near emotionally laden locations such as the corner where a gang member was shot by the intruding gang, and posting them on social media or sending them to rivals.[74] Rivals then see the videos as a sign of disrespect that calls for retaliation.

In the wake of a spate of gang shootings in July in Los Angeles that left one dead and others wounded, warnings of revenge posted on Instagram and Twitter under the hashtags #PrayforLA and #100days100nights spurred widespread fear.[75] Police reinforced patrols and called on interventionists and others in the community to quell rumors and threats. No violence was reported.

Gangs' use of social media is prompting law enforcement officials to use more sophisticated strategies to track gang movements. Many big cities have established "real-time crime centers," where analysts follow Internet gang chatter on giant monitors, trying to decode messages to anticipate where violence may break out, specialists say.

Technology to aid that analysis is under development. The Massachusetts Institute of Technology is crafting

Denver juvenile probation officer Deborah Garcia-Sandoval leads Johnson Elementary School students on March 15, 2015, in a pledge not to join gangs as part of the city's G.R.E.A.T (Gang Resistance Education and Training) program.

methods to parse Internet traffic for certain words and phrases that might denote escalating threats.[76]

The Internet is also a source of evidence that can be used in court. In Los Angeles, detectives found a photo of a gun posted on a Facebook page that showed the weapon's serial number. When they "ran" the number, it turned out to be the firearm used in a murder.[77] Defense attorneys say they routinely check clients' online presence for any photos or postings that police could use against them.[78]

However, experts note, gangs are getting smarter about what they post on the Internet.

Policy Progress

After years of policies that emphasized punishment, policymakers are focusing on prevention and intervention as strategies to reduce gang membership among youths. In Congress, two languishing juvenile justice bills have gained the backing of conservatives and now stand a better chance of passage, observers say.[79]

The Youth PROMISE Act, which would fund gang violence prevention and intervention programs, was introduced for the fifth time this past May. But the latest effort has a new conservative sponsor, Rep. Trey Gowdy, R-S.C., signaling more support for the measure from the far right.[80] Rep. Bobby Scott, D-Va., first introduced the bill in 2007. Other sponsors include fellow Democrat Tony Cárdenas of California and a moderate Republican, Walter Jones of North Carolina.

Gowdy said he joined the bill's sponsorship because it would improve services to at-risk youths and save taxpayer dollars by reducing the number of people sent to prison. "As a former federal prosecutor who saw the immense human toll and suffering at the backend of crime, I am convinced we must be committed to stopping crime before it happens," Gowdy said in a statement.[81]

The bill would create community panels to select local delinquency prevention and intervention programs and fund them through grants to local governments from the Department of Justice's Office of Juvenile Justice and Delinquency Prevention. The programs would work in such areas as early-childhood development, teen parenting, substance abuse, street outreach and mental health. The bill awaits action in the House Education and Workforce Committee.[82]

Another bill aimed at juvenile justice reform, the Redeem Act, was reintroduced this spring in the Senate under another bipartisan sponsorship that could increase the measure's chance of passing.

The bill, sponsored by Sens. Cory Booker, a liberal Democrat from New Jersey, and Rand Paul, a conservative Republican from Kentucky and presidential hopeful, would give incentives to states to keep minors out of adult courts and seal criminal records of youths who commit nonviolent crimes before the age of 15 so their chances in life would not be affected by poor youthful decisions. It also aims to reduce recidivism by allowing courts to seal the records of adults convicted of nonviolent crimes; that would boost their chances of gaining employment, and it would allow certain low-level drug offenders to receive food stamps and other federal aid.[83]

Meanwhile, Democratic and Republican negotiators in the Senate reached a deal on Oct. 1 that would shorten the lengths of mandatory prison sentences for drug convictions and end the three-strikes provision. Booker praised the compromise as an important step forward for the nation, although he and other Democrats said they wished the agreement had gone further to reduce mandatory minimums.[84]

With conservatives and liberals reaching consensus on criminal justice reform, observers hope Congress will finally act. "When you see conservatives who've traditionally been very pro-law enforcement changing their

AT ISSUE

Are injunctions that ban gangs from congregating effective?

YES — Lawrence Rosenthal
Law Professor, Chapman University

Written for *CQ Researcher*, October 2015

For decades, big-city police favored policing by reactive patrol. Police cars drove through a "beat" waiting to respond to calls for help.

The 1980s crack epidemic exposed the deficiencies in reactive policing. Drug sales stopped when police appeared, then resumed when police left. Undercover officers arrested drug dealers, but other dealers took their place. Violent competition in drug markets ran unchecked.

In the early 1990s, New York City adopted a new strategy featuring aggressive stop-and-frisk tactics targeting "hot spots" of crime. Stop-and-frisk, done in volume, makes it too risky to carry drugs or guns in those hot spots. These tactics drive criminals indoors, where they are less vulnerable to stop-and-frisk. When crime is driven indoors, the risk of violent confrontations — to both participants and bystanders — declines.

In the following decade, New York experienced a decline in crimes tracked by the FBI roughly twice that experienced in the rest of the country. The city's homicide rate dropped by more than two-thirds, dramatically exceeding the decline in other big cities. These declines have proved enduring.

Gang injunctions (the banning of gang members from congregating in public) can be effective for the same reasons as other forms of aggressive patrol. Crime does not decline because a judge signs an injunction, but because it is enforced in a way that makes it risky to carry guns and drugs in public. Gang injunctions, when targeting crime hot spots, can facilitate aggressive patrol and preventive policing.

Although unduly broad injunctions may compromise civil liberties and unduly narrow injunctions may prove ineffective, gang injunctions can be effective for the same reason that New York's tactics worked so well. They have the additional virtue of increasing transparency.

The process of putting a case for an injunction together requires community input, gathering of evidence and identification of witnesses. When the injunction is issued, the community is able to understand the enforcement strategy that follows.

In this fashion, gang injunctions can avoid the biggest weakness of the New York model: policing that does not involve the community and where the rationale for enforcement strategy may be opaque from the community's standpoint.

However, there is no substitute for an aggressive police presence at hot spots. Those who advocate a passive police presence in high-crime communities are also sentencing those communities to continued instability.

NO — Caitlin Sanderson
Staff Attorney, American Civil Liberties Union of Southern California

Written for *CQ Researcher*, October 2015

Given the unrelenting bias and systemic racism recently exposed in our criminal justice system, do we really want to let anti-gang cops and prosecutors decide whose rights will be permanently restricted?

That is exactly what happens with civil injunctions against gangs. They are blunt instruments, often wielded indiscriminately with never-ending prohibitions against even innocuous, daily behavior.

While gang injunctions have been found to be constitutional, they nonetheless severely restrict civil liberties without adequate due process. Once someone is on an injunction, activities such as hanging out in public with friends or relatives (if police think they are gang members too), wearing certain colors or being out at night violates the injunction and subjects them to arrest.

And those who are enjoined are rarely allowed to challenge their inclusion under the injunction beforehand. They have no right to appointed counsel in civil proceedings, meaning that to fight the injunctions they must represent themselves in court or hire an attorney.

Most often, however, an injunction is obtained against the gang itself, and the police and district attorney or city attorney — without court oversight — decide how to enforce it and against whom.

Meanwhile, the injunctions do not curb gang violence. Instead, they become a ticket to the prison pipeline for some young people who have never committed a crime, and they shred relations between the police and communities of color.

An uglier consequence of these injunctions comes from studies showing that police in anti-gang units have a greater bias against youths of color than other officers. Gang officers see indicators of gang membership everywhere and cannot distinguish between youths growing up in neighborhoods where gangs exist and those who are actually involved in gang crime. These officers also are more likely to label individuals as gang members, arrest them for alleged gang activity and use violence while doing so.

Gang crime and gang violence are very real problems for many communities. But the question we should ask is, how do we want to spend limited public resources to combat this problem?

A better approach would use after-school programs, job training and early intervention — strategies proved effective at addressing the root causes of gangs and gang violence. Constitutionally problematic injunctions with little data to support their justification, while increasing the risk of police violence and criminalizing youths, are not the answer.

Blanca Kling, a Hispanic outreach worker for the Montgomery County Police Department in Maryland, comforts Maxima Saenz-Sorto as she talks about her murdered 15-year-old son Dennys. He was kidnapped and killed by the 18th Street gang, which mistakenly thought he belonged to the rival MS-13 gang, also known as Mara Salvatrucha.

views and questioning sentencing rates, or the cost of mass incarceration, then you know something's really happening," said Paul Larkin, senior legal research fellow at the Heritage Foundation, a conservative think tank in Washington.[85]

"And because conservatives and liberals both agree that sentencing and corrections reform are really pressing issues that deserve our full attention, I think that right now is a unique time for this issue," he said.[86]

The Department of Justice is also targeting gangs by extending its Violence Reduction Network program, which provides federal resources and guidance to law enforcement in violence-ridden communities, to another four cities: West Memphis, Ark.; Compton, Calif.; Flint, Mich.; and Newark, N.J. They join the inaugural sites of Detroit; Chicago; Camden, N.J.; Wilmington, Del.; Little Rock; and Oakland and Richmond, Calif.[87]

"While we're still early in this process with the five cities we announced last year, we're encouraged by the progress we've made so far," said Deputy Attorney General Sally Quillian Yates in September.[88]

Over the past year, for example, Camden acquired police ballistic equipment and training to aid investigations; Wilmington police created a homicide unit that increased its homicide clearance rate from less than 10 percent to more than 50 percent with advice from federal law enforcement agents; and Oakland police received training on gathering gang intelligence from social networks.[89]

OUTLOOK

Growing Sophistication

Gangs may fluctuate in membership, location and criminal activities, but experts agree they will remain a driving force behind crime for years to come.

"The outlook is not good for getting a handle on the gang problem," says Knox of the National Gang Crime Research Center. "There's no policy or direction."

Experts say gangs' criminal portfolios will continue to evolve as they search for new ways to make money, especially those activities that law enforcement deems low priority. Their increasing use of the Internet, social media and technology points to more sophisticated gangs in the future, according to specialists. Gangs will recruit members on social media, commit cybercrimes such as hacking and identity theft and use pilotless drones to smuggle drugs and surveil police, they say, and technology will make it easier to conduct transnational crime.

This growing off-the-street activity will make it harder for law enforcement to track gang crimes and make arrests, especially in smaller cities and outlying areas where police lack resources and expertise, says McBride of the gang investigators' association.

Budget constraints will force police to focus on violent gangs, the "2013 National Gang Report" said. "As such, gangs that are more violent will likely receive more attention from law enforcement — as they pose the more immediate and overt threat — while gangs that are less violent and perhaps more profit-oriented — will be better positioned to prosper."[90]

Experts see gangs continuing to rely on the high-risk, high-reward narcotics trade as their main business, although the type of drugs may change according to the tastes of U.S. drug users and drug policy. The increasing legalization of marijuana will further cut profits on that drug, while the demand for heroin will continue to widen, these experts say. Other new drugs will undoubtedly be created or will re-emerge for gangs to sell; violence will accompany those developments as gangs battle over turf to distribute the drugs, gang experts say.

With the United States an ongoing magnet for immigrants, gang formation by incoming groups is likely to continue, along with gang involvement in human smuggling. Impoverished immigrants from violent or unstable regions, such as northern Africa, are particularly likely to create gangs. "Changes in immigrant populations, which are susceptible to victimization and recruitment by street gangs, may have the most profound effect on street gang membership," said the National Gang Intelligence Center.[91]

The fact that decades of arrests and legal maneuvers, such as federal indictments and street-corner bans, have not slowed the growth of criminal gangs shows that a different tack is needed, say both gang researchers and law enforcement officers.

Prosecutors have repeatedly targeted some gangs using different tactics to no avail, says Los Angeles gang researcher Alonso. "They're still there, strong as ever," he says.

LAPD's Woodle notes that he's seen multiple generations of gang members from the same family in his three decades on the streets. To prevent youths from joining gangs in the first place, he says, more is needed to improve living conditions and educational and employment opportunities.

"I thought we were doing a damn good job putting handcuffs on them and throwing them in my back seat, but [arrests] haven't changed anything," Woodle says.

McBride, a retired three-decade gang investigator for the Los Angeles County Sheriff's Department, agrees that policing can't single-handedly solve the problem.

"I've never seen a gang wiped out because of law enforcement alone," he says. "You've got to bring the whole toolbox."

Experts concur: To lessen the threat, society must deal with the underlying reasons people join gangs.

"Unless we deal with the core reasons why gangs exist — underperforming schools, poverty, jobs — they're always going to be there," says Leap of UCLA.

NOTES

1. Steve Lieberman, "Street gangs embracing white-collar crime, authorities say," *Journal News*, Nov. 1, 2014, http://tinyurl.com/oxf5aor.

2. "2011 National Gang Threat Assessment," National Gang Intelligence Center, pp. 9, 11, http://tinyurl.com/nvo2enk. "The Gang Threat," Federal Bureau of Investigation, Feb. 6, 2009, http://tinyurl.com/qx2j6qq.

3. "2013 National Gang Report," National Gang Intelligence Center, 2013, p. 6, http://tinyurl.com/pdg694w.

4. Monica Davey and Mitch Smith, "Murder Rates Rising Sharply in Many U.S. Cities," *The New York Times*, Aug. 31, 2015, http://tinyurl.com/ndf8kfj.

5. Will Greenberg, "Police chiefs from around the country meet in D.C. to discuss violent summer," *The Washington Post*, Aug. 3, 2015, http://tinyurl.com/nck6aga.

6. *Ibid.*

7. Davey and Smith, *op. cit.*

8. Nicole Santa Cruz and Kate Mather, "Deadliest August in Los Angelese in 8 years," *Los Angeles Times*, Sept. 4, 2015, http://tinyurl.com/psaqrnu.

9. Cleve R. Wootson Jr., "Putney: Police suspect gangs in weekend shootings in Charlotte," *The Charlotte Observer*, Sept. 8, 2015, http://tinyurl.com/o5n7vfx.

10. Dan Sullivan, "Young, violent, organized: The Trouble with Gangs," *Tampa Bay Times*, Sept. 19, 2015, http://tinyurl.com/ppsued2.

11. "Brief Review of Federal and State Definitions," National Gang Center, undated, http://tinyurl.com/qc6s2vx.

12. "2013 National Gang Report," *op. cit.*, p. 19.

13. "OMGS and the Military 2014," Bureau of Alcohol, Tobacco and Firearms, July 2014, http://tinyurl.com/negr22l.

14. For background, see Barbara Mantel, "Far-Right Extremism," *CQ Researcher*, Sept. 18, 2015, pp. 769-792.

15. "2013 National Gang Report," *op. cit.*, pp. 13-14.

16. Matthew O'Deane and Stephen Morreale, "Gang Injunctions A Tool to Control Gang Activity," Law Enforcement Executive Forum, 2012, p. 1, http://tinyurl.com/o45rqa9.

17. Sara Lynn von Hofwegen, "A Critical Look at California's STEP Act," *Southern California Interdisciplinary Law Journal*, 2009, p. 682, http://tinyurl.com/q37ld7s.

18. "Project Safe Neighborhoods," Office of Justice Programs, undated, accessed Oct. 2, 2015, http://tinyurl.com/7lhvhyc.

19. "2014 Texas Gang Threat Assessment Report," Texas Department of Public Safety, April 2014, p. 29, http://tinyurl.com/oovhfh9.

20. "2013 National Gang Report," *op. cit.*, p. 43.

21. "2014 Texas Gang Threat Assessment Report," *op. cit.*, p. 29.

22. "Street Gangs & Modern Slavery," GlobalCenturion.org, http://tinyurl.com/pa27u6p.

23. Laura Lederer, "Sold for Sex: The Link between Street Gangs and Trafficking of Persons," *Protection Project Journal of Human Rights and Civil Society*, February 2010, p. 9, http://tinyurl.com/p23kwup.

24. Cheryl L. Maxson, Karen C. Hennigan and David L. Sloane, "It's Getting Crazy Out There: Can a Civil Gang Injunction Change a Community?" *Criminology & Public Policy*, April 2005, http://tinyurl.com/nkydbod.

25. O'Deane and Morreale, *op. cit.*

26. Jeffrey Grogger, "The Effects of Civil Gang Injunctions on Reported Violent Crime: Evidence From Los Angeles County," *Journal of Law and Economics*, April 2002, http://tinyurl.com/p2jz6pa.

27. O'Deane and Morreale, *op. cit.*

28. Max Shiner, "Civil Gang Injunctions: A Guide for Prosecutors," National District Attorneys Association, June 2009, p. 17, http://tinyurl.com/opsy9ku.

29. Adolfo Flores, "Federal appeals court rules against O.C. gang injunction," *Los Angeles Times*, Nov. 6, 2013, http://tinyurl.com/plna62z.

30. Kevin Rector and Justin Fenton, "East Baltimore anti-violence group work suspended after guns, drugs found in raid," *The Baltimore Sun*, July 14, 2015, http://tinyurl.com/nkwzsy7. Justin George and Justin Fenton, "W. Baltimore Safe Streets work suspended amid criminal allegations," *The Baltimore Sun*, Dec. 11, 2013, http://tinyurl.com/pmo9e83.

31. Rector and Fenton, *op. cit.*

32. Sarah Childress, "Chicago Drops CeaseFire from Anti-Violence Strategy," "Frontline," Oct. 17, 2013, http://tinyurl.com/kjmvwnv.

33. Andrew Blankstein and Richard Winton, "Some anti-gang workers tempted into old lifestyle," *Los Angeles Times*, Jan. 13, 2009, http://tinyurl.com/oqd5emy; Scott Gold, "Trouble with a South L.A. gang-intervention agency," *Los Angeles Times*, Aug. 2, 2009, http://tinyurl.com/qadyu6j; Christina Hoag, "LA's ex-gangsters train to go against gang life," The Associated Press, April 18, 2010, http://tinyurl.com/o4pkloj.

34. Wesley Skogan *et al.*, "Evaluation of CeaseFire-Chicago," National Institute of Justice, March 2009, pp. 7-9, http://tinyurl.com/ogxwg7a.

35. James Howell and John Moore, "A History of Street Gangs in the United States," *National Gang Center Bulletin*, May 2010, http://tinyurl.com/8xhlx75.

36. Luc Sante, *Low Life: Lures and Snares of Old New York* (1991), pp. 199-201, http://tinyurl.com/o2j4yk3.

37. James C. Howell, *Gangs in America's Communities* (2012), pp. 2-5, http://tinyurl.com/palbtfq.

38. Sante, *op. cit.*, pp. 199-201.
39. Howell, *op. cit.*, p. 9.
40. *Ibid.*
41. Dennis McLellan, "Defendant in notorious Sleepy Lagoon murder case was unjustly convicted," *Los Angeles Times*, March 7, 2008, http://tinyurl.com/p2467o5.
42. George Coroian, "Zoot Suit Riots," *Encyclopedia Britannica*, http://tinyurl.com/p86tmey.
43. Alex A. Alonso, "Racialized Identities and the Formation of Black Gangs in Los Angeles," *Urban Geography*, 2004, pp. 664-666, http://tinyurl.com/q4koaba.
44. Howell and Moore, *op. cit.*, p. 7.
45. Sudhir Venkatesh, *Gang Leader for a Day: A Rogue Sociologist Takes to the Streets* (2008), p. 37.
46. "2013 National Gang Report," *op. cit.*, p. 15.
47. Randy James, "A Brief History of the Hells Angels," *Time*, Aug. 3, 2009, http://tinyurl.com/p4nvh23.
48. Howell, *op. cit.*, p. 20.
49. Alonso, *op. cit.*, p. 669.
50. Howell, *op. cit.*, p. 13.
51. *Ibid.*, p. 146.
52. Jeremy Gorner and Annie Sweeney, "A tale of 3 cities: LA and NYC outpace Chicago in curbing violence," *Chicago Tribune*, Sept. 18, 2015, http://tinyurl.com/onrgkut.
53. "Street gangs in New York City," undated, accessed Oct. 2, 2015, http://tinyurl.com/o22hvk9.
54. Howell, *op. cit.*, p. 20; "2011 National Gang Threat Assessment," *op. cit.*, p. 3.
55. For background, see Peter Katel, "Central American Gangs," *CQ Researcher*, Jan. 30, 2015, pp. 97-120.
56. Roland G. Fryer *et al.*, "Measuring the Impact of Crack Cocaine," National Bureau of Economic Research, May 2005, p. 3, http://tinyurl.com/qf3tzom.
57. For background, see Patrick Marshall, "Three-Strikes Laws," *CQ Researcher*, May 10, 2002, pp. 417-432; and Sarah Glazer, "Sentencing Reform," *CQ Researcher*, Jan. 10, 2014, pp. 25-48.
58. Key Statistic: Total Correctional Population, Bureau of Justice, http://tinyurl.com/pfvg9hx. Also see David Masci, "Prison-Building Boom," *CQ Researcher*, Sept. 17, 1999, pp. 801-824.
59. Katel, *op. cit.*, pp. 102, 106-108.
60. "2011 National Gang Threat Assessment," *op. cit.*, pp. 18-19.
61. "2013 National Gang Report," *op. cit.*, pp. 21-23.
62. "Global Study on Homicide 2013," United Nations Office on Drugs and Crime, p. 126, http://tinyurl.com/npyxq7w.
63. "Total Unaccompanied Alien Children Apprehensions by Month," U.S. Border Patrol, undated, accessed Oct. 2, 2015, http://tinyurl.com/pgcky04; "Southwest Border Unaccompanied Children," U.S. Customs and Border Protection, undated, accessed Oct. 2, 2015, https://tinyurl.com/p3xm4sx.
64. David Starbuck, James C. Howell and Donna J. Lindquist, "Hybrid and Other Modern Gangs," *Juvenile Justice Bulletin*, December 2001, http://tinyurl.com/qghufu3.
65. *Ibid.*
66. 2011 National Gang Threat Assessment, *op. cit.*, p. 21.
67. "2015 Texas Gang Threat Assessment Report," Texas Department of Public Safety, September 2015, p. 30, http://tinyurl.com/nt8rp8h.
68. *Ibid.*, p. 18.
69. "2013 Gang Threat Assessment," *op. cit.*, p. 4.
70. Stevie Borrello, "More than 20 Bronx gang members indicted on 97 counts, including murder," ABC7NY.com, Sept. 16, 2015, http://tinyurl.com/pbb2det.
71. Annie Sweeney, "Gangs increasingly challenge rivals online with postings, videos," *Chicago Tribune*, Aug. 17, 2015, http://tinyurl.com/nu5h4ga.

72. Nicole Santa Cruz, Kate Mather and Javier Panzar, "#100days100nights: Gang threats of violence on social media draw fear," *Los Angeles Times*, July 27, 2015, http://tinyurl.com/p4xmp9k.

73. Dave Roberts, "Social media fueling gang violence in Omaha," WKETV.com, Nov. 3, 2014, http://tinyurl.com/oa5o7r8.

74. Sweeney, *op. cit.*

75. Santa Cruz, Mathers and Panzar, *op. cit.*

76. Sweeney, *op. cit.*

77. Santa Cruz, Mathers and Panzar, *op. cit.*

78. Sweeney, *op. cit.*

79. For background, see Christina L. Lyons, "Reforming Juvenile Justice," *CQ Researcher*, Sept. 11, 2015, pp. 745-768.

80. Christina Wilkie, "A Bill To Keep Kids Out Of Prison Has A New Lease On Life, Thanks To Conservatives," *The Huffington Post*, May 7, 2015, http://tinyurl.com/nqktvnp.

81. "Scott, Jones, Gowdy and Cárdenas Introduce Youth PROMISE Act," House Committee on Education and the Workforce, May 1, 2015, http://tinyurl.com/o73gb39.

82. H.R.2197 "Youth Promise Act," Congress.gov, http://tinyurl.com/njkw7x4.

83. Jonathan D. Salant, "Cory Booker, Rand Paul push to overhaul criminal justice system," N.J. Advance Media, March 9, 2015, http://tinyurl.com/q7bdjzx.

84. Wesley Lowery, "Senators unveil long-awaited compromise on criminal justice reform," *The Washington Post*, Oct. 1, 2015, http://tinyurl.com/q8k8zn2.

85. Wilkie, *op. cit.*

86. *Ibid.*

87. "DOJ expands Violence Reduction Network to Little Rock, 4 other cities," U.S. Department of Justice, Sept. 28, 2015, http://tinyurl.com/okpe6oo.

88. *Ibid.*

89. *Ibid.*

90. "2013 National Gang Report", *op. cit.*, p. 52.

91. "2011 National Threat Assessment Report," *op. cit.*, p. 45.

BIBLIOGRAPHY

Selected Sources

Books

Barker, Tom, *North American Criminal Gangs: Street, Prison, Outlaw Motorcycle and Drug Trafficking Organizations,* **Carolina Academic Press, 2012.**
A professor at Eastern Kentucky University details how gangs have formed national and international alliances to strengthen their criminal activities.

Blatchford, Chris, *The Black Hand: The Story of Rene "Boxer" Enriquez and His Life in the Mexican Mafia,* **Harper, 2009.**
A former member of la Eme reveals how the Mexican supergang operates inside and outside prison.

Boyle, Gregory, *Tattoos from the Heart: The Power of Boundless Compassion,* **Free Press, 2010.**
A Jesuit priest describes his mission to rehabilitate gang members by starting businesses to employ them.

Howell, James C., *The History of Street Gangs in the United States: Their Origins and Transformations,* **Lexington Books, 2015.**
A senior research associate at the National Gang Center in Florida analyzes the emergence and evolution of street gangs.

O'Deane, Matthew, *Gang Investigator's Handbook: A Law-Enforcement Guide to Identifying and Combating Violent Street Gangs,* **Paladin Press, 2008.**
A gang investigator details strategies for identifying and suppressing street gangs.

Articles

Alarcon, Daniel, "How Do You Define a Gang Member?" *The New York Times Magazine*, May 31, 2015, http://tinyurl.com/n9kq26j.
In addition to criminal charges, gang members are being prosecuted for being in gangs, a prosecutorial strategy that can significantly increase their prison sentences. But many argue the tactic is unfair.

Quinones, Sam, "The End of Gangs," *Pacific Standard Magazine*, Dec. 29, 2014, http://tinyurl.com/ocg9yml.
Formerly gang-riddled neighborhoods in Los Angeles are making a comeback as gang presence and influence dwindles in the face of federal and state indictments and injunctions against gang members congregating in public.

Sweeney, Annie, "Gangs increasingly challenge rivals online with postings, videos," *Chicago Tribune*, Aug 17, 2015, http://tinyurl.com/nu5h4ga.
Gangs are using the Internet and social media to drive the cycle of violent retaliation among rivals.

Wallace-Wells, Benjamin, "The Plot From Solitary," *New York Magazine*, Feb. 26, 2014, http://tinyurl.com/p8g6nux.
Four gang leaders held in solitary confinement at a California prison were able to organize a 30,000-inmate hunger strike throughout California prisons that forced officials to end indefinite isolation in cells.

Winter, Jana, and Jordan Smith, "Leaked Report Profiles Military, Police Members of Outlaw Motorcycle Gangs," *The Intercept*, May 22, 2015, http://tinyurl.com/pnj2md6.
A U.S. Bureau of Alcohol, Tobacco and Firearms report details links between the military and other government institutions and biker gangs.

Reports and Studies

"National Gang Report 2013," The National Gang Intelligence Center, 2014, http://tinyurl.com/ocnrtbb.
A government survey, compiled by the FBI and other agencies, shows that street gangs constitute 88 percent of total gang membership; prison gangs, 9.5 percent, and outlaw motorcycle gangs, 2.5 percent.

Alpert, Geoff, et al., "Perceptions of Criminal and Gang Involvement Among College-Student Athletes," *Journal of Applied Sport Management*, Summer 2013, http://tinyurl.com/p66dug9.
Researchers find delinquent behavior by gang members who are college athletes, but athletic directors are reluctant to conduct criminal background checks.

Decker, Scott H., David C. Pyrooz and Richard K. Moule Jr., "Disengagement from Gangs as Role Transitions," *Journal of Research on Adolescence*, June 2014, http://tinyurl.com/p2kr7g8.
Sociologists interview ex-gang members to determine the factors that caused them to exit gang life.

Moule, Richard K. Jr., David C. Pyrooz and Scott H. Decker, "Internet Adoption and Online Behaviour Among American Street Gangs," *British Journal of Criminology*, July 19, 2014, http://tinyurl.com/nk9oqgj.
Gang members use the Internet and social media to challenge rivals and brag about their exploits, but not to recruit members.

O'Deane, Matthew D., and Stephen A. Morreale, "Gang Injunctions: A Tool to Control Gang Activity," *Law Enforcement Executive Forum*, March 2012, http://tinyurl.com/q257hfy.
A study finds that using restraining orders to prevent gang members from congregating in public are effective at suppressing gang activity, but says the police must enforce the injunctions.

For More Information

Homeboy Industries, 130 W. Bruno St., Los Angeles, CA 90012; 323-526-1254; www.homeboyindustries.org. Nonprofit run by a Jesuit priest that provides jobs, counseling and tattoo removal to those who want to leave gangs.

National Alliance of Gang Investigators' Associations, PO Box 574, Queens Creek, AZ 85142; 602-223-2569; www.ngia.org. Law enforcement group that works to reduce gang violence by sharing intelligence, monitoring legislation and increasing awareness.

National Gang Center, Institute for Intergovernmental Research, PO Box 12729, Tallahassee, FL 32317; 850-385-0600; www.nationalgangcenter.gov. Project financed by the U.S. Department of Justice's Office of Juvenile Justice and Delinquency Prevention and the Bureau of Justice Assistance to provide information on street gangs for researchers and policymakers.

National Gang Crime Research Center, PO Box 990, Peotone, IL 60468-0990; 708-258-9111; www.ngcrc.com. Nonprofit that conducts research and consults on gangs, publishes reports and organizes an annual gang investigator training conference.

Organized Crime and Gangs Section, Criminal Division, U.S. Department of Justice, 1301 New York Ave., N.W., Washington, DC 20005; 202-514-3594; www.justice.gov/criminal-ocgs. Federal entity responsible for monitoring and prosecuting gang crime.

Professional Community Intervention Training Institute, 3010 Wilshire Blvd., Suite 256, Los Angeles, CA 90010; 323-275-1904; www.maximumforceenterprises.org. Nonprofit that trains former gang members and others as interventionists and peacekeepers.

8 Racial Conflict

Peter Katel

Following a hung jury in December, Baltimore police officer William G. Porter, right, here with his lawyer, will be retried on charges stemming from the death of Freddie Gray, 25, last April. Gray died from spinal cord injuries allegedly sustained while he was being transported in a police van after his arrest for carrying a pocket knife. Porter is one of six officers charged in Gray's death.

From *CQ Researcher*,
January 8, 2016.

Chicago's Magnificent Mile, a 13-block stretch of upscale shops, sleek office towers and tony hotels, usually buzzes with post-Thanksgiving holiday shopping. But late last year it became a focal point of perhaps the most urgent social issue wracking the nation: relations between whites and minorities, particularly African-Americans.

"Sixteen shots! Thirteen months!" demonstrators shouted as they virtually shut down "Black Friday" commerce in Chicago's main shopping zone. The catalyst was a just-released video showing a Chicago police officer shooting 17-year-old Laquan McDonald 16 times on a city street, killing him. City officials had kept the video under wraps for 13 months until a reporter forced its release through a freedom-of-information request.[1]

Then, one day after Christmas, Chicago police accidentally shot and killed an unarmed grandmother while also fatally shooting an allegedly mentally troubled 19-year-old college student who was reportedly threatening family members with a baseball bat. The Chicago events followed other deadly incidents — in Ferguson, Mo., New York City, North Charleston, S.C., and elsewhere — in which white police officers used deadly force against black suspects, many of them unarmed. Tensions over these deaths ratcheted up again at year's end when a Cleveland grand jury declined to indict a policeman who shot to death 12-year-old Tamir Rice, who had been holding a toy replica of a pistol. What's more, those incidents have followed decades of frustration over large gaps between African-Americans and whites in household wealth, housing, education and employment.[2]

More than 50 years after the official end of segregation and efforts by the Rev. Martin Luther King Jr. and other leaders to protect minorities' civil rights, many activists and some scholars charge that nothing less than institutional racism still grip the nation.

"We still have segregation across America geospatially, with housing practices and banking practices that actually retarded if not prevented integration opportunities," says Maya Rockeymoore, president and CEO of Global Policy Solutions, an advocacy think tank on racial and economic inequality. "And students who have been systematically impoverished are attending impoverished schools in inner-city neighborhoods [and] are never prepared to even qualify to get into higher education. They are victims of structural barriers to opportunity."

Others deny that racism is institutionalized, saying such characterizations are designed to mask the black community's failure to meet the challenges that came after legal discrimination ended in the 1960s. They note that as the nation's first African-American president winds up his second term, a record 48 black lawmakers are serving in Congress and countless more African-Americans preside as big-city mayors, police chiefs and even the U.S. attorney general.[3]

"There is no de jure [legal] segregation in the United States anymore," says Walter E. Williams, an African-American economics professor at George Mason University in Fairfax, Va. "At one time, black Americans did not have the guarantees that everyone else did, but the civil rights struggle is over and won. That does not mean there are not major problems in the black community. When blacks were no more than a generation or more out of slavery, there was greater family stability and there weren't all these problems we see among black folks today."

Wealth Gap Divides Whites, Minorities

The median net worth of white households in 2013 was more than 10 times that of Hispanics and nearly 13 times that of blacks, according to the latest federal data.

Median Household Net Worth by Race/Ethnicity, 2013

White: $141,900
Black: $11,000
Hispanic: $13,700

Source: Rakesh Kochhar and Richard Fry, "Wealth inequality has widened along racial, ethnic lines since end of Great Recession," Pew Research Center, Dec. 12, 2014, http://tinyurl.com/kww2vpoa

As the debate continues, a new generation of activists is challenging racial inequities that have lingered long after pundits declared a "post-racial America" following Barack Obama's 2008 election. Police encounters with black citizen are only one impetus for renewed activism. Also key, advocates say, are the socioeconomic differences between black and white Americans:

• The $11,000 median net worth of black households is about 13 times less than the median white household net worth of $141,900.
• African-Americans die 3.6 years earlier, on average, than whites.
• Only 22 percent of African-Americans earn college degrees, compared with 34 percent of whites.
• About one in 12 black men ages 25–54 are in jail or prison, versus one in 60 white men; and
• Black Americans are almost eight times more likely than white Americans to die by homicide.[4]

For the activists, these outcomes show that America has not shaken off a legacy of race-based oppression. "The [1965] Voting Rights Act and desegregation gave [blacks] more access to a still-racist system," says DeRay Mckesson, a Baltimore-based organizer with the Black Lives Matter movement, which emerged in response to widely publicized cellphone videos of police shootings or violent arrests of African-Americans in the past year.

In a year-long investigation of nearly 1,000 fatal shootings by police in the United States in 2015 (as of late December) *The Washington Post* showed stark racial disproportion in the use of deadly force. Although African-American males account for only 6 percent of the U.S. population, they represent 40 percent — or 37 — of the

90 unarmed men shot to death by police, *The Post* reported. Overall, however, fatal shootings of unarmed black men by white officers accounted for less than 4 percent of such events. (*The Guardian*, a London newspaper, reported its own figure of 1,134 deaths at police hands — including deaths from Taser stun guns and deaths in custody — with African-American 15-to-34-year-old males accounting for 15 percent of the deaths.)[5]

Cellphone, dashboard and other videos, however, do not convey the complexities of America's racial history, many scholars say. They point to what they see as a systematic preference for whites encoded in America's institutional DNA.

Joe R. Feagin, a sociology professor at Texas A&M University, traces the socioeconomic racial divide to centuries of government policies that implicitly or explicitly provided preferential treatment for whites, especially when it came to land grants, government-guaranteed mortgages and college tuition aid — government largesse that has been the foundation of upward mobility for millions of families.

"We white families have had 20 generations to unjustly enrich ourselves," Feagin says. "Even whites who came from working-class backgrounds like mine had access to the marvelous aspects of this country — programs and services."[6]

Many black conservatives, however, reject the notion of present-day institutional racism. "Many times, people use the term when they can't find a racist," Williams says. "A lot of times they can't show you a live, breathing individual or company, so now they call it institutionalized racism." Williams continues, "Next year, I'll be 80 years old. I saw racial discrimination."

Williams blames "the welfare state" for many problems in the black community, saying that government assistance to single mothers "has done what slavery and Jim Crow could not have done: destroy the black family and create a high rate of illegitimacy and family breakdown."

He and other African-American conservatives say that with racial discrimination outlawed for a half-century, ongoing law enforcement issues and poverty in black communities stem from a breakdown of values. "One of the reasons that relations between police and poor blacks are so bad," says Derryck Green, a doctoral candidate at Azusa Pacific University, near Los Angeles, and a member of the National Leadership Network of Black Conservatives, an online think tank for the African-American political right, "is the number of children who grow up in families without a male authority figure."

Jack Hunter, a white libertarian conservative and the political editor of the online news site *Rare*, says many conservatives "cannot wrap their heads around" discriminatory police practices. "Part of that is a lack of recognition that black Americans do have it worse — something that many conservative Republicans are not willing to accept."

For example, "young white men and black men use marijuana at the same rate," he says. "But young black men are jailed at four times the rate for whites" for marijuana violations.[7]

Some scholars cite historical and economic forces for concentrated black poverty, including deficient schools and a loss of manufacturing jobs that once provided a decent living to people with limited education — leaving criminal activities as a major alternative. "Youth unemployment is not some magical problem that dropped from the sky," Feagin says. "When you suffer discrimination on a large scale, where do you go for a job? The crime economy."

In the view of some liberal academics, think tanks and Democratic presidential candidates, government programs to boost employment, educational opportunities and homeownership for all low-income Americans are among the antidotes to racial inequality. And generations of activists and writers — most recently best-selling African-American author Ta-Nehisi Coates — have proposed preferential programs (or reparations) for victims of past institutional discrimination in the distribution of land, home mortgage guarantees and college tuition grants.[8]

But providing racial preferences in anti-poverty programs is widely seen as politically impossible — and unfair, given that many poor people are white. The standard white American's response to racially based criteria would be, "'My tax dollars shouldn't be used to fix something I'm not responsible for,'" says Leslie Hinkson, a sociology professor at Georgetown University in Washington. Hinkson says most people do not know that "structural racism . . . limits the life chances of people because of their race."

Blacks Highest in Police Stops

African-Americans make up less than a third of Chicago's population but represented nearly three-fourths of the people stopped and frisked by Chicago police over a four-month period in 2014. In New York City, where blacks make up less than a fourth of the population, they accounted for more than half of police stops.

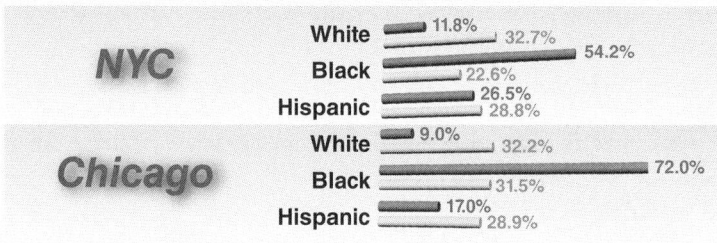

Percentage of Whites, Blacks and Hispanics Stopped and Frisked in Chicago and New York City (from May-August 2014)

	Percentage of People Stopped	Percentage of Population
NYC White	11.8%	32.7%
NYC Black	54.2%	22.6%
NYC Hispanic	26.5%	28.8%
Chicago White	9.0%	32.2%
Chicago Black	72.0%	31.5%
Chicago Hispanic	17.0%	28.9%

Sources: Chicago stop-and-frisk data from ACLU Chicago affiliate, http://tinyurl.com/zpepgmd; New York City stop-and-frisk data from ACLU New York City affiliate, http://tinyurl.com/8vuhkp2; population data from 2014 American Community Survey, U.S. Census Bureau, http://tinyurl.com/o8op597

That idea had wide acceptance in the mid-1960s. The landmark civil rights laws enacted then "helped a lot of black middle-class folks, but didn't do much for the urban black poor," says Michael Javen Fortner, urban studies director at the City University of New York's School of Professional Studies. "Middle-class people could use . . . laws and policies to leave neighborhoods, to get into schools that in the past they couldn't get into."

Paradoxically, the renewed attention to black-white racial tensions comes as the non-Hispanic white majority is becoming a minority.[9] Hispanics have long endured discrimination (reflected in a history of 547 documented lynchings of Mexicans and Mexican-Americans between 1848–1928 in the West and Midwest), and American Indians have been the targets of military campaigns, mass removals and massacres that modern tribal leaders call genocide.[10]

But the African-American experience occupies a unique place in U.S. life because of slavery's legacy and the fact that the nation's culture is partly a black creation. The Smithsonian National Museum of African American History and Culture, due to open this fall on the National Mall in Washington, is designed to introduce a mass audience to that often-hidden side of the American story.[11]

As activists, scholars and others debate race relations, here are some of the questions being asked:

Would improving police interactions with African-Americans significantly advance race relations in America?

Today's conflicts between police and African-Americans have stirred debate about the larger issue of race in America, just as urban riots in the 1960s — often triggered by confrontations between police and black citizens — led to similar soul-searching.[12]

With cellphone video now ubiquitous, the public is seeing what happens in police-citizen interactions that turn ugly. In the past year alone, videos have shown, among other incidents:

• A white police officer at a Columbia, S.C., school overturning an allegedly disobedient black student's chair with her in it before handcuffing her;

• A white officer in McKinney, Texas, slamming a black, bikini-clad girl to the ground at a pool party, then drawing his gun on her companions; and

• A white, Charlotte, N.C., officer shooting and killing an unarmed black man after a one-car accident.[13]

Videos, or "the C-Span of the streets," according to Paul Butler, a professor at Georgetown University Law School and a former prosecutor, corroborate "what African-Americans have been saying for years."[14]

Some police chiefs have accepted video as evidence of misconduct. In South Carolina, the North Charleston chief — saying he was "sickened" by the video of a cop shooting an unarmed black to death — fired the officer, who was later charged with murder.[15]

But videos also can be used unfairly against officers, said Bill Johnson, executive director of the National Association of Police Organizations. "Even if we do everything right, if we do it by the law and the investigation shows that we did, we can still just be so dragged through the mud unfairly and inaccurately by community activists, by the media," he said.[16]

Johnson said the omnipresence of videos today makes police reluctant to be "as aggressive as we used to be," something FBI Director James Comey has said might be causing an uptick in crime. But Comey conceded that police can fall into a habit of linking criminal behavior to race. "The two young black men on one side of the street look like so many others the officer has locked up," Comey said in a speech last February. "Two white men on the other side of the street — even in the same clothes — do not."[17]

Despite the outrage generated by videos, some in the Black Lives Matter movement — which emerged after the 2014 police shooting of Michael Brown, 18, in Ferguson, Mo. — say discriminatory law enforcement is not the worst problem facing African-Americans.[18] Schools, health care and other structures and institutions affect people "along the lines of race and class," says Black Lives activist Mckesson, who has co-authored a plan to limit police use of deadly force.[19]

Nevertheless, Mckesson says, the potentially deadly consequences of confrontations with police make changing relations with cops a priority. "The impact of the criminal justice system, because it means jail for people, means the police are violently interacting with your body. That is a loss of freedom and safety right now."

Some black conservatives argue that confrontations between police and African-Americans typically reflect high crime rates and moral decay in black communities. Williams of George Mason cites statistics showing that most homicide victims are black people killed by other African-Americans.[20] From 1980 to 2008, according to FBI data, 93 percent of black homicide victims were killed by other African-Americans. Overall, 28 percent of the FBI's "known offenders" are black, significantly above the black population share, the data show.[21]

"This is not a civil rights problem," Williams says. "It's not the Klan murdering blacks."

But for others, the high crime rates in poor black neighborhoods do not justify discriminatory police action. Rockeymoore of Global Policy Solutions says police and others in the criminal justice system often automatically link race with criminality. "You have

Brandon Risher is comforted at the casket of his grandmother, Ethel Lance, 70, who was one of nine victims killed in a mass shooting at historic Emanuel African Methodist Episcopal Church in Charleston, S.C., on June 17, 2015. Dylann Roof, 21, a white supremacist, is accused in the shootings, which occurred during a prayer meeting.

situations where innocents are being slaughtered or wrongly arrested," she says.

Last October, *The New York Times* — using data from police traffic stops and arrests in Greensboro, N.C. — concluded that African-Americans accounted for 54 percent of drivers pulled over even though they made up only 39 percent of the city's driving-age population. Cars driven by blacks were searched more than twice as often as cars driven by whites, and force was used more frequently with blacks than with whites. Statistics from six other states showed similar results.[22]

Nevertheless, Rockeymoore, who lives in Baltimore — a black-majority city plagued by violence — acknowledges that the high crime rates in poor, African-American neighborhoods mean those neighborhoods need more police. "It's not a function of race, but of class," she says. "When you combine poor people with primary needs and no way to meet those immediate needs outside of what they perceive as criminality, . . . that increases the rate of people wanting and needing police officers."

Lisa L. Miller, a political scientist at Rutgers University in New Brunswick, N.J., who specializes in crime and race, goes further, arguing that the Black Lives Matter movement's intense focus on policing reinforces fundamental distrust of government, a vision that doesn't match the concerns of people in impoverished minority communities. "My worry about the fixation on state violence is that it reinforces the anti-statist narrative," Miller says. "But we don't need the state to do less; we need it to do more."

Would new laws and government programs reduce institutional racism?

Experts representing all political persuasions agree that the landmark 1954 Supreme Court decision *Brown v. Board of Education* outlawing school segregation, along with three major civil rights laws of the 1960s, were essential to correcting injustices that persisted 100 years after slavery ended.*

But experts are divided over how the government can narrow today's racial gaps in education and employment.

Hillary Clinton, the leading candidate for the Democratic presidential nomination, debated the issue in New Hampshire last summer during a meeting with Black Lives Matter activists.

Clinton acknowledged that a 1994 crime law — endorsed by her husband, President Bill Clinton — brought unintended negative consequences, including a vast increase in imprisonment, especially for African-Americans convicted of drug use.

After candidate Clinton's comments, activist Julius Jones of Worcester, Mass., referring to racism's historical roots, said: "America's first drug [was] free black labor. . . . Until someone . . . speaks that truth to white people in this country so that we can finally take on anti-blackness as a founding problem in this country, I don't believe there's going to be a solution."[23]

Clinton said that approach would accomplish little because too many whites would say, "We get it, we get it, we're going to be nicer." But she added, "That's not enough in my book, that's not how I see politics."

To address racial inequality, Clinton has called for measures intended to fight poverty and reduce income inequality — measures, she says, that would begin to curb disparities in the criminal justice system. Mass incarceration condemns ex-prisoners and their families to poverty, Clinton said.[24]

But citing persistent housing segregation despite the 1968 Fair Housing Act, which banned racial discrimination in housing, Hinkson of Georgetown says, "Hillary Clinton believes too much in the power of the law to effect substantial change. With laws, you have a possibility of change, but you can't have actual change without having mechanisms in place to ensure that the law is upheld."

Furthermore, she continued, "you also need to effect cultural shifts so that people don't feel, 'You're forcing me to do something. I'm going to find ways around it.'"[25]

Without white acknowledgment of racism, Hinkson argues, the majority white view will continue to be: "Sure we understand that racism exists, but we're not willing to have our government do anything to alleviate it because we have this understanding that if I do not overtly discriminate against someone because of their race, then I do not contribute to racism."

Even during slavery times, official, systematic discrimination has led some to argue that the government owes compensation to black victims of government policies. In more recent decades, some activists and politicians have called for "reparations." But even author Coates, among the latest to take up the cause, acknowledges that getting today's lawmakers to agree on a compensation system might be impossible — though, he writes, the debate would be worth it.[26]

Global Policy Solutions, Rockeymoore's organization, proposes a series of government programs aimed at closing the racial wealth gap, including financing infrastructure projects that would provide jobs and subcontracts in the African-American community. But the programs, despite their racial-justice impulse, would be open to all, regardless of color. "I don't think that there has been much political will or public will for racially specific solutions," Rockeymoore says.

Nevertheless, another of the center's proposals calls for reviving the "10–20-30 plan" — a provision of the American Recovery and Reinvestment Act of 2009.[27] The so-called "economic stimulus" poured federal money into food stamps and other aid, as well as infrastructure projects that designated 10 percent of stimulus money toward communities with at least 20 percent of the population living below the poverty line for at least 30 years.

But Green of the National Leadership Network of Black Conservatives, organized by the conservative advocacy group the National Center for Public Policy Research, which supports environmental deregulation, opposes expanding government-funded health care and works to get black conservatives elected, doubts that programs and laws will do much good. "Racism and racial

---

* The three laws were the Civil Rights Act of 1964, the Voting Rights act of 1965 and the Fair Housing Act of 1968.

discrimination are a manifestation of sin," he says. "We have to deal with it from a moral perspective."

Green dismisses a major liberal policy proposal — raising the minimum wage nationally to $15 an hour — because, he says, doing so would kill jobs. "Increasing the minimum wage increases the unemployment of black people, whether teens or adults," he says. "If you increased to $15 for entry-level workers, business owners are not going to hire those who need employment the most. . . . [So] how are they going to develop work skills and overcome the socioeconomic differences between black and white?"

Those who favor government activism acknowledge that government programs can hurt some intended beneficiaries. "The ghetto has become a slum," says William Sampson, chair of the public policy studies department at DePaul University in Chicago. "When it was a ghetto, everybody black lived in it; it didn't matter if you were a lawyer or a dentist or on welfare, the folkways and mores were determined by the middle-income folks. Integration allowed them to leave, and they did, which took away the role models and compass of those communities."

Sampson stresses that he doesn't mean ending legal segregation was bad. "But there was a downside," he says. Some of that negative effect could be counteracted by a massive government program to train families in effective child-rearing techniques, he says.

"Kids who do well in school have quiet, orderly, structured home environments," Sampson says, "and are disciplined, with high self-esteem, internally controlled and responsible."

Does government need to recommit to school desegregation?

Desegregation of public schools, a major victory of the 20th-century civil rights movement, essentially ended after 1991, when the Supreme Court allowed the termination of plans based on busing students to schools outside their neighborhoods to achieve racial balance.[28]

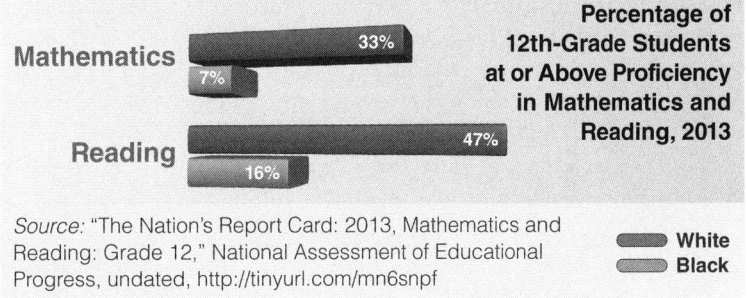

Black Students Lag in Math, Reading

Only 7 percent of black 12th-graders performed at or above proficiency in mathematics in 2013, compared to a third of white students, the latest federal data show. A wider gap existed in reading, with nearly half of white students proficient, compared with only about one-sixth of black students.

Percentage of 12th-Grade Students at or Above Proficiency in Mathematics and Reading, 2013

Mathematics: White 33%, Black 7%
Reading: White 47%, Black 16%

Source: "The Nation's Report Card: 2013, Mathematics and Reading: Grade 12," National Assessment of Educational Progress, undated, http://tinyurl.com/mn6snpf

School integration levels began dropping after the decision, in part because blacks and whites remained residentially segregated. But by 1997, even black families who moved to suburbs found public schools there increasingly divided by race.[29]

As a result, according to the Civil Rights Project, a research organization at the University of California, Los Angeles, a statistically typical white student's class of 30 in 2011–12 had 22 whites, two blacks and four Latinos, while the class of a typical black or Latino student had at least 20 blacks or Latinos and eight whites.[30]

"Black and Latino students tend to be in schools with a substantial majority of poor children," a research report concluded, "but white and Asian students are typically in middle-class schools."[31]

Standardized test results also reflect sharp racial divisions. The most recent report of the National Assessment of Educational Progress shows that in 2013, only 7 percent of black 12th-graders — compared with 33 percent of their white counterparts — were at or above proficiency in math. In reading, 16 percent of black students were proficient, compared with 47 percent of whites.[32]

Some education experts link blacks' poor academic performance to the resegregation of public schools. Sampson of DePaul says schools serving black and Latino students don't get the same level of resources that go to predominantly white schools. "White parents can move" if they are dissatisfied with their children's schools, he says. "Black and Latino parents can't."

George Theoharis, chair of the teaching department at Syracuse University's School of Education and a former Wisconsin school principal, advocates integration. "Certainly, there are other things that matter," he says. "Teaching matters, curriculum matters, leadership matters. But we have disregarded the fact that desegregation really matters. We have enough history in this country of being unable to achieve separate but equal schools."

But rather than pushing for reintegrating public schools, some education experts call for more publicly financed charter schools or more school vouchers, which currently provide subsidies for private-school tuition for low-income and special-needs students in 13 states and Washington, D.C.

Charter schools typically focus on trying to raise academic performance rather than on integration. "Charter schools make no bones" about their focus on academics over race, says Theoharis, who sees charter schools as "part of the whole reform agenda of the past 30 years that has really moved away from desegregation."

Proponents of charter schools, in fact, call those institutions the best way to eliminate academic-performance gaps. Charter schools provide "exciting and viable education in an inclusive, individual manner," said the Center for Education Reform, a leading charter-advocacy organization, citing statistics that show charter students in New York City outperform their public school counterparts.[33]

"In theory, charter schools make some sense," Sampson says. "In practice, they're horrible. They take only the best students. But charter schools on the whole don't outperform public schools." Lotteries that some school districts hold for charter school admissions don't avoid that selection bias, he says, because parents who enter lotteries are by definition more involved in looking for the best schools for their children.

Sampson says having black and white students mix is socially positive for all the students. Georgetown's Hinkson also supports reintegration, pointing out that in her doctoral research at Princeton she found that in the armed forces — often called the most integrated part of America — racial test score gaps at schools for children of military personnel "were smaller there than in any other state in this country."[34]

But Williams of George Mason says, "There is no evidence that in order for black kids to get a high-quality education, we have to capture white kids to sit beside them."

Theoharis says resuming desegregation would be difficult, although "magnet" schools — public schools devoted to one field — could help accomplish more integration, he says, if they were available to all students.

Williams says the need for alternatives is far more urgent than changing schools' racial makeup. He favors school vouchers or tuition tax credits so black parents could have "some kind of alternative to these rotten public schools in many of these neighborhoods."

Green of the National Leadership Network of Black Conservatives argues that public schools should get the kind of scrutiny that Sampson applied to charters. "Some charter schools are going to be terrible and should fail," he says, "and [bad] public schools should fail, too."

BACKGROUND
Slavery and Jim Crow

Today's racial tensions were born in the trans-Atlantic slave trade, which forcibly brought as many as 388,000 Africans to colonial America and the United States between 1619 and 1865, when Congress abolished slavery nationwide by passing the 13th Amendment to the Constitution.[35]

Seventy-eight years earlier, when delegates gathered in Philadelphia in 1787 to write the Constitution, they compromised on slavery in order to keep the South in the Union. Delegates from the North, where several states had banned slavery within their borders years before the constitutional convention convened, wanted to end the trans-Atlantic slave trade. But Southerners refused to accept an immediate ban. The compromise allowed the trade to continue until 1808 and slavery to survive in states where it already existed.[36]

Historians still debate whether the United States was founded as a "slave" nation. Sean Wilentz of Princeton University argued that toleration of regional slavery "did not sanction slavery in national law, as a national institution."[37] But Patrick Rael, of Bowdoin College in Brunswick, Maine, wrote: "If slavery was not legal in every state, it was nonetheless 'national law,' protected and upheld by the Constitution."[38]

The Constitution did contain sections favorable to slave owners, particularly Article 4, Section 2, which held that slaves who escaped to states that had abolished slavery remained slaves and had to be returned to their owners.[39] In 1850 Congress passed a law strengthening slave owners' rights to seize their fugitive "property."[40] Then, in 1857, the Supreme Court ruled in the *Dred Scott* decision that Scott, a slave born in Virginia, did not become free when his master took him temporarily to the free states of Illinois and Wisconsin because he was not a U.S. citizen — nor was any other person of African ancestry.[41]

During the Civil War, President Abraham Lincoln issued the Emancipation Proclamation of 1863, freeing the slaves in Confederate states. In 1865 the 13th Amendment abolishing slavery was ratified, followed three years later by the 14th Amendment, defining anyone born in the United States as a citizen entitled to "equal protection of the laws."[42]

Lincoln's successor, President Andrew Johnson, embarked on Reconstruction, the attempt to establish social and political racial equality in the South. But white resistance won out, with the acquiescence or support of some Northern politicians and judges. The post-Civil War system of white domination became known in the 1890s as Jim Crow. Southern state governments also adopted laws that decreed the arrest of all jobless black people. The penalty was forced labor — essentially, slavery.[43]

In response to white resistance, President Ulysses S. Grant stationed federal troops in nine South Carolina counties.[44] And in 1870 Congress adopted the 15th Amendment, prohibiting states from denying or limiting the right to vote because of "race, color, or previous condition of servitude." Congress followed up with the Enforcement Act, which defined racist violence as a federal crime.[45]

But anti-black violence continued, and in the 1870s, the national political tide shifted against Reconstruction, as Southern white resistance solidified and many Northern politicians proved unwilling to crush the opposition.[46] In 1877, disputed presidential election results led to a Democratic-Republican deal: The Democrats would recognize Republican Rutherford B. Hayes as the winner, and Hayes would pull federal troops out of Louisiana and South Carolina. As a result, white-supremacist politicians' power was cemented throughout the South.[47]

The end of Reconstruction took a deadly toll: Nearly 4,000 blacks were lynched in 12 Southern states between 1887 and 1950, according to the Equal Justice Initiative in Montgomery, Ala.[48]

In several Deep South states — notably Alabama, Florida and Georgia — a forced-labor system was developed in which thousands of black men were worked, often to death, in mines, steel mills and lumber camps. *Slavery by Another Name*, a Pulitzer Prize-winning 2008 book by reporter Douglas A. Blackmon, chronicled how black men were trapped in the labor system by arrests for crimes such as "vagrancy," then "leased" to companies by county sheriffs.[49]

'White Affirmative Action'

After Democrat Franklin D. Roosevelt became president in 1933, his administration's "New Deal" sought to revive the Depression-crippled economy and protect workers' rights through such laws and regulations as the Social Security Act, the Fair Labor Standards Act, the Civilian Conservation Corps, the Works Project Administration and dozens of other efforts.[50]

But whites were the primary beneficiaries, according to historians such as Ira Katznelson of Columbia University, author of the 2005 book, *When Affirmative Action Was White*. Maids and farmworkers — the two kinds of jobs disproportionately held by black people — were excluded from laws protecting unionization and establishing minimum wages and work hours as well as coverage under the new Social Security system. Social Security did not cover those two job categories until the 1950s.[51]

Although Roosevelt and many Northern Democrats didn't share Southerners' racial prejudices, the administration accommodated their racial attitudes because FDR needed support from Southern Democrats to pass New Deal measures.[52] The black press argued that African-Americans were paying the price for the New Deal. Nonetheless, some black commentators did credit FDR and his allies — particularly his wife, Eleanor — with trying to advance racial equality.[53]

After World War II, the GI Bill of Rights — which financed college educations, home mortgages and business ventures — vastly expanded the American middle class.[54] But the bill ensured that Southern black veterans received only minimal benefits — if any. Moreover, blacks were significantly under-represented in the armed forces during

CHRONOLOGY

1789-1863 *Founders compromise on slavery; issue eventually tears country apart.*

1789 Constitution allows slavery and return of fugitive slaves as "property."

1857 Supreme Court rules in *Dred Scott* case that slaves are not citizens.

1863 In midst of Civil War, President Abraham Lincoln issues Emancipation Proclamation, freeing slaves in 10 Confederate states.

1865-1940 *Civil War ends; racist Jim Crow regime in South survives New Deal labor and welfare laws.*

1865 13th Amendment frees all slaves. As Reconstruction attempts to establish racial equality in the South, ex-Confederate Gen. Nathan Bedford Forrest founds Ku Klux Klan to terrorize black population.

1877 Rutherford B. Hayes is recognized as the winner of presidential election in return for pulling federal troops from the South; Jim Crow system follows.

1915 African-Americans begin their "Great Migration" out of the South; the number eventually reaches 6 million.

1933 Compromises with segregationist Southern Democrats restrict black access to New Deal labor benefits.

1940 The number of African-Americans lynched in the South since 1887 approaches 4,000.

1944-1980 *Anger over obstacles to black access to veterans' benefits helps fuel civil rights movement, which wins landmark legislation.*

1944 Local administrators restrict black access to veterans' education grants and business and mortgage loans.

1954 Supreme Court unanimously rules school segregation unconstitutional in *Brown v. Board of Education*.

1964 Civil Rights Act outlaws job, school and public facilities discrimination.

1965 Voting Rights Act prohibits discriminatory obstructions to voting.

1967 Civil disorders erupt in 160 cities.

1968 National commission studying causes of urban riots concludes the nation is moving toward two "separate and unequal" societies. . . . Civil rights leader Rev. Martin Luther King Jr. is assassinated, sparking urban riots. . . . Congress passes Fair Housing Act, banning racial discrimination in housing. . . . Richard M. Nixon is elected president on promise to restore law and order to cities.

1974 Supreme Court rules against combining urban and suburban school districts to desegregate, dealing a blow to desegregation plans.

1994-Present *Crack epidemic prompts harsher sentencing laws for drug-related crimes, later viewed as impetus to mass incarceration of African-Americans.*

1994 Congress and states pass tough anti-crime bills.

2000 Incarcerated population reaches nearly 2 million, up from 474,000 in 1980, with disproportionally high black imprisonment rate.

2008 Democratic Sen. Barack Obama of Illinois is elected president, leading to hopes that America had overcome its racist past.

2012 A neighborhood watch volunteer kills black teenager Trayvon Martin in Florida, focusing new attention on dangers to black males.

2014 Death of Michael Brown at the hands of police in Missouri sparks Black Lives Matter protests and "All Lives Matter" backlash.

2015 President Obama defends Black Lives Matter slogan and movement. . . . Black Lives activists disrupt Democratic candidates' primary speeches, force changes in their campaigns. . . . Demonstrations at the University of Missouri, Yale and elsewhere raise issues of racial discrimination on campus. . . . Chicago police officer is charged with murder in shooting death of 17-year-old Laquan McDonald. . . . Justice Department opens investigation of Chicago police. . . . Chicago Mayor Rahm Emanuel fires police chief; protesters call for Emanuel's resignation.

World War II, with only half of military-age African-Americans serving. The military, which remained segregated until 1948, cited poor performance on health, literacy and aptitude tests for many of the rejections, although the all-black 477th Bombardment Group of airmen performed with distinction.[55]

Three years after the GI Bill was enacted, a report on how black vets were faring said it was "as though the GI Bill had been earmarked 'For White Veterans Only.'"[56]

While the South remained the African-American heartland, about 6 million blacks fled Jim Crow to cities in other regions during the "Great Migration" of 1915 to 1970. The politics and culture of Chicago, New York, Detroit, Los Angeles and many other cities soon reflected the effects of this massive population shift.[57]

In some places, the GI Bill was more equitably administered than in the South. But well into the 1960s, federal housing policy effectively blocked black homeownership — even outside the South — by preventing homes in those areas from qualifying for government-backed mortgages.

"Neighborhoods where black people lived . . . were usually considered ineligible for FHA [Federal Housing Administration] backing," journalist Coates wrote last year, centering his reporting on Chicago. In effect, black people were denied access to mortgages or sometimes forced to rely on extortionate "contract" home purchases, which allowed the sellers to evict families for missing a single payment, leaving the buyers with no equity in the property, Coates reported.[58]

Civil Rights

In the 1950s, the civil rights movement gained fresh momentum, spurred in part by the Supreme Court's 1954 *Brown v. Board of Education* ruling, which called segregated schools inherently unequal.[59]

Then African-Americans and their white allies began a campaign of nonviolent disobedience against state segregation laws, with marches, boycotts and sit-ins that sought to register black voters and end discriminatory practices that, among other things, forced blacks to sit in backs of buses and prevented them from getting served at lunch counters.[60] By the mid-1960s, the movement was challenging racist housing, school and job policies and laws throughout the country.

Within five years of the epic 1963 March on Washington, when 250,000 white and black Americans gathered on the National Mall to demand an end to segregation and job discrimination, Congress had passed the three landmark civil rights laws. They prohibited discrimination in employment, housing, schools and all other public facilities, and mandated that states provide equal access to the polls, with Justice Department prior review — or preclearance — required of any laws that might impede voting in four Deep South states.*[61]

School desegregation efforts begun after the *Brown v. Board of Education* ruling prompted major resistance, including in the North. In Boston, years of sometimes violent protests followed a federal court order in 1974 that both white and black students be bused to schools outside their neighborhoods in order to achieve racial integration.[62]

The busing order was based on a 1970 Supreme Court decision. But four years after the 1974 court order, the high court blocked lower courts from combining city and suburban school districts as part of desegregation plans.[63] Because housing patterns were often racially defined, neighborhood schools remained largely segregated by race.[64]

While residential patterns changed little, national politics were transformed because of the civil rights movement. Democratic President Lyndon B. Johnson, a Texan proud of his Southern roots, championed civil rights and pushed the landmark legislation through a Democratic-controlled Congress; as a result, his party became identified with the movement, and Republicans successfully appealed to Southern white Democrats to switch political allegiances.[65]

"The more Negroes who register as Democrats in the South, the sooner the Negrophobe whites will quit the Democrats and become Republicans," a strategist for Republican President Richard M. Nixon, elected in 1968, later told *The New York Times*. "That's where the votes are."[66] By the 1980s, Republican presidential candidates were winning an average of 67 percent of the white Southern vote.[67]

A major factor in the anti-civil rights backlash was riots in largely black and poor inner-city districts that erupted in Los Angeles, Newark, Detroit and about 160 other cities in 1967. A report by a commission appointed

---

* This "preclearance" requirement was later extended to Alaska and Arizona and selected counties and townships in California, New York and Michigan.

'Black Lives Matter' Slogan Praised and Condemned

Backers point to police brutality, but critics say the slogan is anti-cop.

Three words — Black Lives Matter — have sparked a new argument over race in America. Demonstrators chanting and tweeting that slogan have protested the deaths of African-Americans, many of them unarmed, at the hands of police officers — most of them white — in cities across the country in the past two years. As Black Lives Matter activist Melina Abdullah, Pan-African studies chair at California State University in Los Angeles, said on CNN, the slogan first showed up in media reports of demonstrations after the Aug. 9, 2014, shooting death of black teenager Michael Brown by then-Ferguson, Mo., police officer Darren Wilson.[1]

A series of ensuing demonstrations evolved into the Black Lives Matter movement after unarmed black men or boys were killed by police in New York City; Beavercreek, Ohio; North Charleston, S.C.; and Baltimore. Then, a young white supremacist was charged in the shooting deaths of nine parishioners at a historic African-American church in Charleston, S.C., last July.[2]

The slogan reflects reality, says Leslie L. Hinkson, a sociology professor at Georgetown University in Washington. "We're told in so many ways that 'no, your lives don't matter,'" she says, "You don't have good services, your schools are horrible. There are constant reminders."

Some police officials and political conservatives argue, however, that the slogan and movement behind it are anti-cop. Even some sympathizers say the movement is ignoring the fact that most black homicides are perpetrated by African-Americans (as most homicides of whites are white-on-white).[3]

President Obama has defended the slogan, saying the organizers used the phrase "not because . . . they were suggesting nobody else's lives matter. Rather, what they were suggesting was there is a specific problem that is happening in the African-American community that's not happening in other communities. And that is a legitimate issue that we've got to address."[4]

Criticism of the movement, however, grew more heated after a handful of African-Americans were accused of attacking police. Those incidents included the December 2014 killing of two New York City officers and the September 2015 shooting death of Houston Deputy Sheriff Darren Goforth. "Police Lives Matter" was the rallying cry for a memorial march in his honor.[5]

"Black Lives Matter has blood on their hands . . . blue blood on their hands," Fox News host Eric Bolling said in November, accusing the movement of stoking violence against police.[6]

On the political front, the slogan has given Democratic presidential primary candidates some trouble. In June, at a speech to a black church audience in Missouri, Hillary Clinton said, paraphrasing her mother, "All lives matter." After push-back from activists, she was embracing the slogan by July. "This is not just a slogan, this should be a guiding principle," Clinton said in South Carolina. "We have some serious problems with race and justice and systemic racism."[7]

Among Republican primary candidates, the strongest reaction to Black Lives Matter has come from New Jersey Gov. Chris Christie, who accused members of calling for the killing of police officers, apparently a reference to a chant during a Minneapolis demonstration that one activist said was a joke.[8]

But some conservatives back the slogan. Jack Hunter, a libertarian former aide to Republican presidential primary candidate Rand Paul, says Obama had it right. "It's not that all lives don't matter," Hunter says. "Black Lives Matter is saying that there is something specifically wrong with our society, our criminal justice system, and that is a fact. That is what that phrase means."

Still, the movement could trigger a backlash if critics persuade enough non-African-Americans that the slogan means that only black lives matter, and only when black people are killed or injured by police.

Citing the high death-by-homicide rate for African-Americans at the hands of African-Americans, Hinkson of Georgetown asks, "Don't people within the [black] community also need to be reminded that black lives matter?"

John McWhorter, a linguistics professor at Columbia University in New York, agreed. Calling himself sympathetic to the movement, he said the movement should also direct its "fierceness" at preventing the "minority of black men from killing one another all the time."⁹

Filmmaker Spike Lee spoke in even tougher terms. "We as a people can't talk only about Black Lives Matter," he told *Chicago* magazine, "and then not talk about this self-inflicted genocide. . . . Only by talking about both and addressing both can we bring change."¹⁰

About two weeks after Lee's interview, a 9-year-old Chicago boy, TyShawn Lee, was shot to death in an alley in the city's largely black South Side. Police said the boy was executed because of his father's alleged gang ties; they later charged 27-year-old African-American gang member Corey Morgan with first-degree murder.¹¹

Then attention shifted back to police killings after the release of a video showing a Chicago police officer fatally shooting a black 17-year-old, Laquan McDonald, 16 times; protests led to the early December firing of the police chief.¹²

Black Lives activist DeRay Mckesson, organizer of "Campaign Zero," which advocates new restrictions on police use of force and related measures, says Lee and McWhorter are missing the point. "To see people with such exposure and intellect not be able to grasp the fundamental difference between community violence and police violence is nothing short of stunning," he says. "Police are powerful not only because they have guns but because they are allowed to use guns and have protection when they use them. That makes them different from anyone else."¹³

— *Peter Katel*

A demonstrator on the National Mall on Oct.10, 2015, holds a sign that answers critics who see racism in the Black Lives Matter slogan. The Justice or Else! rally was held to commemorate the 20th anniversary of the Million Man March.

¹"CNN Newsroom," Oct. 2, 2015, Nexis.

²Matt Apuzzo, "Dylann Roof, Charleston Shooting Suspect, Is Indicted on Federal Hate Crime Charges," *The New York Times*, July 22, 2015, http://tinyurl.com/qcwlj8b; Sheryl Gay Stolberg, "Trial Set for First of 6 Baltimore Officers Charged in Freddie Gray Case," *The New York Times*, Sept. 29, 2015, http://tinyurl.com/pnfc22m; Al Baker, J. David Goodman and Benjamin Mueller, "Beyond the Chokehold: The Path to Eric Garner's Death," *The New York Times*, June 13, 2015, http://tinyurl.com/nflggzh. For background, see Barbara Mantel, "Far-right Extremism," *CQ Researcher*, Sept. 18, 2015, pp. 769-792.

³Amy Sherman, "An updated look at statistics on black-on-black murders," *Politifact Florida*, May 21, 2015, http://tinyurl.com/nmvpj4l.

⁴"Remarks by the President in Arm Chair Discussion on Criminal Justice with Law Enforcement Leaders," the White House, Oct. 22, 2015, http://tinyurl.com/qguv37k.

⁵Radley Balko, "Once again: There is no 'war on cops,'" *The Washington Post*, Sept. 10, 2015, http://tinyurl.com/ohbeune; "Community holds 'Police Lives Matter' march in memory of slain deputy," KHOU-TV, *USA Today*, Sept. 12, 2015, http://tinyurl.com/q5lz2ho; Larry Celona et al., "Gunman executes 2 NYPD cops in Garner 'revenge,'" *New York Post*, Dec. 20, 2014, http://tinyurl.com/lgubufb.

⁶"Quentin Tarantino defends anti-cop comments," Fox News, Nov. 5, 2015, http://tinyurl.com/pzrd7te.

⁷Cameron Joseph, "'Black Lives Matter': Hillary Clinton addresses nation's racial inequality in meeting with South Carolina Democrats," *New York Daily News*, July 23, 2015, http://tinyurl.com/otyrq4m; Tamara Keith, "Hillary Clinton's 3-Word Misstep: 'All Lives Matter,'" NPR, June 24, 2015, http://tinyurl.com/nc4ndro.

⁸Quoted in Caitlin Dickson, "Chris Christie doubles down on Black Lives Matter claims," Yahoo News, Oct. 31, 2015, http://tinyurl.com/h4pa59v; "Black Lives Matter Activist: 'Pigs in a Blanket' Chant was 'More Playful Than Anything,'" *Breitbart*, Sept. 1, 2015, http://tinyurl.com/phsasgl; Rich Zeoli, "Executive Director of the FOP: Comey Wrong About Ferguson Effect," CBS News, Oct. 28, 2015, http://tinyurl.com/hp7r9d3.

⁹"CNN Tonight," CNN, Sept. 29, 2015; John McWhorter, "Black Lives Matter should also take on 'black-on-black crime,'" *The Washington Post*, Oct. 22, 2015, http://tinyurl.com/jjfqpys.

¹⁰Bryan Smith, "Spike Lee Sounds Off on Chi-Raq, Gun Violence, and Rahm," *Chicago* magazine, Oct. 22, 2015, http://tinyurl.com/zsmlhsv.

¹¹Sarah Kaplan, "Chicago police: Slain 9-year-old was targeted, lured into alley," *The Washington Post*, Nov. 6, 2015, http://tinyurl.com/hts7spv. See also Jason Keyser, "Charges Filed In Murder Of 9-Year-Old Chicago Boy Tyshawn Lee," The Associated Press, *The Huffington Post*, Nov. 29, 2015, http://tinyurl.com/qfm62o6.

¹²"Chicago mayor fires police chief in wake of video release," The Associated Press, Yahoo! News, Dec. 1, 2015, http://tinyurl.com/j7z7zxx.

¹³"Campaign Zero," undated, http://tinyurl.com/p6vknog.

Race Becomes Big Issue in Upcoming Primaries

Activists demand more action from Democrats.

Race is becoming — again — a headline issue in U.S. life just as the two main political parties are preparing to nominate presidential candidates.

Democratic candidates' speeches have been interrupted by demonstrators demanding more responsiveness on race questions, prompting some changes in how the Hillary Clinton and Bernie Sanders campaigns deal with the issue.

Most members of the larger Republican field have devoted little time to the causes associated with Black Lives Matter — above all, the issue of law enforcement in minority communities.

Nevertheless, the only black candidate from either party is Republican Ben Carson, a retired pediatric neurosurgeon. He had written earlier in his career that blacks and whites received different treatment from the law enforcement system. Now, he is calling the focus on criminal justice a mistake. "I just don't agree that that's where the emphasis needs to be," he said.[1]

The Democratic Party's relations with the black community, forged in the civil rights battles of a half century ago, have not guaranteed an easy ride with the new generation of activists.

Since Democratic front-runner Clinton argued politely with Black Lives Matter activists last summer, she has stepped up her attacks on racial inequities. "Race still plays a significant role in determining who gets ahead in America and who gets left behind," Clinton said in a speech in Atlanta in October. "Racial profiling is wrong." Her campaign website does not single out racial inequality as an issue. But, in her criminal justice proposals she calls for legislation to end racial profiling by federal, state and local law enforcement officials.[2]

Clinton's leading primary opponent, Sen. Sanders of Vermont, a "democratic socialist," had his own tussles with Black Lives Matter activists. He started his campaign by stating that more jobs are the answer to racial injustice. But after activists disrupted some of his speeches, Sanders unveiled a criminal justice policy to address "violence waged against black and brown Americans: physical, political, legal and economic." He advocates "community policing," which promotes closer ties between officers and neighborhood residents; more racial and ethnic diversity on police forces; and aggressive prosecution of lawbreaking police.[3]

Clinton and Sanders' decisions to embrace the activists' cause was good politics, some analysts say. "For Democrats to win the White House in 2016, African-Americans must give 90 to 95 percent of our votes to that party's nominee," wrote Van Jones, the president of two social justice advocacy groups, Dream Corps and Rebuild the Dream, which promote innovative solutions for America's economy. "Given that fact, younger African-Americans rightfully expect each and every Democratic candidate to explicitly, loudly and enthusiastically address the pain and needs of black lives — to their satisfaction."[4]

Donald Trump, the New York real estate developer who has polled highest among the GOP candidates, has a troubled history on racial matters. In July, he reprised his past support of the conspiracy theory — embraced by white supremacists — that President Obama was not U.S.-born.[5]

When Trump opened his presidential campaign in June, he said of Mexican immigrants: "They're bringing drugs, they're bringing crime, they're rapists."[6]

Then in November, Trump defended the punching of a Black Lives Matter protester who disrupted a speech by the candidate in Birmingham, Ala. "Maybe he should have been roughed up because it was absolutely disgusting what he was doing," Trump said after the incident.[7]

Soon after, Trump announced that 100 black ministers and religious leaders would endorse him at a public event.

to investigate the cause of the riots concluded: "Our nation is moving toward two societies, one black, one white — separate and unequal."[68]

Just after the report was issued, more riots broke out, following the April assassination of the Rev. King, the unquestioned leader of the civil rights movement. Within

But the event instead became a private meeting with a smaller group, where the beating of the protester was discussed. After the session, Trump got one endorsement, from the Rev. Darrell Scott, a Cleveland-area pastor who had helped organize the event.[8]

Before the meeting, the Rev. Al Sharpton, a prominent black civil rights activist, cited the candidate's recent comments about undocumented Mexican immigrants as a reason not to attend. "I don't know how you preach Jesus, a refugee, on Sunday and then deal with a refugee-basher on Monday," Sharpton said.[9]

Two Republican candidates stand apart from their competitors on racial issues. Sen. Marco Rubio of Florida spoke sympathetically of protests against discriminatory policing. "This is a legitimate issue," he said on Fox News in August. "It is a fact that in the African-American community around this country there has been, for a number of years now, a growing resentment toward the way law enforcement and the criminal justice system interacts with the community."[10]

Sen. Rand Paul of Kentucky, spoke along similar lines. "There's no justification for violence, but there is anger," he said, also on Fox. "I am starting to understand where the anger comes from, and that we need to fix things . . . in our system, because [justice] isn't being meted out fairly."[11]

But one other Republican candidate's statements on racial matters have been characterized by some as insulting or hostile. Former Florida Gov. Jeb Bush, asked during a South Carolina appearance how he would attract black voters, said: "Our message is one of hope and aspiration. It isn't one of division and 'get in line and we'll take care of you with free stuff.'"[12] Bush immediately came under fire for seemingly echoing a conservative view that government aid has sapped African-Americans' initiative.

Statistics on race and party affiliation give Republicans little political incentive to reach out to black voters in primary races. Only 11 percent of the black population "lean" Republican, according to a 2015 study by the Pew Research Center. By contrast, 80 percent of African-Americans lean Democratic.[13]

Nevertheless, candidates from both parties have been invited to two February town hall meetings on race-related issues. DeRay Mckesson, an African-American activist who is helping to organize the sessions, says, "Whoever the next president is will need to engage on a range of issues, including those that don't necessarily align with their viewpoint."

— *Peter Katel*

---

[1] Quoted in Kelefa Sanneh, "A Wing and a Prayer," *The New Yorker*, Nov. 30, 2015, http://tinyurl.com/pu9vdsh.

[2] Sabrina Siddiqui, "Black Lives Matter protest interrupts Clinton speech on criminal justice," *The Guardian*, Oct. 30, 2015, http://tinyurl.com/p8dvba3; "Our criminal justice system is out of balance," hillaryclinton.com, undated, http://tinyurl.com/pfneqjb.

[3] "Racial Justice," Bernie 2016, http://tinyurl.com/pp8bfja; Brandon Ellington Patterson, "Black Lives Matter Just Officially Became Part of the Democratic Primary," *Mother Jones*, Oct. 21, 2015, http://tinyurl.com/onc9sjm.

[4] Van Jones, "Disrupting Bernie Sanders and the Democrats: 5 lessons," CNN, Aug. 13, 2015, http://tinyurl.com/ouubgf7.

[5] Meghan Keneally, "Donald Trump's History of Raising Birther Questions About President Obama," ABC News, Sept. 18, 2015, http://tinyurl.com/qdtdlu5; Evan Osnos, "The Fearful and the Frustrated," *The New Yorker*, Aug. 31, 2015, http://tinyurl.com/q4dhgs9.

[6] Adam B. Lerner, "The 10 best lines from Donald Trump's announcement speech," *Politico*, June 16, 2015, http://tinyurl.com/or9bsht.

[7] Jeremy Diamond, "Trump on protester: 'Maybe he should have been roughed up,'" CNN Politics, Nov. 23, 2015.

[8] Michael Barbaro and John Corrales, "'Love' and Disbelief Follow Donald Trump Meeting With Black Leaders," *The New York Times*, Nov. 30, 2015, http://tinyurl.com/osd7opc.

[9] *Ibid.*

[10] German Lopez, "Marco Rubio shows other Republicans how to respond to Black Lives Matter," *Vox*, Sept. 30, 2015, http://tinyurl.com/otdbvzb.

[11] Katherine Krueger, "Rand Paul: 'Not A Big Fan' Of Black Lives Matter, But I Get 'The Anger,'" TPM Livewire, Oct. 23, 2015, http://tinyurl.com/og9j74m.

[12] Sean Sullivan, "Jeb Bush: Win black voters with aspiration, not 'free stuff,'" *The Washington Post*, Sept. 24, 2015, http://tinyurl.com/nbpnpz8.

[13] "A Deep Dive Into Party Affiliation," Pew Research Center, April 7, 2015, http://tinyurl.com/lbed829.

---

a week, at Johnson's urging, Congress had passed the Fair Housing Act, outlawing housing discrimination based on race, religion, sex or national origin.

But Nixon — elected months later on a "law and order" platform — blocked efforts by Housing and Urban Development Secretary George Romney to use the new

Acclaimed author Ta-Nehisi Coates, right, discusses racial issues with sociology professor Bruce Western at Harvard University's John F. Kennedy School of Government on Nov. 11, 2015. A MacArthur fellow and national correspondent for The Atlantic, Coates won the 2015 National Book Award for Between *the World and Me*, about the centuries-old legacy of violence inflicted upon African-Americans.

law to "affirmatively further" housing integration. Romney considered the nation's segregated housing patterns a "high-income white noose" around black inner cities and saw poverty in black ghettos as a major cause of the 1967 urban riots.[69]

"Equal opportunity for all Americans in education and housing is essential if we are going to keep our nation from being torn apart," Romney wrote at the time, according to a 2014 investigation by the public interest journalism organization Pro Publica. Romney ordered HUD to reject applications for federal water, sewer and highway projects in places that fostered segregated housing.[70] Nixon promptly shut down Romney's program, explaining in a memo: "I am convinced that while legal segregation is totally wrong, . . . forced integration of housing or education is just as wrong." He acknowledged that his decision would leave blacks and whites living apart and attending separate schools.[71]

Economic Shifts

Major economic shifts followed the civil rights victories of the 1960s. Labor-intensive manufacturing, including textile mills in the South, began moving to Asia and Mexico, putting many unskilled blacks out of work. Many well-paying, blue-collar jobs migrated to predominantly white suburbs.[72]

Drugs, already a presence in some black urban areas, provided steady — albeit illegal — work for some individuals in urban neighborhoods. As addiction spread, so did robberies and burglaries committed by addicts, prompting demands for tougher penalties for users and dealers. In 1973, with strong support from some in the black community, New York Gov. Nelson Rockefeller, a Republican, pushed through tough, new anti-drug laws, the first major attempt to deal with the drug scourge by ratcheting up prison sentences.[73]

Urban crime skyrocketed during a crack cocaine boom in the late 1980s: In Washington, D.C., alone, the rate of homicide deaths of black men jumped eightfold between 1985 and 1991.[74] Congress reacted in 1994 by passing the largest anti-crime bill in U.S. history, mandating life imprisonment without parole after three violent or drug-trafficking convictions and providing nearly $10 billion for prisons.[75]

States adopted similar measures, spurring a major increase in the prison population. From 1990 to 2000, the number of inmates in prisons and jails more than quadrupled, from 474,000 to nearly 2 million. As the prison population rose, so did racial disparity. In 1993, the imprisonment rate among blacks was seven times that of whites. By 2000, nearly 10 percent of all black males ages 25–29 were in prison, compared with 1.1 percent of whites in the same age range.[76]

The skyrocketing prison population led Michelle Alexander, an Ohio State University law professor, to dub the U.S. criminal justice system "the new Jim Crow."[77] She was referring to, among other things, police racial profiling and over-focusing on drug enforcement in African-American communities.[78]

In a forerunner of today's police-violence cellphone videos, a civilian in 1991 recorded four Los Angeles police officers repeatedly kicking and striking an unarmed black motorist, Rodney King, after a high-speed car chase. The video, showing King being struck 56 times with metal batons, aroused nationwide outrage, and the officers were charged with assault and use of excessive force. In 1992, however, an all-white jury acquitted three of them and deadlocked on the fourth, setting off five days of riots in predominantly black South Los Angeles. More than 60 people died in the mayhem. A federal grand jury later indicted the officers on charges of violating King's civil rights; two were convicted and went to prison, and two were acquitted.[79]

Fifteen years later, Obama's election aroused hopes the country had moved into a post-racial era, but reality proved otherwise. A long-running effort on the right to challenge Obama's U.S. citizenship — joined by current Republican presidential candidate Donald Trump — was seen by commentator Fareed Zakaria as "shame[ful] coded racism," a view shared by many others.[80]

Then a series of deaths of black people, mostly at police hands (and one, Trayvon Martin, 17, killed by a neighborhood watch volunteer in Sanford, Fla.), propelled racial issues back to the top of the national agenda.

CURRENT SITUATION
Police on Trial

Police officers face criminal charges in the deaths of two young black men in separate incidents in Baltimore and Chicago. The deaths sparked shock across the nation, riots in Baltimore, dismissal of the Chicago police chief and demands that Chicago's mayor resign.

In Baltimore, six police officers face charges in connection with the death of Freddie Gray, 25, arrested for carrying a knife after running from patrol officers on April 12, 2015. A video showed Gray being dragged, groaning, to a police van, where his hands and legs were shackled but he was not secured with a seatbelt. Hospitalized after losing consciousness, he died from spinal cord injuries allegedly sustained in the van.[81]

In December, William G. Porter was the first officer to go on trial on charges of manslaughter, assault and reckless endangerment — all stemming from his failure to secure Gray with a seatbelt. In mid-December, a mistrial was declared after a jury of seven blacks and five whites deadlocked. Prosecutors said they will retry the officer. The van's driver faces second-degree murder charges, while two other officers are accused of manslaughter and two others with second-degree assault.[82]

Porter's defense focused on his testimony that he had asked Gray if he needed a medic and helped him onto a van bench.[83]

The McDonald shooting in Chicago presents an even starker picture of what can happen in interactions between police and residents of poor, tough neighborhoods. The 17-year-old was shot in Chicago's predominantly black South Side on Oct. 20, 2014, by police responding to a call that a man had punctured a car tire with a knife.

Police reports at the time depicted McDonald advancing on officer Jason Van Dyke and threatening violence by attempting to get up from the ground after being shot.[84]

But a police car dashcam video, released more than a year later, showed McDonald walking away from police and then spinning around and collapsing as he is hit by the first of Van Dyke's 16 bullets.[85] The video became public after a journalist sued to get it released and only hours after Van Dyke was charged with first-degree murder in the death. He was freed on bail, and in late December pleaded not guilty.[86]

A week later, as protests of police practices grew, Mayor Rahm Emanuel fired Police Superintendent Garry F. McCarthy, saying he "had become an issue rather than dealing with the issue." Emanuel later apologized for the killing and took responsibility for it. But protesters demanded that he resign.[87]

Pressure on Emanuel increased again after the post-Christmas police killings of a grandmother and college student. The mayor announced "a major overhaul" of use-of-force policies. Every officer assigned to respond to incidents will be required, by June 1, to carry a non-lethal electric stun gun (Taser).

Meanwhile, new revelations have emerged about the department's treatment of African-Americans. The Cook County prosecutor released another long-held video, of a police shooting of Ronald Johnson III, 25, fatally shot in the back a week before the McDonald incident. Another video, from 2012, showed officers using a stun gun against a jail inmate, then dragging him down a hallway by his handcuffed wrists. The prisoner, Philip Coleman, a University of Chicago graduate with a master's degree from the University of Illinois, was suffering from a mental health crisis when he died in custody, according to his family.[88]

Chicago police shot and killed 70 people, most of them black, in a five-year period ending in 2014 — more than any other of the nation's 10 largest cities, *The New York Times* reported. The city's police oversight panel upheld misconduct claims in only two cases out of more than 400 police shootings since 2007. But the city has paid out more than $500 million since 2004 to settle lawsuits or complaints involving police.[89]

In late December, Dean Angelo Sr., president of the Chicago chapter of the Fraternal Order of Police, pointed to the level of violence in some parts of the city, noting

AT ISSUE

Is Black Lives Matter a valid slogan?

YES — Jack Hunter
Editor, Rare Politics

Written for CQ Researcher, January 2016

If I told my fellow allies in the fight against abortion that "unborn lives matter," few would think I was saying that other lives didn't matter. It's hard to imagine abortion opponents even being offended at such an assertion.

They would implicitly understand that I was saying certain lives seem to matter less under our legal system and in our society. If some anti-abortion activists showed poor judgment or even committed violent acts in the name of their cause, few of the like-minded would suggest that this kind of behavior discredited the cause itself.

"Black Lives Matter" makes the same important point.

Overall, it doesn't matter if Black Lives Matter leaders sometimes do questionable things. It doesn't matter if some who champion this slogan sometimes take things to unnecessary and even deplorable extremes.

Those exceptions do not discount certain realities.

Black Lives Matter is an answer to a long-standing societal question: Why are African-Americans targeted and incarcerated at disproportionate rates compared with any other racial group? Why are they more often the victims of police brutality?

And why do more Americans not realize this is happening?

From Ferguson, Mo., and the killing of Michael Brown, to Baltimore, Md., and the death of Freddie Gray, to Charleston, S.C., and the deadly police shooting of Walter Scott, to a Staten Island, N.Y., sidewalk where Eric Garner was choked to death by the police for selling "loose" cigarettes, Americans continue to see incidents, time and again, where black lives do seem to be valued less than others.

Not all of these high-profile incidents are the same. Some are murkier than others, such as in Ferguson. Some are quite clear, such as in Charleston, where a police officer now sits in jail, charged with murder.

But there is a pattern, one that is repeated too often. Many of these incidents that have captured the national imagination and begun important conversations about race have been caught on smartphone cameras.

Smartphone cameras are relatively new, but black Americans are trying to tell us that this type of brutality is not new. These problems did not begin with the advent of smartphones.

What critics like to portray as a movement needlessly stoking racial division is really just an abused minority finally giving voice to the violence they have long faced.

Black Lives Matter is an integral part of the ongoing fight to right unpardonable wrongs.

NO — Derryck Green
Member of Project 21, the National Leadership Network of Black Conservatives

Written for CQ Researcher, January 2016

Black Lives Matter is neither a valid slogan nor a legitimate protest movement. The slogan's implication and the movement's emphasis are incongruent; it's an intentional mischaracterization. When one hears the slogan Black Lives Matter, one is led to think of an all-inclusive phrase and social movement that's focused on several pressing issues that have a direct and immediate impact on improving the quality of black lives.

But that's not the intention of the motto. Black Lives Matter isn't all-inclusive. It's very selective, because the only black lives that matter to this protest movement are blacks who were shot and killed by white police officers. Members and supporters continue to propagate the belief, with little evidence, that cops are systematically targeting and unjustly killing black people.

This perspective is thoroughly problematic. First, police shoot more white suspects than black suspects. Second, most of the black suspects who were shot and killed by police in the past year — many of whom were defended by Black Lives Matter — were criminals resisting arrest. Defending black criminals legitimizes and glorifies black criminality. Sanctifying black criminals killed by cops largely comes at the expense of black victims — and the movement's credibility — especially when more serious issues desperately need addressing.

Furthermore, the desire to be singularly identified as people who are targeted only because they're black is to embrace victimization. Black Lives Matter doesn't want any other group intruding on or minimizing its claims of victimhood, which explains the petulant indignation to the phrase "all lives matter." If "all lives matter," blacks' special status as victims is negated and the transparent and dishonest rationale for the existence of this movement is destroyed. The movement uses victimization as leverage for its dishonesty.

The disproportionate focus on the rare, alleged cases of police brutality and shootings intentionally diverts attention from the significant difficulties blacks face. Black women accounted for 37 percent of all abortions in 2012. Black illegitimacy is at 72 percent. Black children are disproportionately trapped in substandard and underperforming schools, preserving the educational gap between black and white students. Black unemployment is twice the national rate. Blacks kill 90 percent of black homicide victims. Don't black lives suffering from these problems matter?

The selective moral outrage that favors black criminals over black lives in general invalidates the social and moral credibility of Black Lives Matter.

that officers seize thousands of guns a year. The department took 6,714 illegal guns off the street as of mid-December, 2015. "That is good policing," he said. "But nobody looks at it that way." Politicians are "throwing us under the bus," he added.[90]

Homicides in Chicago and Baltimore have spiked in recent years. By the end of 2015, Baltimore had suffered 344 homicides, the highest number since 1993, when the city had a population of 100,000 more people. Chicago's homicide number rose by 12.6 percent to 468.[91]

Later, at a meeting of mayors and police chiefs in Washington, Emanuel blamed the rising homicide rate on police second-guessing themselves due to fear of being accused of misconduct. Angelo denied Emanuel's accusation, saying police were "out there working their buns off." But his Baltimore counterpart had said following the Freddie Gray incident that officers were "more afraid of going to jail than getting shot and killed right now."[92]

Campus Revolts

Protests against racism are surging at public and private universities.

At the University of Missouri in Columbia, the entire football team, blacks and whites, refused to play unless university President Tim Wolfe quit or was fired. The players were backing black protesters outraged at what they called Wolfe's failure to respond to their concerns over threats and insults against black students. Wolfe resigned in early November, acknowledging his "inaction" in the face of growing unrest. Chancellor R. Bowen Loftin, who supervised the Columbia campus, stepped down as well (but took another job at the university).[93]

Similar protests spread beyond "Mizzou." At Yale, more than 1,000 students marched in early November after several racially tinged incidents, including the alleged exclusion of students of color from a "White Girls Only" fraternity party — denied by Sigma Alpha Epsilon — and a controversy over a student panel's request that students not don racially or ethnically offensive Halloween costumes, such as blackface or feathered headdresses.[94]

Buildings named for former college presidents whose racism is no longer considered acceptable have become a rallying point for many students. At Georgetown, students held a sit-in over plans to rename two buildings after former Georgetown presidents who had organized slave sales in the 19th century. The university canceled the renamings.[95]

At the University of Maryland in College Park, the state Board of Regents acceded to student demands to remove from the football stadium the name of a former university president, Harry C. Byrd, who had opposed admitting black students.[96]

At Princeton, black students objected to the use of U.S. President Woodrow Wilson's name on several university facilities. Wilson, a former Princeton president, purged many African-Americans from the federal civil service during his years in the White House. In November Princeton President Christopher Eisgruber agreed to consider renaming the facilities, among them the Woodrow Wilson School of International Affairs.[97]

Some see name removal as retroactive judgment. "I don't like Woodrow Wilson any more than they do, but we can't impose modern values on historical figures," said Josh Zuckerman, a Princeton senior and the editor-in-chief of the conservative college magazine, the *Princeton Tory*.[98]

But lawyer Gordon J. Davis of the Venable law firm in New York argued in a *New York Times* op-ed that Wilson's race policies had real and lasting consequences, including for his grandfather, who lost his civil service job. Wilson "ruined the lives of countless talented African-Americans and their families," Davis wrote.[99]

OUTLOOK

Hope and Fear

Those who study race view the near-term future with a mix of hope and fear. For many, the country's demographic shift — already underway — is the key change on the horizon.

By 2060 non-Hispanic whites are expected to decrease from 62 percent of the population to less than 44 percent, as Hispanics come to represent more than one-quarter of the country. African-Americans are expected to be only slightly above their current 13 percent level.[100]

For Texas A&M's Feagin, the demographic transformation and what he sees as stepped-up white hostility toward African-Americans and other nonwhites are "like two trains on the same track headed toward each other," illustrated by what he calls "this dramatic increase in white protectionism to protect our privileges that you see so dramatically in Republican candidates."

Trump's incendiary language about Mexican immigrants is a danger sign for all people of color, Feagin says. "We've had coded language, but to call Mexican immigrants rapists — ordinary working people accused of being rapists — forget all the subtle stuff," he says. "This reflects the levels of white fear of losing privilege and income and wealth."

Yet one view from abroad is that Americans are facing up to their racial issues, in sharp contrast to Western Europe, which has failed to integrate Arab and African immigrants, many of them Muslims who have lived in Europe for three generations. Continuing tensions in Parisian suburbs with big immigrant populations since riots in 2005, and recent anti-immigrant violence in Germany, are only the most obvious signs of the strained relations, aggravated by recent terrorist attacks in France and Belgium.[101]

Damaso Reyes, a black Dominican-American photojournalist from New York now based in Barcelona, says the United States is far more willing than Europe to confront race in its social, political and cultural dimensions. "Black people, white people, brown people are all having conversations about race all the time, in social media, schools and history books," he says. "When a Texas history book says that 'workers' were brought to America from Africa, there is a huge outcry: 'Call slavery, slavery.' To me, that is a positive thing."[102]

For Rockeymoore of Global Policy Solutions, solving institutional racism is the most urgent task facing today's activists. "If we don't address structural racism in this country, within 40 to 50 years we'll look like apartheid South Africa or pre-1950 America in terms of opportunity or lack thereof," she says.

Georgetown's Hinkson doesn't think much is going to change in the next 20 years with regard to deep-seated patterns of racial separation. "The very fact that we haven't been able to say that integrating schools by race and class is the best way to eliminate gaps" in academic performance "tells you that as far as our schools being less segregated 20 years from now, that is not going to happen."

Fortner, of City University of New York, is somewhat more hopeful. "I'm a perpetual optimist when it comes to the American project," he says. However, he adds, he doesn't think improvement will come rapidly, given the polarization and gridlock in the political system.

"Washington is broken. If we find a way out of the current political morass, we could race to a much better future," Fortner says. "But if the system remains so gridlocked, it's going to be a slow walk to progress."

NOTES

1. Quoted in Monica Davey and Mitch Smith, "Anger Over Killing by Police Halts Shopping in Chicago," *The New York Times*, Nov. 27, 2015, http://tinyurl.com/pppahla.

2. "Chicago Mayor Cutting Short Cuba Vacation After Police Shooting," Reuters, *The New York Times*, Dec. 28, 2015, http://tinyurl.com/nhdf5cg; "Prosecutors Defend Urging No Charges in Tamir Rice Shooting," The Associated Press, *The New York Times*, Dec. 30, 2015, http://tinyurl.com/ns9eghq.

3. Maya Rhodan, "Congress Now Has More Black Lawmakers Than Ever Before," *Time*, Jan. 6, 2015, http://tinyurl.com/jqawbw3.

4. Nate Silver, "Black Americans Are Killed At 12 Times The Rate of People In Other Developed Countries," *FiveThirtyEight:Politics*, June 18, 2015, http://tinyurl.com/q6o4n38; Justin Wolfers, David Leonhardt, Kevin Quealy, "1.5 Million Missing Black Men," *The Upshot* blog, *The New York Times*, April 20, 2015, http://tinyurl.com/z7f954b; "Digest of Education Statistics," National Center for Education Statistics, 2014, http://tinyurl.com/qerhs5c; Kenneth D. Kochanek, Elizabeth Arias and Robert N. Anderson, "Leading Causes of Death Contributing to Decrease in Life Expectancy Gap Between Black and White Populations: United States, 1999–2013," U.S. Centers for Disease Control and Prevention, "NCHS Data Brief No 218," November 2015, http://tinyurl.com/jcntjbk; and Rakesh Kochhar and Richard Fry, "Wealth inequality has widened along racial, ethnic lines since end of Great Recession," Pew Research Center, Dec. 12, 2014, http://tinyurl.com/kww2vpo.

5. Kimberly Kindy *et al.*, "A Year of Reckoning: Police fatally Shoot Nearly 1,000," *The Washington Post*, Dec. 26, 2015, http://tinyurl.com/zx95ptf; (with updated statistics) http://tinyurl.com/nrsl3xr; Jon Swaine *et al.*, "Young black men killed by US police

at highest rate in year of 1,134 deaths," *The Guardian*, Dec. 31, 2015, http://tinyurl.com/zc39qv2.

6. Kochhar and Fry, *ibid.*

7. "The War on Marijuana in Black and White," American Civil Liberties Union, June, 2013, p. 49, http://tinyurl.com/jycxybp; David Weigel, "The Avenger Without a Mask," *Slate*, Aug. 5, 2014, http://tinyurl.com/jvc9jkn.

8. Ta-Nehisi Coates, "The Case for Reparations," *The Atlantic*, June 2014, http://tinyurl.com/nopprgt.

9. Sandra L. Colby and Jennifer M. Ortman, "Projections of the Size and Composition of the U.S. Population: 2014 to 2060," U.S. Census Bureau, March 2015, p. 9, http://tinyurl.com/zvobj4q.

10. "National American Indian Holocaust Museum," National Congress of American Indians, Resolution #TUL-13–005, 2013, http://tinyurl.com/j2g4hay; Guenter Lewy, "Were American Indians the Victims of Genocide?" History News Network, September 2004, http://tinyurl.com/nhuz248. William D. Carrigan and Clive Webb, "When Americans Lynched Mexicans," *The New York Times*, Feb. 20, 2015, http://tinyurl.com/n2yruap.

11. "National Museum of African American History and Culture," *Smithsonian*, updated Oct. 2, 2015, http://tinyurl.com/mrxe8b.

12. "Report of the National Advisory Commission on Civil Disorders, Summary, Chapter 2," Homeland Security Digital Library, 1968, http://tinyurl.com/jzsccqz.

13. Eliott C. McLaughlin, John Murgatroyd and Kevin Conlon, "Charlotte jury hears vastly different accounts of Jonathan Ferrell's death," CNN, Aug. 6, 2015, http://tinyurl.com/gv54r2g; Peter Holley, "New video shows Texas police officer pulling gun on teenagers at pool party," *The Washington Post*, June 8, 2015, http://tinyurl.com/okvksap; Emma Brown, T. Rees Shapiro and Elahe Izadi, "S.C. sheriff fires officer who threw student across a classroom," *The Washington Post*, Oct. 28, 2015, http://tinyurl.com/hch2ajo.

14. Quoted in Richard Pérez-Peña and Timothy Williams, "Glare of Video is Shifting Public's View of Police," *The New York Times*, July 30, 2015, http://tinyurl.com/nf57czh.

15. Quoted in Alan Blinder and Marc Santora, "Officer Who Killed Walter Scott Is Fired, and Police Chief Denounces Shooting," *The New York Times*, April 8, 2015, http://tinyurl.com/pow99ay.

16. Quoted in Melanie Eversley and Jessica Estepa, "Across the USA, videos of police killings spark protests, drive conversation," *USA Today*, Dec. 8, 2015, http://tinyurl.com/grt92oq.

17. James B. Comey, Georgetown University, Washington, D.C., Feb. 12, 2015, http://tinyurl.com/mckgtf4.

18. For background, see Peter Katel, "Race Relations," *CQ Researcher*, "Hot Topic" report, May 20, 2015.

19. "We The Protesters, Campaign Zero," Campaign Zero, http://tinyurl.com/p6vknog.

20. According to the most recent statistics, 51 percent of 12,253 homicide victims in 2013 were African-American: "Crime in the United States, 2013," FBI, undated, http://tinyurl.com/oxo5mhu.

21. "FBI Releases 2013 Crime Statistics from the National Incident-Based Reporting System," FBI press release, Dec. 22, 2014, http://tinyurl.com/optoe5d; Amy Sherman, "An updated look at statistics on black-on-black murders," *Politifact Florida*, May 21, 2015, http://tinyurl.com/nmvpj4l.

22. Sharon LaFraniere and Andrew W. Lehren, "The Disproportionate Risks of Driving While Black," *The New York Times*, Oct. 24, 2015, http://tinyurl.com/pj9ukke.

23. "Full Video: Hillary Clinton meets Black Lives Matter," "The Rachel Maddow Show," Aug. 20, 2015, http://tinyurl.com/pn9s2ex.

24. David McCabe, "Clinton focuses on race, inequality," *The Hill*, April 29, 2015, http://tinyurl.com/pfkw3rb.

25. For background, see Kenneth Jost, "Housing Discrimination," *CQ Researcher*, Nov. 6, 2015, pp. 937–960.

26. Coates, *op. cit.*; Joe R. Feagin, *Racist America: Roots, Current Realities, and Future Reparations* (2014 3rd. ed.), pp. 306–308.

27. "A Policy Agenda for Closing the Racial Wealth Gap," Center for Global Policy Solutions, 2015, http://tinyurl.com/ov256s5.

28. *Board of Education of Oklahoma City Public Schools v. Dowell*, 498 U.S. 239 (1991), http://tinyurl.com/qc73rxq; Linda Greenhouse, "Justices Rule Mandatory Busing May Go, Even if Races Stay Apart," *The New York Times*, Jan. 16, 1991, http://tinyurl.com/nbrlw6d.

29. Peter Applebome, "Schools See Re-emergence Of 'Separate but Equal,'" *The New York Times*, April 8, 1997, http://tinyurl.com/om4gtqc.

30. Gary Orfield *et al.*, "Brown at 60: Great Progress, a Long Retreat and an Uncertain Future," The Civil Rights Project, UCLA, May 15, 2014, p. 12, http://tinyurl.com/n9cok4e; for background, see Reed Karaim, "Race and Education," *CQ Researcher*, Sept. 5, 2014, pp. 721–744.

31. *Ibid.*, p. 2.

32. "The Nation's Report Card: 2013 Mathematics and Reading: Grade 12 Assessment," Nation's Assessment of Educational Progress, undated, http://tinyurl.com/mn6snpf.

33. "Why Charter Schools Work," Center for Education Reform, undated, http://tinyurl.com/qdmokdf.

34. Leslie Hinkson, "Racial Issues in Urban Schools," TEDx Talks, Nov. 24, 2015, http://tinyurl.com/oxjklhx.

35. Hugh Thomas, *The Slave Trade: The Story of the Atlantic Slave Trade: 1440–1870* (1997), pp. 804–805; "The Abolition of the Slave Trade," undated, The Schomburg Center for Research in Black Culture, http://tinyurl.com/osj9pn9.

36. *Ibid.*, Thomas, pp. 501–502.

37. Sean Wilentz, "Constitutionally, Slavery Is No National Institution," *The New York Times*, Sept. 16, 2015, http://tinyurl.com/nb99yrp.

38. Patrick Rael, "Sean Wilentz is wrong about the Founders, Slavery, and the Constitution," African American Intellectual History Society, Sept. 29, 2015, http://tinyurl.com/q4oe3jb.

39. James McPherson, *Battle Cry of Freedom: The Civil War Era* (1988), p. 73.

40. *Ibid.*, pp. 78–79.

41. Elizabeth R. Varon, *Disunion! The Coming of the American Civil War, 1789–1859* (2008), pp. 298–304.

42. F. Michael Higginbotham, *Ghosts of Jim Crow: Ending Racism in Post-Racial America* (2013), pp. 64–66.

43. *Ibid.*, p. 64.

44. *Ibid.*, pp. 68–69.

45. Charles Lane, *The Day Freedom Died: The Colfax Massacre, the Supreme Court, and the Betrayal of Reconstruction* (2008), Kindle edition, no page numbers.

46. *Ibid.*

47. *Ibid.*

48. "Lynching in America: Confronting the Legacy of Racial Terror, Report Summary," Equal Justice Initiative, 2015, http://tinyurl.com/pu8gqwd.

49. Douglas Blackmon, *Slavery by Another Name: The Re-Enslavement of Black Americans from the Civil War to World War II* (2008), pp. 395–396.

50. Ira Katznelson, *When Affirmative Action Was White* (2005), pp. 24–52.

51. *Ibid.*, pp. 24–25.

52. *Ibid.*, p. 26.

53. *Ibid.*, p. 29.

54. "History and Timeline," U.S. Department of Veterans Affairs, undated, http://tinyurl.com/mgx7vzu.

55. Katznelson, *op. cit.*, pp. 126, 129. Also see J. Todd Moye, *Freedom Flyers: The Tuskegee Airmen of World War II* (2012).

56. *Ibid.*, Katznelson, p. 115.

57. Isabel Wilkerson, *The Warmth of Other Suns: The Epic Story of America's Great Migration* (2010), pp. 8–11.

58. Coates, *op. cit.*

59. *Brown v. Board of Education of Topeka*, 237 US 483 (1954), http://tinyurl.com/o2cl9o9.

60. Taylor Branch, *Parting the Waters: America in the King Years, 1954–1963* (1988).

61. For background, see Kenneth Jost, "Voting Controversies," *CQ Researcher*, Feb. 21, 2014, pp. 169–192.

62. Bridget Murphy, "Effects of Desegregation Busing Battles Linger in Boston," The Associated Press, in

The Huffington Post, April 7, 2013, http://tinyurl.com/p6pwxqj.

63. For background, see Kenneth Jost, "Supreme Court Controversies," *CQ Researcher*, Sept. 28, 2012, pp. 813–840.

64. Reed Jordan, "America's public schools remain highly segregated," Urban Institute, Aug. 27, 2014, http://tinyurl.com/pp79kye.

65. "President Johnson's Special Message to Congress: The American Promise," LBJ Presidential Library, March 15, 1965, http://tinyurl.com/qaq4l6p.

66. Quoted in James Boyd, "Nixon's southern strategy: 'It's All in the Charts,'" *The New York Times Magazine*, May 17, 1970, http://tinyurl.com/nuusnn8.

67. Earl Black and Merle Black, *The Rise of Southern Republicans* (2003), p. 220.

68. "Report of the National Advisory Commission on Civil Disorders," *op. cit.*, "Summary, Introduction."

69. See Nikole Hannah-Jones, "Living Apart: How the Government Betrayed a Landmark Civil Rights Law," *ProPublica*, June 25, 2015, http://tinyurl.com/8jzwt3w.

70. *Ibid.*

71. *Ibid.*

72. Orlando Patterson, with Ethan Fosse, eds., *The Cultural Matrix: Understanding Black Youth* (2015), p. 127.

73. Michael Javen Fortner, *Black Silent Majority: The Rockefeller Drug Laws and the Politics of Punishment* (2015), Kindle edition, no page numbers.

74. For background, see Peter Katel, "Fighting Crime," *CQ Researcher*, Feb. 8, 2008, pp. 121–144.

75. JoAnne O'Bryant, "Crime Control: The Federal Response," Congressional Research Service, updated March 5, 2003, pp. 3–4, http://tinyurl.com/7x9hhdr.

76. "The Punishing Decade: Prison and Jail Estimates at the Millennium," Justice Policy Institute, May 2000, http://tinyurl.com/cp2xa84; Allen J. Beck and Paige M. Harrison, "Prisoners in 2000," *Bureau of Justice Statistics Bulletin*, August 2001, p. 11, http://tinyurl.com/hpucn5l; Allen J. Beck and Darrell K. Gilliard, "Prisoners in 1994," Bureau of Justice Statistics, August 1995, p. 1, http://tinyurl.com/z9s6a4q.

77. Michelle Alexander, *The New Jim Crow: Mass Incarceration in the Age of Colorblindness* (2010).

78. *Ibid.*, pp. 58–88.

79. Lou Cannon, "National Guard Called to Stem Violence After L.A. Officers' Acquittal in Beating," *The Washington Post*, April 30, 1992, http://tinyurl.com/zocva6x; "A timeline of events in Rodney King's life," CNN, June 17, 2012, http://tinyurl.com/zle595t.

80. Ben Smith and Byron Tau, "Birtherism: Where it all began," *Politico*, April 24, 2011, http://tinyurl.com/qcm7uuq; Ari Melber, "The Nation: Confronting Trump's Coded Racism," *The Nation* (NPR), April 27, 2011, http://tinyurl.com/3qfp93p.

81. "The Latest: Medical Examiner: Gray's spine was 'kinked,'" The Associated Press, Dec. 4, 2015, tinyurl.com/1o428x7o; Justin Jouvenal, Lynh Bui and DeNeen L. Brown, "First trial in death of Freddie Gray begins in a city still on edge," *The Washington Post*, Nov. 30, 2015, http://tinyurl.com/j38wwhm.

82. Sheryl Gay Stolberg, "Police Officers Charged in Freddie Gray's Death to Be Tried in Baltimore," *The New York Times*, Sept. 10, 2015, http://tinyurl.com/nanbfwv; Justin Jouvenal and Lynh Bui, "New trial date isn't set for Baltimore officer accused in Freddie Gray's death," *The Washington Post*, Dec. 17, 2015, http://tinyurl.com/hyz9wss.

83. Peter Hermann, "Friends and neighbors remember Freddie Gray," *The Washington Post*, April 24, 2015, http://tinyurl.com/mmbvo7p.

84. "Laquan McDonald police reports differ dramatically from video," *Chicago Tribune*, Dec. 5, 2015, http://tinyurl.com/nmo4my5; "Crime Trends in Archer Heights," *Chicago Tribune*, Nov. 19-Dec. 19, 2015, http://tinyurl.com/gwnlerx.

85. Jason Meisner, Jeremy Gorner and Steve Schmadeke, "Chicago releases dash-cam video of fatal shooting after cop charged with murder," *Chicago Tribune*, Nov. 24, 2015, http://tinyurl.com/nfhhx98. "Changes to Be Announced in Chicago Police Training, Tasers," The Associated Press, *The New*

York Times, Dec. 30, 2015, http://tinyurl.com/oqgh2d3.

86. Ashley Southall, "Reporter Who Forced Release of Laquan McDonald Video Is Barred From News Event," *The New York Times*, Nov. 25, 2015, http://tinyurl.com/q6gl2g2.

87. Rick Pearson, Bill Ruthhart and John Byrne, "Emanuel recall bill, council hearing, show political flank-covering in McDonald case," *Chicago Tribune*, Dec. 16, 2015, http://tinyurl.com/joe2523; Amber Phillips, "Rahm Emanuel is in deep, deep trouble," *The Washington Post*, Dec. 10, 2015, http://tinyurl.com/nhg5kos.

88. Don Babwin, "1 After Another, Chicago Police Videos Made Public," The Associated Press, Dec. 10, 2015, http://tinyurl.com/nlhs8em.

89. Monica Davey and Timothy Williams, "Chicago Pays Millions but Punishes Few in Killings by Police," *The New York Times*, Dec. 17, 2015, http://tinyurl.com/ot78klo.

90. Quoted in *ibid.*, "Changes to Be Announced in Chicago Police Training, Tasers."

91. "Josh Sanburn, "Chicago Shootings and Murders Surged in 2015," *Time*, Jan. 2, 2016, http://tinyurl.com/os3q9ay; Kevin Rector, "Deadliest year in Baltimore history ends with 344 homicides," *The Baltimore Sun*, Jan. 1, 2016, http://tinyurl.com/z9dxs5s.

92. Quoted in John Byrne, "Emanuel blames Chicago crime uptick on officers second-guessing themselves," *Chicago Tribune*, Oct. 13, 2015, http://tinyurl.com/ofxw9wp; Josh Sanburn, "What's Behind Baltimore's Record-Setting Rise in Homicides," *Time*, June 2, 2015, http://tinyurl.com/ngdg4pw.

93. Susan Svrluga, "U. Missouri president, chancellor resign over handling of racial incidents," *The Washington Post*, Nov. 9, 2015, http://tinyurl.com/jv6p7kp.

94. Avianne Tan, "The Allegations of Racism at Yale That Culminated in Over 1,000 Marching for Justice on Campus," ABC News, Nov. 10, 2015, http://tinyurl.com/pkcn35y. Liam Stack, "Yale's Halloween Advice Stokes a Racially Charged Debate," *The New York Times*, Nov. 8, 2015, http://tinyurl.com/oxu7y3o.

95. Katherine Shaver, "Georgetown University to rename two buildings that reflect school's ties to slavery," *The Washington Post*, Nov 15, 2015, http://tinyurl.com/jsj3pdq.

96. Yvonne Wenger, "Byrd Stadium to become Maryland Stadium after regents vote," *The Baltimore Sun*, Dec. 11, 2015, http://tinyurl.com/zapmvgb.

97. Mary Hui, "After protests, Princeton debates Woodrow Wilson's legacy," *The Washington Post*, Nov. 23, 2015, http://tinyurl.com/hplwgqs; William Keylor, "The long-forgotten racial attitudes and policies of Woodrow Wilson," *Professor Voices*, Boston University, March 4, 2013, http://tinyurl.com/nas8ok9.

98. Quoted in Hui, *op. cit*.

99. Gordon J. Davis, "What Woodrow Wilson Cost My Grandfather," *The New York Times*, Nov. 24, 2015, http://tinyurl.com/p36bvol.

100. Colby and Ortman, *op. cit.*

101. Angelique Chrisafis, "'Nothing's changed': 10 years after French riots, banlieues remain in crisis," *The Guardian*, Oct. 22, 2015, http://tinyurl.com/ngd7rerj; Alison Smale, "Anti-Immigrant Violence in Germany Spurs New Debate on Hate Speech," *The New York Times*, Oct. 21, 2015, http://tinyurl.com/oxu7y3o.

102. Manny Fernandez and Christine Hauser, "Texas Mother Teaches Textbook Company a Lesson on Accuracy," *The New York Times*, Oct. 5, 2015, http://tinyurl.com/pwpe3oe.

BIBLIOGRAPHY

Selected Sources
Books

Alexander, Michelle, *The New Jim Crow: Mass Incarceration in the Age of Colorblindness*, The New Press, 2010.
An Ohio State University law professor's book helped spur efforts to change the nation's criminal justice system.

Coates, Ta-Nehisi, *Between the World and Me*, Spiegel & Grau, 2015.

A journalist's brief but searing memoir-essay explores life as a black man in today's America.

Feagin, Joe R., *Racist America: Roots, Current Realities, and Future Reparations,* **Routledge,** 2014.
A Texas A&M sociologist specializing in race, describes government policies that implicitly or explicitly provided preferential treatment for whites.

Fortner, Michael Javen, *Black Silent Majority: The Rockefeller Drug Laws and the Politics of Punishment,* **Harvard University Press,** 2015.
Examining the impact of the country's first drug-crackdown laws, a City University of New York professor of urban studies analyzes anti-crime sentiment in the African-American community.

Oliver, Melvin L., and Thomas M. Shapiro, *Black Wealth/White Wealth: A New Perspective on Racial Inequality,* **Routledge Taylor & Francis,** 2006.
Sociologists from the University of California, Santa Barbara, and Brandeis University, respectively, updated a 1995 book that drew attention to how profoundly discriminatory practices have affected black asset-building.

Riley, Jason L., *Please Stop Helping Us: How Liberals Make It Harder for Blacks to Succeed,* **Encounter Books,** 2014.
A senior fellow at the center-right Manhattan Institute sums up the black conservative vision: Personal choices and a culture of "victimhood" — rather than historical and economic forces — explain conditions in poor African-American neighborhoods.

Articles

Domenech, Ben, "Are Republicans For Freedom Or White Identity Politics?" *The Federalist,* **Aug. 21, 2015, http://tinyurl.com/nny5h66.**
The publisher of a conservative magazine worries that Republican presidential candidate Donald Trump's focus on white grievances could push his party into European-style semi-fascist populism.

Mckesson, DeRay, "Reflections on Meeting with Senator Bernie Sanders and Secretary Hillary Clinton, and the #DemDebate," *Medium,* **Oct. 15, 2015, http://tinyurl.com/o5tumj4.**
A leading activist reports on how top Democratic candidates greeted proposals from members of the Black Lives Matter protest movement.

Rutenberg, Jim, "A Dream Undone," *The New York Times Magazine,* **July 29, 2015, http://tinyurl.com/p8hmfdt.**
A veteran correspondent chronicles a long campaign to weaken the 1965 Voting Rights Act based on the argument that discriminatory conditions have changed in the South.

Smith, Jamil, "BlackLivesMatter Protesters Are Not the Problem," *The New Republic,* **Aug. 10, 2015, http://tinyurl.com/p5b473e.**
An editor at a liberal magazine argues that activists are justified in confronting friendly presidential candidates on racial justice issues.

Walk-Morris, Tatiana, "Blacks Are Challenged to Buy From Black-Owned Businesses to Close Gap," *The New York Times,* **Nov. 15, 2015, http://tinyurl.com/pmasdk3.**
A Chicago lawyer bought only from black-owned businesses for one year, prompting an examination of the effectiveness of grassroots efforts to close the black-white wealth gap.

Williams, Vanessa, "For Clinton, a challenge to keep black voters energized about her campaign," *The Washington Post,* **Nov. 1, 2015, http://tinyurl.com/oxaxqbu.**
A political reporter chronicles the Democratic front-runner's efforts to maintain support of a vital part of the party's constituency.

Reports and Studies

Azerrad, David, and Rea S. Hederman Jr., "Defending the Dream: Why Income Inequality Doesn't Threaten Opportunity," *Heritage Foundation,* **Sept. 13, 2012, http://tinyurl.com/d28ppb7.**
Two staff members of a conservative think tank conclude that the high rate of single-parent households among African-Americans explains the black-white wealth gap.

Orfield, Gary, *et al.,* **"Brown at 60: Great Progress, a Long Retreat and an Uncertain Future,"** *The Civil*

Rights Project, University of California, Los Angeles, May 15, 2014, http://tinyurl.com/q8v3t6b.
Four education scholars conclude that public schools increasingly are segregated by race and class, even though legally mandated segregation has disappeared.

Traub, Amy, and Catherine Ruetschlin, "The Racial Wealth Gap: Why Policy Matters," *Demos*, March 10, 2015, http://tinyurl.com/mxltzn5.
A liberal think tank analyzes government policies that contribute to the wealth gap and others that could narrow the divide.

For More Information

ACLU, 125 Broad St., New York, NY 10004; 212-549-2500; https://www.aclu.org/issues/racial-justice. Litigates on a variety of race-related issues, including discrimination in school discipline and racial profiling by police.

Campaign Zero, www.joincampaignzero.org/#vision. An outgrowth of the Black Lives Matter movement; has proposed ways to help curb police use of force.

Global Policy Solutions, 1300 L St., N.W., Washington, DC 20005; 202-265-5111; http://globalpolicysolutions.com. A research and advocacy organization that focuses on equality of economic opportunity, including racial equity.

Project 21, National Leadership Network of Black Conservatives, www.nationalcenter.org/P21Index.html. Provides an outlet for commentary by African-Americans of the political right on topics such as affirmative action and immigration.

Scholars Network on Black Masculinity, University of Michigan, Department of Sociology, 500 South State St., Ann Arbor, MI 48109; 734-647-4444; http://thescholarsnetwork.org/index.html. Studies how to improve life possibilities for black men.

The Sentencing Project, 1705 DeSales St., N.W., Washington, DC 20036; 202-628-0871; www.sentencingproject.org. A criminal justice reform advocacy think tank.

9

Housing the Homeless

Peter Katel

A Times Square church offers sanctuary from the cold to a homeless man in New York City. Street people represent only the public face of homelessness. Since the early 1980s, large numbers of single-parent families, veterans and mentally ill people have become homeless.

From *CQ Researcher*, October 10, 2014.

Kimberly Mahan had just spent her remaining $3 on a large package of Ramen noodles. It was 2012, and Mahan was stuck in Farmington, N.M., pushing a stroller stuffed with six clothes-filled backpacks for herself and her two young children.

Mahan realized she had no idea how to reach Albuquerque, the state's biggest city, where she hoped to restart her life. She also had no idea of what she was going to do once she got there. "I looked up to the sky and said, 'OK, God, what am I supposed to do?'" she remembers.

A few days later, Mahan made it to Albuquerque, thanks to strangers who gave her rides and money after spotting the family on roadsides. Police officers picked up Mahan and her children and took them to Joy Junction, an evangelical Christian family shelter that provides food, clothing and Bible-based counseling.

Mahan's 180-mile journey began when her husband left, she says, depriving the family of its breadwinner. Mahan, 40, had worked for years in stores and fast-food restaurants but quit after her second child was born. Now, after nearly two years at Joy Junction, she wants to land a job and rent an apartment.

"I hope to have me and my kids back on our feet pretty soon," she says, citing the shelter's policy of allowing residents time to rebuild their lives.

"Typically, you're not going to see [homeless families] on the street," says Carmela J. DeCandia, director of the National Center on Family Homelessness, a think tank in Waltham, Mass.

Majority of Homeless Lives in 5 States

California accounted for more than 20 percent of the nation's homeless population in 2013, and 13 percent lived in New York. Collectively, those two states, along with Florida (8 percent), Texas (5 percent) and Massachusetts (3 percent), had 51 percent of the total.

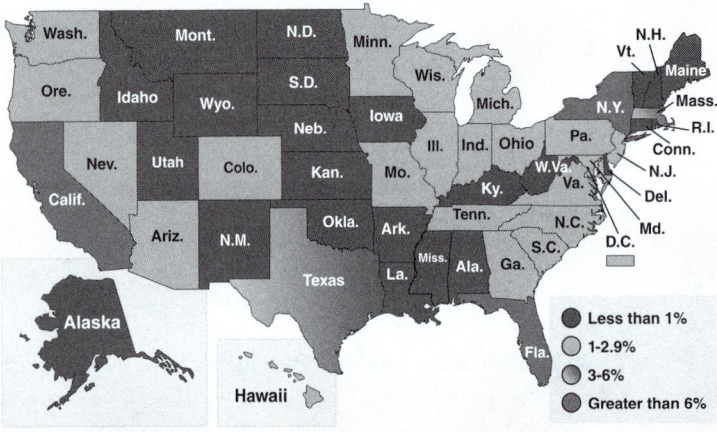

State Shares of National Homeless Population, 2013

Source: Meghan Henry, Alvaro Cortes and Sean Morris, "The 2013 Annual Homeless Assessment Report (AHAR) to Congress: Part 1 Point-in-Time Estimates of Homelessness," U.S. Department of Housing and Urban Development, November 2013, p. 8, http://tinyurl.com/qd89wa8

Homeless single people, on the other hand, can be found in the streets and parks of cities big and small, often to the despair and outrage of residents, business owners and politicians. In the tourism mecca of Honolulu, Mayor Kirk Caldwell calls street people a threat.

"It's time to declare a war on homelessness, which is evolving into a crisis," Caldwell, a Democrat, wrote in *The Honolulu Star-Advertiser* in June. "We cannot let homelessness ruin our economy and take over our city."[1]

But street people represent only the public face of a socioeconomic tragedy that has been intensifying since the early 1980s, when several developments came together. Those include a punishing recession; rises in the divorce rate and number of single-parent families; and changes in mental health care that resulted in more mentally ill people becoming homeless.

Ambitious goals set in the 2000s by the George W. Bush administration to end chronic homelessness within 10 years remain unfulfilled, in part because of the steep recession of 2007-09.

With homelessness entrenched in the national landscape, the debate has focused on the most basic of questions: What exactly is homelessness? Should the definition be limited to street people or include those temporarily living with friends or relatives? The answers lead to an even bigger question: How can homelessness be ended?

Counting the homeless population remains an inexact science. The U.S. Department of Housing and Urban Development (HUD) conducts an annual one-night "point-in-time" count of the homeless. According to HUD's figures, about 610,000 Americans were homeless on a single night in 2013 — a 9.2 percent drop from 2007. HUD also found that between 2012 and 2013 the homeless population fell 3.7 percent.[2]

According to another HUD assessment, nearly 1.5 million Americans used a homeless shelter at some point in 2012 — down since 2007, despite a jump between 2009 and 2010. And 36 percent of those were homeless families — the same percentage that showed up in the "point in time" census.[3]

But HUD's point-in-time count "underestimates the scope of the problem because it misses many people who have found their own refuges outside of formal shelters," says Marybeth Shinn, a social psychologist and the chair of the Human & Organizational Development Department at Vanderbilt University's Peabody College of Education and Human Development in Nashville, Tenn., because it misses many people who have found their own refuges outside of formal shelters.

Shinn helped conduct a study that concluded a point-in-time count in New York City in 2005 missed up to 41 percent of homeless people who were not living in shelters.[4]

HUD itself acknowledges that its numbers fall short of producing a full picture. While HUD-funded housing programs — from shelters to permanent housing — aid more than 1 million people a year, "the total number of persons who experience homelessness may be twice as high," HUD said.[5]

Apart from the difficulties of physically counting the homeless, the HUD numbers reflect a definition of homelessness that some consider too narrow. HUD includes people who are:

- Living in dwellings unfit for human habitation, in emergency shelters or in temporary housing; or
- Leaving such a place;
- Facing loss of their housing within 14 days;
- Living in families with children or unaccompanied youths who haven't had a lease in the past 60 days and have moved two or more times during that period;
- Fleeing domestic violence.[6]

"HUD does not include . . . people who are doubled up," says Nan Roman, president and CEO of the National Alliance to End Homelessness, a Washington-based advocacy and research organization, using the term for people who lose their homes and move in with family or friends. "It includes people in imminent risk of homelessness, but we just haven't figured out a way to count people who would have to leave where they are within 14 days."

Yet, for many people, doubling up is the last step before homelessness. HUD's 2012 annual shelter-based count noted that 66 percent of homeless adults with children had lived with family or friends before entering shelters.[7]

Although not counted by HUD, some of those doubled-up people are tallied by the U.S. Department of Education, which reported that 1.3 million children were homeless during the 2012-13 school year, the most recent figure available. Seventy-five percent of those were doubled-up, 6 percent were in motels and 16 percent in shelters.[8]

"It's a subterranean problem," says Lauren Voyer, a senior vice president at HAPHousing, a Springfield, Mass.-based nonprofit that helps people rent or buy affordable housing. "A lot of families working in low-wage situations who can't get the money together to get an apartment are living in motels. If you are in that situation, you are living without a home."

But others worry that expanding HUD's definition to include doubled-up people could overwhelm the capacity of programs for the homeless. "Doubled-up is its own problem," says Dennis Culhane, a professor of social policy and psychology at the University of Pennsylvania in Philadelphia. "Calling it homeless doesn't solve it. We have a lot of people in this country living in unaffordable, crowded housing," he continues. And relabeling it would only increase "the competition for the tiny resources we have."

Scarce resources, in fact, are the core problem, experts agree. "We still don't have enough affordable housing," says Eric Tars, senior attorney at the National Law Center on Homelessness & Poverty, an advocacy and research organization in Washington. However, as his organization and others advocate, if the federal income tax deduction for mortgage interest were reduced, as has been proposed by some economists, "we could take the savings and reinvest them in affordable-housing programs."

The Obama administration is trying several things aimed at reducing homelessness. On a broad scale, its "Opening Doors" strategy — a sequel to the Bush administration's plan to end homelessness in 10 years — calls for eliminating family homelessness by 2020 by providing affordable or subsidized housing in various forms. It also calls for veterans and homeless individuals who have spent years on the streets to be housed by the end of next year, mainly by placing them in facilities with mental-health and other services.[9]

For the "chronically" homeless, HUD's Housing First doctrine makes providing permanent housing as quickly as possible the top priority, with no qualifying requirements, such as first achieving sobriety. Housing First programs also provide mental health and other services.

Lori Thomas, a professor of social work at the University of North Carolina, Charlotte, says data from Housing First programs for chronically homeless adults show that getting them from shelters into real homes should be the first step. "They need housing to stabilize them to get them working on substance abuse and other issues," she says. "They could never get to that before, because their basic needs were not being met."

Thomas has been assessing the results of a "permanent supportive housing" operation in Charlotte aimed at helping chronically homeless men. That model, with on-site services, embodies the Housing First approach for permanently disabled people. By contrast, other

Homelessness Fell Despite Economic Woes

The number of homeless Americans fell from nearly 672,000 in 2007 to 610,000 in 2013, a decline of 9 percent, despite the 18-month recession that began in December 2007.

Number of Homeless People in the U.S., 2007-2013*

* Calculated as "point-in-time counts," which are one-night estimates of both sheltered and unsheltered homeless populations measured during the last week of January each year.

Source: Meghan Henry, Alvaro Cortes and Sean Morris, "The 2013 Annual Homeless Assessment Report (AHAR) to Congress: Part 1 Point-in-Time Estimates of Homelessness," U.S. Department of Housing and Urban Development, November 2013, p. 6, http://tinyurl.com/qd89wa8

programs — called transitional housing — offer short-term housing aid for up to two years to individuals and families.[10]

Back in Albuquerque, Mahan has now found a part-time job and is hoping for a range of help as she seeks a home for herself and her kids. She stresses she'll need rental assistance from somewhere, as well as psychological aid. "Before I leave here," she says, "I need a support system."

As lawmakers, homeless advocates and academics try to end homelessness, here are some of the questions they are debating:

Does unemployment cause most homelessness?

Experts agree that poverty is the main cause of homelessness. But poverty has many dimensions. Economic factors, including a combination of poor education and joblessness or underemployment, can lead to poverty and homelessness. And social problems such as substance abuse or mental illness can make it difficult to keep a job or afford housing.

An interim HUD report last year on an ongoing study of 2,307 homeless families showed that only 17 percent of the adults were working at the outset of the study, and many of those were working 30 hours a week or less. Likewise, a 1999 study by the Urban Institute, a nonpartisan think tank in Washington, found that only 29 percent of homeless families had paid work in the past month.[11]

Shinn of Vanderbilt University says economic factors — particularly income inequality and rising housing costs — drive many into homelessness. "There are lots of people who are very poor and paying way too much of their income toward rent or are doubled up with other people because they can't afford independent housing," she says.

Data on what causes family homelessness are inconclusive, says Shinn, a principal researcher in the ongoing HUD study. But homelessness became a bigger national issue some 30 years ago, when economic conditions changed, she notes. Many economists say Reagan-era tax cuts contributed to widening disparities in income as the economy continued its march from an industrial model with plenty of well-paid union jobs to an economy dominated by non-union service-oriented jobs. "The change is income inequality and the rising cost of housing," Shinn says. "Anything you can do to raise incomes at the bottom and lower housing costs at the bottom will reduce homelessness."

Peter Gagliardi, president and CEO of HAPHousing, the Springfield nonprofit, notes the loss of traditional jobs that used to define once-thriving factory towns in New England and elsewhere. In Springfield, for instance, several "big employers in the heart of the city that allowed people to walk to work" are now gone, he says. Those employers included board-game-maker Milton Bradley and the Springfield Armory, a then-government-owned firearms manufacturer. Nowadays, he says, "when jobs exist they don't pay enough to cover housing, food and health care. There is a huge, almost unseen, group of families who are in the worst-case housing situation."

Yet, social factors are important, too. DeCandia of the National Center on Family Homelessness says economic trends only partly explain homelessness. "There is a complex interplay between factors like lack of housing and poverty and trauma, domestic violence," she says.

Having a disability or a disabled family member can keep a homeless adult from working, contributing to the low employment rate among adults in homeless families. One study found that 39 percent of homeless adults in families were themselves disabled and/or caring for a relative with a disability that limited the caretaker's ability to work, compared with only 4.5 percent of adults ages 18-44 in the population as a whole.[12]

DeCandia says some families "don't report major mental health issues or major trauma," but they can be "really struggling on the poverty cliff." One thing, she says, "can send them over the edge: loss of a job, or they're hit with a health crisis in the family and can't work regularly." Her organization studied 294 female-headed homeless families in four metropolitan areas of upstate New York and found that 93 percent of the mothers had a history of trauma, most the result of physical assault.[13]

Jessica Williams, who is staying at Albuquerque's Joy Junction with her husband, their newborn son and two older sons, says low wages, combined with a landlord's dishonesty, played a part in their homelessness. "He was going to rent us a house," she says, "and he took our $500 deposit and called us later and said he'd found somebody else."

Williams acknowledged that she had been addicted to cough syrup with codeine, which hurt her employability. Still, both she and her husband found jobs in stores, which allowed them to stay in motels for several weeks. At one, she says, she met someone else who had lost money to an unscrupulous landlord.

"If it's not addiction," she says, "if it's not the economy, it's people."

Is Housing First the best way to keep people from reverting to homelessness?

The name of the doctrine sounds common-sensical and humane. "Housing First" programs are based on the belief that problems a homeless individual or family faces cannot be solved until they are no longer living in the street or a crowded shelter. Hence, people should not be subject to sobriety or drug tests or other requirements as a condition of obtaining housing.[14]

The strategy originated in New York City in 1992 with a program called Pathways to Housing, which provided subsidized permanent housing combined with psychiatric care or drug treatment for chronically homeless individuals. The model later was extended to other categories of homeless persons.[15]

Housing First helps people find long-term housing — other than shelters — as soon as possible and sees that as essential to preventing them from remaining homeless or returning to homelessness. Under that broad concept, a more tactically focused approach, called Rapid Re-Housing, provides short-term financial assistance to allow homeless people or families to acquire temporary housing within 30 days of becoming homeless and to enter a homeless assistance program. The idea is to deal with the immediate burden that finding a rental can place on financially stretched people. Subsidies can be a flat amount or income-based, with households paying a fixed percentage of their earnings for rent. Subsidies typically run for four to six months.[16]

HUD and other agencies — among them the Justice Department, which helps homeless victims of domestic violence and related crimes — use both the Housing First and Rapid Re-Housing approaches. HUD alone serves about 1 million people, including chronically homeless adults and families at imminent risk of homelessness.[17]

Thomas, of the University of North Carolina, says shelters can be counterproductive because of the lack of privacy and the mandatory schedules that participants must abide by. "I've had people tell me they'd rather be in the street," she says. In shelters, "people surrender a lot of their dignity" because of strict rules.

The fundamental idea behind Housing First and Rapid Re-Housing, Thomas says, is that homeless people "need housing to stabilize them, to get them working on substance abuse or other issues. We are going to try to get [you] into housing that you can stay in for the rest of your life, not contingent on following anything but minimal rules — no harm to yourself or others."

But families struggling with poverty, employability and lack of education don't qualify for lifetime supportive housing, so rapidly rehousing them may not keep them from another bout of homelessness, some experts argue.

Ralph da Costa Nunez, president and CEO of the Institute for Children, Poverty & Homelessness in New York City, says Housing First does not work as a

Formerly homeless Air Force veteran Barbara Barnes once slept in one of these bunks at the women's quarters at the New England Center for Homeless Veterans in Boston. Nationwide, nearly 140,000 vets stayed in shelters at one time or another in 2012, down from nearly 150,000 in 2009. The administration is planning to expand its programs for veterans housing to serve 200,000 vets annually. "We're not going to stop until every veteran who has defended America has a home in America," President Obama said in August.

Homelessness agencies can connect people with services, he adds. But he argues against trying to duplicate those services by, for example, setting up dental clinics in homeless shelters. "The homeless system's job should be to solve the homeless problem," Culhane says. "The person is without shelter and should then be returned to some kind of housing."

DeCandia of the National Center on Family Homelessness takes the opposite stance. "Homelessness is not just about lack of housing," she says. "It is embedded in a pattern of residential instability. It is a crisis of housing, but it is not separate from other issues."

Debate should not center on where services are provided, DeCandia says. "There are things that a shelter system and a homeless system can do in the way they create an environment that supports people when they move on, whether that is in a week or three months."

Should homeless families receive bigger or longer-lasting housing subsidies?

The inability of people at the bottom of the socioeconomic ladder to afford housing is at the heart of homelessness, whatever the other contributing factors may be.

one-size-fits-all strategy. "Housing First is terrific for those ready to be housed first," he says. "Eighteen to 22 percent of families in shelters are working poor, with a long work history, and you'll never see them again." Another group of families needs help polishing their job skills and can move into permanent housing relatively quickly, Nunez continues.

But he sees an inherent problem with the relatively short-term nature of assistance available under Rapid Re-Housing models. "The hard-core group churns through the system forever, and it's growing larger and larger," says Nunez, who advocates turning shelters into temporary housing with educational, job-training and other services on-site. "We do them an injustice by simply putting them in housing and seeing them come back. This is not simply a homeless issue; we have to face that."

Culhane of the University of Pennsylvania responds that homelessness is exactly what the word says. "The homeless system is not equipped to solve the problems of poverty," he says, even though homeless people, and poor people in general, may have acute needs, ranging from mental and physical health care to education and financial-management advice.

Federal Section 8 programs — created in 1974 to provide subsidies for low-income renters — and similar, smaller-scale subsidy programs have only enough funds to help about 23 percent of the population that is eligible for assistance, according to two Washington think tanks: the liberal Center on Budget and Policy Priorities and the centrist Bipartisan Policy Center.[18]

In Massachusetts, for instance, 5,400 families are at the end of their two-year state-funded HomeBASE rental assistance. "If I could figure out a way to pay market rate, I would," a homeless Boston mother of two, Altia Taylor, told a state legislative committee last year. "If I could own my own home, I would. I would have done it a long time ago."[19]

Waiting lists for state-administered Section 8 funds are years long. To solve that problem, Republican and Democratic members of a housing strategy panel assembled by the Bipartisan Policy Center recommended last year that "our most vulnerable households, those with extremely low incomes . . . [be] assured access to housing assistance if they need it."[20]

Many congressional Republicans disagree. "Yes, there are some people that probably need and do need housing assistance," Rep. Randy Neugebauer, R-Texas, said last year at a hearing of the House Financial Services Committee. "But this [Section 8] program is on a course that's not sustainable." He cited a 10 percent increase between 2003 and 2013 — from 3 million to 3.3 million — in the number of families participating in the two main Section 8 programs.[21]

Advocating tax cuts and rollbacks of federal regulations on business as ways to stimulate economic growth — and criticizing Democrats for opposing such measures — Neugebauer said, "More and more people are falling off the economic ladder. . . . And so just making the net bigger and bigger is not the long-term solution for many of those families." The long-term solution for those families, he said, "is to keep them on the economic ladder, so that they don't need a safety net."[22]

Democrats on the committee insisted that immediate prevention of homelessness should take priority over longer-term anti-poverty measures. "Full funding of these programs will help keep impoverished Americans, most especially the future of our country, our children, from being pushed onto the streets or forced to live out of cars," said Rep. Carolyn Maloney, D-N.Y.[23]

Maloney denied that Democrats oppose easing regulations on business, but said that leaning too far in that direction, by loosening supervision of the financial industry, could lead to a repeat of the stock market crash of 2008 and thus increase poverty. In any case, she said, homeless people are not in a position to pull themselves up the ladder. "If you don't have and you can't afford housing," she said, "you can't afford going to school."

Others homeless advocates question whether Section 8 subsidies by themselves can do anything more than ensure housing. "I'd like to say that we just need more housing subsidies," says Gagliardi of HAPHousing. "But, ultimately, the solution has to be to address poverty head-on."

That effort, he says, must involve creating or teaching skills for jobs that pay more than minimum wage. "A McDonald's job, a Wal-Mart job — if it's a second job, it's sustaining, but if it's the only one, it doesn't work," he says. Citing the Massachusetts minimum hourly wage of $8, he adds, "You just have to do the math."

Those concerns aside, some homelessness and housing experts argue that experimenting with various forms and levels of rent subsidies, including temporary subsidies to families under Rapid Re-Housing programs, could expand the beneficiary pool.

However, Shinn of Vanderbilt University asks: "Is a short-term subsidy enough?

"Wouldn't it be nice if that were true; then there would be much more to go around."

Shinn urges researchers to look into whether smaller subsidies, which provide less assistance than Section 8, would keep beneficiaries housed while allowing more people to enter the program. The idea, she acknowledges, is "heresy" among advocates for the homeless. But, she says, "I think it's worth experimenting with different structures."

BACKGROUND

"I Ain't Got No Home"

In Elizabethan England, they were known as the strolling poor: vagabonds who took to the highways in search of food, shelter and jobs. In colonial America, village watchmen were responsible for shooing away the wandering

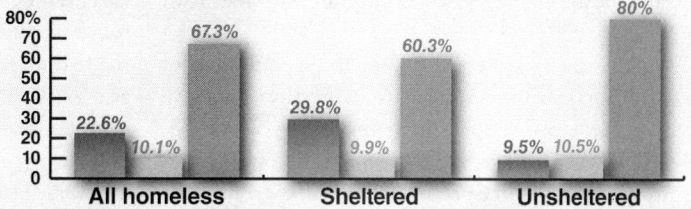

Over One-Fifth of Homeless Are Children

Nearly 23 percent of all homeless people in the United States in 2013 were under 18, and teenagers and children made up nearly a third of those living in shelters. Eighty percent of those living on the street were 25 or older.

Share of U.S. Homeless Population by Age Group, 2013

Source: Meghan Henry, Alvaro Cortes and Sean Morris, "The 2013 Annual Homeless Assessment Report (AHAR) to Congress: Part 1 Point-in-Time Estimates of Homelessness," HUD, November 2013, p. 6, http://tinyurl.com/qd89wa8

poor before they could enter town and become a burden to town charities.[24]

Things were little better in an industrializing America, which saw the emergence of large slums populated by growing numbers of homeless migrants and workers. Single men labeled as "tramps" and "hobos" — the latter looking for work, the former uninterested in working — traveled throughout the country in the late 19th century.

After the stock market crashed in 1929, thousands of banks failed, causing the Great Depression, massive unemployment and a spike in homelessness. By 1933, 1.2 million people were without homes, according to a nationwide census by the private National Center on Care of the Transient and Homeless.[25]

Nature added to the misery: The Dust Bowl — a combination of drought, heat and howling wind that struck the Great Plains — destroyed farms and led some 400,000 people from Oklahoma, Texas, Arkansas and Missouri to flee to California's fertile Central Valley in the mid-1930s.[26] Californians reacted much as their colonial forebears: They tried to keep out the migrants, whom authorities lumped together as "Okies" and "Dust Bowl refugees."

Even without formal anti-Okie policies, police in California earned a reputation for brutal treatment of homeless migrants. In the words of folk singer Woody Guthrie, who together with novelist John Steinbeck, was one of the best-known chroniclers of the migration: "I ain't got no home, I'm just a-roamin' 'round/Just a wandrin' worker, I go from town to town/And the police make it hard wherever I may go/And I ain't got no home in this world anymore."[27]

In 1939, three California district attorneys began enforcing a 1933 state law, the Indigent Act, which made it illegal to help destitute persons enter the state. The U.S. Supreme Court in 1941 overturned that law, making clear that states could not bar people from entry.[28]

Elsewhere in America, the Roosevelt administration's "New Deal" recovery measures financed federal construction projects that would provide shelter and jobs for millions of unemployed "transients" roaming the countryside.[29] Perhaps the best-known was the Civilian Conservation Corps (CCC), open to boys and men ages 16 to 24, as well as up to 25,000 World War I veterans. Participants received housing in newly built camps, food and a small wage for working on flood protection, dams, road-building and other infrastructure projects. By the time the program ended in 1942, about 3 million had served in the CCC.[30]

In a second anti-homelessness measure, Congress appropriated $500 million for grants to states to provide shelter, jobs and other "necessities of life to persons in need . . . whether resident, transient, or homeless." The latter phrase, writes Neil Larry Shumsky, a history professor at Virginia Tech in Blacksburg, marked the first time the federal government explicitly recognized homelessness as a social ill, and it authorized states to help people who were not residents of those states.[31]

The law setting up the fund also created the Federal Transient Program, designed to help states establish relief projects. The program created camps similar to those established by the CCC, but it was a short-lived effort, lasting only until 1935.

Emptying Asylums

In the 1950s, a time of relative prosperity, homelessness again was seen as a problem largely confined to alcoholic single men. President John F. Kennedy undertook some anti-poverty programs in the early 1960s, and his successor, Lyndon B. Johnson, expanded those efforts into his signature War on Poverty program.

Under the program, defined by large-scale nationwide anti-poverty efforts, private and public agencies attempted to end homelessness by broadening the range of services available to the predominantly male homeless population. But projects to reduce the number of people living in poverty took precedence.

Those efforts coincided with another government initiative: decreasing reliance on state psychiatric hospitals (known as "insane asylums" and "mental institutions") for treating mentally ill people. Often dubbed "snake pits," the hospitals had reputations for squalor and abuse or neglect of patients, making legislators increasingly reluctant to fund them. Meanwhile, doctors' associations were promising that new-generation tranquilizers would make hospitalization unnecessary for most patients.

However, "deinstitutionalization," as the process became known, had the unintended consequence of significantly increasing the homeless population.[32] The effort was championed by Kennedy, who had a developmentally disabled sister. The Mental Retardation Facilities and Community Mental Health Centers Construction Act of

1963 sought to replace "custodial mental institutions" with "therapeutic centers," Kennedy said when signing the legislation.[33]

Experts viewed the initial results of the statute and subsequent similar measures as successful. From 1956 to 1980, the hospital population of mentally ill patients dropped from 559,000 to 154,000.[34] But the strategy depended on the availability of space in community-based treatment centers. And by the 1970s, evidence was mounting that nonhospital mental health treatment facilities were in short supply. Two big states, New York and California, saw motels, boarding houses, jails and streets fill up with people discharged from psychiatric hospitals.[35]

In late 1980, shortly before losing his re-election bid, President Jimmy Carter signed the Mental Health Systems Act, designed to expand the number of community mental health centers. But upon taking office in 1981, President Ronald Reagan got Congress to repeal the law. Funds destined for federal mental health centers were combined with other mental health care grants into "block grants" to states, with few conditions for the states to meet. The Reagan administration also launched a review of disability-payment cases, leading to the removal of about 500,000 people from the rolls, many of them mentally ill. However, Congress passed the Disability Benefits Reform Act of 1984, which made such removals more difficult.[36]

Reagan was skeptical of community mental health centers and of services for homeless people, whose situations, he suspected, often reflected personal choice rather than underlying economic or psychological problems.[37]

But the number of homeless people continued to climb due to the effects of deinstitutionalization and the cutback in community mental health services. By 1988, the National Institute of Mental Health reported that between 125,000 and 300,000 people with chronic mental illness were homeless.[38]

Myriad economic problems and profound socioeconomic shifts during the early 1980s added to the homelessness problem. The recession of 1981-82 —the most severe since the 1930s — saw the unemployment rate soar to 10.8 percent in late 1982. Meanwhile, high interest rates and, later in the decade, the failure of more than 700 of the nation's savings and loans institutions made homeownership even tougher for the working poor.[39]

Homeless people sleep on the sidewalk in the Skid Row area of Los Angeles. The city's new anti-homelessness initiative, Operation Healthy Streets, marks a break with Los Angeles' past and the enforcement-heavy anti-homelessness approaches taken by other cities. The initiative provides immediate services for homeless people, such as mental health appointments and enrollment in Medicaid.

Reagan and Congress responded to the recession and the subsequent economic boom by cutting taxes in a series of measures culminating in the Tax Reform Act of 1986. The same period saw the beginning of the widely documented growth in income inequality, though experts argue over whether the new tax structure created the trend, or — as some say — failed to soften the effects of changes occurring in the economy.

At the same time, the number of single-mother families was increasing at a time when the number of manufacturing jobs was decreasing. Plus, a rising divorce rate and widespread adoption of no-fault divorce laws left many divorcees destitute if they lacked marketable job skills.[40]

The "New Homeless"

As the 1990s began, cities began filling up with homeless people to an extent not seen since the Depression. A 1991 study led by Martha Burt, a longtime researcher on homelessness at the Urban Institute, found that between 1981 and 1989 the overall homelessness rate, based on the availability of shelter space, in the nation's 182 largest cities (with populations of 100,000 or more) tripled — from 5 per 10,000 residents to 15 per 10,000. By 1989,

CHRONOLOGY

1933-1941 *Great Depression causes mass homelessness, triggering government programs to combat it.*

1933 With some 1.2 million people homeless, Congress creates, at the request of President Franklin D. Roosevelt, the Civilian Conservation Corps, putting jobless men to work on federally funded projects. . . . Congress provides $500 million for state programs to aid the needy.

1935 Families made homeless by the Depression and the Dust Bowl begin trekking to California.

1939 Three California prosecutors begin enforcing a law prohibiting indigent people from entering the state.

1941 U.S. Supreme Court strikes down California law barring indigents.

1963-1984 *Deinstitutionalization of the mentally ill and cuts to safety-net programs for the poor lead to surge in homelessness.*

1963 President John F. Kennedy signs Mental Retardation Facilities and Community Mental Health Centers Construction Act, designed to treat the mentally ill in community clinics instead of "insane asylums."

1970s As deinstitutionalization takes effect, New York and California see formerly hospitalized people flood cheap lodgings, jails and streets.

1979 New York State Supreme Court rules the state must provide shelter for the homeless.

1980 President Jimmy Carter signs Mental Health Systems Act to expand community mental health centers to treat deinstitutionalized patients.

1981 At the urging of President Ronald Reagan, Congress repeals the community mental health centers law, consolidating all mental health program funding into block grants for states to administer.

1984 Reagan says some people are homeless "by choice."

1987-1996 *Homelessness becomes part of national landscape, prompting various aid measures.*

1987 Growth in homelessness prompts Congress to pass McKinney-Vento Homeless Assistance Act, designed to help the homeless find housing by creating job-training programs.

1988 Up to 300,000 mentally ill people are homeless, the National Institute of Mental Health reports.

1991 Urban Institute says that homelessness tripled between 1981-89.

1992 A New York program pioneers Housing First strategy, combining permanent housing with mental health treatment.

1996 Ninth U.S. Circuit Court of Appeals upholds Seattle ordinances against sitting or lying on downtown sidewalks at certain hours.

2002-Present *Wars in Iraq and Afghanistan focus new attention on homeless veterans, as federal strategy shifts to ending homelessness.*

2002 George W. Bush administration establishes strategy of ending chronic homelessness in 10 years.

2010 Obama administration continues the end-homelessness strategy, vowing to end chronic and veteran homelessness by the end of 2015, and family homelessness by 2020.

2012 Department of Housing and Urban Development reports the number of people using homeless shelters is down 6.3 percent since 2007. . . . Department of Education counts 1.1 million homeless public school students in 2011-12 school year.

2013 One-night "point-in-time" count shows 7 percent drop in number of homeless veterans and a 3.7 percent overall decline in homelessness.

2014 Hawaii's Oahu enacts ordinances designed to keep homeless people out of tourist areas. . . . Police in Albuquerque, N.M., kill homeless schizophrenic man who was camping illegally. . . . Homeless Iraq veteran is arrested for trying to break into the White House.

45 cities had rates higher than 20 per 10,000, and seven (including Washington, D.C., and New York) had rates of more than 40.[41]

The rise in homelessness spawned political and legal movements to provide services, prevent homelessness and protect the homeless from what advocates considered repressive police measures. As early as 1972, the U.S. Supreme Court had ruled that vagrancy laws, long used as an enforcement tool against the homeless, encouraged "arbitrary and erratic arrests and convictions."[42]

In 1979, when New York City was experiencing the first effects of what would become a national trend of growing homelessness, lawyer Robert Hayes won a crucial class-action lawsuit on behalf of six homeless men. The suit — which attacked a city policy of forcing homeless people to find shelter — cited a Depression-era amendment to the state constitution that said "aid, care and support of the needy are public concerns and shall be provided by the state and . . . its subdivisions."[43] The initial court victory led the city to acknowledge its obligation to provide shelter to all homeless men (and, later, women). By 1988, New York shelters could take in up to 10,000 people.[44]

In 1987, advocacy campaigns coupled with the growth in homelessness led to passage of the McKinney-Vento Homeless Assistance Act, which created so-called Continuum of Care programs designed to help the homeless acquire housing.[45]

But the law was based on a definition of homelessness that some experts criticized as too limited. It defined a homeless person as someone without a "fixed, regular and adequate nighttime residence," or someone of low income whose nighttime residence was a shelter. That definition excluded "doubled-up" persons living with relatives or friends. The definition did include people at imminent risk of losing their homes within seven days, but advocates argued that many at-risk people did not meet that seven-day requirement. In effect, that definition severely limited programs designed to help people who were at risk of becoming homeless.[46]

New Strategies

The first major new anti-homelessness initiative since the 1987 McKinney-Vento Act was adopted in 2002. Borrowing the idea from a 2000 proposal by the National Alliance to End Homelessness, the George W. Bush administration declared a goal of ending one form of homelessness — chronic homelessness — within 10 years. It assigned this ambitious task to a revived U.S. Interagency Council on Homelessness, which had been inactive for six years.[47]

The council's director, Philip F. Mangano, enthusiastically adopted the Housing First doctrine, to the applause of some mayors whose cities were struggling with homelessness. "When you ask the consumer what they want," he said at the end of the Bush administration, "they don't simply say a bed, blanket and a bowl of soup. They say they want a place to live."[48]

For chronically homeless individuals, permanent supportive housing — low-rent dwellings with access to substance-abuse counseling and mental health treatment — was seen as the best approach. HUD adopted a policy, still in effect, of favoring Homeless Assistance Grant applicantions from organizations or agencies that provide permanent supportive housing for disabled individuals or families with a disabled adult. That policy effectively addressed the chronically homeless, the nonpartisan Congressional Research Service found, because individuals with a disability are often the ones who are homeless for long, recurring periods.[49]

But Bush's overall housing policy also included efforts to increase homeownership for low- and moderate-income people. Those efforts, supported by Democrats and the lending industry, eventually helped to trigger a housing bubble and the financial crisis of 2007-09, when home prices and the mortgage market collapsed and 2.8 million homes were foreclosed in 2009 alone.[50]

The number of people in homeless shelters rose less drastically, by 2.2 percent between 2009 and 2010, largely because those who lost their homes initially went to rental housing or to stay with friends or family.[51] "We didn't see a lot of foreclosed families ending up in shelters," says Gagliardi of HAPHousing.

However, later research showed that about 20 percent of foreclosures hit rental properties, and 40 percent of families facing eviction from foreclosed apartment buildings were renters, the National Center on Homelessness & Poverty said in 2012. "The problem may only continue to worsen as renters represent a rising segment of the U.S. population," the center concluded.[52]

For children, consequences of foreclosures include frequent moves that tend to lower academic performance, as well as family stress that can bring on "negative behaviors,"

Albuquerque Struggles to Help the Homeless

Needs far exceed the capacity of current services.

On a hot September morning in Albuquerque's hardscrabble South Valley, a group of 30 homeless men and women sit in a large dining hall at a family shelter and talk about how Jesus is helping them rebuild their lives.

"I'm still healing," says a woman in her 40s. "God has shown me how wonderful and merciful he is; my addiction and behaviors made me lose a lot." The shelter's chaplain, Gene Shiplet, leads the program from his desk on the stage, reading Bible passages about leaving bad associates behind. He encourages his flock to participate, complimenting them on their testimonies.

Welcome to the "Life Recovery" program at Joy Junction, New Mexico's largest shelter for homeless families. Staff of the donor-funded project, which opened in 1986, say they won't turn away non-Christians or the nonreligious. But for those who stay, the religious message is unavoidable.

"Things get so bad in peoples' lives that they turn to abuse of alcohol or drugs to escape the pain and dull their senses," says founder and CEO Jeremy Reynalds. "You have to give someone a replacement, a reason for living, someone or something they can turn to to make life worth living. For us as evangelicals, that means having a relationship with Jesus Christ."

A few miles north, in downtown Albuquerque, the head of the state's biggest service center for the homeless is also a man of God. But the Rev. Russell "Rusty" Smith, an Episcopal priest and the executive director of St. Martin's Hospitality Center, takes a secular approach to the center's work.

"Religion doesn't belong in basic human care," Smith says at a coffee shop staffed by a St. Martin's client who is learning job skills. "This is a human response to a human need. I am so opposed to introducing preaching to people in need."

Regardless of whether help comes with Bible readings, no one disputes the need for homeless services in New Mexico's biggest city. Its history has been intertwined with homelessness since the 1930s, when the city was a key stop on Route 66, the fabled highway used in the 1930s by migrants heading to California to escape the Dust Bowl.[1]

"66 is the mother road, the road of flight," John Steinbeck wrote in *The Grapes of Wrath*, as he traced the highway from Arkansas to California, where it wound through "Tucumcari and Santa Rosa and into the New Mexican mountains to Albuquerque, where the road comes down from Santa Fe."

But the Dust Bowl refugees were only passing through. This year in Albuquerque, a schizophrenic homeless man, James Boyd, was shot dead by police, and two homeless Navajo men, Allison Gorman and Kee Thompson, were bludgeoned to death, allegedly by teenagers, as they slept.[2]

Extraordinarily, one of the accused teenagers had been homeless himself. "It's so hard that he could do that to someone where . . . I mean, like I said, we came from

a former poverty specialist at the federal Health and Human Services Department concluded in a report for the Brookings Institution think tank.[53]

Congress responded in 2009 with the Helping Families Save Their Homes Act, which expanded the definition of homelessness to include people staying in motels or hotels at the expense of a government agency or a charity.[54] Under the new definition, unsuitable places to sleep included cars, parks, abandoned buildings, bus and train stations and campgrounds. And the seven-day limit on loss-of-housing risk was doubled to 14 days. People fleeing domestic violence, sexual assault or other such dangers, and who were unable to find new housing immediately, also were added to the definition.[55]

The increase in homelessness in 2008-09 prompted the Obama administration to adopt and expand its predecessor's objective of ending homelessness. In a 2010 strategy document, "Opening Doors," the administration set a five-year timetable for ending homelessness among the chronically homeless, as well as veterans. The administration also announced a plan to end homelessness in 10 years for families, youth and children.[56]

there," Victor Prieto, the father of a 15-year-old who is charged with killing the Navajo men, told Albuquerque's KOB-TV.[3]

According to the city's count, Albuquerque typically had 1,170 homeless people on any one night last year — in a city with about 556,000 people — down 28 percent from 2011. But under the U.S. Department of Education's more expansive definition of homelessness, Albuquerque's public schools enrolled more than 6,000 homeless students during the 2011-12 academic year, according to the school system's Homelessness Project.[4]

Support services in Albuquerque are "highly fragmented [and] underfunded," making it difficult for people to navigate multiple services, according to the New Mexico Coalition to End Homelessness, which includes St. Martin's.

Substance-abuse counseling is one of those services. Reynalds says nearly everyone who shows up at Joy Junction comes with a tormented personal history that usually involves alcohol or drugs. "The BBC came to do a segment retracing *The Grapes of Wrath*, and they wanted to find people who were at Joy Junction purely for lack of money," he says. "We were able to scrape up three people."

For the homeless, Smith argues, substance abuse can be a vital form of survival. "If I was living on the streets, I'd be blitzed every day," he says. "Eating pizza from a dumpster, you can only do that if you're drinking."

St. Martin's offers substance-abuse counseling and other mental health services, along with a day lounge, showers, a laundry and storage space. However, says Monet Silva-Caldwell, the center's development director, "that is not what St. Martin's is all about. We want to get them into housing."

To that end, St. Martin's screens willing clients for a variety of small-scale housing programs that are available. They include "permanent supportive housing" — 142 apartments with mental health services on-site — and subsidized housing for as long as two years in 10 two-bedroom apartments. A new program funded by United Way offers three months of rental assistance and job-search help to people in imminent danger of homelessness.

But the staff at both St. Martin's and Joy Junction say the needs far exceed the capacity of current services. St. Martin's has registered 6,200 people for its day services since August 2013. Joy Junction houses about 300 men, women and children a night.

While Reynalds acknowledges the evangelical nature of Joy Junction's therapeutic services, he draws some lines. "There is a proclivity in some religious missions to say, 'Have your gospel, and then we'll feed you,'" he says. "I have always been strongly opposed to that. We want to take care of your physical needs and then feed you spiritually."

— *Peter Katel*

---

[1] John Steinbeck, *Grapes of Wrath* (1939), http://tinyurl.com/nyas79c.

[2] Ryan Boetel, "Teenage attacker to homeless victims, 'Eat mud,'" *Albuquerque Journal*, July 23, 2014, http://tinyurl.com/ly6mg5j; Rick Nathanson, "James Boyd's dark journey," *Albuquerque Journal*, March 30, 2014, http://tinyurl.com/knkw5rr.

[3] Quoted in Lindsey Bever, "One teen charged with killing two homeless men was once homeless himself, his father said," *The Washington Post*, July 22, 2014, http://tinyurl.com/mge76l4/.

[4] "A Community Response to Homelessness in Albuquerque 2013-2017," New Mexico Coalition to End Homelessness, updated September 2014, p. 5, http://tinyurl.com/mv5h6fq.

"In many respects, this current period of economic hardship mirrors the early 1980s, when widespread homelessness reappeared for the first time since the Great Depression," the strategy document said.[57]

The administration also has focused on reducing homelessness among veterans, through services such as HUD's Veterans Affairs Supportive Housing program (VASH).

"Since 2008, we've housed more than 73,000 veterans through the HUD-VASH program, which provides housing vouchers to help homeless veterans pay for permanent, stable housing," first lady Michelle Obama wrote in an op-ed in July.[58] Nearly 140,000 veterans stayed in shelters at one time or another in 2012, down from nearly 150,000 in 2009.[59]

But that number is still large. And, at a time when 1.4 million Afghanistan and Iraq vets are no longer on active duty, studies of past veteran cohorts show that psychological effects of wartime service often show up as late as 10 years after leaving the military.[60]

Culhane of the University of Pennsylvania, who is a consultant to the Department of Veterans Affairs, says the agency is planning to expand VASH and other

Motels Become Transitional Housing

"Families crowd into rooms, living week to week."

When the Democratic Party held its national convention in Charlotte, N.C., in 2012, homeless shelters saw a sudden influx of families. "We had a big displacement of homeless families," says social work professor Lori Thomas of the University of North Carolina, Charlotte, because they were shut out of where they'd been living — motels. As anyone involved in the world of the homeless knows, motels play an important role for those who have lost their housing.

"Over the years, I've seen motels end up becoming their housing," says Carmela J. DeCandia, director of the National Center on Family Homelessness in Waltham, Mass., "because they can pay night to night or week to week and because there is no security deposit or credit check."

"People in motels are shelter people," says Ralph da Costa Nunez, president and CEO of the Institute for Children, Poverty & Homelessness in New York City.

But Nan Roman, president and CEO of the National Alliance to End Homelessness in Washington, says families with no resources who can't find room at a shelter are likely to sleep at a friend's or relative's house, or in a car. "People in motels have got money, though they've probably got a cash flow problem," she says. "They need help but probably have income."

The motel-living trend got national exposure three years ago, when "60 Minutes" ran a hard-hitting piece on families in Central Florida whose incomes were too low for them to live anywhere except in motels. "In Seminole County, near Orlando, so many kids have lost their homes that school buses now stop at dozens of cheap motels where families crowd into rooms, living week to week," CBS reporter Scott Pelley said.[1]

In Albuquerque, N.M., as in Orlando, some incomes leave people very close to the edge. Jeremy Reynalds, a pastor and the director of Joy Junction, an Albuquerque family shelter that sends a food truck to serve families living in local motels, says some of those who eat the free meals have only enough to pay for lodging. Jessica Williams, a Joy Junction resident with her husband and their newborn, says they stayed at a Motel 6 "until we ran out of money and came here."

The Albuquerque mayor's office cracked down on substandard motels in 2008, reducing, at least for a while, the stock of available motel housing, Reynalds remembers.[2] "I sympathized with what they were doing," he says, because some of the motels had safety hazards. But he adds, "It's like payday loans; they take advantage of the poor, but if they weren't there, what would take their place?"

No one knows how many homeless people are living in motels nationwide. The closest thing to a census of that population is the U.S. Department of Education's count of 64,930 public school students living in hotels and motels during the 2011-12 school year. That figure does not include the students' parents and preschool-age siblings, or any motel-dwellers not attending school.[3]

Massachusetts appears to have the best data of the states, because a state law guarantees homeless families a "right to shelter," and Massachusetts turned to motels when shelters filled up. Last year, the state was housing more than 2,000

programs to serve 200,000 people a year. Results so far show that "homelessness has gone down dramatically among veterans," he says.

"We're not going to stop until every American who has defended America has a home in America," President Obama said in a speech to the American Legion in August.[61] The administration's goal is to end homelessness among veterans next year.

But some congressional Republicans and homelessness experts doubt that target can be met and question how much progress is being made. "There has been an incredible outlay of resources, and other than VA statistics, we really don't have specifics on the programs' effectiveness, outcomes and sustainability," Rep. Jeff Miller, R-Fla., chairman of the House Veterans' Affairs Committee, told *The New York Times*.[62]

In the fiscal year ending this past September, the VA has budgeted $5.4 billion for clinical health services for homeless vets, and $1.4 billion on other programs for the homeless. For the new fiscal year, the administration wants

families, including 2,008 school-age children, in motels and hotels, at a cost of $48.1 million, according to the New England Center for Investigative Reporting.⁴

The nine-member family of Sergio and Rosa Serrano was living in a Days Inn in Shrewsbury. For the children, "it's not good, but what are you going to do?" Sergio Serrano, an unemployed and partially disabled construction worker, told the center. "They want to be outside, but they can't. They have no place to play."⁵

New York City also requires that the homeless have shelter. The city, which has the state's greatest number of homeless residents, at one point took over buildings whose owners were in default on tax obligations. One shelter near John F. Kennedy International Airport is a former Best Western motel.⁶

At the other end of the country, San Jose, Calif. — another city with a large homeless population and high housing costs — is planning to pay motel bills for "transitionally homeless" people. The motel subsidies could last up to one year for those with good employment prospects who have qualified for rental-assistance vouchers but can't find a place to live.⁷

The paucity of affordable housing in places like New York, Massachusetts and San Jose, which as home to the lucrative high-tech industry has famously high housing costs, makes it difficult for families working at the low end of the job market.

"We have a lot of families working in low-wage situations who can't get the money together to get into an apartment, and who are living in motels," says Lauren Voyer, a senior vice president at HAPHousing, a Springfield, Mass.-based nonprofit that helps people rent or buy affordable housing. "If you're in that situation, you're living without a home."

— *Peter Katel*

Theresa Muller, a homeless woman in Kissimmee, Fla., prepares to move out of the cluttered motel room she shared with her boyfriend, father and three children. They were planning in August to move to a home in a neighboring county.

¹Scott Pelley, "Homeless Children: The Hard Times Generation," "60 Minutes," June 20, 2011, http://tinyurl.com/pwwvmwc.

²Dan Mckay, "Mayor Brings in New Team," *Albuquerque Journal*, July 8, 2008, http://tinyurl.com/ntp79r2.

³"Education for Homeless Children and Youth Program," U.S. Department of Education, updated August 2013, http://tinyurl.com/osbmbwq. For background, see Marcia Clemmitt, "Homeless Students: Should Aid Programs Be Expanded?" *CQ Researcher*, April 5, 2013, pp. 305-328.

⁴Rupa Shenoy, "Homeless in motels: How some families are hanging on," New England Center for Investigative Reporting (in the *Worcester Telegram & Gazette*), Feb. 23, 2014, http://tinyurl.com/qdfnafk.

⁵Quoted in *ibid*.

⁶Ian Frazier, "Hidden City," *The New Yorker*, Oct. 28, 2013, http://tinyurl.com/npr83gk.

⁷Alice Yin, "Homeless Programs Take Different Paths to Address Crisis," *San Jose Inside*, Aug. 27, 2014, http://tinyurl.com/ndulwu5.

---

a 17.8 percent increase for the VA's homelessness efforts, including $1.64 billion for housing and homelessness-prevention programs. Overall, since 2010, the administration has spent $4 billion on homeless-vet housing programs, including apartment rentals.⁶³

Homelessness among veterans has been an embarrassing issue since the Vietnam War ended. VA research based on 2009 data concluded that veterans were overrepresented among the homeless, and that the possibility of a veteran becoming homeless rose after the draft ended in 1973. Male veterans were 1.25 times more likely to be homeless than non-veterans, and women veterans were 2.1 times more likely than non-veteran women.⁶⁴

The most extensive research so far on veteran homelessness is several decades old and focused on Vietnam vets, the Congressional Research Service reported. That 1984-88 study did not find a direct connection between post-traumatic stress disorder (PTSD) and homelessness. However, some of the issues contributing to

PTSD — including substance abuse and unemployment — were risk factors for homelessness.

Data on the mental health of Afghanistan and Iraq veterans do point to a high potential for homelessness in their ranks. Two studies found that between 14 percent and 17 percent of those veterans showed signs of PTSD and depression.[65]

CURRENT SITUATION

Arresting the Problem

Several new ordinances in Hawaii aim to crack down on the growing number of homeless people, seen as a threat to tourism — the economic lifeblood of Oahu Island, home to Honolulu, Pearl Harbor and the famous Waikiki beaches.

One law makes it a crime to sit or lie on sidewalks in the Waikiki area, punishable by a $1,000 fine and up to 30 days in jail. Another law makes it a petty misdemeanor to urinate or defecate on Waikiki's streets or in other public places on the island.

These realities clash with the island paradise image promoted by tourism business leaders. "There's an expectation for Waikiki, for Hawaii. It's a dream," said Helene "Sam" Shenkus, marketing director of the Royal Hawaiian Center, a popular shopping mall. "And because they're families, and it's their money, they don't have to come here."[66]

Honolulu Mayor Kirk Caldwell pushed through the ordinances after announcing measures to open more public restrooms and add more shelter space for homeless people. Still, Oahu has 4,400 beds for an estimated homeless population of 4,700.

The County of Honolulu, which includes the entire island, is planning to expand homeless shelter space, and when proposing the measures Caldwell described them in humane, rather than punitive, terms. But the American Civil Liberties Union of Hawaii said the "sit-lie" ordinance criminalizes "basic human functions [and] in the absence of options for shelter violates the Eight Amendment prohibition against cruel and unusual punishment."[67]

While Honolulu's status as a tourism mecca made its homelessness crackdown newsworthy, less glamorous cities have been adopting similar measures for years, especially after the Ninth U.S. Circuit Court of Appeals in 1996 rejected a challenge to Seattle's ordinance banning aggressive panhandling and sitting or lying on downtown sidewalks at certain times.[68]

According to the National Law Center on Homelessness & Poverty, 53 percent of U.S. cities now ban sitting or lying in certain public places; 65 percent prohibit loitering in specific places; 43 percent prohibit sleeping in vehicles; 57 percent bar camping in certain public places and 34 percent ban all camping within city limits.

Although such anti-homelessness laws may restore some degree of order in cities, they can have other consequences. A mentally ill homeless man shot and killed by police in Albuquerque last March was illegally camping in the Sandia Mountain foothills at the eastern edge of town. The shooting of James Boyd, 38, added to discontent over the police department's reliance on force and raised questions about the effectiveness of services for homeless people with mental illness.[69]

The Rev. Russell "Rusty" Smith, an Episcopal priest who is executive director of the St. Martin's Hospitality Center in Albuquerque, which offers a variety of aid to the homeless, but not overnight shelter, said Boyd had frequented the center but had refused services. Smith said he couldn't disclose details of Boyd's history. But schizophrenics who take medication often quit when they feel better, Smith added. In any event, "the reason that he was up in the hills is that he felt safe there," Smith said.

Ordinances designed to keep the homeless out of downtowns and parks often are enacted in response to citizens who say they feel threatened by the proximity of large numbers of homeless people. In San Francisco, enforcement of the city's anti-homelessness ordinances is lax, and public urination and defecation and screaming at passersby is common, according to the *San Francisco Chronicle*. "If you're very tolerant of inappropriate behavior, you're pretty likely to keep getting more of it," Bill McConnell, a former behavioral health division staffer for the city, told the newspaper in June.[70]

But Tars of the National Law Center on Homelessness & Poverty says, "Criminalizing [homelessness] is at least three times as costly as providing shelter or housing." However, officials would have to allocate a budget line to housing or shelter, he points out, while the costs of

AT ISSUE

Is Housing First the best approach to ending homelessness?

YES   **Nan Roman**
President and CEO, National Alliance to End Homelessness

Written for *CQ Researcher*, October 2014

Research indicates that Housing First is the most effective and least costly way to end homelessness for a majority of people. The strategy, which helps people experiencing homelessness to quickly obtain housing, supported with rental assistance and services, eliminates lengthy and costly stays in homeless programs. Data indicate that Housing First prevents relapses into homelessness better than any other approach.

Housing First is based on two premises: that homelessness is traumatic and damaging and should be as brief as possible, and that all people benefit from the stability of a home. The importance of a home is backed by evidence. The Centers for Disease Control and Prevention found that housing is essential to good health. Children do better in school when they have a permanent place to live, and services and treatment are more effective when people are in a home.

For families, homelessness is typically an economic issue. They are poor, and housing is expensive. In the past we addressed their homelessness by providing a temporary place to stay and social services that did little to help them with their immediate problem — the lack of a home. Today, Housing First for families reverses this process by helping families move back into housing after a short stay in a shelter and then providing them with services. It works. Housing First shortens the time families are homeless by up to 50 percent and does a better job of preventing returns to shelter than any other approach we have tried.

Housing First also works for those with more persistent problems. A minority of homeless people, mostly single adults, are disabled. It is neither realistic nor humane to expect them to address their challenges while living in shelters or on the streets. Housing First gets them into permanent supportive housing — housing with services attached — and studies indicate that it is significantly less expensive than leaving them on the street ($29,000 a year per person less in one Seattle cost study).

There is, of course, no one-size-fits-all solution to any problem, and Housing First is no exception. Youths and young parents experiencing homelessness, as well as people who need a sober recovery environment and some victims of domestic violence, may benefit from specialized transitional housing.

But on the whole, people who become homeless want, and need, to be housed again. And that is exactly what Housing First does.

NO   **Ralph da Costa Nunez**
President and CEO, Institute for Children, Poverty & Homelessness

Written for *CQ Researcher*, October 2014

As an across-the-board solution to the problem of homelessness, no. Individuals and families become homeless for a variety of reasons, and to assume that one approach is going to work for everyone is misguided.

Housing First is a well-intentioned approach: get people out of shelter and into housing as quickly as possible. However, the implementation of a Housing First approach has varied widely between communities and among various populations, and it has had some unintended consequences.

For chronically homeless individuals, Housing First has usually meant placement into housing with long-term assistance, such as permanent supportive housing with ongoing services. Once placed, individuals have a reasonable expectation that they will be able to remain housed.

However, for families, this is simply not the case. For them, Housing First has generally taken the form of rapid rehousing: usually a voucher or subsidy that offers short-term rental support, as well as help finding housing. Services are usually limited in scope and duration, if they exist at all, and rarely address the underlying causes of their homelessness. For some families, this is the right amount of support. But for many others who struggle with limited educations and job skills, domestic violence or mental health challenges, rapid rehousing offers at best only brief stability.

New York City has spent almost 10 years and unknown millions of dollars rapidly rehousing families. There is daily proof that this approach does not work. Two-thirds of all families who enter a shelter have been there before. It is hard to argue that these families were ever truly helped or cost-effectively rehoused the first time around.

Although proponents of rapid rehousing often claim impressive success rates, these outcomes are usually conveniently measured at the six- or 12-month mark, while rental supports are still in place. The real proof of success will be if these families remain housed over the long term. Until those results are measured, governments will continue spending millions of dollars on an unproven idea. Only time and data will tell.

Sadly, the unintended consequences of Housing First for America's 1.8 million homeless children are yet to come. Housing instability has proven not only to have negative effects on their education and health, but also increases the likelihood that they may themselves become homeless as adults. When Housing First puts the long-term needs of families last, the more important question to ask is, Can we afford to pay that price?

criminalization can be hidden in police, court and emergency room budgets.

In any case, not all municipal enforcement efforts to curb homelessness are successful in the courts. In June, the Ninth U.S. Circuit Court of Appeals threw out a Los Angeles ban on living in vehicles.[71]

Alternate Approach

Los Angeles, as it happens, has embarked on an anti-homelessness strategy that marks a break with its own past and with enforcement-heavy options chosen by other cities.

"I don't consider homelessness breaking the law," Los Angeles Police Capt. Mike Oreb told the *Los Angeles Times*. "We're not the homeless police."[72]

In September, a month after Los Angeles city and county launched a drive to remove health hazards and provide immediate help to the 3,500 homeless people who live on Skid Row, officials said the effort had succeeded in providing emergency housing for 42 people; removing 3.5 tons of waste and hazardous material, including syringes, needles and knives; and granting approval for six people to obtain permanent housing.[73]

The Skid Row sweep also identified 80 people who needed immediate medical care and 27 who required mental health attention.[74]

The Operation Healthy Streets project will involve further sweeps of the area, both to remove trash and provide immediate services such as mental health appointments and enrollment in Medicaid, the state-run, federally subsidized health insurance program for low-income Americans.[75]

Some experienced police officers had been calling for a new approach, one that doesn't rely on police to be mental health workers. "The police have been asked for years to be the answer to the issues stemming from mental illness in the communities we serve," Deon Joseph, a Los Angeles Police Department senior lead officer with 16 years' service on Skid Row, wrote in the *Los Angeles Downtown News*.

"It is not the LAPD that has failed the mentally ill or the public," he wrote. "It is our society that has failed them. A society that has closed down hospitals. A system that is slow to create more housing-plus-care locations."[76]

OUTLOOK
"A Human Right"

Homelessness experts have accumulated vast experience in human suffering. But some of them are hopeful, citing the new federal emphasis on ending homelessness as a recognition that homelessness should not be seen as an unsolvable problem.

"We have been doing a lot of work on housing as a human right, and after many years of feeling that we were banging our heads against the wall, the federal government has become more responsive [to our argument]," says Tars of the National Law Center on Homelessness & Poverty. He cites the U.S. Interagency Council on Homelessness' adoption of the doctrine.[77]

Eventually, Tars says, acknowledgment of housing as a fundamental right will combine with the pressure created by the shortage of affordable housing to force the government to fill the gap. "We don't have to go all the way to subsidized housing or public housing for every American," he says. "It can be done in a market-based system, with a safety net that ensures that no one is without that essential human need."

Tars and others advocate getting the business sector involved by providing incentives for builders to construct affordable rental housing — similar to the mortgage interest income tax deduction that encourages taxpayers to buy a house.

"The private sector is very good at building housing," Sheila Crowley, president and CEO of the National Low Income Housing Coalition, said in a telephone conference call for journalists in March. But under current conditions, she added, "if you could make money housing people [with very low incomes], somebody would have figured out how to do that by now. You can't make money at it. It has to have a public subsidy in order to be able to achieve that goal."

If the amount homeowners can deduct in mortgage interest payments were reduced even slightly, she said, the resulting increased revenues could be used to "solve the housing problems of the very poorest."[78]

Other developments are perhaps more promising. Smith of St. Martin's Hospitality Center said the Affordable Care Act (ACA) — known as "Obamacare" — has made an enormous and immediate difference to the homeless men and women he sees by expanding eligibility for access to Medicaid, reducing reliance on a local nonprofit, Albuquerque Health-Care for the Homeless. "It has been life-changing," he says. "A year and a half ago, most of our clients received medical care through Health-Care for the Homeless and the emergency room, and when they were dealing with a chronic illness they didn't go. Now, at least 30 percent of our clients have signed up with the ACA."

Gagliardi of HAPHousing in Springfield, Mass., points to a small resurgence of jobs that pay more than minimum wage. "This area used to be known for precision manufacturing, then it all went away," he says. "Now it's coming back, and they can't find enough qualified people. Community colleges and vocational schools are out to produce them. If, in fact, there really is a return to work for people at a decent wage, that will make a huge difference."

Culhane of the University of Pennsylvania praises the development of rapid rehousing and permanent supportive housing projects. "From the treatment perspective, these are very good cures," he says. "We need to scale that up, and we are seeing that happen incrementally every year."

Da Costa Nunez of the Institute for Children, Poverty & Homelessness in New York is similarly optimistic about the centers operated by Homes for the Homeless, a nonprofit that he also heads, which combine transitional housing with after-school and jobs programs. The nonprofit already operates four "family inns" along those lines for New York City.

The institute also is building a major center in the Bronx, whose job training efforts will include an on-site culinary training institute as well as educational and childcare programs open to the surrounding community. "We are not building shelters," he says. "We are building something that is part of the community. It's time to take the word 'shelter' out and think of it as a residential community resource center."

Yet the poverty underlying homelessness remains severe. "We need to revisit the adequacy of welfare payments to families, especially those with preschool-age kids," Culhane says. "Poverty among young families remains a problem. But these are things that can be solved."

Others stress the need to expand the stock of affordable housing. "If we don't do something about that, people are going to keep losing housing and being homeless,"

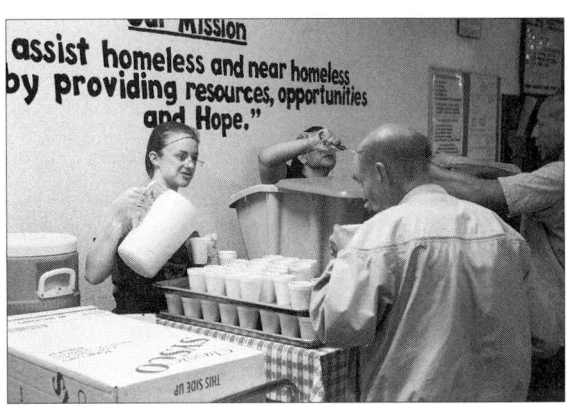

St. Martin's Hospitality Center in Albuquerque, N.M., the state's biggest service center for the homeless, does not provide housing but offers other assistance, such as hot meals and substance-abuse counseling.

says Roman of the National Alliance to End Homelessness. "But I do think we could end homelessness in the way we know it now, and make it a very brief, rare one-time-only event."

NOTES

1. Quoted in Adam Nagourney, "Honolulu Shores Up Tourism With Crackdown on Homeless," *The New York Times*, June 22, 2014, http://tinyurl.com/pcmuvcm.

2. "The 2013 Annual Homelessness Assessment Report (AHAR) to Congress: Part 1, Point-in-Time Estimates of Homelessness," U.S. Department of Housing and Urban Development, p. 7, http://tinyurl.com/qd89wa8.

3. "2012 Annual Homeless Assessment Report (AHAR) to Congress, Volume II," U.S. Department of Housing and Urban Development, September 2013, pp. 1-7, 3-7, http://tinyurl.com/l6j268s.

4. Kim Hopper, *et al.*, "Estimating Numbers of Unsheltered Homeless People Through Plant-Capture and Postcount Survey Methods," *American Journal of Public Health*, August 2008, http://tinyurl.com/oan68g3.

5. "Homelessness Assistance," U.S. Department of Housing and Urban Development, undated, http://tinyurl.com/d5kejj3.

6. "Changes in the HUD Definition of 'Homeless,'" National Alliance to End Homelessness, Jan. 18, 2012, http://tinyurl.com/pswbcak. For background, see Marcia Clemmitt, "Homeless Students," *CQ Researcher*, April 5, 2013, pp. 305-328.

7. *Ibid.* "Changes in the HUD Definition," p. 41; "The 2012 Annual Homeless Assessment Report to Congress," Vol. II, *op. cit.*, pp. 3-14.

8. "Education for Homeless Children and Youth Program: Consolidated State Performance Report Data," National Center for Homeless Education, September 2014, http://tinyurl.com/ktbhbhh; "Laws & Guidance/Elementary & Secondary Education — Part C — Homeless Education," U.S. Department of Education, updated Sept. 15, 2004, http://tinyurl.com/36jhv5x.

9. "Opening Doors: Federal Strategic Plan to Prevent and End Homelessness," U.S. Interagency Council on Homelessness, 2010, p. 4, http://tinyurl.com/n6z52dn.

10. "Homeless Emergency Assistance and Rapid Transition to Housing: Continuum of Care Program, A Rule by the Housing and Urban Development Department on 7/31/2012," *Federal Register*, July 31, 2012, http://tinyurl.com/pro9rwa.

11. "Interim Report: Family Options Study," U.S. Department of Housing and Urban Development, March 2013, p. xiv, http://tinyurl.com/mtohsek; Martha R. Burt, *et al.*, "Homelessness: Programs and the People They Serve," Urban Institute, August 1999, p. 29, http://tinyurl.com/lx7o62u.

12. *Ibid.*, "Interim Report," p. 56.

13. Maureen A. Hayes, Megan Zonneville and Ellen Bassuk, "The SHIFT Study: Final Report," National Center on Family Homelessness, 2010, pp. 18-19, http://tinyurl.com/m3t9uhc.

14. "Rapid Re-Housing: A History and Core Components," National Alliance to End Homelessness, April 22, 2014, http://tinyurl.com/n8u5w7p.

15. Libby Perl, *et al.*, "Homelessness: Targeted Federal Programs and Recent Legislation," Congressional Research Service, Feb. 3, 2014, p. 23, http://tinyurl.com/l5x3tma; "Housing First," National Alliance to End Homelessness, undated, http://tinyurl.com/qcu7qvw; "McKinney-Vento Homeless Assistance Success Stories," National Alliance to End Homelessness, February 2006, http://tinyurl.com/n3ubo5q.

16. "Rapid Re-Housing: A History and Core Components," National Alliance to End Homelessness, April 22, 2014, http://tinyurl.com/n8u5w7p; "Rapid Re-Housing: Creating Programs that Work," National Alliance to End Homelessness, July 2009, pp. 41-43, http://tinyurl.com/k887hp5.

17. "Homelessness Assistance," U.S. Housing and Urban Development Department, *op. cit.*; Perl, *et al.*, *op. cit.*, summary, p. 13.

18. "Chart Book: Federal Housing Spending Is Poorly Matched to Need," Center on Budget and Policy Priorities, Dec. 18, 2013, http://tinyurl.com/nxgpdyc; "Housing America's Future: New Directions for National Policy," Housing Commission, Bipartisan Policy Center, February 2013, pp. 10-11, http://tinyurl.com/mm9tum6.

19. Quoted in Steve LeBlanc, "In Mass., A Tough Quest to End Family Homelessness," The Associated Press, Jan. 1, 2014, http://tinyurl.com/k435udf.

20. "Housing America's Future," *op. cit.*, p. 11; "Policy Basics: Section 8 Project-Based Rental Assistance," Center on Budget and Policy Priorities, Jan. 25, 2013, http://tinyurl.com/qe4x8eo; "Policy Basics: The Housing Choice Voucher Program," Center on Budget and Policy Priorities, May 14, 2014, http://tinyurl.com/mrjcxkm.

21. "Rep. Jeb Hensarling Holds a Hearing on Sustainable Housing Finance System," House Committee on Financial Services, CQ Transcriptions, July 18, 2013.

22. *Ibid.*

23. *Ibid.*

24. Peter Charles Hoffer, *Law and People in Colonial America* (1998), p. 8.

25. Martha R. Burt, *Over the Edge: The Growth of Homelessness in the 1980s* (1993), p. 3.

26. James N. Gregory, " 'The Dust Bowl Migration' Poverty Stories, Race Stories," http://faculty.washington.edu/gregoryj/dust%20bowl%20migration.htm.

27. Woody Guthrie, "I Ain't Got No Home," 1938, http://tinyurl.com/plt3dp6; John Steinbeck, *The Grapes of Wrath* (1939).

28. James N. Gregory, *American Exodus: The Dust Bowl Migration and Okie Culture in California* (1989), pp. 98-99; *Edwards v. California*, 314 U.S. 160 (1941), http://tinyurl.com/mbbzyha.

29. Ella Howard, *Homeless: Poverty and Place in Urban America* (2013), Kindle edition, no page numbers.

30. Neil Larry Shumsky, *Homelessness: A Documentary and Reference Guide* (2012), pp. 147-151; "CCC Brief History," CCC Legacy, undated, http://tinyurl.com/cbgc6oz.

31. Quoted in *ibid.*, p. 150.

32. Chris Koyanagi, "Learning From History: Deinstitutionalization of People with Mental Illness As Precursor to Long-Term Care Reform," Henry J. Kaiser Family Foundation, August 2007, http://tinyurl.com/lxmwgp6; Richard D. Lyons, "How Release of Mental Patients Began," *The New York Times*, Oct. 30, 1984, http://tinyurl.com/b894wpq.

33. "Remarks on signing mental retardation facilities and community health centers construction bill, Oct. 31, 1963," John F. Kennedy Presidential Library and Museum, http://tinyurl.com/lget9yx; Martin Weil, "Rosemary Kennedy, 86; President's Disabled Sister," *The Washington Post*, Jan. 8, 2005, http://tinyurl.com/yb47jgo.

34. Koyangi, *op. cit.*, p. 4.

35. E. Fuller Torrey, "Ronald Reagan's shameful legacy: Violence, the homeless, mental illness," Salon, Sept. 29, 2013, http://tinyurl.com/lr4s422.

36. *Ibid.*; for background see Barbara Mantel, "Mental Health Policy," *CQ Researcher*, May 10, 2013, pp. 425-448.

37. Quoted in Howard, *op. cit.*

38. Torrey, *op. cit.*

39. For background, see "The S&L Crisis: A Chrono-Bibliography," Federal Deposit Insurance Corporation, http://tinyurl.com/masdhwx.

40. Howard, *op. cit.*; Marc Labonte, "The 2007-2009 Recession: Similarities to and Differences from the Past," Congressional Research Service, Oct. 6, 2010, http://tinyurl.com/msqquca; David Kocieniewski, "Since 1980s, the Kindest of Tax Cuts for the Rich," *The New York Times*, Jan. 18, 2012, http://tinyurl.com/ou3tg6e; William A. Galston, "Stop Blaming the Tax Code for America's Inequality Problem," *The New Republic*, via Brookings Institution, April 19, 2012, http://tinyurl.com/qgzmp78; "History of the US Tax System," U.S. Department of the Treasury, undated, http://tinyurl.com/79oer4b.

41. Martha R. Burt, "Causes of the Growth of Homelessness During the 1980s," 1991, from "Understanding Homelessness: New Policy and Research Perspectives," Fannie Mae Foundation, 1991, 1997, pp. 182-183, http://tinyurl.com/lrzckm2.

42. *Papachristou v. City of Jacksonville*, 405 U.S. 156 (1972), http://tinyurl.com/mh95nlp; ibid., Burt, "Causes of the Growth."

43. Quoted in Ian Frazier, "Hidden City," *The New Yorker*, Oct. 28, 2013, http://tinyurl.com/npr83gk; for background, see Peter Katel, "Housing the Homeless," *CQ Researcher*, Dec. 18, 2009, pp. 1053-1076.

44. *Ibid.*, Katel.

45. Shumsky, *op. cit.*, pp. 234-235; "Continuum of Care (CoC) Program," HUD Exchange, U.S. Housing and Urban Development Department, undated, http://tinyurl.com/o2myeut.

46. Rosemary Chapin, *Social Policy for Effective Practice: A Strengths Approach* (2010), p. 177; Maria Foscarinis, "Homelessness in America: A Human Rights Crisis," *Journal of Law in Society*, Wayne State University, 2012, p. 517, http://tinyurl.com/of6rrl2.

47. Libby Perl, *et al.*, "Homelessness: Targeted Federal Programs and Recent Legislation," Congressional Research Service, Feb. 3, 2014, pp. 22-24, http://tinyurl.com/l5x3tma.

48. Quoted in Derek Kravitz, "Homelessness Official Wins Praise With Focus on Permanent Housing," *The Washington Post*, Dec. 30, 2008, http://tinyurl.com/lbd766q.

49. *Ibid.*, pp. 23-24.

50. Jo Becker, Sheryl Gay Stolberg and Stephen Labaton, "Bush drive for home ownership fueled

housing bubble," *The New York Times*, Dec. 21, 2008, http://tinyurl.com/7emvj3z.

51. "Foreclosure to Homelessness 2009: the forgotten victims of the subprime crisis," National Coalition for the Homeless, 2009, http://tinyurl.com/mknpp3.

52. "Eviction (Without) Notice: Renters and the Foreclosure Crisis," National Law Center on Homelessness & Poverty, December 2012, p. 6, http://tinyurl.com/l7ebrxa. Les Christie, "Record 3 million households hit with foreclosure in 2009," CNN Money, Jan. 14, 2010, http://tinyurl.com/ybqrkje.

53. Julia B. Isaacs, "The Ongoing Impact of Foreclosures on Children," Brookings Institution, April 2012, pp. 5-6, http://tinyurl.com/pw8feh3; Julia Isaacs, [professional biography], Urban Institute, http://tinyurl.com/jvqauv7.

54. *Ibid.*, pp. 4-5; Christie, *op. cit.*

55. Perl, *et al.*, pp. 5-6.

56. *Ibid.*, pp. 24-25; "Opening Doors," *op. cit.*, p. 4.

57. *Ibid.*, "Opening Doors."

58. Michelle Obama, "Let's end veteran homelessness once and for all," McClatchy Newspapers, July 30, 2014, www.mcclatchydc.com/2014/07/30/234885_lets-end-veteran-homelessness.html?rh=1.

59. "The 2012 Annual Homeless Assessment Report to Congress, Vol. II," *op. cit.*, pp. 4-7.

60. Libby Perl, "Veterans and Homelessness," Congressional Research Service, Nov. 29, 2013, p. 39, http://tinyurl.com/n6sncq4.

61. Quoted in Erica E. Phillips and Ben Kesling, "Number of Homeless Veterans in the U.S. Falls Over Past Four Years," *The Wall Street Journal*, Aug. 26, 2014, http://tinyurl.com/mhw5dv2.

62. Quoted in Dave Philipps, "Many Veterans Adapt to a Strange World, One With Walls," *The New York Times*, Sept. 20, 2014, http://tinyurl.com/lfokh8h.

63. *Ibid.*; Phillips and Kesling, *op. cit.*; "Proposed Fiscal year 2015 Budget Fact Sheet: Homelessness Assistance, U.S. Interagency Council on Homelessness, undated, http://tinyurl.com/lnmb8lg.

64. Perl, "Veterans and Homelessness," *op. cit.*, pp. 12-14.

65. *Ibid.*, pp. 16-17.

66. Quoted in Cathy Bussewitz, "Honolulu Approves Plan to Move Homeless," The Associated Press (via *Minneapolis Star-Tribune*), Sept. 11, 2014, http://tinyurl.com/mnen5hz; Mileka Lincoln, "Mayor Caldwell signs homeless bills into law," KGMB, KHNL, Sep. 17, 2014, http://tinyurl.com/n22pxv7.

67. Quoted in Lincoln, *ibid.*, "Mayor Caldwell"; Kirk Caldwell, "Together we can resolve problem of homelessness in Honolulu," *Honolulu Star-Advertiser*, June 1, 2014, http://tinyurl.com/ok2g4rt; Bussewitz, *ibid.*

68. "A Dream Denied: The Criminalization of Homelessness in U.S. Cities, Case Summaries," National Coalition for the Homeless, National Law Center on Homelessness & Poverty, January 2006, http://tinyurl.com/ol32u9y; Heather Knight, "San Francisco looks to Seattle: Did sidewalk sitting ban help?" *San Francisco Chronicle*, in *Seattle Post-Intelligencer*, March 29, 2010, http://tinyurl.com/ohyjxef.

69. Russell Contreras, "Albuquerque Police Release New Video of James Boyd Shooting," The Associated Press (via *The Huffington Post*), June 12, 2014, http://tinyurl.com/qdozuvc; Rick Nathanson, "James Boyd's dark journey," *Albuquerque Journal*, March 30, 2014, http://tinyurl.com/knkw5rr.

70. Quoted in Heather Knight, "A decade of homelessness: Thousands in S.F, remain in crisis," *San Francisco Chronicle*, June 28, 2014, http://tinyurl.com/ncb94my.

71. Quoted in Maura Dolan and Gale Holland, "Appeals court panel ends L.A. ban on homeless living in vehicles," *Los Angeles Times*, June 19, 2014, http://tinyurl.com/oxfye5v.

72. Quoted in Gale Holland, "L.A. leaders are crafting new plan to help homeless on skid row," *Los Angeles Times*, July 15, 2014, http://tinyurl.com/kmsh8rg.

73. Gale Holland, "Skid row sweep finds many homeless with medical, psychiatric needs," *Los Angeles Times*, Sept. 11, 2014, http://tinyurl.com/o7c5d4p.

74. *Ibid.*

75. Holland, "L.A. leaders," *op. cit.*

76. Deon Joseph, "Skid Row Cop: Downtown Is in a Mental Health State of Emergency," *Los Angeles Downtown News*, June 30, 2014, http://tinyurl.com/nbh5ckq.

77. "U.S. Department of Housing and Urban Development Statement on the U.S. Participation in the United Nations' Universal Periodic Review," U.S. Department of Housing and Urban Development, 2010, http://tinyurl.com/qhec7kq.

78. "The National Low Income Housing Coalition Holds a Teleconference on a Report Regarding the Affordable Rental Housing Shortage," *SEC Wire*, March 24, 2014 (via Nexis).

BIBLIOGRAPHY
Selected Sources
Books

Howard, Ella, *Homeless: Poverty and Place in Urban America*, **University of Pennsylvania Press, 2013.**
A history professor at Armstrong State University in Savannah, Ga., chronicles homelessness and government responses to it from the late 19th century on, focusing on New York's Bowery.

Reynalds, Jeremy, *A Sheltered Life: Take It to the Streets*, **West Bow Press, 2013.**
The English-born founder of a homeless shelter in Albuquerque recounts his own brief homelessness and describes the lives of some of the people he and his colleagues have helped.

Shumsky, Neil Larry, *Homelessness: A Documentary and Reference Guide*, **Greenwood, 2012.**
A history professor at Virginia Tech in Blacksburg depicts the course of homelessness throughout the country's history.

Articles

Frazier, Ian, "Hidden City," *The New Yorker*, **Oct. 28, 2013, http://tinyurl.com/npr83gk.**
A detailed first-person account by a magazine writer describes the lives of New York City's homeless.

Joseph, Deon, "Skid Row Cop: Downtown Is in a Mental Health State of Emergency," *Los Angeles Downtown News*, **June 30, 2014, http://tinyurl.com/nbh5ckq.**
A Los Angeles police officer writes about the horrific conditions in which thousands of the city's mentally ill homeless people live, calling it an indictment of American society.

Knight, Heather, "A decade of homelessness: Thousands in S.F. remain in crisis," *San Francisco Chronicle*, **June 27, 2014, http://tinyurl.com/l8s7bye.**
Despite a 10-year-old pledge by the city's then-mayor to end homelessness, San Francisco continues to struggle with the problem.

Nathanson, Rick, "James Boyd's dark journey," *Albuquerque Journal*, **March 30, 2014, http://tinyurl.com/knkw5rr.**
A mentally ill homeless man shot to death by Albuquerque police had shuttled between jails and a psychiatric hospital for years.

Olsen, Hanna Brooks, "Homelessness and the Impossibility of a Good Night's Sleep," *The Atlantic*, **Aug. 14, 2014, http://tinyurl.com/oykcjn7.**
A Seattle writer explores an unknown facet of homelessness: the debilitating effects of never getting a restful night's sleep, whether the person is in a shelter or on the street.

Phillips, Erica E., and Ben Kesling, "Number of Homeless Veterans in the U.S. Falls Over Past Four Years," *The Wall Street Journal*, **Aug. 26, 2014, http://tinyurl.com/mhw5dv2.**
The number of homeless veterans has dropped sharply, but ending it by next year (as the Obama administration wants) seems unlikely.

Shenoy, Rupa, "Homeless in motels: How some families are hanging on," New England Center for Investigative Reporting, in the *Worcester Telegram & Gazette*, **Feb. 23, 2014, http://tinyurl.com/qdfnafk.**
Journalists investigate the difficulties of family life in a motel room and the Massachusetts state government's attempts to meet its obligation to shelter homeless families.

Reports and Studies

"Meeting the Child Care Needs of Homeless Families — How Do States Stack Up?" Institute for Children, Poverty

& Homelessness, July 2014, http://tinyurl.com/lz8zsr2.
A New York-based think tank reports that child care, needed by homeless mothers who must work to acquire housing, receives little attention in most states' homelessness programs.

"No Safe Place: The Criminalization of Homelessness in U.S. Cities," National Law Center on Homelessness & Poverty, July 2014, http://tinyurl.com/plgfed2.
Cities are passing laws that effectively penalize homelessness, reports a Washington-based advocacy organization that opposes the trend both as inhumane and a waste of money.

Abt Associates, "Family Options Study, Interim Report," U.S. Housing and Urban Development Department, March 2013, http://tinyurl.com/l9cxnpx.
The first installment of a study of more than 2,300 homeless families reports on their characteristics and the services that are available to them. A second installment is intended to provide data on which services are most effective as permanent solutions to homelessness.

Henry, Meghan, Dr. Alvaro Cortes, and Sean Morris, "The 2013 Annual Homeless Assessment Report to Congress, Part I: Point-in-Time Estimates of Homelessness," http://tinyurl.com/qd89wa8, and "The 2012 Annual Homeless Assessment Report to Congress, Vol. II: Estimates of Homelessness in the United States," Office of Community Planning and Development, U.S. Department of Housing and Urban Development, September 2013, http://tinyurl.com/l6j268s.
These annual reports detail point-in-time counts and data on shelter use.

For More Information

Institute for Children, Poverty & Homelessness, 44 Cooper Square, New York, NY 10003; 212-358-8086; www.icphusa.org. Think tank that researches links between homelessness and poverty and its effects on families.

National Alliance to End Homelessness, 1518 K St., N.W., 2nd Floor, Washington, DC 20005; 202-638-1526; www.endhomelessness.org. Advocacy group and research center that helped popularize the idea of ending homelessness, rather than simply sheltering the homeless.

National Center on Family Homelessness, c/o American Institutes for Research, 201 Jones Rd., Waltham, MA 02451; 781-373-7080; familyhomelessness.org. Think tank that explores causes and effects of homelessness on parents (single mothers, for the most part) and children, and effectiveness of treatment methods.

National Law Center on Homelessness & Poverty, 2000 M St., N.W., Washington, DC 20036; 202-638-2535; www.nlchp.org. Opposes laws that penalize homeless people; advocates that housing be defined as a human right.

U.S. Department of Veterans Affairs, 810 Vermont Ave., N.W., Washington, DC 20420; 877-424-3838; www.va.gov/homeless. Runs a separate site with information on programs aimed at homeless vets.

U.S. Interagency Council on Homelessness, 1275 1st St., N.E., Washington, DC 20002; 202-708-4663; www.uscih.gov. The coordinating arm of federal anti-homelessness efforts that publishes updates of strategy on fighting homelessness.

10 Wealth and Inequality

Sarah Glazer

An Occupy Wall Street demonstrator protests against economic inequality at a rally in New York City on May 1, 2012. The top 1 percent of the world's richest people own about half of all global wealth, and the bottom half less than 5 percent. President Obama has proposed steps to help struggling Americans climb the income ladder, including raising the minimum wage and ending tax loopholes for the richest Americans. But conservative economists say such measures would punish entrepreneurship and stifle economic growth.

From *CQ Researcher*,
April 18, 2014; updated May 2016.

The excavation machines are busy these days in London's most fashionable neighborhoods, digging several stories under historic mansions to create the swimming pools, wine cellars and bowling alleys demanded by their wealthy owners.[1]

Yet many of these houses will remain empty most of the year, as their owners divide their time among other homes in Europe, Asia, or the Middle East, according to real estate agents. London's prime homes are becoming a "global reserve currency" where the world's richest people can park their money, in the words of London journalist Michael Goldfarb. He mourned the loss of neighbors joining the exodus of middle-class families no longer able to afford the city.[2]

In Miami, an apartment in a new luxury building designed by world-renowned architect Zaha Hadid gets the buyer a roof-top helipad and a private vault for storing precious jewelry and artwork. Prices start at $5 million and go up to $45 million for the duplex, six-bedroom penthouse, whose 15,207 square feet include an indoor pool, media room, library, gym, staff quarters, and more than 1,000 square feet of terrace.

These are just some of the more ostentatious signals that the very rich in the United States and around the world have been doing very well since the recession, even though many middle-class households still struggle. The astounding rise in wealth of the very few continues to make international headlines: The latest report by the anti-poverty charity Oxfam finds that the wealth of the world's 62 richest billionaires now equals that of the poorest half of the world's population.[3]

Once the backwater of economics and the concern of a few public-interest groups, the issue of income inequality — the term used for the growing disparity between the incomes of society's poorest and wealthiest sectors — is getting new attention on the national and international scene. The World Economic Forum, which sponsors the annual Davos gathering of the world's economic glitterati, declared the worsening wealth gap the problem most likely to pose a risk on a global scale, based on its survey of 700 experts.[4] The concern raised at Davos that increasing inequality threatens the political and financial stability of nations has also become a new focus of the 189-nation International Monetary Fund, which lends money to countries in trouble.[5]

"The reason we worry about inequality is [that] it's not a good thing to be a plutocracy," says liberal University of Texas-Austin economist James K. Galbraith.

Scott Winship, a senior fellow at the conservative Manhattan Institute think tank, has suggested the popular preoccupation with equality is related to economic anxiety during and following the recession. "I do believe if the economy picks up and unemployment goes back down to 5 percent, the interest in income inequality will go away again," he told CQ Researcher in March 2014 when the unemployment rate was above 6 percent.

Yet even though the unemployment rate has dropped since then, hovering at or below 5 percent since October of last year, inequality has become a defining issue in the current presidential election campaign.[6]

One reason may be that even if you're employed, your wages have barely kept up with the cost of living — a syndrome known as wage stagnation. Wages have essentially remained flat or declined for most workers since the recession, adjusted for inflation, according to the Economic Policy Institute, a pro-labor think tank.[7]

Since the 1970s, wages for the bottom 70 percent of earners barely grew even as corporate profits rose and as income for the top 1 percent increased 156 percent, according to the Institute.[8] Hourly wages for the typical worker increased only 9 percent, adjusted for inflation, between 1973 and 2014.[9]

The candidate who made inequality the centerpiece of his campaign for the Democratic nomination, Sen. Bernie Sanders of Vermont, blamed much of that divide on wage stagnation.

"Despite huge advancements in technology and productivity, millions of Americans are working longer hours for lower wages," he stated on his campaign website. "The reality is that since the mid-1980s there has been an enormous transfer of wealth from the middle class and the poor to the wealthiest people in this country," Sanders said, repeatedly citing the figure that the Americans in the top 1 percent of the income ladder's richest 1 percent own as much as the bottom 90 percent.[10]

Sanders' ability to draw support from young and white working class voters during the primary campaign pushed Democratic presidential candidate Hillary Clinton to refocus her message on inequality, as well, in the view of seasoned political observers. By August 2015, the former Secretary of State expressed willingness to consider taxes on the wealthy to pay for the shortfall in Social Security, a shift from her earlier centrist position.[11]

"The deck is stacked in favor of those at the top," she declared in campaign advertisements. At a New Hampshire campaign rally in 2015, she already sounded much like Sanders, saying, "The top 25 hedge-fund managers earn more than all the kindergarten teachers in America combined," even as Sanders was questioning her ties to Wall Street.[12]

Clinton's prescription for curing inequality looks similar to Sanders' original agenda, while somewhat more moderate: raising the minimum wage, increasing taxes on the wealthy, and providing universal pre-K.

Republican presidential candidate Donald Trump, a millionaire real estate developer and reality TV star, has also honed in on wage stagnation in his speeches. But in the early stages of the campaign he focused the blame mainly on free trade agreements with China and Mexico for taking away factory jobs and undercutting wages. By May 2016, Trump seemed to be "taking a page from the Sanders playbook," *The New York Times* noted — attacking Wall Street, expressing willingness to raise the minimum wage, and suggesting he would make the wealthy pay higher taxes than in his original proposal.[13]

Providing statistical and scholarly support for many of these political claims about inequality is the widely discussed 2014 best-seller, *Capital in the Twenty-First Century* by Thomas Piketty, a professor at the Paris School of Economics. In his book, Piketty warns that rising inequality could threaten the very fabric of democracy and proposes confiscatory taxes on the rich.

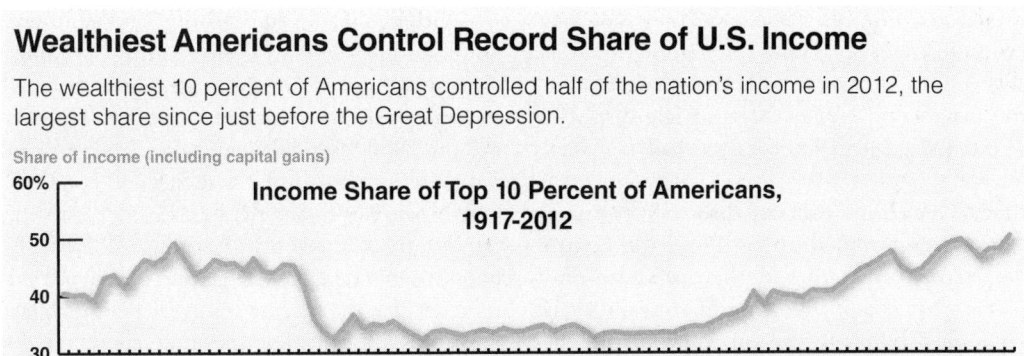

Wealthiest Americans Control Record Share of U.S. Income

The wealthiest 10 percent of Americans controlled half of the nation's income in 2012, the largest share since just before the Great Depression.

Source: Emmanuel Saez, "Striking it Richer: The Evolution of Top Incomes in the United States (Updated with 2012 preliminary estimates)," University of California-Berkeley, Sept. 3, 2013, http://elsa.berkeley.edu/~saez/saez-UStopincomes-2012.pdf; data from http://elsa.berkeley.edu/~saez/TabFig2012prel.xls

Piketty argues that invested capital has been growing faster than earned income, permitting those who own capital — like money, real estate, and stocks — to see their wealth grow faster than those trying to get by on wages alone. The result is a cycle leading to an ever-widening divide between the rich and everyone else, he has contended.

Some academic experts are describing a similar syndrome in the United States. "All the costs and risks of capitalism seem to have been shifted largely to those who work rather than those who invest," Harvard Professor of Social Policy Christopher Jencks told the *Harvard Gazette* in February 2016.[14]

Tax-increase proposals targeting the rich — whether the very high taxes backed by Piketty or less extreme versions proposed by Democrats, including Hillary Clinton — are strongly opposed by conservatives, who say high taxes stifle growth. Those critics argue that rising wealth at the top doesn't hurt those at the bottom, because as long as the economy is growing overall, all will benefit.

Liberal economist Paul Krugman, a *New York Times* columnist and Nobel Prize winner, is among those referring to the current era as a new Gilded Age, harking back to the 19th century, when so-called "robber barons" such as J. P. Morgan and John D. Rockefeller were accused of accumulating enormous wealth at the expense of the new industrial working class.[15]

In the United States, research shows inequality has been growing, with the richest 10 percent of families now capturing half of all personal income, a level not seen since 1917 and even greater than the Roaring '20s, according to University of California-Berkeley economist Emmanuel Saez.[16]

Even starker is how far the richest households in America have pulled ahead of everyone else since the 2007-2009 recession. The top 1 percent — those with annual incomes of more than $394,000 — saw their incomes grow by 31 percent in the three years following the end of the recession, compared with a less than 1 percent gain for the other 99 percent. As a result, that upper stratum captured 95 percent of the nation's income gains during the recovery, Saez calculates.[17]

The United States reflects a global trend toward concentration of wealth, according to Piketty's new book. Worldwide, inequality now appears comparable to that of stratified Europe in 1900-1910, with the top 1 percent holding about half of global wealth, and the rest of the population owning less than 5 percent, according to Piketty.[18]

"[T]he poorer half of the population are as poor today as they were in the past," Piketty writes, making the comparison to 1910, when the poor held barely 5 percent of total wealth. "Basically, all the middle class managed to get its hands on was a few crumbs."[19]

Yet in 1910, few homes had indoor tap water — something even the poorest American households take for granted today. If indoor plumbing, refrigerators, TV and medical advances like penicillin could be measured to reflect their true worth, "they would probably show how much richer everyone has become," economist Tim Kane, a research fellow at Stanford University's Hoover Institution, wrote in a May 2016 article disputing Piketty's claim that inequality is just as bad as it was a hundred years ago.[20]

President Obama has contrasted today's stagnating middle-class incomes with the post–World War II years, when wages rose along with the nation's economy. "[F]or some, that meant following in your old man's footsteps at the local plant, and you knew that a blue-collar job would let you buy a home, and a car, maybe a vacation once in a while, health care, a reliable pension," Obama said.[21]

Conservative economists and some liberals say that rosy period of middle-income growth in the 1950s to the 1970s was unique — before American manufacturing faced global competition and before a high-tech economy required more than a high school education to support a family.

Those factors drove down wages for the less educated: "This is part of globalization and all these changing things about society you can't put back in the bottle," says Salim Furth, senior policy analyst in macroeconomics at the Heritage Foundation, a conservative think tank in Washington. "If [employers] are going to compete, they have to pay global wages."

Yet it is those downsides of globalization that Trump has capitalized on to reach disaffected workers, even promising to put the free trade genie back into the bottle. He has said he would renegotiate and "probably terminate" the North American Free Trade Agreement, which has allowed free trade between the United States, Canada, and Mexico since the mid-1990s, and would renegotiate China's admittance to the World Trade Organization (WTO), which took place under President Clinton in 2000.[22]

"Since China joined the WTO, Americans have witnessed the closure of more than 50,000 factories and the loss of tens of millions of jobs. It was not a good deal for America then and it's a bad deal now," his campaign website says.[23]

In a debate in August 2015, Trump said, "We don't beat China in trade. We don't beat Japan, with their millions and millions of cars coming into this country, in trade. We can't beat Mexico, at the border or in trade."[24]

Writing in the op-ed pages of *The Wall Street Journal*, commentator Mickey Kaus, author of *The End of Equality*, suggested Americans are more concerned about social inequality than income inequality. "Do we remember the 1950s as a halcyon egalitarian era because the rich weren't rich — or because rich and poor had served together in World War II?" he asked. He questioned the growing preoccupation with income differences: "If the poor and middle class were getting steadily richer, would it matter that the rich are getting richer much faster?"[25]

Like Kaus, others on the more conservative end of the spectrum who have studied recent trends tend to agree that income inequality has increased, though some experts say it has increased less drastically than Piketty claims.

Piketty has "overstated" the differences between growth in wealth among the richest and poorest because he failed to include safety net programs such as food stamps for the poor, according to the Manhattan Institute's Winship. He points to a calculation by the Congressional Budget Office that finds — after taxes and employer fringe benefits are accounted for — that the top 1 percent increased their share of national income between 1979 and 2007 from 7 to 17 percent, less than Piketty's 10 to 24 percent.[26]

Even when conservatives accept the general direction of Piketty's findings, they tend to disagree with the implication — that a growing share at the top means less wealth for those below. In testimony before the congressional Joint Economic Committee in January 2014, Winship said living standards have improved for the middle class even as income inequality has grown. "Inequality was high and rising during the late 1990s," he noted, "but because the growing economy was largely benefiting everyone, few people were worried about income concentration at the top."[27]

Liberals such as Yale political science professor Jacob S. Hacker argue that middle-class incomes have stalled mainly because of government policies supported by the rich: "Government rewrote the rules," in three areas, he says: weakening unions, weakening oversight of financial markets, and looking the other way on exploding executive pay.

However, Winship points out that the pace of economic growth has slowed not only in the United States but also in Japan and Europe. "We are talking about global economic trends that are not specific to the U.S.," he says, citing global competition and a freer labor market. "It's not that we crushed unions and that's the whole story," he says, or that pro-union European countries have done a lot better.

"We are the 99 percent," the 2011 slogan of the protest movement Occupy Wall Street, called attention to the advantages of the wealthiest 1 percent, and in the last few years some politicians have taken up the cry. New York City Mayor Bill de Blasio, elected in 2013 after promising to reduce the gap between rich and poor, advocated increased taxes on the wealthy to fund universal pre-kindergarten. On the federal level, Obama has also proposed increasing taxes on the wealthiest Americans.

Yet conservatives warn that raising taxes on the rich would hurt the entire economy because the wealthy would have less money to invest in job-producing activities that benefit the rest of the population. "There is a large literature that high tax rates clearly hurt growth," says the Heritage Foundation's Furth.

Experts and the public remain deeply divided about growing wealth at the top and its implications for everyone else. Here are some of the questions being debated in the press, academia and the political arena:

Does income inequality hamper economic growth?

Middle-class stores like Sears and JCPenney have been closing down in malls and downtowns across America, and midpriced restaurants like Olive Garden and Red Lobster have been struggling.[28] Meanwhile upscale dining chains like Capital Grille are thriving as the rich account for a bigger slice of U.S. consumption.[29]

Some economists say the shrinking of middle-class consumption could seriously hurt economic growth — and that reduced consumer demand may have contributed to the country's slow recovery from the 2007-09 recession.

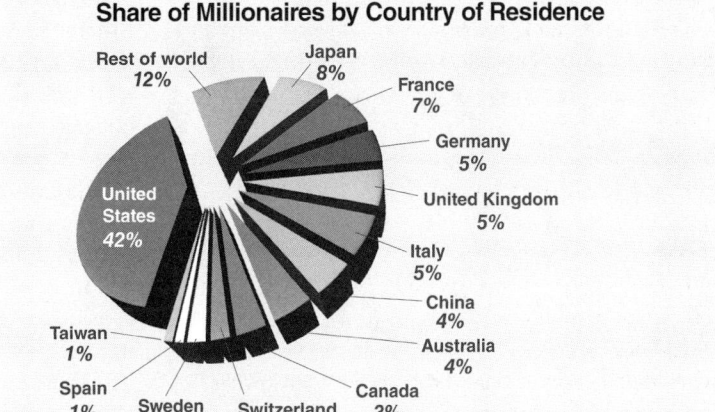

U.S. Has Highest Share of Millionaires

Of the world's millionaires, 42 percent are from the United States, by far the largest share. Canada, France, Germany, Italy, Japan and the U.K. account for a combined 33 percent share of the global total.

Share of Millionaires by Country of Residence

- United States 42%
- Rest of world 12%
- Japan 8%
- France 7%
- Germany 5%
- United Kingdom 5%
- Italy 5%
- China 4%
- Australia 4%
- Canada 3%
- Switzerland 2%
- Sweden 2%
- Spain 1%
- Taiwan 1%

Note: Percentages do not add to 100 because of rounding.

Source: "Global Wealth Report 2013," Credit Suisse, p. 23, https://publications.credit-suisse.com/tasks/render/file/?fileID=CDB1364-A105-0560-1332EC9100FF5C83

The top 5 percent of U.S. earners were responsible for an outsized chunk of domestic consumption in 2012, 38 percent up from 28 percent in 1995, according to a study by two economists from the Weidenbaum Center at Washington University in St. Louis, and their consumption has risen much faster than that of the less well-heeled. Since 2009, spending by those top earners rose 17 percent, compared with 1 percent growth among the bottom 95 percent.[30]

Some economists and activists blame this phenomenon on stagnating middle-class wages since 1980. A middle-income family would have had $18,897 more to spend in 2007, the year before the recession, if there "had been no growth in income disparities since 1979," according to the Economic Policy Institute, a liberal think tank in Washington that focuses on working Americans.[31] More spending from those families would have helped stimulate the economy, argues Princeton economist Alan Krueger, who was a top economic adviser to Obama from 2009 to 2013.

If the shift in income to top earners in recent years had been more evenly distributed, Krueger calculates that annual consumption would be $400 billion to $500

French economist Thomas Piketty warns in a widely discussed book that rising inequality could threaten the very fabric of democracy and proposes high taxes on the rich. His book, *Capital in the Twenty-First Century*, argues that the United States reflects a global trend toward concentration of wealth and that inequality worldwide now appears comparable to stratified Europe in the early 20th century.

billion higher today, equal to 3.5 percent of gross domestic product (GDP).[32]

Conservatives counter that investment is just as important as consumption to a growing economy and that more wealth at the top means more investment, with benefits trickling down in the form of new jobs. "The combination of more investment, innovation and risk-taking at the top that's been facilitated by rising income" has contributed to continued economic growth, says the Manhattan Institute's Winship.

Winship estimates that the increase in the top 1 percent's share of national income between 1979 and 2007 raised GDP during that period and therefore increased household income for the middle class.[33]

"If the top 1 percent continues to get a bigger share of a pie that grows fast enough, then the middle class and poor may receive pretty big gains themselves," he says. The rising share of national income going to the wealthiest — the statistic cited by Piketty that has attracted so much recent attention — "may be the wrong indicator to focus on," Winship says.

One reason the United States may have more inequality than other rich countries is that "we honor entrepreneurs more," says Heritage's Furth. When a young unknown like Bill Gates suddenly becomes a millionaire, he pulls far ahead of everyone else.

"I don't think there's any evidence that inequality hurts growth," says Furth. "The United States has remained at the top of GDP-per-capita charts for large countries for 60 to 80 years," he says, pointing out that the median household in the United States earns more than its counterparts in countries including Great Britain, France, Italy, and Spain.

But others say the pie is being divided unfairly even amid growth. "As long as productivity is growing, someone's getting the money; it just ain't America's middle class," says Heather Boushey, executive director of the Washington Center for Equitable Progress, a project studying inequality at the Center for American Progress, a liberal think tank in Washington.

From 1973 to 2014, the nation's net productivity surged by 72 percent, but the hourly pay of a typical worker grew by only 9 percent, according the Economic Policy Institute.[34] If all workers' wages had risen in line with productivity growth, as they did in the three decades prior to World War II, an American earning $50,000 today would instead be earning close to $75,000, the institute calculates.[35]

Economists generally agree that some amount of inequality is inevitable once a country shifts from a mainly agrarian economy, where most people are living at a more or less equal subsistence level, to an industrialized economy.[36]

That theory was first advanced by the influential American economist Simon Kuznets in the 1950s and 1960s. As Piketty explains, Kuznets theorized that as countries shifted to industrialized economies, the disparities between those living off the land and those in factory jobs would increase, "because only a minority of people would be prepared to benefit from the new wealth." In later stages of a country's development, Kuznets believed, inequality would automatically decrease as a larger and larger fraction of the population shared in economic growth.[37]

"For any kind of functioning economy, you wouldn't want inequality to be zero," says UT-Austin's Galbraith. However, he adds, "It's like blood pressure. . . . When inequality is going up rapidly, it's a sign you have trouble."

An international comparison by the International Monetary Fund (IMF) finds countries that have lower inequality, after taking into account taxes and welfare benefits, tend to have "faster and more durable growth."[38]

An earlier study from the IMF, one of the most frequently cited in this debate, found recovery from downturns was slower in countries with high inequality. But the study's "boosters generally fail to note that only developing nations are examined," says Winship.[39]

"To generalize from that to industrialized countries and the U.S. is egregious," Winship says. Instead, he cites another study supporting his view that "economic growth has benefited from rising inequality" by leaving poor and middle-class households "with a smaller share of a bigger economic pie and no worse off for it."[40]

With so many studies on both sides of the debate, and with conclusions that vary depending on which countries and periods of time they examine, there probably isn't a one-for-one relationship between inequality and growth, concludes Hacker, the Yale political scientist. "The more relevant question is, 'Does income inequality hamper middle-class income growth?'" he says. "In the U.S., you had a big increase in average incomes, but most of that's driven by the rise at the very top."

Increasingly, experts on both right and left have been pointing to America's highly unequal educational system, in which affluent suburbs provide far better public schools than struggling inner cities, as a root cause of income inequality. However, they disagree on the solutions — Republicans favor school choice, while Democrats advocate universal free pre-kindergarten.

That educational gap between rich and poor hurts the economy because the nation doesn't make the most of all its talented citizens, most experts agree. And the gap between low-income and upper-income children in obtaining a college education is large and widening.[41]

"Talent is evenly spread throughout our country. Opportunity is not," according to Harvard Graduate School of Education Dean James Ryan. "Right now, there exists an almost ironclad link between a child's ZIP code and her chances of success."[42]

Liberal economist Krugman has called that educational divide "a huge and growing waste of human potential — a waste that surely acts as a powerful if invisible drag on economic growth."[43]

Are parental background and inheritance becoming more important for success?

In his book, economist Piketty finds that today's trends echo the aristocratic class system described in the 19th-century novels of British writer Jane Austen and French writer Honoré de Balzac: Inherited wealth in some European countries is becoming as important for individual financial success as it was in the 19th century, he writes. Inherited wealth accounts for nearly half of the total amount of the largest fortunes worldwide, he estimates.[44]

Even in the United States, where inheritance has historically been less important than in Europe, wealth is providing an ever-more cumulative advantage, Piketty argues, because capital begets more wealth once invested and has been growing at a faster rate than wages.

According to Forbes' global billionaires list, the top wealth holders have seen their holdings rise at 6 to 7 percent per year from 1987 to 2013, a rate more than three times faster than the growth in income and output at the global level. That means rich people can accumulate wealth at far higher rates than the majority of workers, whose wages grow no faster than the economy or their own productivity, Piketty argues.

In an interview, Piketty explained, "If wealth is rising three times as fast as the economy and this goes on for several decades, it means the middle class is vanishing and a rising fraction of national wealth will be taken by a small fraction" of people at the very top.

"It's not sustainable unless you are able to accept an oligarchic concentration of wealth, which is not fully compatible with the democratic idea," says Piketty, whose solution is a global tax on wealth combined with higher income taxes on the richest in the United States.

"Growing income and wealth inequality is skewing our democracy: We're supposed to have a system where every vote counts but where increasingly money counts," says Lawrence Mishel, president of the Economic Policy Institute, a liberal think tank in Washington.

"Upward mobility has stalled," Obama declared in his January 2014 State of the Union speech and he stressed the need to build "ladders of opportunity into the middle class."[45] Even Conservative Republicans Rep. Paul Ryan of Wisconsin and Florida Sen. Marco Rubio bewailed social immobility and said there should be more reward for people who work hard.[46]

But a 2014 study found upward mobility in the United States has not slowed and is actually similar to its level a generation ago.[47]

A roving bus in New York City in December 2013 offered British-style tea and biscuits to promote season four of the hit period drama *Downton Abbey*. In the United States, unlike in the early-20th-century England portrayed in the popular PBS series, the very wealthy tend to be the "working rich," rather than aristocrats who inherited their fortunes.

According to the study, led by Harvard economist Raj Chetty, the probability that a child born in 1971 in the bottom fifth of incomes would make it to the top fifth was 8 percent; for children born in 1986 it was 9 percent.[48] Yet, many don't see that as good news because it still means most families at the bottom never make it to the top.

And mobility in the U.S. is about half that in some Scandinavian countries. In Denmark, a poor child has twice the chance of making it to the top fifth as in America.[49]

A study by University of California-Davis economist Gregory Clark finds the elite status of aristocratic families is amazingly resilient over generations even in a country like Sweden, famous for its income equality.[50] His finding runs counter to most previous studies, which find more upward mobility in Europe and Scandinavia than in the United States.

The American dream of upward mobility for all "is clearly a myth," he told a London audience, based on his study of the persistence of elite families in professions like medicine and law.

Clark uses an unconventional method — tracking elite surnames over centuries — and comes to an unconventional conclusion: "We can't find any society that is achieving high rates of social mobility," he says, concluding, "It's not going to be worthwhile making massive social investments in trying to improve social mobility." But he does favor Scandinavian-style welfare to produce more income equality.

There's no question that Sweden's system of welfare benefits evens out differences in income, making that nation one of the most equal of rich countries. Surprisingly, Sweden actually starts out similar to the United States in inequality if one counts solely incomes paid by employers — before taxes and welfare benefits. In the United States, "The really big story is [that] we redistribute much less," says Janet Gornick, director of the Luxembourg Income Study Center, of Luxembourg and New York.

Many policymakers maintain there are ways to boost social mobility in America without recreating a Swedish welfare state. Ron Haskins helped design 1996 welfare reform legislation as a Republican congressional staffer, later serving as a White House adviser to Republican President George W. Bush, and currently is a senior fellow in economic studies at the centrist Brookings Institution think tank. He says that with a college diploma, young people born into low-income families can quadruple their chance of making it to the top of the income ladder — from 5 percent to 20 percent.

However, Haskins stresses the role of personal responsibility. In 2009, he analyzed census data to see how adult Americans were doing if they followed three norms of modern society: finishing high school, getting a full-time job, and waiting until age 21 to get married before having children. Young adults who followed all three had only a 2 percent chance of winding up in poverty; they had a 74 percent chance of reaching the middle class, he found.[51]

"Liberals are very reluctant to talk about personal responsibility because it's blaming the victim," Haskins says.

Unlike the wealthiest families of 19th-century Europe or even those of early 20th-century England portrayed on the PBS series *Downton Abbey*, the very wealthy in the United States tend to be the "working rich"; and there hasn't been a big increase in inherited wealth since the 1980s. In fact, intergenerational wealth transfers as a proportion of net worth have fallen from 29 percent to 19 percent between 1989 and 2007.[52]

That's a big contrast to Europe, where French economist Piketty finds inheritance is reaching levels not seen since the 19th century as a share of national income.[53]

However, when Piketty looks more broadly at accumulated wealth globally, not just inheritance, he finds it comparable to the levels in Europe in 1900 to 1910, during France's so-called Belle Époque, when industrialists were accumulating wealth and there was a large underclass. Today, the top 1 percent owns about half of all global wealth and the bottom half less than 5 percent, Piketty calculates.[54]

Wealth, inherited or not, is a huge advantage in becoming even wealthier, Piketty says, because the wealthy have financial advisers and can afford high-risk, high-return investments, compared with the small saver, who can't afford to risk any part of a nest egg.

Yet, Americans still believe in the rags-to-riches American dream, polls by the Pew Charitable Trusts find.[55] That may be because most families (84 percent) are making more than their parents, notes Erin Currier, director of economic mobility research for Pew. But the glass is only half full. "For families at the bottom, yes, they have more money than their parents, but often the increase is so small that it's not enough to move them out of the bottom," she says. Seventy percent of children born into families in the bottom 20 percent never even make it to the middle class as working adults, according to Pew.[56]

Should the wealthy be taxed more?

Imposing higher taxes on the rich has received renewed attention as Democratic presidential candidates Bernie Sanders and Hillary Clinton joined Obama in calling on the wealthy to share more of the burden.

Sanders declared his campaign was "sending a message to the billionaire class . . . You can't get huge tax breaks while children in this country go hungry."[57]

By contrast, Trump has proposed tax cuts at all income levels with the largest benefits going to the highest-income households.[58]

The ability of the super-rich to hide their wealth from the taxman also came into the spotlight following the leaks of the so-called "Panama Papers" in April 2016; they revealed billions of dollars hidden in more than 200,000 offshore entities, traced to political leaders and wealthy individuals in countries as far-flung as the United States, Russia, Saudi Arabia, Syria, and Iceland.

"Inequality is one of the defining issues of our time," the anonymous source of the leaks, known only as John Doe, wrote in a May 2016 blog post. As for why inequality's "sudden acceleration" has many people "helpless to stop its steady growth," he concluded, "The Panama Papers provide a compelling answer to these questions: massive, pervasive corruption."[59]

A controversial proposal by French economist Piketty to impose a global tax on "wealth" — including all assets such as trusts, partnerships and stocks — has also stimulated debate. To keep the rich from evading the tax by moving their money abroad to offshore tax havens, such a tax should be global, Piketty argues. While conceding that it is probably utopian to think all governments would agree to that measure, he suggests it would "realistic" for Europe.

For Piketty, his brash proposal is a way to draw attention to his central concern: Accumulating capital is conferring unfair advantages on the rich in a cycle that could eventually see the disappearance of the middle class. "The point is not just to raise taxation — it's to help the diffusion of wealth and make sure the wealth of the middle class expands rather than continues to shrink," he says.

And he thinks this is a more effective way to tax the rich than solely through income tax, considering how much is hidden offshore "If some people are taxed on the basis of declared incomes that are only 1 percent of actual incomes, then nothing is accomplished by raising income tax rates to 50 or even 98 percent," he writes.[60]

Heritage Foundation conservative Furth objects that taxing capital would penalize the modest Swedish millionaire who invests his capital to create jobs and drives a beat-up Saab. Instead it would favor the decadent consumption of a "Wolf of Wall Street"-style millionaire who merely spends his money.[61] "Investment helps everyone else, consumption only helps you. If you want to help labor, tax capital at zero," he advises.

In a critique of Piketty's book published in *The Wall Street Journal*, Christopher DeMuth, Republican President Ronald Reagan's deregulation czar in the 1980s and now a distinguished fellow at the conservative Hudson Institute, argued that in practice income redistributed by government often ends up in the hands of the powerful rather than the needy. The pro-government "intellectual imagines redistributing capital profits while leaving owners with the losses," he wrote. Yet

Americans Divided on Action to Curb Inequality

A majority of Americans belonging to both political parties agree that economic inequality has worsened over the past decade, according to a recent survey. However, 90 percent of Democrats interviewed say the government should take "a lot" or "some" action to reduce the gap, compared with 69 percent of independents and 45 percent of Republicans.

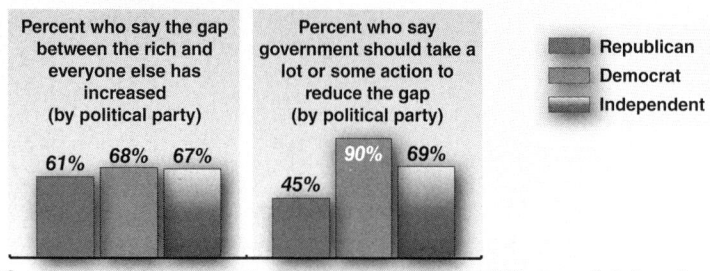

Source: "Most See Inequality Growing, but Partisans Differ over Solutions," Pew Research Center, Jan. 23, 2014, www.people-press.org/2014/01/23/most-see-inequality-growing-but-partisans-differ-over-solutions/

"the opposite — profits for owners and managers, losses for taxpayers — has been frequently observed in the wild."[62]

Some concerned about inequality in the United States have proposed raising income tax rates on the rich — now at 39.6 percent on the highest income bracket. Political scientist Hacker says that rate kicks in well below the richest of the rich. He has proposed raising the top rate on the truly rich — to 45 percent for those with annual incomes between $1 million and $10 million and to 49 percent for those with income of $1 billion or more.[63]

Hacker argues that the prospect of such high taxation would stem extremely high corporate pay packages — which have skyrocketed in recent years — because so much would get taxed away. He predicts "companies would pay slightly smaller packages and plow some of that into firm investment or salaries for the rank and file. But the main reason to do it is to raise money and assure the tax code is progressive all the way up the income distribution." (A progressive income tax is one in which the tax rate increases as the payer's income increases.)

Arguments for taxing the rich often stem from "a misguided belief that the economy is a zero-sum game and that reducing the position of the top 1 percent automatically improves everyone else's," Sendhil Mullainathan, a professor of economics at Harvard, cautioned in *The New York Times*.[64]

In a public debate on the issue, conservative supply-side economist Arthur Laffer argued that the rich already pay enough — more of the nation's income tax than anyone else. He also argued, "You aren't going to get the money from these guys. They can hire lawyers, they can hire accountants. . . . they can hire congressmen, . . . senators."[65]

Former Labor Secretary Robert Reich, who served in the administration of Democratic President Bill Clinton, countered that the country's budget deficits require tax increases and that those ought to come mostly from people at the top because "people at the top have never had it so good."[66]

Conservatives like Furth cite findings that high taxes on the rich remove incentives to continue working and thus ultimately hurt growth. "I'd argue incentive effects matter. Even if the rich have a Learjet, they want more money and are willing to work for it and create more businesses," he says.

That was the argument of Reagan, under whose administration top rates were lowered, as recommended by Laffer. But, says the University of Texas' Galbraith, "We taxed the rich a lot less 34 years ago and got no more investment."

Rather than a high income tax, Galbraith favors a high estate tax to "actively discourage dynasty building." Piketty does not: "Life is very long these days," he says. "If you wait until people die to regulate the consumption of wealth it will be too long; you need a lifetime wealth tax."

Ultimately, the argument comes back to whether the income of the wealthy should be redistributed through the tax system to counter inequality. Haskins of Brookings argues that on that score the "government is already fighting inequality dramatically." Households at the bottom of the ladder, earning $25,400 a year, received almost $9,600 in government benefits in 2013, including Social Security and Medicare, according to the Congressional Budget Office.[67]

However, those transfers still leave the United States far behind Scandinavia and some European countries on equality measures, because those countries have far more generous welfare benefits.

A self-described budget hawk like Haskins questions how much more the government can afford to do. "After all, we're spending $1 trillion between the federal government and the states on benefit programs, and our tax system is hugely progressive: The upper 20 percent pay over 90 percent of federal income taxes," he says.[68] "You want the rich to pay 96 percent of federal income taxes?"

Even some liberal activists who are calling attention to growing inequality say they're more interested in seeing changes that create more opportunity — like a higher minimum wage, more jobs and more bargaining power for workers. "I think we need to have more taxes on the best-off, but I think what matters for me is what happens in the marketplace," says the Economic Policy Institute's Mishel.

Pointing to trends such as the growing competitiveness of foreign workers and the education gap between rich and poor, Urban Institute tax expert Eugene Steuerle, who served in four White House administrations, both Republican and Democratic, cautions, "The forces in society that are leading to inequality are much larger" than the solutions currently proposed such as "nipping at the taxes the rich pay or bumping up the transfers that low-income people receive."

President Theodore Roosevelt addresses a crowd from the back of a train, circa 1907. President from 1901 to 1909, Roosevelt championed an estate tax in 1910 to prevent extreme accumulation of wealth. "The absence of effective state . . . restraint upon unfair money-getting has tended to create a small class of enormously wealthy and economically powerful men, whose chief object is to hold and increase their power," he charged.

BACKGROUND

'Fatal Ailment'

Ancient philosophers and their Enlightenment heirs believed that democracy required not a utopian form of equality but rather laws that would limit the excesses of the wealthy. "An imbalance between rich and poor is the oldest and most fatal ailment of all republics," the Greek philosopher Plutarch (A.D. 45-120) declared.[69]

The French Enlightenment philosopher Montesquieu (1689-1755) identified "real equality" as the soul of democracy, but acknowledged that in practice republics could only "fix the differences to a certain point."[70]

Similarly, the architects of American democracy shared a concern that political factions arising from deep class divisions and "unequal distribution of property," in the words of Founding Father James Madison, could undermine democracy. Madison stressed that the new American republic would derive its powers from the people, not from aristocratic or hereditary privileges as in England.[71]

Fear of coming to resemble old Europe was part of American interest in imposing progressive taxes. Throughout the 19th century, the United States had no income tax. But the industrial revolution, which created a small class of American plutocrats, changed that.

During that era, some of the rich flaunted their wealth: At an 1897 costume ball in New York, the mother of millionaire John Jacob Astor came as Marie Antoinette in a dress adorned with $250,000 in jewels.[72]

CHRONOLOGY

1870s-1900s *Gilded Age sees rising inequality; progressives call for taxes on the rich.*

1913 States ratify 16th Amendment to U.S. Constitution, allowing Congress to institute income tax.

1916 U.S. Congress incorporates estate tax into tax code.

1920s-1930s *FDR's Depression-era New Deal creates social programs; increases taxes on the rich.*

1929-1933 Great Depression; U.S. unemployment nears 25 percent.

1933 Under President Franklin D. Roosevelt, top U.S. tax rate increases to 63 percent.

1940s-1970s *World War II brings highest U.S. tax rates on the rich.*

1941 U.S. enters World War II.

1942 Congress raises top tax rate to 88 percent to pay for war effort; Nation's wealthiest 10 percent see their share of U.S. income drop from about 45 percent to 33 percent, where it stays into the 1970s.

1944 Congress raises top rate again to 94 percent on income over $200,000 — $27 million in current dollars.

1954 Union membership peaks at more than one in three workers.

1974 Union membership drops to less than one in four workers — plummeting to 11 percent in 2013.

Late 1970s-1990s *Conservatives support tax cuts as key to growth; middle-class income growth falls behind productivity growth.*

1979-1980 *Supply-side economics advocates Margaret Thatcher and Ronald Reagan elected to top positions in Britain and the United States.*

1981 Economic Recovery Tax Act reduces top U.S. tax rates.

1986 Tax Reform Act of 1986 reduces top income tax rate from 50 percent to 28 percent.

1992-2000 *Average income grows 32 percent as economy expands; income of bottom 99 percent grows 20 percent; income of wealthiest 1 percent grows 99 percent.*

1992 After 1990-91 recession, President Bill Clinton elected.

2000 Unemployment drops to 20-year low of 4 percent from peak of 7.5 percent in 1992.

2000s-Present *Financial collapse leads to new financial regulation; average family income drops during Great Recession (2007-2009).*

2001 Under President George W. Bush, tax cuts adopted despite budget deficit; taxes cut again in 2003.

2008 Global financial crisis follows subprime mortgage collapse.

2010 Dodd-Frank Wall Street reform law increases financial regulation as well as reporting of executive pay.

2012 Top 10 percent capture more than 50 percent of U.S. income — highest share since 1917, according to Berkeley economists.

2013 Berkeley researchers say top 1 percent of earners captured 95 percent of income gains since 2009 recovery; Bill de Blasio elected New York City mayor promising to tax rich to pay for pre-kindergarten; Bush tax cut expires; top tax rates raised from 35 percent to 39.6 percent.

2014 Senate hearings find thousands of U.S. taxpayers hiding money in offshore havens; President Obama sends budget to Congress urging taxes on rich, expanded preschool; Credit Suisse fined for helping U.S. taxpayers evade taxes.

2015 Bernie Sanders pushes inequality to forefront of presidential Democratic primary campaign; Hillary Clinton takes up the cry, vowing to raise minimum wage, provide free preschool, and help with college tuition. Republican candidate Donald Trump vows to renegotiate trade agreements to save American jobs.

2016 Panama Papers leaks reveal thousands of offshore entities hiding wealth of individuals and companies from taxes; President Obama proposes legislation requiring companies to report offshore income to U.S. government; Obama administration extends overtime to millions of workers.

Between 1870 and 1914, an era known as the Gilded Age, the increasing concentration of wealth at the top created extreme inequality. As late as 1919, Irving Fisher, president of the American Economic Association, expressed alarm that the top 2 percent owned more than 50 percent of the wealth while two-thirds of the population "owns almost nothing."[73]

Politicians calling themselves *Progressives*, including Republican Theodore Roosevelt, railed against monopolies for stifling competition and for treating workers badly. "The absence of effective state . . . restraint upon unfair money-getting has tended to create a small class of enormously wealthy and economically powerful men, whose chief object is to hold and increase their power," charged Roosevelt in 1910.[74]

Roosevelt, president from 1901 to 1909, championed an estate tax in 1910 to prevent extreme accumulation of wealth, which, along with a graduated income tax, became a key plank of the Republican Party.

In 1913, the states ratified the 16th Amendment to the Constitution, giving Congress the power to collect income taxes; in October of that year, Congress passed a law creating the first permanent U.S. income tax.[75] In 1916, seven years after Roosevelt left office, Congress incorporated an estate tax into the federal code.[76]

Between World War I and World War II, the United States was the first country to try very high tax rates — 70 percent on the top tier of income in 1919-22 and 70 percent on estates in 1937. The purpose was to put an end to such large incomes and estates — not to raise revenue, writes Piketty.[77]

After World War I, many countries adopted a progressive income tax, including Britain (1909), France (1914), India (1922), and Argentina (1932).

During the Roaring '20s, an era of rising fortunes, the top income tax rate was cut to 25 percent and again to 24 percent in 1929.

Coming to power during the Great Depression, President Franklin D. Roosevelt immediately moved to raise the top tax rate — and succeeded in raising rates on the wealthiest, first to 63 percent in 1933, then to 79 percent in 1937, surpassing the 1919 record.

As FDR expressed it in 1936, "For too many of us the political equality we once had was meaningless in the face of economic inequality. A small group had concentrated . . . an almost complete control over other people's property, money . . . labor . . . lives."[78]

As part of FDR's program to make sure the excesses that led to the Depression were not repeated, banks were regulated and deposits insured. The securities industry was placed under new tight restrictions; higher taxes were levied on the rich.[79]

Roosevelt's economic officials also supported measures that gave labor unions greater power to organize. Old-age and unemployment insurance provided workers with economic protection.

Top U.S. income tax rates reached their highest points during World War II: The 1942 Victory Tax Act raised the top rate to 88 percent; in 1944, Congress raised the rate again to 94 percent on annual income over $200,000 — $27 million in current dollars.[80]

Postwar Prosperity

Following World War II, all developed countries including the United States enjoyed high economic-growth rates. Americans' income grew at roughly the same rate no matter how much money they made.

The traditional economic view promoted by American economist Kuznets in the 1950s held that the post–WWII period represented an inevitable trend toward increasing equality and greater upward mobility, which would continue indefinitely.[81]

More recently, conservatives have argued that there's no returning to a time when an unskilled worker with only a high school education could support a family. In 1992, economists John Bound and George Johnson pointed to "skill-based technological change" and globalization as the main reasons wages stopped growing at the same rate after the 1970s.[82]

That argument has been debated by liberal economists such as Hacker, Galbraith, and Mishel who say government policies after 1978 were more important in retarding wage growth. They point to the declining power of U.S. unions; from a peak of one in three workers after World War II, union membership has declined to one in ten — a decline they say was abetted by anti-union government policies.[83]

Yale political science professor Hacker charges that by breaking the air-traffic-controllers strike in 1981 and appointing a National Labor Relations Board heavily in favor of management, Reagan contributed to the increasingly aggressive posture of business against unions and helped create a political vacuum that unions once filled as advocates for middle-class concerns.[84]

Tax Havens Shelter Trillions

"The current estimates of inequality are massively understated."

An estimated $21 trillion to $32 trillion is squirreled away in offshore bank accounts, largely untaxed, by the world's 10 million richest people, estimates the British advocacy group Tax Justice Network.[1]

"The current estimates of inequality are massively understated because they exclude offshore wealth," says John Christensen, director of the network. Most people with assets of more than $4 million "hold much if not the majority of their wealth offshore — and therefore outside the national statistics."

Offshore tax havens are loosely defined as places that permit individuals and companies to escape their home jurisdiction's laws and regulations — especially those involving taxes —"using secrecy as a prime tool," according to the Tax Justice Network.

The U.S. Foreign Account Tax Compliance Act (FATCA), passed in 2010, requires all foreign banks to inform the U.S. Treasury Department about bank accounts held abroad by U.S. taxpayers. The penalty for noncompliant banks is a 30 percent surtax on the banks' U.S. income, which Christensen describes as the "big American stick."

The law is far stricter than a 2003 European Union directive that called for information exchange to ensure proper taxation of interest-bearing accounts, which French economist Thomas Piketty has called "timid . . . meaningless . . . not enforced." (A directive is a legal action that tells European member nations what goal they must achieve, but does not dictate the means.)[2] But even FATCA is not sufficient in Piketty's view. It's not comprehensive enough to cover all taxpayers, such as certain trust funds and foundations, he writes, and the penalties against banks may not be enough of a deterrent.[3]

In 2013, the leaders of eight of the world's major industrialized economies, known as the G8, called for tax authorities around the world, including those in smaller countries, to share information automatically to crack down on tax evasion.[4]

Following that action, and catalyzed by America's new law, famed tax havens such as the Cayman Islands, Luxembourg, and Jersey were among more than 40 jurisdictions that agreed in February 2014 to pioneer a system of automatic information exchange for offshore bank accounts. Tax Justice Network hailed the move as "the first big step in putting together the nuts and bolts of real change."[5]

"If we were able to put into place effective information-exchange cooperation among countries, the ability to evade taxes would be massively diminished," says Christensen.

Over 100 countries and jurisdictions have committed to introducing such automatic information exchanges within the next two years and reporting investors' tax details to their home governments, under a plan developed by the Paris-based Organisation for Economic Co-operation and Development (OECD).[6]

However, activists from groups like the Tax Justice Network have questioned the OECD's claim that this effort will end tax havens, saying governments like Britain haven't collected the necessary information on companies, while others criticized the information for not being made public.[7]

Governments around the world have been criticized for not doing enough to crack down on tax evaders ever since the leak in April 2016 of millions of documents showing how a Panamanian law firm had helped thousands of individuals hide their money offshore. In the wake of the so-called "Panama Papers" leaks, the European Union (EU) stepped up its campaign against aggressive tax avoidance.

An open letter to world leaders signed by 300 economists, including equality guru Thomas Piketty and Columbia University professor Jeffrey Sachs, urged governments to go further — to set global rules for companies to report their income in every country where they operate and to make the information public. Sachs charged that recent rules changes initiated by the OECD and others still contained too many loopholes. He urged the United States, the United Kingdom, and the EU to take the lead in closing such loopholes.

"I think these governments don't really want to do much because their powerful backers, whether it is in the city of London, or on Wall Street, are fighting very, very hard to keep these loopholes open," he told BBC radio in

May 2016. "This is a system that has been created over time for the convenience of very rich and powerful people."[8]

The economists' letter was timed to influence an anti-corruption summit of world leaders meeting in London in May 2016. At the summit, the United States came in for criticism for failing to create a register of the real owners of so-called shell companies, which often hide money — and their genuine owners — by setting themselves up in low-regulation tax haven states like Delaware.[9]

The Obama administration announced the same month that it was submitting a legislative proposal to Congress requiring such companies to report their real ownership to the Treasury.[10]

Critics said Congressional approval would be difficult to obtain, and the legislation would not make the information public, as tax reform activists have been urging.[11]

The methods that wealthy American taxpayers use to hide their money from the taxman became the focus of attention at Congressional hearings in 2014.

The Senate Permanent Subcommittee on Investigations released a report that year accusing Swiss banks and the Swiss government of helping to hide billions of U.S. taxpayer dollars in offshore accounts. Zurich-based Credit Suisse was one of 14 Swiss banks then under investigation by the U.S. government for helping Americans evade taxes.[12]

The subcommittee reported that Credit Suisse bank employees traveled to the United States to recruit wealthy customers and engaged in secret-agent style transactions — even handing over a customer's bank statements hidden in a *Sports Illustrated* magazine.[13]

In November 2014, Credit Suisse was sentenced to conspiracy to aid U.S. taxpayers in filing false income tax returns and was ordered to pay $2.6 billion in fines and restitution to the United States.[14] The Justice Department has signed agreements with 80 Swiss banks that have admitted to criminal conduct and that have paid more than $1.3 billion in penalties.[15]

As the recent Panama Papers scandal illustrates, it has been so easy for kleptocrats and politicians from Russia to the Middle East to shift billions of dollars' worth of wealth out of their home countries, that, in Christensen's words, "this has created a criminogenic global financial market, where it is more profitable for lawyers, bankers and accountants to engage in criminal activity on behalf of clients than to do their job properly."

— *Sarah Glazer*

[1] "Inequality and Tax Havens," Tax Justice Network, no date, http://tinyurl.com/n49w879.

[2] European Commission, "What are EU directives?," no date, http://europa.eu/eu-law/decision-making/legal-acts/index_en.htm.

[3] Thomas Piketty, *Capital in the Twenty-First Century* (Cambridge, MA: Belknap Press, 2014), p. 522.

[4] George Parker and Vanessa Houlder, "G8 Seeks Rewrite of Global Tax Rules," *Financial Times*, June 18, 2013, http://tinyurl.com/lk3xblg.

[5] Vanessa Houlder, "Global Tax Standard Attracts 42 Countries," *Financial Times*, February 13, 2014, http://tinyurl.com/k6y2etk.

[6] OECD statement: "Statement from OECD President Secretary-General Angel Gurria on the 'Panama Papers,'" April 4, 2016, http://www.oecd.org/tax/statement-from-oecd-secretary-general-angel-gurria-on-the-panama-papers.htm.

For updated figure of 101 jurisdictions, see OECD, "Automatic Exchange Commitment and Monitoring Process," May 9, 2016, http://www.oecd.org/tax/automatic-exchange/commitment-and-monitoring-process/AEOI-commitments.pdf.

[7] "Tax havens will end in 2018, says OECD," *The Times*, October 31, 2014, http://www.thetimes.co.uk/tto/money/tax/article4253248.ece.

[8] Patrick Wintour, "Tax Havens have no economic justification, say top economists," *Guardian*, May 9, 2016, http://www.theguardian.com/world/2016/may/09/tax-havens-have-no-economic-justification-say-top-economists?CMP=Share_iOSApp_Other.

[9] Henry Mance and Tom Burgis, "Offshore centres hit at US financial transparency 'hypocrisy,'" *Financial Times*, May 12, 2016, http://www.ft.com/cms/s/0/39a8a40c-1859-11e6-bb7d-ee563a5a1cc1.html?siteedition=uk.

[10] White House, "President Obama's Efforts on Financial Transparency and Anti-Corruption," May 6, 2016, https://www.whitehouse.gov/blog/2016/05/06/president-obamas-efforts-promote-financial-transparency-and-combat-corruption-what.

[11] Mance and Burgis, op. cit.

[12] Gina Chon, Kara Scannell and James Shotter, "Credit Suisse 'Helped U.S. Tax Evaders,'" *Financial Times*, February 25, 2014, http://tinyurl.com/jvnpzx8.

[13] "Opening Statement of Sen. Carl Levin," Senate Permanent Subcommittee on Investigations Hearing: Offshore Tax Evasion, February 26, 2014, http://tinyurl.com/lnn782o.

[14] U.S. Department of Justice, "Credit Suisse Sentenced for Conspiring to Help U.S. Taxpayers Hide Offshore Accounts from Internal Revenue Service," November 21, 2014, https://www.justice.gov/opa/pr/credit-suisse-sentenced-conspiracy-help-us-taxpayers-hide-offshore-accounts-internal-revenue.

[15] White House, op. cit.

Luxury Homes Are Hot in London — and Controversial

The world's wealthy spend millions, while locals are priced out.

What do you get for $45 million in London's fashionable Mayfair neighborhood? That was the asking price in March 2014 for a narrow four-story house tucked into a mews, one of many cobblestone alleys that once served as the rear quarters for the servants and horses of grand townhouses, but are now enjoying a revival for their charm and proximity to luxury shopping.

Newly built to mimic the 18th-century style of the original house that stood on the lot, this home packs six bedrooms plus a servant's room into 6,500 square feet. And it comes with all the amenities one might expect from the price tag: gym, screening room, separate his-and-hers bathrooms and dressing rooms as well as walk-in closets for each of the main guest rooms.

Increasingly the foreign buyers who dominate London's high-end market also are looking for Versailles-quality workmanship and prepackaged British taste right down to the candlesticks, according to a real estate agent and developer specializing in the luxury market who led this reporter on a walk-through.

Included in the price tag were the bespoke furniture and the carefully displayed *objets*, from the signed Picasso ceramics to an antique volume of the Encyclopedia Britannica. A chandelier specially designed for the soaring stairwell required two weeks of assembly by a team of eight working with 800 crystal pieces.

For most prospective buyers, this is their third or fourth home, so they're not interested in furnishing and decorating yet another house, explains Sanjay Sharma, a former investment banker. He cofounded luxury developer Fenton Whelan in 2010 with another London banker to build and renovate luxury homes and to provide investors with "record prices and exceptional returns on capital," according to the company's website.

The antiques and old-fashioned ceiling moldings like those that Fenton Whelan supplies fulfill the "zeitgeist of the moment — the desire to feel they're buying something British rather than generic," says Richard Cutt, an agent specializing in the city's luxury market for London-based international real estate firm Knight Frank.

Growth in the number of super-rich individuals around the world, particularly in emerging markets such as China, has been driving London's hot luxury housing market in recent years, where prices soared 65 percent between March 2009 and the market's peak in 2014, according to Knight Frank.[1] Globally, the number of individuals with net assets of at least $30 million ballooned by 59 percent from 2003 to 2013; in aggregate, their assets totaled $20 trillion, according to the firm.

Skyrocketing housing prices for low- and middle-income Londoners coupled with a housing supply shortage have intensified hostility toward new luxury homes. In April 2014, Prince Charles said climbing prices would drive young people away from the city, noting the average London house price had reached 10 times an elementary school teacher's salary. His Foundation for Building Community released a report criticizing the tendency for the majority of new housing to serve those in the highest income bracket. The report urged more building of affordable five- to eight-story apartment buildings rather than luxury residential towers.[2]

Several newspaper investigations finding mansions left empty by wealthy overseas owners intensified criticism. Central London "is fast becoming a ghost-town where absentee investors park their wealth" while creative types are pushed to the periphery, London club owner Alex Proud wrote in *The Telegraph*. "Tax empty houses? Why no. We wouldn't want to upset some ex-KGB thug who looted the Kazakh treasury in the mid-1990s."[3]

An investigation by the *Evening Standard* found more than 700 expensive homes standing empty throughout London. Many of the owners were offshore investors parking their wealth in mansions and hiding behind anonymous overseas post office boxes, the newspaper reported.

On "Billionaires' Row," the latest moniker of The Bishops Avenue near fashionable Hampstead Heath, once known as Millionaires' Row, mansions owned by Saudi royals and oil magnates are valued at up to 65 million British pounds ($109 million). In a separate investigation, *The Guardian* found one-third standing derelict and empty.[4]

The Guardian expressed indignation at the avenue's 120 vacant bedrooms at a time when more than 6,000 Londoners were homeless and more than 300,000 families were on waiting lists for public housing. The cost of rising house prices is "borne by those lower down on the chain," wrote *Guardian* columnist Aditya Chakrabortty.[5]

In response, liberals called for a "mansion" tax.[6] The British government compromised by expanding taxes on luxury homes bought through a corporate structure, citing concerns that rich individuals were using this avenue to avoid taxes.[7]

But some real estate agents say such moves are a xenophobic reaction to the fact that the city is becoming more cosmopolitan. "An Italian banker who is living here five years, renting, and then buys a house — is he a foreign buyer?" asks Liam Bailey, global head of residential research at Knight Frank.

After years of vigorous growth, however, prices on luxury homes have been declining in recent months, the *Financial Times* reported in in April 2016.[8]

In March 2016, prices in central London's most luxurious residential areas had dropped 6.7 percent from their 2014 peak, real estate agent Savills reported. Some of the factors cited for dampening demand include higher taxes on the sales of luxury homes introduced since December 2014, downturns in some emerging market economies that spawned some of the earlier luxury homebuyers and worries about the June 2016 vote on whether Britain should leave the European Union.[9]

However, the new trend doesn't seem to have slowed the rush to build new luxury housing in London — nor the complaints from residents about noise from expensive renovations. In May 2016, the number of new homes under construction in expensive inner London had risen by more than 40 percent in 18 months as developers pushed ahead with schemes aimed at the very rich.[10]

— *Sarah Glazer*

The table is set with crystal service for 10 and fresh flowers at a house in London's fashionable Mayfair district that was offered for sale for $45 million — tableware included.

---

[1] Knight Frank, "The Wealth Report," March 2014, http://tinyurl.com/ntseto9.

[2] Prince's Foundation for Building Community, "Housing London: A Mid-Rise Solution," March 2014, http://tinyurl.com/p3zokr7. Also see, op. cit., "Prince Charles: We Need More Homes for Londoners."

[3] Alex Proud, "'Cool London' is Dead, and the Rich Kids Are to Blame," *The Telegraph*, April 7, 2014, http://tinyurl.com/nlqneju.

[4] Robert Booth, "Inside 'Billionaires' Row,'" *The Guardian*, January 31, 2014, http://tinyurl.com/qhugbjl.

[5] Aditya Chakrabortty, "How to Handle the Hoarding of Houses on 'Billionaires' Row,'" *The Guardian*, February 3, 2014, http://tinyurl.com/pl4u82z.

[6] James Kirkup, "Liberal Democrats would tax the rich to clear deficits, says Nick Clegg," *The Telegraph*, February 10, 2014, http://tinyurl.com/paz2hwk.

[7] "Budget 2014: Upmarket Property Ripe for Raiding," *Financial Times*, March 19, 2014, http://tinyurl.com/pw2vq8w.

[8] Judith Evans, "Top London homes being sold at a discount," *Financial Times*, April 21, 2016, http://www.ft.com/cms/s/0/7157843c-0c82-11e6-b0f1-61f222853ff3.html#axzz47nT5s8Uj.

[9] Ibid.

[10] Judith Evans, "Prime London sees 40% rise in new housebuilding," *Financial Times*, May 6, 2016, http://www.ft.com/cms/s/0/95c1bd8a-139c-11e6-839f-2922947098f0.html#axzz48q1uTRaM.

The Great Switch

Much of the increase in the very highest incomes in the United States and the United Kingdom came after 1980, following the elections of conservatives Reagan and British Prime Minister Thatcher.

In the United States, the highest tax brackets had averaged 83 percent from 1932 through 1980, according to Piketty, in contrast with continental Europe. In France and Germany, for instance, the top rate in those years never exceeded 30 to 40 percent. Rates in the United Kingdom were closer to those in the United States. In the 1980s, both the United States and United Kingdom cut rates sharply — U.S. top rates fell to 28 percent after the Reagan tax reform in 1986.[85]

According to Piketty, the "spectacular decrease" in the progressivity of income tax rates during those years probably explains much of the increasing fortunes at the top that followed.

However, in his book *Winner-Take-All Politics*, Hacker chooses 1978, when Democrat Jimmy Carter was still president, as "the great switch point."

In 1978, Congress passed a bill with deep cuts in the capital gains tax, mainly benefiting the wealthy, which was signed by Democratic President Jimmy Carter. Congress also sharply raised payroll taxes, a levy that hits workers' pockets hardest, marking the beginning of a pronounced reversal in federal tax policy, Hacker argues.[86] By 1981, under the Reagan administration, the tax debate had degenerated into a "frenzied bidding war" between Republicans and Democrats to shower benefits on business, writes Hacker.[87] As Reagan budget director Dave Stockman recalled, "the hogs were really feeding."[88]

Under the 1981 Economic Recovery Tax Act, top income tax rates came down sharply, and the tax on multimillion-dollar estates was cut from 70 percent to 50 percent.[89] Hacker's book argues that in the ensuing years, the wealthy have had an outsized influence on government policies and politicians of both parties, noting that in the 1980s and 1990s, senators voted with the interests of the wealthiest upper third of their constituents.[90]

Continuing into the presidency of Bill Clinton, politicians from both parties increasingly accepted the view that excessive regulation impedes economic growth. During the 1990s, financial deregulation swept across national borders, and by 2001, Piketty writes, the owners of capital were prospering as they hadn't since 1913.

Under President George W. Bush in 2001, a huge tax cut bill was supported by Republicans advocating tax cuts even in the face of big deficits in order to stimulate the economy; more cuts followed in 2003, bringing down top tax rates further.[91]

According to analysts, the Bush tax cuts mainly benefited the wealthy and increased inequality but also cut taxes for the middle class.[92]

In March 2008, the investment bank Bear Stearns collapsed, the start of a worldwide financial crisis and recession. While volumes have been written on the causes of the crisis, liberal economists like Boushey and Hacker blame income inequality for driving excessive borrowing by those who couldn't afford it, abetted by lax oversight of the financial industry.

The tax legislation passed at the start of 2013, under Obama, permanently extended the Bush-era tax cuts for most people, but also added a top marginal tax rate of 39.6 percent for those at higher incomes — $400,000 for single filers, $450,000 for married couples filing jointly and $425,000 for heads of household. For tax years 2012 and earlier the highest tax bracket had been 35 percent.[93]

However, some critics say the very rich rarely pay that 39.6 percent because of numerous loopholes, including a provision that lets hedge fund and private-equity firm managers count some income as capital gains, which is taxed at a lower rate — a loophole known as the "carried-interest" provision.

Although it is often dubbed the "hedge-fund loophole," the provision has been far more beneficial to private-equity firms — formerly known as leveraged buy-out firms — which buy companies, then cut their costs or improve their operations and sell them at a profit. The tax break has helped private equity become one of the most well-paid sectors of the financial industry, according to experts, creating private-equity executives worth billions of dollars. Victor Fleischer, a tax-law professor at the University of San Diego School of Law, has argued that the loophole is an important contributor to inequality by boosting the income of financiers in the top 1 percent of the richest 1 percent.[94]

In November 2013, Bill de Blasio swept into office as mayor of New York City on a platform that vowed to fix the gap between the city's haves and have-nots. He proposed to tax the rich to fund universal free pre-K education, which he dubbed a crucial weapon against inequality.

De Blasio's proposed tax became a lightning rod for conservative criticism and a stand-in for the larger debate about whether the rich should be taxed further to cure inequality.

Democratic New York Gov. Andrew Cuomo announced a budget agreement in March 2014 that rejected the mayor's proposed tax on high earners but provided most of the money de Blasio said he needed to create pre-kindergarten for every child in the city.[95]

Haskins of Brookings cautions that most preschool programs aren't good enough to get the sterling results touted by advocates citing studies of high-quality early education. "If we really think preschool is going to bring these kids to the starting line of public schools roughly equal to their more advantaged peers, we need much better teachers, which means we have to pay a lot more money," he says.

While conservatives tend to agree with liberals that unequal education is a root cause of inequality, their solutions differ: Conservatives such as Furth back approaches that give parents more choice in picking schools, such as vouchers and charter schools.

The budget that Obama sent to Congress in 2014 echoed many of the solutions to inequality proposed by liberals — from more taxes on the rich to funding preschool for the less advantaged.

"As a country, we've got to make a decision if we're going to protect tax breaks for the wealthiest Americans, or if we're going to make smart investments necessary to create jobs and grow our economy, and expand opportunity for every American," the president said.[96]

But noting the increasing emphasis on raising taxes and redistributing wealth coming from Obama and international organizations such as the International Monetary Fund (IMF), Dan Henninger, deputy editorial page director of *The Wall Street Journal*, wrote, "What's unacceptable about the income-inequality agenda of the Obama Democrats, the United Nations and the IMF is that all assume that the U.S.'s historic century of strong, capital-driven growth is over, and that it must reorder its priorities to admit the reality of reduced long-term economic performance. In short, it's time to slow down and divide up what pie we've got." That's what Europe and Russia did, he added. "That's what the United States would be nuts to do."[97]

Even supporters of Obama's proposals to expand pre-kindergarten and tax credits for low-income workers predicted that Republicans would resist "every dollar" of the $651 billion the president asked for over the next decade, in the words of a *New York Times* editorial. That partisan opposition has doomed most of Obama's legislative efforts to remedy inequality in a Republican-controlled Congress.[98]

The conservative Heritage Foundation, which instantly pronounced the budget "dead on arrival,"[99] called a proposed cap on deductions for high earners "troubling" because it would apply to retirement savings, health insurance, and municipal bond income.

And it singled out Obama's proposal to implement the so-called "Buffet rule" originally put forward by billionaire businessman Warren Buffet, who said he paid a lower tax rate than his secretary. Buffet said millionaires should pay no less a share of their income than middle-class households. The Obama proposal, originally put forward in 2011, would require those making more than $1 million a year to pay no less than 30 percent of their income in taxes after charitable contributions.[100] Heritage said most top earners already meet that bar.[101]

CURRENT SITUATION
Proposed Fixes

Taxing the rich once again became a major issue in the 2016 presidential campaign. Bernie Sanders set a high bar by proposing to dramatically increase taxes on the very rich. Under his campaign proposal the top 0.1 percent of earners would have seen their tax burden increase by an average of $3 million in 2017.[102]

Similarly, nearly all of Hillary Clinton's proposed tax increases would fall on the top 1 percent, according to the Tax Policy Center, the non-partisan tax research arm of the Urban Institute and the Brookings Institution.[103]

By contrast, Trump has advocated across-the-board tax cuts at all income levels. However, the largest benefits from his proposed cuts, in dollar and percentage terms, would go to the highest-income households, according to the Tax Policy Center. Trump would slash the current top income tax rate from 39.6 percent to 25 percent, lavishing the top 0.1 percent with a tax cut of $1.3 million on average by 2017, the Center calculates.[104]

President Obama calls for a hike in the minimum wage to $10.10 during an address at a Costco store in Lanham, Md., on Jan. 29, 2014. In his State of the Union address, Obama said upward mobility had stalled and stressed the need to build "ladders of opportunity" to the middle class.

Like Sanders and Clinton, Trump has criticized the existing tax breaks for hedge fund managers, saying they "are getting away with murder" and "they'll pay more." Like Sanders and Clinton, Trump says he would make these high-income individuals pay the ordinary income tax rate on the chunk of their profits, known as "carried interest," which is now taxed at the lower capital gains tax rate.[105]

But in the final analysis Trump's overall tax plan actually wouldn't raise taxes on wealthy hedge fund managers, largely because he's also proposing to cut ordinary income tax rates for their top tax bracket, according to James Pethokoukis, a scholar at the conservative American Enterprise Institute. Trump's tax package "supposedly tries to sock it to the undeserving wealthy but will actually reduce their tax burden," he wrote.[106]

The massive size of Trump's proposed tax cuts — a reduction of $9.5 trillion in federal revenues over a decade according to the Tax Policy Center — came in for criticism both from liberals and from conservative analysts like Pethokoukis, who said the increases in the national debt could swallow up any economic growth they might generate.

In May 2016, Trump suggested he was open to higher taxes on the rich, saying his published campaign position was just a starting point for bargaining with Congress. "On my plan they're [taxes for the rich] going down. But by the time it's negotiated, they'll go up," the presumptive Republican presidential nominee said on ABC's *This Week*. "I am willing to pay more," said the real estate mogul, who describes himself as "very rich," although experts have disputed his claims of net worth in the billions. "And you know what? The wealthy are willing to pay more. We've had a very good run."[107]

Yet in a later interview with CNN in May, Trump said he only meant the rich would pay more than his original proposal but would still pay less than they do now.[108]

Several ideas put forward by the Obama administration that have failed to receive congressional approval, such as universal pre-K, got more attention during the campaign, with both Clinton and Sanders saying they supported it. Both candidates underscored universal pre-K and access to a college education as crucial to creating more income equality.

On college education, Sanders went the furthest of any of the candidates, saying he wanted to make tuition free at public colleges and universities, to be paid for by a tax on Wall Street speculators.[109]

Hillary Clinton has said that she is committed to making public colleges debt free for students and to cutting interest rates for people struggling with debt from loans taken out to pay for college.[110]

As late as May 2016, Donald Trump's website had no standalone section on education. However, he has said he would consider getting rid of the federal Department of Education. In an analysis of his stance on education, *Education Week* pointed out that his Trump University wasn't a university at all and was targeted by numerous lawsuits claiming misleading advertising.[111]

As part of his agenda for tackling inequality, Obama has for several years proposed an increase in the federal minimum wage — from $7.25 to $10.10 an hour.

In his January 2015 State of the Union address, Obama said, "to everyone in this Congress who still

AT ISSUE

Do the rich pay enough in taxes?

YES
Curtis Dubay
Research Fellow, Tax and Economic policy, Heritage Foundation

Written for *CQ Researcher*, April 2014

When it comes to the rich paying taxes, how much is enough? Because everyone defines *enough* differently, for the debate to move forward, we need to ask better questions.

One "better" question is, Do taxes overall need to rise at all? According to the Congressional Budget Office (CBO), tax receipts, as a share of the economy, will hover around 18 percent for the next 10 years — the historical average. Because tax revenues are running at the standard, operational level, it's difficult to argue that there's a crying need to extract more money from current taxpayers, be they rich or otherwise.

The next logical question is, Do the rich pay their fair share of the current tax burden? This, of course, is a more subjective question, but looking at the data can provide some guidance. Again, according to the most recent analysis by CBO, the top 1 percent of households earned just under 15 percent of all income in 2010. Yet they paid 39 percent of all federal income taxes — and more than 24 percent of all federal taxes that year.

These taxpayers paid an average tax rate of 29.4 percent. In other words, President Obama's Buffett Rule, which calls for a minimum tax rate of 30 percent on those who make more than $1 million a year, is essentially already in effect.

What if we broaden the definition of *rich* to the top 10 percent of U.S. households? They paid more than three-quarters of all federal income taxes — or more than half of all federal taxes in 2010.

Any way you slice it, the rich pay the lion's share of the taxes. Still, some may want to gouge the rich more, simply to satisfy their unique sense of fairness. So what would happen if we jacked up taxes on the rich, just to be "fair"? The rich would pay more, certainly. But the non-rich would feel the pain. High-earners also happen to be business owners, investors and entrepreneurs — the people who take risks that create opportunities for the rest of us. Raising their taxes reduces the resources they have to invest and their incentive to do so. Restricted capital means fewer jobs and lower wages.

Do the rich pay enough in taxes? If you think there is too much economic opportunity in America, the answer is "no." Otherwise, you'd have to agree that they already pay more than enough.

NO
Peter Diamond
Professor of Economics, Emeritus, Massachusetts Institute of Technology

Written for *CQ Researcher*, April 2014

Whatever level of federal government spending comes from the political process, that spending must be covered by taxes. In paying for that spending, the more tax revenue that comes from those with the highest incomes, the less needs to come from everyone else.

In choosing how much to collect from the richest, we need to consider the impact on the economy and the differences in abilities to pay between those at the top and those with less, often much less. While views differ on what makes a tax fair, there should be a greater willingness for higher taxes on the highest incomes since income distribution has become dramatically more unequal over recent decades.

To consider the impact on the economy, we need to recognize that throughout the income distribution, taxes affect behavior — through changes in work and saving, changes in (legal) tax avoidance, and changes in (illegal) tax evasion. These responses affect the efficiency of the economy and affect the level of revenue collected with a given tax structure. Tax avoidance and tax evasion can be reduced by changes in tax rules and changes in tax enforcement, enhancing the ability to collect taxes more fairly and efficiently. And this approach permits more of tax collection to come from those with the greatest ability to pay.

We cannot run controlled experiments on the economy to estimate the additional revenues from tax changes, but we do have many studies of the effects from past tax changes.

While studies differ in their findings, overall, they shed considerable light on the revenue and efficiency implications of tax changes. The evidence supports the view that we can considerably increase the revenues currently being collected by taxes on the highest incomes, while having limited impacts on the functioning of the economy.

In light of this empirical evidence, I favor a federal tax rate on the highest incomes within the historical range from 50 percent (the 1982-86 level under President Reagan) to 70 percent (the level from 1965 to 1981, under Presidents Johnson, Nixon, Ford, and Carter).

Collecting these extra revenues can help finance more public investments to enhance our country's future and can help limit the need for higher taxes on those with lower incomes as we deal with our sizable public debt.

New York City Mayor Bill de Blasio visits with a pre-kindergarten student studying worms at P.S. 1 on April 3, 2014. Democrat de Blasio was elected after promising to reduce the gap between rich and poor. He advocated raising taxes on the wealthy to help pay for pre-K programs for all the city's children.

refuses to raise the minimum wage, I say this: If you truly believe you could work full-time and support a family on less than $15,000 a year, go try it. If not, vote to give millions of the hardest-working people in America a raise."[112]

Even strong supporters of Obama's proposal never expected a minimum wage raise to get past Washington's partisan gridlock. But the issue was newly energized by the "Fight for $15" movement, which sprung up in cities around the country after 200 fast food workers in New York City staged a one-day strike for $15 an hour in 2012. Since then, workers' frustration over stagnating wages has helped fuel similar protests in 150 cities. Seattle, Los Angeles, and San Francisco have since passed measures to raise their minimum wage to $15.[113]

In March, California became the first state to pass the $15 threshold; New York became the second state hours later with a budget agreement to raise the minimum wage in New York City to $15 by the end of 2018, followed by slower increases in other parts of the state.[114]

Since Obama first proposed a raise in 2013, 18 states and Washington, D.C., as well as about 40 cities and localities have raised their minimum wage by some amount, if not to $15, according to the White House.[115]

The issue got new visibility as the Democratic candidates sparred over who supported a higher minimum wage. Sanders charged, "When this campaign began, I said we have to end the starvation minimum wage of $7.25, raise it to $15. Secretary Clinton said let's raise it to $12."

Clinton's official position is that she prefers a $12 federal minimum wage, but views it as a floor, allowing cities and states to go further.[116]

Donald Trump opposed raising the minimum wage in the early stages of the campaign, saying, "Our wages are too high."[117]

Later in the campaign, he called for a higher minimum wage but said the issue should be left to the states rather than a federal increase.[118]

Faced with a Republican-controlled Congress blocking his legislative proposals aimed at improving workers' status, Obama has used his executive powers to promulgate rules that don't require Congressional approval.[119]

In the waning months of his presidency, the administration issued a regulation granting nearly 2 million home care workers minimum wage and overtime rights and issued guidelines suggesting many employers were misclassifying workers as contractors and thus depriving them of basic workplace protections.[120]

On May 17, 2016, the Obama administration announced a new rule broadening eligibility for overtime pay, which it said would cover 4.2 million new workers. Under the new rule, workers making up to $47,476 a year must be paid time-and-a-half for hours worked over 40 hours during a week. The previous cut-off for overtime pay, set in 2004, was $23,660.[121]

"The middle class is getting clobbered," said Vice President Joseph Biden, noting that more than 60 percent of salaried workers qualified for overtime pay in 1975, but only 7 percent do today.[122]

The pro-labor Economic Policy Institute had pushed for the new rule as a major strike against inequality and stalled wages. One reason Americans' paychecks are not keeping pace with overall productivity is that millions of Americans are working overtime and not getting paid for it, the institute contends.[123]

Supporters of the new rule predicted it would spur employers to give millions of workers a raise over the new threshold to avoid paying overtime and to hire additional workers after reducing the hours of other workers to 40 hours a week.[124]

"This is a big deal to be able to help that many working people without Congress having to pass a new law," said Ross Eisenbrey, vice president of the Economic Policy Institute. "It's really restoring rights that people had for decades and lost."[125]

The Institute estimated that over 12 million workers — even more workers than the administration estimated — would benefit, with millennials, workers ages 16 to 34, constituting more than a third of directly benefiting workers.[126]

However, the center-right research organization American Action Forum said the rule provided minimal worker benefits at major costs to business, saying businesses would face nearly $3 billion in compliance costs.[127]

Republican lawmakers, many of whom support industries critical of the new rule, vowed to block the rule during a mandated congressional review period.[128]

Executive Pay

Wall Street's 2008 financial meltdown and the accompanying recession focused new scrutiny on executive salaries. The pay for top executives has grown to 300 times that of the rank and file worker in recent years. In 1965, it was just 20 times as high.[129]

As part of the 2010 Dodd-Frank Wall Street reform law that grew out of the crisis, regulators at the Securities and Exchange Commission (SEC) issued a rule in August 2015 that will require public companies to disclose the ratio of their chief executive officer's earnings to their rank-and-file workers' pay starting in 2017. The SEC rule, originally proposed in September 2013, ran into opposition from businesses, which objected that it imposed a heavy logistical burden on companies with employees around the globe. The SEC said its final rule addresses such concerns by allowing companies to exclude some non-U.S. employees under certain circumstances and to determine the pay of their median employee only once every three years.[130]

The new rule is designed to inform shareholders when voting on executive pay compensation under the so-called "say on pay" rule previously issued by the SEC. Say-on-pay allows shareholders a nonbinding vote on executive pay packages: Since the passage of Dodd Frank, say-on-pay may have given some investors new fortitude to question executive pay: Citigroup shareholders rejected a $15 million pay package in 2012 for the bank's chief executive, Vikram Pandit.[131]

Limiting executive pay could allow more of a firm's profits to go to its workers or be plowed back into the company, advocates hope. Yet some, like Yale's Hacker, are skeptical that the current rules go far enough, calling the say-on-pay rule's nonbinding vote a "weak" weapon.

Most recently, a May 2016 report by business information firm Equilar suggested that average executive pay may have peaked, having fallen by 15 percent in 2015. But the gulf between chief executive and worker compensation remains huge; and, as *The New York Times* notes, "it is still too early to call this decline a trend."[132]

OUTLOOK
'Oligarchic Evolution'

While some advocates and politicians continue pushing for policies they say would help middle-class incomes grow again as they did pre-1980, others say such rapid growth is unlikely to reappear in developed economies as population growth slows.

French economist Piketty predicts a slow-growth future and that presents a potentially apocalyptic scenario if the richest continue claiming a growing share of income. "This risk of oligarchic evolution is something of concern — not just in Russia and China, but also in America and Europe. There is no natural economic mechanism that prevents such an extreme thing from happening," he says.

Conservatives tend to be more optimistic that the economy will pick up again and that workers will share in the benefits. James Sherk, a senior labor policy analyst at the Heritage Foundation, predicts worker pay will grow robustly as the economy picks up again. Policymakers, he says, "should look for ways to make less-skilled workers more productive, such as reducing the cost of higher education. Market forces will then force employers to increase compensation."¹³³

Supporting Sherk's optimistic view, in 2015 hourly wages, adjusted for inflation, grew across the board. But this growth was largely due to a sharp dip in inflation, which the Economic Policy Institute said is "unlikely to be a durably source of future real wage gains." And wage growth was fastest for those already at the top, the institute said, "illustrating that wage inequality continued its 35-year rise last year."¹³⁴

Until recently, higher population growth in the United States reduced the relative importance of inherited wealth compared with a more static Europe. But that could soon change. The aging of baby boomers should bring a sudden boom in inheritances and potentially a "flood of princelings," as an article in *The New York Times* put it, peaking in 2031. Economists such as Piketty are predicting that this trend will contribute even further to growing wealth inequality in the United States.¹³⁵

"We have more income inequality, and that means that down the road, we are bound to have more wealth inequality and more inequality of inherited wealth," predicted Piketty.¹³⁶

Since the 1980s, the value of inheritance has drifted upward only slightly, and wealth transfers in the United States as a share of net worth have fallen. But experts say that trend could reverse drastically as baby boomers hand on their wealth to the next generation.

A lot of multimillionaires are men of age 60 or 70, said David Friedman of Wealth-X, an international research firm that studies habits of the wealthy. "They're sensing their mortality now. And there's a growing wave of liquidity that's going to fuel luxury and fuel philanthropy in a way that the market's never seen."¹³⁷

But scholars who study social cohesion in America say they find this growing divide between rich and poor deeply troubling. "There's an increasing sense that . . . we're moving toward an America that none of us has ever lived in, a world of two Americas, a completely economically divided country," said Harvard Professor of Public Policy Robert Putnam, whose 2000 book, *Bowling Alone*, warned Americans were losing their sense of community. "That's not an America I want my grandchildren to grow up in. And I think there are lots of people in America who, if they stop and think about it, would say, 'No, that's not really us.'"¹³⁸

NOTES

1. Eoghan Macguire, "Swimming Pools and Golf Ranges in London's Insane Luxury Basements," CNN, January 24, 2014, http://tinyurl.com/kqx4m7d.
2. Michael Goldfarb, "London's Great Exodus," *The New York Times*, October 12, 2013, http://tinyurl.com/l33hjbq.
3. Oxfam Press Release, "62 people own same as half the world—Oxfam," January 18, 2016, http://www.oxfam.org.uk/media-centre/press-releases/2016/01/62-people-own-same-as-half-world-says-oxfam-inequality-report-davos-world-economic-forum.
4. "Worsening Wealth Gap Seen as Biggest Risk Facing the World in 2014," press release, World Economic Forum, 2014, http://tinyurl.com/n8mpa8c.
5. Eduardo Porter, "In New Tack, I.M.F. Aims at Income Inequality," *The New York Times*, April 8, 2014, http://tinyurl.com/mqdjpjx.
6. Bureau of Labor Statistics, Graphics for Economic News Releases, "Civilian Unemployment Rate," May 2016, http://www.bls.gov/charts/employment-situation/civilian-unemployment-rate.htm#.
7. Lawrence Mishel, "Causes of Wage Stagnation," Economic Policy Institute, January 6, 2015, http://www.epi.org/publication/causes-of-wage-stagnation/.
8. Alvin Powell, "The Costs of Inequality," *Harvard Gazette*, February 1, 2016, http://news.harvard.edu/gazette/story/2016/02/the-costs-of-inequality-when-a-fair-shake-isnt/.
9. Economic Policy Institute, "The Productivity Pay Gap," Updated September 2015, http://www.epi.org/productivity-pay-gap/.
10. Bernie Sanders Campaign: "Income and Wealth Inequality," https://berniesanders.com/issues/income-and-wealth-inequality/.
11. Max Erhenfreund, "How Hillary Clinton's positions have changed as she's run against Bernie Sanders,"

Washington Post, April 29, 2016, https://www.washingtonpost.com/news/wonk/wp/2016/04/29/how-hillary-clintons-positions-have-changed-while-running-against-bernie-sanders/.

12. George Kynaston, "How inequality became the defining issue of the 2016 presidential campaign," *New Statesman*, October 15, 2015, http://www.newstatesman.com/culture/observations/2015/10/how-inequality-became-defining-issue-2016-us-presidential-campaign.

13. Ashley Parker and Jonathan Martin, "Donald Trump Borrows from Bernie Sanders's Playbook to Woo Democrats," *The New York Times*, May 17, 2016, http://www.nytimes.com/2016/05/18/us/politics/donald-trump-bernie-sanders-campaign.html?version=meter+at+0&contentId=&mediaId=&referrer=http%3A%2F%2Fwww.nytimes.com%2F%2F%3Foref%3Dlogin&priority=true&action=click&contentCollection=Politics&module=RelatedCoverage&region=EndOfArticle&pgtype=article.

14. Christina Pazzanese, "The Costs of Inequality: Increasingly, it's the rich and the rest," *Harvard Gazette*, February 8, 2016, http://news.harvard.edu/gazette/story/2016/02/the-costs-of-inequality-increasingly-its-the-rich-and-the-rest/.

15. Paul Krugman, "Liberty, Equality, Efficiency," *The New York Times*, March 9, 2014, http://tinyurl.com/q8y2grc.

16. Emmanuel Saez, "Striking it Richer: The Evolution of Top Incomes in the United States," University of California, Berkeley, September 3, 2013, p. 3, http://tinyurl.com/o7zo3mm.

17. Ibid., p. 3.

18. Thomas Piketty, *Capital in the Twenty-First Century* (Cambridge, MA: Belknap Press, 2014), p. 438.

19. Thomas Piketty, *Capital in the Twenty-First Century* (2014), http://dowbor.org/blog/wp-content/uploads/2014/06/14Thomas-Piketty.pdf.

20. Tim Kane, "Piketty's Crumbs," Commentary, May 2016, pp. 31-38, https://www.commentarymagazine.com/articles/pikettys-crumbs/.

21. "Remarks by the President on Economic Mobility," White House, December 4, 2013, http://tinyurl.com/mk4qe7n.

22. Parker and Martin, op. cit.

23. Donald Trump Campaign Website, "Reforming The U.S.-China Trade Relationship To Make America Great Again," https://www.donaldjtrump.com/positions/us-china-trade-reform.

24. "Donald Trump on Free Trade," On the Issues, http://www.ontheissues.org/Celeb/Donald_Trump_Free_Trade.htm.

25. Mickey Kaus, "The Other Kind of Inequality," *The Wall Street Journal*, January 26, 2014, http://tinyurl.com/ms2op6h.

26. Scott Winship, "Inequality Testimony before the Joint Economic Committee," E21: Economic Policies for the 21st Century, Manhattan Institute, January 15, 2014, http://tinyurl.com/lwy9kjm.

27. Ibid.

28. Phil Wahba, "Sears Closing Flagship Chicago Store As It Eyes More Focus On Online Retail" The Huffington Post, January 21, 2014, updated March 24, 2014, http://www.huffingtonpost.com/2014/01/22/sears-closing-flagship-store_n_4640634.

29. For revenue trends of Capital Grille and Olive Garden, see Market Realist, "What You Need to Know about Darden Restaurants," March 17, 2015, http://marketrealist.com/2015/03/business-overview-darden-restaurants/.

30. Nelson D. Schwartz, "The Middle Class Is Steadily Eroding. Just Ask the Business World.," *The New York Times,* February 2, 2014, http://tinyurl.com/l7fwj86.

31. *The State of Working America, 12th Edition*, Economic Policy Institute, March 17, 2014, http://tinyurl.com/4vb2ct.

32. Nelson D. Schwartz, "How Eroding the Middle Hits Economic Growth," Economix blog, *The New York Times*, February 5, 2014, http://tinyurl.com/mlo6hnb.

33. Winship, op. cit.

34. Economic Policy Institute, "The Productivity–Pay Gap," updated September 2015, http://www.epi.org/productivity-pay-gap/.

35. Elise Gould, "Wage Inequality Continued its 35-year Rise in 2015," Economic Policy Institute, March 10, 2016, http://www.epi.org/publication/wage-inequality-continued-its-35-year-rise-in-2015/#epi-toc-2

36. See for example, Andrew G. Berg and Jonathan D. Ostry, "Inequality and Unsustainable Growth: Two Sides of the Same Coin?" International Monetary Fund, April 8, 2011, http://tinyurl.com/445a8t6.

37. Piketty, op. cit., p. 13.

38. Jonathan D. Ostry, Andrew Berg, and Charalambos G. Tsangarides, "Redistribution, Inequality and Growth," February 2014, International Monetary Fund, http://tinyurl.com/q5qz6l6.

39. Berg and Ostry, op. cit. Also see Winship, op. cit. http://tinyurl.com/q5qz6l6.

40. Winship, op. cit.

41. College completion rates increased only 4 percentage points from the generation of low-income children born in the early 1960s to those born in the 1980s. For high-income children the increase was 18 percentage points, according to Martha Bailey and Susan Dynarski writing in "Gains and Gaps: Changing Inequality in U.S. College Entry and Completion" (NBER Working Paper No. 17633), National Bureau of Economic Research, March 10, 2014, http://tinyurl.com/kp49o9y.

42. Alvin Powell, "The Costs of Inequality: When a fair shake isn't*,*" *Harvard Gazette*, February 1, 2016, http://news.harvard.edu/gazette/story/2016/02/the-costs-of-inequality-when-a-fair-shake-isnt/

43. Krugman, op. cit.

44. Piketty, op. cit., pp. 438-440.

45. "President Barack Obama's State of the Union Address," White House, January 28, 2014, http://tinyurl.com/kemgt7x.

46. Sean McElwee, "Republicans Suddenly Can't Stop Talking about 'Mobility,' " The New Republic, February 19, 2014, http://tinyurl.com/lfwxxg8.

47. "Class in America: Mobility Measured," The Economist, February 1, 2014, http://tinyurl.com/n9t3ar7.

48. Raj Chetty, Nathaniel Hendren, Patrick Kline, Emmanuel Saez, and Nicholas Turner, "Is the United States Still a Land of Opportunity?" National Bureau of Economic Research, January 2014, http://tinyurl.com/lphlkz2.

49. "Class in America," op. cit.

50. Gregory Clark, The Son Also Rises: Surnames and the History of Social Mobility (2014).

51. Cited in Ron Haskins, "Mobility Is a Problem: Now What?" Dec. 23, 2011, http://tinyurl.com/mnuuezj. The data was published in a book written by Haskins and Isabel Sawhill, Creating an Opportunity Society (2009).

52. Annie Lowrey, "What Comes after Rich Baby Boomers?" *The New York Times Magazine*, March 11, 2014, http://tinyurl.com/l2xa7lv.

53. Inheritance as a share of national income in France was 20 percent from 1840 to 1914, declined to a low of 5 percent in the 1950s and rose to 15 percent in 2010. See Piketty, op. cit., pp. 380-381.

54. Piketty, op. cit., p. 438.

55. Pew Charitable Trusts, "Economic Mobility and the American Dream," May 2011, http://tinyurl.com/l5l4rc2.

56. "Pursuing the American Dream: Economic Mobility Across Generations," Pew Charitable Trusts, July 9, 2012, http://tinyurl.com/872oy5z.

57. Bernie Sanders Campaign: "Income and Wealth Inequality," https://berniesanders.com/issues/income-and-wealth-inequality/

58. Tax Policy Center, "Analysis of Donald Trump's Tax Plan," Dec. 22, 2015, http://www.taxpolicycenter.org/publications/analysis-donald-trumps-tax-plan

59. Louise Dewast, ABC News, "300 Economists sign open letter against offshore tax havens after 'Panama Papers,'" May 9, 2016, http://abcnews.go.com/International/300-economists-sign-open-letter-offshore-tax-havens/story?id=38980820.

60. Piketty, op. cit., p. 525.

61. The Oscar-nominated film *Wolf of Wall Street* is based on the story of Jordan Belfort, who served 22 months in prison for security fraud between 2004 and 2006. See, "Real-life Wolf of Wall Street says his life of debauchery 'even worse' than in film," *The Guardian*, February 28, 2014, http://tinyurl.com/o6oo3vs.

62. Christopher DeMuth, "Capital for the Masses," *The Wall Street Journal*, April 7, 2014, http://tinyurl.com/keenuwn.

63. Jacob S. Hacker and Nate Loewenthal, "Prosperity Economics," (2012), p. 48.

64. Sendhil Mullainathan, "A Top-Heavy Focus on Income Inequality," *The New York Times*, March 8, 2014, http://tinyurl.com/qdqkddd.

65. "The Rich are Taxed Enough," Intelligence Squared U.S., October 24, 2012, p. 16, http://tinyurl.com/lb9q58c.

66. Ibid.

67. "The Distribution of Household Income and Federal Taxes, 2010," Congressional Budget Office, December 2013, p. 7, http://tinyurl.com/pxzutsz.

68. Households in the highest quintile paid 93 percent of federal income taxes in 2010, ibid., p. 13.

69. Jacob C. Hacker and Paul Pierson, *Winner-Take-All Politics* (New York: Simon & Schuster, 2010), p. 75.

70. Ibid.

71. Ibid., p. 76.

72. Chrystia Freeland, *Plutocrats: The Rise of the New Global Rich and the Fall of Everyone Else* (New York: Penguin, 2012), p. 6.

73. Piketty, op. cit., p. 506.

74. "From the Archives: President Teddy Roosevelt's New Nationalism Speech," https://www.whitehouse.gov/blog/2011/12/06/archives-president-teddy-roosevelts-new-nationalism-speech.

75. Jennifer Rosenberg, "History of Income Tax in the U.S.," about.com, updated November 20, 2015, http://tinyurl.com/n2wep8k.

76. Tim Rutten, "And the Rich Get Richer," *Los Angeles Times*, December 18, 2010, http://tinyurl.com/37ku7aq.

77. Piketty, op. cit., p. 507.

78. Hacker, op. cit., p. 87.

79. Ibid., p. 88.

80. History of Federal Individual Income Bottom and Top Bracket Rates, National Taxpayers Union, undated, http://www.ntu.org/foundation/page/how-have-the-top-and-bottom-income-tax-brackets-changed-over-timeCalculation of current dollars, http://www.dollartimes.com/inflation/inflation.php?amount=200000&year=1944.

81. Eduardo Porter, "Free Market is no Remedy for Disparity," *International New York Times*, March 13, 2014, p. 15.

82. American Economic Review, cited in James K. Galbraith, *Inequality and Instability* (New York: Oxford University Press, 2012), p. 125.

83. Ana Swanson, "The incredible decline of American unions, in one animated map," *Washington Post*, February 24, 2015, https://www.washingtonpost.com/news/wonk/wp/2015/02/24/the-incredible-decline-of-american-unions-in-one-animated-map/.

84. Hacker, op. cit., pp. 56-57.

85. Piketty, op. cit., pp. 507-509.

86. Hacker, op. cit., pp. 99-100 and pp. 133-134. The capital gains tax, which taxes profits such as those from the sale of stock or business assets, was cut from 48 percent to 28 percent.

87. Ibid., p. 134.

88. William Greider, "The Education of David Stockman," *The Atlantic*, December 1981, http://tinyurl.com/d43yal3.

89. "General Explanation of the Economic Recovery Tax Act of 1981," Joint Committee on Taxation, December 29, 1981, p. 229, http://tinyurl.com/lf9w9pd.

90. Hacker, op. cit., p. 111. The research cited is by political scientist Larry Bartels.

91. Hacker, op. cit., p. 217.

92. Zachary A. Goldfarb, "The legacy of the bush tax cuts, in four charts," *The Washington Post*, January 2, 2013, http://tinyurl.com/b9l5vca.

93. "Federal Income Tax Table," http://tinyurl.com/cnrhnns. Also see, "New 39.6 Percent Tax Bracket for wealthiest people," Politico, January 22, 2014, http://tinyurl.com/kb3nwob.

94. Alec MacGillis, "The Billionaires' Loophole," *New Yorker*, March 14, 2016, http://www.newyorker.com/magazine/2016/03/14/david-rubenstein-and-the-carried-interest-dilemma.

95. Thomas Kaplan and Javier C. Hernandez, "State Budget Deal Reached, $300 Million for New York City Pre-K," *The New York Times*, March 29, 2014, http://tinyurl.com/mofuy4s.

96. "Remarks by the President Announcing the FY 2015 Budget," White House, March 4, 2014, http://tinyurl.com/kapxcj6.

97. Dan Henninger, "The Income-Inequality Love Train," *The Wall Street Journal*, April 2, 2014, http://tinyurl.com/l4xgwmt.

98. Editorial, "The What-Might-Have-Been Budget," *The New York Times*, March 4, 2014, http://tinyurl.com/ktgyugc.

99. Stephen Moore, "Why Obama's Budget Should Be Dead on Arrival," Heritage Foundation, March 4, 2014, http://tinyurl.com/mfa2grw.

100. "The Budget for Fiscal Year 2015," White House, http://tinyurl.com/oo6gsdd.

101. Katrina Trinko, "Live Analysis: Heritage Experts Weigh In On Obama's 2015 Budget," Heritage Foundation, March 4, 2014, http://tinyurl.com/n3poqup.

102. Frank Sammartino, James R. Nunns, Leonard E. Burman, Jeffrey Rohaly, and Joseph Rosenberg, Tax Policy Center, "An Analysis of Senator Bernie Sanders's Tax Proposals," March 4, 2016, http://www.taxpolicycenter.org/publications/analysis-senator-bernie-sanderss-tax-proposals.

103. Sammartino et al., Tax Policy Center, "An Analysis of Hilary Clinton's Tax Proposals" March 3, 2016, http://www.taxpolicycenter.org/publications/analysis-hillary-clintons-tax-proposals.

104. Sammartino et al., Tax Policy Center, "Analysis of Donald Trump's Tax Plan," December 22, 2015, http://www.taxpolicycenter.org/publications/analysis-donald-trumps-tax-plan.

105. James Pethokoukis, "Taking Trump Seriously on Taxes," Commentary, April 15, 2016, https://www.commentarymagazine.com/articles/taking-trump-seriously-taxes/.

106. Ibid.

107. Sahil Kapur, "Tax Shift Marks Trump's Latest Test of Conservative Orthodoxy," Bloomberg Politics, May 9, 2016, http://www.bloomberg.com/politics/articles/2016-05-09/tax-shift-marks-trump-s-latest-rejection-of-conservative-orthodoxy.

108. Tami Luhby, "Here are the massive tax breaks Trump is proposing for the rich," CNN Monday, May 9, 2016, http://money.cnn.com/2016/05/09/news/economy/trump-tax-rich/.

109. Bernie Sanders Campaign, "It's Time to Make College Tuition Free and Debt Free," https://berniesanders.com/issues/its-time-to-make-college-tuition-free-and-debt-free/.

110. Tyler Bishop, "Hillary Clinton's Smorgasbord Approach to Student Loans," The Atlantic, August 12, 2015, http://www.theatlantic.com/politics/archive/2015/08/hillary-clinton-student-loans/401171/.

111. "Presidential Candidates on Education: Election Guide," Education Week, updated May 12, 2016, http://www.edweek.org/ew/section/multimedia/election-guide-5-education-takeaways-from-candidates.html.

112. White House, "Raise the Wage," https://www.whitehouse.gov/raise-the-wage.
113. Steven Greenhouse, "How the $15 Minimum Wage Went from Laughable to Viable," *The New York Times*, April 1, 2016, http://www.nytimes.com/2016/04/03/sunday-review/how-the15-minimum-wage-went-from-laughable-to-viable.html?_r=0.
114. Jesse McKinley and Vivian Yee, "New York Budget Deal with Higher Minimum Wage is Reached," *The New York Times*, March 31, 2015, http://www.nytimes.com/2016/04/01/nyregion/new-york-budget-deal-with-higher-minimum-wage-is-reached.html?hp=&action=click&pgtype=article&clickSource=story-heading&module=meterLinks&region=top-news&WT.nav=top-news&_r=0&version=meter+at+0&contentId=&mediaId=&referrer=https%3A%2F%2Fwww.google.co.uk&priority=true&contentCollection=meter-links-click.
115. Ibid.
116. Lauren Carroll, "Does Hillary Clinton want a $15 or $12 minimum wage?" Politifact, April 15, 2016, http://www.politifact.com/truth-o-meter/statements/2016/apr/15/bernie-s/does-hillary-clinton-want-15-or-12-minimum-wage/.
117. Maggie Haberman, "First Draft: Donald Trump Insists that Wages are 'Too High,'" *The New York Times*, November 11, 2015. http://www.nytimes.com/politics/first-draft/2015/11/11/donald-trump-insists-that-wages-are-too-high/.
118. Parker and Martin, op. cit.
119. Noam Schieber, "As His Term Wanes, Obama Champions Workers' Rights," *The New York Times*, August 31, 2015, http://www.nytimes.com/2015/09/01/business/economy/as-his-term-wanes-obama-restores-workers-rights.html?version=meter+at+0&contentId=&mediaId=&referrer=http%3A%2F%2Fwww.nytimes.com%2F%3Foref%3Dlogin&priority=true&action=click&contentCollection=Business%20Day&module=RelatedCoverage&region=EndOfArticle&pgtype=article.
120. Ibid.
121. Noam Scheiber, "White House Increases Overtime Eligibility by Millions," *The New York Times*, May 17, 2015, http://www.nytimes.com/2016/05/18/business/white-house-increases-overtime-eligibility-by-millions.html?hp&action=click&pgtype=Homepage&clickSource=story-heading&module=first-column-region&region=top-news&WT.nav=top-news&_r=0.
122. Ibid.
123. Economic Policy Institute, "Why it's time to update overtime pay rules," August 4, 2015, http://www.epi.org/publication/time-update-overtime-pay-rules-answers-frequently/.
124. Ross Eisenbrey, "Universities, inequality and the overtime rule," Economic Policy Institute, April 20, 2016, http://www.epi.org/blog/universities-overtime-rule/.
125. Scheiber, op. cit.
126. Ross Eisenbrey, "The new overtime rule will directly benefit 12.5 million working people," Economic Policy Institute, May 17, 2016, http://www.epi.org/publication/who-benefits-from-new-overtime-threshold/.
127. Ben Gitis and Dan Goldbeck, "Final Overtime Rule: Minimal Benefits and Major Costs," May 19, 2016, http://www.americanactionforum.org/research/final-overtime-rule-minimal-benefits-major-costs/.
128. Scheiber, op. cit.
129. Patrick Jenkins, "Why it is time to curb the madness of executive pay," *Financial Times*, May 9, 2016, http://www.ft.com/cms/s/0/b3cee000-15d1-11e6-9d98-00386a18e39d.html#axzz48Fym1qrT.
130. U.S. Securities and Exchange Commission, Press Release, "SEC Adopts Rule for Pay Ratio Disclosure," August 5, 2015, http://www.sec.gov/news/pressrelease/2015-160.html.

131. Editorial, "The Boss and Everyone Else," *The New York Times*, May 2, 2012, http://tinyurl.com/74dxau6.

132. David Gelles, "Top C.E.O. Pay Fell—Yes, Fell—in 2015," *The New York Times*, May 27, 2016, http://www.nytimes.com/2016/05/29/business/top-ceo-pay-fell-yes-fell-in-2015.html.

133. James Sherk, "Productivity and Compensation: Growing Together," Heritage Foundation, July 17, 2013, http://tinyurl.com/mv2rh9g.

134. Elise Gould, "Wage inequality continued its 35-year rise in 2015," Economic Policy Institute, March 10, 2016, http://www.epi.org/publication/wage-inequality-continued-its-35-year-rise-in-2015/.

135. Lowrey, op. cit.

136. Ibid.

137. Ibid.

138. Christina Pazzanese, "The Costs of Inequality: Increasingly, it's the rich and the rest," *Harvard Gazette*, February 8, 2016, http://news.harvard.edu/gazette/story/2016/02/the-costs-of-inequality-increasingly-its-the-rich-and-the-rest/.

BIBLIOGRAPHY

Books

Clark, Gregory, *The Son Also Rises: Surnames and the History of Social Mobility*, Princeton University Press, 2014.
A University of California-Davis economist finds movement up the social ladder has changed little over eight centuries, even in highly equal countries such as Sweden.

Freeland, Chrystia, *Plutocrats: The Rise of the New Global Rich and the Fall of Everyone Else*, Penguin Books, 2012.
While a Reuters economics reporter, Freeland, now a member of the Canadian Parliament, wrote this book describing the world of today's global super-rich and their historic rise.

Galbraith, James K., *Inequality and Instability: A Study of the World Economy Just Before the Great Crisis*, Oxford University Press, 2012.
A University of Texas-Austin economist argues that the rise of inequality mirrors the rise of finance and free-market policies.

Hacker, Jacob S., and Paul Pierson, *Winner-Take-All Politics: How Washington Made the Rich Richer — and Turned its Back on the Middle Class*, Simon & Schuster, 2010.
A Yale political scientist (Hacker) and a University of California-Berkeley political scientist argue that the American political system has been hijacked by the very rich, leading to government policies favoring the wealthy.

Piketty, Thomas, *Capital in the Twenty-First Century*, Belknap Press, 2014.
In this much-discussed study of 20 countries over 300 years, a professor at the Paris School of Economics argues that wealth is becoming too concentrated at the top and advocates a global wealth tax.

Articles

DeMuth, Christopher, "Capital for the Masses," *The Wall Street Journal*, April 7, 2014, http://tinyurl.com/keenuwn.
A conservative critique of Thomas Piketty's *Capital in the Twenty-First Century* says the book bolsters arguments for privatizing retirement systems such as Social Security.

Krugman, Paul, "Liberty, Equality, Efficiency," *The New York Times*, March 9, 2014, http://tinyurl.com/q8y2grc.
A liberal economist asks whether redistribution of economic wealth hurts growth — and answers in the negative.

Lowrey, Annie, "What Comes after Rich Baby Boomers? Kids With a Big Inheritance," *The New York Times Magazine*, March 11, 2014, http://tinyurl.com/l2xa7lv.

An economics reporter forecasts a new wave of well-to-do "princelings" will inherit wealth from the aging baby boomers.

Mullainathan, Sendhil, "A Top-Heavy Focus on Income Inequality," *The New York Times*, March 8, 2014, http://tinyurl.com/qdqkddd.
A Harvard economist argues that reducing income for the wealthy through higher taxes does not necessarily mean more for everyone else.

Saez, Emmanuel, "Striking it Richer: The Evolution of Top Incomes in the United States," September 3, 2013, p. 3, http://tinyurl.com/o7zo3mm.
This unpublished paper by a University of California-Berkeley economist has been widely cited for its chart showing that the upper 10 percent now command an even greater share of national income than in the 1920s.

Pazzanese, Christina, "The Costs of Inequality: Increasingly, it's the rich and the rest," *Harvard Gazette*, February 8, 2016, http://news.harvard.edu/gazette/story/2016/02/the-costs-of-inequality-increasingly-its-the-rich-and-the-rest/.
Several Harvard professors express concern that rising income inequality is leading to less equal educational opportunities for those without money and greater political influence for those who have it.

Reports and Studies

"Moving on Up: Why Do Some Americans Leave the Bottom of the Economic Ladder, but Not Others?" Pew Charitable Trusts, November 2013, http://www.pewtrusts.org/en/research-and analysis/reports/0001/01/01/moving-on-up.
The research group examines why some Americans move up the social ladder and others do not, finding that college education greatly increases one's chances.

"Offshore Tax Evasion: The Effort to Collect Unpaid Taxes on Billions in Hidden Offshore Accounts," U.S. Senate Permanent Subcommittee on Investigations, Feb. 26, 2014, http://tinyurl.com/lnn782o.
The Senate subcommittee, which found thousands of U.S. taxpayers hiding billions of dollars in offshore tax accounts, criticized the Swiss government and Credit Suisse for secrecy.

"The Distribution of Household Income and Federal Taxes, 2013," Congressional Budget Office, June 2016, https://www.cbo.gov/publication/51361. The nonpartisan agency looks at the incomes of a range groups in the United States both before and after taxes.

The State of Working America, 12th Edition, Economic Policy Institute, March 17, 2014, http://tinyurl.com/4vb2ct.
A book-length report analyzes data on income, mobility, wages, jobs, wealth and poverty.

"An Economy for the 1%: How privilege and power in the economy drive extreme inequality and how this can be stopped," Oxfam, Jan. 18, 2016, http://policy-practice.oxfam.org.uk/publications/an-economy-for-the-1-how-privilege-and-power-in-the-economy-drive-extreme-inequ-592643.
An anti-poverty charity finds the world's 62 richest billionaires have combined fortunes equal to those of the world's poorest half.

For More Information

Brookings Institution, 1775 Massachusetts Ave., N.W., Washington, D.C. 20036; 202-797-6000; http://www.brookings.edu. Think tank that covers a wide range of topics, with scholars who are generally moderate to liberal.

Economic Mobility Project, Pew Charitable Trusts, 901 E St., N.W., Washington, D.C. 20004; 202-552-2000; http://www.pewtrusts.org/en/archived-projects/economic-mobility-project. Research project investigating U.S. economic mobility.

Economic Policy Institute, 1225 Eye St. NW, Suite 600, Washington, D.C. 20005; 202-775-8810; http://www.epi.org. Think tank that studies low- and middle-income workers.

Heritage Foundation, 214 Massachusetts Ave., N.E., Washington, D.C. 20002; 202-546-4400; http://www.heritage.org. Think tank that promotes conservative policies based on free enterprise.

Oxfam, 226 Causeway St., Boston, MA 02114; 800-776-9326; https://www.oxfamamerica.org. Antipoverty charity that recently released a report on the global rich.

Tax Policy Center, Urban Institute, 2100 M St., N.W., Washington, D.C. 20037; 202-833-7200; http://www.taxpolicycenter.org. Joint project with the Brookings Institution that provides nonpartisan analyses of tax legislation.

Urban Institute, 2100 M St. N.W., Washington, D.C. 20037, 202-833-7200; http://www.urban.org. Think tank that focuses on U.S. social and economic issues.

Washington Center for Equitable Growth, 1500 K Street, NW, 8th Floor,, Washington, D.C. 20005; 202-682-1611; http://equitablegrowth.org. Project housed at the liberal Center for American Progress that investigates the effect of inequality on economic growth.

11

Housing Discrimination

Kenneth Jost

Demonstrators march in Baltimore in May, a day after authorities said criminal charges would be filed against six police officers in connection with the death of 25-year-old Freddie Gray. Explosive clashes between inner-city residents and police in Baltimore, Ferguson, Mo., and other cities have been linked to the isolation of African-Americans in racially segregated, high-poverty neighborhoods.

From *CQ Researcher*, November 16, 2015.

Kimberly grew up in public housing in the 1990s in one of Baltimore's predominantly African-American neighborhoods with her single, drug-abusing mother. Two decades later, living in a modest home in a racially mixed Baltimore suburb, she looks back on those years unhappily.

"My mom got me into the public housing system," Kimberly (whose last name was not made public) told researchers studying the court-ordered Baltimore Housing Mobility Program, which was aimed at breaking up racially based housing patterns in one of the nation's most segregated cities. "I don't want that for my children."[1]

Kimberly had a troubled adolescence in the kind of dysfunctional social system characteristic of many of the barracks-style public housing projects. She was expelled from school, got pregnant at 15 and moved from one housing project to another.

Kimberly left the inner city for a suburban single-family home thanks to a lawsuit under the federal Fair Housing Act (FHA), the landmark 1968 law prohibiting discrimination in the sale or rental of housing. The law has helped reduce, but by no means eliminate, racial segregation in U.S. cities and suburbs. Enforcement of the law by the U.S. Department of Housing and Urban Development (HUD) and local public housing authorities has lagged. Experts blamed inadequate funding and political opposition at the local level to demographic changes viewed as threatening the character of established, predominantly white neighborhoods.

Public housing tenants in Baltimore had joined in a federal lawsuit in 1995 charging HUD, the Baltimore housing authority and other city officials with perpetuating racial segregation by

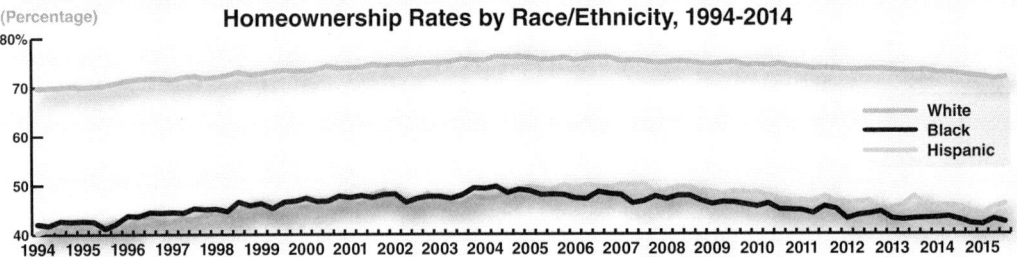

Homeownership Highest for Whites

Seventy-two percent of non-Hispanic white Americans own homes, compared with 46 percent of Hispanics and 43 percent of African-Americans. The gap between white and Hispanic homeownership rates narrowed over the past two decades, while the gap between whites and blacks widened. Ownership rates have fallen more for both minority groups than for whites since the beginning of the 2007-09 recession.

Source: Graphic from "Where You Live Matters: 2015 Fair Housing Trends Report," National Fair Housing Alliance, April 30, 2015, p. 9, http://tinyurl.com/neuq462; data downloaded from "Housing Vacancies and Homeownership" Historical Tables, Table 16, U.S. Census Bureau, http://tinyurl.com/kxxz82g

concentrating public housing in predominantly African-American neighborhoods. The suit, *Thompson v. HUD*, resulted in 2003 in the creation of a program to provide federal housing vouchers to low-income families to move from the crime-ridden projects to low-poverty, racially mixed neighborhoods.[2]

Kimberly hesitated when she first heard about the Section 8 voucher program but eventually decided to participate, as did 2,400 others in Baltimore so far. Today, Kimberly lives with her two daughters, a half-sister and her grandfather and says she feels more in control of her life. "It's only in leaving that I started growing and wanting to do different things, learn different things and be something different," she told the researchers.

The Baltimore anti-discrimination suit was one of more than a dozen filed in the 1990s, aimed at breaking up persistent patterns of black-white residential segregation in the United States. Housing advocates and experts across the ideological spectrum agree that the federal government bears much of the blame for the growth of housing segregation in the first half of the 20th century by steering tax-supported housing to minority neighborhoods. And most also fault the government for doing too little to promote desegregation after passage of the 1968 law.

"There is a broad consensus that intentional discrimination is unlawful and immoral, but there's also a growing understanding that government policy and institutional structures have fostered segregation in this country," says Philip Tegeler, executive director of the Poverty & Race Research Action Council in Washington, a civil rights think tank. "But I don't think there's political will really to confront that legacy of segregation and do what needs to be done to reverse it."

The Fair Housing Act prohibits discrimination in the sale, rental or financing of housing on the basis of race, national origin or other characteristics. One provision, largely disregarded until now, according to critics, requires HUD to administer its programs in a manner that "affirmatively" furthers the law's goals.[3]

In a report issued in 2008 on the 40th anniversary of the law, a bipartisan commission convened by four major civil rights groups described HUD's enforcement efforts as "failing." The seven-member commission was co-chaired by two former HUD secretaries: Republican Jack Kemp and Democrat Henry Cisneros.[4]

In the Baltimore case, U.S. District Judge Marvin Garbis found HUD guilty of consigning the poor to the inner city instead of dispersing public housing throughout the region. "It is high time that HUD live up to its statutory mandate to consider the effect of its policies on the racial and socio-economic composition of the surrounding area," Garbis wrote in a stinging decision.[5]

Fair-housing advocates blame the private sector as well for the lagging progress in combating residential segregation. "We still have barriers in the real estate market," says Lisa Rice, executive vice president of the National Fair Housing Alliance (NFHA), a consortium of fair-housing groups. "We still have barriers in the lending market. We have barriers in the rental market."

Rice says housing authorities have mixed records in promoting racial integration. "Some housing authorities have not done what they should, and some are doing exactly what they should," she says." The "mosaic of housing authorities" in most cities also prevents breaking up urban segregation and diversification in the suburbs, according to Jacob Vigdor, a professor of public policy and governance at the University of Washington in Seattle.

In the pre-civil rights era, the real estate industry openly blocked African-Americans from moving into predominantly white neighborhoods either as homeowners or renters. The federal government created a program in 1934 to promote homeownership by insuring home mortgages, thus lowering interest rates on the loans. But the program effectively blocked use of the loans in African-American neighborhoods by "redlining" those areas — designating them on maps in red as credit-unworthy. White Americans used those loans after World War II to create suburbs, which then adopted restrictive zoning laws that still effectively operate to make many homes unaffordable for lower-income black families.

On the positive side, residential segregation has been declining since fair housing became law nationwide. The number of metropolitan areas categorized by one of the leading experts as either highly or, in his terminology, "hypersegregated" has declined from 40 in 1970 to 21 in 2010. Still, Douglas Massey, a professor of sociology at

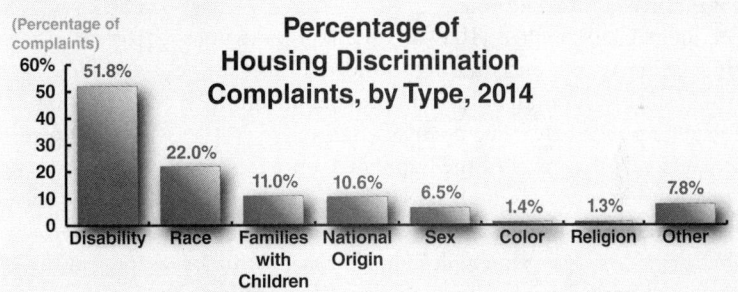

Disability Complaints Most Common

Allegations of discrimination against people with disabilities represented more than half of complaints filed in 2014 with local, state and federal housing agencies, private fair-housing groups or the U.S. Department of Justice. Complaints alleging racial discrimination accounted for about 20 percent of the total.

Percentage of Housing Discrimination Complaints, by Type, 2014

(Percentage of complaints)
- Disability: 51.8%
- Race: 22.0%
- Families with Children: 11.0%
- National Origin: 10.6%
- Sex: 6.5%
- Color: 1.4%
- Religion: 1.3%
- Other: 7.8%

* Percentages add to more than 100 because some complaints involve multiple categories.

Source: "Where You Live Matters: 2015 Fair Housing Trends Report," National Fair Housing Alliance, April 30, 2015, p. 21, http://tinyurl.com/neuq462

Princeton University, says one-third of all African-American city dwellers were living in highly or hypersegregated neighborhoods as of 2010.[6]

Despite the decline, "Many of our metro areas remain largely segregated," says Bryan Greene, a 25-year HUD veteran now serving as deputy assistant secretary for fair housing and equal opportunity.

Recent HUD enforcement actions indicate that tenants and homebuyers still encounter discrimination. HUD won settlements with housing authorities in Medina, Ohio, over alleged discrimination in administering the Section 8 voucher program and in Hazelton, Pa., over restrictive terms on would-be Hispanic tenants. The Wisconsin-based Associated Bank agreed in May to provide minority customers $200 million in mortgage loans to settle charges of redlining.[7]

Massey and others link the recent explosive clashes with police in Baltimore and Ferguson, Mo., to the isolation of African-Americans in cities. The riots and protests "have occurred in racially segregated, high-poverty neighborhoods," writes Paul Jargowsky, a professor of public policy at Rutgers University in Camden, N.J.[8]

The decline in segregation has coincided with a shift in public housing policies away from construction of large, publicly owned "projects." Instead, the government began providing the Section 8 subsidies for private rentals for the poor and tax credits to encourage developers to build affordable housing. The low-income housing tax credits (LIHTCs, pronounced lie-techs) required developers to build a certain percentage of units for low-income tenants, with rents no more than 30 percent of the area's median income.

Judge Garbis faulted HUD and the Baltimore housing authority for concentrating subsidized units in the inner city, even as the old-style projects in minority neighborhoods were being demolished.

In a case that reached the Supreme Court this year, fair-housing advocates in Dallas similarly challenged the Texas state housing agency for awarding tax credits primarily to developers who built in predominantly minority neighborhoods. The issue in *Texas Department of Housing and Community Affairs v. Inclusive Communities Project, Inc.* was whether to apply the Fair Housing Act not only to intentional discrimination but also to government policies that adversely affect minorities — so-called disparate impact.[9]

The justices appeared to have a strong interest in re-examining lower court decisions that had adopted the broader disparate-impact view of discrimination under the housing law. Twice the court had accepted cases posing the issue, in 2011 and 2012, but the cases settled instead. Fair-housing advocates were pleased in June when the court issued a 5–4 decision reaffirming the broader view of the law.

"Recognition of disparate-impact claims is consistent with the FHA's central purpose," Justice Anthony M. Kennedy wrote in the June 25 decision joined by the court's four liberal members. "It permits plaintiffs to counteract unconscious prejudices and disguised animus that escape easy classification as disparate treatment [intentional discrimination]."[10]

Just two weeks later, on July 8, HUD issued a long-awaited rule requiring state and local housing agencies to "affirmatively further" the fair-housing law's goals of banning housing discrimination and promoting housing desegregation. HUD Secretary Julián Castro called the rule "the most serious effort" ever to require communities to reduce housing segregation.[11]

As HUD implements the new regulation, the National Association of Housing and Redevelopment Officials (NAHRO), which opposed the rule, continues to criticize it. The Republican-controlled House of Representatives voted on June 9 to block implementation of the rule on grounds that it would threaten local control of housing issues.

Fair-housing advocates applaud the rule but continue to fault HUD for what they see as its lagging enforcement of the law. Federal programs are "perpetuating this long pattern of segregation," Tegeler says. HUD relies on state and local housing authorities and private fair-housing groups to bring most individual cases. Interestingly, just over 50 percent of complaints received in 2014 involved possible discrimination against persons with disabilities — coverage added to the law in 1988.

With racial issues in U.S. cities still roiling, here are some of the fair-housing questions being debated:

Are current government policies contributing to residential segregation?

Texas' Department of Housing and Community Affairs is responsible for approving applications from builders for the federal tax credits for building low-income housing. Over the 10-year period from 1999 to 2008, 92 percent of the tax-credit units built in the Dallas area were in mostly nonwhite neighborhoods. The state agency, applying a complex formula, approved just under half of the applications to build in areas with 90 percent minority populations but only 37 percent of the applications in areas with 90 percent or more white population.

U.S. District Judge Sidney Fitzwater made those findings as part of his March 2012 ruling that the state agency had failed to justify the concentration of housing built with tax credits in minority neighborhoods. The Supreme Court's decision in the case left those findings in place but sent the case back to Fitzwater for further proceedings.[12]

Demetria McCain, executive vice president of the Inclusive Communities Project (ICP), the plaintiff in the case, says the state used the tax credits "not only to recreate racial segregation but to make it worse. It will be a long time before there's even a modicum of units in white areas," she says.

Tegeler, with the poverty research group, says the Texas pattern can be found nationwide. "The vast majority of housing programs are steering housing to minority neighborhoods," he says.

In defending its policies, the Texas agency noted that federal law requires housing agencies to give a preference to tax-credit applicants proposing to build in low-income areas. The state said it was neutrally applying a set of factors in acting on applications for the tax credits, including a state provision that a project's financial viability was to be the major criterion. In his ruling, however, Fitzwater ordered the state to give additional points for projects in areas with good schools and to disqualify projects proposed in high-crime areas or near landfills.

Commenting after the Supreme Court decision, a lawyer with the Washington Legal Foundation, a conservative public-interest law firm that backed Texas in the case, continued to defend concentrating affordable housing in low-income neighborhoods. Cory Andrews, a senior legal counsel at the foundation, argued that it makes sense to allocate tax credits to lower- instead of higher-income communities — "where, presumably, fewer low-income minorities will stand to benefit. If the goal is to provide affordable housing to people," Andrews explains, "you would presumably provide it in places where those people live."[13]

In its comment after the ruling, the National Association of Housing and Redevelopment Officials emphasized portions of Kennedy's majority opinion upholding housing authorities' discretion in policy priorities. "Disparate-impact theory does not override the permissibility of basing decisions on market factors, issues that contribute to quality of life, or other legitimate business interests," NAHRO said in a written statement.

Housing advocates and experts across the ideological spectrum join in condemning the federal policies that cut African-Americans out of federally subsidized home loans in the 1930s and during the critical post-World War II years. In a recent appearance on NPR's "The Diane Rehm Show," Richard Rothstein, a research associate with the liberal Economic Policy Institute, noted that the Federal Housing Administration insured loans for homebuyers "on the explicit condition" that no loans be approved for African-Americans. On the same program, Edward Pinto, a housing expert with the conservative American Enterprise Institute (AEI), called the policies of that era "abhorrent."[14]

Even after passage of the Fair Housing Act, the federal government failed to develop policies to affirmatively promote desegregation, according to Rutgers professor

A joyous Sallie Sanders stands in front of her new home in Hamtramck, Mich., in March 2010, more than 50 years after her family was forced out of their rental home in the same suburban Detroit neighborhood. In 1971, a federal judge found that Hamtramck officials had used urban-renewal projects to raze black areas, displacing Sanders' family and hundreds of others. After years of delays following the ruling, the city has built more than a hundred homes for the children and grandchildren of the displaced Hamtramck residents who initially sued the city.

Jargowski. "They could have required every new suburban community to have some element of affordable housing," Jargowski says. "We could have desegregated as we suburbanized. That's not what happened."

HUD now has a critical role to play in getting state and local housing authorities to break down segregated housing patterns, according to Fred Underwood, director of diversity at the National Association of Realtors. "The proof is going to be in how HUD and the local communities handle it," says Underwood, who previously worked on fair-housing enforcement for HUD and a private civil rights group. The test, he says, is whether policies "really do focus on a more holistic approach. It's not simply enforcing the law."

HUD official Greene says the department's new rule is intended to help housing authorities comply with the law. "Communities need for HUD to inform them what is necessary to meet these requirements," he says. In explaining the rule, however, HUD Secretary Julián Castro said that cutting off funds to agencies that fail to comply would be a "last resort."[15]

Rice, of the National Fair Housing Alliance, says her organization is working with local agencies to develop policies to promote integration. "We are making

Federal Discrimination Investigations Decline

The Department of Housing and Urban Development (HUD) investigated 1,710 housing-discrimination complaints in 2014, roughly 20 percent of all those received. It was the fewest investigations since HUD was given additional enforcement authority under 1988 amendments to the Fair Housing Act. Investigations declined sharply from 1992 to 1997 as HUD increasingly referred complaints to state and local housing agencies for investigation.

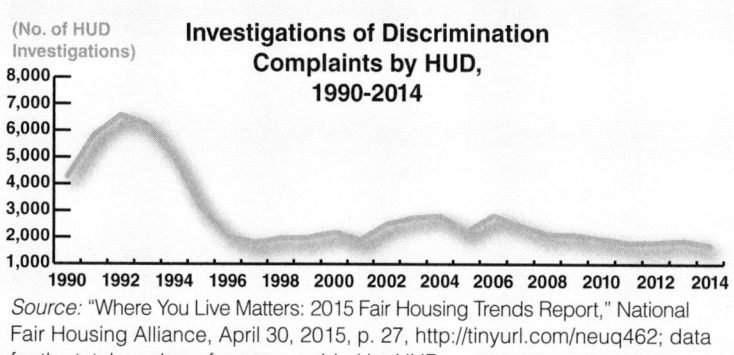

Source: "Where You Live Matters: 2015 Fair Housing Trends Report," National Fair Housing Alliance, April 30, 2015, p. 27, http://tinyurl.com/neuq462; data for the total number of cases provided by HUD

progress," Rice says. "The government is moving in the right direction." But institutional inertia and lack of funds hamper progress at the local level, she says.

"You're trying to change the way that these agencies do business," Rice says. "That's a heavy lift. That heavy lift becomes even heavier if those agencies don't have the funding to implement them."

Are current real estate and lending practices contributing to residential segregation?

New Jersey's largest savings bank agreed in September to pay $32.5 million to settle federal charges that it violated the Fair Housing Act by concentrating branches and mortgage loans in white neighborhoods while avoiding predominantly black and Hispanic areas.

"Redlining is not a vestige of the past," Vanita Gupta, head of the Justice Department's Civil Rights Division, told reporters in announcing the action against Hudson City Savings Bank.[16]

Rice, with the fair-housing alliance, is especially critical of what she sees as continued redlining of minority communities by mainstream lenders. "There's never been a time in U.S. history when the mainstream credit market has been the primary provider of credit for certain communities of color," she says.

"Redlining was very much practiced as official policy," HUD official Greene says. "Those kinds of practices don't go away overnight."

Minorities also continue to face discrimination at the hands of real estate brokers who screen racial and ethnic minorities from buying or renting in non-minority areas, according to a HUD-commissioned study released in 2013. Researchers from the Washington-based Urban Institute, a nonpartisan research organization, found that racial and ethnic minorities continue to face "subtle forms of housing denial" by real estate brokers and apartment owners, even though "blatant" acts of racial discrimination are declining.

"Discrimination still persists," HUD's then-secretary, Shaun Donovan, told reporters in releasing the study in mid-June.[17]

Minority communities also "got flooded with subprime loans" offered by so-called predatory lenders during the housing bubble and subsequent financial crisis of 2007–09, according to Gregory Squires, a professor of sociology and public policy at George Washington University in Washington, D.C. "And minority communities were hardest hit by foreclosures when the housing bubble burst."

In response, Pete Mills, a senior vice president with the Mortgage Bankers Association, says the industry has taken "dramatic steps . . . in strengthening its fair-lending performance," and the government has "ample tools" to ensure compliance with nondiscriminatory lending laws. But Mills says credit-tightening rules adopted after the financial crisis now put lenders at risk of running afoul of HUD's disparate-impact rule.

The regulations require lenders to closely examine factors such as a borrower's income and debt levels, which indicate an applicant's ability to repay, Mills explains. "The unintended consequence, he says, "is that these factors are often correlated by race, ethnicity and some of the other prohibited factors."

Real estate brokers often are caught up in small-scale HUD enforcement actions, many of them resulting from the use of black and white "testers" to uncover different treatment of would-be customers based on race. In one recent example, the Philadelphia real estate firm Brotman Enterprise agreed in June 2014 to pay $25,000 in damages to settle charges that it referred the white testers posing as customers to a "safe" neighborhood while the supposed customers who were black were shown properties in a less desirable, high-crime area.

To conduct such testing, HUD contracts with private groups such as the National Fair Housing Alliance (NFHA), which filed the complaint in the Brotman case. "Testing remains one of our most effective tools for exposing unlawful housing discrimination," Greene said in a release announcing the settlement.[18]

The 2013 study was based on similar testing in 28 metropolitan areas. It found that African-Americans, Hispanics and Asians seeking apartments to rent were told about or shown fewer units than white testers. Among would-be homebuyers, African-Americans and Asians were shown fewer houses than whites, with no difference between Hispanics and whites.

Rice, the NFHA executive director, says discrimination by real estate agents is hard to detect. "It's discrimination with a smile," Rice says. "It's no one telling you that they're not going to service you because you're a person of color. It's discrimination that happens behind cloak and veil."

On the industry side, National Association of Realtors' official Underwood acknowledges that violations still occur and says violators should be punished. "There is a strong commitment to eliminating discrimination in the market," he says.

Underwood says, however, that the incidence of "bad actors" is decreasing. "The focus on one particular point of the transaction obviously will uncover problems as long as problems exist in our society," Underwood says. "The question is how impactful are those situations."

Rice acknowledges that the real estate industry is itself increasingly diversified and calls the Realtors' commitment to fair housing "genuine." But she says fair-housing enforcement is difficult because victims may not recognize discrimination when it occurs or may simply move on to another broker without ever filing a complaint.

She agrees with HUD that using testers is an important tool, but complains that Congress does not provide enough funding for the purpose. "There is a funding problem," Rice says. "Congress doesn't want to appropriate the funds necessary to deal with this particular issue."

Housing activists in New York City hold a "die-in" on Sept. 17, 2015, to demand more affordable housing options for the homeless and the poor. Public-housing policies in the United States have shifted away from the construction of large, publicly owned "projects." Instead, the federal government began providing Section 8 subsidies for private rentals for the poor and tax credits to encourage developers to build affordable housing.

The Office of Fair Housing and Equal Opportunity budget for fiscal 2015 was $63.2 million — down from a peak of $71.3 million in 2011, according to a spokesman in the agency's press office.

Can local officials do more to reduce racial segregation in housing?

Crystal Wade had hoped to use a federal housing voucher to move out of her run-down townhouse in Ferguson, the predominantly black St. Louis suburb roiled by police-citizen tensions over the past year, and into a better neighborhood elsewhere in St. Louis County. But after looking all over the county this summer for a big enough place that was affordable and available to tenants paying with Section 8 vouchers, she came up mostly empty.

Wade, who lives with her boyfriend and three daughters, ended up with a house in somewhat better condition but in another racially segregated neighborhood with a higher crime rate, although one with fewer vacant lots. Boyfriend Bryant Goston was philosophical about the move. "I can adapt, yeah," he told a *New York Times* reporter. "Because, to be honest, that's what all black people have to do."[19]

Many housing policy experts on both sides of the ideological fence are similarly downbeat about the short-term potential for desegregating U.S. cities. "Inserting subsidized housing into suburban neighborhoods is going to be a drop in the bucket," says Peter Salins, a professor of political science at Stony Brook University in New York and a senior fellow at the Manhattan Institute, a conservative think tank.

"Massive investments went into creating segregated housing," Sherilyn Ifill, president and director-counsel of the NAACP Legal Defense and Educational Fund, said on "The Diane Rehm Show." "You cannot undo the damage simply by no longer making those investments."

The Section 8 housing voucher program — now officially called the Housing Choice Voucher Program — has built-in limitations, with a long waiting list — 25,000 in the city of St. Louis — and a $2,200-per-month rental cap, which limits options for finding housing in better neighborhoods. In addition, landlords are generally under no obligation to accept Section 8 tenants. The city of St. Louis has a law requiring landlords to accept Section 8 vouchers, but the county does not.

Some housing experts also suggest that many people in minority neighborhoods are reluctant to move from familiar surroundings into majority-white neighborhoods. "While expanding choice has a lot of appeal," University of Washington professor Vigdor explains, "it doesn't necessarily mean they're going to make different choices."

The researchers who studied the Baltimore program argue, however, that "intensive counseling" can overcome that reluctance. "Residential preferences can shift over time as a function of living in higher-opportunity neighborhoods," they write.[20]

Political obstacles, including resistance from majority-white neighborhoods, may also limit the potential for desegregation. "If you allow this to be a purely local decision about where to put these projects," Vigdor says, "there's just going to be a natural gravitation toward neighborhoods that offer the least amount of resistance."

Jargowsky, the Rutgers professor, says HUD itself has lacked the political will to force desegregation on communities. "They work so much with the housing authority, and the housing authority works with the developers," he says. "Over time, many of the programs that were designed to make housing more dispersed, they ended up replicating the existing patterns."

HUD official Greene concedes that the statutory command to "affirmatively further fair housing" is "probably the greatest unfinished business" at the department. "It's a new rule but not a new requirement," he explains, citing the language from the original 1968 law. "HUD had an obligation to affirmatively further fair housing, and by extension recipients of federal financial assistance from HUD had an obligation." The new regulation, Greene says, "is intended to make sure that communities know the path forward and to help communities make sure that they're dotting their i's and crossing their t's." But the housing authorities' national organization views the rule less favorably.

In comments submitted to HUD in mid-August, NAHRO said the new rule and the related "Assessment of Fair Housing" tool, which housing authorities must complete to show their compliance with the law, create "administrative burdens" while ignoring local community conditions. "Program participants are being pressured to set goals that do not fully reflect the needs and priorities of their communities and ignore the real-world constraints under which they operate," NAHRO argued.

At the Supreme Court, NAHRO joined a brief that said housing authorities risked facing legal liability whether they placed affordable housing in minority neighborhoods or in majority-white communities. NFHA executive director Rice says the fear is misplaced, however.

"You have to have a multipronged approach to achieving fair housing," Rice says. "The law makes it clear it's not either-or," she says. "You have do both."

Greene agrees. "HUD has steadfastly maintained that communities need to pursue a balanced approach," he says.

BACKGROUND
Separate Worlds

White and black Americans have lived mostly in separate worlds from the post-slavery era until at least the mid-20th century. After slavery was outlawed, residential segregation resulted from law, custom and market forces as well as, significantly, mid-20th-century federal policies promoting homeownership and urban renewal that benefited whites but significantly disadvantaged blacks. The passage of the Fair Housing Act in 1968 made racial discrimination illegal, but racially identifiable neighborhoods continued to be the norm in U.S. cities and suburbs.

African-American slaves lived side by side with white slave owners, but they had no legal rights and gained neither income nor wealth from the fruits of their labor. Despite the abolition of slavery in 1865, most blacks in the South continued to live in a form of indentured servitude, many as sharecroppers on the onetime slave plantations. They still effectively were denied legal, political or economic rights. Few African-Americans lived in the North before the Civil War, and immediately after the war their numbers grew only slightly. Some migrated westward along with white settlers seeking land and new lives in the American frontier.

After emancipation, some self-segregated themselves, establishing about 60 all-black townships across the country.[21] Two of those communities were destroyed by white rioters in the early 1920s following accusations of interracial sexual assaults. The Greenwood district in Tulsa, Okla. — proudly proclaimed as "the Black Wall Street" — was burned to the ground in a 15-hour assault that lasted from May 31 to June 1, 1921. The official death toll of 36 is believed to be low. Two years later, the all-black community of Rosewood, Fla., was razed in an incident known as the Rosewood massacre. The official death count of six blacks and two whites is similarly thought to be low.[22]

In the 20th century, the lure of jobs in the industrialized North and Midwest, combined with the harshness of the Jim Crow era, led more than 6 million African-Americans to move out of the South in a phenomenon now called the Great Migration.[23] But law, custom and market forces continued to limit black Americans' ability to choose where to live.

Some cities enacted ordinances segregating neighborhoods by race — ostensibly to preserve racial harmony — although the Supreme Court ruled such ordinances unconstitutional in a 1917 Louisville, Ky., case.[24] Smaller communities — "sundown towns" — enforced, by custom, rules requiring African-Americans to leave by nightfall.[25] And real estate firms continued to use racial covenants, contractual terms that prohibited the sale of a property to African-Americans or, in some instances, to Jews. Only in 1948 did the Supreme Court rule that those restrictions could not be enforced in court.[26]

Racial segregation in housing also was enforced by anti-black intimidation and in some instances violent confrontations. A riot broke out in the all-white Chicago suburb of Cicero on July 11–12, 1951, after an

Demonstrators at U.S. District Court in Manhattan on Aug. 8, 1988, protest a judge's decision to heavily fine Yonkers, N.Y., because its City Council refused to accept his housing desegregation order. Judge Leonard Sand ordered Yonkers to build public housing for minority residents in a white section, but the city resisted right up to the brink of municipal bankruptcy. More than 200 new townhouses for low-income minority families were finally opened for occupancy in 1992.

African-American family moved into an apartment building. There were no deaths, but the building suffered at least $20,000 in damage. A Cook County grand jury indicted the apartment owner for inciting a riot, but the charges were eventually dropped. The police chief and two officers were convicted in federal court for failing to protect the family's rights.[27]

The federal government undertook major policies to promote homeownership as part of President Franklin D. Roosevelt's New Deal, but the policies fortified patterns of residential segregation. The federal Home Ownership Loan Corp.'s practice of designating predominantly minority neighborhoods in red as uncreditworthy created the new word "redlining." The Federal Housing Administration and Veterans Administration (VA) adopted the same practice, limiting the availability of federally insured home mortgages for African-Americans. Federal support for urban renewal in the post-World War II era cleared predominantly minority slums in many cities, but the displaced minorities got little by way of relocation assistance. Meanwhile, the real estate and credit industries continued many of the practices that disadvantaged would-be African-American tenants or homebuyers even after the demise of legally enforceable racial covenants.[28]

The midcentury civil rights revolution brought housing discrimination issues to the fore. President John F. Kennedy

CHRONOLOGY

1930s–1950s *Racial segregation in housing is legal, widespread and buttressed by federal policy.*

1933–34 Federal government establishes home loan assistance programs; "redlining" limits loans to African-Americans.

1948 In a landmark ruling, Supreme Court holds that courts cannot enforce racial covenants on real estate.

1951 A race riot breaks out in Cicero, Ill., when an African-American family moves into an apartment building, drawing worldwide condemnation after being broadcast on television.

1960s–1970s *Government moves to bar racial discrimination in housing.*

1962 President John F. Kennedy issues executive order prohibiting racial discrimination in housing owned or financed by federal government.

1968 President Lyndon B. Johnson signs Fair Housing Act into law one week after assassination of the Rev. Martin Luther King Jr. . . . Supreme Court says racial discrimination in housing had been illegal under Civil Rights Act of 1866.

1974 Fair Housing Act is amended to prohibit gender-based discrimination. . . . Equal Credit Opportunity Act broadly prohibits discrimination by lenders. . . . Section 8 program is established to provide subsidies for low-income renters.

1975 Home Mortgage Disclosure Act is enacted to gather demographic data from mortgage lenders.

1977 Community Reinvestment Act requires federally regulated financial institutions to meet the credit needs of their communities.

1980s–1990s *Congress strengthens fair-housing enforcement.*

1985 Federal judge orders Yonkers, N.Y., to build public housing for minorities in a predominantly white neighborhood; the homes open for occupancy in 1992.

1986 Low-Income Housing Tax Credit program is created under the Tax Reform Act of 1986 to help finance construction of low-income housing.

1988 Fair Housing Act is amended to cover familial status, disabilities; amendments also strengthen Department of Housing and Urban Development's (HUD) enforcement authority.

1995 Public housing tenants sue HUD and Baltimore officials for concentrating public housing in minority neighborhoods; similar suits are filed in more than a dozen cities during the decade.

2000–Present *Residential segregation declines overall, but persists in many U.S. cities.*

2005 Federal judge finds HUD guilty in Baltimore case of failing to disperse affordable housing throughout the metropolitan region.

2008 Bipartisan commission calls for reorienting federal housing programs to help minorities move to less racially and economically segregated communities.

2009 Federal judge says Westchester County, N.Y., misrepresented desegregation efforts in seeking federal funds.

2012 Federal judge faults Texas housing agency for awarding tax credits for low-income housing mostly in minority neighborhoods in Dallas; state's appeal eventually reaches Supreme Court. . . . Wells Fargo agrees to pay $175 million to settle charges that it discriminated against minorities in its mortgage lending practices.

2013 A HUD-commissioned study finds racial screening by real estate brokers is still widespread.

2015 Supreme Court upholds "disparate impact" liability for housing policies that result in segregation. . . . HUD issues "Affirmatively Furthering Fair Housing" rule to enforce long-standing obligation under 1968 law; National Association of Housing and Redevelopment Officials calls for rule to be scrapped. . . . New Jersey's largest savings bank agrees to pay more than $30 million to settle "redlining" charges. . . . Judge in Dallas housing case sets briefing schedule for further proceedings.

issued an executive order in 1962 directing federal agencies to prevent racial discrimination in housing owned or financed by the federal government. It took six more years for Congress to pass and President Lyndon B. Johnson to sign the Fair Housing Act. The legislation stalled even after the passage of the omnibus Civil Rights Act of 1964 and the Voting Rights Act of 1965, but Johnson helped push it across the congressional finish line just one week after the assassination of the Rev. Martin Luther King Jr. in April 1968. King had helped dramatize the issue by focusing on fair housing as one of the goals after he allied with the grassroots Chicago Freedom Movement, beginning in late 1965.[29]

The Fair Housing Act prohibited private discrimination in housing on the basis of race, religion or national origin, with some exceptions — for example, for small boarding houses. It included a provision requiring local governments to affirmatively further integration, but gave HUD only limited enforcement authority. In an ironic postscript, the Supreme Court ruled two months later that private discrimination in housing had been illegal for more than a century under the Civil Rights Act of 1866, which guaranteed blacks the same contract rights as white persons.[30]

Slow Changes

Congress and the federal judiciary expanded fair-housing protections under federal law through a succession of statutes and judicial decisions beginning in the 1970s. Over time, enforcement combined with voluntary compliance and affirmative efforts by some local housing authorities to reduce black-white residential segregation somewhat, but most African-Americans still lived in highly segregated metropolitan neighborhoods. And resistance to integration persisted, as demonstrated by one high-profile clash over public housing in Yonkers, N.Y.

The Supreme Court set the stage for strengthening fair-housing enforcement by interpreting the job discrimination provisions of the Civil Rights Act of 1964 to cover not only intentional discrimination but also employment practices that had an adverse or disparate impact based on race. The 1971 ruling in *Griggs v. Duke Power Co.* allowed a civil rights challenge to a supposedly race-neutral job requirement for a high school diploma — without adequate justification — based on its adverse impact on African-Americans. Over the next four decades, federal appeals courts uniformly held that practices by housing authorities, real estate firms or lenders could similarly be challenged under a theory of disparate-impact liability without proof of intentional discrimination.

Earlier, however, President Richard M. Nixon had squelched a politically treacherous plan by his housing secretary, George Romney, to use HUD funds to force cities, counties and states to try to break up residential segregation. Romney ordered HUD officials to withhold grants for water, sewer or highway projects from jurisdictions with policies that fostered segregation. Once opposition reached the Oval Office, Nixon ordered the policy rescinded in a 1972 memo to his domestic policy director, John Ehrlichman.[31]

Congress expanded the Fair Housing Act in 1974 to prohibit discrimination on the basis of sex and again in 1988 to prohibit discrimination on the basis of family status or disabilities. HUD used the sex and family status provisions as the basis of a non-statutory regulation issued in 2012 to prohibit discrimination on the basis of sexual orientation or gender identity in HUD-assisted housing.[32] The disabilities provision required builders to construct new, multifamily dwellings to meet specified adaptability and accessibility requirements. The 1988 law also authorized HUD to file discrimination complaints, gave individuals more time to file an administrative complaint or a lawsuit and somewhat expanded available remedies. Significantly for the eventual Supreme Court case, the law included language that appeared to adopt judicial decisions recognizing disparate-impact liability under the law.

HUD's major low-income housing programs began taking shape in the 1970s and '80s. The Housing and Community Development Act of 1976 replaced an existing rent-subsidy program with the Section 8 voucher program. Qualified low-income tenants found their own housing but had to pay no more than 30 percent of their adjusted gross income for rent; public housing authorities made up the difference with direct payment to landlords. A decade later, Congress aimed at the supply side of the issue by authorizing, as part of the Tax Reform Act of 1986, dollar-for-dollar tax credits for developers to build or rehabilitate affordable housing. Over time, it was estimated that the tax credits were responsible for 90 percent of the affordable housing built in the country.

Meanwhile, Congress strengthened fair-housing protections with three laws aimed at preventing discrimination in the mortgage industry. The Equal Credit Opportunity Act, enacted in 1974, prohibited discrimination in the

Fewer Metro Areas Seens as "Hypersegregated"

All-white neighborhoods "extinct," but inner-city poverty worsens.

Residential segregation along racial lines has declined in the United States since passage of the Fair Housing Act in 1968, but experts who have crunched the numbers disagree on exactly how much.

One leading researcher using 2010 census figures counts 21 U.S. metropolitan areas as "hypersegregated," or extremely segregated, down from 40 in 1970.

"Despite evidence of progress in many metropolitan areas, therefore, the United States has not become a race-blind society," concluded Princeton University sociology professor Douglas Massey. The United States "has not been able to eradicate hypersegregation from its urban areas."[1] Massey defined the degree of residential segregation in an area using a methodology that weighs several criteria, rather than setting specific percentages of people of varying races.

Two other researchers, using a different methodology to analyze the same census figures, proclaimed "the end of the segregated century."[2] Harvard economics professor Edward Glaeser and University of Washington public policy professor Jacob Vigdor say all-white neighborhoods in nonrural areas used to be common but are now "effectively extinct." The scholars, affiliated with the free market-oriented Manhattan Institute, cite as evidence the migration to the suburbs of higher-income African-Americans.

"There's been a dramatic change in the number of neighborhoods where you find exactly zero African-American residents," says Vigdor. "These used to be very common and are very rare now."

Massey and co-author Jonathan Tannen, a PhD student in urban and population policy at Princeton, say 26 percent of the nation's African-Americans live in hypersegregated metropolitan areas, compared with 47 percent in 1970.

Residential segregation can be quantified in five different ways. The most commonly used method calculates the relative number of blacks and whites who would have to exchange neighborhoods to achieve an even distribution. On average, in the eight most segregated cities, seven out of every 10 blacks and seven out of every 10 whites would have to swap neighborhoods to have an even residential distribution. Other methods calculate the relative isolation of African-Americans, the degree of clustering around racially defined neighborhoods, the relative amounts of space occupied by whites and blacks and the degree of racial concentration around the metropolitan center.

In Massey's calculation, eight cities are hypersegregated on all five of those measures and 13 others on four of the five. Together, those 21 cities account for about one-third of African-Americans living in metropolitan areas. Six of the eight most segregated cities are in the Midwest's Rust Belt: Milwaukee, Detroit, St. Louis, Chicago, Cleveland and Flint, Mich. The two others also are once heavily industrialized cities: Birmingham, Ala., and Baltimore.[3]

Hispanics and Asians have not experienced anywhere near the high degree of residential segregation from whites experienced by African-Americans, according to Massey. The 2010 census figures show that three-fourths of urban

---

approval of credit applications on the basis of race, sex national origin, marital status or receipt of public assistance. Adopted a year later, the Home Mortgage Disclosure Act required lenders to disclose data on loan applications and approvals to address the concern about credit shortages in some urban neighborhoods. The Community Reinvestment Act, passed in 1977, added an affirmative obligation for federally regulated financial institutions to address financing needs of communities they served.

Over time, Americans generally came to accept the principle of fair housing, but concrete steps to integrate neighborhoods still stirred controversy. In one dramatic example, a federal judge provoked a political standoff in Yonkers, an exurban area just north of the Bronx in New York; Judge Leonard Sand found the city guilty of discrimination in 1985 because all public housing was sited in a small, predominantly African-American section. Sand ordered the city to build public housing for minority residents in a white section, but the city resisted right up to the brink of municipal bankruptcy. The 230 townhouses were finally opened for occupancy in 1992; they now house about 200 low-income minority families.[33]

The nation's demographics were changing rapidly in the late 20th century because of increased immigration

Hispanics and 100 percent of Asian urbanites are in cities with moderate or low segregation. Those figures "underscor[e] the continued distinctiveness of black segregation in metropolitan America," Massey and Tannen write.

Another leading expert on the issue criticizes Glaeser's and Vigdor's decision to use the migration of Asians and Hispanics into predominantly black neighborhoods to suggest reduced segregation. "They calculated segregation as black versus non-black," says Paul Jargowsky, a professor of public policy at Rutgers University in Camden, N.J. "I feel that when we're talking about segregation, what we're really concerned about is how segregated a particular minority group is from the majority."

All of the experts agree that despite reduced segregation, predominantly black neighborhoods are suffering from increased concentration of poverty. "Once the barriers to free housing choice were lessened, the first to leave these neighborhoods were the more affluent," Vigdor says.

Jargowsky calculated that the number of people living in high-poverty ghettos, barrios and slums has nearly doubled since 2000 — from 7.2 million to 13.8 million today. "We are witnessing a nationwide return of concentrated poverty that is racial in nature," he wrote in an article for The Century Foundation, a liberal think tank in Washington.[4]

In their article, Massey and Tannen say poverty is particularly concentrated in hypersegregated areas. "Owing to the important role that it plays in concentrating poverty," they wrote, "segregation is critical to understanding racial stratification in the United States today."

— *Kenneth Jost*

Harvard economics professor Edward Glaeser contends all-white neighborhoods in nonrural areas, once common, are now "effectively extinct." Other experts disagree, saying many cities are still extremely segregated.

[1] See Douglas S. Massey and Jonathan Tannen, "A Research Note on Trends in Black Hypersegregation," *Demography*, Population Association of America, June 2015 [published online March 20, 2015], http://tinyurl.com/odta3bf.

[2] Edward Glaeser and Jacob Vigdor, "The End of the Segregated Century: Racial Separation in America's Neighborhoods, 1890-2010," *Civic Report, No. 66*, Manhattan Institute, January 2012, http://tinyurl.com/7sz2hjh.

[3] For a complete list of the cities designated as "hypersegregated" in 1970 and in 2010, see Tanvi Misra, "America Has Half as Many Hypersegregated Metros as It Did in 1970," *City Lab* (blog of *TheAtlantic.com*), May 21, 2015, http://tinyurl.com/oca9f7s.

[4] Paul A. Jargowsky, "Architecture of Segregation: Civil Unrest, the Concentration of Poverty, and Public Policy," The Century Foundation, Aug. 7, 2015, http:// tinyurl.com/q2uzvyt.

from Latin America and Asia under liberalized country-of-origin rules enacted by the landmark Immigration and Nationality Act of 1965.

With the Fair Housing Act in effect, the newly arriving Latino- and Asian-Americans encountered less overt discrimination than immigrants had experienced in the past; some found homes in predominantly white neighborhoods, but many moved into predominantly black neighborhoods. By the end of the century, black-white residential segregation had also decreased, but only slowly. The number of "hypersegregated" metropolitan areas in the United States declined from 40 as of 1970 to 21 in 2010, according to Massey, and within those areas, the degree of black-white segregation had fallen only slightly.[34]

Unsettled Times

Racial segregation in housing decreased further in the 21st century, but migration patterns combined with an economic downturn to leave many cities with significantly higher degrees of concentrated poverty in predominantly minority neighborhoods. Fair-housing advocates complained about lagging federal enforcement under President George W. Bush and about the disproportionate effect that the 2007–09 housing bust had on minority

Pet-Policy Dispute Lands in Court

Tenants with disabilities have right to "support animals."

Armed with a prescription from her doctor, Chelsy Walsh called one of the owners of her Sioux Falls, S.D., apartment complex in January 2014 to say she would be buying a dog as a "support animal" for her mental health. But Linda Christensen told Walsh that animals were not allowed at the Viking Villas and warned Walsh that she would have trouble finding another place to live because she was receiving a federal subsidy under the Section 8 voucher program.

Today, the seemingly everyday landlord-tenant dispute over pets is literally a federal case after the Department of Housing and Urban Development (HUD) charged Linda and her husband Robert with violating the Fair Housing Act by discriminating against Walsh on the basis of her disability. The Christensens are disputing the charge, which is pending in a federal court in South Dakota.

Congress expanded the landmark 1968 law in 1988 by also prohibiting discrimination based on disabilities. The law initially prohibited discrimination in the sale, rental or financing of housing on the basis of race, national origin or other characteristic. Today, disability-related claims account for just over half of the Fair Housing Act complaints received by HUD, state or local agencies or nongovernmental organizations that fight housing discrimination.[1] A majority of the complaints — 57 percent — stem from allegations that landlords or apartment owners failed to make "reasonable accommodation" for individuals with disabilities, as the law requires, according to HUD statistics.[2]

"I don't think that housing providers even this far after the Fair Housing Act have totally realized that people with disabilities are a protected class and they can't be discriminated against," says Kenneth Shiotani, a senior staff attorney with the Washington-based National Disability Rights Network, an umbrella organization for state and local disability rights groups.

The National Apartment Association says it "strongly supports" the right of tenants with disabilities to request reasonable accommodations, but says requests for emotional support animals are "a particular area of concern." "A lack of clarity in the law . . . allows for abuse and imposes an unfair burden on property owners," the association told *CQ Researcher* in a written statement supplied on request.

Walsh, who suffers from post-traumatic stress disorder and bipolar disorder, formalized her phone call with a written request a week later and then filed an administrative complaint with HUD. In June she bought a seven-year-old, 10.5-pound shih tzu-lhasa apso mix.

Robert Christensen allegedly responded by asking Walsh to sign a "Companion Animal/Pet Policy Agreement"

neighborhoods. Those groups cheered, however, when the Supreme Court in June upheld the broader, disparate-impact definition of housing discrimination and HUD issued its rule in July detailing local governments' affirmative duty to promote integrated housing.

The number of discrimination complaints filed by HUD "spiraled downward" during the Bush administration, according to data in the 2008 report of the private National Commission on Fair Housing, a bipartisan group convened by civil rights organizations and headed by two former HUD secretaries: Democrat Henry Cisneros and Republican Jack Kemp. The number had fallen under President Bill Clinton from 125 in fiscal 1995 to 88 in fiscal 2001, and then fell sharply under Bush to only 31 in fiscal 2007. Data from the fair-housing alliance showed the number rose under President Obama to a peak of 55 in fiscal 2011 but fell by more than half to only 27 in fiscal 2014. Both reports faulted HUD for its slow pace in processing complaints.[35]

Meanwhile, federal judges had signaled impatience with housing desegregation efforts in two high-profile cases on the East Coast. In his 2005 ruling in the Baltimore case, Garbis accused HUD of "effectively wearing blinders" by placing low-income housing only in minority neighborhoods. Four years later, U.S. District Judge Denise Cote faulted suburban Westchester County, N.Y., for misrepresenting its desegregation efforts when applying for federal funds by leaving the location of low-income housing up to individual villages and towns. The county settled the case six months later by promising to site low-income

that included inspection and property damage provisions and allowed the owners to revoke permission for the animal at their "sole discretion." Walsh considered the agreement overly burdensome and moved out.

After failing to conciliate the dispute, HUD turned the case over to the Justice Department, which filed the federal suit on Sept. 15 seeking damages for Walsh and an injunction to prevent the Christensens from future discrimination on the basis of disability.

Michael Paulson, an attorney representing the Christensens, says the dispute resulted from "a communication issue" with Walsh. "My clients have done absolutely all that they can to make reasonable accommodations," Paulson says. The lawyer also agrees with the apartment owners' association that the disabilities provision is subject to abuse because the language is vague and the requirements for proving a disability too lax.

Requests for service or emotional support animals are "a fairly routine problem," according to Shiotani, a 10-year veteran with the disability rights network. Under the law, tenants with disabilities cannot be denied permission or charged a fee for having a service or support animal live with them. Among other examples, HUD's website explanation of the law says apartment owners cannot refuse to rent because they are uncomfortable with an individual's disability and can be required to make such accommodations as a reserved parking space or some structural modifications at the resident's expense.[3]

The HUD summary also explains that most multifamily buildings constructed after March 13, 1991, must meet seven design and construction requirements, including accessible entrances and common spaces. Individual units must have "usable doors" — that is, wide enough for a wheelchair; "usable" kitchens and bathrooms; reinforced bathroom walls and accessible light switches and other controls. Construction-related complaints account for under 5 percent of all cases, according to HUD statistics.[4]

The increasing number of disability-related fair-housing complaints reflects the effect of education and outreach efforts by HUD itself and advocacy organizations, according to Bryan Greene, HUD's deputy assistant secretary for fair housing.

"Discrimination against people with disabilities remains much more in the open than many other forms of discrimination," he says. "It's very important for people with disabilities that you stand up for your fair-housing rights."

— *Kenneth Jost*

[1] "Where You Live Matters: 2015 Fair Housing Trends Report," National Fair Housing Alliance, April 30, 2015, http://tinyurl.com/neuq462.

[2] "Annual Report on Fair Housing," U.S. Department of Housing and Urban Development, November 2014, p. 6, http://tinyurl.com/o4mxboh.

[3] See "Disability Rights in Housing," U.S. Department of Housing and Urban Development, undated, http://tinyurl.com/3ujp6fx.

[4] "Annual Report on Fair Housing," *op. cit.*

---

housing in predominantly white neighborhoods, but the county is now facing possible penalties for failing to follow through on the accord.[36]

The big housing story of the early 21st century, however, was the foreclosure crisis, brought on by the bursting of a decades-long housing bubble. African-Americans were hurt the worst, according to experts and advocacy groups, because mainstream lenders made them targets for risky subprime loans. In the 2008 report, the national commission charged that "predatory lenders" had steered minority homebuyers into subprime loans, with appealing but ultimately risky features, even when they could have qualified with mainstream mortgage lenders. The commission urged a federal crackdown on unscrupulous lenders. In 2012, Wells Fargo, the nation's largest mortgage lender, agreed to pay $175 million to settle charges that its independent brokers discriminated against black and Hispanic borrowers.[37]

Over time, the Supreme Court generally upheld broad applications of the Fair Housing Act — for example, in a 1982 decision allowing "testers" to sue real estate firms for racial screening.[38] The court's unsuccessful moves in the 2011 and 2012 to reconsider the question of disparate-impact liability stirred fears that the conservative majority was about to limit the law to intentional discrimination. Civil rights forces instead applauded the 5–4 decision, issued on June 25, to uphold the broader definition.

The Legal Defense Fund's Ifill called the ruling "a crucial victory for all Americans who care about the continuing impact of segregation." But Roger Clegg,

Tracy Carrithers and Carla Cathion search for suitable rental housing in Chicago on June 27, 2015. The two women planned to pay their rent with vouchers from the federal government's Section 8 program for low-income families. The program has built-in limitations, including long waiting lists and a $2,200-per-month rental cap, which limits options for finding housing in better neighborhoods. In addition, landlords generally are not obligated to accept Section 8 vouchers.

general counsel of the conservative Center for Equal Opportunity, warned the decision would encourage "race-based decision-making in the housing area, exactly what the Fair Housing Act was meant to prohibit."[39]

Two weeks after the Supreme Court decision, HUD announced its long-under-development rule aimed at strengthening the requirement that state and local agencies affirmatively reduce residential segregation. Speaking to *The New York Times*, HUD Secretary Castro stressed cooperation over confrontation as the goal in dealing with local agencies. Enforcement "is possible," Castro said, "but our preference is to work cooperatively and steadfastly with communities."[40]

The Republican-controlled House of Representatives voted 239–191 on June 9 to try to block implementation of the rule, and Republicans and conservatives renewed criticism of the rule after it was issued. The Senate has not acted on the House measure.

Pinto, of the American Enterprise Institute, called the rule "the latest of a series of attempts by HUD to social-engineer the American people." But Marc Morial, president of the National Urban League, a New York-based civil rights organization, called it "a serious effort by the administration to, in effect, enforce one of the legacy civil rights laws."

CURRENT SITUATION
Stepping Up Efforts

HUD's fair-housing enforcement unit is stepping up efforts to desegregate U.S. cities, even as its staffing has fallen to historically low levels and it is outsourcing many of its cases to state and local civil rights agencies.

"Our numbers and staff have been declining," says Greene, second in command in HUD's Office of Fair Housing and Equal Opportunity. "We do have a great challenge ahead of us, and it's very much on the resource effort."

"There is a funding problem," says NFHA Executive Director Rice. "Congress doesn't want to appropriate the funds necessary to deal with this particular issue."

Congress authorized funds in fiscal 2015 for only 516 employees at the fair-housing office, the lowest number since HUD was given additional enforcement authority in 1988 and far below the 750 recommended by the Kemp-Cisneros commission in 2008, according to NFHA's most recent annual report. The understaffing "has increased the number of aged cases, delaying justice for victims of discrimination and resolution for respondents," the alliance states.[41]

The alliance also faults as "insufficient" the funding for HUD's Fair Housing Initiatives Program, which awards grants to private organizations for education, outreach, testing, investigation and mediation. During the Obama administration, funding for the program has risen from $27.5 million in fiscal 2009 to $40.1 million in fiscal 2015 — far short of the $75.4 million in applications from fair-housing groups in fiscal 2009. The amount still is insufficient to "monitor local housing markets or address the overall incidence of housing discrimination," the alliance says.[42]

Greene says present-day discrimination is more subtle and thus harder to detect or even recognize than the blatant refusal to sell or rent in the days before the Fair Housing Act. "Our tools to uncover that kind of discrimination have to be sharper today," he says.

AT ISSUE

Should Congress block HUD's new fair-housing rule?

YES
Rep. Paul Gosar, R-Ariz.
Written for *CQ Researcher*, November 2015

As President Obama reaches the end of his second term, he has made it clear that his top priority during his waning days is to further his far-left political agenda by forcing big government programs on the American people. The calling card of this administration has been to use overreaching executive mandates and regulations to force American families, businesses and consumers into complying with its misguided utopian ideology.

The Affirmatively Furthering Fair Housing (AFFH) rule, introduced by the Department of Housing and Urban Development (HUD) this past July, is no different. This overreaching new rule is an attempt to extort communities into giving up control of local zoning decisions and reengineer the makeup of our neighborhoods. Important federal housing grants will be stripped away if communities do not fit the racial and economic standards concocted by D.C. bureaucrats. Just as the president has used the Department of Justice, Internal Revenue Service and Department of Homeland Security as a political weapon, he has now expanded his arsenal to include HUD as a way of punishing neighborhoods that don't fall in line with his liberal view of where Americans should live.

Let me be clear: This new Washington mandate has nothing to do with race, as housing discrimination has been illegal for more than 40 years. The 1968 Fair Housing Act already makes discrimination illegal in the "sale, rental and financing of dwellings based on race, religion, sex or national origin." Apparently, it's not enough to provide everyone with equal opportunity in housing matters. What the Obama administration wants is equal outcomes, and the only possible way to produce this is for the federal government to force itself upon local jurisdictions.

Similar to other big-government policies from this administration, the flawed AFFH rule will result in more harm than good by way of increased taxes, depressed property values and further harm to impoverished communities. Local zoning decisions have always been, and should always be, made by local communities and municipalities. American citizens should be free to choose where they would like to live and not be subject to neighborhood engineering and gerrymandering at the behest of an overreaching federal government. Congress must remain vigilant in opposing this new edict, and I am pleased that, so far, many of my colleagues have recognized the perils associated with this looming threat that will negatively impact homeownership.

NO
Rep. Keith Ellison, D-Minn.
Written for *CQ Researcher*, November 2015

For decades, our nation has prohibited housing discrimination based on race, sex, religion, national origin and disability. The law prohibits landlords from discriminating and precludes discrimination by towns, cities, counties and states receiving federal housing funds.

Our nation faces an alarming rental-housing crisis. Our limited federal housing assistance must provide more than shelter; it must provide opportunities for families to thrive in communities with jobs and access to high quality education, health care and transportation.

Despite having more than 11 million households spending more than 50 percent of their income on rent, fewer than one in four who qualify for housing assistance receive it. Limited federal housing funds should provide housing and reduce racial segregation and concentrated poverty.

HBO's miniseries "Show Me a Hero" vividly depicted what happens when federal housing dollars are spent exclusively in low-income and minority communities. These communities are at a higher risk for crime, poor schools and limited access to jobs and health care.

The Affirmatively Furthering Fair Housing rule requires local governments to use their funds to actively increase fair housing. They must provide options for those who receive housing assistance to live in supportive communities that provide opportunities to their families. Federal housing funds should afford low-income families, people with disabilities and the elderly access to community resources. By providing low-income families access to jobs, health care and good schools, we can reduce racial segregation and concentrated poverty.

We must resist Republican attacks to end the Fair Housing requirements for federal funds. Despite arguments that fair-housing rules are about "unrealistic utopian ideas of what every community should resemble," we must be proactive and use limited housing resources to reduce segregation. Everyone benefits when people with disabilities, African-Americans, Latino Americans, families with children, immigrant families and the elderly live in safe communities with access to jobs and quality services.

For too long, ZIP codes have been the defining factor in determining access to quality education, jobs and health care. Unequal access to vital resources results in unequal access to opportunity, undermining our nation's prosperity and success. We should expand housing assistance and ensure that our families and communities can thrive.

Many subtle real estate practices of old continue, Greene explains. "Many of the people in the real estate industry were trained under the old guidelines," he says. Testing evidence "amply illustrates some of the practices that go on today," Greene adds.

Redlining by lenders also continues, Greene says, with some banks choosing not to make loans or establish offices in minority neighborhoods. He cites the pending Hudson City case as an example. He notes that the complaint quotes Hudson City executives as favoring European or Asian ethnic groups when opening offices on predominantly white Staten Island, and ignoring African-Americans and Hispanics.

HUD itself had come under criticism in the 2008 Kemp-Cisneros commission report. The three major federal programs — Section 8 vouchers, public housing and low-income housing tax credits (LIHTCs) — "do very little to further fair housing and, in some cases, work to create and/or maintain segregated housing patterns," the report stated. "These programs must be reoriented to focus, in part, on helping families move to less racially and economically segregated communities."[43]

The report also said HUD had "failed" in ensuring that state and local recipients of federal housing assistance comply with the obligation to "affirmatively further" fair housing. The new rule is aimed in that direction, but NAHRO, the housing officials' organization, is unhappy with HUD's promise of help in meeting the obligation.

NAHRO noted in its mid-August statement that HUD is promising to supply some data for the new Assessment of Fair Housing tool, but it called the information "unwieldy and hard to understand." Some of the information "relies on complex social science indices . . . whose meaning is largely unintelligible to most users," NAHRO added.

Even as NAHRO and other groups are calling for rewriting the rule, the Dallas fair-housing group Inclusive Communities Project hopes the new rule will help reorient housing policies there. ICP vice president McCain says she hopes HUD will get "very serious" about enforcing the rule — by withholding federal funds if necessary.

Squaring Off in Court

The Inclusive Communities Project is back before a federal trial judge in Dallas challenging the Texas Department of Housing and Community Affairs (TDHCA) to award more federal tax credits for affordable housing in white neighborhoods.

The Supreme Court's decision to recognize disparate-impact liability under the Fair Housing Act sent the seven-year-old case back for a decision on the merits of ICP's allegation that state policies were causing discrimination against African-Americans. But Justice Kennedy's opinion for the majority included several comments and instructions that could help housing authorities or private developers being sued on the grounds of disparate impact.

ICP and the state squared off over how Judge Fitzwater should conduct future proceedings. As part of a Sept. 10 joint status report, ICP argued that it had already proved, "using uncontested evidence," the discriminatory effect of the housing authority's policies. The only remaining issues, the group argued, were whether the state could justify its policies or there were fewer discriminatory alternatives.

The TDHCA, however, said the judge should reconsider his earlier summary judgment in ICP's favor, noting that the Supreme Court had "repeatedly questioned" whether ICP had even alleged a disparate-impact claim and had "strongly suggested" that the state had "a valid defense." The agency said Fitzwater "did not have the benefit of the Supreme Court's explanation of what is required to establish a disparate-impact cause of action" when he made his earlier ruling.

On Oct. 8, Fitzwater said he would reconsider whether ICP had established a prima facie case of discrimination, needed to proceed to the other issues, and said either side could present additional evidence. "The judge is trying to be eminently fair," says Michael Daniel, the attorney representing ICP. In his opinion, Kennedy stressed that housing authorities and private developers should be given "leeway to state and explain the valid interest served by their policies" when sued on the grounds of disparate impact. "Entrepreneurs must be given latitude to consider market factors," he explained, and zoning officials must consider "a mix of factors" affecting a community's "quality of life."

Kennedy also said a statistical disparity alone was insufficient to make a case unless a plaintiff could cite policies by the defendant causing the disparity. The TDHCA reasserted that federal law, not its own policies, create a preference for building tax-credit units in minority neighborhoods. But ICP says the state agency's formula failed to give points to developments that would further what it called "a concerted community revitalization plan."

Fitzwater's eventual ruling could be delayed until 2016. The losing party will probably appeal his decision to the Fifth Circuit appeals court.

Meanwhile, ICP has a separate lawsuit pending against the U.S. Department of the Treasury and the Office of Comptroller of the Currency for allegedly failing to promote fair housing in its policies regarding low-income housing tax credits. Treasury administers the LIHTC program; the Comptroller oversees portions of it to make sure national banks don't invest in LIHTC projects unless they would primarily promote the public welfare, including housing for low- and moderate-income families.

ICP's complaint, filed in August 2014, alleges that neither Treasury nor the Comptroller has regulations related to the perpetuation or elimination of racial segregation. The two sought to have the case dismissed, but Fitzwater issued an opinion on Aug. 4, allowing most of the suit to proceed. The government's answer on the merits was to be filed on Oct. 30.[44]

OUTLOOK

Political Challenges

As mayor of Seattle, Ed Murray is pushing a multipronged plan to provide affordable housing in a city now ranked among the 10 most expensive in the United States. Murray's plan includes an array of tax breaks and land use changes, but he retreated in the face of strong political opposition from a proposal to allow multifamily buildings in parts of the city now zoned for single-family houses only.[45]

Murray's about-face on the so-called upzoning proposal underscores the volatile nature of housing policy debates even when race is not an explicit issue. As Stony Brook professor Salins notes, the low-density zoning laws that created the modern American suburb lead inevitably to higher housing prices and thus economic segregation.

Salins favors easing those zoning restrictions but cautions against linking any changes to breaking down residential segregation. 'If you want to kill any chance of economic integration and racial integration," he says, "tie the two together."

Despite progress on fair housing, experts and advocates alike agree that institutional barriers to residential desegregation are still daunting. "We've come quite a bit of a way in terms of achieving fair housing, but we still have a long way to go," says NFHA Executive Director Rice.

Rothstein, the Economic Policy Institute researcher, agrees with HUD official Greene that case-by-case enforcement of fair-housing laws is not enough to break down the barriers that created and now to some extent maintain residential segregation. "Prohibiting ongoing discrimination can't undo that," Rothstein remarked on "The Diane Rehm Show." Legal Defense Fund President Ifill said on the same program: "If you have massively invested in the creation of white suburbs . . . you cannot undo the damage of that simply by no longer making those investments."[46]

The housing officials group's opposition to the new HUD rule indicates that the government can expect local resistance as it seeks to enforce the long-standing obligation to affirmatively further fair housing. Political opposition seems certain if communities are required to put housing that minority buyers and tenants can afford into predominantly white neighborhoods. "The greatest opposition is going to be from neighborhoods that don't have any of that housing yet," says Vigdor, the University of Washington professor.

"We have a long way to go," says Tegeler, with the Poverty & Race Research Action Council. "These structures are not easy to undo. They require a lot of courage from officials and a lot of work from people at the local and regional level."

Like others, Vigdor and Tegeler profess at least a measure of cautious optimism about future trends. At HUD, Greene sees reason for optimism in changing preferences across racial and ethnic lines about where to live. "I'm very hopeful that we're going to see the dial turn toward more integrated communities in this country," Greene says. "I see more people moving into cities because they want to live in an integrated community."

In its annual report, the fair-housing alliance stressed that housing patterns have far-reaching consequences — on schools, air quality, access to jobs and transportation and the ability to accumulate wealth through homeownership.

"Inequality persists in all of these areas along racial and ethnic lines," Shanna Smith, the group's president and CEO, wrote in an accompanying press release, "which means that we need an all-out strategy to build up neighborhoods and provide a range of safe and affordable housing options for all Americans."[47]

NOTES

1. All quotes and background drawn from Stefanie DeLuca and Jessi Stafford, "Voices of the Baltimore Housing Mobility Program," The Century Foundation, March 2014, http://tinyurl.com/p9tajgt. Kimberly's last name and other details were omitted in the multimedia presentation. For an academic paper based on the investigation, see Jennifer Darrah and Stefanie DeLuca, "'Living Here Has Changed My Whole Perspective': How Escaping Inner-City Poverty Shapes Neighborhood and Housing Choice," *Journal of Policy Analysis and Management*, Vol. 33, Issue 2 (spring 2014), http://tinyurl.com/qyu5x56 ($$). A pre-publication version of the article is available at http://tinyurl.com/pwyhvxv. For a more positive view about public housing, see David Madden, "Five Myths About Public Housing," *The Washington Post*, Sept. 13, 2015, p. B3, http://tinyurl.com/oltzg8l.

2. The suit was filed initially by the American Civil Liberties Union of Maryland (ACLU) and joined by the NAACP Legal Defense and Educational Fund (LDF). For legal and other materials, see the ACLU's website, http://tinyurl.com/nlqjer7, or the LDF's website, http://tinyurl.com/pc8f7x6.

3. The law is codified at 42 U.S.C. §§3601–3619, http://tinyurl.com/ph2td8b; the "affirmatively further" provision is section 3608(e)(5).

4. "The Future of Fair Housing: Report of the National Commission on Fair Housing and Equal Opportunity," http://tinyurl.com/qaeunt5. The commission was convened by the Lawyers' Committee for Civil Rights Under Law, the Leadership Conference on Civil Rights, the NAACP Legal Defense and Educational Fund and the National Fair Housing Alliance.

5. The full text of the decision is at: http://tinyurl.com/pe85hx4. For coverage, see Eric Siegel, "Judge criticizes pooling poor in city," *The Baltimore Sun*, Jan. 7, 2005, http://tinyurl.com/p7jx4vj.

6. Douglas S. Massey and Jonathan Tannen, "A Research Note on Trends in Black Hypersegregation," *Demography*, Population Association of America, June 2015 (published online March 20, 2015), http://tinyurl.com/odta3bf.

7. See "Fair Housing and Equal Opportunity," undated, accessed October 2015, http://tinyurl.com/4a9ku8b.

8. Paul A. Jargowsky, "Architecture of Segregation: Civil Unrest, the Concentration of Poverty, and Public Policy," The Century Foundation, Aug. 7, 2015, http://tinyurl.com/q2uzvyt.

9. For an account, see Kenneth Jost, "Fair Housing Law Held to Apply Broadly," in *Supreme Court Yearbook 2014–2015*. http://tinyurl.com/po8ks9n. For case materials and pre- and post-decision coverage, see *SCOTUSblog*, http://tinyurl.com/n2o892m.

10. *Texas Department of Housing and Community Affairs v. Inclusive Communities Project, Inc.*, http://tinyurl.com/o5xfdsk. Kennedy's opinion was joined by Justices Ruth Bader Ginsburg, Stephen G. Breyer, Sonia Sotomayor and Elena Kagan; the main dissenting opinion was written by Justice Samuel A. Alito Jr. and joined by Chief Justice John G. Roberts Jr. and Justices Antonin Scalia and Clarence Thomas.

11. See "HUD Announces Final Rule on Affirmatively Furthering Fair Housing," http://tinyurl.com/ov4z4j5. The press release includes a link to the text of the rule. Castro is quoted in Emily Badger, "Long-awaited rules aim to strengthen housing act," *The Washington Post*, July 8, 2015, http://tinyurl.com/qcd8eck.

12. For comprehensive compilation of materials from plaintiff's side, see the website of the law firm Daniel & Beshara, http://tinyurl.com/ofhvejh.

13. Cory Andrews, "Supreme Court's Victory for Disparate Impact Includes a Cautionary Tale," *SCOTUSblog*, June 25, 2015, http://tinyurl.com/nkd3pf6.

14. "Housing Discrimination, Racial Segregation, and Poverty in America," The Diane Rehm Show, Sept. 16, 2015, http://tinyurl.com/ou4ysbf.

15. See Julie Hirschfeld Davis and Binyamin Appelbaum, "Obama Unveils Stricter Rules on Fair Housing," *The New York Times*, July 9, 2015, http://tinyurl.com/px3xqf4.

16. "CFPB and DOJ Order Hudson City Savings Bank to Pay $27 Million to Increase Mortgage Credit

Access in Communities Illegally Redlined," Consumer Financial Protection Bureau, Sept. 24, 2015, http://tinyurl.com/q9uec68. The settlement also includes a $5.5 million penalty. The press release includes links to the complaint and proposed consent decree. For coverage, see Richard Newman, "Hudson City Settling Case," *Herald News* (Passaic County, N.J.), Sept. 25, 2015, http://tinyurl.com/nnvnff7.

17. Margery Austin Turner et al., "Housing Discrimination Against Racial and Ethnic Minorities 2012," Urban Institute, prepared for U.S. Department of Housing and Urban Development, June 2013, http://tinyurl.com/oqn74wl. For coverage, see Shaila Dewan, "Discrimination in Housing Against Nonwhites Persists Quietly, U.S. Study Finds," *The New York Times*, June 12, 2013, p. B3; web version: http://tinyurl.com/p83kolr.

18. "HUD, Philadelphia-Area Real Estate Company Reach Agreement Resolving Racial Steering Allegations," U.S. Department of Housing and Urban Development, June 24, 2014, http://tinyurl.com/ncue7lu.

19. John Eligon, "An Indelible Black-and-White Line," *The New York Times*, Aug. 9, 2015, http://tinyurl.com/pnlfczv.

20. Darrah and DeLuca, *op. cit.*

21. "The Black Towns Project," http://tinyurl.com/np8jppc; Larry O'Dell, "All-Black Towns," *Encyclopedia of the Great Plains*, The University of Nebraska Lincoln, 2011, http://tinyurl.com/q2g3mhj.

22. James H. Hirsch, *Riot and Remembrance: The Tulsa Race War and Its Legacy* (2002); R. Thomas Dye, "Rosewood, Florida: The Destruction of an African American Community," *The Historian*, Vol. 58, No. 3 (spring 1996), pp. 605–622.

23. For a compelling account, see Isabel Wilkerson, *The Warmth of Other Suns: The Epic Story of America's Great Migration* (2010).

24. The decision is *Buchanan v. Warley*, 245 U.S. 60 (1917). The Supreme Court's unanimous decision sustained a challenge to the ordinance brought by a white property owner who had sought to sell his home to an African-American.

25. For an account, see James W. Loewen, *Sundown Towns: A Hidden Dimension of American Racism* (2005).

26. The decision is *Shelley v. Kraemer*, 334 U.S. 1 (1948).

27. See Arnold R. Hirsch, *Making the Second Ghetto: Race and Housing in Chicago 1940–1960* (1998).

28. For an overview, see Ta-Nehisi Coates, "The Case for Reparations," *The Atlantic*, June 2014, http://tinyurl.com/nopprgt.

29. HUD's website has a celebratory account of the enactment: "History of Fair Housing," http://tinyurl.com/6f7exxg.

30. The decision is *Jones v. Alfred H. Mayer Co.*, 392 U.S. 409 (1968).

31. Account drawn from Nikole Hannah-Jones, "Living Apart: How the Government Betrayed a Landmark Civil Rights Law," *ProPublica*, Oct. 29, 2012 (updated June 25, 2015), http://tinyurl.com/8jzwt3w. See also Christopher Bonastia, *Knocking on the Door: The Federal Government's Attempt to Desegregate the Suburbs* (2006).

32. The statutes have been codified as indicated: Equal Credit Opportunity Act, 15 U.S.C. §§1691 et seq.; http://tinyurl.com/pvhrt53; Home Mortgage Disclosure Act, 12 U.S.C. §§ 2801 et seq., http://tinyurl.com/2wb8xpx; Community Reinvestment Act, 12 U.S.C. §§ 2901 et seq., http://tinyurl.com/4w74td. The LGBT rule, formally entitled "Equal Access to Housing in HUD Programs — Regardless of Sexual Orientation or Gender Identity," was issued on Jan. 27, 2012, and took effect after formal publication on March 5, 2012, http://tinyurl.com/6s3jj8p.

33. See Lisa Belkin, "The Painful Lessons of the Yonkers Housing Crisis," *The New York Times*, Aug. 14, 2015, http://tinyurl.com/nhnqpg7.

34. Massey and Tannen, *op. cit.*

35. See "Fair Housing Enforcement at HUD Is Failing," in "The Future of Fair Housing: Report of the National Commission on Fair Housing and Equal Opportunity," December 2008, http://tinyurl.com/phzn4c6; National Fair Housing Alliance, "Where You Live Matters: 2015 Fair Housing Trends Report," April 30, 2015, p. 28, http://tinyurl.com/neuq462.

36. See Fernanda Santos, "Judge Faults Westchester County on Desegregation Efforts," *The New York Times*, Feb. 27, 2009, http://tinyurl.com/pyho9ja; Sam Roberts, "Housing Accord in Westchester," *The*

New York Times, Aug. 11, 2009, http://tinyurl.com/lgl36q; Mark Lungariello, "Feds: Housing accord violated," *The Journal News* (Westchester County, N.Y.), July 23, 2015, http://tinyurl.com/ph8osw3.

37. See "Fair Housing and the Foreclosure Crisis," Future of Fair Housing, *op. cit.*, http://tinyurl.com/czpj9b; Charlie Savage, "Wells Fargo Will Settle Mortgage Bias Charges," *The New York Times*, July 13, 2012, http://tinyurl.com/mdoqvqo.

38. The decision is *Havens Realty Corp. v. Coleman*, 455 U.S. 363 (1982).

39. Quoted in Jost, *op. cit.*

40. Davis and Appelbaum, *op. cit.*

41. "Where You Live," *op. cit.*, pp. 41–42.

42. *Ibid.*, pp. 43–44.

43. See "Summary of Recommendations," in Future of Fair Housing, *op. cit.*

44. For text of complaint and other materials, see website of the law firm Daniel & Beshara, http://tinyurl.com/o6ruldg.

45. See Daniel Beekman, "Mayor Murray backs off plan to increase density in single-family zones," *The Seattle Times*, July 30, 2015, http://tinyurl.com/pnsn9r2. Seattle ranked 7th in a list of the United States' 25 most expensive cities compiled by Vanessa Ho, "The 25 most expensive cities in the United States," *Expatistan*, Jan. 25, 2014, http://tinyurl.com/n2pzjkf.

46. "Housing Discrimination, Racial Segregation, and Poverty in America," *op. cit.*

47. "National Fair Housing Alliance Report Links Fair Housing to Health, Education, Transit, Wealth, and Job Opportunities," April 30, 2015, http://tinyurl.com/q2r77nd.

BIBLIOGRAPHY

Selected Sources

Books

Jackson, Kenneth T., *The Crabgrass Frontier: The Suburbanization of the United States*, **Oxford University Press, 1985.**
This comprehensive history of the development of the modern American suburb by a professor of history and social science at Columbia University traces some of the barriers that contributed to residential segregation in metropolitan areas. Includes detailed notes.

Oliver, Melvin L., and Thomas M. Shapiro, *Black Wealth/White Wealth: A New Perspective on Racial Inequality*, **Routledge, 2006 (10th anniversary edition).**
The authors link homeownership patterns to the persistent wealth inequality between white and black Americans. Includes detailed notes, list of references. Oliver is professor of sociology and dean of social sciences at the University of California, Santa Barbara; Shapiro is a professor of law and social policy at the Heller School for Social Policy and Management at Brandeis University.

Sharkey, Patrick, *Stuck in Place: Urban Neighborhoods and the End of Progress toward Racial Equality*, **University of Chicago Press, 2013.**
An associate professor of sociology at New York University details political decisions and social policies that he says have led to severe disinvestment from African-American neighborhoods, persistent segregation and declining economic opportunities. Includes detailed notes, list of references.

Articles

Bridegam, Martha, "Fair Housing: Talking Past Each Other About Cities and Segregation," *California Planning & Development Report*, **Aug. 30, 2015, http://tinyurl.com/oh4o87l.**
The article discusses the conflicting reactions to the Supreme Court's decision recognizing "disparate impact" liability for housing policies by government or the private sector that contribute to racial or ethnic segregation.

Coates, Ta-Nehisi, "The Case for Reparations," *The Atlantic*, **June 2014, http://tinyurl.com/nopprgt.**
A senior writer for *The Atlantic* details what he calls "35 years of racist housing policy" in a widely noticed call for compensatory payments to African-Americans.

Eligon, John, "A Year After Ferguson, Housing Segregation Defies Tools to Erase It," *The New York Times*, **Aug. 8, 2015, http://tinyurl.com/pnlfczv.**

A journalist examines efforts to reduce residential segregation in St. Louis against the backdrop of police-citizen clashes in the predominantly black suburb of Ferguson and indicates that barriers "remain very much a thing of the present."

Hannah-Jones, Nikole, "Living Apart: How the Government Betrayed a Landmark Law," *ProPublica*, **June 25, 2015 (originally published Oct. 29, 2012), http://tinyurl.com/8jzwt3w.**

The nonprofit investigative-reporting website critically examines the lagging enforcement of the Fair Housing Act under both Republican and Democratic presidents.

Reports and Studies

Glaeser, Edward, and Jacob Vigdor, "The End of the Segregated Century: Racial Separation in America's Neighborhoods, 1890–2010," Manhattan Institute, January 2012, http://tinyurl.com/7sz2hjh.

The report by the conservative, New York City-based think tank finds U.S. cities more integrated today than at any time since 1910 and all-white neighborhoods all but nonexistent. Glaeser is a senior fellow at the institute and an economics professor at Harvard University; Vigdor is an adjunct fellow at the institute and a professor of public policy and governance at the University of Washington.

Jargowsky, Paul A., "The Architecture of Segregation: Civil Unrest, the Concentration of Poverty, and Public Policy," The Century Foundation, August 2015, http://tinyurl.com/pbjyqhe.

A Rutgers University professor describes the increasing concentration of poverty in racially and ethnically segregated ghettos and barrios in U.S. cities and links the trend to the increased civil unrest in the wake of violent confrontations between police and residents.

Massey, Douglas, and Jonathan Tannen, "A Research Note on Trends in Black Hypersegregation," *Demography*, **Population Association of America, June 2015, http://tinyurl.com/odta3bf.**

The number of "hypersegregated" cities has declined since 1970, the researchers find, but those cities house one-third of the country's black city dwellers. Massey is a professor of sociology and Tannen a Ph.D. candidate at Princeton University.

Rothstein, Richard, "From Ferguson to Baltimore: The Fruits of Government-Sponsored Segregation," Working Economics Blog (Economic Policy Institute), April 29, 2015, http://tinyurl.com/nqs2q5x.

A researcher with the liberal think tank traces the history of government-sponsored residential segregation in Baltimore.

Swarns, Rachel L., "Biased Lending Evolves, and Blacks Face Trouble Getting Mortgages," The New York Times, Oct. 30, 2015, http://tinyurl.com/qcuxtj5.

The article recounts the increased attention to racial discrimination in the mortgage industry in the wake of the 2007–2009 recession.

For More Information

Housing and Civil Enforcement Section, NWB, Civil Rights Division, U.S. Department of Justice, 950 Pennsylvania Ave., N.W., Washington, DC 20530; 202-514-4713; www.justice.gov/crt/housing-and-civil-enforcement-section. Enforces the Fair Housing Act, the Fair Lending Act and the public accommodations provisions in Title II of the Civil Rights Act of 1964.

Manhattan Institute for Policy Research, 52 Vanderbilt Ave., New York, NY 10017; 212-599-7000; www.manhattan-institute.org. A conservative think tank, renamed in 1981 from the International Center for Economic Policy Studies, that supports market-oriented policies in, among other areas, housing and land use.

Mortgage Bankers Association, 1919 M St., N.W., 5th floor, Washington, DC; 20036; 202-557-2700; www.mba.org. Represents all segments of the real estate finance industry on legislative and regulatory issues and works to develop open and fair standards and practices for the industry.

NAACP Legal Defense and Educational Fund, 40 Rector St., 5th floor, New York, NY 10006; 212-965-2200; www.naacpldf.org. Civil rights organization that has been involved in fair-housing litigation through much of its history.

National Association of Housing and Redevelopment Officials, 630 I St., N.W., Washington, DC 20001; 202-289-3500; www.nahro.org. Represents housing and redevelopment officials who administer federal housing programs, including public housing and section 8 housing choice vouchers.

National Association of Realtors, 500 New Jersey Ave., N.W., Washington, DC 20001; 202-383-1000; www.realtor.org. An influential trade association with 1 million members in the commercial and residential real estate industries.

National Disability Rights Network, 820 1st St., N.E., Suite 740, Washington, DC 20002; 202-408-9514; www.ndrn.org. Advocates for basic rights for persons with disabilities, including nondiscrimination in housing.

National Fair Housing Alliance, 1101 Vermont Ave., N.W., #710, Washington, DC 20005; 202-898-1661; www.nationalfairhousing.org. A consortium of more than 220 private, nonprofit fair housing organizations, state and local civil rights agencies and individuals.

Office of Fair Housing and Equal Opportunity, U.S. Department of Housing and Urban Development, 451 7th St., S.W., Washington, DC 20410; 800-669-9777; www.hud.gov/fairhousing. The office responsible for the administration, enforcement, development and public understanding of federal fair-housing provisions.

Poverty & Race Research Action Council, 1200 18th St., N.W., #200, Washington, DC 20036; 202-906-8023; www.prrac.org. Civil rights policy organization convened by major civil rights, civil liberties and anti-poverty groups in 1989-90 to connect social science research to advocacy in those fields.

12 Fighting Urban Poverty

Jane Fullerton Lemons

Philadelphia child-care worker Tianna Gaines-Turner, here with her husband Marcus, left, and uncle Steve, told the House Budget Committee last year that the hourly wages she and Marcus earn are not enough to support them and their three children. "No one who lives in poverty wants to stay on government assistance programs," she testified. An estimated 45 million Americans have annual earnings below the federal poverty line — $24,250 for a family of four.

From *CQ Researcher*,
July 17, 2015.

To begin to understand urban poverty, consider the lives of Tianna Gaines-Turner and her husband.

They both have jobs but live in public housing in inner-city Philadelphia, one of the most impoverished big cities in the United States. He earns $8.25 an hour working full time at a grocery deli counter; she earns $10.88 an hour working part-time providing child care. Together they typically bring home about $300 a week.

As Gaines-Turner told the House Budget Committee last year, that's not enough to cover living expenses for themselves and their three children, all of whom have medical problems. The family must supplement its income with food benefits provided by the Supplemental Nutrition Assistance Program, formerly known as the food stamp program.[1]

"No one who lives in poverty wants to stay on government assistance programs," she testified. "We want to be independent. We want to work hard — and believe in the American Dream that if I work every day, get up at 7 in the morning, and my husband gets up, and we work, that we'll have the same jobs benefits, wages, paid sick leave as everyone else."[2]

That's long been the dream not only of Gaines-Turner but also of the estimated 45 million Americans throughout the nation who subsist on annual incomes below the federal poverty line, this year defined as $24,250 for a family of four.[3]

Yet, 50 years after President Lyndon B. Johnson declared a "war on poverty" and mustered an arsenal of federal programs to wage it, urban poverty — much of it deep, concentrated and seemingly

Poverty Rose Nationwide in 2000s

The proportion of Americans living in poverty rose from just over 11 percent in 2000 to 14.5 percent in 2013. The Midwest experienced the biggest shift, with the poverty rate climbing 3.6 percentage points. Poverty remained highest in the South, increasing to more than 16 percent. Nearly 15 percent of Westerners lived in poverty in 2013, as did nearly 13 percent of Northeasterners.

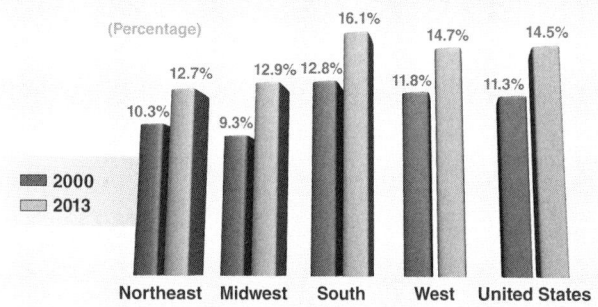

U.S. Poverty Rates, by Region, 2000 and 2013

Source: "Table 9. Poverty, by Region," Historical Poverty Tables, U.S. Census Bureau, located at http://tinyurl.com/csklehg

intractable — persists in neighborhoods stretching from New York, Philadelphia, Los Angeles and Seattle to Rust Belt Midwest cities struggling with job losses and blight in the wake of the 2007-09 recession.

According to a study by City Observatory, an urban policy think tank in Portland, Ore., the number of high-poverty urban neighborhoods in the nation's 51 largest cities tripled — to 3,100 — between 1970 and 2010.[4] Moreover, the number of poor persons living in those areas doubled over the 40 years, the study found. And two-thirds of the tracts defined as high poverty areas in 1970 remained so in 2010.[5]

"Poverty rates are still much higher than they should be, inexcusably high," says Valerie Wilson, director of the Program on Race, Ethnicity and the Economy at the Economic Policy Institute, a liberal think tank in Washington. "That's partly due to the Great Recession and the slow pace of recovery."

Sociologists Karl Alexander and Linda Olson of Johns Hopkins University note that "poverty is colorblind" and extends beyond the urban black community. "Many whites live side by side African-Americans in some of the country's poorest urban neighborhoods," they said.[6]

Still, poverty hits blacks hardest. In 2013, the latest year for which federal figures are available, the poverty level for blacks was 27.2 percent and 23.5 percent for Hispanics — roughly twice the 12.3 percent rate for whites.[7]

The federal data also show that black children are four times more likely to be living in poverty than white or Asian children, according to a new study.[8]

Overall, the analysis found that 20 percent of U.S. children, or 14.7 million, lived in poverty in 2013. At the same time, the poverty rate declined for Hispanic, white and Asian children. The rate for black children held steady at about 38 percent, making them significantly more likely than other demographic groups to live in poverty. In addition, the total number of impoverished black children (4.2 million) appears to have surpassed the total number of impoverished white children (4.1 million), even though there are three times as many white children as black children.[9]

In the South, 16.1 percent of the population lived under the poverty threshold in 2013. The rate in the West was 14.7 percent; Midwest, 12.9 percent; and Northeast, 12.7 percent.[10]

In recent months, urban poverty has made front-page headlines as a backdrop to civil unrest following allegations of police misconduct against African-Americans in Ferguson, Mo., Baltimore, Cleveland, Oakland, Calif., and elsewhere. But what experts define as the underlying causes of poverty — racism, crime, unemployment, poor schools, family breakdown, high incarceration rates among black men, and urban blight, among them — long predate those recent episodes. And solutions offered by advocacy groups, policy analysts and political candidates remain elusive.

Historically, ideas for reducing poverty have broken along partisan and ideological lines, with liberals typically advocating more social programs and federal spending, and conservatives calling for greater personal responsibility and a smaller governmental role. Both sides agree, however, that alleviating urban poverty depends significantly on economic growth and the nation's ability to provide more, and better-paying, jobs.

Six years after the end of the 2007-09 recession, unemployment remains high in many impoverished urban areas, where, according to one study, 83 percent of the short-term unemployed and 87 percent of the long-term unemployed live.[11]

It's been nearly half a century since a Johnson initiative, the National Advisory Commission on Civil Disorders, commonly known as the Kerner Commission, looked into the causes of violence and civil unrest that had been ravaging cities in the 1960s.[12]

That commission made its famous observation that "our nation is moving toward two societies, one black, one white — separate and unequal." It offered recommendations for addressing the problems of urban poverty and unrest, but they never gained much political traction.[13]

In the years following the Kerner Commission's report, the nation began a decades-long crackdown on crime that led to longer sentences, often for drug crimes, that fell disproportionately on urban black men. "Blacks are much more likely to be arrested for drugs and other offenses, and they are now about five times more likely to go to prison than whites, a disparity far out of proportion to racial differences in criminal offending," wrote Bruce Western, a professor of sociology and criminal justice at Harvard University.[14]

In a study of the "prison-to-poverty" cycle, University of Washington sociologist Becky Pettit documented how poverty leads to crime and how prisons in turn fuel poverty. The cycle is particularly pronounced among black men. In 1980, some 10 percent of young African-American men who dropped out of high school were in prison or jail, according to the study. By 2008, the rate was 37 percent.[15]

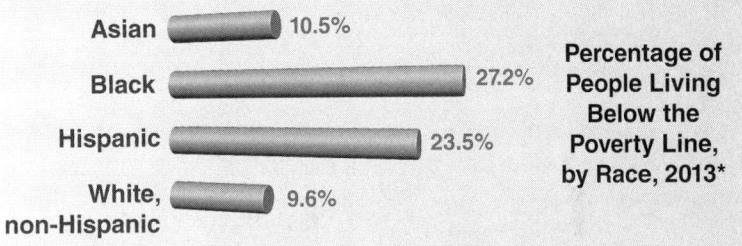

Black Poverty Rate Twice That of Whites, Asians

More than one in four blacks lived below the poverty line in 2013, more than twice the rate of non-Hispanic whites and Asians, according to a Census Bureau survey. Poverty among Hispanics was nearly as high as for blacks.

Percentage of People Living Below the Poverty Line, by Race, 2013*

- Asian: 10.5%
- Black: 27.2%
- Hispanic: 23.5%
- White, non-Hispanic: 9.6%

* The 2013 poverty line was an annual income of $23,834 or less for a family of four.

Source: Carmen DeNavas-Walt and Bernadette D. Proctor, "Income and Poverty in the United States: 2013," U.S. Census Bureau, September 2014, p. 13, http://tinyurl.com/ppj9y43

"While elected officials talked tough on crime, economic catastrophe unfolded in American cities," Western said. "Urban employment in manufacturing declined. When the jobs left, people followed, often leaving behind neighborhoods of concentrated poverty. In Baltimore from 1978 to 2014, the population dropped from 815,000 to 620,000. The city lost 90,000 jobs. Four years after the 2008 recession, a third of the city's population, mostly African American, was on food stamps."

In Detroit, the city's poverty rate is 38 percent, but a United Way study found the rate is even higher when the cost of living — for housing, child care, food, transportation and health care — is factored in. Among families in Detroit, which has been hit hard by job losses in the auto industry, massive population outflows and grinding urban blight, 67 percent live under the poverty line or are "asset-limited."[16]

By asset-limited, the United Way study is referring to households like Gaines-Turner's that have working members who are one missed paycheck from poverty. "The core of the problem is that these jobs do not pay enough to afford the basics of housing, child care, food, health care, and transportation," the study said.

As economists, politicians and others debate urban poverty, here are some of the questions being asked:

Earned Income Tax Credit Garners Bipartisan Support

Forty-year-old program aided 28 million workers in 2013.

One of the federal government's key programs for helping workers with low or moderate incomes is the Earned Income Tax Credit, or EITC.

"A tax credit means more money in your pocket. It reduces the amount of tax you owe and may also give you a refund," according to the Internal Revenue Service (IRS).[1]

To claim the credit, single filers or heads of households with no children must earn less than $14,820 a year (income limits are higher for those with dependent children). For tax year 2013, nearly 28 million taxpayers received more than $66 billion in EITC credits. The average credit was $2,407.[2]

In addition to the federal credit, 25 states and the District of Columbia have their own versions of the EITC.[3]

Congress must renew the tax credit when it expires in 2017, and most observers say it enjoys bipartisan support and will likely be reapproved. The EITC's critics, however, question its cost and note it has a high "error" rate that leads to waste.

The EITC was instituted in 1975 under Republican President Gerald Ford as an alternative to cash welfare and was expanded under Republican Ronald Reagan and Democrat Bill Clinton. While liberals (and some conservatives) support it as a supplement to other safety-net programs, conservatives (and some liberals) back it because it rewards work.[4]

Scott Winship, a senior fellow at the Manhattan Institute, a conservative think tank in New York that seeks to encourage economic choice, calls the EITC a successful example of how tax policy can change behavior and encourage upward mobility. "It sends a real strong signal that working is going to pay to a much better degree than it has before," he says.

An analysis by the Congressional Research Service, which provides impartial advice to Congress, found the EITC "has encouraged single mothers to enter the workforce and it has reduced poverty among families with children."[5]

In addition, research by the Brookings Institution, a centrist Washington think tank, has tracked the geographic distribution of EITC recipients. It found that in 2007, low-income workers claimed $47.5 billion through the EITC, with 60 percent of that going to residents of the 100 largest metropolitan areas.[6]

Jon Hartley, co-founder of a financial information firm, said the EITC also helps the broader economy by expanding the labor supply, thus lifting the labor force participation rate from its near record low of 62.8 percent in 2013 to 63 percent in 2014, and reducing wealth inequality. Unlike some policies implemented to strengthen the economy after the recession of 2007-09, Hartley wrote in a blog, "pro-growth fiscal policies, like an expanded EITC, are the best policy options to reduce wealth inequality by giving economic mobility to low- and middle-income workers. Such a pro-growth policy regime would be a winning anti-poverty strategy."[7]

Billionaire investor Warren Buffett argued recently that an expanded EITC would benefit low-wage workers more than a

Would more federal aid reduce poverty in urban areas?

Ten major anti-poverty programs and tax credits account for about one-sixth of all federal spending, according to the Congressional Budget Office.[17]

During the past 40 years, federal spending for these programs — cash payments for, or assistance in, obtaining health care, food, housing or education — has more than tripled as a share of gross domestic product. Adjusted for inflation, total spending for low-income people rose from $55 billion in 1972 (when just five of the 10 programs existed) to $588 billion in 2012.[18]

The urban poor face problems that differ from those of low-income residents of rural and suburban areas.

"We have yet to win the war on urban poverty, and several challenges persist for poor city residents,

higher minimum wage. "In essence, the EITC rewards work and provides an incentive for workers to improve their skills. Equally important, it does not distort market forces, thereby maximizing employment."[8]

President Obama has proposed expanding the EITC to include more workers without children, a plan endorsed by Rep. Paul Ryan, R-Wis., chairman of the powerful House Ways and Means Committee which controls tax legislation.[9] Although a bill has not yet been introduced, Congress will have to take action on extending and enlarging key provisions of the EITC, which are set to run out in 2017.[10]

But others question the cost of expanding the EITC and note its high rate of errors, which critics often characterize as fraud.

The Government Accountability Office (GAO), an independent federal agency that provides auditing and investigative services to Congress, found that the EITC program had an "improper payment error rate" of 24 percent, costing $14.5 billion in fiscal 2013. The GAO did not use the term "fraud" but said the error rate represents "duplicate or erroneous payments, payments to ineligible recipients, or payments for ineligible services," which also would include taxpayer filing errors and IRS processing errors.[11]

At the American Enterprise Institute, a conservative think tank in Washington that studies the economy and social welfare, poverty studies fellow Robert Doar and research fellow Angela Rachidi said Congress must consider the cost and problems associated with the EITC before expanding it.[12]

"It is rare in American politics that lawmakers from both sides of the aisle support a similar policy proposal, let alone one that costs billions of dollars," they wrote. "But before jumping on board, lawmakers should consider these issues and determine whether the trade-offs are worth the expense."

— *Jane Fullerton Lemons*

[1]"EITC, Earned Income Tax Credit, Questions and Answers," Internal Revenue Service, undated, accessed June 30, 2015, http://tinyurl.com/q58zwtb.

[2]"Earned Income Tax Credit and Other Refundable Credits," Internal Revenue Service, undated, accessed June 30, 2015, http://tinyurl.com/o2b2t3q.

[3]Jake Grovum, "A Renewed Push for Earned Income Tax Credit in States," Pew Charitable Trusts, Feb. 11, 2014, http://tinyurl.com/or793l6; "Policy Basics: State Earned Income Tax Credits," Center on Budget and Policy Priorities, Jan. 28, 2015, http://tinyurl.com/p55qb2n.

[4]Jonathan Chait, "Obama to Republicans: You're Right, Let's Expand the Earned Income Tax Credit," *New York*, March 4, 2014, http://tinyurl.com/omdxcus.

[5]Margot L. Crandall-Hollick, "The Earned Income Tax Credit (EITC): An Economic Analysis," Congressional Research Service, June 2, 2015, http://tinyurl.com/pd98o6c.

[6]Emily Garr and Elizabeth Kneebone, "Responding to the New Geography of Poverty: Metropolitan Trends in the Earned Income Tax Credit," Brookings Institution, Feb. 17, 2011, http://tinyurl.com/og6whek.

[7]Jon Hartley, "How Federal Reserve Quantitative Easing Expanded Wealth Inequality," *Forbes* blog, June 25, 2015, http://tinyurl.com/ncaf62t; for more on labor force participation rates, see Bureau of Labor Statistics, July 7, 2015, http://tinyurl.com/3o3g52o.

[8]Warren Buffett, "Better Than Raising the Minimum Wage," *The Wall Street Journal*, May 21, 2015, http://tinyurl.com/nzrd3n3.

[9]"Paul Ryan Looking for Common Ground with Democrats on Taxes," "Meet the Press," NBC, Feb. 1, 2015, http://tinyurl.com/oz58dp4.

[10]Chuck Marr and Chye-Ching Huang, "Strengthening the EITC for Childless Workers Would Promote Work and Reduce Poverty," Center on Budget and Policy Priorities, Feb. 20, 2015, http://tinyurl.com/o687no5.

[11]"Improper Payments: Inspector General Reporting of Agency Compliance under the Improper Payments Elimination and Recovery Act," Government Accountability Office, Dec. 9, 2014, http://tinyurl.com/o7h4y57.

[12]Robert Doar and Angela Rachidi, "Are the costs of the EITC worth it?" American Enterprise Institute, June 26, 2015, http://tinyurl.com/ogjxkku.

---

including concentrated poverty, crime, affordable-housing shortages, a lack of investment in good public-transit systems, job loss and segregation," according to Tracey Ross, a senior policy analyst at the Center for American Progress, a liberal Washington think tank.[19]

Although analysts generally agree that government has a role to play in combating urban poverty, they disagree — largely along ideological lines — about what that role should be and how much it should cost.

"While government anti-poverty programs have had many successes, more can clearly be done," says Arloc Sherman, a senior fellow at the Center on Budget and Policy Priorities, a Washington think tank that analyzes government spending. "This is particularly important because we know poverty affects people's present well-being and future opportunities to succeed and contribute to society."

Sherman points to studies that show safety net programs — such as Social Security, housing subsidies, tax credits and food stamps — have lifted millions of Americans above the poverty line.[20]

Michael Tanner, a senior fellow at the libertarian Cato Institute, agrees government has a role but says, "It's not the one we're pursuing, of just giving money to people."

Says Tanner, "We haven't done a very good job of helping people get out of poverty." The focus should be on helping people prepare for and find jobs by providing job training, encouraging education, and discouraging pregnancy outside of marriage, he says. That is "not a moral judgment — it's an economic one," he adds, because households headed by a single mother are more likely to be poor compared with married-couple families.

Many conservatives make similar arguments, particularly about the need to focus on family structure. Promoting work and restoring marriage "would be a better battle plan for eradicating poverty in America than spending more money on failed programs," said Robert Rector, a senior research fellow at the conservative Heritage Foundation think tank in Washington.[21]

Even those who agree with that premise believe the government must put its focus on employment. Current policies fail to help people become self-sufficient, says Robert Doar, a fellow in poverty studies at the American Enterprise Institute, a conservative think tank in Washington. "I have become more and more focused on programs that build human capital" — particularly job-training and education programs that help prepare young people for work — "that address not just the symptoms but the causes of poverty," Doar says.

Liberals point to studies showing that poor people do work. David Cooper, an economic analyst at the Economic Policy Institute, cites research showing that 63 percent of those below the federal poverty threshold work, with 44 percent holding full-time jobs.[22]

The key problem, liberals say, is low pay.

"The majority of the folks that can work, do work," Cooper says. "A lot of these folks are just not getting enough money from their time in the labor market to escape poverty. That means we need to be strengthening the safety net supports that the government provides. But we also need to be finding ways to make work more rewarding" in terms of pay and benefits.

For liberals, that means pursuing policies that boost wages. To boost wage-growth and reduce poverty rates, a policy agenda must include provisions to raise the minimum wage, raise the overtime threshold and strengthen workers' collective-bargaining rights, said a study by the Economic Policy Institute.[23]

Do federal housing programs alleviate urban poverty?

Housing is most Americans' largest monthly expense. According to the Department of Housing and Urban Development (HUD), "families who spend more than 30 percent of their income on rent or mortgage payments are considered cost burdened and may have difficulty affording necessities such as food, clothing, transportation and medical care." The department estimates 12 million households pay more than 50 percent of their annual income for housing.[24]

The federal government's three largest rental assistance programs provide more than 4.5 million units of assisted housing. Of those, the vast majority — 87 percent — are in metro areas.[25]

Sherman, of the Center on Budget and Policy Priorities, says federal housing programs have a demonstrable effect on poverty rates. "Current housing programs lift a particularly high share of those they serve above the poverty line by our estimates but serve a particularly low share of families poor enough to be eligible," he says.

In 2010, about 10 million Americans in 5 million low-income households received housing assistance, according to Sherman's research. Although the number of recipients is lower than for other federal safety net programs, the reach is greater: 37 percent of those recipients were lifted above the poverty line because of the housing assistance.[26]

Sherman says housing programs could be strengthened by expanding the number of government-funded vouchers, which provide the poor with financial help to secure housing.

Providing the opportunity to move into better neighborhoods was at the heart of a Supreme Court case this year concerning the 1968 Fair Housing Act, which made it illegal to refuse to sell or rent dwellings to individuals because of their race, religion, sex or national origin.

A Texas group that helps lower-income black families find housing in the Dallas suburbs had accused state officials of violating the act: The families rely on housing vouchers, and landlords receiving federal low-income tax credits are required to accept the vouchers. The fair housing group argued that Texas officials violated the Fair Housing Act when they gave a disproportionate share of the tax credits to landlords in minority neighborhoods, which had the effect of concentrating minorities in low-income areas.

The argument before the Supreme Court was whether people suing under the Fair Housing Act must prove intentional discrimination or merely show that the challenged practice had produced a "disparate impact," as occurred in Texas. In a 5-4 decision, the court ruled June 25 that lawsuits can proceed even if the purported discrimination was unintentional.[27]

Civil rights groups applauded the decision, saying a looser interpretation of the law is crucial to fighting housing discrimination, while critics said the ruling makes it too easy to get claims into court.[28]

Richard Rothstein, a research associate at the Economic Policy Institute, has studied how government policies at all levels have contributed to housing segregation and urban poverty.[29] "We have a myth today that the ghettos in metropolitan areas around the country are what the Supreme Court calls 'de-facto' — just the accident of the fact that people have not enough income to move into middle class neighborhoods or because real estate agents steered black and white families to different neighborhoods or because there was white flight," Rothstein said.[30] Practices that contributed to racially segregated ghettos included restrictive covenants that barred minorities from moving into white neighborhoods and the construction of large public housing projects that concentrated minority tenants in blighted areas.[31]

In the wake of the Supreme Court decision, the Obama administration said it will require cities and towns to show they are complying with the Fair Housing Act and to set goals for how they will reduce residential segregation.[32]

Building more low-income housing in middle-class and affluent neighborhoods would give more children in low-income families a chance at better educational

Number of High-Poverty Neighborhoods Rose

The urban poor are increasingly living in neighborhoods of concentrated poverty, according to a 2014 study. In 1970, 28 percent lived in a "high-poverty" area, defined as a neighborhood with a poverty rate of 30 percent or more. In 2010, 39 percent did. Moreover, the number of high-poverty neighborhoods tripled and their populations doubled during the 40-year period.

Growth in High-Poverty Tracts in 15 U.S. Metro Areas, 1970-2010

Metro Area	Population of High-Poverty Tracts, 1970	High-Poverty Tracts, 1970	Population of High-Poverty Tracts, 2010	High-Poverty Tracts, 2010
Atlanta	47,035	26	83,594	76
Baltimore	71,252	38	52,593	55
Boston	19,211	17	63,797	54
Chicago	159,379	77	211,889	199
Cleveland	42,435	22	96,651	113
Dallas	40,257	18	116,002	72
Denver	20,343	16	69,460	48
Detroit	38,589	20	228,450	211
District of Columbia	26,201	19	46,419	41
Kansas City, Mo-Kan.	18,469	15	56,441	64
Los Angeles	84,119	76	309,683	210
New York	404,587	198	632,754	387
Philadelphia	92,825	45	240,577	149
Phoenix	24,510	24	145,537	96
Portland, Ore.	7,615	8	22,961	18

Source: Joe Cortright, "Lost in Place," City Observatory, Sept. 12, 2014, http://tinyurl.com/p2v22jg

Faith Calhoun and her 9-year-old daughter Olivia, waiting for a bus in Denver, have lived for two years at the Crossing, a transitional housing program for families. The poverty rate in the West rose from 11.8 percent in 2010 to 14.7 percent in 2013.

opportunities and more diverse social networks, says Kristen Lewis, co-director of Measure of America, a Brooklyn, N.Y., advocacy group that uses statistical data to track the nation's well-being.[33]

"Housing is more than just a house," Lewis said. "It's a fulcrum of opportunity because where you live determines where you go to school, who your neighbors are, how safe your streets are, how easy it is to get to your job, how hard it is to exercise and get healthy foods. It even determines the air you're breathing every day."

Another challenge facing low-income housing advocates is gentrification because it can force low-income residents out of affordable urban areas when higher-income homeowners move in. Some big-city mayors are seeking to minimize gentrification's effects. One study, though, says fears of gentrification are overblown and may be obscuring more significant trends in urban poverty, the most important being the concentration of poverty.[34]

"There are certainly examples of neighborhoods where poor residents have been displaced from their homes by rising prices," wrote economist Joe Cortright of Impresa, an economic consulting firm. He co-authored the City Observatory report, which concluded that the persistence and spread of poverty — not gentrification — are the biggest issues facing cities. "While such instances of neighborhood change are striking, our study shows they are actually quite rare."[35]

Should the business community play a larger role in solving urban poverty?

Many analysts see private efforts as essential to creating jobs, improving wages and benefits and fostering economic growth.

"There are no silver bullets," says Jeffrey Buchanan, senior domestic policy adviser at Oxfam America, the U.S. branch of an international organization seeking solutions to poverty. "But with all these things, certainly there's connectivity. There's a lot of great examples of companies stepping up and making private commitments to increase their wages or to change their benefit structure to support low-wage working families."

Buchanan cited Facebook changing its policy to require its service contractors — "the folks cleaning the office at night or working in the cafeteria or the security guards" — to pay a $15 minimum wage.[36]

"As more companies do that," he added, "it's going to put pressure on other companies that don't pay their workers well, that pay poverty level wages, to consider increasing their wages to compete."

A Microsoft official agreed. "More broadly in the country, obviously there's been more of a discussion about income inequality, wages and benefits," said Bradford L. Smith, general counsel of Microsoft, which said in March it would require many of its contract workers to receive 15 paid sick and vacation days. "In this area of paid time off, we've concluded that it's not just good for people, but good for business."[37]

Companies that have said they will raise their starting pay above the federal minimum wage include Wal-Mart, Target, McDonald's, Gap and Ikea.[38]

Some analysts say, however, that increasing the minimum wage could, over the long term, harm the very people it is designed to help.

"Unless higher wages translate into higher productivity, the cost of paying higher wages will tend to lead to higher prices in sectors that employ large numbers of low-wage workers," which could ultimately lead to job losses, said Reihan Salam, executive editor of the *National Review*, a conservative magazine.[39]

But liberals point out that the low minimum wage means workers have to rely on public assistance; one study noted workers in the bottom 20 percent of wage earners receive more than $45 billion in government assistance each year from the six primary means-tested income-support programs.*[40]

The private sector can help impoverished urban neighborhoods in other ways, researchers say. They note the importance of "anchor institutions" — large entities that provide goods and services, create jobs and foster community relations in poor neighborhoods. That could mean opening a department store or supermarket, a hospital or other health care facility, or a school or university.[41] In fact, big-box stores — such as Wal-Mart, Target and Home Depot — have begun to locate in poorer urban areas.

According to *Governing*, a magazine about state and local government, "The country's largest retailers have oversaturated rural and suburban America, and companies view urban centers as huge, largely untapped markets. Meanwhile, cities are desperate for the property and sales tax revenue the stores can generate, not to mention the jobs they'll create and the access to fresh food they can provide at a time when the issue of food deserts has become a national concern."[42]

"It's like having an anchor in a shopping mall," said Ed McMahon, senior resident fellow with the Urban Land Institute, a research group in Washington that focuses on land use. "It's bringing people into the neighborhood."[43]

In Baltimore, the importance of CVS pharmacies to impoverished neighborhoods became apparent after two of its stores were badly damaged by rioters following the funeral of Freddie Gray, a black man whose death protesters blamed on police negligence. Residents and city officials worried that CVS would pull out, eliminating jobs and leaving customers with no convenient place to get medicines. Baltimore City Health Commissioner Leana Wen told NBC News "hundreds, if not thousands" of residents had been affected by the closures of the CVS and other neighboring pharmacies. For many individuals it's a case of life and death."

---

*The six programs are the Earned Income Tax Credit (EITC); the Supplemental Nutrition Assistance Program (SNAP), also known as food stamps; the Low Income Home Energy Assistance Program (LIHEAP); the Supplemental Nutrition Program for Women, Infants, and Children (WIC); the Section 8 Housing Choice Voucher program; and the Temporary Assistance for Needy Families program (TANF) or equivalent state and/or local cash assistance programs.

In May, CVS announced it will reopen the stores and donate $50,000 to the United Way's Maryland Unites Fund and the Baltimore Community Foundation's Fund for Rebuilding Baltimore.[44]

Doar, of the American Enterprise Institute, says businesses can not only provide employment to urban residents but also offer workforce training.

"The businesses that are really interested in developing their workforce — in other words, they're willing to take a chance on person A, who they will pay, but they'll also train and nurture and help grow — are very effective in helping alleviate poverty," Doar says. "And they're more effective than businesses that just provide a job."

Obama's My Brother's Keeper Alliance, announced in February 2014, seeks to encourage such training. A private effort funded by American Express and other companies, it provides education, job training and mentoring to young men of color.[45]

Robert Woodson, a black conservative and longtime activist who founded the Washington-based Center for Neighborhood Enterprise in 1981, advocates a "third way" of addressing poverty: investing private capital in alliances focused on creating jobs and getting results.[46]

As he explained in a newspaper column, "The most powerful means to accomplish this goal was not through government programs or large-scale associations and organizations but by identifying indigenous groups that live in the low-income communities and linking them to sources of support and recognition."[47]

His group assists community and faith-based organizations with training and technical assistance so that low-income residents can address the needs of their impoverished neighborhoods. One of its programs — designed to prevent youth violence — has been adapted in more than 30 schools nationwide.[48]

BACKGROUND

Expanding Slums

In 1890, social reformer Jacob Riis' landmark exposé of life in New York City tenements, *How the Other Half Lives*, opened the eyes of many Americans to the appalling conditions overtaking the nation's cities.

Policies enacted during the Clinton administration contributed to the nation's high incarceration rates by mandating lengthy prison sentences, particularly for drug crimes. The House Judiciary Committee has begun studying ways to improve criminal justice, including changing laws seen as over-criminalizing certain behaviors. University of Washington sociologist Becky Pettit has documented how poverty leads to crime and prison, especially for black men. In 1980, some 10 percent of young African-American men who dropped out of high school were in prison or jail, according to the study. By 2008, the rate was 37 percent. Above, the California state prison at Chino.

"Today three-fourths of [New York] people live in the tenements, and the nineteenth century drift of the population to the cities is sending ever increasing multitudes to crowd them," he wrote. "The fifteen thousand tenant houses that were the despair of the sanitarian in the past generation have swelled into thirty-seven thousand."[49]

Riis' book came at a pivotal time in the history of urban America. Industrialization led to rapid population growth in the cities, as rural residents and European immigrants sought better jobs and pay in urban factories.

As Riis and others documented, overcrowding, disease and crime plagued many urban neighborhoods, and slums expanded.[50] But the Progressive era (about 1890 to 1920) led to measures aimed at alleviating urban poverty: Congress passed legislation to improve sanitation, establish the eight-hour workday, ban child labor and require workers' compensation for federal employees.

However, not all Americans shared equally in these advances. Nine in 10 African-Americans lived in the South at the turn of the century, where Jim Crow laws legalized entrenched segregation. The Supreme Court in 1896 had upheld the power of states to create two "separate but equal" societies in its infamous *Plessy v. Ferguson* ruling.[51]

The South's racial violence, oppression and lack of jobs spurred the "Great Migration" of about 5 million blacks from the region to Northern and Western states between 1915 and 1960; before World War II, the majority moved to Northern cities such as Chicago and Detroit; after World War II, the most popular destinations became Western cities such as Los Angeles and San Francisco.[52]

But racial conditions were not much better in the North and West. In his research into state-sponsored residential segregation, Rothstein of the Economic Policy Institute has tallied the barriers people of color faced through the years, including zoning rules that classified white neighborhoods as residential and black neighborhoods as commercial or industrial; segregated public housing projects that replaced integrated low-income areas; and suburban racial homogeneity enforced by the Federal Housing Administration with policies such as denying mortgage insurance to blacks or backing developments with racially restrictive deed covenants.[53]

While blacks in the South had long experienced white hostility, they often received similar treatment in the North, both before the Great Migration and for decades thereafter. In Baltimore, when a black lawyer tried to move into a white neighborhood in 1910, the city council and mayor responded to white protests by passing a residential segregation ordinance. Baltimore's mayor explained: "Blacks should be quarantined in isolated slums in order to reduce the incidence of civil disturbance, to prevent the spread of communicable disease into the nearby White neighborhoods, and to protect property values among the White majority."[54]

Depression Era

The federal government began efforts to alleviate poverty in the 1930s with the onset of the Great Depression. When President Franklin D. Roosevelt took office in 1933, more than 13 million people, nearly 25 percent of the workforce, were unemployed, including about half of African-Americans. He responded with the New Deal — a series of measures designed to reinvigorate the economy.[55]

CHRONOLOGY

1876-1929 *Industrialization leads to rapid urban growth, fueling poverty and sparking reform efforts.*

1876 Fifteenth Amendment grants suffrage to African-American men. . . . First "Jim Crow" segregation law passed in Tennessee, mandating separation of blacks and whites, a policy upheld by the Supreme Court in *Plessy v. Ferguson* (1896).

1900 Some 30 million people, or 30 percent of the U.S. population, live in cities, many in slums.

1907 A record 1.25 million immigrants arrive at Ellis Island in New York.

1911 Triangle Shirtwaist Factory fire in New York City kills 146, mostly young women, propelling movement to improve working conditions.

1915 "Great Migration" of blacks from the South to Northern cities begins.

1929-1964 *Great Depression hits; World War II spurs economic recovery, but poverty persists.*

1929 Stock market crashes.

1932 Half of black Americans are unemployed.

1933 Franklin D. Roosevelt becomes president and initiates the New Deal.

1938 Fair Labor Standards Act establishes minimum wage and overtime pay.

1941 U.S. entry into World War II leads to creation of 17 million jobs and spurs recovery from the Depression.

1954 Supreme Court overturns "separate but equal" doctrine with landmark *Brown v. Board of Education* ruling, helping set the stage for the civil rights movement.

1964 President Lyndon B. Johnson declares "war on poverty," launches Great Society programs.

1964 Food stamp program becomes permanent.

1965 Medicare, a health care program for the elderly, and Medicaid, for the poor, established.

1968 Kerner Commission concludes that America is moving toward racially separate societies. . . . Martin Luther King Jr. and Robert F. Kennedy assassinated; widespread unrest follows. . . . Civil Rights and Fair Housing acts passed.

1975-2007 *Social programs come under scrutiny.*

1975 Earned Income Tax Credit provides alternative to cash welfare.

1981 President Ronald Reagan takes office, calls for welfare cuts.

1993 Bill Clinton becomes president after campaigning "to end welfare as we know it."

1994 Clinton signs Violent Crime Control and Law Enforcement Act, later criticized for fueling mass incarceration.

1996 Clinton signs major welfare overhaul that replaces Aid to Families with Dependent Children with Temporary Assistance for Needy Families (TANF).

2009-Present *Massive job losses and plunge in home values occur amid steep recession.*

2009 Congress raises minimum wage to $7.25 an hour. . . . Unemployment peaks at 10 percent, hitting double digits for the first time in 26 years.

2010 Long-term unemployment reaches a historic high of 6.7 million people, or 45 percent of the unemployed.

2014 Fourteen states and the District of Columbia enact minimum wage increases.

2015 President Obama calls for raising the minimum wage from $7.25 to $10.10 an hour and guaranteeing paid sick leave for workers. . . . Supreme Court reaffirms Fair Housing Act, and Obama administration says it will enforce the act by requiring cities to scrutinize their housing patterns for racial bias.

Jobs Program Helps Men Reform Their Lives

"Our core belief is that work works."

At age 39, Nazerine Griffin recalled, he was using and selling drugs and living in a homeless shelter in New York City.[1]

Then Griffin joined the transitional jobs program Ready, Willing & Able (RWA), which mainly helps formerly homeless or incarcerated men. In New York City, the program's "men in blue," wearing distinctive uniforms, regularly clean 150 miles of city streets. In Philadelphia, they tend Fairmount and LOVE parks and Rittenhouse Square.[2]

Now, after completing the nine- to 12-month program and working his way up at RWA, Griffin is director of the Brooklyn center where he once was a client.[3]

"We do all we can to give these men the tools they need to live a better, a healthier, a more productive life, one that brings them some happiness," he said. "Our core belief . . . is that work works. Our men need a job, they need a home, and they need the ability to deal effectively with the changes and challenges that life throws at them."[4]

RWA was founded in 1990 by George and Harriett McDonald's Doe Fund, which provides jobs, housing and food to the needy, coupled with social services, job training and career development. George McDonald was an apparel industry executive when he started the fund during an upturn in homelessness; it now operates three shelters in New York and one in Philadelphia. Participants are barred from using drugs or alcohol, a policy enforced through random drug testing.

RWA also has low-income housing programs as well as programs for youths and veterans. The Doe Fund operates several so-called enterprise projects designed to provide jobs and training. All the programs combined serve more than 1,000 people a day. Funding comes from a variety of sources — 33 percent from private donations, 41 percent from city contracts, 10 percent from government grants and the rest from other sources, including revenue from enterprise projects.[5]

Those projects put RWA's clients in the workforce, provide services and generate income that goes back into the programs' coffers. The men operate a pest management company, collect leftover cooking oil that is recycled into biodiesel and operate a "one-stop shop" that provides business services such as direct mail, data processing and market research.[6]

RWA began by serving the homeless, but it has evolved to take in men recently released from prison who have nowhere to live. A 2010 Harvard University study found the RWA program reduced criminal recidivism by 60 percent.[7]

The program is "targeted at the hardest group in America right now, which is men and urban men," says Robert Doar, a fellow in poverty studies at the American

---

When Roosevelt delivered his second Inaugural Address in 1937 — declaring that "I see one-third of a nation ill-housed, ill-clad, ill-nourished" — no official measurement existed for what constituted poverty.[56] The Depression led to assisted housing programs to shelter the needy and to create construction jobs. In addition, the minimum wage, labor standards and the rights of unions to bargain collectively for wages and benefits also appeared.[57]

In 1954, the Supreme Court's *Brown v. Board of Education* ruling overturned the "separate but equal" policy in education, paving the way for the 1960s civil rights movement that would coincide with efforts to alleviate urban poverty.

"War on Poverty"

Just months before his assassination in November 1963, President John F. Kennedy directed his Council of Economic Advisers to recommend ways to fight domestic poverty.[58]

His successor, President Johnson, took up the mantle by launching the so-called War on Poverty in his first State of the Union address on Jan. 8, 1964. He called for many of the same programs that advocates push for today: better

Enterprise Institute, a conservative think tank in Washington.

Doar became familiar with RWA through his previous job as commissioner of New York City's Human Resources Administration, where he observed many approaches to alleviating poverty. In 2014, Doar called RWA a model for other anti-poverty initiatives.[8]

"The program they run," Doar said, "is based on a clear contract between the shelter managers and the homeless men. 'You get up every day and go to work and stay drug free — and we will pay you and house you and feed you.'"

That's exactly what Griffin says he needed. "I used to think it was corny to go to work from 9 to 5," he said. "I ridiculed my father because I thought he lived such a boring life. That's what I was running away from. By the end of my run, all I wanted was to go to work."[9]

McDonald said similar programs could help alleviate the poverty and unemployment underlying the rioting that took place this year in Ferguson, Mo., and Baltimore after unarmed black men died amid allegations of police misconduct. After news media reported that Ferguson's unemployment rate for black men ages 20 to 24 was 46 percent, he said unemployment leads to "a terrible, aggressive form of social decay."[10]

— *Jane Fullerton Lemons*

It's graduation day at the Doe Fund's Ready, Willing & Able program, which provides housing and essential jobs for men who are homeless or recently released from prison.

[1] "Success Story: Nazerine Griffin," Ready, Willing & Able: The Doe Fund, undated, accessed June 30, 2015, http://tinyurl.com/pa2t3cg.

[2] For background, see the Ready, Willing & Able website, www.doe.org.

[3] "Success Story," *op. cit.*

[4] Nazerine Griffin, "Breaking the Cycle of Homelessness: Nazerine Griffin of the Doe Fund | David Lynch Foundation," YouTube, Jan. 31, 2011, http://tinyurl.com/p9nv6gj.

[5] "Financial Information," The Doe Fund, undated, accessed July 9, 2015, http://tinyurl.com/pl865u2.

[6] "Social Enterprises," The Doe Fund, undated, accessed July 9, 2015, http://tinyurl.com/qa4zokr.

[7] Catherine Sirois and Bruce Western, "An Evaluation Of 'Ready, Willing & Able,'" Harvard University, May 14, 2010, http://tinyurl.com/onbyses.

[8] Robert Doar, "The Path to Responsibility Can Start With a Broom and a Paycheck," *The Wall Street Journal*, Feb. 28, 2014, http://tinyurl.com/o3o9xv6.

[9] "Success Story," *op. cit.*

[10] "Ferguson's Crisis of Opportunity," Ready, Willing & Able: The Doe Fund, Aug. 27, 2014, http://tinyurl.com/pwufzoh.

---

schools and housing, better health care and job training. "Very often a lack of jobs and money is not the cause of poverty, but the symptom," Johnson said.[59]

The cornerstone of the War on Poverty was the Economic Opportunity Act of 1964, which established Head Start, Job Corps, Community Action, Legal Services and other programs. During this era, Medicare, a federal health care plan for the elderly, and Medicaid, for the poor and disabled, were established, and food stamps became permanent.[60]

Some of the programs took aim at urban poverty, including legislation to build low-income housing and prohibit racial discrimination there. Critics contended the efforts to build public housing exacerbated the problems they sought to alleviate by warehousing urban poor in ghettos.

Charles Murray, a libertarian scholar at the American Enterprise Institute, contended in his 1984 book, *Losing Ground: American Social Policy, 1950-1980* that as spending on the poor increased, progress against poverty decreased. "We tried to provide more for the poor and produced more poor instead," Murray wrote. "We tried to remove the barriers to escape from poverty, and inadvertently built a trap."[61]

A protester throws a bottle at police during riots in Baltimore on April 27, 2015, following the death of Freddie Gray, a 25-year-old African-American who died from injuries sustained after his arrest. On May 1, Gray's death was ruled a homicide and charges were issued against the six officers allegedly involved in the incident. In recent months, urban poverty has made front-page headlines as a backdrop to civil unrest following allegations of police misconduct against African-Americans in other cities, including Cleveland, Oakland, Calif., and Ferguson, Mo.

Harvard University sociologist William Julius Wilson offered a different analysis in his 1996 book, *When Work Disappears: The World of the New Urban Poor*, contending the problems are rooted in society's structures rather than the poor themselves. Dramatic changes in employment patterns and the globalization of the economy also must be taken into account, he wrote, because the loss of industrial jobs, the movement of jobs overseas, the movement of jobs from inner cities to suburbs and other factors have reduced employment opportunities.[62]

Race riots in Chicago, Detroit, Washington and elsewhere that followed the 1968 assassination of Martin Luther King Jr. in some ways presaged what happened this year in places such as Ferguson, Mo., where entrenched poverty and a lack of jobs fueled protesters' rage.

As a June 3, 2015, report by the *Baltimore Afro-American* stated, "The seeds of disillusionment, hurt and frustration that gave birth to the '68 riots were in many ways responsible for the unrest that bloomed almost 50 years later."[63]

President Johnson's War on Poverty continued under Republican President Richard M. Nixon, whose administration created the Aid to Families with Dependent Children (AFDC) program, which provided cash assistance to needy families. In addition, the food stamp program begun during the John F. Kennedy-Johnson era was expanded.[64]

High unemployment in the mid-1970s led to the creation of large-scale public service employment programs, the first such government job-creation effort since the Depression-era Civilian Conservation Corps and Works Progress Administration.

In addition, the 1970s saw several other anti-poverty efforts, including:

• The Supplemental Security Income program, which provides stipends to the needy aged, blind, and disabled.
• Section 8 rental housing assistance for the poor.
• The Earned Income Tax Credit (EITC) for low-wage workers.[65]

The anti-poverty programs begun during the Johnson era came under fire in the 1980s from Republican President Ronald Reagan. "My friends, some years ago, the federal government declared war on poverty, and poverty won," Reagan said in his 1988 State of the Union address.[66]

According to a Congressional Research Service report, the 1980s saw rising concerns about an urban "underclass," defined as a group excluded from the mainstream of society, suffering from "behavioral as well as income deficiencies." Attention focused on the inner cities, where high rates of poverty, crime, single parenting and welfare use disproportionately affected African-Americans living there.[67]

When Democrat Bill Clinton campaigned for president in the early 1990s, he called for changes in the welfare system coupled with greater personal responsibility. In 1996, he signed a sweeping overhaul of the nation's welfare programs — the Personal Responsibility and Work Opportunity Reconciliation Act. The act started the Temporary Assistance to Needy Families program, which placed time limits on welfare assistance, and made other changes to the welfare system including stricter conditions for food stamps eligibility, reductions in immigrant welfare assistance, and work requirements for welfare recipients.

But another Clinton-era policy, a major crime bill, contributed to high incarceration rates because it mandated lengthy prison sentences, particularly for drug crimes. As the links between incarceration and poverty have become clearer, Democrats and Republicans alike have called for criminal justice reforms as a key to providing the opportunities needed to alleviate the kind of entrenched urban poverty that is creating unrest.[68]

Recession Takes Root

In the first decade of the 21st century, the United States plunged into the most severe economic downturn since the Depression, a recession that lasted from December 2007 to June 2009.[69]

During the crisis, housing values plummeted, job losses mounted and unemployment increased. Long-term unemployment — those out of work for more than 27 weeks — reached historical levels, peaking at 6.7 million — or 45.1 percent of the unemployed — in 2010.[70] In response, Congress expanded federal aid for low-income Americans.

But most anti-poverty policies have not been significantly modified since the 1990s.[71]

Although the economy is improving, unemployment remains high in cities, where 83 percent of the short-term unemployed and 87 percent of the long-term unemployed live. Since 2010, the share of urban residents who have been unemployed long term has increased, widening the gap between rural and urban unemployment.[72]

The problem is acute for black Americans. In 2013, the nation's overall unemployment rate was 7.4 percent; for African-Americans, 13.1 percent. And blacks had the highest rates among adult men (12.9 percent), adult women (11.3 percent) and teens (38.8 percent).[73]

The pace of the recovery has been slow, leading to calls from the Rev. Dr. Martin Luther King Jr.'s family, Democratic presidential candidate Hillary Rodham Clinton and others for a Cabinet-level "poverty czar" who would coordinate anti-poverty efforts across the government's various agencies. "As my father often said, 'The time is always right to do what is right,'" Martin Luther King III said.[74]

CURRENT SITUATION

Promise Zones

Obama in 2013 introduced "Promise Zones," a program that awards grants, technical assistance and tax incentives

Housing and Urban Development Secretary Julián Castro announces new policies aimed at promoting racially integrated neighborhoods on July 8, 2015, in Chicago. Providing the opportunity to move into better neighborhoods was at the heart of a Supreme Court case this year concerning the 1968 Fair Housing Act, which made it illegal to refuse to sell or rent dwellings to individuals because of their race, religion, sex or national origin. Castro said the Obama administration will require cities and towns to show they are complying with the act and to set goals for how they will reduce residential segregation.

to impoverished communities. Under the program, Obama said, "the federal government will partner with and invest in communities to . . . create jobs, leverage private investment, increase economic activity, expand educational opportunities, and reduce violent crime."[75]

In 2014, the first zones were established in San Antonio, Philadelphia, Los Angeles, southeastern Kentucky and the Choctaw Nation of Oklahoma; in April 2015, Obama announced eight more zones.

In Philadelphia, the zone attracted approximately $30 million in federal, state and private funding, according to HUD. The money went to, among other things, career training and placement for youths who have been involved in the criminal justice system, loans for food-based entrepreneurs and the renovation of 48 homes at Mt. Vernon Manor, a nonprofit affordable housing community, HUD said.[76]

The construction of public housing complexes like this one in New York City exacerbated the problems of the urban poor by warehousing poor people in blighted neighborhoods, many critics contend. Building more low-income housing in middle-class and affluent neighborhoods would give more children in low-income families a chance at better educational opportunities and more diverse social networks, says Kristen Lewis, co-director of Measure of America, a Brooklyn advocacy group.

Critics, however, deride the Obama effort as inadequately funded and say it's a pale imitation of former Republican HUD Secretary Jack Kemp's "enterprise zones." The 1980s Republican approach offered tax incentives and regulatory relief for businesses that would provide jobs and commerce in impoverished inner-city and rural areas.

In addition to the "Promise Zone" idea, Obama, in his Jan. 20 State of the Union address, called on Congress to pass several measures that advocates say would help the working and urban poor.[77] They include:

- Raising the federal minimum wage from $7.25 to $10.10 an hour.
- Guaranteeing paid sick leave along with expanding paid family and medical leave.
- Eliminating the gender gap in pay for women.
- Revising federal overtime rules.

In April, Rep. Robert "Bobby" Scott, D-Va., introduced the Raise the Wage Act to increase the federal minimum wage to $12 by 2020, which would raise the pay of nearly 38 million American workers.[78] In the Senate, the measure is sponsored by Patty Murray, D-Wash., and has the backing of the Democratic leadership. It has 32 co-sponsors in the Senate and 160 co-sponsors in the House — all Democrats. Republicans generally have opposed increasing the minimum wage because they contend it would raise costs for business that could lead to job cuts — ultimately hurting the people intended for help.[79]

In an analysis by congressional district of how many workers would benefit from a higher minimum wage, Oxfam America found a "remarkably diverse" mix of urban and rural locales. Among the urban areas with the highest concentrations of low-wage workers: East Los Angeles, Dallas-Fort Worth and the Bronx, N.Y.[80]

Some metro regions — including Los Angeles, San Francisco and New York — had areas with both the highest and lowest concentrations of low-wage workers.

The U.S. minimum wage ranks third-lowest among the 34 member countries of the Organisation for Economic Co-Operation and Development (OECD), which seeks to stimulate growth among high-income economies. Talking with reporters in October 2014, Labor Secretary Tom Perez called the situation embarrassing.[81]

Some states and cities are not waiting for their federal counterparts to act on the minimum wage. Currently, 29 states and the District of Columbia mandate a higher minimum than does the federal government.[82]

Connecticut, Delaware, Hawaii, Maryland, Massachusetts, Michigan, Minnesota, Rhode Island, Vermont, West Virginia and the District of Columbia enacted minimum wage increases during their 2014 legislative sessions.

In addition, voters in Alaska, Arkansas, Nebraska and South Dakota approved minimum wage increases through ballot initiatives.[83]

Workplace Issues

Other issues with ramifications for urban areas include:

- Reforming the criminal justice system. The House Judiciary Committee has begun looking at ways to improve criminal justice, including changing laws that allegedly over-criminalize certain behaviors, revamping sentencing guidelines, improving prisons and protecting citizens through improved criminal procedures and policing strategies — all issues stemming from the police incidents in Ferguson and Baltimore.[84]

AT ISSUE

Would raising the minimum wage help alleviate poverty?

YES David Cooper
Senior Economic Analyst, Economic Policy Institute

Written for *CQ Researcher*, July 2015

The federal minimum wage is one of our country's basic protections against poverty. It ensures that regular work — regardless of the type of job, the worker's circumstances or macroeconomic conditions — is a means to a decent quality of life.

But because the federal government sets the minimum wage at a specific amount, its buying power erodes each year as prices increase. This means more workers face falling into poverty unless policymakers raise the minimum wage.

Research has consistently confirmed that raising the minimum wage to keep up with inflation significantly reduces poverty. Researchers at the University of Massachusetts, Amherst, reviewed all the existing literature on the topic since the 1990s. Their conclusion: All but one study found that raising the minimum wage significantly and sizably reduced the poverty rate. The paper's empirical analysis concluded that every 10 percent increase in the minimum wage reduced the share of the population living in poverty by 2.9 percent.

The findings suggest that increasing the federal minimum wage from the current $7.25 to $10 or more would reduce the number of people living in poverty by millions.

Critics of raising the minimum wage sometimes contend that it is ineffective at combating poverty because many poor people do not work. This claim is misleading. A significant portion — roughly 42 percent — of those in poverty are either children under age 18 or persons age 65 or older.

Among employable working-age adults — individuals ages 18 to 64 who are not retired, in school or disabled — nearly two-thirds (63 percent) work, and more than 40 percent work full time. For these individuals, raising the minimum wage will directly increase their incomes.

Moreover, because many poor children have a parent who works in a low-wage job, increasing the minimum wage simultaneously reduces both the adult poverty rate and the child poverty rate.

Raising low-wage workers' pay will also reduce some families' need for public assistance, freeing up resources that can then be used to strengthen anti-poverty programs, or make investments in public infrastructure, research and education that will help grow the economy over the long term.

Effectively fighting poverty requires a two-pronged approach: social safety net programs that provide resources to those either unable to work or who have fallen on hard times and labor standards like the minimum wage that ensure work remains adequately rewarding.

NO Michael Tanner
Senior Fellow, Cato Institute

Written for *CQ Researcher*, July 2015

Good intentions must often confront economic reality. Trying to reduce poverty by raising the minimum wage is a case in point.

A minimum wage increase would help surprisingly few poor people. Fewer than 5 percent of minimum wage earners are adults working full time to support a family. Minimum wage earners might not be just college kids earning summer beer money anymore, but neither are they hard-pressed single parents. In fact, the average annual family income for a minimum wage worker is $53,000. Perhaps that is why, according to research by Joseph Sabia and Richard Burkhauser for the Employment Policies Institute in Washington, federal minimum wage increases between 2003 and 2007 had no effect on state poverty rates.

At the same time, a minimum wage increase could reduce the number of entry-level jobs available to poor people with few job skills, effectively cutting the first rungs off the economic ladder. After all, we know that a job — any job — is the surest route out of poverty, and even a minimum wage job can be a start. Of those beginning at minimum wage, two-thirds will be earning a higher wage within a year.

The amount of compensation workers receive is more or less a function of their productivity. As Greg Mankiw, chairman and professor of economics at Harvard University, explains, "Economic theory says that the wage a worker earns, measured in units of output, equals the amount of output the worker can produce." This is somewhat oversimplified, of course. Other factors are involved. But one can't just arbitrarily declare a worker's "value." Increasing the minimum wage simply tries to ignore this economic reality.

The academic evidence is pretty clear. A review of more than 100 studies on the minimum wage for the National Bureau of Economic Research in Cambridge, Mass., concluded that 85 percent of studies found raising the minimum wage led to negative employment effects. Neumark and Wascher wrote that the preponderance of evidence shows that a higher wage leads to "disemployment" — fewer jobs — especially for the least-skilled groups.

If we really want to reduce poverty, some more effective things we can do including reduce taxes and regulation to increase job creation, reform education, reduce overcriminalization and incarceration of the poor and stabilize family formation. But raising the minimum wage is simply good intention gone bad.

- Raising the overtime threshold. Obama recently announced proposed changes to federal regulations on overtime pay. The Labor Department estimates the move could raise the wages of nearly 5 million people making up to $50,440 a year who work more than 40 hours a week.[85]

Many employees now receiving as little as $455 a week, or $23,660 a year — below the federal poverty line for a family of four — currently don't receive overtime pay because they are classified as managers.[86] "This is probably the most significant step they can take to raise wages for millions of workers," said Bill Samuel, director of legislative affairs for the AFL-CIO.[87]

- Requiring predictable scheduling. In November 2014, San Francisco became the first jurisdiction to regulate how employers provide schedules for hourly workers.[88]

The difficulties of living without a predictable work schedule — such as arranging child care, holding a second job or taking classes — have been documented by studies and by those living in such situations. And those issues can have an impact on earnings.[89]

"This variability of work hours contributes to income instability and thus adversely affects not only household consumption but general macroeconomic performance," concluded a study from the Economic Policy Institute.[90]

Other jurisdictions considering following San Francisco's lead include Delaware, the District of Columbia, Michigan and New York, where the state attorney general has investigated retailers for their "on-call" scheduling practices.[91]

Meanwhile, 17 American companies, led by international coffee chain Starbucks and including Microsoft, CVS Health and Walmart, announced plans in July to collectively employ 100,000 more young Americans over the next three years. Companies participating in the so-called 100,000 Opportunities Initiative will create new full-time positions and internship programs and participate in citywide job fairs aimed at Americans ages 16 to 24.[92]

A number of participating companies, such as Hilton Worldwide and Walgreen's, have developed programs to employ thousands of young Americans in their respective sectors. Starbucks CEO Howard Schultz donated $3.4 million from his company and his and his wife's foundation in 2014 to coffee barista and retail training for at risk youth around the country.[93]

"As business leaders, I believe we have a critical role to play in hiring more Opportunity Youth" — those not employed or in school — "and offering these young people excellent training, and the chance to dream big and reach their aspirations," said Starbucks CEO Howard Schultz.[94]

In a separate op-ed, Schultz and his wife, Sheri, highlighted how the successes of former participants from their foundation's programs showed that teaching workplace skills could enable youth to overcome economic hardships and stay in school. "While some have lost hope in this population, blaming them and their families for creating their own problems, we believe these young people represent a significant untapped resource of productivity and talent," they wrote.[95]

Presidential Candidates

The incendiary incidents involving the deaths of black men in Baltimore, Ferguson and elsewhere have prompted the 2016 presidential candidates to begin discussing crime and poverty, though mostly in general terms.[96]

Following the racially motivated shooting deaths of nine people in a South Carolina church in June, Hillary Clinton said, "Despite our best efforts and our highest hopes, America's long struggle with race is far from finished. We can't hide from hard truths about race and justice. We have to name them, own them and change them."[97]

Clinton made her remarks in a Missouri church not far from Ferguson, where the police shooting of Michael Brown, an 18-year-old unarmed black man less than a year earlier led to days of sometimes violent protests that sparked a national discussion about police tactics, urban poverty and the relationship between the two.

Democrat Martin O'Malley, a former mayor of Baltimore and governor of Maryland, has defended his tough-on-crime record that some contend contributed to the protests in that city.[98]

On the Republican side, former Florida Gov. Jeb Bush so far has focused his poverty message on calling for two-parent families and reforming education.[99]

Sen. Marco Rubio of Florida has said he would consolidate federal funding for anti-poverty programs into one agency and turn those funds over to the states.[100]

Sen. Rand Paul of Kentucky has long advocated criminal justice reforms such as rolling back mandatory sentences and restoring voting rights for felons, along with creating "economic freedom zones" that would lower individual, corporate and payroll tax rates in impoverished areas in an attempt to attract businesses.[101]

Issues surrounding poverty and income inequality don't typically rise to the top of the agenda for presidential candidates, but advocates hope they will during the 2016 election cycle.[102]

Says Melissa Boteach, vice president of the Poverty to Prosperity Program at the Center for American Progress, "It's up to citizens to hold their elected officials accountable to debate these issues and act on these issues as part of the next election cycle."

OUTLOOK

Economy Is Key

Although poverty, particularly urban poverty, has garnered renewed public attention, the outlook ultimately depends on one factor — the economy.

"Poverty alleviation is very dependent on job availability and economic growth," says Doar of the conservative American Enterprise Institute.

"When the economy was growing, the wind was at our back and we were able to help a lot more people," he says. "And when it's not growing, when jobs are scarce, you can have the nicest program in the world, but if you can't find people work, they're going to be struggling."

Cooper of the liberal Economic Policy Institute agrees that progress depends on how the economy fares as it recovers from the recession. If conditions keep getting better, more jobs and higher wages — key factors needed to combat urban poverty — should follow.

"If the economy continues to stay on course, then we should, in theory, start to see poverty go back down again," he says.

With Obama and the 2016 candidates discussing urban poverty, Cooper says he expects the political spotlight to remain on poverty and income inequality.[103]

"These questions focusing on trying to raise pay, trying to raise incomes for folks, are going to be the primary discussion, absent some other major challenge that the country faces, for the foreseeable future,"
he says. "Whoever is elected president in 2016 is still going to be dealing with this question of how do we raise wages, how do we reduce income inequality."

Woodson, the neighborhood activist, has grown weary of the partisan battles and hopes the country can move beyond them when it comes to helping the urban poor. He has accompanied Rep. Ryan to impoverished areas so the Wisconsin congressman could see firsthand what urban poverty looks like.[104]

"I've got renewed enthusiasm that change is possible," Woodson says. "I don't care about the history of racism, I don't care about what people's motivations are," he says. "It's essential to move beyond the ideological divide, Woodson said. While that may prove difficult in an election-year climate, he acknowledges, "I'm eternally optimistic. I believe that we can make anything happen that we choose."

NOTES

1. Tianna Gaines-Turner, written testimony submitted to the House Budget Committee, July 9, 2014, http://tinyurl.com/psgpsof.

2. "Poverty and Working Families," House Budget Committee Hearing, July 9, 2014, http://tinyurl.com/ohljgck.

3. "Poverty Main," U.S. Census Bureau, http://tinyurl.com/p98nlcv; see also "2015 Poverty Guidelines," Department of Health and Human Services, http://tinyurl.com/lhen3u2.

4. Joe Cortright and Dillon Mahmoudi, "Lost in Place: Why the persistence and spread of concentrated poverty — not gentrification — is our biggest urban challenge," City Observatory, December 2014, http://tinyurl.com/p2v22jg.

5. Jonathan Grabinsky and Stuart M. Butler, "The Anti-Poverty Case for 'Smart' Gentrification, Part 1," Brookings Institution, Feb. 10, 2015, http://tinyurl.com/nf2ghg8.

6. Karl Alexander and Linda Olson, "Urban poverty, in black and white," CNN, July 11, 2014, http://tinyurl.com/ptg7bct.

7. Current Population Survey, 2013 and 2014 Annual Social and Economic Supplements, U.S. Census Bureau, p. 1, http://tinyurl.com/3p9ynr3.

8. Sabrina Tavernise, "Black Children in U.S. Are Much More Likely to Live in Poverty, Study Finds," *The New York Times*, July 14, 2015, http://tinyurl.com/qb3ujnh.

9. Eileen Patten and Jens Manuel Krogstad, "Black child poverty rate holds steady, even as other groups see declines," Pew Research Center, July 14, 2015, http://tinyurl.com/p6s6jqj.

10. "Table 9. Poverty, by Region," Historical Poverty Tables, U.S. Census Bureau, located at http://tinyurl.com/csklehg.

11. Andrew Schaefer, "The Long-Term Unemployed in the Wake of the Great Recession," Carsey Institute, University of New Hampshire, winter 2014, http://tinyurl.com/o5943yj.

12. John Herbers, "Panel on Civil Disorders Calls for Drastic Action to Avoid 2-Society Nation," *The New York Times*, Feb. 29, 1968, http://tinyurl.com/og9haky.

13. "Report of the National Advisory Commission On Civil Disorders, Summary of Report," University of Washington Department of History, http://tinyurl.com/pp54cvw.

14. Bruce Western, "The Man Who Foresaw Baltimore," *Politico Magazine*, April 30, 2015, http://tinyurl.com/o76tzol.

15. Sasha Abramsky, "Toxic Persons: New research shows precisely how the prison-to-poverty cycle does its damage," *Slate*, Oct. 8, 2010, http://tinyurl.com/q6lh8e5; Bruce Western and Becky Pettit, "Incarceration & social inequality," *Dædalus*, summer 2010, http://tinyurl.com/3qupux4.

16. "ALICE: Study of Financial Hardship, Michigan," the United Way, 2014, http://tinyurl.com/okdh9ht; Kate Abbey-Lambertz, "Most Detroit Families Can't Afford Their Basic Needs: Report," *The Huffington Post*, Sept. 4, 2014, http://tinyurl.com/o4zqafl.

17. "Growth in Means-Tested Programs and Tax Credits for Low-Income Households," Congressional Budget Office, Feb. 11, 2013, http://tinyurl.com/q6pmxuk.

18. *Ibid.*

19. Tracey Ross, "Addressing Urban Poverty in America Must Remain a Priority," Center for American Progress, June 5, 2015, http://tinyurl.com/nqrkrjj.

20. Arloc Sherman and Danilo Trisi, "Safety Net More Effective Against Poverty Than Previously Thought," Center on Budget and Policy Priorities, May 6, 2015, http://tinyurl.com/phklw4a.

21. Robert Rector, "How the War on Poverty Was Lost," *The Wall Street Journal*, Jan. 7, 2014, http://tinyurl.com/p663tgc.

22. Elise Gould, "Poor People Work: A Majority of Poor People Who Can Work Do," Economic Policy Institute, May 19, 2015, http://tinyurl.com/lo49h2y.

23. *Ibid.*

24. "Affordable Housing," Department of Housing and Urban Development, undated, accessed July 10, 2015, http://tinyurl.com/ndclokg.

25. "Rental Assistance in Urban and Rural Areas," Center on Budget and Policy Priorities, May 12, 2015, http://tinyurl.com/oopacs6.

26. Sherman and Trisi, *op. cit.*

27. Adam Liptak, "Justices Back Broad Interpretation of Housing Law," *The New York Times*, June 25, 2015, http://tinyurl.com/ozyjvpb.

28. Jess Bravin and Robbie Whelan, "Supreme Court Upholds Tool for Fighting Housing Bias," *The Wall Street Journal*, June 25, 2015. http://tinyurl.com/orm6kut; "Texas Department Of Housing And Community Affairs *et al.* v. Inclusive Communities Project, Inc., *et al.*," Supreme Court, June 25, 2015, http://tinyurl.com/pjpcpos.

29. Richard Rothstein, "The Making of Ferguson: Public Policies at the Root of its Troubles," Economic Policy Institute, Oct. 15, 2014, http://tinyurl.com/qcqgpop.

30. "Historian Says Don't 'Sanitize' How Our Government Created Ghettos," Fresh Air, NPR, May 14, 2015, http://tinyurl.com/o77rv2c.

31. Emily Badger, "Obama administration to unveil major new rules targeting segregation across U.S.," *The Washington Post*, July 8, 2015, http://tinyurl.com/pnhboaj.

32. *Ibid.*
33. "Opportunity Index 2014: Where is Opportunity in America?" Measure of America, 2014, http://tinyurl.com/nmmgvxf.
34. Cortright and Mahmoudi, *op. cit.* For more on gentrification, see Alan Greenblatt, "Gentrification: Are the Young and the Wealthy Displacing the Poor?" *CQ Researcher*, Feb. 20, 2015, pp. 169-192.
35. John Buntin, "The Myth of Gentrification," *Slate*, Jan. 14, 2015, http://tinyurl.com/pgwhfgd. Joe Cortright, "More People in Cities Today Live in Poverty Than in 1970," *Next City*, Dec. 5, 2014, http://tinyurl.com/mr8dz3b.
36. Don Reisinger, "Facebook boosts minimum wage for contract workers to $15 an hour," Cnet, May 13, 2015, http://tinyurl.com/nc8m95z.
37. Claire Cain Miller, "New Momentum on Paid Leave, in Business and Politics," *The New York Times*, June 22, 2015, http://tinyurl.com/okcxjly.
38. Laurie Kulikowski, "McDonald's, Wal-Mart and 10 Other Big Companies That Pay Above Minimum Wage," *TheStreet*, April 2, 2015, http://tinyurl.com/qzz2tw4.
38. Reihan Salam, "Don't Let Facebook Determine Our Minimum-Wage Policy," *National Review*, May 14, 2015, http://tinyurl.com/q5b6296.
40. David Cooper, "Raising the Federal Minimum Wage to $10.10 Would Save Safety Net Programs Billions and Help Ensure Businesses Are Doing Their Fair Share," Economic Policy Institute, Oct 16, 2014, http://tinyurl.com/mrdebv4.
41. Tracey Ross, "Eds, Meds, and the Feds: How the Federal Government Can Foster the Role of Anchor Institutions in Community Revitalization," Center for American Progress, Oct. 24, 2014, http://tinyurl.com/o9r8fxe.
42. Ryan Holeywell, "Walmart Makes Its Urban Debut," *Governing*, June 2012, http://tinyurl.com/czlldur.
43. *Ibid.*
44. Daniella Silva, "CVS Health to Rebuild Burned Stores Burned in Baltimore Riots," NBC News, May 6, 2015, http://tinyurl.com/oocqq4d.
45. Mara Liasson, "'My Brother's Keeper' To Expand Opportunities For Young Men Of Color," NPR, May 5, 2015, http://tinyurl.com/q52oyof.
46. Jason L. Riley, "A Black Conservative's War on Poverty," *The Wall Street Journal*, April 18, 2014, http://tinyurl.com/p9jrlk8.
47. Robert L. Woodson Sr., "How to triumph over poverty," *Milwaukee Journal Sentinel*, March 29, 2014, http://tinyurl.com/op7ek43.
48. "Reducing Youth Violence: The Violence-Free Zone," Center for Neighborhood Enterprise, undated, accessed July 10, 2015, http://tinyurl.com/osxo2mt.
49. Jacob Riis, *How the Other Half Lives: Studies Among the Tenements of New York* (1890).
50. "From the Countryside to the City," U.S. History, Pre-Columbian to the New Millennium, Independence Hall Association, UShistory.org, http://tinyurl.com/q3f4458.
51. "Booker T. Washington," U.S. History, Pre-Columbian to the New Millennium, UShistory.org, Independence Hall Association, http://tinyurl.com/nmmmdz9; "Plessy v. Fergsuon — Case Brief Summary," Lawnix, undated, accessed July 10, 2015, http://tinyurl.com/bpzbzp.
52. "The Great Migration (1915-1960)," BlackPast.org, http://tinyurl.com/kkker7e.
53. Rothstein, *op. cit.*
54. Cortright, *op. cit.* See also Department of Labor, http://tinyurl.com/nvhn5zd.
55. "The New Deal," Roosevelt Institute, undated, accessed July 10, 2015, http://tinyurl.com/c6hr7c4; "Great Depression and World War II, 1929-1945: Race Relations in the 1930s and 1940s," Library of Congress, undated, accessed July 10, 2015, http://tinyurl.com/bptlkjg.
56. Franklin D. Roosevelt, 1937 Inaugural Address, Joint Congressional Committee on Inaugural Ceremonies, http://tinyurl.com/oab87bq.
57. Gene Falk and Karen Spar, "Poverty: Major Themes in Past Debates and Current Proposals," Congressional Research Service, Sept. 18, 2014, http://tinyurl.com/q9y3udf.

58. See H. B. Shaffer, "Status of War on Poverty," in *Editorial Research Reports*, Jan. 25, 1967, available at *CQ Researcher Plus Archive*, www.cqpress.com.
59. Lyndon B. Johnson, "State of the Union address," Jan. 8, 1964, http://tinyurl.com/kwcvpnp.
60. Falk and Spar, *op. cit.*
61. Charles Murray, *Losing Ground: American Social Policy, 1950-1980* (1984).
62. William Julius Wilson, *When Work Disappears: The World of the New Urban Poor* (1996), p. 9.
63. Zenitha Prince, "Riot Redux: 2015 Mirrored 1968 Unrest," *Afro-American Newspapers*, June 3, 2015, http://tinyurl.com/q4blsbs.
64. Falk and Spar, *op. cit.*
65. *Ibid.*
66. Ronald Reagan, State of the Union address, Jan. 25, 1988, http://tinyurl.com/p3g8v4a.
67. Falk and Spar, *op. cit.*
68. Justin Wolfers, David Leonhardt and Kevin Quealy, "1.5 Million Missing Black Men," *The New York Times*, April 20, 2015, http://tinyurl.com/jw5xnfg.
69. "Chart Book: The Legacy of the Great Recession," Center on Budget and Policy Priorities, June 25, 2015, http://tinyurl.com/oo82soj.
70. Karen Kosanovich and Eleni Theodossiou Sherman, "Trends in long-term unemployment," Bureau of Labor Statistics, March 2015, http://tinyurl.com/pzdlhpa.
71. Falk and Spar, *op. cit.*, p. 10.
72. Schaefer, *op. cit.*
73. "Labor Force Characteristics by Race and Ethnicity, 2013," "BLS Report," Bureau of Labor Statistics, August 2014, http://tinyurl.com/qzo4jmg.
74. Jesse Byrnes, "Obama pressed to appoint poverty czar," *The Hill*, May 19, 2015, http://tinyurl.com/noe9wwr.
75. "Promise Zones Overview," Department of Housing and Urban Development, http://tinyurl.com/nmaarar.
76. "Promise Zones First Round Designees," HUD Exchange, undated, accessed July 10, 2015, http://tinyurl.com/mju8rme.
77. Remarks by the President in State of the Union Address, Jan. 20, 2015, http://tinyurl.com/mp3tjpb.
78. "H.R.2150, Raise the Wage Act," Congress.gov., undated, accessed July 10, 2015, http://tinyurl.com/nrrykm9.
79. Tim Devaney, "Dems bet 2016 on $12 minimum wage," *The Hill*, May 5, 2015, http://tinyurl.com/p94vsma.
80. "Working Poor In America," Oxfam America, June 11, 2014, http://tinyurl.com/k8fm7fr.
81. Eric Morath, "U.S. Minimum-Wage Employees Must Work 50 Hours a Week to Escape Poverty, OECD Says," Real Time Economics blog, *The Wall Street Journal*, May 6, 2015, http://tinyurl.com/l8gzz2r. Kathleen Hunter, "Christie Has 'Head in Sand' on Minimum Wage, Labor Chief Say," Bloomberg, Oct. 23, 2014, http://tinyurl.com/pcg4asr.
82. "Minimum Wage Laws in the States — January 1, 2015," Department of Labor, http://tinyurl.com/yh6mqwz.
83. "2015 Minimum Wage By State," National Conference of State Legislatures, June 30, 2015, http://tinyurl.com/kxsuowu.
84. "House Judiciary Committee Announces Criminal Justice Reform Initiative," House Judiciary Committee, June 10, 2015, http://tinyurl.com/q25o5jg.
85. "Notice of Proposed Rulemaking: Overtime," Department of Labor, undated, accessed July 10, 2015, http://tinyurl.com/q9yo4yx. Noam Scheiber, "Obama Making Millions More Americans Eligible for Overtime," *The New York Times*, June 29, 2015, http://tinyurl.com/pthrvhc.
86. "Mike Dorning, "Obama Plans to Expand Overtime Eligibility for Millions," *Bloomberg News*, June 29, 2015, http://tinyurl.com/q9qrjmx.
87. Marianne Levine, "Barack Obama poised to hike wages for millions," *Politico*, June 8, 2015, http://tinyurl.com/prayts9.
88. Marianne Levine, "San Francisco passes first-in-nation limits on worker schedules," *Politico*, Nov. 25, 2014, http://tinyurl.com/odxfe5q.

89. Jodi Kantor, "Working Anything but 9 to 5," *The New York Times*, Aug. 13, 2014, http://tinyurl.com/morpl8b; Gillian B. White, "The Very Real Hardship of Unpredictable Work Schedules," *The Atlantic*, April 15, 2015, http://tinyurl.com/mv86fq2.

90. Lonnie Golden, "Irregular Work Scheduling and Its Consequences," Economic Policy Institute, April 9, 2015, http://tinyurl.com/pwg4t2l.

91. Lauren Weber, "Retailers Are Under Fire for Work Schedules," *The Wall Street Journal*, April 12, 2015, http://tinyurl.com/oxt5xcr.

92. Nelson D. Schwartz, "Starbucks and Other Corporations to Announce Plan to Curb Unemployment of Young People," *The New York Times*, July 13, 2015, http://tinyurl.com/ne74485.

93. *Ibid.*; Ángel González, "Schultz Foundation, Starbucks launch training program for at-risk youth," *The Seattle Times*, Sept. 8, 2014, http://tinyurl.com/pku85zn.

94. "Top U.S.-Based Companies Launch the "100,000 Opportunities Initiative," news release, Starbucks, July 13, 2015, http://tinyurl.com/pku85zn.

95. Howard Schultz and Sheri Schultz, "Connecting Young People With Jobs," *The New York Times*, July 13, 2015, http://tinyurl.com/plhjpnv.

96. Danny Vinik, "Is It Inequality or Mobility? Neither Economists nor GOP Candidates Can Decide," *The New Republic*, April 7, 2015, http://tinyurl.com/p8pdtr2; Charles D. Ellison, "Baltimore Just Became a Political Epicenter for 2016," *The Root*, May 6, 2015, http://tinyurl.com/nbf2t2f.

97. Annie Karni, "Hillary Clinton, near Ferguson, calls for confronting 'hard truths' about race," *Politico*, June 23, 2015, http://tinyurl.com/naagqmm.

98. Jason Horowitz, "Martin O'Malley Embraces Baltimore, for Better or Worse, in Long-Shot Presidential Bid," *The New York Times*, April 30, 2015, http://tinyurl.com/oxxwefp.

99. Akilah Johnson, "N.H. voters alert to issues involving race, urban ills," *The Boston Globe*, May 12, 2015, http://tinyurl.com/o2c7d7x; Jeb Bush, "Commentary: Jeb Bush's War on Poverty revamp," *Chicago Tribune*, May 6, 2015, http://tinyurl.com/p5b4esa.

100. Jackie Kucinich, "Rubio: War on Poverty has been lost," *The Washington Post*, Jan. 8, 2014, http://tinyurl.com/p6mpv9b; Julie Pace, "Problems facing the poor inch into 2016 presidential race," Associated Press via PBS Newshour, May 2, 2015, http://tinyurl.com/ne7jalg.

101. Ovetta Wiggins, "At GOP fundraiser in Maryland, Rand Paul decries racial injustice, champions diversity," *The Washington Post*, June 10, 2015, http://tinyurl.com/o2gabhh; "Economic Freedom Zones," Sen. Rand Paul, undated, accessed July 10, 2015, http://tinyurl.com/kv9cdbk.

102. David Lauter, "Income inequality emerges as key issue in 2016 presidential campaign," *Los Angeles Times*, Feb. 5, 2015, http://tinyurl.com/ohreb4l.

103. Jill LePore, "Richer and Poorer," *The New Yorker*, March 16, 2015, http://tinyurl.com/maq4o4s.

104. "The Politico 50, Paul Ryan & Bob Woodson," *Politico Magazine*, 2014, http://tinyurl.com/ouu2ho2.

BIBLIOGRAPHY

Selected Sources

Books

Harrington, Michael, *The Other America, Poverty in the United States*, **Macmillan, 1962.**
A political scientist's landmark study of poverty in post–World War II America helped spur the War on Poverty.

Putnam, Robert, *Our Kids: The American Dream in Crisis*, **Simon & Schuster, 2015.**
An eminent Harvard University social scientist examines how widening income gaps affect upward mobility.

Shipler, David K., *The Working Poor: Invisible in America*, **Penguin Random House, 2005.**
A Pulitzer Prize-winning journalist chronicles the lives of the working poor as they try to escape poverty.

Wilson, William Julius, *The Truly Disadvantaged: The Inner City, the Underclass, and Public Policy*, **2nd ed., University of Chicago Press, 2012.**
A Harvard University sociologist rejects both liberal and conservative theories in an examination of the social

structures underlying urban ghettos and the convergence of race and poverty.

Articles

Dukmasova, Maya, "Our Impoverished Debate About Housing Segregation," *Slate*, July 7, 2015, http://tinyurl.com/qxme99h.
The writer contends those looking for solutions to poverty should understand the structural causes and change the language surrounding the discussion.

Kantor, Jodi, "Working Anything but 9 to 5," *The New York Times*, Aug. 13, 2014, http://tinyurl.com/nm5fr9s.
A journalist explains how workplace technology has created havoc in the private lives of low-wage workers with no set schedules.

Keller, Bill, "David Simon on Baltimore's Anguish," The Marshall Project, April 29, 2015, http://tinyurl.com/qbhwyxa.
The former executive editor of *The New York Times* interviews the creator of HBO's Baltimore-focused "The Wire" to provide context about the policies, policing and poverty in the city leading up to and following the death of Freddie Gray.

Leonhardt, David, Amanda Cox and Claire Cain Miller, "An Atlas of Upward Mobility Shows Path Out of Poverty," *The New York Times*, May 4, 2015, http://tinyurl.com/oc3pupa.
University research illustrates that children who move from poor areas have better chances of escaping poverty than children who stay.

Thompson, Derek, "The Curse of Segregation," *The Atlantic*, May 2015, http://tinyurl.com/ncst9p3.
Studies show that the chances for income mobility for poor children in the city of Baltimore are worse than in any large county in America.

Reports and Studies

"The Effects of a Minimum-Wage Increase on Employment and Family Income," Congressional Budget Office, Feb. 18, 2014, http://tinyurl.com/pf7yjqf.
The nonpartisan research agency examines the impact of raising the minimum wage.

Boteach, Melissa, et al., "The War on Poverty: Then and Now," Center for American Progress, January 2014, http://tinyurl.com/nbnskuq.
A liberal Washington public policy group evaluates the War on Poverty's legacy.

Chetty, Raj, and Nathaniel Hendren, "The Impacts of Neighborhoods on Intergenerational Mobility: Childhood Exposure Effects and County-Level Estimates," Harvard University, 2015, http://tinyurl.com/oofkcyy.
Researchers conclude that moving from impoverished areas can have positive outcomes for children later in life.

Eberstadt, Nicholas, "The Great Society at 50: The triumph and the tragedy," American Enterprise Institute, May 19, 2014, http://tinyurl.com/pey3coz.
A scholar with the conservative Washington think tank evaluates the legacy of President Lyndon B. Johnson's Great Society programs.

Kneebone, Elizabeth, "The Growth and Spread of Concentrated Poverty, 2000 to 2008-2012," Brookings Institution, July 31, 2014, http://tinyurl.com/q3gusqw.
A report by the centrist Washington think tank shows that while poverty has spread beyond urban areas, it has become more concentrated in inner-city neighborhoods.

Lewis, Kristen, and Sarah Burd-Sharps, "Zeroing In on Place and Race," Measure of America, June 10, 2015, http://tinyurl.com/nj63ouo.
Researchers from an initiative of the Social Science Research Council analyze how "disconnected" youth are faring in impoverished American cities.

Rothstein, Richard, "The Making of Ferguson: Public Policies at the Root of its Troubles," Economic Policy Institute, Oct. 15, 2014, http://tinyurl.com/o6lvr3h.
A scholar with the liberal Washington think tank contends deliberate segregationist policies were at the root of recent events in Ferguson.

For More Information

Baltimore CASH Campaign, 217 E. Redwood St., Suite 1500, Baltimore, MD 21202; 443-692-9487; www.baltimorecashcampaign.org/. Coalition that provides free tax preparation and financial advice for low-income individuals and families.

Brookings Institution, 1775 Massachusetts Ave., N.W., Washington, DC 20036; 202-797-6000; www.brookings.edu/research/topics/metropolitan-areas. Centrist think tank that conducts research on urban and poverty issues.

Center for American Progress, 1333 H St., N.W., 10th Floor, Washington, DC 20005; 202-682-1611; www.americanprogress.org/issues/poverty/view. Liberal think tank that studies a wide range of policy topics, including poverty.

Center for Neighborhood Enterprise, 1625 K St., N.W., Suite 1200, Washington, DC 20006; 202-518-6500; www.cneonline.org. A nonprofit that helps residents of low-income neighborhoods address the problems of their communities.

Center on Budget and Policy Priorities, 820 First St., N.E., Suite 510, Washington, DC 20002; 202-408-1080; www.cbpp.org/topics/poverty-and-inequality. Liberal think tank that analyzes economic policy implications for low- and moderate-income families.

Doe Fund: Ready, Willing & Able, 232 E. 84th St., New York, NY 10028; 212-628-5207; www.doe.org/index.cfm. Nonprofit that works to find employment for homeless and recently paroled men.

Druid Heights Community Development Corp., 2140 McCulloh St., Baltimore, MD 21201; 410-523-1350; druidheights.com/. Offers housing, educational and other programs in its Baltimore neighborhood.

Economic Policy Institute, 1333 H St., N.W., Suite 300, East Tower, Washington, DC 20005; 202-775-8810; www.epi.org/research/inequality-and-poverty. Liberal think tank focusing on the economic conditions of low- and middle-income Americans.

Oxfam America, 1101 17th St., N.W., Suite 1300, Washington, DC 20036; 800-776-9326; policy-practice.oxfamamerica.org/work/poverty-in-the-us/. U.S. branch of an international confederation of organizations focusing on poverty and injustice.